Negotiating a Settlement in Northern Ireland, 1969–2019

The Good Friday Agreement of 1998 ended a protracted violent conflict in Northern Ireland and became an international reference point for peace-building. *Negotiating a Settlement in Northern Ireland, 1969–2019* traces the roots and out-workings of the Agreement, focussing on the British and Irish governments, their changing policy paradigms, and their extended negotiations, from the Sunningdale conference of 1973 to the St Andrews Agreement of 2006. It identifies three dimensions of change that paved the way for agreement: in the evolution of elite understanding of sovereignty, in the development of wide-ranging and complex modes of power-sharing, and in the interrelated emergence of substantial equality in the socio-economic, cultural, and political domains. The book combines wide-ranging analysis with unparalleled use of witness seminars and interviews where the most senior British and Irish politicians, civil servants, and advisors discuss the process of coming to agreement. In tracing the processes by which British and Irish perspectives converged to address the Northern Ireland conflict, the book provides a benchmark against which the ongoing impact of Brexit on the Good Friday Agreement can be assessed.

John Coakley is a Fellow of the Geary Institute for Public Policy at University College Dublin.

Jennifer Todd is a Fellow of the Geary Institute for Public Policy at University College Dublin.

Negotiating a Settlement in Northern Ireland, 1969–2019

JOHN COAKLEY AND JENNIFER TODD

OXFORD
UNIVERSITY PRESS

OXFORD
UNIVERSITY PRESS

Great Clarendon Street, Oxford, OX2 6DP,
United Kingdom

Oxford University Press is a department of the University of Oxford.
It furthers the University's objective of excellence in research, scholarship,
and education by publishing worldwide. Oxford is a registered trade mark of
Oxford University Press in the UK and in certain other countries

© John Coakley and Jennifer Todd 2020

The moral rights of the authors have been asserted

First published 2020
First published in paperback 2023

Published in the United States of America by Oxford University Press
198 Madison Avenue, New York, NY 10016, United States of America

British Library Cataloguing in Publication Data
Data available

Library of Congress Cataloging in Publication Data
Data available

ISBN 978-0-19-884138-8 (Hbk.)
ISBN 978-0-19-888282-4 (Pbk.)

DOI: 10.1093/oso/9780198841388.001.0001

Preface

The Northern Ireland conflict and settlement provide a very rich source of comparative and historical insight. The conflict spanned a quarter of a century, preoccupied the British and Irish states, generated a sequence of state-initiated settlement attempts, and finally led to the Good Friday Agreement of 1998, which has produced an extended period of peace and relative stability. The manner in which the two states managed the process, the circumstances that made it so difficult, and the preconditions for settlement are the topic of this book.

The book has two aims. First, we seek to make an original contribution to the analysis of the peace and settlement process, one that builds on a very wide range of primary source material and that engages with key themes in the literature on the institutions of peace building. Second, we provide the reader with selections of this primary data. At the centre of the book are edited extracts from long witness seminars and interviews with the senior civil servants and politicians who undertook the negotiations. These are framed within analytical discussions about the context, process, and significance of the negotiations and agreements. The primary source material is complemented by an extensive collection of documents that formed the basis of negotiation and were discussed in the witness seminars. Thus the volume provides a distinctive perspective on the Northern Ireland conflict and on the efforts to resolve it. It provides not simply in-depth analysis of negotiations and agreements, but also direct evidence of the elite perspectives and reasoning processes involved, and of the outcomes—the drafts rejected and the agreements ultimately reached. Readers are provided not just with the questions, theories, and conclusions of analysis, but also with the evidence, and with alternative perspectives on events, so that they may engage reflexively in the analysis of the meaning, significance, and lessons of the process.

The oral testimony included in this volume is based on four witness seminars organized by the Institute for British–Irish Studies at University College Dublin, covering the Sunningdale Agreement (1973), the Anglo-Irish Agreement (1985), the Downing Street Declaration (1993), and the implementation of the Good Friday Agreement (1998–2006). The book also includes a series of interviews, conducted between 1998 and 2017, focusing on the negotiations leading to the Frameworks Documents (1995), the Good Friday Agreement (1998), and the St Andrews Agreement (2006). It makes no claim to be comprehensive in its choice or coverage of these episodes, or in the selection of participants. A wider but still far from comprehensive range of perspectives in witness seminars and interviews is lodged in the UCD Archives. The material in this volume is chosen so as to open the door on the inner workings of the states, and to show how the differential perspectives, traditions, and imperatives of the British and Irish states were brought to convergence on Northern Ireland. It shows the hidden and little-acknowledged work—largely by civil servants in conjunction with politicians and advisors—that prepared the ground for the later major political agreements, and for the settlement itself. This is of incomparable intrinsic value. It also forms a focus for our analysis of the patterns and impact of the negotiations, and for reflection and debate by readers.

We have incurred a large number of debts in bringing this book to completion. The book developed from two research projects led by the authors. First, in 1998–2002, a collection of interviews with sixty-five politicians and civil servants involved in the process that led to the Good Friday Agreement was put together by Jennifer Todd. It was funded by the John Whyte Trust Fund and the Joseph Rowntree Charitable Trust. Part of this collection forms the basis of Chapter 5.

Second, in 2007–10, the authors directed a more extensive and systematic project, 'Breaking the Patterns of Conflict', involving key participants in the negotiating process—eighty-eight in one-to-one interviews and fifty-four in six 'witness seminars'. It was funded by the Irish Research Council for the Humanities and Social Sciences (now the Irish Research Council). Four of the witness seminars formed the main source for the oral material presented in the book.

The recordings and transcripts of these interviews and seminars have been deposited in the UCD Archive for use by other scholars, and we are indebted to the funding agencies just mentioned for making this possible. We are also grateful for the support of the UCD College of Social Sciences and Law, the UCD Geary Institute, the UCD School of Politics and International Relations, and the UCD Institute for British–Irish Studies; the School of History, Anthropology, Philosophy and Politics, Queen's University Belfast; and the Political Studies Association of Ireland.

It is a pleasure also to record our warm thanks to the several colleagues and researchers who gave their time so generously to work on this project, always with commitment and dedication. Those who assisted in this way by helping to organize, conduct, transcribe, or edit the interviews and seminars include Michael Anderson, Lauryn Cash, Sophie Clingan-Darack, Jessica Leigh Doyle, Anne Alexandra Fournier, Theo Honohan, Jennifer Jackson, Cliona Kealy, Edwin Kelly, Ronan Kennedy, Kevin LaBarge, Robert Mauro, Susan McDermott, Ricki Schoen, and Heidi Riley, and, in the earlier period, Mark Crystall, Claire Mitchell, Muiris MacCarthaigh, and Adrian Millar. We are particularly indebted to Dara Gannon, manager of the Institute for British–Irish Studies, for her crucial work in coordinating the project, to Christopher Farrington, who played a major role in planning and launching it, and to the late Ronan Fanning, who brought his own erudition to the seminars.

Other colleagues, civil servants, and politicians with inside knowledge of the process helped us in a range of ways. These include a number of serving and retired British and Irish civil servants whose advice was invaluable. We thank Kate Manning for her work in preparing the entire collection of material for deposit in UCD Archives, and the staff of the Irish National Archives, the Public Record Office of Northern Ireland, the National Archives, Kew, the Linenhall Library, Belfast, and the libraries of University College Dublin and Queen's University Belfast for their assistance.

Most of all, however, we wish to record our thanks to the participants in the witness seminars and interviews that form the central part of this book: Bertie Ahern, †Antony Alcock, Lord Robert Armstrong, Lord Robin Butler, Austin Currie, Sir Jeffrey Donaldson, Seán Donlon, Noel Dorr, Mark Durkan, Seán Farren, †Garret FitzGerald, †Sir David Goodall, Lord Peter Hain, Ted Hallett, †Mahon Hayes, Walter Kirwan, Colm Larkin, Michael Lillis, Hugh Logue, †Muiris Mac Conghail, Sir John Major, Tony McCusker, †Frank Murray, †Dermot Nally, Seán Ó hUiginn, John Swift, and Sir Quentin Thomas. They generously gave their time, and dealt untiringly, courteously, and patiently with our many queries.

In particular, we would like to thank Noel Dorr, a former Chair of the Institute for British–Irish Studies, for correcting not just his own contributions but also those of the late Dermot Nally and Garret FitzGerald, whose families also approved the project. We owe special thanks to Seán Donlon and Walter Kirwan for contributing notes on the development of key institutions on the Irish side; to Michael Kennedy, Chris Maccabe, CB, and Martin Mansergh for advice and assistance on a range of matters, and to the late Sir George Quigley, also a former Chair of the Institute for British-Irish Studies, for his encouragement.

Finally, we would like to thank those who helped to bring this book to completion: Dominic Byatt, Olivia Wells and Céline Louasli of Oxford University Press, Priyanka Swansi who oversaw its production, and Hilary Walford for her exemplary work as copy editor.

Contents

List of Figures

List of Tables

List of Appendices and Documents

Appendices

Documents

Abbreviations

AIIC	Anglo-Irish Intergovernmental Council
AIIGC	Anglo-Irish Intergovernmental Conference
ANC	African National Congress
BIC	British–Irish Council
BIIGC	British–Irish Intergovernmental Conference
BSE	bovine spongiform encephalopathy ('mad cow disease')
CAP	Common Agricultural Policy
CIÉ	Córas Iompair Éireann (Irish state transport authority)
DCAL	Department of Culture, Arts and Leisure
DFA	Department of Foreign Affairs
DUP	Democratic Unionist Party
EC	European Community
ECHR	European Convention on Human Rights
EEC	European Economic Community
EPU	Economic Policy Unit
EU	European Union
FÁS	Foras Áiseanna Saothair (Irish state employment training agency)
FCO	Foreign and Commonwealth Office
FEC	Fair Employment Commission
FF	Fianna Fáil
FG	Fine Gael
GAA	Gaelic Athletic Association
GOC	General Officer Commanding
IDA	Industrial Development Authority (Republic of Ireland)
IDB	Industrial Development Board (Northern Ireland)
IDU	Inter-Departmental Unit on the North of Ireland/Northern Ireland
INLA	Irish National Liberation Army
Interreg	EU programme supporting regional cooperation
IRA	Irish Republican Army
MLA	Member of the Legislative Assembly
MOD	Ministry of Defence
NAI	National Archives of Ireland
NI	Northern Ireland
NIHRC	Northern Ireland Human Rights Commission
NIO	Northern Ireland Office
NORAID	Irish Northern Aid Committee (US-based republican support group)
NSMC	North/South Ministerial Council
OFM/DFM	Office of First Minister and Deputy First Minister
PSNI	Police Service of Northern Ireland

PUP	Progressive Unionist Party
RIC	Royal Irish Constabulary
RUC	Royal Ulster Constabulary
RTÉ	Raidió Teilifís Éireann (Irish state broadcasting authority)
SACHR	Standing Advisory Committee on Human Rights
SDLP	Social Democratic and Labour Party
STV	single transferable vote
SOLAS	Irish further education and training agency
TD	Teachta Dála (Dáil deputy; plural, Teachtaí Dála)
UCD	University College Dublin
UCDA	University College Dublin Archives
UDP	Ulster Democratic Party
UDR	Ulster Defence Regiment
UUP	Ulster Unionist Party
UWC	Ulster Workers' Council

Note on Documents

In selecting documents for inclusion in this book, we have in each case sought to use the most authoritative or the most appropriate version of the text (there are commonly minor differences between versions). We have retained spelling, punctuation and capitalization as in the original, except where there was an obvious and serious misprint, punctuation error or inconsistency in capitalization. Dashes, quotation marks and bulleted and numbered lists have been standardized. Editorial interventions are where appropriate indicated by use of square brackets, but square brackets were in some cases part of the original document; we have indicated the significance of these in a note at the end of any document where this applies.

1

Introduction: Defining Moments in the British-Irish Relationship

1.1. Introduction

The Good Friday Agreement of 1998 was one of the great achievements of the late twentieth century. It helped bring peace to the island of Ireland. It had symbolic importance for other divided societies, as a model of how the remaking of interstate relations can help resolve the most difficult of conflicts, a lesson centrally important for the European Union. It was made possible by a decades-long process of British–Irish negotiations and state realignments. This book focuses on these negotiations, outlining the processes by which successive agreements were reached, and analysing the principles and practices that underlay them.

The implications of the Good Friday Agreement and the mechanisms needed to uphold it have come into focus again two decades later. As the consequences of the UK's imminent departure from the European Union were assessed throughout all its member states and institutions, it became clear that this was likely to endanger the Agreement.[1] While struggling to finalize a draft agreement for Brexit, therefore, the European Council and Commission stressed the need to safeguard another, the Good Friday Agreement.[2] The outworkings of this commitment have generated intense debates in the British parliament and sequential crises in the Brexit negotiations into 2019. Whatever the eventual outcome, relations between communities within Northern Ireland, between Northern Ireland and the UK government, between the two parts of the island of Ireland, and between Britain and Ireland have been profoundly disrupted. It is therefore all the more important to understand the principles and processes that made possible the 1998 Agreement and that sustained it.

---

[1] For analyses and assessments of the impact of Brexit on Northern Ireland, see Doyle and Connolly (2017); Harvey (2018); Hayward and Murphy (2018); Humphreys (2018); Mars et al (2018); Murphy (2014); Murphy (2018) Phinnemore and Hayward (2017); Stevenson (2017); Tannam (2018); Todd (2015); Tonge (2017).

[2] In April 2017 the European Council adopted a solemn commitment in its Brexit negotiating guidelines, noting its consistent support for 'the goal of peace and reconciliation enshrined in the Good Friday Agreement in all its parts', and pledging itself to protect 'the achievements, benefits and commitments of the peace process'; see Special meeting of the European Council (art. 50) (29 April 2017)—Guidelines; <www.consilium.europa.eu/media/21763/29-euco-art50-guidelinesen.pdf> (accessed 9 May 2019).

Negotiating a Settlement in Northern Ireland, 1969–2019.
John Coakley and Jennifer Todd, Oxford University Press (2020). © John Coakley and Jennifer Todd.
DOI: 10.1093/oso/9780198841388.001.0001

The Good Friday Agreement was concluded following seven months of intense negotiations. But these months were preceded by over four years during which paramilitary ceasefires were negotiated, and by three decades of intermittent discussions between governments and parties. In the two decades after the Agreement, the British and Irish governments acted together to implement its provisions, strengthen its institutions, and incentivize the Northern Ireland parties to participate in them. This book gives unprecedented access to the thinking of some of the major actors in the British–Irish relationship over almost a half century, while contextualizing and analysing the impact of the long process of interstate negotiation and change. It provides an outline of the achievements of successive British–Irish agreements, and their outworking in Northern Ireland. It thus lays out the benchmarks of successful conflict management against which changes in contemporary British politics and British–Irish processes can be assessed, and in respect of which their impact on Northern Ireland can be evaluated.

The settlement of the Northern Ireland conflict was a singular achievement brought about in important part by the efforts of the British and Irish states.[3] The governments' successive rounds of negotiations changed the geopolitical context so as to provide the conflicting political parties with windows of opportunity for compromise. Interstate negotiations led directly and indirectly to changes in policy priorities, and in particular to a determination to secure a regime of equality and rights in Northern Ireland. Thus the series of negotiations between the British and Irish governments generated outcomes that changed the sociopolitical structure and the assumptions of the parties in Northern Ireland in ways that made settlement possible.

The Northern Ireland peace and settlement process has attracted a very large literature, which we will discuss further. In this book, however, we adopt a distinctive approach, presenting the 'view from within', in the words of the state actors themselves. Chapters 2–6 of the book provide edited transcripts of discussions (in witness seminars and interviews) about intergovernmental and inter-party negotiations by those involved in them. They focus on critical points in the evolution of the British–Irish relationship since the beginning of the 1970s: the Sunningdale Agreement (1973), the Anglo-Irish Agreement (1985), the Downing Street Declaration and the Framework Documents that followed (1993 and 1995), the making of the Good Friday Agreement (1998), and the path towards its implementation through supplementary agreements (1998–2006). We keep these edited discussions separate from our own contextualization and analysis, which are presented in Chapters 1 and 7, and in the introductory sections of Chapters 2–6. To these chapters we have added appendices reproducing selected

---

[3] This was, of course, in association with the political parties and interests in Northern Ireland.

relevant documents, mainly obtained from the Irish and British national archives, in order to provide further context for the discussions of the participants.

We have deliberately chosen to focus on one aspect of the negotiations and discussions, that involving British and Irish politicians and civil servants, and in some cases their Northern Irish counterparts. This shines light down the dark tunnel of interstate negotiation. There are other tunnels, some even darker: relations within and between more militant parties, for example, and relations between these parties and the governments. Here we focus only on one part of the story, one for which we have been able to assemble a formidable amount of original material that offers new insights into important developments in the peace and settlement process. This material comprises the recollections and interpretations, as recorded in witness seminars and interviews, of those centrally involved in the negotiation process at selected critical junctures—principally officials and advisors, and sometimes politicians.[4] Collectively, their discussions document an evolution in thinking in relation to constitutional matters, a shift in perspectives on access to and sharing of power, and a new recognition of the importance of equality and rights in every field. These discussions by those at the centre of the state provide unparalleled insight into how subtle but important changes in state policy paradigms and practices take place.

In this introductory chapter, we set the context for the five chapters that follow, each of which focuses on one specific moment in the British–Irish negotiation process since 1973; the final chapter discusses the lessons of the process and returns to the analytical themes raised in this introduction. We begin by presenting the broad historical pattern that formed the context for the episodes discussed in detail in the chapters that follow. We continue by outlining the methods through which we organized the witness seminars and interviews that form the core of our information base, and by assessing the value of oral evidence in social scientific research. We conclude by discussing the institutional context within which the contributors to this process were embedded—the framework that defined the position of the *dramatis personae* in the course of the negotiations.

1.2. The Conflict and its Context

The road to peace in Northern Ireland is important not just as an instance of successful conflict management, but also as a model for possible application elsewhere. The conflict spanned a quarter century, cost more than 3,500 lives, caused tens of thousands of injuries, and placed an exceptional and costly burden on the British and Irish states. It also generated a sequence of state-initiated

---

[4] For biographical notes on those whose contributions are included in the present volume, see Appendix 1.2.

settlement attempts, most significantly the Good Friday (Belfast) Agreement of 1998, which has led to an extended period of peace and relative stability. The manner in which the two states managed the process, the circumstances that made it so difficult, and the preconditions for settlement remain topics of a very extensive descriptive and analytical literature.[5]

In this chapter, we contextualize the events discussed in witness seminars and interviews and show how the evidence presented in them can help to advance analysis of the negotiating process and its impact on conflict. The rest of this section addresses five broad topics:

- the evolution of the British–Irish relationship in the decades before the civil unrest began;
- the series of initiatives taken by governments and parties in pursuing an accommodation;
- the long-term political trends that underlay the negotiating process;
- the shifting demographic and socioeconomic relationships that provided momentum for the negotiations; and
- the recurring themes that characterized the content and course of conflict, that partly defined the shape of settlement, and that remained important in subsequent years.

We return to these themes in the final chapter, which draws lessons from the process.

1.2.1. The British–Irish Relationship after Partition

When the Irish and British governments first began to engage together in addressing the Northern Ireland conflict in the early 1970s, their respective positions were conditioned by a half-century of mutual antagonism. In the aftermath of partition in 1921 and the creation of the Irish Free State in 1922, two big issues remained unresolved. The first was partition itself. Irish nationalists intuitively and unquestioningly equated the nation with the population of the island of Ireland. But the Government of Ireland Act of 1920 and the Anglo-Irish Treaty of 1921 had provided for the secession of the six counties of Northern Ireland, and this was confirmed by a trilateral agreement in 1925, by which the Irish, British, and Northern Irish governments confirmed the existing location of

---

[5] For recent introductory and analytical accounts of the conflict and settlement, see Aughey (2005); McGrattan (2010); McKittrick (2012); Tonge (2002, 2005). For a useful chronology, see Bew and Gillespie (1999); for a directory of organizations and individuals, Elliott and Flackes (1999); and for comprehensive background information, the CAIN website (CAIN 2019). Comprehensive interpretations, including those of the authors, are referred to below.

the border.[6] At the level of the Irish constitution, the partition issue was 'resolved' in 1937, when article 2 of the new constitution defined the 'national territory' as comprising 'the island of Ireland, its islands, and the territorial seas', though article 3 acknowledged that the state's jurisdiction did not extend over this. At the level of political rhetoric, the territorial claim was articulated periodically and often stridently, if also ineffectually. Strong nationalist demands, indeed, often had an effect opposite to that intended. Thus the British response to the declaration of the Republic of Ireland in 1948–9 was enactment of the Ireland Act, 1949, which reinforced Northern Ireland's position as part of the United Kingdom, by providing that 'in no event will Northern Ireland or any part thereof cease to be part of His Majesty's dominions and of the United Kingdom without the consent of the Parliament of Northern Ireland'.

The second big issue was the political subordination of the new state to its larger neighbour. The 1921 Treaty had conceded no more than dominion status, not independent statehood, to the Irish Free State. Although its government sought, with some success, to expand its independence as far as possible within this constraint, the consolidation of independence took place only gradually. The Executive Authority (External Relations) Act, 1936, used the occasion of the abdication of King Edward VIII to remove the crown from domestic Irish politics. The constitution of 1937 emphasized the de facto independence of the state—for example, by replacing the governor-general by a directly elected president, whose functions, however, were confined to the domestic arena. The Anglo-Irish Agreements of 1938 brought an 'economic war' with the UK to an end and handed British naval facilities in counties Cork, Kerry, and Donegal to the Irish (thus facilitating the country's wartime neutrality). The Republic of Ireland Act, 1948, terminated the role of the king in Ireland's external affairs and severed the link with the Commonwealth. Disparity in size, a heritage of economic dependence, and the persistence of post-colonial attitudes nevertheless sustained inequality and asymmetry in the Irish–British relationship until the latter part of the twentieth century. One of the most far-reaching developments in promoting Irish 'catch-up' was the 1972 treaty of accession to the European Economic Community (EEC), which admitted the two states on a basis of formal equality to membership of what would eventually become the European Union.

When civil unrest broke out in Northern Ireland in 1968, neither state had developed a clear analysis of the problem or a strategy for dealing with it (see Prince 2018; Purdie 1990; Williamson 2017). The British government had adopted a policy of not intervening in any matter that fell under the jurisdiction of the Northern Ireland government, a jurisdiction whose scope was interpreted as extending over a very wide range of issues; and a parliamentary convention in

---

[6] The 1925 agreement also terminated embryonic institutionalized political links between North and South through a Council of Ireland and made certain financial concessions to the Irish Free State.

Westminster precluded MPs from raising any matter for which responsibility had been devolved (Gibbons 2018). Meanwhile, notwithstanding articles 2 and 3 of the Irish constitution, the Irish government had no role or presence north of the border, was rigorously excluded from any involvement in the affairs of Northern Ireland, had few avenues of information, and had no developed policy (Dorr 2017: 35–49; Ivory 2014; Ó Beacháin 2019).

With the exception of a few episodes of cooperation, formal relations between the two sovereign states tended to be poor (Kennedy 2000).[7] This was not altogether surprising, considering the geopolitical and cultural dynamics of relationships between a great power and an adjacent former subject territory. The problems in the relationship ranged from the capacity of the dominant state to exercise real power in matters affecting its smaller neighbour to everyday irritants that had limited policy implications. To the former belonged such momentous policy developments as the decision to seek EEC membership (given its economic dependence on trade with the United Kingdom, Ireland had little choice other than to follow the British lead). To the latter belonged the refusal by each state to accept even the name of the other. From Dublin's perspective, the expression 'United Kingdom of Great Britain and Northern Ireland' was unacceptable, since it implied a right to rule Northern Ireland (which, in any case, was usually described in Dublin as the 'Six Counties').[8] From London's perspective, the name of the other state was 'Eire', or perhaps the 'Irish Republic', or maybe even the 'Republic of Ireland'—but never 'Ireland' simpliciter, the name on which Irish diplomats insisted (Coakley 2009a).

The traditional pattern of relations between the British and Irish governments was severely jolted by the social and political turmoil that began in Northern Ireland in the late 1960s and that quickly developed into organized and widespread violence in the early 1970s. The instability and eventual demise of the old regime led to a new, intense set of interactions and negotiations. The civil-rights marches of 1968 and the popular unrest and political violence that escalated in the early 1970s convinced Irish governments that, without prejudice to constitutional principle, some form of practical engagement with political forces in Northern Ireland was essential to prevent further escalation of conflict and inevitable overspill across the border. These same factors, and the obvious incapacity of

[7] So too did relations between Northern Ireland and the Republic of Ireland, with the exception of two meetings between the heads of government–Seán Lemass and Terence O'Neill–in early 1965, and two meetings in late 1967 and early 1968 between O'Neill and Lemass's successor as Taoiseach, Jack Lynch.

[8] This practice changed only in the early 1970s, when 'Northern Ireland' gradually replaced 'The Six Counties' in official references to the northern state. This change in nomenclature is reflected in official publications, as illustrated by the case of the Central Statistics Office. Its annual *Statistical Abstract of Ireland* included an appendix on 'The Six Counties' until its 1969 edition (published in 1971). In the next edition (for 1970–1, published in 1974), and subsequently, this appendix was headed 'Northern Ireland'. References to the same territory in the monthly *Trade Statistics of Ireland* used 'The Six Counties' until December 1972, but then switched to 'Northern Ireland' in January 1973.

the Northern Ireland regime to sustain itself, persuaded British governments of the need to reach a *modus vivendi* with the Irish side in the pursuit of a longer-term solution.

1.2.2. The Pursuit of a Constitutional Settlement

The collapse of the old regime in Northern Ireland, with the suspension of the devolved institutions in March 1972, followed more than three years of public unrest, civil protest, and armed violence. Legally and constitutionally, responsibility rested with the British government, but from an early stage Irish government involvement was accepted in practice by the British side. This was a response to the need to encourage moderate nationalists in Northern Ireland to accept the legitimacy of the new regime, and it also recognized the implications of the conflict for political, social, and economic life in the Republic.

Almost from the beginning, it became clear that three conditions would have to underlie any new set of structures designed to replace those that had collapsed: the new arrangements would have to be based on a sharing of power between the two communities in Northern Ireland; they would have to incorporate an 'Irish dimension' (implying institutionalized links between North and South); and they would have to respect the 'principle of consent' (interpreted as meaning that a united Ireland would come about only with the democratic consent of a majority in Northern Ireland). Although the Irish constitution of 1937 embodied a commitment to unity as an ideal, successive Irish governments now began to accept the 'principle of consent' as a requirement in practice. Indeed, while the two governments wavered from time to time in the extent to which they insisted on each of these three conditions, the conditions have remained central in subsequent efforts to devise a solution. They are frequently referred to in the witness seminars in later chapters.

Before going on to look at the political forces and socioeconomic pressures that defined the context of the negotiation process, it is worth offering an overview of the shape of this process itself. We may summarize efforts since 1972 to arrive at a political settlement by highlighting twelve specific episodes (the chapters that follow demonstrate the threads of continuity that run through these).[9]

- The Sunningdale Agreement (1973): a commitment to establish a North–South Council of Ireland based on certain other trade-offs including recognition of the 'principle of consent'; it was preceded by several months of talks, the election of an assembly and the provisional designation of a

---

[9] For overviews of the negotiation and peace process from a number of perspectives, see Cochrane (2013); Gilligan and Tonge (1997); Kerr (2011); Mitchell (2015); and Wilford (2001).

power-sharing executive; the initiative collapsed when the executive was forced to resign following a political strike organized by unionists in May 1974.

- The Constitutional Convention (1975): a body elected in Northern Ireland to devise new government structures there compatible with the three fundamental conditions already outlined; it came to an end in 1976 without succeeding in this.
- The Atkins Talks (1980): a set of meetings between the Northern Ireland parties convened by Northern Ireland Secretary Humphrey Atkins in an effort to establish common ground between them and to assess possible solutions; they failed to produce agreement.
- The Prior 'Rolling Devolution' Initiative (1982): a plan to use a Northern Ireland assembly elected initially as a deliberative body as one to which power would be progressively devolved in areas where substantial consensus emerged; boycotted by nationalists, the experiment made little progress, but was not formally wound up until 1986.
- The Anglo-Irish Agreement (1985): an international agreement between the British and Irish governments that did not involve the Northern Ireland parties; it offered the Irish government an institutional voice in the internal affairs of Northern Ireland through a new Anglo-Irish Intergovernmental Conference.
- The Brooke–Mayhew Talks (1991–2): a set of talks convened initially by Northern Ireland Secretary Peter Brooke, and involving the Northern Ireland political parties (excluding Sinn Féin) and the British and Irish governments; they were continued by his successor, Sir Patrick Mayhew, but concluded in November 1992 without yielding agreement.
- The Downing Street Declaration (1993): a document agreed by the British and Irish governments and announced by Prime Minister John Major and Taoiseach Albert Reynolds, stating the principles on which the governments would attempt to negotiate a settlement to the Northern Ireland conflict; it was intended to assist in bringing about an IRA ceasefire.
- The Framework Documents (1995): two blueprints for the future of Northern Ireland; one, drawn up by the British and Irish governments and announced by Prime Minister John Major and Taoiseach John Bruton, dealt with the North–South and East–West relationships; the other, announced by the British government, proposed structures for the future internal government of Northern Ireland.
- The Multiparty Talks (1996–8) and the Good Friday (Belfast) Agreement (1998): a comprehensive effort to settle the conflict not only by incorporating three parameters from past negotiations (power-sharing, the Irish dimension, and consent) but by addressing the full range of issues in dispute, from security to transborder institutions, from equality and cultural rights to the position of victims; it incorporated a formal British–Irish agreement that in turn included all of the provisions of the multi-party agreement.

- The St Andrews Agreement (2006): a compromise package that made minor adjustments to the Good Friday Agreement with a view to securing acceptance by the Democratic Unionist Party (DUP) and to removing Sinn Féin reservations about policing, and to encouraging these parties to play a leading role in the Northern Ireland Executive.
- The Hillsborough Castle Agreement (2010): a supplementary deal that addressed certain outstanding matters and provided for the devolution of responsibility for policing and justice.
- The Stormont House Agreement (2014): an accord between the governments and most of the parties on certain legacy issues (notably identity-related and historical ones), and also on some new matters (including welfare reform); it was followed by a 'Fresh Start' Agreement (2015) intended to secure implementation of this.

While these were the most important initiatives designed to devise agreed new structures of government for Northern Ireland, account should be taken of other deliberative exercises that sought to feed into perspectives on constitutional options. Four of these played a significant role in shaping the thinking of individuals and parties. The New Ireland Forum (1983–4) was a structure created by the Irish government to consider constitutional options for the island of Ireland; although initially intended as inclusive, only the representatives of the three main southern parties (Fianna Fáil, Fine Gael, and Labour) and the main nationalist party in Northern Ireland (the Social Democratic and Labour Party (SDLP)) fully participated; the Forum identified three institutional models for the future relationship of Northern Ireland with the Republic. The Kilbrandon Committee (1984) was a private initiative that brought academic and political figures together to explore the practical implications of the options identified by the New Ireland Forum.[10] The Opsahl Commission (1992–3), created by a group of individuals concerned at the absence of political progress in Northern Ireland, sought to provide a voice for ordinary citizens rather than offering a specific constitutional or institutional solution. The Forum for Peace and Reconciliation (1994–6) was an Irish government initiative to bring together the main political parties on the island to review constitutional options (although once again the unionist parties did not attend); one of its central contributions was to offer a space for Sinn Féin to become involved in the political talks process.[11]

[10] This is not to be confused with the Kilbrandon Commission, a royal commission of inquiry into the territorial government of the United Kingdom chaired by the same person (1969–73).
[11] Two of these bodies were named after their chairs, Lord Kilbrandon, a Scottish judge (1906–89), and Torkel Opsahl, a Norwegian human-rights lawyer (1931–93). The New Ireland Forum was chaired by Colm Ó hEocha, President of University College Galway (1926–97), and the Forum for Peace and Reconciliation by Catherine McGuinness, then a Circuit Court judge (b. 1934).

1.2.3. The Political Context

The initiatives just described took place within a context of uneven political change in Northern Ireland. This was to lead ultimately to a transformation of political relations within and between the two communities in Northern Ireland, and awareness of these changes shaped the mentalities of participants in the talks processes.

The first and most visible change was in the area of security. Loyalist paramilitaries were responsible for three murders already in 1966. The outbreak of civil unrest in 1969 resulted in a spiral of violence that escalated rapidly. The data are summarized starkly in Table 1.1, which groups them into five relatively clearly defined periods:

- 1969–70, escalating disorder: civil unrest aggravated by loyalist and republican paramilitary activity;
- 1971–6, peak violence: republican mobilization and bombing campaign followed by loyalist reaction and sectarian murders;
- 1977–93, contained violence: tapering-off of level of violence, and stalemate between the contending groups, but continuing paramilitary campaigns;
- 1994–2005, disturbed peace: formal ceasefires by the major groups but continuing activities by dissident paramilitary groups and others;
- 2006–17, nonviolent coexistence: formal peace boosted by IRA decommissioning and renewed agreement.

Table 1.1. Phases in political violence in Northern Ireland, 1969–2017

Period	Shootings	Bomb devices	Fatalities
Number			
1969–70	286	180	42
1971–6	24,325	7,828	1,752
1977–93	10,099	6,653	1,519
1994–2005	2,672	1,765	242
2006–17	737	589	31
1969–2017 (all)	38,119	17,015	3,586
Annual average			
1969–70	143	90	21
1971–6	4,054	1,305	292
1977–93	594	391	89
1994–2005	223	147	20
2006–17	61	49	3
1969–2017 (all)	778	347	73

Note: Data refer to incidents in Northern Ireland only.

Source: Computed from Police Service of Northern Ireland (2018).

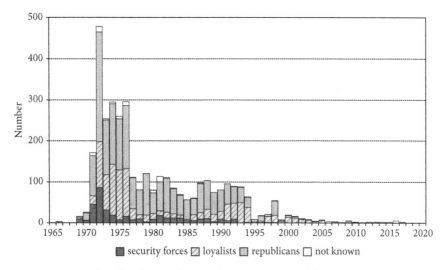

Figure 1.1. Deaths related to civil unrest by group responsible, 1966–2018

Source: Derived from Malcolm Sutton database at <cain.ulst.ac.uk/sutton/>, updated by data on the CAIN website (CAIN 2019) and the website of the Police Service of Northern Ireland (Police Service of Northern Ireland 2019).

The peak period (1971–6) accounted for 64 per cent of the 38,000 shooting incidents over the period 1969–2017, 46 per cent of the bomb devices used or located over the same period, and 49 per cent of the 3,586 deaths resulting from the associated civil conflict.

The profile of deaths arising from the civil unrest may be explored in greater detail as an indicator of changing levels of political violence. Figure 1.1 illustrates this pattern from 1966 to 2017.[12] It summarizes the security background at the time when the political initiatives just listed took place: the first two at a time of intense violence, the middle six (mainly talks processes) at a period of reduced but significant conflict, and the remainder following a major reduction in violence in the aftermath of the 1994 ceasefires. There was, of course, a symbiotic relationship between intensity of violence and potential for political progress: high levels of violence and associated bitterness undermined the capacity for successful negotiation, while negotiated agreements that made a real difference to Northern Ireland helped to reduce the intensity of violence. The diminution of violence in the early twenty-first century attests to the success of the initiatives discussed in this volume in bringing peace to Northern Ireland.

The path towards a political resolution in Northern Ireland was shaped not so much by violence as by efforts to sideline this or to channel it into conventional

---

[12] The first deaths in the late twentieth century that may be related to the tension underlying the later civil conflict took place in 1966, before the outbreak of sustained unrest.

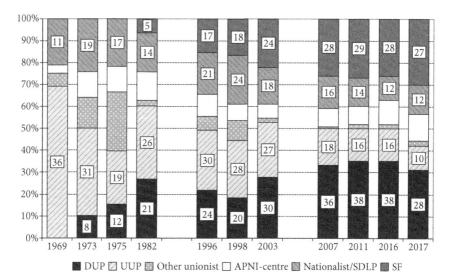

Figure 1.2. Party composition of Northern Ireland representative bodies, 1969–2017

Note: Figures refer to numbers of seats for the four largest parties. 'UUP' includes also, in 1969, 13 'Anti-O'Neill' members and in 1973 9 'Anti-White Paper' members; 'Other unionist' includes the Vanguard Unionist Party (9 seats in 1973, 14 in 1975) and the Unionist Party of Northern Ireland (5 seats in 1975) as well as smaller unionist parties; 'APNI-centre' includes the Alliance Party and other minor parties of the centre; 'Nationalist/SDLP' includes 6 members of the Nationalist Party and 5 others in 1969. The total number of seats was 52 (House of Commons, 1969), 78 (Assembly, Convention and new Assembly, 1973–82), 110 (Forum, 1996), 108 (Assembly, 1998–2016), and 90 (Assembly, 2017).

Source: ARK (2019); Elliott (1973).

political activity. The shape of political opinion was critical in determining the character and relative strength of the parties engaged in negotiations. Figure 1.2 reports the results of elections to each representative body at Northern Ireland level since 1969, indicating the number of seats won by the several parties.

Four broad trends are worth noting. First, there was initially a marked fragmentation of unionism, all the more surprising given its political monopoly in this part of Ireland since 1885. Already by 1969 the long-standing dominance of the Ulster Unionist Party (UUP), which had always eclipsed the venerable party that represented Catholic interests, the Nationalist Party, was being challenged within the unionist bloc, as the traditional two-party system was replaced by a multiparty one. The DUP ultimately supplanted the UUP in 2003 as the dominant force within the Protestant community, and it subsequently consolidated this position. Second, precisely as unionism was splintering in the 1970s, Catholic support (traditionally fragmented) was consolidating around the SDLP. As Sinn Féin embarked down a political path in the 1980s, it was able first strongly to challenge and then, also in 2003, to replace the SDLP as the main nationalist party. Like the DUP, it subsequently reinforced this position of communal dominance. Third, notwithstanding the polarization of the party system, there was always sizeable support for cross-communal politics. With the demise of the Northern Ireland Labour Party in the 1970s, this position was taken by the Alliance Party; the Women's Coalition and the Green Party also played an important role in representing a middle ground. Finally, there is a long-term decline in unionist electoral support, with near parity between nationalists and unionists recorded at the 2017 Assembly election.

1.2.4. The Demographic and Socioeconomic Contexts

The shifting balance of political power—both between and within blocs—reflects underlying patterns of demographic and socioeconomic development. Most evident among these has been the gradual increase in the Catholic share of the population recorded since the 1971 census. The 2011 census showed Catholics (by community background) as accounting for 45 per cent of the population, and Protestants for 48 per cent, and the trends suggest that the next census, in 2021, will record substantial parity between these two groups. As matters stand, Catholics outnumber Protestants in all five-year age cohorts below the age of 40, pointing to a time in the near future when Catholics will outnumber Protestants first in the overall population and later in the electorate.

The resurgence of the Catholic population extends also to the labour force, where Catholics were traditionally associated with lower-status positions and economic sectors, and with higher levels of unemployment. Early attempts to overcome the profound inequalities that characterized the Northern Ireland labour market made direct discrimination illegal and sought to ensure equality of opportunity (the Fair Employment Act, 1976, which provided for a new Fair Employment Agency, is an example). But this had limited impact. A more interventionist strategy was adopted later, when new legislation, the Fair Employment Act, 1989, led to the targeting of indirect as well as direct discrimination and to the creation of a Fair Employment Commission with enhanced powers, including a remit to monitor the religious background of the employed workforce. A still more powerful Equality Commission replaced the Fair Employment Commission in 1999 in the aftermath of the Good Friday Agreement.

The effect of these measures is to be seen in Figure 1.3, which looks at changes in the overall composition of the working-age population and at selected components of the monitored workforce.[13] The gap between the two top lines (Catholics

---

[13] The monitored workforce data refer to Catholics as a percentage of all those whose community background can be established (thus producing higher percentages than if expressed as a proportion of the total population or workforce); for consistency, the working-age population data use the same measurement system.

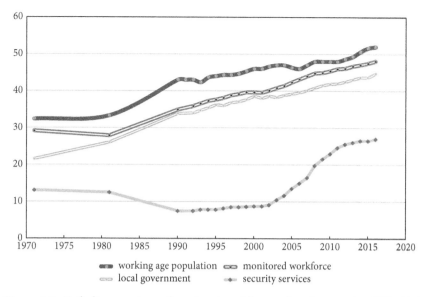

Figure 1.3. Catholic percentage of employed workforce, selected categories, 1971–2017

Note: 'Working-age population' refers to those aged 15–64 (1971–81) and to a similar (but not identical) category subsequently; the data from 1991 onwards are three-year moving averages. The three other lines refer to employed population (1971, 1981) and to monitored employed workforce (1990–2017), and are not precisely comparable across these two groups. All percentages refer to Catholics as a proportion of the total number of Catholics and Protestants.

Source: Computed from Equality Commission for Northern Ireland (2002–17), Executive Office (2018), Northern Ireland General Register Office (1975), and Northern Ireland Registrar General (1984); and associated Excel tables (see <https://www.equalityni.org/> (accessed 21 May 2019)).

as part of the working-age population, and in the monitored workforce) reflects differences in participation in the workforce (for example, because of a high proportion of Catholics in education) as well as long-term unemployment patterns. For important sectors of the workforce, the Catholic percentage is so close to the overall percentage that the resulting lines would be invisible if these were reported in Figure 1.3. For example, over the ten-year period 2007–16 the proportion of Catholics in private-sector employment was only 0.2 per cent below the overall proportion, and the corresponding figure for the civil service was just 0.4 per cent below the overall figure. The continuing under-representation of Catholics in the local-government sector and in particular in the security services (which include not just police but also support staff and other security employees) is clear.[14] With these notable exceptions, the general picture is one of steady growth in the proportion of Catholics both in the working-age population and

---

[14] Note that the percentage of Catholics in the police service is slightly higher than that in the wider security services reported here, which include support staff and other security employees, areas where Catholics are less well represented.

in the workforce, to the point where parity between the two communities has effectively been reached.

Even more telling shifts have been taking place within particular employment sectors, as the traditional position of Catholic over-representation in the lower, less prestigious, and less influential positions was replaced by greater access to senior posts. The 1971 census showed that 'Protestants control the top positions of economic and political power . . . Catholics are concentrated in lower status occupations, generally with minimal political influence or strategic significance'. This meant that, put more vividly, 'while a clerk may be a Catholic, it is more likely that the office manager will be a Protestant; while a skilled craftsman may be a Catholic, it is more likely that the supervisor will be a Protestant; and while a nurse may be a Catholic, it is more likely that the doctor will be a Protestant' (Aunger 1975: 8).

This pattern of what might be described as a 'denominational division of labour' changed sharply after the 1989 Fair Employment Act and had almost disappeared by the 2010s. The proportion of Catholics in managerial positions increased from 16 per cent in 1971 to 44 per cent in 2010; and the percentage of Catholics in the most senior civil-service positions increased from 7 per cent in 1980 to 35 per cent in 2010, and to 44 per cent in 2018. There was also enhanced educational attainment; the Catholic share of those with a degree qualification or higher increased from 27 per cent in 1971 to 44 per cent in 2011. The long-standing disproportionate clustering of Catholics among the ranks of the unemployed has also changed. In 1971, the Catholic male unemployment rate was 17 per cent, by comparison with a Protestant rate of 7 per cent; by 2011 the Catholic rate had dropped to 12 per cent, while the Protestant rate remained at 7 per cent; and by 2016 the Catholic male unemployment rate, at 8 per cent, was only two percentage points greater than the corresponding Protestant rate, 6 per cent.[15]

Steady improvement in the socioeconomic position of Catholics seems to have promoted a softening of Catholic grievance. Thus, in 1968 74 per cent of Catholics reported feeling that they were discriminated against or treated unfairly; by 2012 this had dropped to 14 per cent (Northern Ireland Life and Times Survey 2012; Rose 1971: 272). Meanwhile the political opposition of Protestants to power-sharing has softened. Willingness to contemplate power-sharing or to accept institutional or constitutional arrangements that were traditionally objectionable to one community or the other has, of course, varied over time. So, for example, there was considerably more flexibility in constitutional attitudes in 1967–8 than in the following years

---

[15] These data are calculated from a variety of sources including the censuses of 1971 and 2011 (Northern Ireland 1975; Northern Ireland Statistics and Research Agency 2019), the 2016 labour force survey (Executive Office 2018) and the report on equality statistics for the civil service (Northern Ireland Statistics and Research Agency 2018); see also Gallagher, Osborne, and Cormack (1995); Harbison and Hodges (1991: 189); Osborne and Shuttleworth (2004: 4, 82). In the case of data on the civil service, the base category in 1980 was the top 121 positions (assistant under-secretary or higher); in 2010 the top 300 positions (SOC1); and in 2016 the top 212 positions (grade 5 or higher).

(Whyte 1990: 79), and in attitudes to power-sharing in 1973 than in 1974. Among Protestants, traditionally most opposed to power-sharing, Whyte (1990: 82) notes that only 10–20 per cent positively preferred it in the 1970s and 1980s, although around a half found it acceptable. By 2000, 40 per cent of Protestants supported power-sharing and only 18 per cent opposed it, while by 2011 nearly three-quarters of DUP supporters, and over 80 per cent of other unionists supported this.[16] The momentum towards a willingness to share power seems now to be irreversible.

This pattern of socioeconomic change has transformed fundamentally the power resources at the disposal of the two communities. The shift was in part a consequence of demographic change, in part driven by advances in government policies, and in part a product of shifting global economic processes. These changing relative power resources provided incentives to parties for political compromise, since nationalists could now hope to achieve significant progress politically, and unionists had to compromise to gain some control over the process of change (Ruane and Todd 2007, 2014).

1.2.5. The Parameters of Debate

The negotiations that are discussed in the following chapters varied greatly in their form, in their detailed content, and in those who participated. There were, however, marked continuities in the substance of the talks. These focused on broad sets of issues concerning sovereignty, democracy, and inequality that touched on issues of political principle as well as of social and political interest. These three sets of issues run through the half-century of change covered in this book. Each was eventually resolved, though not necessarily completely, in part through negotiated British–Irish and multi-party agreements, and also through changing policy paradigms on the part of the two states. These sets of issues arise frequently in this book, and we return to them in Chapter 7:

- *competing conceptions of sovereignty and self-determination*, with a steady but by no means unanimous transformation in approaches;
- *clashing images of democracy and governance*, with a prolonged debate about the relative merits of majoritarian democracy and the principles of 'soft' or 'hard' power-sharing;
- *conflicting interpretations of equality and rights*, with disagreements about the appropriate response to inequality (equality of opportunity or of condition, affirmative action or positive discrimination), about the relative balance of rights and security, and about the appropriate content of any bill of rights.

---

[16] See Hayes and McAllister (2013: 141). The general source for the public opinion data quoted here is the annual *Northern Ireland Life and Times Survey* (see Northern Ireland Life and Times 1998–2017).

The question of sovereignty lies only barely beneath the surface in a large number of arenas of dispute in Northern Ireland, and is often revealed in telling form when that surface is scratched. It lies hidden behind disputes over the display of flags and emblems, over parades and marches, and even over the question of tariffs on trade between Northern Ireland and Great Britain that arose during the Brexit negotiations. It has an important bearing on perceptions of legitimacy: on the legitimacy of the rule of the unionist government of Northern Ireland before 1972, on the legitimate existence of Northern Ireland as a unit, on the legitimacy of British sovereignty over Northern Ireland, and on the legitimacy of nationalist opposition to this constitutional configuration (Guelke 1988; McGarry and O'Leary 1995). In the late twentieth century the sovereignty question became increasingly entwined with the 'principle of consent', a deceptively euphemistic label for a fundamentally problematic formula for legitimizing state boundaries, to which we return in Chapter 7. With the Good Friday Agreement, there has been an attempt to move the debate over sovereignty from the question of which state is in control to the question of the sovereign sources of authority and the principles that should govern the behaviour and policies of any state or political system in Northern Ireland (Morison 1999, 2001). Questions about sovereignty in Northern Ireland have acquired renewed salience in the light of the British debate on sovereignty sparked by the Brexit campaign. This is a central thread in all of the chapters that follow.

Contention about forms of democracy may also be deeply divisive. The civil-rights movement in the late 1960s had focused on deficiencies in Northern Ireland's existing system of democracy—for example, gerrymandering of electoral boundaries and restrictions on the franchise at local level that disproportionately affected Catholics. There had long been suspicions that the abolition of proportional representation in the 1920s had been designed to give an advantage to unionists.[17] The suitability of Westminster-style majoritarian democracy for Northern Ireland came into question from 1969 onwards.[18] Successive unionist governments had secured their power by expanding their economic dominance, their monopoly position in the civil service and judiciary, their control over local government and public culture, and their direction of the security forces against nationalist dissent (O'Leary and McGarry 1996; Ruane and Todd 1996).

[17] The reintroduction of the plurality system in Stormont elections in 1929 appears to have been designed to protect the Unionist Party against threats from independent unionists and the Northern Ireland Labour Party, while leaving nationalist representation largely undisturbed but confined to no more than a quarter of all parliamentary seats; Coakley (2009b: 257–8). However, at the level of local elections, the reintroduction of the plurality system, the gerrymandering of electoral boundaries, and the retention of old franchise arrangements were designed to secure unionist majorities in as many areas as possible.
[18] Power-sharing was first suggested by a leading journalist, John Cole, in 1969, and a 'Swiss-style' system of allocation of ministries in proportion to parliamentary seats was advocated by a prominent academic, John Whyte, in 1971; Coakley (2011: 479–80); New Ulster Movement (1971).

Passionate defenders of the 'Westminster model' took the procedures of the 'mother of parliaments' as paradigmatically democratic, thus justifying the systematic exclusion of the nationalist minority from government. But, as the debate moved on, models of power-sharing became more elaborate and more demanding. Power-sharing was understood in 1972–4 primarily as a form of party-political coalition government between the more moderate parties from each bloc and the cross-community Alliance Party. Over time, the international understanding of what was necessary for party-political power-sharing to work was implicitly broadened to include a wide-ranging notion of proportionality in public-sector and security force personnel and resource allocation (Hartzell and Hoddie 2007). By 1998, the understanding of power-sharing government had changed from voluntary and middle-ground coalition to an all-party government where parties' inclusion was determined by their strength in the Assembly (McGarry and O'Leary 2004).

The debate over equality and rights was a reaction to the systematic inequality and discrimination across economic, political, and cultural spheres that had been a central feature of the old regime (Ruane and Todd 1996: 116–203). By 1968, civil-rights opposition to the unionist regime was focused on public policy (electoral gerrymandering, housing and public employment), the security forces (the B-Specials), and the legal apparatus (the Special Powers Act). British outlawing of direct discrimination, as already discussed, had little effect on employment equality in the workplace. It was only following the introduction in 1989 of strong fair employment legislation, which led to monitoring and effective action against indirect discrimination, that communal inequality in employment was substantially reduced. On another front, the Report of the New Ireland Forum (1984) asserted the goal of cultural and national equality in the public sphere (equality of institutional recognition and expression of the two 'traditions' and identities). This aim, though strongly resisted by unionists, merged into a wider 'equality agenda' in the 1990s. This agenda was strengthened by the Good Friday Agreement, but it has remained contested and only partly implemented. Notwithstanding a full overhaul of the policing system, Catholics remain under-represented in the police service, and cultural rights remain in dispute. Although a Human Rights Commission created in 1999 was tasked to devise a bill of rights for Northern Ireland, no such bill was enacted. There was very uneven success in the regulation of cultural equality in such areas as the display of flags and the status of the Irish language.

These three sets of issues were recurrent topics in the negotiations discussed in this book and were key to political debates between nationalists and unionists within Northern Ireland. A fourth set of issues cut across the nationalist–unionist dimension, dividing instead 'hardliners' and moderates in each bloc, and was recurrent in analyses of the Northern Ireland conflict. This set of questions addressed the willingness of the British state seriously to address nationalist grievances and their capacity to broker a lasting settlement between the communities.[19] It centred on the question whether a state-led incremental approach to reform could transform political relations in Northern Ireland. The failure of the Sunningdale experiment in 1974 suggested the incapacity or unwillingness of the British state to push forward with egalitarian reforms; instead, even after direct rule, successive British governments appeared unwilling to disrupt their long-term alliance with the Protestant and unionist local administrators in Northern Ireland (Ruane and Todd 1996: 30–3, 133–4, 226–9). The subsequent three decades showed incremental change in British practices, paradigms, and policies. By the 1990s it was increasingly plausible even to republicans that significant reform and even constitutional change could take place within a changing British state. This perception had transformative effects on conflict. Later chapters of this book show how such change took place, with what effects, and within what limits.

Chapter 7 returns explicitly to these four sets of issues, benchmarking the progress towards agreement, demonstrating the process by which compromise became possible, and showing the limits of its institutionalization. Thus it returns to the lessons learned from the Northern Ireland process and their wider significance for the negotiation of agreements where there are conflicting perspectives on sovereignty, democracy, and equality, and opposed judgements on the potential for reform within existing state structures.

1.3. Analysing the Changing British–Irish Relationship

The long-running conflict in Northern Ireland that began in response to the events of 1968, though sharing features with ethnic conflicts elsewhere, is unusual in persisting over such a long period and within the bounds of a powerful British state. It also stands out in the manner in which a settlement was found through negotiation, beginning with a path towards establishing common positions between the British and Irish governments. This in turn formed the basis for inter-party negotiations. In the chapters that follow the focus is on the slow, often behind-the-scenes process by which the British–Irish relationship was redefined, with knock-on effects on policies and ultimately on peace in Northern Ireland. In the rest of this section we look in turn at the challenges of researching this negotiating process; the methods by which the primary data used in this book were generated; and the basis on which we have selected extracts from this material for inclusion in this book.

---

[19] This question divided the 'internal-conflict' theorists Darby (1976) and Whyte (1990, 194–205) from those who emphasized the British (and Irish) causes of conflict, Guelke (1988), O'Leary and McGarry (1996), Ruane and Todd (1996), and Wright (1987). Politically it divided nationalists from republicans, and unionists who were willing to try for compromise from those who thought nationalism must first be defeated.

1.3.1. The Challenge

This book analyses the efforts of British and Irish goverments and parties to resolve the Northern Ireland conflict. Its primary data consist of the perspectives of 'insiders': the civil servants, advisors, and politicians who assessed the options, narrowed down the choices to be made by political leaders, and carried forward the decisions made by the latter.

A central objective of the book is analytical: to define the parameters that guided the actors in reaching agreement, the assumptions they made and revised, and the aims that they thought possible to achieve. This is central to understanding not just the letter but also the meaning and spirit of the sequence of agreements. The parameters of the past may no longer be relevant today, but only by identifying them can we grasp the nature of the institutions set in place, with all their ambiguities and contradictions. In a context where highly politicized readings of past agreements are common, it is all the more important to provide evidence that allows for a dispassionate understanding of these compromises, the processes that led to them and their impact on conflict.

A second objective in the book is to open to the wider community of researchers and to other interested readers some of these important intra- and interstate perspectives. The need to record the memories of the central participants in the various rounds of negotiations, their recollections of events, and their interpretations of motivations, is a pressing one. While archives in Dublin, Belfast, London, and elsewhere contain an abundance of material produced by civil servants, politicians, and others that documents the negotiating process, these rarely tell the full story. The unwritten memories and perspectives of the central actors are a crucial resource that needs to be tapped. In this book we report on one major initiative to do precisely this by creating a major oral archive. The book itself reproduces only a small part of this archive.

The raw material on which this book is based comprises first-hand discussions by those high-level British and Irish officials and politicians who negotiated the sequence of British–Irish agreements and Northern Irish initiatives from 1973 to 2006. This allows us to observe closely some of the policy learning and institutional patterns that characterized the sequence of British–Irish negotiations and agreements. Policy learning is not always cumulative, nor is it always unidirectional. The story told in this book is of challenges, partial reversals, and leaps forward to new prospects of agreement.

The book's focus on the perspectives of high-ranking officials and politicians in Britain and Ireland (and between 1998 and 2003 in Northern Ireland) is important in providing insight into what Bulpitt (1983) called the 'habits of statecraft' in Britain and Ireland and, in the immediate aftermath of the Good Friday Agreement, in Northern Ireland. It shows how actors high in the state apparatus saw the Northern Ireland conflict, how they believed it could be ameliorated or resolved, and how they understood their mutual relations and their own state's interests in regard to these. It also traces patterns of change and evolution in these interpretations and relationships. It allows us to trace how these influential actors discussed issues that touched on highly contested concepts such as sovereignty and self-determination, sought formulas to deal with conflicts over cross-border relations and power-sharing, and pursued reform to promote equality and rights. It reveals their perceptions of the debates within their own governing institutions about them. It shows, too, when and how far these actors took public attitudes into account in their deliberations.

By introducing evidence of the political actors' own understandings of the contests over sovereignty, democracy, and inequality, and their own perceptions of the limits of reform, we show why agreements were worded as they were, why particular forms of institutional design were chosen, and when and why conflicts over implementation of agreements and functioning of agreed institutions were likely. Taking seriously the standpoints of the most powerful actors allows richer analyses of the functioning of the institutions that they set in place. Thus it is directly relevant to a whole set of scholarly debates: on the role of the British and Irish states in the Northern Ireland conflict and settlement, on the character and extent of their co-management of conflict, and on the nature and functioning of power-sharing institutions in Northern Ireland.[20] It is also relevant to more general debates on issues such as the constitutional framework of settlements, the functioning and malfunctioning of power-sharing institutions, the role of horizontal inequality in conflict and the ways it can be reformed, the manner in which states change, and the varying understanding of sovereignty in the contemporary world.[21] We return to these debates in the final chapter.

1.3.2. The Material

In studying the role of the state, where so much happens in secret, a range of data sources is needed. These sources include relatively accessible public material, such as constitutional and legal documentation, parliamentary debates, other official documents, press releases, newspaper reports, and media coverage. They include less widely available sources, such as confidential government or civil-service documents, briefing statements, private contemporaneous notes made by officials, and other written documents that are to be found in government archives.

---

[20] For further perspectives, see Arthur (2000); Bew, Gibbon, and Patterson (1996); Coakley and Todd (2014b); Garry (2016); Guelke (1988); O'Leary and McGarry (1996); Jarrett (2018); McGarry and O'Leary (2004); O'Duffy (2007); O'Kane (2007); Ruane and Todd (1996, 2007); Taylor (2009); White (2018). Other dimensions also need to be considered—e.g. the influence exerted by successive American presidents; Cooper (2017).
[21] See Brown, Langer, and Stewart (2012); Choudhry (2008); Keating (2001); Kissane (2011); McGarry, (2017); Mahoney and Thelen (2015); Morison (2001); Stewart (2008); White (2017).

They also include sources of a kind that we rely on here: material that has been assembled from oral sources, such as elite interviews and witness seminars. Interviews have been used to question individual actors about their part in particular processes of negotiation or implementation of agreements. Witness seminars involve a small group of elite respondents who participated in major historical episodes spending an extended period (in our research, a full day) engaged in discussion with a number of academic observers. This allows for intensive questioning and confrontation of viewpoints on the nature and meaning of the negotiation process, and offers unique insights into the obstacles to the making and implementation of agreements.

A first tranche of semi-structured interviews was carried out over the years 1998–2002 with sixty-five participants (politicians and civil servants) in the process that led to the Good Friday Agreement, with support from the John Whyte Trust Fund and from the Joseph Rowntree Charitable Trust. The collection has been named the 'John Whyte Oral Archive of the Northern Ireland Peace Process' to honour the role of the late Professor John Whyte as a pioneering analyst of the Northern Ireland conflict.[22] A major programme to expand this research to cover a longer time period was launched in 2007 by the Institute for British–Irish Studies at University College Dublin, with the support of the Irish Research Council for the Humanities and Social Sciences (now incorporated in the Irish Research Council), led by the authors.[23] This programme involved a second tranche of interviews and witness seminars with those involved in defining moments in the British–Irish relationship from the Sunningdale Agreement of 1973 to the St Andrews Agreement of 2006. These were collected by two principal means: one-to-one interviews with eighty-eight participants in the negotiating process and six 'witness seminars' involving fifty-four participants. The latter included four witness seminars addressing critical episodes: the Sunningdale Agreement (1973), the Anglo-Irish Agreement (1985), the Downing Street Declaration (1993), and the implementation of the Good Friday Agreement (1998 and later). Two further witness seminars focused on business relations between North and South.[24]

---

[22] John Henry Whyte (1928–90) was successively lecturer in history, Makerere University College, Uganda, 1958–61; lecturer in politics, University College Dublin, 1961–6; lecturer, reader and professor of politics in Queen's University Belfast, 1966–84; and professor of politics at University College Dublin, 1984–90.

[23] The project, formally entitled 'Breaking the Patterns of Conflict', operated during the years 2007–10 and was designed to provide an archive for scholars by capturing the recollections and perspectives of contributors to the Irish peace process.

[24] This new material has been deposited in an expanded John Whyte Archive in the UCD Archives in the form of digital recordings of the original interviews and witness seminars, together with transcripts of these approved by the participants. The original materials are subject to embargoes of varying (and sometimes indefinite) duration, depending on the basis on which they have been cleared by participants; they are being released in stages. A seventh witness seminar, on the implementation of the Anglo-Irish Agreement in the Maryfield Secretariat, was undertaken by the team in 2016 on the initiative and with the support of Michael Lillis. It has been published in the *Dublin Review of Books* (see Lillis 2016).

In organizing the witness seminars, we took as models the set of witness seminars at the Institute of Contemporary British History, now at King's College London, which explored a wide range of major developments in the contemporary period.[25] We adapted this methodology to the British–Irish and Northern Ireland context and to the continuing sensitivity and confidentiality of much of the material. For example, we decided not to foreground security issues, where the truth about what the states knew and agreed remains highly sensitive and is unlikely to be revealed fully. Instead, we explored the negotiation, interpretation, and implementation of British–Irish agreements. The final agreement in each case was publicly promulgated, and sometimes registered as an international treaty. However, the processes by which they were agreed, interpreted, and implemented were behind the scenes, and thus the frank discussion by participants in the witness seminars brings important new insight.

Considerable research was undertaken prior to each witness seminar and interview. This allowed us to define broad themes and a set of more specific questions that formed the framework for the witness seminar (or interview), which was then supplemented by more specific questions, depending on the course of discussion. In the interviews on the Good Friday Agreement, for example, a set of very general topics and questions on each strand of the negotiations was defined, and the focus in each interview was on the areas in which the respondent had personally participated.

For each of the witness seminars, we faced the question whether to draw participants from one 'side', which promised to allow significant freedom of discussion, or from both, which offered to reveal more about converging and conflicting perspectives. Our decisions in the end were largely pragmatic. The Sunningdale seminar involved only Irish and nationalist participants because it was not possible to convene an equal number of similarly senior British and unionist participants. For both the Anglo-Irish Agreement and the Downing Street Declaration seminars, a balanced two-sided participation was possible, not least because so few individuals had been involved in the processes. For the final (Good Friday) implementation seminar we tried and failed to gain a balanced unionist–nationalist participation and, in view of the impending end of the funded project, went ahead with a group involving civil servants from Northern Ireland and the Republic, and nationalist politicians and advisors. In each case the discussion was intense, energetic, and insightful, and determined efforts were made to ensure that the process of recording exchanges was both unobtrusive and accurate.[26]

---

[25] One of these seminars is discussed at length by Peter Rose (2000) and forms the data for his book on British political perspectives at the very start of the Northern Ireland troubles.

[26] Very great care was taken in recording; small recording devices were placed on several parts of the table. Outline notes were taken to help with the eventual transcription. An academic chair was designated and was usually changed for morning and afternoon sessions; his or her task was to keep the discussion moving and to ensure that important issues were not left out. It was neither easy nor

1.3.3. The Selection

The vast collection of oral material just described is sufficiently rich to provide a basis for many books. In this one, we focus on the dynamics of the negotiation process. Research to date has tended to be based on information given confidentially by a relatively small number of individual civil servants, though with some significant efforts to present the views of policymakers in their own words (see, e.g., Spencer 2015). The research of which this book forms a part allowed us to choose from discussions with over two hundred civil servants and politicians. For the purposes of the volume, we have selected five critical initiatives, which were the subject of witness seminars and/or of interviews, and which are addressed in the five chapters that follow:

- the Sunningdale Agreement of 1973 (the first major effort to resolve the conflict following the fall of the institutions established in 1921);
- the Anglo-Irish Agreement of 1985 (an arrangement later absorbed by the Good Friday Agreement, but itself critical in promoting that accord);
- the Downing Street Declaration of 1993 and the Framework Documents that followed in 1995 (a major initiative in bringing about paramilitary ceasefires and in creating the conditions for a negotiated settlement);
- the negotiation of the Good Friday Agreement of 1998 (the culmination of efforts to reach an inclusive agreement—a process involving very many parties and negotiators);
- the implementation of the Good Friday Agreement and supplementary agreements (the process of steady institutionalization of the principles of the Agreement, from the immediate post-agreement period through the St Andrews Agreement of 2006 and its successors).

In each case except the negotiation of the Good Friday Agreement, the core of the chapter comprises a witness seminar, supplemented where appropriate by interview material. On the negotiation of the Good Friday Agreement, we have relied entirely on interviews, which we have edited and presented in such a way that they too can provide multi-perspective insights into the processes of negotiation.

In producing the present text from the original transcripts of the witness seminars and interviews, we have been guided by the following four principles:

---

indeed always appropriate to impose 'order' on talkative and engaged participants. Discussion continued over coffee and lunch. This could not be recorded, but important issues raised in informal discussion during breaks were brought up again in the afternoon session by the academic questioners.

- in selecting the content, we have prioritized those sections of the witness seminar or interview where there was extended discussion of important political issues in which ideas, perspectives, and processes were elaborated, questioned, and clarified;
- in organizing the material, we have taken some liberties with the order in which the various points of discussion took place, occasionally reorganizing sequences with a view to optimizing thematic coherence;
- in editing the text, we have sometimes rephrased sentences to ensure maximum clarity, while ensuring that the edited text would represent fully the views of the speaker;
- in finalizing the document, the approval of the participants for the version of the transcripts included here has been obtained.[27]

In preparing the edited transcripts for publication, we have removed hesitations, and sometimes revised sentence structure to conform with norms in a written text. We have added supplementary information in the form of clarificatory notes (for example, identifying who a particular figure was, which book was being referred to, or what specific little-known incident or episode was being discussed). We have added an appendix to each chapter with additional information and documentation that helps in interpreting and understanding the content of these exchanges.

Notwithstanding their value in supplementing—and occasionally correcting—other data sources, both interviews and witness seminars have limitations whose implications for this book need to be noted. To start with, there may be issues of reliability. Elites do not always know, recall accurately or at all, or wish to reveal information about the past, and they do not have privileged insight into causal processes. They may not have (or be willing to reveal) insight into their own past motivations, and they may forget or conceal the manner in which institutions functioned in practice, and how decisions were actually made. Yet, by triangulating interviews together with other evidence and—in the witness seminars—bringing together a number of participants who are willing to correct each other and emphasize different aspects of the process, some of these limitations can be overcome (Natow 2019). Of course, like all data sources, interviews and witness seminars need to be used alongside other sources, and they need to be checked both against each other and against independently sourced data. With these provisos in place, they are of irreplaceable value.

---

[27] The late Dermot Nally, Garret FitzGerald, and Mahon Hayes corrected early versions of the text and approved the project, and their families have been shown the final version, on which other participants also commented. The late David Goodall, Muiris Mac Conghail, and Frank Murray, and the remaining living participants, also approved the edited transcripts reproduced here. Mrs Mary Alcock approved the inclusion of the interview with her husband, the late Antony Alcock.

In addition, there may be issues of selection bias. This book was a product of the large data collection and archival project already described. Thus the dataset is at once much more extensive and varied than can possibly be covered in a single book, and the specific research questions that arose in the process of analysis are not always fully addressed in each of the individual interviews or witness seminars. Given the richness of the data, there is more than enough material to explore these questions. But there are three aspects of potential selection bias that require comment.

First, the fact that the focus of the book is on the perspectives of state actors—officials, politicians, and advisors—substantially removes other key players from the story and may appear to sideline their roles. Thus, for example, we do not document the crucial talks between republicans and representatives of the British and Irish governments in the 1970s or in the 1990s (for this, see Ó Dochartaigh 2015). Neither do we engage with the debates within and between the Northern Irish political parties (on this, see Bloomfield 1998, 2001; Tonge et al. 2014; Hennessey et al, 2019). Most importantly, the book does not seek to address the positions of two parties whose political role became increasingly important in the twenty-first century, Sinn Féin and the DUP.[28] To deal thoroughly with their contributions to peace and settlement would require a different book. This book, then, consciously focuses on just one aspect of the peace and settlement process. It is constrained by the available data, which, though rich, are also limited. The book is not a comprehensive overview of all viewpoints, but is designed to cover a broad, but far from total, range of related perspectives.

Second, while our interviews range across British and Irish participants, and unionist and nationalist ones, only two of the four witness seminars had mainland British participants, and, although Northern Irish civil servants, advisors and politicians participated, unionists did not. This reflects the practical constraints of organization: for example, almost all of the main Irish protagonists in 1973–4 were available to attend the first (Sunningdale) witness seminar, but almost none of the main British ones could participate, so we decided to focus only on the Irish participants.

Third, the participants were overwhelmingly men. This relates to a political reality of the late twentieth century: the fact that the great majority of senior policymakers and politicians were male. Some women were centrally involved—not least Margaret Thatcher, who was, however, unable to participate in the research. We interviewed several female participants in the negotiation processes, but the material that they covered was less relevant to the theme of this book than that of some of their male colleagues, whether because of time constraints or because of their position outside the main party structures. Other women came to political prominence after 2007, beyond the scope of our interviews and witness seminars. Most of all,

---

[28] One of those interviewed in 1998, Jeffrey Donaldson, was a UUP member at the time, but he left the UUP and in 2004 joined the DUP.

however, the fact that all of the respondents in this book are men reflects the almost exclusively male character of the political elite in these years.

1.4. The Institutional Context

Finally, to appreciate the significance of the exchanges that follow in subsequent chapters, we set the participants in the broader institutional context within which they operated. In this, there was a significant difference between the Irish and British sides, given their asymmetrical standing in relation to Northern Ireland, with one side formally aspiring to sovereignty over it, and the other exercising sovereignty and responsible for all aspects of its government. Here, we provide an overview of the institutional framework and of its personnel.

1.4.1. Institutional Evolution

On the British side, relations with Ireland had originally been managed (under the formal mandate of the Lord Lieutenant of Ireland) by the Chief Secretary for Ireland, who was normally a cabinet member, and whose office in Dublin Castle was supplemented by the Irish Office in London. After partition, relations with the Irish Free State and its successors were managed in turn by the Colonial Office, the Dominions Office, and the Foreign Office (now the Foreign and Commonwealth Office) in London. In the early years of the independent Irish state, the British government was effectively without representation in Dublin. In other dominions, it was possible to rely on the office of governor-general; but in the Irish Free State the holder of this office was marginalized by the Irish government from the outset, and rendered almost invisible after 1932 (Coakley 2012). The appointment in 1939 of the first British 'Representative' in Dublin, Sir John Maffey (later, Lord Rugby), was therefore of considerable significance; in 1950 his office became that of the British ambassador.

The relationship of Northern Ireland to the United Kingdom was completely different after 1921. Following the disappearance of the Irish Office after 1922, oversight of Northern Ireland's affairs became the responsibility of the Home Office. The introduction of direct rule in 1972 required a revision of this arrangement, reflecting the more interventionist role the British government was now required to play. In addition to the new post of Secretary of State for Northern Ireland, a new department, the Northern Ireland Office, was created. This absorbed Northern Ireland's own Home Affairs department, and expanded in response to changing security needs and political pressures. The Northern Ireland responsibilities of other British departments and agencies also increased, and the prime minister's office developed a growing interest in and expertise on Northern Ireland.

On the Irish side, the Department of External Affairs (later, Department of Foreign Affairs) managed relations with the UK through the Irish High Commission (later, Embassy) in London. For a long time there was no machinery for liaising with Northern Ireland. Governments used the North-East Boundary Bureau (1922–6) and the All-Party Anti-Partition Conference, commonly known as the Mansion House Committee (1949–71), for limited political purposes. With the escalation of civil unrest, however, a small 'Inter-Departmental Unit on the North of Ireland' was established in May 1970. Two departments began to play an increasingly active role in relation to Northern Ireland: the Department of Foreign Affairs (within which an Anglo-Irish Division was established in 1972) and the Department of the Taoiseach (which also developed a Northern Ireland Division in the 1970s; see Appendices 1.3 and 1.4).

The main (but by no means only) political players in defining the British–Irish relationship were, then, the Prime Minister, the Northern Ireland Secretary and the Foreign Secretary on the British side, together with their respective offices, and the Taoiseach and the Minister for Foreign Affairs (and their departments) on the Irish side. On specific sectoral issues, such as security, other agencies might well be involved—in this case, the British Home Office and Ministry of Defence, and the Irish Department of Justice.

A number of bodies that grew out of the evolving British–Irish relationship also constituted important nodes for developing these relations and undertaking negotiation and policymaking. Those who had positions within them (for example, the joint secretaries of the Anglo-Irish Intergovernmental Conference from 1985 to 1999 and of the British–Irish Intergovernmental Conference since 1999) were well placed to observe British–Irish and North–South relations and to take them forward through the implementation of policy. In addition, and particularly from the 1990s, the position of 'advisor' became more important as successive taoisigh and prime ministers brought in experts whom they could trust. Martin Mansergh served in this role for Charles Haughey, Albert Reynolds and Bertie Ahern; Seán Donlon did so for John Bruton; and, in the UK, Jonathan Powell (Tony Blair's chief of staff) and Alastair Campbell (his press secretary) were just two of several important policy advisors.

1.4.2. Personnel

No formal institutional map can adequately describe the influence of officials, or their positioning at the heart of the events that changed British–Irish relations and led to a redefinition of political relations in Northern Ireland. Irish ambassadors to the United States, for example, frequently played a crucial role and, as Seán Donlon records, often provided very complete written information on government priorities.[29] Particular officials, formally or informally, might be assigned Northern Ireland duties, as were the successive 'travellers' in the Irish Department of Foreign Affairs, whose business it was to keep the Irish government in touch with thinking and experience on the ground in Northern Ireland. At some points in time, legal experts (the Attorney General and officials in his or her office) were key in formulating policy, for example on the extradition of accused persons from one jurisdiction to another, while at other times the Department of Justice was at the centre of North–South networks and dialogue.

There was an even greater range of influential players on the British side. The asymmetrical relationship between senior political and administrative posts in the two sovereign states was made more complex by the legacy of devolution in Northern Ireland. The most obvious and enduring expression of this was the survival of a separate Northern Ireland civil service even after the introduction of direct rule in 1972. While Northern Ireland civil servants indeed played a role in the negotiation process in 1972–4, and again between 1998 and 2002, for most of the period discussed in this book they remained almost entirely outside this framework. Instead, a central position was occupied by the Northern Ireland Office, a branch of the UK civil service, as discussed above. Headed, like other UK government departments, by a permanent under secretary, it absorbed the old Northern Ireland Home Affairs department. Two deputy undersecretaries were responsible for security and for political matters, and were based respectively in Belfast and London. The latter played an important role in the negotiation process, and was in turn supported by two assistant undersecretaries, one of whom also functioned as joint secretary of the Anglo-Irish (and later British–Irish) Intergovernmental Conference. These posts were later retitled, but the most significant change took place after 2010, when agreement on the devolution of policing and security led to a radical reduction in the functions and size of the Northern Ireland Office.

Given this bureaucratic complexity, it is not easy to determine where to begin and end in listing the officials who were most important in driving the British–Irish relationship. We adopt a formal approach in the tables in the appendix to this chapter, which list the occupants of certain important positions during the years covered here. The first table shows the political administrations that have held office on the Irish side since 1969, listing the Taoiseach and the Minister for External/ Foreign Affairs. This is followed by lists of those occupying four important civil-service positions on the Irish side: the Secretary or Secretary General of the Department of Foreign Affairs, the Irish ambassador in London, the head of the Anglo-Irish Division in the Department of Foreign Affairs, and the Irish Joint Secretary of the Anglo-Irish (and later British–Irish) Intergovernmental Conference.

---

[29] See Subsection 3.3.7.

The appendix continues with lists of corresponding political or civil-service figures on the British side: prime ministers and secretaries of state for Northern Ireland, heads of the Northern Ireland Office, British ambassadors in Dublin, political directors and under secretaries (political) in the Northern Ireland Office, and British Joint Secretaries of the Anglo-Irish and British–Irish Intergovernmental Conference. Confining the appendix lists to these categories inevitably omits some important office-holders who played a crucial role, such as officials in the Department of the Taoiseach and Foreign Office officials in the UK. In particular, certain cabinet officials and Downing Street advisors, including but not limited to those who have participated in this volume, played a central role in the negotiating process.[30]

Most important of all were the knowledge and experience that these officials brought to the processes of negotiation, policymaking and implementation. It is clear that all major policy shifts in British–Irish relations were ultimately put forward by the prime minister and his or her Irish counterpart. But, if they made the final decisions, these leading politicians were not the people who formulated the detail of policy, who ensured that anticipated outcomes met the interests of each state, who were charged with responsibility for policy implementation, and who were required to address the unanticipated obstacles to and the sometimes unexpected consequences of implementation. By focusing on the role of senior civil servants who did confront these problems, this set of witness seminars and interviews offers a perspective on the major political decisions and agreements that differs from that which has been recounted elsewhere. It presents a novel multi-perspective view of changing intergovernmental relations from the inside, allowing a measured assessment of the nature of their impact on the parties and communities within Northern Ireland.

1.5. Conclusion

Two decades on, when some of the European underpinnings of the Good Friday Agreement are being challenged, it is important to go back to examine the assumptions, aims, and principles that underlay the sets of negotiations that paved the way for the Agreement and that informed its implementation. In a slow process that began in 1972–3, British and Irish perspectives came to converge in the 1990s and 2000s in aims, principles, and strategies with respect to Northern Ireland. In tracing this evolving process, this book provides a benchmark by which the rolling-out of British–Irish, North–South, and internal Northern Irish relations in the

---

[30] So, e.g., in the 1990s Sir Roderic Lyne, Private Secretary to the Prime Minister, 1993–7, and Martin Mansergh, senior advisor to the Taoiseach, worked together in the negotiation process and played crucially important roles.

contemporary context can be assessed. It does this by presenting the perspectives on the conflict of those inside the Irish and British states: the perceptions of the political leaders who defined broad policy guidelines, and the senior civil servants and advisors who negotiated, drafted, and implemented various aspects of the resulting agreements. It provides an analytical commentary on these perspectives and returns in the final chapter to assess the extent of change achieved by 2006, the uneven progress since then, and the prospects of sustaining the principles of agreement, as a divided UK struggles with the extended process of leaving the European Union.

Appendices

Appendix 1.1. Bibliographical Note on Additional Source Material

This book necessarily restricts itself to only a small portion of the extensive source material on the Northern Ireland conflict and its settlement. Important additional material will be found in the major public archives (The National Archives in Kew, the Irish National Archives in Dublin, and the Public Record Office of Northern Ireland), and we have drawn extensively on this. Since 1997, a major online resource of exceptional value has been maintained in Ulster University's 'Conflict Archive on the Internet' <cain.ulster.ac.uk> (accessed 9 May 2019); this contains not just important documents but also chronologies, guides, and information on background events and developments. Of direct relevance to the discussions in this volume are the collections held in the University College Dublin (UCD) Archives, including the papers of Dermot Nally (UCDA P254), Garret Fitzgerald (UCDA P215), and a set of papers circulated in the Department of Foreign Affairs (DFA) by John Swift (UCDA P207). A wide range of autobiographical or similar material also supplements the accounts we present in the chapters that follow, and we discuss this further in this appendix, theme by theme.

The Sunningdale Agreement

Autobiographical writings by Irish politicians are rare, but the role of Jack Lynch in the early years of the conflict is discussed in Keogh (2008: 138–357). The Sunningdale negotiations, their context, and their later outworkings are discussed in two autobiographical works by the Irish foreign minister at the time, Garret FitzGerald (1991: 196–263; 2010: 244–57). Political autobiographies are much more common on the British side. The Sunningdale episode has been discussed by two prime ministers, Ted Heath (1998: 420–45) and Harold Wilson (1979: 66–79). Heath's role at this time is discussed also by his official biographer, Philip Ziegler (2010: 298–317). The Agreement, its context, and its later failure feature also in the autobiographical writings of successive home secretaries: Callaghan (1973), which records the author's role in dealing with the old Stormont administration, and Maudling (1978: 178–88). It is also addressed in autobiographies of

Northern Ireland secretaries William Whitelaw (1989: 77–122) and Merlyn Rees (1985: 7–35); the latter was shadow secretary of state during the Sunningdale talks, and Northern Ireland Secretary during the final months of the power-sharing executive. Other participants in the Sunningdale conference have also discussed the conference and its context in autobiographical works: Sir Kenneth Bloomfield (1994: 168–223), Austin Currie (2004: 205–301), Paddy Devlin (1993: 172–251), Brian Faulkner (1978: 203–50), Maurice Hayes (1995: 161–204), Basil McIvor (1998: 85–123), and Conor Cruise O'Brien (1999: 348–59). Sir Kenneth Bloomfield (2007: 30–49) also later offered the analytical perspective of an informed insider. A particularly important contribution by an Irish official offers a wealth of documentation and analysis (Dorr 2017).

The Anglo-Irish Agreement

As in the case of Sunningdale, British political memoirs entirely overshadow Irish auto-biographical writing for the period of the negotiation and implementation of the Anglo-Irish Agreement. The background is discussed in detail in the autobiography of the Taoiseach, Garret FitzGerald (1991: 494–575). Margaret Thatcher's account of her years as prime minister include a description of her approach to Northern Ireland, and especially of the negotiation of the Anglo-Irish Agreement (Thatcher 1993: 379–415); her part in the negotiations is also discussed in detail by her official biographer (Moore 2015: 298–342). The two secretaries of state in office during the negotiations have also left an account of their involvement: James Prior (1986: 177–246) and Douglas Hurd (2003: 295–314). Some of the security dimensions are discussed in the autobiography of Chief Constable Sir John Hermon (1997: 179–82). Of particular note are two 'insider' accounts of the negotiation of the Anglo-Irish Agreement, by Michael Lillis and Sir David Goodall (2010); see also Lillis 2009. A vivid account of life in Maryfield, the well-fortified secretariat of the Anglo-Irish Intergovernmental Conference, is available in a witness seminar that records the experience of Irish officials in the early years there (Lillis 2016).

The Downing Street Declaration and Framework Documents

Relatively little autobiographical insight is available from the main participants in the negotiation of the Downing Street Declaration. The autobiography of Albert Reynolds (Reynolds with Arlon 2009: 213–427) discusses this period, as does that of his British counterpart, John Major (1999: 431–94). Among the several biographies of Reynolds's predecessor, Charles Haughey, one focuses specifically on his role in relation to Northern Ireland and offers a brief analysis of his involvement in the early stages of the drafting of the Declaration (Kelly 2016a: 340–45). The memoirs of political advisors Fergus Finlay (1998: 180–204) and Seán Duignan (1995: 96–128) offer the perspectives of two close observers. John Hume and Gerry Adams were also principal actors, whose involvement was at one remove, and they have left little published discussion of their role, but this is covered briefly in Gerry Adams's autobiography (Adams 2003: 136–50), and, among several studies of the contribution of John Hume, Peter McLoughlin (2010) provides a valuable overview of his formative contribution to shifting political perspectives within nationalism.

The Good Friday Agreement: Negotiation

Reflections on the negotiation process are available in autobiographical works by the two prime ministers who were party to the Good Friday Agreement, Bertie Ahern (Ahern with Aldous 2009: 210–30) and Tony Blair (2010: 152–80). Northern Ireland Secretary Mo Mowlam (2002) covered the negotiation process in detail, as did Tony Blair's advisor Jonathan Powell (2008). Alastair Campbell's very detailed diaries (especially vol. ii, which covers the period 1997–9; see Campbell and Hagerty 2010–12) are an important work of reference; the Irish sections of the diaries are collected and published separately in Campbell 2013. The two most significant external parties have discussed their involvement in Northern Ireland: President Bill Clinton (2004: *passim*) and Senator George Mitchell (2000). The Sinn Féin perspective on the negotiations is covered in Adams (2003: 302–68). Perspectives of the political parties involved are described in the case of the Ulster Unionists in Godson's biographical work (2004) on Trimble, while several of those involved in the talks process have provided insider accounts, often overlapping with academic analysis. Examples include Mallon 2019: 89–108; Farren and Mulvihill 2000: 161–200; Hennessey 2000; Mansergh 2003; and Morgan 2000. A series of articles in the *Fordham International Law Journal*, 22/4 (April 1999), 1136–1344, illustrate a range of political perspectives, including those of George Mitchell, David Trimble, John Hume, Gerry Adams, Bertie Ahern, John Bruton, David Byrne (Irish Attorney General), and contributors from the various political parties involved: Stephen Farry and Sean Neeson (Alliance Party of Northern Ireland), Kate Fearon and Monica McWilliams (Northern Ireland Womens Coalition), Ian Paisley (DUP), and Duncan Shipley Dalton (UUP).

The Good Friday Agreement: Implementation

Several of the works discussed in the previous section (notably Ahern and Aldous 2009: 231–6, 263–7, 296–301, 308–14; Blair 2010: 181–99; Mallon 2019: 109–40; Campbell and Hagerty 2010–12; Campbell 2013; and, more briefly, Clinton 2004: *passim*) also cover issues of implementation, as do some of the other works to which reference is made there. In addition, two Northern Ireland secretaries have written about their experience in Belfast in the aftermath of the Good Friday Agreement: Peter Mandelson (2010: 284–315) and Peter Hain (2012, 2015). Former prime minister David Cameron (2019: 303–12) has also written briefly of his involvement in Northern Ireland. The question of police reform in Northern Ireland is addressed in the work of the Chair of the Independent Commission on Policing, Northern Ireland (1998–9), Chris Patten (2017: 157–81).

Appendix 1.2. Biographical Notes on Participants

Ahern, Bertie. Born Dublin, 1951; educated College of Commerce, Rathmines; Fianna Fáil TD, 1977–2011; leader of Fianna Fáil, 1994–2008; minister of state, 1982; government minister, 1987–94; Taoiseach, 1997–2008.

Alcock, Antony. Born Malta, 1936; educated Harrow, McGill, Stanford, and Geneva; Senior Lecturer and later Professor, New University of Ulster, Coleraine (from 1984, University of Ulster); specialist on minority rights and the South Tyrol question; member Vanguard

Unionist Party in the 1970s; member of the Northern Ireland Forum and Ulster Unionist talks team, 1996–8; died 2 September 2006.

Armstrong, Robert. Born 1927; educated Eton, Christ Church, Oxford. Principal Private Secretary to the Prime Minister, 1970–5; Permanent Secretary to the Home Office, 1977–9; Secretary of the Cabinet, 1979–87; Head of Civil Service, 1981–7; knighted, 1978; created a peer, 1988.

Butler, Robin. Born Lancashire, 1938; educated Harrow, University College, Oxford; Private Secretary to British Prime Ministers Edward Heath and Harold Wilson, 1972–5; Principal Private Secretary to Margaret Thatcher, 1982–5; Secretary of the Cabinet and Head of Civil Service, 1988–98; Master of University College, Oxford, 1998–2008; knighted, 1988; created a peer, 1998.

Currie, Austin. Born Coalisland, Co. Tyrone, 1939; educated St Patrick's Academy Dungannon, Queen's University Belfast; Nationalist MP for East Tyrone, 1964–70; founder member of SDLP, 1970, and member of Assembly (1973–4), Convention (1975–6) and Assembly (1982–6); negotiator at Sunningdale conference, 1973; Minister of Housing, Planning and Local Government, Northern Ireland Executive, 1974; Fine Gael TD for Dublin West, 1989–2002; Minister of State, Fine Gael–Labour coalition, 1994–7.

Donaldson, Jeffrey. Born Kilkeel, Co. Down, 1962; educated Kilkeel High School, Castlereagh College; Ulster Unionist member of the Northern Ireland Assembly, 1995–6; member of the Northern Ireland Forum and Ulster Unionist talks team, 1996–8; MP for Lagan Valley since 1997; member of the Assembly, 2003–10; junior minister in the Office of First Minister and Deputy First Minister, 2008–9; left the inter-party talks on Good Friday in protest at the agreement; joined the DUP, 2004; appointed to the Privy Council, 2007; knighted 2016.

Donlon, Seán. Born Athboy, Co. Meath, 1940; educated St Finian's College Mullingar, University College Dublin; Assistant Secretary in the Department of Foreign Affairs specializing in Anglo-Irish affairs, 1971–8; Ambassador of Ireland to the United States, 1978–81; Secretary General of the Department of Foreign Affairs, 1981–7; private sector, 1987–94; Special Advisor to the Taoiseach, John Bruton, 1994–7.

Dorr, Noel. Born Limerick, 1933; educated St Nathy's College Ballaghadereen, University College Galway, Georgetown University; joined Irish diplomatic service, 1960; Irish Permanent Representative to the United Nations in New York, 1980–3; Irish Ambassador in London, 1983–7; Secretary General of the Department of Foreign Affairs, 1987–95; later served as Irish representative in the negotiation of the Amsterdam and Nice treaties.

Durkan, Mark. Born Derry, 1961; educated St Columb's College, Queen's University Belfast; joined the SDLP, 1981; party chair, 1990–5, and party leader, 2001–10; member of the Assembly, 1998–2010; MP for Foyle, 2005–17; Minister for Finance and Personnel, 1999–2001; Deputy First Minister, 2001–2.

Farren, Seán. Born Dublin, 1939; educated University College Dublin, University of Essex, University of Ulster; joined the SDLP in 1973; Chair of the SDLP, 1980–4; elected to Assembly, 1982–6; member of Assembly, 1998–2007; Minister for Employment and Learning, 1999–2001; Minister for Finance and Personnel, 2001–2.

FitzGerald, Garret. Born Dublin, 1926; educated Belvedere College, University College Dublin, and King's Inns; worked as a research and schedules manager in Aer Lingus and later as Lecturer in Political Economy, University College Dublin; Fine Gael senator, 1965–9, and TD 1969–92; leader of Fine Gael, 1977–87; government minister, 1973–7; Taoiseach, 1981–2 and 1982–7; died 18 May 2011.

Goodall, David. Born 1931; educated Ampleforth, Trinity College, Oxford; joined British diplomatic service, 1956; seconded to the Cabinet Office as Deputy Secretary, 1982–4; High Commissioner to India, 1987–91; knighted 1991; died 22 July 2016.

Hain, Peter. Born 1950; spent childhood in Pretoria until anti-apartheid parents exiled in 1966; educated Pretoria, London, Queen Mary College, and Sussex University; prominent in the Anti-Apartheid Movement and initially Young Liberals; joined Labour Party, 1977; MP for Neath, 1991–2015; after serving in several junior ministerial posts since 1997, he became Secretary of State for Wales, 2002–8 and 2009–10, Leader of the Commons, 2003–5, and Secretary of State for Northern Ireland, 2005–7; among other senior posts he held was that of Secretary of State for Work and Pensions, 2007–8; created a peer, 2015.

Hallett, Ted. Born 1947; research analyst on Irish matters, Foreign and Commonwealth Office, 1984–2003; Head of Western Europe Research Group, FCO, 1995–2003; seconded to Northern Ireland Office, 1988–91; Deputy Head of Mission, British Embassy, Dublin, 2003–6.

Hayes, Mahon. Born Cork, 1930; educated CBS Thurles, University College Dublin, the Institute of Public Administration, and King's Inns; worked in the Land Registry and Department of Justice, 1960–5; joined the legal division of the Department of External Affairs in 1965; legal advisor, Department of Foreign Affairs, 1970–7; Ambassador to Denmark, Norway, and Iceland, 1977–81; Permanent Representative to the United Nations in Geneva, 1981–7; Deputy Secretary of the Department of Foreign Affairs, 1987–9; Permanent Representative to the United Nations in New York, 1989–95; died 27 June 2011.

Kirwan, Walter. Born Dublin, 1944; educated O'Connell Schools, University College Dublin, Trinity College Dublin; served as the Assistant Secretary General in the Department of the Taoiseach under seven taoisigh; responsible for the Northern Ireland Division from 1978; coordinator of the secretariat of the New Ireland Forum, 1983–4, Secretary General of the Forum for Peace and Reconciliation, 1994–6; member of the Irish government delegation throughout Multi-Party talks, 1996-8; Secretary General of the National Forum on Europe, 2001–4.

Larkin, Colm. Born Co. Derry, 1949; educated St Patrick's College Armagh, Balliol College Oxford; European Commission official, 1974–2004; posts held included Deputy Chef de Cabinet to Peter Sutherland, Chef de Cabinet to Ray McSharry and Director of the Commission Representation to Ireland; special advisor to Seamus Mallon in the Office of the First Minister and Deputy First Minister, 1998–2001; member of the Northern Ireland Human Rights Commission, 2007–11.

Lillis, Michael. Educated at University College Dublin; joined the Irish diplomatic service, 1966; counsellor (political) in the Irish Embassy in Washington, DC, 1976–9; diplomatic advisor to the Taoiseach, 1981; head of the Anglo-Irish Division of the Department of Foreign Affairs, 1983–5; Irish Joint Secretary of the Anglo-Irish Secretariat, Maryfield, Belfast, 1985–6; Ambassador to the UN in Geneva, 1986–8; retired from the diplomatic service in 1988 and has since pursued business interests mainly in Latin America.

Logue, Hugh. Born Claudy, Co. Derry, 1949; executive member of Northern Ireland Civil Rights Association; founder member of the SDLP, 1970, and elected for SDLP to Northern

Ireland Assembly and Convention for the Derry constituency in 1973, 1975, and 1981; joined the European Commission in 1984; Chairman of the Northern Ireland Group in Brussels, 1991–4; special advisor in the Office of the First Minister and Deputy First Minister in Northern Ireland, 1999–2003; Board of InterTrade Ireland, 2008–11.

Mac Conghail, Muiris. Born Dublin, 1941; educated University College Dublin, Maynooth, King's Inns; joined Radió Teilifís Éireann (RTÉ) as a broadcaster in 1964; Head of Features and Current Affairs, Radio, 1971–3, and Controller of Programmes, RTÉ Television, 1977–86; Assistant Secretary at the Department of the Taoiseach and Head of the Government Information Service, 1973–5; died 26 November 2019.

McCusker, Tony. Born and educated in Portadown; former Northern Ireland civil servant; served in former Northern Ireland Assembly and Departments of Education and Environment; advisor to Mo Mowlam; aide to David Trimble; retired from the Northern Ireland civil service in 2005 and has been the Chairman of the Community Foundation for Northern Ireland and the Rural Development Council, and a board member of the UK Community Foundations.

Major, John. Born Surrey, 1943; educated Rutlish School London; active in Young Conservatives from the age of 16; MP for Huntingdonshire, 1979–83 and for Huntingdon, 1983–2001; served in a number of government posts before joining the cabinet as Chief Secretary to the Treasury, 1987–9; Secretary of State for Foreign and Commonwealth Affairs, 1989; Chancellor of the Exchequer, 1989–90; Leader of the Conservative Party, 1990–97; Prime Minister, 1990–97; made Companion of Honour by HM the Queen, 1999; appointed Knight Companion of the Most Noble Order of the Garter by HM the Queen, 2005; awarded The Grand Cordon of The Order of The Rising Sun by the Emperor of Japan in 2012.

Murray, Frank. Born Carrick-on-Shannon, 1941; educated Carrick-on-Shannon, University College Dublin; joined civil service, 1960; Private Secretary to Taoiseach Liam Cosgrave, 1973–7; worked on Northern Ireland desk in the Department of Taoiseach, 1977–83; Assistant Secretary to the Irish Government, 1983–93; retired from the Department of the Taoiseach in 2000 and held a number of varied public-service positions; appointed Co-Commissioner of the Independent Commission for the Location of Victims Remains in 2006; died 31 March 2018.

Nally, Dermot. Born Dublin, 1927; educated CBS Synge Street, Belvedere College Dublin, University College Dublin, London University; joined the civil service, 1947, and served in a variety of departmental roles; Assistant Secretary in the Department of the Taoiseach, 1973–80; Secretary to the Government, 1980–93; chairman of the group of Irish officials negotiating the Anglo-Irish Agreement; served under five taoisigh; following his retirement, returned as a negotiator; died 30 December 2009.

Ó hUiginn, Seán. Born Co. Mayo, 1944; educated St Jarlath's College Tuam, University College Galway, and University of Bordeaux; joined Department of External Affairs, 1969; Irish Joint Secretary of the Anglo-Irish Secretariat in Belfast, 1987–90; Head of the Anglo-Irish Division, Department of Foreign Affairs, 1991–7; served in a number of ambassadorial posts, including Ambassador to the USA, 1997–2002, and to Germany, 2002–6.

Swift, John. Born Dublin, 1941; educated Synge Street CBS and University College Dublin; joined Department of Foreign Affairs, 1962; worked in Anglo-Irish Division, 1972–4, and as Press and Information Officer, 1974–6; later postings included Deputy Permanent

Representative to EEC, Head of EEC, Economic and Development Cooperation Divisions, Permanent Representative, UN (Geneva), Ambassador to the Netherlands, and Ambassador to Cyprus.

Thomas, Quentin. Born 1944; educated Cambridge University; British civil servant serving in Home Office, Northern Ireland Office, and Cabinet Office; joined Northern Ireland Office as Under Secretary (Political) in 1988; Political Director in Northern Ireland Office, 1991–8; headed Constitution Secretariat, 1998–9; President of the British Board of Film Classification, 2002–12; knighted, 1999.

Appendix 1.3. The Anglo-Irish Division in the Department of Foreign Affairs

THE CREATION OF THE ANGLO-IRISH DIVISION IN THE DEPARTMENT OF FOREIGN AFFAIRS, 1970: A NOTE BY SEÁN DONLON, NOVEMBER 2011

When I joined the Department of External Affairs in 1963, no section or individual was actively involved in dealing with Northern Ireland matters.[31] The O'Neill–Lemass meetings were, on the Irish side, organized by T. K. Whitaker of the Department of Finance. Issues that arose in Anglo-Irish relations, for example repatriation of Casement's remains, were handled by the Political Division, whose main focus, however, was on Ireland's UN membership. I was stationed in the embassy in Bonn, Federal Republic of Germany, from 1964 to 1969, and when I became aware of pamphlets produced by the Dungannon-based Campaign for Social Justice in Northern Ireland, I asked the department to let me have copies. The reply was that these were of 'a political nature' and had not been approved by the minister for distribution to or by embassies.

In as far as there was Northern Ireland-related activity in the department in the early days of the 'troubles', it was in the Press and Information section, where, successively, Florrie O'Riordan, Denis Holmes, and Noel Dorr were in charge. Theoretically they were not a policymaking unit, and in normal circumstances their role would have been confined to dealing with the foreign and domestic media and preparing speeches and articles on the basis of known policy. In the absence of alternatives, however, the section played an important policy-formulation role, especially when Noel Dorr was involved.

In July 1968, Eamonn Gallagher returned from a posting in the embassy in Paris and was assigned as a first secretary in the Trade section of the department. He began to spend weekends with his sister, Anna, in Letterkenny, where he had been raised and gone to school.

In August 1969, Gallagher had his first meeting with John Hume. It happened on Gallagher's initiative. Anna was friendly with a Derry-based couple, Conor and Kathleen Desmond, who were friendly with the Humes. Towards the end of the month, Conor Desmond brought Gallagher to meet Hume at Hume's then family home in Derry. Gallagher introduced himself as a representative of the Irish government. Hume

---

[31] In preparing this note, I have consulted Joe Small and Noel Dorr.

subsequently introduced Gallagher to other civil-rights people and Nationalist Party people, initially in the Derry area.[32]

Gallagher began writing reports on the Northern Ireland situation and submitting them to the Secretary of the Department, Hugh J. McCann, who in turn passed them to the minister, P. J. Hillery, and the Taoiseach, Jack Lynch. The first such report that I am aware of is dated November 1969, but it is possible that there are earlier reports. By Christmas 1969, Gallagher's role was recognized at least to the extent that Miss Dempsey, McCann's private secretary, told him that his claims for travel expenses to Northern Ireland would now be paid.

In March 1970, Gallagher was promoted to Counsellor and assigned to the Political Division, where he headed a new section, which became known as the Anglo-Irish Section. There appears to have been no announcement of this, internally or otherwise. It is likely that the Departments of the Taoiseach and/or Finance were consulted, the latter because sanction to create any new post in the civil service was required. In April 1970, Joe Small was transferred from the embassy in Lagos to be First Secretary reporting to Gallagher. Two newly recruited Third Secretaries, Donal Kelly and Jim Brennan, were assigned to the section.

At about the same time, an Inter-Departmental Unit on Northern Ireland (the IDU) was set up. It comprised senior officials from the Departments of the Taoiseach, Finance, and Foreign Affairs and was chaired by the secretary of the Department of the Taoiseach, Dan O'Sullivan. J.F. McInerney represented Finance, and Gallagher represented Foreign Affairs. Joe Small was its secretary. Among its projects was the elaboration of rules and standing orders for the Assembly of the Northern Irish People and a study of possible functions for a Council of Ireland. With the passage of time personnel changed. Dermot Nally took over from O'Sullivan, Maurice Doyle from McInerney, and Bob McDonagh from Gallagher.

Immediately following the introduction of internment in Northern Ireland in August 1971, I was assigned, on a temporary basis, to the Anglo-Irish section from my post as Consul General in Boston. I was told by Gallagher that my main function was to go to Northern Ireland and collect whatever information I could on the circumstances surrounding the introduction of internment. By the end of November that year, it was clear that the information which was gathered and which continued to be gathered would form the basis of the Strasbourg human-rights case. This would obviously take time, and I was permanently transferred from Boston to Dublin. I continued to travel in Northern Ireland, mainly on the human-rights case, through 1972 and early 1973.

On 1 February 1972, a new division was created in the Department of Foreign Affairs with Bob McDonagh as its assistant secretary—that is, head of division. The division had three sections, Anglo-Irish Political, Press and Information, and Cultural (Gallagher was promoted but transferred to the EEC division). My role on the human-rights case continued, but I also took on a broader intelligence-gathering role since neither McDonagh nor anyone else from the department was travelling in Northern Ireland. My expanded role was formalized when the government changed in March 1973 and Garret FitzGerald became Minister for Foreign Affairs. On his first day in office, he asked who was seeing whom in

---

[32] Details given to me by email from Patricia Hume, John's wife, 17 December 2010.

Northern Ireland. When he heard that our contacts were limited and mainly on the nationalist side, he asked that we (*a*) expand our nationalist contacts but continue to exclude those engaged in violence and (*b*) open contacts with the unionist side. Shortly afterwards, a newly appointed counsellor, John McColgan, was assigned specifically to build relationships with unionists.

McDonagh was succeeded as head of the Anglo-Irish Division by Charlie Whelan, who had been number two in the embassy in London. In 1975, I succeeded Whelan as assistant secretary and head of the division and held that position until my appointment as ambassador to the USA in August 1978.

Appendix 1.4. The Northern Ireland Division in the Department of the Taoiseach

THE CREATION OF THE NORTHERN IRELAND DIVISION IN THE DEPARTMENT OF THE TAOISEACH: A NOTE BY WALTER KIRWAN, DECEMBER 2018

In the run-up to the 'troubles', there was no corporate structure within the Irish civil service to consider policy in relation to Northern Ireland. Individual departments reacted to developments there as circumstances demanded. The Department of Finance, for instance, maintained an interest in cross-border economic development policies and economic planning strategies. Up to the early 1970s, the core function of the Department of the Taoiseach was to provide the secretariat for the government and its meetings and, very broadly and with occasional exceptions, the department's senior officials, who were very few in number, did not advise the Taoiseach on policy matters. Before the 'troubles', it was Ken Whitaker, Secretary of the Department of Finance and himself a Northerner, who took the initiative in organizing the Lemass–O'Neill meetings (1965) and the Lynch–O'Neill ones (1967–8). It was to Whitaker that, on the onset of the Northern Ireland 'troubles', the Taoiseach, Jack Lynch, initially turned, and as long as Lynch was Taoiseach Whitaker remained an important source of advice.

Some limited steps were taken by Lynch to provide a small capacity for policy advice within the Department of the Taoiseach, initially with a strong focus on economic policy in the widest sense. First, in 1970 Dr Martin O'Donoghue was seconded from Trinity College to act as an economic advisor; secondly, in 1973 an official of the Department of Local Government, Dermot Nally, was appointed assistant secretary in the Department of the Taoiseach, with a roving brief but also, at the outset, with a primarily economic focus. As developments in Northern Ireland claimed more attention, Nally's focus turned more and more towards policy relating to the northern 'troubles', and, over time, he became the lead official in the civil service in the South dealing with Northern Ireland until his retirement in 1993.

Steps were also taken to draw on wider sources of potentially useful advice within the civil service. An Inter-Departmental Unit on the North of Ireland (IDU) was established on 28 May 1970 by decision of the government ('North of Ireland' was later replaced by 'Northern Ireland'). Its role was to gather and analyse information and offer advice on 'all aspects of Anglo-Irish relations having a bearing on the Six Counties', to undertake the 'study in depth of possible long-term solutions (e.g., the federal solution), as well as short-term problems', to advise on contact with groups in Northern Ireland and Britain, to coordinate information activity abroad, and to act as a clearing house for departmental contacts with Northern Ireland.

The IDU was made up of representatives of the departments of the Taoiseach, External Affairs (which supplied the chair and the secretariat), and Finance. It attracted some internal criticism initially on the basis that it was too involved in 'fire brigade' activities, and that reporting lines were not clear. In March 1972 responsibility for chairing its meetings was transferred to the Department of the Taoiseach.

Following the collapse of Stormont in March 1972, the IDU engaged in extensive exploration of the political options, and by the end of the year it had produced reports in five areas: on alternatives to the British 'guarantee' to unionists, on the options for a new Northern Ireland administration, on the possible shape of a Council of Ireland, on police reform, and on any constitutional, legal, or other actions that reforms in these areas might require in the Republic. The IDU went on to coordinate a great deal of the research into possible structures and functions of a proposed Council of Ireland in 1973–4, before and after the Sunningdale conference of 6–9 December 1973.

Following the collapse of the power-sharing and Council of Ireland experiments, the IDU was enlarged to include also representatives of the Departments of Defence and Justice, reflecting new concerns about security. A further set of reports on options was drawn up in 1975. These included studies on the management of refugees from Northern Ireland in the context of loyalist attacks, on the treatment of casualties of the conflict there, on the potential role of the Irish army in Northern Ireland, on the implications of negotiated independence for Northern Ireland, and on the form that any negotiated repartition of Northern Ireland might take. As the likelihood of further political change receded and as the policy advice capacity in the Departments of the Taoiseach, Foreign Affairs, and Justice dealing with Northern Ireland Affairs became stronger in the late 1970s, the need for the IDU declined, though it continued to meet.

At the level of personnel, the first step that brought support to the ever more involved assistant secretary, Dermot Nally, flowed from the planned Council of Ireland agreed at Sunningdale in December 1973. It was envisaged that there would be joint secretaries, and that in the South this function would be discharged by an official of Principal Officer rank in the Department of the Taoiseach. Following interdepartmental competition, I was appointed (I was then an official in the Department of Finance). The Council of Ireland never functioned, but as worsening violence led to the declaration of a state of national emergency in 1976, and as the involvement of the offices of prime ministers in the direction of European Affairs intensified following the initiation of the European Council in 1975, I was retained and, indeed, reinforced by the creation of a post at Assistant Principal level.

Although work on Northern Ireland had become an important responsibility of the Department of the Taoiseach, a clearly defined division had not yet emerged. Further steps towards that occurred in 1977 and 1978, as Nally was elevated to deputy secretary general rank, I was appointed to the resulting vacancy at assistant secretary general level, and— following the change of government in 1977—Frank Murray became a principal officer reporting to me and focusing primarily on Northern Ireland issues.

The Northern Ireland Division finally took shape as a relatively clearly defined entity in 1980. This followed further reorganization on Charles Haughey's assumption of office in 1979. This led to the abolition of the Department of Economic Planning and Development.

The senior staff of that department, comprising a secretary, an assistant secretary and four principal officers, together with supporting staff, were reassigned to the Department of the Taoiseach, which now became much more active in the formation of domestic economic and social policy. A dual structure was established, with two co-equal secretaries. The cabinet secretariat and the divisions dealing with Northern Ireland, European affairs, and international affairs reported to Dermot Nally, now promoted to secretary level. All other units became the responsibility of Noel Whelan, previously head of the Department of Economic Planning and Development. Aside from that structure, a second secretary post was created, held by Pádraig Ó hAnnracháin, who acted in an 'at large' manner as, essentially, a special political advisor, with a roving brief, which, from time to time, gave him a role in the formation of policy on Northern Ireland. Nally and I continued to have a deep involvement in Northern Ireland matters but were also heavily involved in European Affairs, where, under Haughey, responsibility for coordination of Irish policy on Europe was transferred from the Department of Foreign Affairs to that of the Taoiseach.

This position continued when Garret FitzGerald became Taoiseach in 1981, but, as he indicated in his memoirs, FitzGerald was uncomfortable with the dimensions of the department he inherited from Haughey and, in respect of Northern Ireland and European matters, he tended to rely more on his own creation as minister in 1973–7: an expanded Department of Foreign Affairs. While retaining Dermot Nally as a key advisor, FitzGerald also developed the concept of special advisors, outside divisional structures, reporting directly to the Taoiseach and, in regard to Northern Ireland, he brought Foreign Affairs official Michael Lillis across to the Taoiseach's Department at assistant-secretary level during his first period of office. Later, on Haughey's return to government in 1987 and under Albert Reynolds and Bertie Ahern, former Foreign Affairs official Dr Martin Mansergh had a very influential role as a special advisor on Northern Ireland.

Since 1979, the considerable variation in the arrangements for dealing with the formation and implementation of government policy has reflected the preferences of the Taoiseach of the day. The key role in respect of Northern Ireland was discharged by the Northern Ireland Division of the Department of the Taoiseach, staffed by permanent officials through a single vertical structure, running from secretary or second secretary through a single assistant secretary, a single principal officer, a single assistant principal to a single administrative officer (the 'secretary' title was changed to 'secretary general' in 1997).

The description of an organizational unit in the civil service or elsewhere as a 'division' would normally connote a larger body embracing a number of branches and/or sections, but the term was used in the Department of the Taoiseach without that connotation. This largely reflected the strongly held view of Dermot Nally, the first policy-oriented official recruited into the department in the early 1970s and, effectively, the division's leader as long as he served. He held that the policy advisory capacity in the office of a head of government should be kept small and that attempts to build empires or to duplicate or 'mark' the staffs of such government departments as Foreign Affairs, Finance, or Justice could only result in incoherence and confusion in policy formation and implementation.

I shared Nally's belief that, in respect of policy and events relating to Northern Ireland and the European Union, the Department of the Taoiseach should work in the closest collaboration with, especially, the Departments of Foreign Affairs and Justice. This was, in fact, the norm throughout the period in question. Despite its restricted staffing complement, the Northern Ireland Division of the Department of the Taoiseach succeeded in contributing effectively to such achievements as the Haughey–Thatcher and FitzGerald–Thatcher summit meetings in the early 1980s; the New Ireland Forum, 1983–4; the Anglo-Irish Agreement, 1985; the Downing Street Declaration, 1993; the Forum for Peace and Reconciliation, 1994–6; the initiation of the Saville Inquiry into events on 'Bloody Sunday' (30 January 1972) in Derry, 1998; the Good Friday Agreement, 1998; and implementation of the Agreement since then.

Appendix 1.5. Tables of Office-Holders

Table 1. Taoiseach and Minister for Foreign Affairs, 1966–2019

Date	Taoiseach	Minister for Foreign Affairs
10 November 1966	Jack Lynch (FF)	Frank Aiken (FF)
2 July 1969		Patrick Hillery (FF)
3 January 1973		Brian Lenihan (FF)
14 March 1973	Liam Cosgrave (FG)	Garret FitzGerald (FG)
5 July 1977	Jack Lynch (FF)	Michael O'Kennedy (FF)
11–12 December 1979	Charles Haughey (FF)	Brian Lenihan (FF)
30 June 1981	Garret FitzGerald (FG)	John M. Kelly (FG)
21 October 1981		James Dooge (FG)
9 March 1982	Charles Haughey (FF)	Gerard Collins (FF)
14 December 1982	Garret FitzGerald (FG)	Peter Barry (FG)
10 March 1987	Charles Haughey (FF)	Brian Lenihan (FF)
12 July 1989		Gerard Collins (FF)
11 February 1992	Albert Reynolds (FF)	David Andrews (FF)
12 January 1993		Dick Spring (Lab)
18 November 1994		Albert Reynolds (FF)
15 December 1994	John Bruton (FG)	Dick Spring (Lab)
26 June 1997	Bertie Ahern (FF)	Ray Burke (FF)
8 October 1997		David Andrews (FF)
27 January 2000		Brian Cowen (FF)
29 September 2004		Dermot Ahern (FF)
7 May 2008	Brian Cowen (FF)	Micheál Martin (FF)
19 January 2011		Brian Cowen (FF)
9 March 2011	Enda Kenny (FG)	Eamon Gilmore (Lab)
11 July 2014		Charles Flanagan (FG)
14 June 2017	Leo Varadkar (FG)	Simon Coveney (FG)

Table 2. Secretary/Secretary General, Department of Foreign Affairs, 1963–2019

Date	Secretary/Secretary-General
1963	Hugh McCann
1974	Paul Keating
1977	Robert McDonagh
1978	Andrew O'Rourke
1981	Seán Donlon
1987	Noel Dorr
1995	Pádraic MacKernan
2001	Dermot Gallagher
2009	David Cooney
2014	Niall Burgess

Table 3. Irish Ambassador to the United Kingdom, 1964–2019

Date	Ambassador
1964	John Molloy
1970	Donal O'Sullivan
1977	Paul Keating
1978	Eamon Kennedy
1983	Noel Dorr
1987	Andrew O'Rourke
1991	Joseph Small
1995	Edward Barrington
2001	Daithí Ó Ceallaigh
2007	David Cooney
2009	Bobby McDonagh
2013	Dan Mulhall
2017	Adrian O'Neill

Table 4. Head, Anglo-Irish Division, Department of Foreign Affairs, 1972–2019

Date	Head, Anglo-Irish Division
1972	Robert McDonagh
1974	Charles Whelan
1975	Seán Donlon
1978	David Neligan
1983	Michael Lillis
1986	Eamon Ó Tuathail
1987	Dermot Gallagher
1991	Seán Ó hUigínn
1997	Dermot Gallagher
2000	Daithí Ó Ceallaigh
2001	Brendan Scannell
2005	Patrick Hennessy
2009	Adrian O'Neill
2010	Niall Burgess
2014	Adrian O'Neill
2017	Fergal Mythen

Table 5. Irish Joint Secretary, Anglo-Irish and British–Irish Intergovernmental Conference, 1985–2019

Date	Joint Secretary
	Anglo-Irish Intergovernmental Conference
1985	Michael Lillis
1987	Seán Ó hUiginn
1990	Declan O'Donovan
1995	David Donoghue
1999	Donal Hamill
	British–Irish Intergovernmental Conference
1999	Donal Hamill
2001	Ray Bassett
2005	Gary Ansbro
2008	Colm Ó Floinn
2010	Kieran Dowling
2012	Barbara Jones
2014	Ruairí de Búrca
2017	Kevin Conmy

Table 6. Prime Minister and Secretary of State for Northern Ireland, 1964–2019

Date	Prime Minister	NI Secretary
16 October 1964	Harold Wilson (Lab.)	
30 November 1967		*James Callaghan (Home Secretary)*
19–20 June 1970	Edward Heath (Con.)	*Reginald Maudling (Home Secretary)*
24 March 1972		William Whitelaw
2 December 1973		Francis Pym
4–5 March 1974	Harold Wilson (Lab.)	Merlyn Rees
5 April 1976	James Callaghan (Lab.)	
10 September 1976		Roy Mason
4–5 May 1979	Margaret Thatcher (Con.)	Humphrey Atkins
14 September 1981		James Prior
11 September 1984		Douglas Hurd
3 September 1985		Tom King
24 July 1989		Peter Brooke
28 November 1990	John Major (Con.)	
10 April 1982		Patrick Mayhew
2–3 May 1997	Tony Blair (Lab.)	Mo Mowlam
11 October 1999		Peter Mandelson
25 January 2001		John Reid
24 October 2002		Paul Murphy
6 May 2005		Peter Hain
27–8 June 2007	Gordon Brown (Lab.)	Shaun Woodward
11–12 May 2010	David Cameron (Con.)	Owen Paterson
4 September 2012		Theresa Villiers
13–14 July 2016	Theresa May (Con.)	James Brokenshire
8 January 2018		Karen Bradley
24 July 2019	Boris Johnson (Con.)	Julian Smith

Note: Several officials on the British side were knighted but are listed here without their titles since these were typically (but not always) acquired some time after their appointments.

Table 7. Head, Northern Ireland Office, 1972–2019

Date	Head
	Permanent Under Secretary
1972	William Nield
1973	Frank Cooper
1976	Brian Cubbon
1979	Kenneth Stowe
1981	Philip Woodfield
1984	Robert Andrew
1988	John Blelloch
1990	John Chilcot
1997	Joseph Pilling
2005	Jonathan Phillips
	Director-General
2010	Hilary Jackson
2012	Julian King
	Permanent Under Secretary
2014	Jonathan Stephens

Table 8. British Ambassador to Ireland, 1964–2019

Date	Ambassador
1964	Geofroy Tory
1967	Andrew Gilchrist
1970	John Peck
1973	Arthur Galsworthy
1976	Christopher Ewart-Biggs
1976	Robin Haydon
1980	Leonard Figg
1983	Alan Goodison
1986	Nicholas Fenn
1991	David Blatherwick
1995	Veronica Sutherland
1999	Ivor Roberts
2003	Stewart Eldon
2006	David Reddaway
2009	Julian King
2012	Dominick Chilcott
2016	Robin Barnett

Table 9. Political Director, Northern Ireland Office, 1972–2011

Date	Political Director
1972	Neil Cairncross
1972	Philip Woodfield
1974	Douglas Janes
1979	John Marshall
1982	Anthony Brennan
1987	Ian Burns
1990	Joseph Pilling
1991	Quentin Thomas
1998	William Jeffrey
2002	Jonathan Phillips
	Director General (Political)
2005	Robert Hannigan
2007	Hilary Jackson

Note: The post was originally designated Deputy Under Secretary (London). It was abolished in 2011. A second post at the same rank, Deputy Under Secretary (Belfast), was responsible for security matters.

Table 10. Under Secretary (Political), Northern Ireland Office, 1979–2008

Date	Under Secretary (Political)
1979	Ian Burns
1984	David Chesterton
1988	Quentin Thomas
1991	Peter Bell
1995	Stephen Leach
1996	Jonathan Stephens
1998	William Fittall
	Political Director (London)
2000	David Cooke
2004	Robert Hannigan
2005	Hilary Jackson
	Political Director (Belfast)
2000	Christopher Maccabe

Note: The post was originally designated Assistant Under Secretary (London), and was answerable to the Deputy Under Secretary (London). In 2000 the additional post of Political Director (Belfast) was created. Both posts were abolished in 2008.

Table 11. British Joint Secretary, Anglo-Irish and British–Irish
Intergovernmental Conference, 1985–2019

Head	Joint Secretary
	Anglo-Irish Intergovernmental Conference
1985	Mark Elliott
1988	Oliver Miles
1990	Robert Alston
1993	Martin Williams
1996	Peter Bell
	British–Irish Intergovernmental Conference
2000	Christopher Maccabe
2008	Mary Madden
2013	Michael McAvoy
2015	Kate Beggs
2017	Clare Sloan

2

The Sunningdale Agreement, 1973

2.1. Introduction

The Sunningdale Agreement of December 1973 provided for North–South institutions that would complete a newly agreed structure of governance for Northern Ireland. This proposed new structure failed at the implementation hurdle, when a central institution, the power-sharing Northern Ireland Executive, collapsed in the face of the loyalist Ulster Workers' Council (UWC) strike of May 1974. Notwithstanding this reversal, the Agreement stands out as a milestone in the British–Irish relationship: after decades of exclusion from any say in the politics of Northern Ireland, the British government had sought the cooperation of the Irish government in devising a solution to political instability and civil unrest there.

The introduction of power-sharing government and provision for recognition of the 'Irish dimension' represented a radical new departure, and these became key features of future settlement initiatives. Formal declarations by the two governments at the time marked an important shift in the traditional position of each; each government solemnly recognized that the future status of Northern Ireland would be determined by the wishes of a majority there. For the Irish government this stance represented a fundamental reorientation of long-standing priorities, which had for decades stressed the 'injustice' of partition and called for Irish unity as the outcome supported by a majority of people on the island of Ireland.

Sunningdale generated radically divergent views and interpretations among the parties and voters in Northern Ireland. In part this reflected uncertainty about how the new institutions were going to function, about whether the remaining imbalance of power resources at the social, economic, and cultural levels would give unionists a continued advantage in the new political institutions, and about whether the aspiration for Irish unity would grow or diminish in strength with increased nationalist political influence in power-sharing government and through North–South links. Yet many politicians and citizens believed that the new institutions could bring political stability. Their collapse pointed to problems that Sunningdale had been unable to tackle.

As is detailed in this chapter, the problems included a series of contingent events—a change of government in London following an election, and a constitutional challenge in Dublin—that provoked a destabilization of the institutions (Dorr 2017: 377–81). Once these had occurred, a set of decisions, most of all the British decision not to intervene to remove the barricades in the initial days of the

Negotiating a Settlement in Northern Ireland, 1969–2019.
John Coakley and Jennifer Todd, Oxford University Press (2020). © John Coakley and Jennifer Todd.
DOI: 10.1093/oso/9780198841388.001.0001

UWC strike in May 1974, sealed the fate of the institutions (Kerr 2006; McCann and McGrattan 2017). But there was, and remains, no consensus as to why bad judgements had such disastrous effects. One argument is that the Agreement was too ambitious in its aspirations for a Council of Ireland, and that it pushed the unionists a bridge too far.[1] This assumes that unionists, unpushed, would have been willing to go the extra mile to compromise with nationalists on internal Northern Ireland affairs: to reform the policing system, to end internment, to remedy economic inequality, and to validate Irish culture in Northern Ireland. Alternatively, it assumes that nationalists would have been willing to accept Protestant and unionist hegemony in these fields into the future. The mechanisms by which a process of consensual reform might have begun—if the Council of Ireland had not so angered unionists—are far from evident.

Another argument is that the Agreement was insufficiently inclusive: that, by leaving the Democratic Unionist Party (DUP) outside the executive and margin-alizing republicans, it reduced its chances of success (see discussion in McGarry and O'Leary 2017). A third argument is that the wider social and political context made any political agreement vulnerable to political contingencies and misjudge-ments and removed its resilience to exogenous shocks (see Ruane and Todd 2014; Wolff 2001). So, for example, neither state was prepared for the long task of reforming the socioeconomic as well as the political institutions of Northern Ireland, and the British elite was disinclined to get too involved in the process of internal reconstruction (Todd 2014). Meanwhile, the significant advantage that the unionist population still held in the economy, in the security forces, in the civil service, and in the political culture encouraged their expectation that they could get rid of the Agreement if they wanted to. At the same time, the Irish government faced its own dilemmas and problems as it redirected its long-standing irredentist rhetoric and began to develop a more pragmatic strategy towards Northern Ireland (Coakley 2017a, b).

The Sunningdale experiment raises important questions as to how the British and Irish governments conceived of the Northern Ireland conflict at this time, what their longer-term strategy was, how it developed, what they believed could be achieved by Sunningdale, and what capacity they thought they had to shape the process. This chapter explores the views of Irish civil servants and policymakers who were party to this process. It shows the developing and shifting Irish views over the period of negotiation, implementation, and collapse, and the choices that they saw for themselves in the face of the British decision not to intervene against the strike. It begins by detailing the context in which the Sunningdale conference took place. In the witness seminar that follows, the Irish participants discuss their perceptions of and perspectives on that conference.

---

[1] See Subsection 2.4.1.

2.1.1. The Northern Ireland Context

The vacuum left by the suspension of the parliament and government of Northern Ireland on 24 March 1972 needed to be filled quickly given the growing intensity of the civil conflict, as discussed in Chapter 1 (see Table 2.1 for a summary of key events). The appointment of William Whitelaw to the new post of Secretary of State for Northern Ireland and the creation of a new Northern Ireland Office were first steps and were followed quickly by efforts to find a more enduring solution. On the one hand, secret talks took place between the IRA and representatives of the British government during the summer of 1972; they failed to reach any agreement. On the other hand, discussions took place with the political parties with a view to devising alternative structures of government. A key development was a meeting in a hotel near Darlington, Durham, England, on 25–8 October 1972 between the Northern Ireland Secretary, the Ulster Unionist Party, the Northern Ireland Labour Party, and the Alliance Party of Northern Ireland. The Social Democratic and Labour Party (SDLP) refused to attend in protest against the policy of internment of suspects without trial, a policy introduced in August 1971 and still in force at that time. The party did, however, publish its own policy proposals, *Towards a New Ireland* (Social Democratic and Labour Party 1972).

Table 2.1. Important political developments, 1969–1974

Date	Development
28 December 1969	Split in IRA and formation of Provisional IRA
30 March 1972	Introduction of direct rule from London to replace Northern Ireland institutions created in 1921
30 October 1972	British government discussion document, *The Future of Northern Ireland* (Green Paper)
20 March 1973	British government policy document, *Northern Ireland Constitutional Proposals* (White Paper)
28 June 1973	Election by proportional representation of new Northern Ireland Assembly
21 November 1973	Three parties (Ulster Unionists, SDLP, Alliance Party) agree on formation of power-sharing executive
9 December 1973	Communiqué announces agreement at end of Sunningdale conference (6–9 December)
1 January 1974	Power-sharing executive takes office
4 January 1974	Ulster Unionist Council rejects Council of Ireland, leading to Faulkner's resignation as party leader (7 January)
28 February 1974	Election to UK House of Commons: anti-agreement unionists win 11 out of 12 Northern Ireland seats; Labour Party replaces Conservative Party in government
14 May 1974	Political strike led by Ulster Workers' Council begins (ends, 29 May)
28 May 1974	Resignation of Unionist ministers leads to collapse of executive

The parties expressed themselves in favour of the following institutional arrangements (Northern Ireland Office 1972):

- Ulster Unionist Party: a unicameral assembly elected by the plurality ('first-past-the-post') system with a set of committees at least half of which would be chaired by opposition members; a prime minister and executive answerable to the assembly; policing and law and order to be a matter for these authorities; a comprehensive bill of rights; and, subject to the outcome of talks to secure agreement on the status of Northern Ireland and on appropriate North–South security cooperation, an Irish Intergovernmental Council to discuss matters of mutual interest, especially in the economic and social areas;
- Alliance Party: a unicameral assembly elected by the single transferable vote (STV) system of proportional representation with a set of committees whose chairs would be proportionally representative of the assembly and would have executive functions; a local police force (controlled by the assembly) alongside one for more serious crimes (the latter, the Royal Ulster Constabulary, would be controlled by Westminster); a bill of rights based on the Universal Declaration of Human Rights; and an advisory Anglo-Irish Council with representatives from the British parliament, the Dáil, and the Northern Ireland assembly;
- Northern Ireland Labour Party: a unicameral assembly elected by proportional representation with a set of committees whose chairs would be proportionally representative of the assembly and would have ministerial functions; policing and law and order to be controlled by Westminster, though with management of the police devolved to the assembly; a bill of rights; and a 'consultative and deliberative' Council of Ireland;
- SDLP: a British declaration in favour of Irish unity and, in the interim, joint sovereignty to be exercised through commissioners representing the British and Irish governments; a unicameral assembly elected by the STV system of proportional representation; an executive elected from the assembly by proportional representation; security to be controlled by the British and Irish commissioners; and a National Senate of Ireland with equal representation from Dublin and Belfast to plan North–South integration.

Immediately after the conference, on 30 October 1972, the British government published a discussion document (Green Paper; Northern Ireland Office 1972) outlining the options and specifying the criteria that would have to be met in any settlement. These included the need to acknowledge the 'Irish dimension', subject to a guarantee to the people of Northern Ireland that the status of Northern Ireland as part of the United Kingdom would not be changed without their consent, and the proviso that any new regional government be based on the involvement of 'minority interests' in the exercise of executive power. A plebiscite was promised to ascertain the electorate's views on the issue of Irish unity. The plebiscite duly took place on 8 March 1973, and, though boycotted by nationalists, it achieved a 57 per cent turnout, with 99 per cent voting to maintain the Union.

Following a further period of consultation, the British government published more specific proposals in a policy document (White Paper; Northern Ireland Office 1973) on 20 March 1973. This proposed an assembly elected by proportional representation, an executive drawn from both sections of the community, and 'institutional arrangements for consultation and co-operation between Northern Ireland and the Republic of Ireland'. The proposals provoked deep divisions within the Ulster Unionist Party, which was still led by Brian Faulkner.[2] Considerable numbers of the party's activists were opposed to the principles embodied in the White Paper but remained within the party; a more militant group with links to loyalist paramilitaries, the 'Vanguard' movement, broke away entirely. Vanguard had been founded on 9 February 1972 by former Home Affairs Minister William Craig and others as a ginger group within the Ulster Unionist Party and reconstituted itself on 30 March 1973 as the Vanguard Unionist Progressive Party. The government nevertheless pushed ahead with its plans, and on 3 May 1973 the Northern Ireland Assembly Act became law.

Even before the election to the new Assembly took place on 28 June 1973, however, the broad shape of the new party system was prefigured in the results of the first elections to the new local authorities on 30 May 1973. These were of great importance as the first elections in the territory of Northern Ireland by proportional representation since 1925, and formed part of a fundamental reform of local government, with the old system of county, rural, urban, and other councils, which had been discredited by widespread practices of electoral gerrymandering, replaced by a new, single-tier system of twenty-six local-government districts. The combination of deep divisions within unionism and the tendency for proportional representation to facilitate multi-party politics resulted in a very fragmented party system (Knight and Baxter-Moore 1973). The Ulster Unionist Party remained the largest party by far, but much of its support moved to the DUP and to smaller unionist and loyalist groups. This was the first electoral outing for the new SDLP and Alliance parties, which had a big impact, largely supplanting the Nationalist Party and the Northern Ireland Labour Party respectively.

These results were broadly confirmed by the Assembly election two months later (Knight 1974; Lawrence, Elliott, and Laver 1975). The Ulster Unionist Party was still the largest, but the DUP and the Vanguard Party performed well, and had allies within the Ulster Unionist Party itself, where a significant minority strongly opposed the provisions of the White Paper (see Table 2.2). The SDLP entirely

---

[2] Faulkner had carried on as party leader even after his position as prime minister of Northern Ireland came to an end on the suspension of the Stormont institutions in 1972.

Table 2.2. Results of election to Northern Ireland Assembly, 1973

Party	Votes	Seats
Ulster Unionist Party*	35.8	31
Vanguard Unionist Party	10.5	7
Democratic Unionist Party	10.8	8
Other unionists	5.1	4
Alliance Party	9.2	8
Northern Ireland Labour Party	2.6	1
Others	0.3	0
SDLP	22.1	19
Republican Clubs	1.8	0
Other nationalists	1.8	0
Total	100.0	78

*Including 'Anti-White Paper' unionists (10.5%, 9 seats).

Source: Computed from ARK (2019); Electoral Office for Northern Ireland (2019).

dominated the nationalist or Catholic vote, with the Alliance Party holding a strong position in the centre. The first meeting of the Assembly took place on 31 July 1973. Prolonged negotiations between the Ulster Unionist Party, the SDLP, and the Alliance Party chaired by the Northern Ireland Secretary resulted in agreement in principle on a power-sharing executive on 21 November 1973.

2.1.2. The British–Irish Dimension

Political changes in London and Dublin formed a crucial background to developments during this period. On the British side, Harold Wilson's Labour administration had been in power during the early years of civil unrest, and the Home Secretary, James Callaghan, was directly responsible for relations with Northern Ireland. At the general election of 18 June 1970, however, Wilson lost to the Conservative Ted Heath, and the new Home Secretary, Reginald Maudling, was responsible for the management of Northern Ireland during the turbulent last years of the old regime there. With the creation of the new office of Secretary of State for Northern Ireland in March 1972, however, responsibility passed to William Whitelaw. At a critical time, on 2 December 1973, Whitelaw was replaced in this position by Francis Pym, who was less familiar with the challenges posed by Northern Ireland. Of particular significance for later developments, though, was the defeat of the Conservative government at the general election of 28 February 1974: it brought in a new Labour government headed by Harold Wilson, with Merlyn Rees as Northern Ireland Secretary—an administration that was less committed to the new institutions that had been so painstakingly crafted.

On the Irish side, Jack Lynch's Fianna Fáil government was in power when civil unrest began in Northern Ireland. In August 1969, following violent disturbances in Derry and Belfast, the Irish government decided to press for a UN peacekeeping force for Northern Ireland, but an appearance before the UN Security Council by the Irish Minister for External Affairs, Patrick Hillery, to seek such a force was unsuccessful. At home, Hillery strongly supported Lynch in facing down internal criticism as he developed a new, more accommodating approach to Northern Ireland. When Hillery left to become a European Commissioner in January 1973, he was succeeded briefly in the post by Brian Lenihan. The general election of 28 February 1973 resulted in a Fine Gael–Labour coalition headed by Liam Cosgrave and Brendan Corish, with Garret FitzGerald as Minister for Foreign Affairs. Unusually for a southern politician, FitzGerald had an intense interest in Northern Ireland and paid particular attention to this part of his brief. The Irish government initially had little knowledge of or expertise on Northern Ireland. The efforts of individual civil servants were, however, soon institutionalized, with the creation of an Inter-Departmental Unit on Northern Ireland (IDU), of a specialist Northern Ireland Division within the Department of External Affairs in 1970, and of a similar Northern Ireland Division within the Department of the Taoiseach, in effect from 1974 (see Chapter 1 and Appendices 1.3 and 1.4).

Alongside the talks between the Northern Ireland parties and the Northern Ireland Secretary that led to agreement in principle on a power-sharing executive in autumn 1973, discussions over new political arrangements for Northern Ireland also involved intensive negotiations between the two governments. These extended over late 1972 and all of 1973, and included meetings between Prime Minister Ted Heath and Taoiseach Jack Lynch in September and December 1972, which were followed by further negotiations between Heath and Lynch's successor, Liam Cosgrave, in July and September 1973. Together with parallel discussions by civil servants, these resulted in a good deal of agreement, making it possible for the British side to produce a substantial draft of a communiqué even before the official final conference had begun (see Document 2.1). Finally, on 6–9 December 1973 teams led by the two prime ministers met the three Northern Ireland parties that had agreed to share power at the civil-service college at Sunningdale, Berkshire, England.[3] There, they agreed on the establishment of a Council of Ireland to complement the power-sharing executive, adopted declarations guaranteeing that the status of Northern Ireland would depend on the wishes of a majority there, and made commitments to tackle serious challenges in the areas of security and human rights (for the text of the Agreement, see Document 2.2).

[3] The talks were chaired by Ted Heath, as British prime minister.

The extent to which the British position was shifting is reflected in the differences between the British draft communiqué and the final version. The British draft echoed the words of the Northern Ireland Constitution Act, 1973, to the effect that Northern Ireland would not cease to be part of the United Kingdom 'without the consent of the majority of the people of Northern Ireland'. This had been designed to transfer to the people of Northern Ireland the guarantee given to the parliament of Northern Ireland in the Ireland Act, 1949. But the draft went rather further, in committing the British government 'to support the wishes of the majority [...] if in the future the majority of the people of Northern Ireland should indicate a wish to become part of the Republic of Ireland'. The final communiqué was a more unreserved endorsement of the 'consent' principle. It was a solemn declaration that

> it was, and would remain, [British government] policy to support the wishes of the majority of the people of Northern Ireland. The present status of Northern Ireland is that it is part of the United Kingdom. If in the future the majority of the people of Northern Ireland should indicate a wish to become part of a united Ireland, the British Government would support that wish.

The Irish government had developed a rough but ambitious blueprint for the kinds of powers and functions that would be transferred to the Council of Ireland. A relatively developed version of this in November 1973 proposed that the number of staff to be transferred from the southern side would be just under 6,000, with a corresponding budget of almost £17m (though at different stages in the evolution of these estimates other numbers of staff—sometimes much larger— were given). The areas proposed for transfer included various agricultural services (2,080 staff, £5m); forestry (1,000 staff, almost £3m); social-welfare administration (800 staff, £2.5m); and three other areas of similar size (with about 300 staff and a cost of about £1m in each case)—the meteorological service, the housing area of local government, and health-service administration.[4] Pressure for full agreement on all details at Sunningdale was, however, reduced by a decision to defer formal ratification of the Agreement to a later conference once the Northern Ireland Executive had taken office. This gave additional time for the negotiation of unresolved matters, such as long-term funding arrangements and the list of functions to be transferred. Importantly, arrangements for the Council of Ireland were linked to two other issues on which agreement was reached in principle: security cooperation and recognition of the status of Northern Ireland. This status was not, however, specified by the Irish government to avoid the possibility of

---

[4] See 'Council of Ireland Financing: Estimates of the Numbers of Staff who would be Transferred from Central Government Departments and of the Costs Involved', 28 November 1973, National Archives of Ireland (NAI) TSCH/2004/21/627.

conflict with the constitution; the Sunningdale communiqué instead used parallel texts to ensure that the Irish government declaration did not appear to endorse the British understanding of 'status').

2.1.3. The Power-Sharing Executive and the UWC Strike

The new executive took office on 1 January 1974. It included six Ulster Unionists (including Brian Faulkner as Chief Executive), four members of the SDLP (including party leader Gerry Fitt as Deputy Chief Executive), and one representative of the Alliance Party. Although the executive itself functioned amicably, with rather good personal relationships between its members despite their conflicting political views, it got little opportunity to establish itself or to root itself within Northern Ireland's fragmented political culture. It came under immediate pressure from Faulkner's unionist critics, who, while also objecting to power-sharing, targeted in particular the Council of Ireland, which they claimed represented a united Ireland in embryo.

A mixture of deep divisions within unionism and contingent external factors undermined the position of the new executive. First, Brian Faulkner was forced to engage in vigorous battle with his opponents in the Ulster Unionist Party, who sought to mobilize the party grassroots against him. At its meeting on 4 January 1974, the Ulster Unionist Council, the central source of authority in the party, rejected the Council of Ireland proposal by 417 votes to 374. This precipitated Faulkner's resignation as party leader. He continued to function as leader of the Ulster Unionist Assembly group, and eventually formed a new party, the Unionist Party of Northern Ireland. The new party, though, lacked the organizational resources of the parent party, which now came under the control of the anti-Sunningdale group. Second, the British general election of 28 February 1974 demonstrated the extent of unionist opposition to the deal. Opponents of the Agreement won eleven of Northern Ireland's twelve Westminster seats, leaving SDLP leader Gerry Fitt as the only MP favouring it, and dealing its supporters a critical morale blow. Third, the election brought to power a new Labour government in London, headed by Harold Wilson, that had little sense of ownership of the Agreement. Fourth, Faulkner's position was weakened by a court case in Dublin. Kevin Boland, a former Fianna Fáil minister who had resigned in 1970 alleging that the Taoiseach, Jack Lynch, was insufficiently supportive of the traditional nationalist position, initiated a constitutional challenge in the High Court, claiming that the Sunningdale Agreement violated articles 2 and 3 of the Irish constitution by accepting the validity of partition. Since the Irish attorney general's defence was that there was no formal agreement to recognize the status of Northern Ireland, a central plank of Faulkner's defence of what he had negotiated at Sunningdale was removed. Finally, violence on the part of the IRA and of loyalist paramilitaries continued, allowing its critics to argue that the Agreement had brought few tangible benefits (see Dorr 2017: 374–86; Hennessey 2015; McCann and McGrattan 2017).

Given a widespread unionist perception that, despite their concessions on the Council of Ireland, they had won little in the form of increased security or of Irish government recognition of Northern Ireland's status, Faulkner encountered considerable difficulty in delivering on the remaining stages of what had been agreed at Sunningdale. A meeting of northern and southern ministers at Hillsborough, Co. Down, on 1 February 1974 failed to make progress. The proposed powers and functions of the Council of Ireland were watered down in successive North–South negotiations—a process that was not necessarily unwelcome to the civil service in Dublin, where there was evidence of resistance to the transfer of functions to the Council (Coakley 2017c: 64; FitzGerald 1991: 203, 225). No agreement was reached on a date for the formal conference that would seal the deal negotiated in general terms in Sunningdale. Opposition finally crystallized on 14 May 1974 in the form of a general strike organized by the Ulster Workers' Council, an umbrella group for a range of loyalist and unionist, political, trade union, and paramilitary interests. Faced with continuing violence, the prospect of a prolonged and costly disruption of the electricity supply, and the passive position adopted by the British government and the security forces, the unionist members of the executive resigned on 28 May 1974. This brought the power-sharing experiment to an end.

2.1.4. The Witness Seminar

The witness seminar, which took place on 7 September 2005 at the Geary Institute in University College Dublin, included Austin Currie, formerly of the SDLP; Seán Donlon, Noel Dorr, Mahon Hayes, and John Swift, formerly of the Department of Foreign Affairs; Garret FitzGerald, former leader of Fine Gael and Taoiseach; Muiris Mac Conghail, journalist and former Head of the Government Information Bureau; and Dermot Nally, formerly of the Taoiseach's department.

Academic questioners included Ronan Fanning, Christopher Farrington, Susan McDermott, and Jennifer Todd.

2.2. Background to the Negotiations

2.2.1. Participant Roles

MUIRIS MAC CONGHAIL: The ground rules that I set for Sunningdale were that I went privately to the head of facilities in RTÉ to disclose to him what was happening at Sunningdale so that I could have a live feed of RTÉ radio brought into the press room, for the Irish correspondents in particular, so that in determining the nature of the coverage they would be responding as much to how Sunningdale was seen from Ireland rather than taking the British media lead in this matter.

DERMOT NALLY: My business was to stay as close as possible to whoever happened to be the Taoiseach, to make sure, as far as possible, that he got all information and briefings as necessary, and to record what happened when he met other prime ministers, in particular Heath and Wilson. There were very full notes of these meetings.[5]

NOEL DORR: From July 1970 to April 1974 I was attached to the Press and Information section in Foreign Affairs. I wrote various speeches and so on for both Jack Lynch and Liam Cosgrave, including the *Foreign Affairs* article which was published under Jack Lynch's name in 1972 in the American journal *Foreign Affairs*.[6] My draft was rather toughened up by my colleague Eamonn Gallagher.[7] In the period up to Sunningdale, under the coalition government, I wrote various speeches which tried to articulate the kind of thing that was envisaged. At Sunningdale itself, though I was Head of Press and Information, when I reflect on it, over the four days I never went to the press centre. I wrote the opening and closing statements for Liam Cosgrave for the conference. Particularly in the opening statement, I tried as best I could to set out the whole rationale, the whole approach to the conference and what the idea behind it was, including the Council of Ireland.

JOHN SWIFT: I was the lowest head on the DFA [Department of Foreign Affairs] totem pole at Sunningdale. Before Sunningdale, I was one of the three or four 'travellers' in Northern Ireland, talking on a regular basis to various people there, including Austin [Currie]. After it, I spent some time as one of the six secretaries of the Anglo-Irish Law Commission, which dealt with extradition, all-Ireland courts, and extraterritorial jurisdiction. Later, Sunningdale became a personal touchstone for me and for my views and interpretations of events and developments in the North.

MAHON HAYES: I think I'm right in saying that there were four of us around this table who were at Sunningdale at counsellor level. For my own part I was legal advisor in the Department of Foreign Affairs from 1970 and I remember much more about the preparations for Sunningdale than Sunningdale itself, about which my recollection is scrappy and anecdotal rather than very significant. Before Sunningdale, the government set up a committee under the chairman-ship of the Attorney General to look at the legal implications of what might or

---

[5] The Nally papers have been deposited in the UCD Archive (UCDA P254).
[6] See Lynch (1972).
[7] Eamonn Gallagher (1926–2009) was an official in the Department of External Affairs who specialized in Northern Ireland policy from 1968 until assuming responsibility for EEC matters in 1972.

might not come out of Sunningdale, and I was a member of that committee. One of the things we looked at was how a Council of Ireland could be set up— how could this be done between the parties, who the parties should be, what the implications would be for the constitution, what legislation would be required. It was mostly Council of Ireland stuff that was the main topic, but there was also a slight look at the question of extradition, and there was consideration of the possibility of a court which could be either attached to the Council, with functions in relation to the Council, and/or an all-Ireland court, and of an all-Ireland court of human rights. I have no recollection of being involved in any discussions of any of this during Sunningdale.

AUSTIN CURRIE: I was a member of the SDLP negotiating team involved at Stormont Castle prior to Sunningdale. When we got to Sunningdale there were significant matters which had already been agreed, but clearly there were certain matters that had not or could not be agreed in advance of the conference. I refer specifically of course to the status declaration, to the Council of Ireland, to extradition, and also, very importantly, to the whole position in relation to policing.[8] After Sunningdale I was a member of the power-sharing executive which was brought down on 28 May 1974.

SEÁN DONLON: I have been involved in Northern Ireland matters since August 1971, when I was asked to assemble and assess information which formed the basis of the interstate human-rights case.[9] From roughly the beginning of 1973 and particularly when the government changed in March of 1973, Garret [FitzGerald] had asked me to maintain very detailed contact with as many people in the political spectrum as possible. Obviously my primary contacts were with people in the SDLP, but I also had contact with community leaders, priests, bishops, and so on, and, on one occasion, with Dermot Nally, I went to see Brian Faulkner—I believe in October 1973.

DERMOT NALLY: We had gooseberry juice before lunch!

SEÁN DONLON: We had gooseberry juice. That meeting in fact had been primarily set up by John Hume. Once the inter-party talks in Stormont had started in October 1973, the SDLP delegation kept me fully informed every step of the way. Normally after a session you would come to a location in West Belfast and [the SDLP would] brief me as to what happened. I would then do my report, go down to Dublin, and come back up again. Most of the serious negotiation at Sunningdale took place at political level and a lot of civil-service

---

[8] The 'status declaration' refers to the constitutional status of Northern Ireland, discussed in Subsection 2.3.3.

[9] Following allegations that fourteen persons detained without trial in Northern Ireland in August 1971 had been tortured, the Irish government took a case against the British government in the European Court of Human Rights in Strasbourg. The court ruled in 1978 that the detainees had been subjected to 'inhuman and degrading treatment', but not torture. The case was reopened on the basis of new evidence in 2014. In 2018 the court reaffirmed the earlier finding; the Irish government was not granted permission to appeal.

time was spent in corridors outside. But Mahon has forgotten one bit. Mahon and I didn't get to go to dinner the night before Sunningdale, and we stayed at the Irish Embassy and we did forty-three redrafts of Articles 2 and 3.

NOEL DORR: Four of us did, at the Irish Embassy. We were told to redraft the status declaration, while everybody else, Garret and Liam Cosgrave and Dermot Nally, went off to have dinner at Downing Street, and we were very disgruntled. First of all we couldn't get any sandwiches or anything in the Embassy. Seán sat down and the first thing he did was to get a piece of paper and he wrote on the top of it, draft number 43 or something like that [...] and then we worked away and we did our best to soften it, which was what we were told to do. The government had agreed a text on the status of Northern Ireland [...] that was to be our negotiating position when Sunningdale started, but somebody, I'm not sure who, at ministerial or Taoiseach level, decided that we would be asked to redraft it somewhat to try a softer version that evening.

GARRET FITZGERALD: What does 'softer' mean?

NOEL DORR: Well, to give a little more to the unionists. And when you all came back from Downing Street at about 12.30 or 1.00 a.m., and some were happier than others, we produced our text and there was general astonishment and disapproval—we were asked what did we mean, officials softening the text that the government had agreed on. That added to our grievance because we had been told to do this and had been deprived of dinner.

SEÁN DONLON: Just to finish then, in summary, before Sunningdale my primary contacts were obviously with the SDLP, some contact with the unionists, some contact with the British through their office in Laneside—James Allen, who had been there since, I would guess 1972–3 (James Allen was probably MI5). Then when the Northern Ireland Office got going, senior people stayed at least Monday to Friday in the Culloden Hotel, just outside Hollywood. So occasionally I would meet with the British in the Culloden Hotel and then after Sunningdale those contacts obviously continued and were probably intensified, particularly in the period during the UWC strike and afterwards.[10]

2.2.2. Expectations

Q: Can I ask what at the time you all thought was happening historically?

GARRET FITZGERALD: We felt we had arrived, the whole thing was settled. Well, you see, the IRA were not involved, and we were thinking obviously about the parties, but it seemed that if we got an agreement, we thought, the IRA would be almost made irrelevant.

---

[10] The Ulster Workers' Council strike is discussed in Subsection 2.1.3.

MUIRIS MAC CONGHAIL: Well I think there's an issue in this, looking at the background, looking exactly at the atmosphere in Ireland at that time, looking at the anniversary of the Treaty and considering the government strategy. This was that it should meet as a government in Sunningdale—it should travel with its complete bag there and not leave anything behind for very obvious reasons, but everybody knew what the obvious reason was.

Noel Dorr and I were down some days previously buying Tom Jones's *Whitehall Diaries*, not because of that, but suddenly this all became relevant.[11] When we went to Sunningdale, it was against a backdrop in which the main political party at Sunningdale from Ireland had also been somewhere else in 1922 or 1921, and this was a very interesting, guiding thing.

Desmond O'Malley says, 'What would you expect of this government on the eve of the anniversary of the signing of the Treaty?' We must put it all into the context of what was happening, the actual chemical make-up of the whole mood as it then was. The government had just won a by-election against the odds in Monaghan, and think about Monaghan and Ernest Blythe in 1933, and Alexander Haslett.[12] Think about that, and the important issue of that occurring in the build-up to Sunningdale, plus, if I may say so, several collections of tensions within the government and between the members of the government about the issues. It would be unfair of us to ignore these tensions between Dr Fitzgerald and Conor Cruise O'Brien and the SDLP.

NOEL DORR: Muiris has introduced a point on the mood and attitude, so to speak, the overall attitude going into Sunningdale. He is certainly right that there was a sense of remembering the Treaty and in this, Tom Jones's diary, Tom Jones being the assistant secretary to Lloyd George...

AUSTIN CURRIE: The dates coincide, 8 December.

NOEL DORR: ...Jones had made a note of everything that passed in the Treaty negotiations, and we had a sense that we were going to the biggest Anglo-Irish negotiations held since the Treaty. That was the whole mood, that we were going into a big negotiation. In fact, it turned into something very different because Heath was not an antagonist across the table but rather a presiding chairman who was willing to accept more or less whatever the two sides [unionist and nationalist] could agree on.

DERMOT NALLY: It was even more complicated than that. I was at all of the meetings of the half of the Irish government that was in Sunningdale—the other half of the government was back in Dublin—and I had an arrangement,

[11] This work (Jones 1971) contains detailed notes taken during the 1921 Treaty negotiations by Jones, who was Assistant Secretary to the Cabinet at the time.

[12] The Monaghan by-election on 27 November 1973 was caused by the election of Erskine Childers (Fianna Fáil) as President of Ireland, and was won by Brendan Toal (Fine Gael). In 1933, Ernest Blythe, a prominent member of Cumann na nGaedheal (shortly to be reborn as Fine Gael), had lost his seat in the same constituency to Alexander Haslett, an independent.

or Dan O'Sullivan had an arrangement with me, to tell him what was going on.[13] And the arrangement was we would speak in Irish, and I would say the opposite of what was intended. And Seán told me afterwards, and I don't know if this is my memory or whether it was a dream, because we went on very very late, he told me that the British had Irish speakers on the switch in Sunningdale.

2.2.3. Development of Irish Government Policy

NOEL DORR: When the North broke apart in 1968–9, both governments reacted first in an outdated way. Over the years from 1969 onwards they gradually came to see the reality of the situation in Northern Ireland. I leave aside the whole business of the arms crisis and the crisis in the Fianna Fáil government.[14] I am just looking at the official policy.

The first step of the Irish government was to try to show that the Stormont model of a parliament didn't work properly; it wasn't suited to Northern Ireland because it meant a permanent majority. There was some stuff written on that, and there was a particular pamphlet called *Stormont: An Assessment* which we wrote in Foreign Affairs which was pushed down the throat of the United Irish Association in London for publication as their document, and a bit was added about partition just to bring them along. It was published under the heading *Stormont: An Assessment*.[15] I always think that had quite an influence.

Dublin was at that stage trying to assert its role. The aim was, under the Fianna Fáil government, to assert a foothold for Dublin, and secondly to discredit the model of a parliament where the unionists were always a permanent majority. In my view that idea, that concept, was accepted in a sense in the British Green Paper of 1972.[16] A key phrase, the 'Irish dimension', was probably intended as one of those phrases that in times of crisis, like 'the legitimate rights of the Palestinian people', are thrown out, so that both sides can play with it for a while. But it was in effect a kind of acceptance that the issue was not between North and South but that in-built into Northern Ireland was an intrinsic aspect which was to be the Irish dimension. If you wanted to put the pieces together in Northern Ireland, you had to cater for an Irish

---

[13] Dan O'Sullivan, the Cabinet Secretary, had a powerful dual role, and was replaced by two people when he retired in 1980: Dermot Nally as Secretary to the Government, and Noel Whelan as Secretary to the Department of the Taoiseach.

[14] The Irish government had been deeply divided since the 'arms crisis' of May 1970, following which several ministers, including future leader Charles Haughey, resigned or were dismissed. The crisis was sparked by attempts by ministers to procure weapons for Northern Ireland nationalists.

[15] United Ireland Association (1972).   [16] See Northern Ireland Office (1972).

dimension. Now that seems to me to have been the key which eventually led to the proposals for a Council of Ireland.

To get on to Sunningdale, I think the key ideas of Sunningdale were an acceptance that you should not now try to decide what the future would be. You had to do something about 'status' to put a floor under the unionist fears, but the key aim was to build structures and institutions which could grow together and bring some kind of reconciliation, and let each stage in the process determine the next stage.[17] I think that was the motivating idea going into Sunningdale.

Liam Cosgrave's opening speech had a point about the Council of Ireland not being just something to appeal to the South; it was an intrinsic and necessary part of the structure in Northern Ireland. In other words, you needed that prop for power-sharing. Also, at that time, I think at least some of us thought that, while the Council had to have the power to evolve, and might bring the two parts of Ireland together, the real progress might come from power-sharing in Northern Ireland, but that you could not have power-sharing put in place […] as far as the SDLP were concerned, and the minority in Northern Ireland, unless you had the reassurance or prop of a Council of Ireland.

AUSTIN CURRIE: Without a Council of Ireland it would have been described as an internal solution. The SDLP obviously was very keen to avoid that accusation, particularly from the republican elements. Indeed, my understanding going to Sunningdale was that the Faulkner Unionists had accepted (1) that there would be a Council of Ireland; (2) that it would be on two levels, even though the second level—they had to be pushed into that and they were thinking more in terms of an inter-parliamentary thing such as had existed between the Northern Ireland parliament and Commonwealth parliaments—they had accepted in principle that there should be a second tier, which was extremely important. Indeed, I can remember that at Sunningdale I felt it necessary, I think it might be on the first day, to remind Brian Faulkner that we had already agreed in relation to these matters, so, as I say, certain progress has been made which was to be built upon.

Q: If I just might quote very briefly from Kelvin White, and this is a note he prepared for Downing Street as to how they had been playing things:[18] '26 October 1973. The present phase […] is a good particular example of what in essence the FCO [Foreign and Commonwealth Office] have been doing throughout the whole Northern Ireland crisis, i.e. bringing the Irish into play if they [the Irish government] are a helpful factor and keeping them at arm's length when, as said so often, and, as now, they are likely to disturb things.'

[17] A reference to the status of Northern Ireland as part of the United Kingdom.
[18] Kelvin White was head of the Irish section of the Foreign and Commonwealth Office.

SEÁN DONLON: Just one general point. There was no Anglo-Irish section in the Department of Foreign Affairs until 1 February 1972. The degree of contact and information that we had, particularly on the unionist side, was very poor. Even going into Sunningdale we were heavily if not exclusively reliant on what we were told by Brian Faulkner himself or by people in the SDLP, particularly by Austin, and John [Hume] and Gerry Fitt. Gerry Fitt was actually quite a good weathervane for us in terms of unionists, but I think it is important to remember there was no Anglo-Irish section and therefore there was no body of information available either in the Department or indeed in the Department of the Taoiseach.

DERMOT NALLY: I came into the Taoiseach's Department in January 1973, and I was thrown into Sunningdale.

SEÁN DONLON: And there was nothing to fall back on. And don't forget all this time the British had a very elaborate intelligence-gathering system, a political intelligence-gathering system in Northern Ireland.

DERMOT NALLY: May I tell a story? I came into the Department and Dan O'Sullivan, who was Secretary to the Government at the time, said 'Welcome, great, go on, there's your office now go around and get a few papers', and then I came back and he said, 'Yeah, I know what you'll do, we'll put you on Northern Ireland', and that was that. And it became clear over the years that nothing happened on Northern Ireland, nothing serious, unless the two prime ministers, Irish and British, were involved.

NOEL DORR: On the question of the Anglo-Irish role in Foreign Affairs, when the troubles broke out in 1969, as I said, everything was out of date. There was no section. As Seán said, I think probably in 1969, maybe early 1970, Eamonn Gallagher, who had been sidelined—he had been in Paris on the economic side—gradually, by going North, by having contacts with John Hume and the SDLP and doing reports in an area that he wasn't assigned to, he gradually established a real credibility. I think he started it on his own and then perhaps was encouraged to do it because his reports were so good in a situation where no reports existed, and gradually he became the guru for Jack Lynch.

SEÁN DONLON: The point I want to make is that the development of policy—I think accidentally—was driven by the SDLP. The SDLP set up something called the Assembly of the Northern Irish People, do you remember that?[19] Eamonn Gallagher asked me to write the rules of procedure on the constitution for the Assembly of the Northern Irish People, which I did with the help of a clerk of the Dáil.

We stayed up all night writing these documents and gave them to the SDLP. The next thing, I was asked by Eamonn Gallagher to write a policy

[19] Known to some as the 'Dungiven Parliament', the Assembly of the Northern Irish People, attended only by nationalists, met in Dungiven on 26 October 1971.

document—what was the Irish government's policy—and I had a bash at it, relying heavily, frankly, on some of the stuff that had come out of Fine Gael— because where else would you look, there was no file. I gave this to Eamonn Gallagher, who, I know, gave it to Paddy Hillery and I think Hillery felt it was just too moderate and it wouldn't wash and it didn't go any further. That was probably September–October 1971.

I think what was happening was a position was emerging, but it wasn't going to become a formally adopted position until something made it happen.

Q: So there's no file saying what Irish government policy was?

SEÁN DONLON: No, there is not.

Q: Well, what Dermot Nally is saying [is that] when he came into the Taoiseach's Department on 15 January 1973 there is no file, there is no formal statement about what Irish policy is on Northern Ireland.

NOEL DORR: There were different stages in coming to a more sensible approach, which was eventually Sunningdale. The first stage for the Fianna Fáil government, as I saw it, was to discredit the idea of a single majority parliament, this sort of static majority, which had led to fifty years of unionist rule.

The second thought at that stage was what they called 'a new Ireland by agreement'. But that phrase, 'by agreement', had an inbuilt ambiguity in it because the question was 'whose agreement?' Was it the agreement of the two governments or was it the agreement of a majority in Northern Ireland? Jack Lynch was invited to write an article for the American journal *Foreign Affairs*. I took on the drafting of it in May 1972 and I did a draft and it was generally accepted. But Eamonn Gallagher being the guru, I had to go through it with him. We sat down together and we argued and discussed various aspects of that, and his input was to toughen it up in various ways towards the idea that I'm talking about, unity by agreement, but not spelling out whose agreement was involved, and this concept of a new Ireland. The article was published in the July 1972 issue of *Foreign Affairs*.

If I might say so, it was historic and it was a fairly broad-minded and irenic statement of the position, but the conclusion in the end would have led basically to a united Ireland. In other words, it argued that the Anglo-Irish question, or the old 'Irish question', had been reopened, and the only way ultimately to settle it was via unity, but unity by agreement, but with that hanging ambiguity as to whose agreement it was.

My sense was that the phrase 'unity by agreement' in itself was an admirable phrase, but I have a thesis that sometimes in difficult political situations you invent a phrase which has possibly ambivalence in it, and this is enough to hold the line for a time. 'Unity by agreement' was thought to be a good phrase; it was desirable and everybody thought 'that's a good thing', but I have a memory of trying to push it towards spelling out whose agreement or consent, and being, so to speak, told 'no, no, we leave it at unity by agreement' in order that it would not be quite clear who had to agree.

Q: But it does speak volumes that Irish foreign policy is enunciated not in the Dáil, not in a speech by the Taoiseach, but in an article in *Foreign Affairs* in the USA. That does say something.

JOHN SWIFT: It is absolutely true that there was no DFA policy file on Northern Ireland, but that doesn't mean there was nothing. There was a whole series of speeches, going back to the earlyish days of Jack Lynch as Taoiseach, that one could cannibalize and pick things out of. For example, the Tralee speech, I remember.[20]

NOEL DORR: But remember, Paddy Hillery had enunciated policy to the [United Nations] Security Council in August 1969. Paddy McKernan wrote it; I wrote part of the next one for the General Assembly that year. In the mid-1960s when I was at the UN there was an Irish American lobby group, there was a man called Heaney who was pressing Frank Aiken to raise Northern Ireland at the UN and we were sort of drafting replies for Aiken, and that was the time of hands across the border and so on. It's not quite correct to say there was no policy on Northern Ireland. Lemass had spoken at the Oxford Union in 1959.[21]

GARRET FITZGERALD: I'm talking of the evolution of the policy that emerged of a constructive engagement based on the idea of power-sharing and a Council of Ireland—that the rethinking of policy (and all the anti-partition rubbish that had gone before), that, really, July 1972 was the beginning of that.

SEÁN DONLON: There was one additional strand in the development of policy which hasn't been mentioned, and that's the influence of Ken Whitaker, particularly on Jack Lynch.

Ken Whitaker, I believe, wrote the Tralee speech.[22] Ken Whitaker maintained contact with quite a number of people in Northern Ireland but notably with Ken Bloomfield,[23] and Ken Bloomfield was involved, I know, in drafting the Green Paper, so that tic-tacking continued probably until Jack Lynch retired from politics.

Q: It is a measure of the kind of thing we are talking about, the absence of policy, nobody knowing what policy is. It's all very well to say 'there's the article in

[20] The speech, made at Tralee on 20 September 1969, sought to accommodate traditional nationalist thinking with a new perspective on Northern Ireland that acknowledged the need for consent on the part of the people of Northern Ireland.

[21] Taoiseach Seán Lemass addressed the Oxford Union on the subject of Irish unity on 15 October 1959, shortly after taking office, in a speech widely regarded as marking a new departure in official Irish thinking (*Irish Times*, 16 October 1959). Frank Aiken and Patrick Hillery were successive Ministers for External Affairs (1966–9 and 1969–73 respectively). Pádraic McKernan was an official (later Secretary General) in the Department of External Affairs.

[22] Kenneth Whitaker (1916–2017) was Secretary of the Irish Department of Finance and an influential economic strategist and policymaker.

[23] Kenneth Bloomfield had been Deputy Secretary to the Northern Ireland Cabinet and later became Secretary to the Northern Ireland Executive.

Foreign Affairs', but that's not ordinarily the way democratic governments frame policy?

NOEL DORR: The way that Irish government policy was made all along was the speech. You'd be asked to do a speech and that was it. You sit down and you try to work out what the policy is, and if it was accepted it becomes policy. It's a method. It was the way it was done for a long time. It wasn't just on Northern Ireland; it was on other things too.

Q: Is this how policy was formulated just on Northern Ireland or just in the Department of Foreign Affairs? Was this the way economic policy was made, for example, the White Paper on economic development?

JOHN SWIFT: It's not confined to Ireland; it's the way policy is sometimes made in the UK.

MUIRIS MAC CONGHAIL: It's how the free education system was declared by Donogh O'Malley.[24]

DERMOT NALLY: The same general principle applies all the time; this was both to Lynch and to you [Garret FitzGerald] and to Liam Cosgrave. You were arguing: 'For God's sake, get things away from what is happening immediately, have an objective of getting the people involved in political action in some way, get the people involved in administration and involve the community.' That is a common theme, and insofar as there was a policy, an Irish government policy, that is it. And Albert Reynolds continued in the same vein.

2.3. The Sunningdale Negotiations

2.3.1. Experience of Negotiation at Sunningdale

DERMOT NALLY: A general comment: I don't know if you appreciate what happened in Sunningdale—the degree to which it was an exercise in exhaustion. It went on for four days and a lot of the night during that time. The negotiation finished, I think, at about 6 or 7 o'clock on the morning of Sunday, 9 December. Faulkner had tremendous objections to working on a Sunday and he was only convinced to go on by the idea, I think, that 'OK, we stopped the clock'. At 2 o'clock on the Sunday morning Cosgrave phoned Heath and said 'Look, I'm going to bed, our crowd are proving difficult', and he just went off to bed. But the argument on policing, I think it was, went on until 4, 5, 6 in the morning.

---

[24] Donogh O'Malley (1921–68) was Irish Minister for Education, 1966–9, and famously broadened access to Irish secondary education by announcing a radical new scheme without getting cabinet approval.

NOEL DORR: I have a series of notes which I dictated during that night for the concluding statement made by Liam Cosgrave when it would have ended. And one is marked 11 p.m., next one 2 a.m., next one 5 a.m., so it was right through the night. We were standing around in the Irish delegation room because there was a lot of to-ing and fro-ing between Heath's people and the Northern Ireland parties, probably the SDLP. My memory is that Sunningdale had a big sort of baronial hall, and we were sitting down in the centre, and you could see the balconies around the rooms, and we were watching people scurrying over and back, but the Irish government delegation was essentially detached enough at that stage. I remember Seán Donlon, at about 4 a.m., sitting in the middle of the floor, started dictating into some kind of a dictaphone, you know, 'we're sitting here in Sunningdale', and Gerry Fitt...

GARRET FITZGERALD: He fell asleep.

NOEL DORR: Very ostentatiously.

GARRET FITZGERALD: Not on the couch but on the back of the couch.

NOEL DORR: At a time when there was a fraught situation between Heath and the SDLP upstairs and a lot of to-ing and fro-ing. Gerry was ostentatiously stretched out in the middle of this big baronial hall and was either asleep or pretending to be asleep, so to speak, for political reasons, to show he wasn't involved in it. Now I don't know if any of you remember that?

GARRET FITZGERALD: He was gradually sliding towards the floor in a big armchair fast asleep, and we actually took bets as to what time he would actually reach the floor.

JOHN SWIFT: And John Hume came in eventually at some small hour in the morning and caught him by the chin and said 'Gerry, time for work' and he got up and went off to the SDLP.

DERMOT NALLY: At the time of Sunningdale, whether it was before or afterwards, I made a summary of what I thought were the main concerns involved, the interests involved:

'The Faulkner and Alliance parties: no Council of Ireland or only when executive formed and functioning, secondly police powers for executive, thirdly extradition, fourthly Northern Ireland not to be submerged—in other words status, that's the Faulkner and Alliance concern. British: no police powers for executive, the Strasbourg human rights case, concern that if the Council of Ireland were conceded the SDLP would hold up the executive [I don't know why they had that idea but they had it] and the unionists would leave the executive.'

AUSTIN CURRIE: A policing function for the executive, yes, that became a very big issue at Sunningdale.

GARRET FITZGERALD: Heath didn't want to give the new executive any policing powers. The British army was abused in Northern Ireland by a provincial government was his attitude, and he wanted it to never happen again, so no policing powers of any kind in Northern Ireland.

AUSTIN CURRIE: You had a situation in Sunningdale whereby the SDLP, the Faulkner Unionists and Alliance were pushing for police powers for the executive and Heath was saying 'oh no, no, no way'.

DERMOT NALLY: Most of the stuff had finished and the people had reported back to the government rooms and the only issue outstanding was the issue of policing, and policing went on and on.

AUSTIN CURRIE: Well, the SDLP deliberately decided at an early stage that we would drag policing out as long as we felt it was necessary and that if we got other things agreed the pressure would then be on for an agreement on policing. And the final wording on policing was agreed in Heath's room at 7.35 p.m. on Sunday evening. The final plenary session commenced at 8.25 [p.m.] so it was policing which delayed everything. It could have ended twenty-four hours earlier except for policing.

GARRET FITZGERALD: It was trilateral—that was the problem.

AUSTIN CURRIE: At 4.35 a.m. most of the SDLP delegation was in the party room when, unannounced, Heath and Frank Cooper walked in.[25] Heath confirmed that he had been to see Faulkner but little progress had been made. Brian, he said, is still hankering after what he lost in 1972 and he is not getting it back. He said he had warned him that if negotiations broke down now Faulkner himself would be blamed; the inference was that the British government would ensure this. It was a remarkably candid exposition of his views and his commitment.

He had hard things to say to us as well, but not as harshly. We were on the cusp of government and it was unacceptable that we were not prepared to accept the forces of law and order. We responded in kind and it took some time for things to calm down. After that things calmed down, and when Heath left us at 4 minutes past 5 we understood he had agreed to fully support nominations to the Police Authorities after consultation with the Council of Ireland, that the Council should also have a role in human-rights protection through an all-Ireland ombudsman, and that he would continue to lean on Faulkner. But what happened then was that the three Northern Ireland parties sort of ganged up together and sort of said to Heath we want the executive to have a role through the Council of Ireland in relation to policing—if only a minimal connection.

NOEL DORR: But it was a sticking point at least, let's agree on that. And then the issue was returned to on Sunday evening, and what was put into the communiqué was the best that could be done to patch up the situation. Now the point of difference between you is who was the problem on that, was it the British?

---

[25] Frank Cooper was Permanent Under-Secretary at the Northern Ireland Office under William Whitelaw and later Merlyn Rees.

GARRET FITZGERALD: The SDLP?

AUSTIN CURRIE: No, the British were. Heath and his attitude to Faulkner and his memory, his very recent memory, of the circumstances in which he suspended Stormont. Remember, he took the security function away from Stormont. Therefore it was nearly impossible for Faulkner to get from Heath even the slightest leaf to cover Faulkner's weaknesses. Down the road, yes, I mean I made the point a good few times at Sunningdale that the Northern Ireland executive without some control over policing matters would be a eunuch. Right?

Later, in the power-sharing executive, as Minister for Housing I had to face the reality that you couldn't do even the most minimal things which required the use of the police except by going through the British Secretary of State. But I was aware of that, and the SDLP was aware of that at Sunningdale, and that's why we joined with Faulkner and the Alliance in putting pressure on Heath to provide the fig leaf.

GARRET FITZGERALD: In relation to what happened during the morning, at some time during Saturday night our friend here [Dermot Nally] said 'play a game, anything to keep awake', so the game was to write down on a piece of paper the four parties—we didn't put down the Alliance—and the four main issues, and to give marks for each party on each issue. What emerged from this, and this was a considerable diversion, was that Conor [Cruise O'Brien] was the most conservative unionist; I came next; Richie Ryan was the most republican at the other end of it. We added all the scores up and what came out was that the British and SDLP were equal and the unionists were a long way behind. So then we went off to bed. We agreed to meet again at 4 o'clock on Sunday afternoon.

So I went to bed and woke up at half past 12, and my mind was clear at this stage. Putting emotion on one side, the question was who really gives in in a negotiation of this kind when it's at the crunch—the parties that have gained most, or the parties that have gained least? In any objective assessment the Irish government and SDLP had gained the most and the unionists the least. Which direction should we give in, in any negotiation at the crunch—by adding something to the package that will help a party or by taking something away that will damage another? Who will have best balance in gain or loss from a breakdown at this point?

The unionists would avoid the immediate and terrible political risks of being destroyed. What type of concessions would be most likely to reduce violence post-talks? To the unionists what would reduce the danger of loyalist violence and above all save Catholic lives? What's involved in a concession to the unionists is merely putting into words, when all are agreed, what would and should happen eventually—devolution of power over a normal police-backed executive.

Then I did a draft statement: 'The British government envisages that, without prejudice to the question of security, control of Northern policing should in due course be vested in the executive. While this is not possible at the present time and this is permitted [. . .]'. I waited outside for the first person to come back to the main building where I had been asleep. I could see Paddy Devlin approaching, and as he arrived I pulled the door open and said 'Paddy, I should give you this,' and I gave it to him and said 'Would you just look at this?' And he went off to the SDLP meeting with that and the SDLP then modified their position.

That's actually what happened. Now that's all on the record.

AUSTIN CURRIE: There were two elements of it, one was that the Council of Ireland would have a say in the appointment of the Policing Authorities North and South.

GARRET FITZGERALD: That was agreed.

AUSTIN CURRIE: That was agreed, and then secondly that at some future stage, when the security situation allowed it, that serious consideration should be given to devolving policing arrangements to a Northern Ireland executive.

DERMOT NALLY: Heath had said at the meeting with Cosgrave on 17 September: 'There's no way we'll give policing because I'm not going to get the British army involved in supporting a police force which they can't control.' I think one of the extraordinary things in all this is the Pauline conversion of Heath, if you think of his meetings with Jack Lynch earlier on, and his dismissive talk.[26]

SEÁN DONLON: At one point someone mentioned Heath's autobiography. I think autobiography [is] notoriously unreliable as a source, but his particularly. There were five or six people engaged either by him or by his publishers, it was long, long overdue and eventually to save his deposit he hired a big team of people, one of whom came to see me at one stage and I was shocked by the level of ignorance. And then when the book came out I was shocked by the poor level of research—a very, very poor book. I would be very cautious about using any bit of it without double-checking somewhere else.[27]

MUIRIS MAC CONGHAIL: But I have to say, I'm not an apologist for Liam Cosgrave, there was one thing in his mind, he was absolutely conscious he was his father's son.[28] He had now become Taoiseach and suddenly, this Sunningdale thing—he knew it was going to be the largest thing in his life, the most important conference ever, and he didn't play around with people in that way nor was he Machiavellian enough to be able to say—not subtle enough I think—to actually do the kind of fine-tuning to which you are referring. It

---

[26] Heath had earlier firmly rejected any role for the Irish government; see Dorr (2017: 87–9).

[27] See Heath (1998).

[28] Liam Cosgrave was a son of William T. Cosgrave (1880–1965), first President of the Executive Council of the Irish Free State (1922–32) and leader of the Cumann na nGaedheal Party, which later became the core of Fine Gael.

was more important also, actually to his credit, to not provide Fianna Fáil with anything which they could use against him subsequently.

NOEL DORR: There was a very important point about Sunningdale that needs to be remembered and we haven't touched on it at all. Sunningdale was only the first part of a two-part conference and that may not be fully understood—the second part never took place. This would be important when we come to why it failed. I will argue at that stage that the judgement was made prematurely on Sunningdale in the election of 1974. There was to be a follow-up formal conference at which all these things would be done and ratified. The Council of Ireland was announced in the Sunningdale communiqué with the broad structures. But it was not given any content, and the content was to be filled out before the formal conference. There was to be a formal conference, 'early in the new year' was the phrase, and after that the Agreement was to be formally ratified and signed and registered with the United Nations as an international treaty. So that's the point you have to keep in mind all the time.

MAHON HAYES: What came out of the first part was a declaration or a communiqué, not an agreement.

JOHN SWIFT: Yes, that was partly to protect the SDLP but also the executive. Until the executive was in function, it couldn't, properly speaking, participate in making what amounted to an international agreement.

2.3.2. Council of Ireland

GARRET FITZGERALD: On the Council of Ireland I decided on the tactic to try and persuade people in our jurisdiction to be willing to give more, because it seemed to me that there were many departments simply thinking it was an alien body to which things were being handed over, so I had the impression of negativity on the part of government departments.

DERMOT NALLY: We produced a report in January or early February 1974 which set out a list of functions which could be given to the Council of Ireland.

SEÁN DONLON: 80,000 civil servants.

DERMOT NALLY: It was only 13,000, 12,000. I think. The total civil service at the time, if you leave out the post office, it was quite small. In other words, I think it was two-thirds or three-quarters of the entire civil service.

NOEL DORR: The Irish side's brief for Sunningdale envisaged just under 6,000 civil servants moving to the Council of Ireland. The brief for Sunningdale spells out 6,000. I have it here; I can produce it for you if you like. To be exact it was 5,980. Thereafter, in the six months before the executive fell, there was a committee under Noël Whelan which produced a figure in a report which was much higher, but even before Sunningdale the official brief going into Sunningdale did use a figure just under 6,000, and it was rounded up to 6,500.

To start with, in perhaps late November–early December 1972 the concept was there, but filling out and putting forward a substantial paper with proposals as to how it might be done, and so on, that began to develop in early 1973. The IDU did a paper on the Council of Ireland—did a number of papers on aspects of the Council of Ireland—and all that was ongoing at the time of the change of government in March 1973.[29]

Finally I have in front of me the unionist proposals, which we were talking about a moment ago, and this is the opening paragraph if you don't mind my reading it: 'We believe that all the people of Ireland have a common interest in the achievement and maintenance of peace, the provisional arrangements whereby no part of the British Isles can provide a haven for terrorists, the coordination of government activities on many social and economic matters and the promotion of mutual understanding and tolerance between the different Irish traditions. We therefore propose that a Council of Ireland shall be set up to assist in achieving these objectives.'

DERMOT NALLY: When Heath met Cosgrave in Baldonnel on 17 September 1973 he had no problem with the Council of Ireland except one, and that one problem was the relationship between the Council and the executive. He said 'if you establish the executive before a Council the SDLP will keep dragging us along week after week and month after month'; that was his comment.

AUSTIN CURRIE: Yes, but Faulkner was very insistent that an executive be formed before the Council of Ireland, because if it was at the same time as the Council of Ireland then unionists would allege that the Irish government had too great an influence.

GARRET FITZGERALD: That row went on for several months.

DERMOT NALLY: The second point there, Austin, was that, if the executive was not formed, then Paisley would have to be invited, because they would have to have all the unionist representation.[30] So, if you form the executive, you had people who were responsible, these are the people who will attend at Sunningdale and would attend the conference and that's why.

Q: Did you actually think you were going to get such a strong Council of Ireland out of it at the end?

VOICES: Yes.

GARRET FITZGERALD: We were naive enough to think so.

Q: When did you stop thinking that?

GARRET FITZGERALD: January 1974—the months January to May . . .

---

[29] See Appendix 1.4.
[30] Revd Ian Paisley (1926–2014) was founding leader of the Democratic Unionist Party, which had won eight of the Assembly's seventy-eight seats in the 1973 election.

MUIRIS MAC CONGHAIL: I don't know, did we? It was the optimism of Dr Fitzgerald about the Council of Ireland that led that on, but I'm not sure I would have shared it at all.

NOEL DORR: There's also this point, that Sunningdale, and the whole effort was a political effort to solve the problem, but once you start putting down the concept of a Council of Ireland you then pass it over to the more technical people—Noel Whelan and the various departments, you have an interdepartmental committee. It escapes from the political framework in which it started, and then it becomes an exercise in how many different things you can find to include in it. Now it's true that there was a reluctance on the part of all departments here to give up some of their functions, and Garret would keep plugging that, but it seemed to me at the time that the 1974 planning exercise was crazy, essentially crazy.

And now I think it was even crazy to think of 6,000, but I said earlier on, and I still say it, that the real importance of the Council of Ireland was not so much what it did as that it allowed—it was the prop that allowed—power-sharing to happen in Northern Ireland and kept it from being a purely internal settlement. The real germination and the real reconciliation would come with power-sharing in Northern Ireland, but that political thinking, that concept, escaped out of the bottle and became 'technicalized', or whatever word you want to use, into a big exercise of finding out all the possible functions for the Council—canals and God knows what.

AUSTIN CURRIE: John Oliver was the most senior civil servant, maybe, and was my permanent secretary, and he was among a group of civil servants who went down to Dublin to discuss functions for the Council of Ireland, and he came back to me and I remember he said, 'Minister', he says, 'are they really serious in the South about the Council of Ireland?', and I said 'Why, John?', and I replied: 'They don't want to give it any powers.'

NOEL DORR: That's true enough too.

AUSTIN CURRIE: But how do you answer them?

JOHN SWIFT: But that's only one side of the story. I mean, it's true, and Garret's book brings it out strongly, with regard to Pat Cooney, for example, he had absolutely firm views. But it is also true that, at a technical level, the Noel Whelan committee tended to load everything they could possibly think of with a North–South link, real or imaginary, into the Council of Ireland. I suppose that is why our figures went up, from a total of 6,000 to approximately 12,000 in all—6,000 civil servants plus a further 6,000 from the semi-state bodies.

AUSTIN CURRIE: Later, in spring 1974, we were unfortunate that, at the same time as the loyalists were building up their strength, we had this discussion which paralysed the executive for quite a while as to the phasing-in of the Council of Ireland, and it was the Faulkner proposal, which in fact was a compromise proposal, which was very moderate in comparison to the attitude that his backbenchers were taking.

The Faulkner proposal was that the Council of Ireland should proceed in two ways, that between then in 1974 and the election that was due in 1977 the Council of Ireland should be consultative, and that after a test of opinion which was effectively the election in 1977 then we could go on to fully implement the Sunningdale proposals.

Now that caused serious trouble for the SDLP. It caused serious internal problems, and those of us who were on the executive agreed to another sort of compromise thing when we brought it to our parliamentary party. We only managed to get eight votes for it, and then Gerry brought in Stan Orme.[31] As a result of that, on his impassioned pleas the minority was reduced to five, but even Paddy Devlin had voted against the compromise the first time out so it was a very, very serious situation for the SDLP at the time when the strike was actually happening—people didn't have electricity, you couldn't get petrol for our bloody official cars.

2.3.3. Constitutional Status

NOEL DORR: The status issue was terribly important—that is what the Irish government could say about the position of Northern Ireland—and has been at subsequent conferences also. The reason was that you needed to put a floor under unionists' fears to give them reassurance.

GARRET FITZGERALD: Without changing the constitution.

NOEL DORR: Now the maximum reassurance that could be achieved at Sunningdale was these parallel declarations. I'll comment in a moment on the text. The texts are interesting in themselves. But then when you come to the Anglo-Irish Agreement in 1985 the two texts which had to be published in parallel in Sunningdale were now incorporated into a single text which was paragraph one of article 1 of the Anglo-Irish Agreement. But that in turn was ambiguous, and if you look at it—we won't go into it now, but I can show you how it's ambiguous. But it held until the Supreme Court held that Irish unity was a 'constitutional imperative', which again drained the agreed text of ambiguity.[32]

---

[31] Stan Orme, MP for Salford West, became a Minister of State at the Northern Ireland Office following Labour's victory at the general election of February 1974.

[32] Two prominent members of the Ulster Unionist Party, Christopher and Michael McGimpsey, took an action in the Irish High Court arguing that the Anglo-Irish Agreement of 1985 was in violation of articles 2 and 3 of the constitution. The High Court found against them in July 1988, and this ruling was upheld in March 1990 by the Supreme Court, which, however, described the constitution's reference to the 'national territory' as 'a claim of legal right', and the reintegration of this territory as 'a constitutional imperative' ('Christopher McGimpsey and Michael McGimpsey, Plaintiffs, v. Ireland, An Taoiseach and Others, Defendants', *Irish Reports*, (1988, 567; 1990 no. 1, 110).

So it's only when you get to the Good Friday Agreement that you can get a full floor under unionist fears.

The 'status issue' in the Agreement was an important point. What was said at Sunningdale did not prove adequate in the end to reassure the unionists against being slid willy-nilly into a united Ireland. Now, if we look at the text, the Irish government 'fully accepted and solemnly declared that there could be no change in the status of Northern Ireland until *a* majority of the people of Northern Ireland desired a change in that status'. Note, it is '*a* majority'. Now if you look at the British side, it is their policy to support the wishes of *the* majority—so that was a very significant difference there.

The Irish government's position was always that it was a question of 'a' majority, whereas, if you say 'the' majority, you're talking by implication about the unionists. Furthermore, the Irish side said there could be no change in the status of Northern Ireland until a majority desired a change; it subsequently dropped down a bit from that because of what was said at the time of the Haughey–Thatcher meetings in 1980, and by the time of the Anglo-Irish Agreement in 1985—article 1—it is there 'would' be no change rather than there 'could' be no change because Haughey had used that word in the 1980 communiqué, as Dermot said earlier. So you have the subtlety of 'could', which is a stronger formulation in Sunningdale than 'would', which was actually used in 1985.

Furthermore, you have on the British side the approach of British governments going back to Lloyd George talking at the Treaty negotiations. Tom Jones's diary records this. Lloyd George is using almost exactly the kind of language that British governments were still using until relatively recently: we will stand aside if you can persuade, but we will not be persuaders ourselves. You'll find an almost exact quotation from him in November 1921 to Collins or Arthur Griffith who were making the nationalist case across the table in almost the same terms as today; it was still being made in the 1970s, and the answer was almost exactly the same.

Q: The reason was that the British were also reading the same papers you were reading, because I [Ronan Fanning] went in the early 1970s to the Public Record Office in London to do research on the archives on the Treaty negotiations and I was told they were all out to the Cabinet Office.

NOEL DORR: Can I just add that the British did go a little bit further in Sunningdale, because—while they had said before 'if the majority so wanted', you know 'if you persuade them'—they go a little bit further, very subtly, saying they would *support* that wish, so it's a slightly advanced stage. So that's all built into these two statements. But they're two different statements, and, as I said, in parallel, that simply wasn't enough to reassure the unionists.

But note the next paragraph, which said the conference agreed that the formal agreement incorporating the declarations of the British and Irish governments would be signed at the formal stage at the conference and registered at the United Nations. Question: would it have still been in parallel, or would they have been incorporated into a single text? I don't know.

DERMOT NALLY: The degree to which British policy is continuous is illustrated by the actions of Robert Armstrong. He was at the September meeting between Cosgrave and Heath, he was at Sunningdale and took Heath's place when Heath had to go for an hour or two. Armstrong was with Mrs Thatcher in Dublin at the 1980 Summit and he was the principal British negotiator in 1985 on the Anglo-Irish Agreement. That's the stream of continuity.

JOHN SWIFT: Noel said that the status declaration at the end proved not enough to prevent unionists developing fears of being railroaded against their will into something they didn't want. My question is: is it significant that, after the brief flurry of interest in the status declaration, it's there in the background, but it never became a political point for the unionists?

DERMOT NALLY: It did.

JOHN SWIFT: In the period between January and May of 1974?

GARRET FITZGERALD: Oh Lord yes. It was the crucial issue.

DERMOT NALLY: I got a phone call; there was a vote in the Unionist Party—this was in the 800-member Ulster Unionist Council, and there was a majority of 53 against Sunningdale, and this was part of the reason. When that vote was taken, Bloomfield got onto me and said 'can we organize a meeting fast between Faulkner and Cosgrave?', and that meeting took place in Baldonnel on 16 January, and in Baldonnel Faulkner said 'the Boland case is destroying us'.[33] It was about status, because the defence in the Boland case was specifically to deny that the Irish government had entered an agreement which was repugnant to the constitution of Ireland. In other words, he said, even if you have what purports to be a constitutional modification in this Agreement, it is only words, this is your defence of this case, you have wrecked our attitude on status.[34]

GARRET FITZGERALD: Unfortunately, a lawyer concerned to protect the Agreement from being impugned by the Supreme Court put in every possible defence, all of which totally undermined the phraseology. I could see that as a disaster. The other thing by the way was that Cosgrave was asked 'Would this

[33] Casement Aerodrome, Baldonnel, is a military airbase in south Dublin that was sometimes used as a secure and accessible location in which sensitive meetings could take place.

[34] The Boland case was an action taken by former Minister for Local Government Kevin Boland (who had resigned from the Lynch government in 1970 in protest at his handling of the 'arms crisis'), alleging that the Sunningdale Agreement was in breach of articles 2 and 3 of the Irish constitution; 'Boland v. an Taoiseach', *Irish Reports*, 1974, pp. 338–72.

lead to Irish unity?', and said 'Yes' in December in a radio broadcast; I mean, if I was asked I would have said 'Yes, if the majority agree', but he didn't say that.

JOHN SWIFT: Of course, there was the Boland case, but what I was trying to say was that the wording of the status declaration as such never became a problem for the unionists. It became a problem for us in court with Justice Murnaghan.[35]

DERMOT NALLY: Faulkner is saying that 'you have destroyed my support, and you have destroyed it in two ways, first of all by your statement on status, and secondly by your Council of Ireland moves'. Now the second was a little bit less vehement than the first.

NOEL DORR: On that point, I was involved in the early 1990s in talks in Stormont under Mayhew when the unionists began for the first time to really hammer articles 2 and 3 and one of the points made, I think, on the SDLP side by John Hume, and on our side, was that it had not been a big feature in the past— articles 2 and 3 as such had not been such a big issue.

But the point, I think, is this, that Faulkner was having to go back and sell a Council of Ireland which sounded like a mechanism to trundle them into a united Ireland; furthermore, there was going to be internal tension or conflict in the Northern Ireland side of the Council. It was going to have a good helping of nationalists, of the SDLP in other words, so it wasn't simply North and South, unionists and nationalists. It would be a northern side which was internally divided, so in order to allow him to sell a Council of Ireland Faulkner needed good reassurance on status. He needed not so much on articles 2 and 3 as such, but he needed something that could prove that the Council of Ireland wasn't going to trundle them willy-nilly into a united Ireland, and that was the function of the status declaration. So it was something to buttress the Council on the unionist side and give reassurance on the unionist side.

AUSTIN CURRIE: Faulkner made two claims after Sunningdale principally, one was that he had achieved something on status which Craig and Brookeborough had not been able to achieve, so he was successful in that. And, secondly—we dealt with this earlier—the reasons why Faulkner was in favour of the Council of Ireland was because he felt that it could, and would, be very helpful on the security side.

As it turned out it wasn't helpful on the security side, and I remember the period of time. He took office on 1 January 1974, and, by the end of April, seventy-four people had lost their lives in Northern Ireland. The IRA escalated its campaign, it went into places like Bangor where it had never been active before, and the loyalists were escalating their campaign as well, so, in fact, the security situation was deteriorating. So, on both of those grounds, Faulkner

---

[35] This is a reference to Mr Justice Murnaghan's ruling in the High Court in the Boland case.

was in trouble: on security because the situation had worsened, and on the status thing because it was being questioned by Boland, and the Irish government in its defence had, as far as Faulkner was concerned, undermined him.

DERMOT NALLY: There was a third concern. The SDLP plus the nationalists in the South would form a majority.

GARRET FITZGERALD: But they would not form a unanimity. The Council of Ministers would act in unanimity.

DERMOT NALLY: It was his concern. He says that you have this majority.

2.3.4. Extradition and Common-Law Enforcement Policy

GARRET FITZGERALD: We thought we had solved the problem with Declan Costello's use of the 1861 Act to charge people with murder in any other state, so extradition was not thought to be necessary—ingenious, although it has only been used once or twice I think.[36]

NOEL DORR: That's not quite the case, if I understand correctly. My memory of that period is this. The 1861 Act provided for the simple backing of warrants between Britain and Ireland when we were part of the United Kingdom; there was no 'extradition' as such. After we became an independent state, the police here just continued the old 1861 Act backing of warrants; it wasn't described as 'extradition'.

The Supreme Court in a particular case—I'm not sure whether in the 1960s or early 1970s—held that this was unconstitutional, so you couldn't use the 1861 Act. But what we then proposed in the context of Sunningdale—we were under strong pressure on extradition—the legal people on our side, Declan Costello particularly, took a very hard line, saying that not alone was non-extradition for political offences *tolerated* in international law, it was a *requirement* of international law, and that was the line we argued.[37]

So what we proposed in the lead-up to Sunningdale was a reciprocal arrangement whereby through new legislation it would be possible to try a person in the South for crimes committed in the North and vice versa. That was the point, not the 1861 Act, which had been shot down by the Supreme Court.

MAHON HAYES: Costello used the wording 'a generally accepted principle of international law', rather than a 'requirement of international law'. I'm not sure whether it was the 1861 Act, but there was certainly an Act, a British Act,

[36] This is a reference to the Offences Against the Person Act, 1861 (24 & 25 Vict., *c.* 100), which consolidated the law in relation to offences of violence and made provision for extraterritorial jurisdiction.

[37] Declan Costello, lawyer and Fine Gael Dáil deputy (TD), served as Attorney General from 1973 to 1977, and was a Judge of the High Court from 1977 to 1997.

not about backing warrants at all but about extraterritorial jurisdiction. So that existed already, and that's what was put forward at Sunningdale as a way to go.

NOEL DORR: What was done at Sunningdale—they couldn't agree on this, so a commission was set up. John [Swift] was on the secretariat of the commission; there were three judges or three lawyers, or four, from the Irish side, and an equal number from the British side to report on possible methods of handling this. They went through the different possibilities, extradition and so on, and miraculously, as you can imagine, it turned out that all the English lawyers thought that extradition for political offences was quite possible and all the Irish lawyers thought it wasn't.[38]

But the common agreed position was that there could be this reciprocal jurisdiction and it was, I think I'm right, thus that the legislation was passed in the South, which allowed us to try to arrest someone in the South for an act of terrorism committed in the North and try them in the South.

MAHON HAYES: The power for extraterritorial jurisdiction was there; but it may be that it only applied to certain offences.

GARRET FITZGERALD: It was for murder only.

MAHON HAYES: Maybe only, and maybe it wasn't wide enough to cover terrorism other than that. That may be the reason for the new legislation.

GARRET FITZGERALD: You're right. Both sides acted politically, and in fact the Northern Ireland Chief Justice, Lowry, complained to me that the whole thing was a ready-up, that he overheard something, a call from Declan Costello to one of our judges who was on the Commission, telling him what to do, literally, and he was very cross about that indeed, very bitter about it. Not to say that it is true.

MAHON HAYES: I think that it is true actually. I took the position before we left Sunningdale. I said to Declan Quigley, 'Listen, we're taking on this, it's untenable in international law, it was based solely on our constitutional provision that our foreign relations would be conducted on the basis of generally accepted principles of international law.'[39]

Now, extradition itself was not a generally accepted principle in international law, it's only established by contract, by agreements between parties and reciprocal arrangements, so to suggest that an exception to extradition could be a general principle in international law seems to be crazy.

JOHN SWIFT: Two brief points. The first is that the Irish view, which Mahon has described, in other words the question of an exception, an exception to an exception, was not maintained fully on our side. There was a marked difference of view within our ranks.

[38] See Law Enforcement Commission (1974).
[39] Declan Quigley was a senior official in the Attorney General's office.

If you read the report of the Law Enforcement Commission, there is a relevant footnote that goes back to one of our Supreme Court justices. Judge Henchy disagreed, but he did not stick out for his point of view. That is to say, he disagreed with the general Irish argument that we were bound by our constitution (article 29) not to extradite for 'political' crimes, because refusal to extradite for politically motivated crimes was a fully accepted principle of international law. Henchy basically did not agree with that, but he did not stand out strongly enough against it.

NOEL DORR: Later, Tom O'Higgins in the Supreme Court essentially decided, or took the line in a particular case, that someone could be extradited because you couldn't call murder 'political'.[40] It's a kind of ingenious argument that doesn't quite work. I mean, he wasn't facing the full problem, but he was getting out of it by saying that murder couldn't be a political offence. But there are other examples in international law—genocide, for instance, and piracy, if I'm right. The Law Commission report, the body that John was on the secretariat of, says that the conferring of extraterritorial jurisdiction on domestic courts would be possible without the enactment of reciprocal legislation, but its effectiveness would be enhanced by reciprocal legislation to facilitate the taking of evidence.

Now that was what was done in 1975, but there was a follow-up to that, because there was no agreement at that time on extradition. My perception of that period was very strongly that neither government—neither Fianna Fáil nor the coalition government—really wanted extradition. Declan Costello was one of the strongest against it. There was a sort of fine legal argument spun about article 29 of the constitution committing us to generally accepted principles of international law. We argued that this was a general principle, therefore you couldn't do it.

DERMOT NALLY: There was also the earlier point that we wanted an all-Ireland court which would try offences committed either in the North or in the South.

GARRET FITZGERALD: Was that in the Sunningdale Agreement?

NOEL DORR: It's in the preparation for Sunningdale, it's in the report. We return to it in 1985, if you remember, in the Anglo-Irish negotiations, and the British side almost bought it at that time.

MAHON HAYES: Declan Costello was very strong on that, in fact Declan Costello at one stage talked in terms of settling the Strasbourg case on the basis of the establishment of an all-Ireland human-rights court, you know.[41]

---

[40] This is a reference to a Supreme Court judgment in December 1982 in the case of a prominent INLA activist who was extradited to Northern Ireland to face a murder charge; see 'Dominic McGlinchey, Plaintiff, v. Laurence Wren, Defendant', *Irish Reports*, 1982, 154.

[41] The Strasbourg case was taken by Ireland against the UK; see n. 9.

DERMOT NALLY: It didn't run.

MAHON HAYES: No, it didn't run. He never pushed it, but he was thinking in those terms.

DERMOT NALLY: Heath's point was that you are arresting people in the South and then you are releasing them on bail, and when they're on bail they turn up in the North and they commit more crimes—can you stop that? He cited actual cases. It seemed like a simple request. There was perhaps some judicial interpretation of something in the constitution.

NOEL DORR: My sense of it was that before Sunningdale there was kind of agreement even with the unionists on some kind of an all-Ireland court for security matters reporting to the Council of Ireland, but that Dublin wanted it also to have a remit in the human-rights area and the unionists were willing to have it as a security-type court only, under the Council of Ireland in some way.

MAHON HAYES: On our side at least, this was looked at from three points of view: (*a*) a court that would be associated with the Council of Ireland which would have the jurisdiction to adjudicate on the orders and actions of the Council of Ireland, of their interpretation, of their validity and that sort of thing, (*b*) that it would have a function in relation to terrorist offences in both parts of the country on the basis of coinciding legislation, and (*c*) that it would have a function—not very well spelt out in relation to human rights—on the basis of the European Convention being part of the domestic law in both parts of the country.

NOEL DORR: Yes, the fact that the court would be dealing with security or crime, if you like, terrorist crime, was something that the government in Dublin were willing to accept. It was coming from the unionist side, but Dublin was willing to accept it if it also covered the human rights—the third of your points.

JOHN SWIFT: If we are coming to the end of this section of the discussion, could I come back to my second point? The introduction to the report of the Law Enforcement Commission has a summary of the solutions considered, and it mentions four:

(1) a common law-enforcement area in which jurisdiction is exercised by an all-Ireland court;
(2) extradition;
(3) the conferring of additional extraterritorial jurisdiction upon the courts of each jurisdiction; and
(4) as a variant of the third solution, the exercise in each country of extraterritorial jurisdiction by special courts consisting of three judges, at least one of whom would be a judge of the other jurisdiction.

Now, the net result of the discussion was that, in very short order, solution number four was put to one side as not practical, and so was solution number one, the all-Ireland court, in spite of the interest on our side in pushing it. All the judges agreed, and I quote, 'we deal with this method very briefly because we are agreed that it is not practicable to deal urgently with the problem by this means'. They gave half a page to it, and that was the end of the all-Ireland court method.

GARRET FITZGERALD: So we were going to be divided again.

NOEL DORR: The summary, the conclusion, said at the end, we are agreed that the mixed court method would confer no legal or procedural advantage over the extraterritorial method as exercised by domestic courts.

GARRET FITZGERALD: The judges didn't want to get involved with each other.

DERMOT NALLY: The real reason was that you couldn't spell 'no extraterritoriality' across a road but you could spell 'no extradition.' Look at the roads and walls in the West: 'No extradition' used to be scrawled on them.

2.4. The Failure of Sunningdale

2.4.1. The Causes of Failure

NOEL DORR: I would suggest that it's a very facile assumption, which is now becoming accepted, partly on Conor Cruise O'Brien's view, and others, perhaps, that the Council of Ireland overloaded Sunningdale and that that brought it down—that is, that it would all have worked if there had been simply the power-sharing executive. But that wouldn't have worked at the time; the pieces wouldn't have fitted together; it wouldn't have held, I think, as Austin would probably confirm for the SDLP; but it seems to me you can trace about five reasons why Sunningdale fell.

The first was that there was to be a second stage, a formal stage in the conference. This was only the first stage, and what it did was that it announced a Council of Ireland with some idea of broad functions, and all that, but it didn't give it any content, so you had a concept launched without content. So the fears of unionists were able to focus on the empty concept rather than on the actual thing, whatever it would be.

Secondly was that when the need (the political need after Sunningdale, as I think is said in the closing speeches and so on) was to go back and sell it as a settlement at last of a long-standing problem, to really put your heart into it, North and South, and Faulkner needed it above all in the North—at just that time Boland took his court action. The government in Dublin were estopped, to use a legal term, I think it's correct, but anyway they were frozen, they were legally advised not to say anything. Faulkner was beginning to gasp for air and look for support, and the government in Dublin were not in a position to say anything. They were gagged by the lawyers, to put it bluntly.

GARRET FITZGERALD: And we never thought of the possibility of such an action.

NOEL DORR: Thirdly, the court action itself: Declan Costello as Attorney General went into the court and, like a good lawyer, he argued the best possible case. But the case that was being made against the Agreement by Boland was that it was contrary to articles 2 and 3 of the constitution and therefore unconstitutional, and the Attorney General's argument against that was, no, it's not, it's merely a statement, it's merely this, it's merely that, there's nothing new after all. Everything that was said in the court diminished the political importance of what had been agreed at the very time when Faulkner's political need in the North was to be told that this is something new, a new departure, Irish nationalism and unionism working together, something new.

The fourth was the fact that an election was called in February 1974, for other reasons altogether, throughout the United Kingdom. The result of that was that the unionist community, being rather fearful about what had been done, and getting very nervous about it, were being asked to make a judgement on the Sunningdale Agreement, such as it was at the first conference, at a premature stage. In other words, if the Agreement and the executive had continued in Northern Ireland, as Austin said, it was working well, and Faulkner said it was working well and so on, and others said that too, it would have settled in perhaps over a year or two, and then an election might have brought a different result. For one thing, the concept would have been fleshed out and we would have had a content to the Council of Ireland, that fearful monster which was just a concept at that stage. So the election meant a premature judgement. The phrase you might use is a judgement on the house while the scaffolding is still around it, and the electorate voted on their fears in that election.

The next point that worked against Sunningdale was that a government came in that 'knew not Joseph', to quote a biblical term. Wilson came in; he didn't have any feel for Sunningdale or what had been done. Heath had lived through it, and we talked earlier about the education of Heath and his conversion, if you want to call it that, and here was Wilson now taking over, and he had no feel for the whole thing. Finally he did two further things: he appointed Merlyn Rees, who was pusillanimous—generally a disaster of a secretary of state—and then, when the loyalist workers called their strike, the British government was unwilling or unable to stand up to it, and a small number of people pulled it down.

I think in any fair analysis of what happened you'd have to take all these points together. For Conor to say, 'Oh, the Council of Ireland overloaded it' is too facile, because the Council of Ireland, as I said many times, was necessary at the time in order to buttress power-sharing in Northern Ireland and to prove that it wasn't an internal settlement.

AUSTIN CURRIE: All of those, all of those five points, plus at least as important was the deteriorating security situation, which totally undermined Faulkner, who from the very beginning had been in favour of the Council of Ireland to handle the security situation.

Q: Was a constitutional challenge not anticipated?

AUSTIN CURRIE: There had been an anticipation that a challenge might be made. What Garret suggested, in terms of putting the two declarations side by side, was to reduce the possibility of a successful challenge, and so therefore it was a matter of some consideration.

GARRET FITZGERALD: But it didn't seem as though it would be a fact, and that our defence would undermine the Agreement.

NOEL DORR: First of all, at Sunningdale it was anticipated there would be a second stage, to take place in early January.

Q: But the second stage did not take place?

NOEL DORR: It didn't take place because the thing began to fray with the Boland case.

AUSTIN CURRIE: Of course, except there was a meeting at Hillsborough.

DERMOT NALLY: There was a meeting in Baldonnel before the meeting in Hillsborough.[42]

NOEL DORR: If you go through the different things as to whether they could have been anticipated at Sunningdale, one was that Sunningdale planned for a second stage early in the new year. That was the way it was thought of. Therefore, the idea of leaving a truncated and a half-baked conference without the full form certainly wasn't anticipated, because it was anticipated it would be, on the contrary, a completed conference eventually. Secondly, one couldn't have anticipated a British election. Thirdly, we had some opposition on the part of Fianna Fáil—the greener wing of Fianna Fáil—that might have been anticipated. Maybe the Boland case might have been thought about, but you couldn't have anticipated the plea that would be made, the way it would be argued. You couldn't have anticipated a change of government in Britain, you couldn't have anticipated Merlyn Rees, you couldn't have anticipated a lot of things.

Q: But the one thing that was anticipated but wasn't factored in was unionist opposition to it.

GARRET FITZGERALD: We knew about the opposition there.

MUIRIS MAC CONGHAIL: The SDLP had just come from a very acrimonious scene in the Assembly in Northern Ireland—jumped over tables or whatever they'd

---

[42] This refers to a meeting between Taoiseach Liam Cosgrave and the Chief Executive of the Northern Ireland Executive, Brian Faulkner, at Casement Aerodrome, Baldonnel, Dublin on 16 January 1974. Northern and Southern ministers met at Hillsborough on 1 February 1974 to discuss the detailed functions of the Council of Ireland.

done. They'd just arrived there, I think it was the previous day, Austin, wasn't it?[43]

AUSTIN CURRIE: It was the Faulknerites that the wrath was directed at by Paisley. Basil McIvor was hit, and there were others attacked in the Assembly, but the one thing that we haven't put enough emphasis on yet is the criticism that was made and continues to be made that we gave Faulkner too much to do in selling the Agreement—that the Council of Ireland made it impossible for Faulkner.

Now that was not Faulkner's view. I had an experience, for which I was grateful afterwards, on the Sunday afternoon, when I had gone to sleep for a few hours. I came out into the grounds and Faulkner was there, and Basil McIvor and a couple of others, walking around, and at this stage we were just waiting for the winding-up; everyone knew what the score was. Faulkner was full of confidence, and he wasn't expressing any negative reservations, he wasn't saying, 'Oh you've given me too much to sell', or anything of that nature—going back to the fact that he claimed credit initially for the Council of Ireland itself.

MAHON HAYES: Sorry, I would add two points to Noel's. They're less important ones than the ones he mentions. First of all I think that Oliver Napier, on New Year's Day, maybe, undermined Faulkner's position by making an attack on the Irish government for not agreeing to change articles 2 and 3.[44] That undermined Faulkner immediately.

On the other side, [Faulkner was also undermined by] the IRA campaign and of course now from the workers' strike, supported by and fomented by the Paisleyites, who were on the outside, just as the IRA was on the outside. The fact was that the British didn't face this down, and my own view, and it's a purely personal view, was that this strike was aimed as much at the power-sharing executive as at the Council of Ireland.

GARRET FITZGERALD: That was Faulkner's view also. We indicated to the British beforehand that we would understand if they had brought some of them along to a meeting or something. We were concerned about the exclusion of Paisleyites—just like the Anglo-Irish Agreement—we wanted the British to have him come along to the beginning of each conference. Each time we were more open to that than the British were.

---

[43] The policy of the 'anti-power-sharing unionists' (mainly the DUP, the Vanguard Unionists, and Faulkner's opponents within his own party) of obstructing the activities of the Assembly had resulted in violent scenes on more than one occasion in the preceding months. On 28 November and 5 December 1973, and 22 January 1974, police had intervened to clear the debating chamber.

[44] Oliver Napier, founding leader of the Alliance Party and a minister designate in the new Northern Ireland executive, addressed a forthright 'open letter to the people of the Republic' on 27 December 1973 in which he questioned the good faith of the Irish government and called for constitutional change; see *Irish Times*, 28 December 1973.

JOHN SWIFT: A very quick question to Austin. Is it a fair criticism that, when Heath called the election for the end of February, the anti-Agreement unionists got their act together very fast, maximized their vote, put up one candidate per constituency, etc.; but on the pro-Agreement side, they were at sixes and sevens?

AUSTIN CURRIE: Take Faulkner, for example. Faulkner had just had to resign as leader of the Unionist Party.

JOHN SWIFT: And he lost his secretariat.

AUSTIN CURRIE: He decided to set up a new party. Faulkner went into that election without any army, and no weapons. He had no weapons at all; the executive had only been set up, it had no opportunity to prove itself, and here he was fighting the election without even a party.

JOHN SWIFT: I suppose it would have been totally out of the question for the pro-Agreement people, across the nationalist–unionist divide, to help one another?

AUSTIN CURRIE: Well, if you can look at it afterwards, it certainly should have happened. The SDLP's position was that we would fight every constituency, but we had our own fish to fry, and the fish we had to fry were Bernadette Devlin and Frank McManus, who were as much anti-Sunningdale as were the unionists.[45] And we had to get rid of them, which was a messy split vote situation in Fermanagh–South Tyrone and Mid-Ulster. And that was our job that we had to do.

DERMOT NALLY: On 5 January 1974, the Ulster Unionist Council voted against Sunningdale with a majority of fifty-three. There was the Boland case which had started, and the defence had been put in. Faulkner got on to Cosgrave, or Bloomfield got on to me, anyway, and said 'Can we meet? We must discuss what is happening—this is an emergency.' And he came in a state almost of panic. First of all he said that Sunningdale was 'the most important political event in Ireland in the last fifty years, and that is my firm belief'. Secondly, he said 'the executive is working extremely well, I have had no experience of any government or any executive where people have come together and obviously worked so cohesively', so he was happy with the executive and he was happy with the total Sunningdale thing, but he said there are two major concerns.

The first concern is status. He said that 'unless something is done about that I'm in deep trouble'. The second concern was the Council of Ireland. He said 'the more the Council of Ireland is pushed the more I lose support, and if I lose support the whole thing will collapse, and I need time'. He says, 'give me a year,

---

[45] Bernadette Devlin and Frank McManus were the sitting MPs in the Mid-Ulster and Fermanagh & South Tyrone constituencies, respectively. Both had been elected under the Unity banner in 1970 (Devlin previously winning her seat in a by-election in 1969), and both were to lose their seats to unionists in the February 1974 election.

give me eighteen months, give me two years and people will see how the executive works and then Sunningdale will be no problem'.

That was on 16 January, and [Faulkner said:] 'We do not have any, any credibility at all', that's a quotation of what he said at that meeting, referring to the Boland case.

GARRET FITZGERALD: How did they react to that? What was Cosgrave's reaction?

DERMOT NALLY: I don't think there was much of a reaction because he couldn't say anything on status, he said that's before the courts.

GARRET FITZGERALD: That was in March. We never thought though that if a case would be taken it would have the effect of immobilizing us politically. Nobody thought that.

NOEL DORR: I happen to have here a paper that I did on 22 March 1974, which is headed, 'Sunningdale'. I tried to analyse this thing, first of all to make a distinction between the basic premises underlying Sunningdale and the actual accommodation reached at Sunningdale. This was in March. The basic premise was that none of the various intermediate but essentially static solutions will work (a federal Ireland, confederal, and all that); the only alternative therefore is an accommodation between the two traditions, which will be the basis not for a static solution of any kind but for a process of growth towards reconciliation in which both commit themselves in good faith, without seeking to predetermine the exact outcome.

And this is relevant: such a settlement depends first on finding a point where the forces in the island are in balance so that the process of reconciliation can begin from the most stable base possible, and then constructing institutions both within Northern Ireland and at an all-Ireland level which will positively encourage cooperation for its own sake and as a way of easing the conflict. This point of equilibrium of forces cannot be established a priori; it must be worked out at the all-Ireland level and within Northern Ireland by elected representatives who between them speak for all the major forces in the island.

And then, I went on, such a settlement will not end violence, but the situation now is such that no settlement will end violence at present. A settlement, however, which is an accommodation worked out between representatives of all the major forces in the island, offers the best hope of reducing violence to the minimum, that is to the hard core—either virtual gangsters or [those] who want trouble for ulterior revolutionary motives, or simply cannot be satisfied because they reject the very idea of compromise, and settlement on their own terms is not possible. That, if you like, is thinking about Paisley and the IRA continuing.

The central idea was to build on the centre and find the point that brings the maximum number of people into the centre, and then you have to deal with the fringes, that was the thinking of the time.

Now I went on to propose at that stage—I had been shocked by either seeing the letter already referred to or hearing about this account of how things were fraying in Northern Ireland—I proposed that the conference go ahead to the second stage, but that it be explicitly stated that the council and all of that would not come into effect until ratified North and South in an election of some kind, let's say another parliamentary election in the North and possibly change in the constitution in the South.

This proposal was perhaps far too ambitious and maybe it was crazy at the time, but the idea was that you needed to say something of the kind. The relevance of bringing it in here is that my sense in March 1974 was that the thing was coming apart, that the distinction between the basic premises and the actual accommodation reached at Sunningdale remained valid, but the actual accommodation was coming apart, and that the only way to save it was to promise some kind of electoral ratification or validation North and South and rush ahead and get the Agreement in place as quickly as you could on the promise of future electoral validation.

AUSTIN CURRIE: To quote myself, 'the basic objective should be to isolate the two Ps of Provisionalism and Paisleyism'—that was the objective. Heath declared the election on 4 February for the 28th [of February]; we had less, we had just a month, right. Now you were talking about validation, I suggested at one stage in a contribution at Sunningdale that we should have a referendum on the Sunningdale Agreement. I didn't push it because it was clear that there wasn't going to be any support for it, and Brian Faulkner thought it was too chancy to be doing, but I don't know, if we had done it immediately afterwards, if we had had a referendum then instead of Heath's bloody election, things might have been different.

Q: Wilson wasn't interested at all; Wilson's talking about when he is going to call an election. Wilson's talking about withdrawal, and Armstrong is arguing very, very forcefully against withdrawal, as strongly as he can against withdrawal.[46]

AUSTIN CURRIE: Merlyn Rees had the best motives but he was so weak and was also in circumstances where the army was determined not to be fighting on two fronts.

NOEL DORR: On 29 October the Irish political correspondents went to Belfast for a briefing at lunch with William Whitelaw and Frank Cooper. On their return they told Muiris what Cooper had said. I sent a note about this subsequently to Garret. I won't read it out but Frank Cooper spoke of 'Garret Fitzgerald and Conor Cruise O'Brien' as 'blank, blank academics'. I won't say what was in the blanks.

GARRET FITZGERALD: 'Third rate'?

---

[46] See Donoughue (2006: 127).

AUSTIN CURRIE: He was very strong and he was quite ruthless. There was one occasion we had discussions with him about the RUC and we even said, 'You're asking the RUC to do something that's going to lead to injury and maybe death'. He said 'That's what they're there for.'

GARRET FITZGERALD: What Shirley Williams said was that the non-intervention in the workers' strike reflected the fact that the government were not sure of the army, and that in the army ever since Suez morale was poor. They were unable to send the army into Rhodesia because they couldn't rely on them to act, and this was a factor in the decision not to act.

When Wilson came back from the Scilly Islands to meet, I think, Merlyn Rees in Cornwall, he invited me, and he was told, 'Whitehall are against any action', which is to say the Ministry of Defence.

In all of this we never mentioned the Ministry of Defence. Throughout the period there has never been actually a coherent response here to Northern Ireland because the Tories would never rein in the army. Labour were afraid to, and I know from senior people in the Foreign Office their view, that the first British government to actually take the army on was the Blair government when it came in in 1997. Until then nobody would take on the army.

So, no matter what, it can be said the army did to protect people from murder, if the army run the place, no one would take them on. So the army, actually, their policy was not under control, they did huge damage in this whole period, and they alienated the nationalists. Britain had no actual policy, or no Northern Ireland policy, because the Ministry of Defence had a separate policy which was to protect the army's morale, that's it.

That's a thing we never talk about; it is shown up of course in the workers' strike. The most extreme example was General Tuzo's attitude then.[47] It's impolite to say the British didn't control their army but that's fundamental to the whole history of Northern Ireland.

NOEL DORR: You mean it's the Curragh Mutiny continued?[48]

MUIRIS MAC CONGHAIL: We also had some problems ourselves during that period. The communiqué wasn't brought back because there wasn't a second stage to the Agreement, to the discussion after Sunningdale, we didn't have it [in] January for reasons already stated. The debate…didn't take place in Dáil Éireann until March, and that was a fatal organizational flaw.

Fianna Fáil dissidents were out there as well, busily knocking away at it at all stages, and undermining, and we became concerned at some point about the fact that it required Fianna Fáil to be in office to come to any constitutional

---

[47]   General Sir Harry Tuzo was commander of British Forces in Northern Ireland, 1971–2.

[48]   The 'Curragh Mutiny' was an incident in March 1914 in which senior army officers based in the Curragh Camp, Co. Kildare, threatened to resign rather than taking military action against the Ulster Volunteer Force.

agreement; otherwise it's 'illegitimate' if another government than Fianna Fáil is in office.

The civil servants as well behave in this way about this issue; they understand that rule absolutely. The issue about that is very, very strange, so we have a problem. It is not discussed by Dáil Éireann, it is not discussed at all, nor do we actually circulate or provide the documentation even in the Dáil record. When you look at it, you look up to discover where the text of the Sunningdale Agreement is to be found, but it's not in the Dáil proceedings. It's important to underline that parliament itself did not get involved in this discourse. It was disastrous from that point of view. No serious parliamentary discussion took place on the Sunningdale Agreement.

DERMOT NALLY: Blaney had a motion for discussion in private members' time, and I think there was real fear that if that motion were discussed there would be quite a lot of fireworks on the floor of the house, and things would be said which would wreck the entire thing.

NOEL DORR: Muiris is perfectly right, and in democratic terms it's an outrage and strange and wrong and so on, but that is all a subset of the basic problem, which is that the government took legal advice and followed it and were frozen, and they were afraid to have a debate.

But there's a general question that's worth perhaps putting to Austin, because a lot of what we're talking about now circles around the question of whether Sunningdale could have been done differently, whether it was overloaded, whether the Council could have been dropped at Sunningdale or after Sunningdale. Can you just make a general comment, Austin, on whether it would have worked at Sunningdale or after Sunningdale if the Irish government had said 'Look, we'll abandon the Council for the moment'. Is my perception wrong on that? My perception is that it wouldn't have been acceptable.

AUSTIN CURRIE: The SDLP couldn't have accepted a power-sharing arrangement without the Council of Ireland. Otherwise, Sunningdale would have been an internal settlement which would have been unacceptable to a party which believed in a united Ireland, and additionally we needed a link between the Council and policing. We wanted a change in the name of the RUC, we wanted a change in uniform, and there were a few other things. The unionists wouldn't have it, or, more importantly, the British government wouldn't have it.

That was clear at Stormont Castle,[49] it was clear at Sunningdale, and in the absence of those things we said 'Well, what else do we have? Is there any other way in which we can secure sufficient identification between the nationalist community and the police force?' And the only way we could think of was

---

[49] The reference is to the talks between the Ulster Unionist Party, the Alliance Party, and the SDLP at Stormont Castle, 5, 9, and 16 October 1973, chaired by William Whitelaw; on 21 November the parties agreed to form a power-sharing executive.

some link-up with the Council of Ireland, so the Council of Ireland was essential—it was essential. By calling an election, Heath put the whole thing in jeopardy, but had he won the election, then the situation certainly wouldn't have been as bad as it became under Wilson.

GARRET FITZGERALD: And Heath said on radio some time afterwards he would have put the army in at the very beginning.

AUSTIN CURRIE: And as far as the strike was concerned, if by the third day the security forces had moved the strike would have gone, and the leaders of the strike recognised that, and to this day recognize that.

MUIRIS MAC CONGHAIL: But the Irish government also weren't prepared, as indeed the general citizenry, including the media, were entirely unprepared, for the stupidity of the Wilson government on coming into office. And the Irish press (with a small 'p') as a whole were entirely unprepared too—after all, this is a good thing, here were the good guys back, except they weren't the good guys anymore. And Merlyn Rees—I had extreme difficulties in explaining to Merlyn Rees the difference between a strike and a *coup d'état*.

JOHN SWIFT: Could I go back to Muiris's point: why was it not discussed in the Dáil? We all know the specific reasons, but doesn't that raise basic questions about our system?

The first point is, we stand on the constitution, and make a big play about it, but if a court case, taken against the government on constitutional grounds, has the effect of paralysing parliament in relation to one of the biggest political developments on the island for years and years, what does that say about our constitution, and/or our way of handling it? It says in substance that our constitution and/or our way of handling it, is a weakness, not a strength.

The second point is for Garret, not Muiris. It seems to me almost incomprehensible that, following Sunningdale, and following the developments immediately after Sunningdale, by the end of December, starting with the court case, there was no discussion in government about what arguments the Attorney General was going to employ in court. The political content here has to be as important as the constitutional content, but, as far as I understand it, this was never discussed.

MAHON HAYES: I have a point about it—what else could have been done at that time? I mean the obvious lawyer's reaction to this is 'OK, we defend it, and we'll use every possible argument', because that's what you do as a lawyer. What was the alternative politically?

Let me ask the question. Is the alternative that the Attorney General would have been instructed by the government that you defend this, but you will only defend it without undermining it, and that if we lose the case we say we go to the country with a referendum to change the constitution?

NOEL DORR: I think it was just left to Declan Costello. On the scandal of parliament not being involved, I think we tend here to assimilate our situation to the British one, where parliament has an existence of its own and there's a need to satisfy parliament.

Here, to be blunt about it, here the Dáil is the creature of the government of the day, and if the government of the day feel themselves stopped or blocked from making a clarification statement they are in a position to say, 'We don't want to debate in the Dáil, it's just too troublesome and we don't have to, we won't do it until after the court case is settled.' It's a different situation from the British parliament; you wouldn't get away with that in London, I think.

2.4.2. The Consequences of Failure

DERMOT NALLY: There's only one further matter now, that Austin raised, that could be added to it, I think. And that's withdrawal. British withdrawal was the shadow. Wilson produced a paper in 1971, and he said why don't we withdraw, more or less, and, OK, finish the subsidy in three years, five years. Then, when he was prime minister in April 1974, he said, the British, and the Conservatives believe, the men in the street believe, that we should pull out and let them cut one another's throats. Any attempt to bring the issue of Northern Ireland into the next election would end in...I wouldn't like to forecast what would happen. Now, if there was ever a threat, that was a threat.

Just to add, Bernard Donoughue came on to me sometime around then—I don't know the exact date, I never made a note of it—but he said 'would you support withdrawal?' I said 'Oh God! No', and you know that, that's my contribution.

GARRET FITZGERALD: He said that he had rung you about something else, he didn't say you, he rang some other person in Dublin about something else, and at the end of it you said—he, by the way, reported to two other people before about the policy, including withdrawal—and you said 'you wouldn't be thinking of doing anything radical would you?' And he was horrified—how did you know that such a thing existed? What did you mean? And you said, 'don't put down the phone'.

In fact that was not the end of it. I mean, John Hume was constantly pressing me to clarify with the British whether they would withdraw. I said 'I will not'; I said if I ask them will they withdraw, and ask them not to withdraw, they will take that as permission to withdraw.

Q: What lessons did you take in 1974 from the failure of Sunningdale?

GARRET FITZGERALD: A sense of impotence because, you know, it failed. Where do you go from there? And how will the British government react to that? I was very conscious of the danger of British withdrawal. Indeed, some of the SDLP were pressing me to clarify with the British government, which it wasn't fair to do, because it would give them the psychological go-ahead.

Merlyn Rees refused to see me throughout 1975. He was negotiating with the IRA, so-called Sinn Féin, in January. The British ambassador came in to Liam Cosgrave three times and gave him different accounts each time, saying 'sorry, I wasn't right the last time', so that at the end of it, we didn't know what the truth was, and certainly we weren't told the truth the first and second time, so we were in total uncertainty.

AUSTIN CURRIE: That period, the end of 1974, 1975, 1976—I don't think we ever came closer to civil war. First of all there was the uncertainty about British intentions, and there was good reason to think that they would withdraw. Then the loyalists had their tails up: they had brought down the power-sharing executive, they had brought down the Council of Ireland, they became more and more involved in sectarian warfare.

The nationalist community was dismayed, afraid, disappointed, frustrated— the feeling of it being hopeless, fearful, because Sunningdale had been such a bright hope, and there it was, brought down because of the joint activity of the loyalists and the IRA. What was the future going to hold? And also, the circumstances where there was an escalation of sectarian killing.

GARRET FITZGERALD: You see, the argument was we knew our army was totally inadequate. The most it could do was get to Newry and Derry, and no further. There's no way we could give help to Belfast or the countryside, and yet if we did anything about strengthening the army that would be seen as a threat by loyalists, so we were in a position of total impotence. We knew we couldn't tackle the situation, and yet we couldn't do anything to make ourselves ready to tackle the situation.

AUSTIN CURRIE: Repartition was more and more being talked about—along the line of the Bann.

DERMOT NALLY: There's a detailed report by the IDU on the question of with-drawal. The point was that the Irish army had 12,000 or 13,000 people. We said 'How many of those could you free for intervention in the North?' 'Oh, there would be 5,000 effective frontline', 'OK, the Guards will increase the numbers, how many could you provide?', and the numbers were infinitesimal.

At the time, as far as I can remember, there were 30,000 troops and police in Northern Ireland and they were trying to keep order in face of dissension arising from the minority community. If we, even with our very, very small resources, were to have to try to keep order in face of dissension arising from the majority community, who were well armed and well skilled, through their work in the B-Specials, UDR, etc., it would have been a total fiasco, we just could not have done it.[50]

---

[50] The 'B-Specials' (formally, the Ulster Special Constabulary) were part of a special constabulary created in 1920 to support the Royal Irish Constabulary (RIC). They continued in a similar support role for the Royal Ulster Constabulary (RUC) after the creation of Northern Ireland; two other categories

Then there was the whole question of the British subvention. I'm not sure of the exact figures but I think it was something like that the total amount of the subvention was more than the total yield of income tax in the country at the time. In other words, what we were facing would be ruin, civil war, God knows what else, but at that time—now this is 1974, towards the end of 1974—Wilson was asking Armstrong and company to look at the question of withdrawal and he said . . .

GARRET FITZGERALD: in May?

Q: The key memorandum from Wilson is 3 June.

DERMOT NALLY: Yes, well they were looking at the question of withdrawal, and we had an inkling of this. The conclusion of that, which was summarized by Armstrong, the conclusion was 'We are looking at direct rule for the foreseeable future.' I said, 'Well, thank God.'

NOEL DORR: There was an idea around in the mid-1970s in very respected thinking in Britain and elsewhere that the only way was to allow the fight go on, and then the forces will find an equilibrium, and then you could find a settlement.

GARRET FITZGERALD: Repartition?

NOEL DORR: No, the boil would have to be lanced. Now on the other side, the Irish side, in 1969—and still kind of vaguely floating around in some people's minds—there had been the idea that the Irish army 'should have gone in and taken' Newry and Derry.

Q: The Blaney line?

NOEL DORR: It now appears that the Irish army had ammunition for half a day at that time. Some people still argued on the basis that the Irish army should have gone in and that that would internationalize it, and the United Nations would step in. The trouble is that the Irish would be the aggressors in that situation, and immediately condemned by everybody.

But what did emerge on the Irish side from the strong, the greener side of Fianna Fáil, was the idea of a declaration of intent to withdraw at a future date. Now the strong argument against that was that that would lead to people grabbing for territory, consolidating their positions, and you would have cantons or whatever would emerge, and you would have civil war sooner rather than later.

GARRET FITZGERALD: We couldn't strengthen the army because it was seen as provocative in the North.

AUSTIN CURRIE: Even for internal security.

(full-time 'A-Specials' and part-time 'C-Specials') disappeared at that time. The B-Specials were almost exlusively Protestant. The force was disbanded in 1970 and replaced by the Ulster Defence Regiment (UDR), created as a regiment within the British army. Many Protestants had received basic training in the B-Specials and later in the UDR.

GARRET FITZGERALD: The fact that we couldn't even strengthen internal security without seeming to say that to the North. That's the extraordinary position that we were in.

AUSTIN CURRIE: Whatever about the diplomatic arguments, the important element was what was going to happen to isolated Catholic communities.

GARRET FITZGERALD: We didn't hear about that.

JOHN SWIFT: But that was an argument that was made back in 1969.

NOEL DORR: The Irish army wouldn't be capable of taking on the B-Specials and the number of trained—and militarily trained—people in Northern Ireland, but the broader relevance is that through the late 1960s and 1970s there was a current around in Dublin, but some perhaps in British thinking, that could possibly have led to civil war. I mean that was the ultimate unthinkable, so to speak—the 'appalling vista'. So you've got to understand a lot of the effort at Sunningdale and afterwards in that context, and Austin has given a very pessimistic account of the aftermath of Sunningdale in 1975.

DERMOT NALLY: There are maps, Austin, which were drawn up at that time by the IDU, or someone in the IDU, which showed the isolated communities which would be at risk in the event of civil war. It wasn't distributed but the maps exist.

GARRET FITZGERALD: But somehow none of this ever penetrated to people generally.

AUSTIN CURRIE: How near we were!

NOEL DORR: I just think that in assessing the success or failure of Sunningdale you've got to look at the longer perspective. It's not just enough to say that, you know, this finished in 1974. I think it was part of a long process of coming to terms realistically with the problems of this island, which began with complete misunderstanding in 1969, in Dublin and London at least, and then worked its way through a series of stages to where we are at today.

Sunningdale was a very important stage in that: the idea of putting institutions in place within Northern Ireland, partnership between North and South, with potential for growth, leaving the future to determine the exact outcome, all of those kinds of ideas. It needed something more, and it got it over the following generation. In 1980 Charlie Haughey and Margaret Thatcher brought out a new dimension, 'the totality of relations'. That is the idea that you build on the Dublin–London relationship in order to ease the tensions in Northern Ireland. Then we go on to the Anglo-Irish Agreement of 1985, the two governments acting together. It was an agreement that provided a potential for devolution, but in the meantime the Dublin government would act as a surrogate voice for the minority in Northern Ireland until and unless there could be power-sharing.

Then finally you come to the Good Friday Agreement, when those basic building blocks I mentioned were eventually put in place in a negotiation which reached out beyond the middle ground, which had been the basis for the previous efforts, and instead tried to bring in everybody, provided that they would cease violence. But that was done in a way that contained a lot of ambiguities in the text, and a lot of possibilities of going in different directions, and we're still living with that. But Sunningdale has to be fitted into that long perspective rather than simply saying it failed or it didn't fail.

GARRET FITZGERALD: But the truth is that there was never any other solution. There was only one solution, which was power-sharing in Northern Ireland and some kind of a North–South link, and full acceptance of the consent principle. We can talk about stages but each time we were just coming back to that. There was never going to be any other solution.

AUSTIN CURRIE: Cast your mind back to 1968 when the civil-rights movement began. The unionists were in total control, about to celebrate fifty years of Stormont, one-party rule, we thought they would go on forever. And yet, that was 1968. On 1 January 1974 we have a power-sharing administration taking over, with the Council of Ireland. I mean, think of the progress that was made in such a short period of time, and the unionist party was really smashed. And it was built on, as Garret has said, it was built on the concept of partnership in the North and partnership between North and South.

Now, 'Sunningdale for slow learners', that was what, twenty-five, thirty years later, that is still what the thing is based on. The weakness I see today—I was in South Africa and when I came back and somebody said, 'Jesus, there are certain parallels between apartheid in South Africa and what is developing in Northern Ireland today'. The similarity is in terms of the original meaning of 'apartheid', which is 'separate development'. That, I fear, is what is happening in Northern Ireland.

My long-held attitude was that, if you could get people together from the two traditions involved in government, then by tackling the economic and political and social and other problems we could bring about reconciliation by tackling these particular problems. But now you've got a situation where you've got the Paisleyites and the Provos in government, which are the two extremes, and also at local government. They'll be looking only after their own areas—already in local government you can see it.

Paisley is not concerned about what the Provos do in the areas that they control, and the Provos aren't that concerned about what the Paisleys are doing in the areas that they control, and you've got the development of an apartheid society in Northern Ireland, where they just look after their own interests and forget about the common good.

NOEL DORR: What I'm saying is that if you think back over a century or more you can see three possible 'agendas' in relation to Ireland. The first would have been Home Rule within the United Kingdom. The UK failed in that, and so we got the Free State and partition. That created a second 'agenda'—this time for

Irish nationalism. Our aspiration to Irish unity would have meant persuading the unionists and finding a way to accommodate them in a future united Ireland. We didn't succeed very well in that. So that left a third possible 'agenda'—this time for unionists in the smaller area of Northern Ireland, which was created in response to their opposition to an independent united Ireland. That would have been to accommodate nationalists and make them feel at home there. They didn't do very well in that either.

Now, since Sunningdale, each successive effort at a settlement has been based on somehow accommodating the nationalist and unionist agendas and allowing them to compete—so long as this was done exclusively by peaceful means.

It hasn't proved possible to build a fully stable foundation so far on these two competing agendas. What Austin seems to be saying is that it's now becoming a question of allowing each to develop its own area rather than which of the two agendas will prevail. The question is, have Sinn Féin really bought into the agenda of making Northern Ireland work, or are they still vigorously pursuing the agenda, as seems to be the case, of a united Ireland, and therefore the two agendas are still in contention?

DERMOT NALLY: If you look at Blair and look at the Belfast Agreement and look at anything that has been done, you could say, in a way, this is a preparation for departure, not now, not I hope suddenly, but a sort of preparation for the medium to long term and, I hope, with agreement and in an orderly fashion.

NOEL DORR: Certainly British officials for a generation at least have been preparing, maybe not to leave, but trying to create a situation where if they did decide to leave it would be possible. That seemed to me the deeper motive behind the 1985 Agreement.

Q: To find a way under which they could ultimately leave without civil war?

GARRET FITZGERALD: And they'd like us to unite peacefully. Grand, yes, OK.

Documents

Document 2.1. Draft Communiqué (British Version), 4 December 1973

[DRAFT] HEADS OF AGREEMENT, 4 DECEMBER 1973

The Conference, comprising representatives of HMG, the Government of the Republic and the Northern Ireland Executive designate, met at Sunningdale from Thursday 6 December to Saturday 8 December 1973. The object of the Conference was to decide on action which will contribute to the restoration of peace and stability throughout Ireland and bring to an end politically motivated violence.

2. [Statement by Government of Republic on the status of Northern Ireland].

3. For their part, HMG solemnly declare that it is their earnest wish that the people of Ireland should live together in peace and harmony and that the increasingly close and friendly relations between the United Kingdom and the Republic of Ireland should continue to prosper. HMG further declare that they will continue to honour to the full their commitment that Northern Ireland will not cease to be part of the United Kingdom without the consent of the majority of the people of Northern Ireland. They recognise that this commitment to support the wishes of the majority would have equal moral force and validity if in the future the majority of the people of Northern Ireland should indicate a wish to become part of the Republic of Ireland.

4. The Conference discussed the setting up of a Council of Ireland and decided upon certain propositions which should govern the nature of its institutions. It was agreed that the Council of Ireland should be confined to representatives of the North and South of Ireland with proper safeguards for HMG's financial and other interests; that it should consist of an equal number of representatives of the Government of the Republic and of the Northern Ireland Executive and also, on a separate advisory and consultative level, of an equal number of representatives from parties in the Dáil and the Northern Ireland Assembly; and that the Council should have its own Secretariat. In order that decisions of the Council should carry the greatest degree of support, they should be taken at governmental level on a basis of unanimity.

5. The functions which might be undertaken by a Council of Ireland were discussed and the Conference agreed that subjects in respect of which it might be suitable for a Council of Ireland to exercise executive responsibilities would include roads, electricity, regional development and tourism. HMG and the Government of the Republic have agreed to make available staff who will jointly undertake an immediate preliminary examination of these matters to see how a Council of Ireland might carry out executive functions in respect of them. As soon as a Northern Ireland Executive has been appointed, the Government of the Republic and the Northern Ireland Executive will nominate persons from their number to form a Council of Ireland. The Council will then appoint a Secretary-General who will be directed to proceed with the recruitment of his own staff and the drawing up of plans for a permanent headquarters. It has been agreed that until a permanent headquarters is ready, facilities should be made available so that a Council of Ireland can meet as soon as possible alternately in the North and South of Ireland.

6. The Conference agreed that a Council of Ireland could, and should, play an important role in the law and order field. It is the view of the Conference that terrorism must be dealt with on an all-Ireland basis if effective steps are to be taken and it was agreed that the establishment of a common law enforcement area throughout the whole of Ireland could contribute significantly to this end. Arrangements are, therefore, to be made to enable the courts both in the North and the South to hear cases in the place where a fugitive from the jurisdiction in which he committed the crime is arrested. The matter is of considerable constitutional and legal difficulty and HMG and the Government of the Republic have agreed to appoint a joint commission to recommend to both Governments what changes in the law are best suited to carry out their agreed objective. Both Governments undertook to bring forward the necessary legislation in their respective legislatures as soon as possible.

7. The Conference also considered the question of policing within Ireland as a whole. HMG reaffirmed its decision that the RUC will continue to provide the police service for Northern Ireland. [The Government of the Republic stated that they must retain responsibility for the Gardai.] It was agreed, however, that there would be great advantage in close links between the RUC and the Gardai. To this end, the Government of the Republic undertook to introduce legislation to set up a police authority for the Gardai and, when this is done, arrangements will be made to establish a Standing Joint Committee including representatives of both police authorities so that there can be a systematic exchange of views on policing in the North and the South. Reports will be made available by the Gardai and the RUC to the Standing Committee. In addition, arrangements will be made for the closest co-operation, under the aegis of a Council of Ireland, between the Gardai and the RUC on operational and other matters, particularly in the field of training and communications.

8. The Conference agreed that a Council of Ireland could also make a significant contribution in the field of human rights. It was agreed that the Council should be invited to examine the legislation in both the North and the South of Ireland related to anti-discrimination and the protection of human rights and to draw attention to any legislative or other measures which might be required either in Northern Ireland or in the Republic of Ireland to provide any necessary protections additional to existing legislation on these matters. The Council of Ireland will be invited to do this in the light of the European Convention on Human Rights to which HMG and the Government of the Republic are signatories.

9. The Conference took note of a reaffirmation by HMG of its firm commitment to bring detention to an end in Northern Ireland for all sections of the community as soon as the security situation permits and noted also that the Secretary of State for Northern Ireland hopes to be able to bring into use his statutory powers of selective release in time for a number of detainees to be released before Christmas.

10. HMG stated that, in the light of the decisions reached at the Conference, it would now seek the authority of Parliament to devolve full powers on the Northern Ireland Executive and Northern Ireland Assembly as from 1 January 1974. The formal appointment of the Northern Ireland Executive would now be made.

11. The Conference agreed that a formal conference would be held early in the New Year at which HMG, the Government of the Republic and the Northern Ireland Executive would meet together to ratify the Agreement reached and to review the work which has been commissioned.

Note: Square brackets in this document are reproduced from the original and do not represent editorial intervention.

Source: appended to memorandum from Robin Butler to Prime Minister, 4 December 1973; TNA: PREM/15/1685.

Document 2.2. Sunningdale Communiqué, 9 December 1973

AGREED COMMUNIQUÉ ISSUED FOLLOWING THE CONFERENCE
BETWEEN THE IRISH AND BRITISH GOVERNMENTS AND THE PARTIES
INVOLVED IN THE NORTHERN IRELAND EXECUTIVE (DESIGNATE) ON
6TH, 7TH, 8TH, AND 9TH DECEMBER, 1973.

1. The Conference between the British and Irish Governments and the parties involved in the Northern Ireland Executive (designate) met at Sunningdale on 6, 7, 8 and 9 December 1973.

2. During the Conference, each delegation stated their position on the status of Northern Ireland.

3. The Taoiseach said that the basic principle of the Conference was that the participants had tried to see what measure of agreement of benefit to all the people concerned could be secured. In doing so, all had reached accommodation with one another on practical arrangements. But none had compromised, and none had asked others to compromise, in relation to basic aspirations. The people of the Republic, together with a minority in Northern Ireland as represented by the SDLP delegation, continued to uphold the aspiration towards a united Ireland. The only unity they wanted to see was a unity established by consent.

4. Mr Brian Faulkner said that delegates from Northern Ireland came to the Conference as representatives of apparently incompatible sets of political aspirations who had found it possible to reach agreement to join together in government because each accepted that in doing so they were not sacrificing principles or aspirations. The desire of the majority of the people of Northern Ireland to remain part of the United Kingdom, as represented by the Unionist and Alliance delegations, remained firm.

5. The Irish Government fully accepted and solemnly declared that there could be no change in the status of Northern Ireland until a majority of the people of Northern Ireland desired a change in that status. The British Government solemnly declared that it was, and would remain, their policy to support the wishes of the majority of the people of Northern Ireland. The present status of Northern Ireland is that it is part of the United Kingdom. If in the future the majority of the people of Northern Ireland should indicate a wish to become part of a united Ireland, the British Government would support that wish.

6. The Conference agreed that a formal agreement incorporating the declarations of the British and Irish Governments would be signed at the formal stage of the Conference and registered at the United Nations.

7. The Conference agreed that a Council of Ireland would be set up. It would be confined to representatives of the two parts of Ireland, with appropriate safeguards for the British Government's financial and other interests. It would comprise a Council of Ministers with

executive and harmonising functions and a consultative role, and a Consultative Assembly with advisory and review functions. The Council of Ministers would act by unanimity, and would comprise a core of seven members of the Irish Government and an equal number of members of the Northern Ireland Executive with provision for the participation of other non-voting members of the Irish Government and the Northern Ireland Executive or Administration when matters within their departmental competence were discussed. The Council of Ministers would control the functions of the Council. The Chairmanship would rotate on an agreed basis between representatives of the Irish Government and of the Northern Ireland Executive. Arrangements would be made for the location of the first meeting, and the location of subsequent meetings would be determined by the Council of Ministers. The Consultative Assembly would consist of 60 members, 30 members from Dáil Éireann chosen by the Dáil on the basis of proportional representation by the single transferable vote, and 30 members from the Northern Ireland Assembly chosen by that Assembly and also on that basis. The members of the Consultative Assembly would be paid allowances. There would be a Secretariat to the Council, which would be kept as small as might be commensurate with efficiency in the operation of the Council. The Secretariat would service the institutions of the Council and would, under the Council of Ministers, supervise the carrying out of the executive and harmonising functions and the consultative role of the Council. The Secretariat would be headed by a Secretary-General. Following the appointment of a Northern Ireland Executive, the Irish Government and the Northern Ireland Executive would nominate their representatives to a Council of Ministers. The Council of Ministers would then appoint a Secretary-General and decide upon the location of its permanent headquarters. The Secretary-General would be directed to proceed with the drawing up of plans for such headquarters. The Council of Ministers would also make arrangements for the recruitment of the staff of the Secretariat in a manner and on conditions which would, as far as is practicable, be consistent with those applying to public servants in the two administrations.

8. In the context of its harmonising functions and consultative role, the Council of Ireland would undertake important work relating, for instance, to the impact of EEC membership. As for executive functions, the first step would be to define and agree these in detail. The Conference therefore decided that, in view of the administrative complexities involved, studies would at once be set in hand to identify and, prior to the formal stage of the conference, report on areas of common interest in relation to which a Council of Ireland would take executive decisions and, in appropriate cases, be responsible for carrying those decisions into effect. In carrying out these studies, and also in determining what should be done by the Council in terms of harmonisation. the objectives to be borne in mind would include the following:

(1) to achieve the best utilisation of scarce skills, expertise and resources;
(2) to avoid, in the interests of economy and efficiency, unnecessary duplication of effort; and
(3) to ensure complementary rather than competitive effort where this is to the advantage of agriculture, commerce and industry.

In particular, these studies would be directed to identifying, for the purposes of executive action by the Council of Ireland, suitable aspects of activities in the following broad fields:

(a) exploitation, conservation and development of natural resources and the environment;

(b) agricultural matters (including agricultural research, animal health and operational aspects of the Common Agriculture Policy), forestry and fisheries;

(c) co-operative ventures in the fields of trade and industry;

(d) electricity generation;

(e) tourism;

(f) roads and transport;

(g) advisory services in the field of public health;

(h) sport, culture and the arts.

It would be for the Oireachtas and the Northern Ireland Assembly to legislate from time to time as to the extent of functions to be devolved to the Council of Ireland. Where necessary, the British Government will cooperate in this devolution of functions. Initially, the functions to be vested would be those identified in accordance with the procedures set out above and decided, at the formal stage of the conference, to be transferred.

9. (i) During the initial period following the establishment of the Council, the revenue of the Council would be provided by means of grants from the two administrations in Ireland towards agreed projects and budgets, according to the nature of the service involved.

(ii) It was also agreed that further studies would be put in hand forthwith and completed as soon as possible of methods of financing the Council after the initial period which would be consonant with the responsibilities and functions assigned to it.

(iii) It was agreed that the cost of the Secretariat of the Council of Ireland would be shared equally, and other services would he financed broadly in proportion to where expenditure or benefit accrues.

(iv) The amount of money required to finance the Council's activities will depend upon the functions assigned to it from time to time.

(v) While Britain continues to pay subsidies to Northern Ireland, such payments would not involve Britain participating in the Council, it being accepted nevertheless that it would be legitimate for Britain to safeguard in an appropriate way her financial involvement in Northern Ireland.

10. It was agreed by all parties that persons committing crimes of violence, however motivated, in any part of Ireland should be brought to trial irrespective of the part of Ireland in which they are located. The concern which large sections of the people of Northern Ireland felt about this problem was in particular forcefully expressed by the representatives of the Unionist and Alliance parties. The representatives of the Irish Government stated that they understood and fully shared this concern. Different ways of solving this problem were discussed; among them were the amendment of legislation

operating in the two jurisdictions on extradition, the creation of a common law enforcement area in which an all-Ireland court would have jurisdiction, and the extension of the jurisdiction of domestic courts so as to enable them to try offences committed outside the jurisdiction. It was agreed that problems of considerable legal complexity were involved, and that the British and Irish Governments would jointly set up a commission to consider all the proposals put forward at the Conference and to recommend as a matter of extreme urgency the most effective means of dealing with those who commit these crimes. The Irish Government undertook to take immediate and effective legal steps so that persons coming within their jurisdiction and accused of murder, however motivated, committed in Northern Ireland will be brought to trial, and it was agreed that any similar reciprocal action that may be needed in Northern Ireland be taken by the appropriate authorities.

11. It was agreed that the Council would be invited to consider in what way the principles of the European Convention on Human Rights and Fundamental Freedoms would be expressed in domestic legislation in each part of Ireland. It would recommend whether further legislation or the creation of other institutions, administrative or judicial, is required in either part or embracing the whole island to provide additional protection in the field of human rights. Such recommendations could include the functions of an Ombudsman or Commissioner for Complaints, or other arrangements of a similar nature which the Council of Ireland might think appropriate.

12. The Conference also discussed the question of policing and the need to ensure public support for and identification with the police service throughout the whole community. It was agreed that no single set of proposals would achieve these aims overnight, and that time would be necessary. The Conference expressed the hope that the wide range of agreement that had been reached, and the consequent formation of a power-sharing Executive, would make a major contribution to the creation of an atmosphere throughout the community where there would be widespread support for and identification with all the institutions of Northern Ireland.

13. It was broadly accepted that the two parts of Ireland are to a considerable extent interdependent in the whole field of law and order, and that the problems of political violence and identification with the police service cannot be solved without taking account of that fact.

14. Accordingly, the British Government stated that, as soon as the security problems were resolved and the new institutions were seen to be working effectively, they would wish to discuss the devolution of responsibility for normal policing and how this might be achieved with the Northern Ireland Executive and the Police.

15. With a view to improving policing throughout the island and developing community identification with and support for the police services, the governments concerned will cooperate under the auspices of a Council of Ireland through their respective police authorities. To this end, the Irish Government would set up a Police Authority, appointments to which would be made after consultation with the Council of Ministers of the Council of Ireland. In the case of the Northern Ireland Police Authority, appointments would be made after consultation with the Northern Ireland Executive, which would

consult with the Council of Ministers of the Council of Ireland. When the two Police Authorities are constituted, they will make their own arrangements to achieve the objectives set out above.

16. An independent complaints procedure for dealing with complaints against the police will be set up.

17. The Secretary of State for Northern Ireland will set up an all-party committee from the Assembly to examine how best to introduce effective policing throughout Northern Ireland with particular reference to the need to achieve public identification with the police.

18. The Conference took note of a reaffirmation by the British Government of their firm commitment to bring detention to an end in Northern Ireland for all sections of the community as soon as the security situation permits, and noted also that the Secretary of State for Northern Ireland hopes to be able to bring into use his statutory powers of selective release in time for a number of detainees to be released before Christmas.

19. The British Government stated that, in the light of the decisions reached at the Conference, they would now seek the authority of Parliament to devolve full powers to the Northern Ireland Executive and Northern Ireland Assembly as soon as possible. The formal appointment of the Northern Ireland Executive would then be made.

20. The Conference agreed that a formal conference would be held early in the New Year at which the British and Irish Governments and the Northern Ireland Executive would meet together to consider reports on the studies which have been commissioned and to sign the agreement reached.

Source: Ireland (1973).

3

The Anglo-Irish Agreement, 1985

3.1. Introduction

The failure of the Sunningdale arrangements and the collapse of the power-sharing executive in May 1974 left a political stalemate and a legacy of failed negotiation that lasted for more than a decade. The Anglo-Irish Agreement of 1985 ended that stalemate and provided a positive model of negotiation. It represented a turning point in the British–Irish relationship, in that for the first time it gave the Irish government a formal voice in the affairs of Northern Ireland. Aside from the direct contribution of the institutions that it established, the Agreement was also instrumental in persuading unionists of the need to negotiate, and in demonstrating to the IRA the potential advantages of the political path.

From the start, there were radically opposed interpretations of the significance of the Anglo-Irish Agreement (Aughey and Gormley-Heenan 2011). Was it primarily of symbolic importance, or did it also represent a new phase in territorial management, marking a sharp break with previous British policy and practice? The phrase 'direct rule with a green tinge' used by Bew, Gibbon, and Patterson (1996: 217) implies limited change. But there is also evidence that the Anglo-Irish Agreement represented a radically new direction in British policy on Northern Ireland, though falling significantly short of joint authority (McGarry and O'Leary 2004; O'Duffy 2007; Ruane and Todd 2007). Indeed, its impact was different and less far-reaching than its makers had intended, but it has been argued that it helped to change British, and also Irish, policy paradigms with respect to Northern Ireland (Todd 2011).

These debates about the meaning and impact of the Agreement touch upon issues of general significance about state change and the role of negotiated agreements in starting new paths of territorial management. The Anglo-Irish Agreement carefully bypassed conflicting British and Irish positions on sovereignty rather than directly confronting them. Did this simply disguise the dominance of the stronger party ('direct rule with a green tinge'), or did it contribute to remaking the very understanding of sovereignty among the political elite (Meehan 2014)? These are not simply academic questions. The witness seminar on the Anglo-Irish Agreement shows senior civil servants and politicians themselves engaging with such issues. While they may have given subtly different answers, they limited the room for reinterpretation and the impact of disagreement by drafting a detailed Anglo-Irish 'catechism' that was to inform both governments'

Negotiating a Settlement in Northern Ireland, 1969–2019.
John Coakley and Jennifer Todd, Oxford University Press (2020). © John Coakley and Jennifer Todd.
DOI: 10.1093/oso/9780198841388.001.0001

statements about the Agreement (see Document 3.5).[1] The views of the participants in the witness seminar thus provide evidence as to how and when states change their strategies and embark on new paths of conflict management, and how they embed these paths. We return to these questions in the final chapter.

3.1.1. Political Context

Following the collapse of the power-sharing executive in May 1974, there was a prolonged delay before inter-party talks were restarted, and an even longer gap before effective intergovernmental negotiations took place. The main developments are summarized in Table 3.1. Three broad patterns are evident. The first is an effort on the British side to pursue an 'internal' settlement of the conflict, both by seeking to revive domestic institutions of government within Northern Ireland and by trying to secure a military defeat of the IRA within the context of direct rule from London. The second pattern is of initial marginalization of the Irish side, followed by efforts by Irish governments and parties to rethink their traditional strategies and aims. The most ambitious expression of this was the New Ireland Forum of 1983–4. Third, and following the failure of the British 'internal' approach, there was a steady convergence in the standpoints of the British and Irish sides in the course of a set of intergovernmental meetings, culminating in the Anglo-Irish Agreement of 1985.

As violence continued following the collapse of the power-sharing executive, one option considered by Harold Wilson in late 1974 and in 1975 was a 'Doomsday scenario': British withdrawal from Northern Ireland, a prospect that was dreaded and resisted by the Irish government (FitzGerald 2006).[2] The Wilson government also sought to keep the idea of devolution alive. Its efforts focused initially on the parties in the Assembly, but, as little progress was made, a new initiative was launched. Rather than seeking to impose a single model, the government opted for a strategy of allowing the parties to negotiate a new framework for government, subject to a requirement that this would have to enjoy cross-community support and recognize the 'Irish dimension'.

---

[1] Several of the questions in the 'catechism' (notably, about the implications for devolved government, extradition, mixed courts, sovereignty, and American support) were indeed asked during the press conference at which the Agreement was formally announced. The two principals were clearly so thoroughly in command of the issues that they were able to develop the prepared answers further in responding to these and other questions (dealing with such topics as the general importance of the Agreement). See report on the press conference, 'Both Leaders Pledge Support for Devolved Government', *Irish Times*, 16 November 1985. Other topics that loomed large in the 'catechism' were less prominent in the press conference (e.g., the role of the New Ireland Forum Report). For a full transcript of the press conference, see 'Joint Press Conference with Irish Prime Minister (Dr Garret FitzGerald)', Margaret Thatcher Foundation Archive <www.margaretthatcher.org/document/106173> (accessed 15 August 2019).
[2] See Subsection 2.4.2.

Table 3.1. Important political developments, 1974–1985

Date	Development
1 May 1975	Election of Northern Ireland Constitutional Convention (dissolved, 5 March 1976)
7 January 1980	Secretary of State Atkins convenes Northern Ireland Constitutional Conference (adjourned indefinitely, 24 March)
21 May 1980	Haughey–Thatcher meeting plans enhanced British–Irish cooperation
8 December 1980	Haughey–Thatcher meeting in Dublin involving other senior ministers plans sectoral studies of British-Irish relations
1 March 1981	Hunger strike by republican prisoners began; called off on 3 October 1981 following deaths of ten prisoners
6 November 1981	FitzGerald–Thatcher meeting agrees to establish the Anglo-Irish Intergovernmental Council
20 October 1982	Elections to Northern Ireland Assembly in line with plan for 'rolling devolution' (Assembly dissolved 23 June 1986)
30 May 1983	Inter-party New Ireland Forum holds first meeting in Dublin
1 March 1984	'Armstrong Proposals' on creation of a border zone presented to Irish negotiators
2 May 1984	New Ireland Forum report outlines constitutional options
11 May 1984	'Nally Proposals' on joint authority presented to British negotiators
19 November 1984	Thatcher dismisses three Forum options as 'out' following a meeting with FitzGerald
17 January 1985	British government produces draft agreement
15 November 1985	Anglo-Irish Agreement

The outcome was a new Constitutional Convention that met for the best part of a year (May 1975–March 1976). Elected on the same basis as the Assembly of 1973, this was dominated by a coalition of three unionist parties (the Ulster Unionist Party, now led by Harry West and controlled by opponents of power-sharing, the Democratic Unionist Party, led by Revd Ian Paisley, and the Vanguard Unionist Party, led by William Craig). Between them, these parties held forty-five of the seventy-eight seats in the Convention, and also had the support of one independent unionist (see Table 3.2).

The report of the Convention on 20 November 1975 (Northern Ireland Constitutional Convention 1975) reflected the political perspective of this unionist coalition. It proposed re-establishing a reformed version of the pre-1972 institutions based on the principle of majority rule, and advocated 'good neighbourly relations' with the Republic of Ireland rather than institutionalized North–South links. The report was not accepted by the British government, and a late initiative by William Craig to explore the possibility of a 'voluntary coalition' with the SDLP resulted only in a fatal split in Craig's own Vanguard Party. The Convention was

Table 3.2. Results of elections to Northern Ireland representative bodies, 1975–1982

Party	Convention, 1975		Assembly, 1982	
	Votes	Seats	Votes	Seats
Ulster Unionist Party	25.4	19	29.7	26
Democratic Unionist Party	14.8	12	23.0	21
Other unionists	*22.3	21	5.7	2
Alliance Party	9.8	8	9.3	10
Others	1.8	1	0.4	0
SDLP	23.7	17	18.8	14
Sinn Féin	.	.	10.1	5
Other nationalists	2.2	0	3.0	0
Total	100.0	78	100.0	78

* Including Vanguard Unionist Party (12.7% of votes, 14 seats) and Unionist Party of Northern Ireland (7.7% of votes, 5 seats) in 1975.

Source: Computed from ARK (2019); Electoral Office for Northern Ireland (2019).

wound up in March 1976, but its report continued to be an important benchmark for the main unionist parties until at least the late 1980s.

With the idea of a British withdrawal from Northern Ireland enjoying little support in any quarter outside the IRA, and the conflict itself continuing, there was a shift in emphasis from political to security strategies on the part of the Labour government (especially under Secretary of State Roy Mason, 1976–9).[3] But, with the advent of Margaret Thatcher's Conservative government in 1979, the new Secretary of State, Humphrey Atkins, once again embarked on a political initiative designed to promote inter-party consensus on a measure of devolved government. He convened a formal Constitutional Conference (January–March 1980) as part of a broader set of discussions with the parties that were dubbed the 'Atkins talks'. The conference, however, simply highlighted the gulf between the parties, with the Ulster Unionist Party refusing to attend it and the SDLP objecting to the absence of the 'Irish dimension' from its agenda.

The British government nevertheless persisted with this approach, and Atkins's successor, James Prior, took the process a stage further by creating a new elected body to act as a forum for discussion, one to which powers could potentially be devolved. The resulting Assembly (November 1982–June 1986) was also elected on the same basis as the 1973 Assembly, but was attended consistently only by the Democratic Unionist Party and the Alliance Party (for its political composition, see Table 3.2). The plan for 'rolling devolution' provided that devolution could take place on a phased basis, as a sufficient level of consensus was achieved, sector by sector; it fell foul of implacable unionist resistance to power-sharing. The

[3] See Subsection 3.1.2.

Assembly ultimately became little more than a forum of discussion and debate, though even this role was compromised by the fact that the nationalist parties did not participate (O'Leary, Elliott, and Wilford 1988).

3.1.2. Security Context

Coinciding with the pursuit of a political solution in the late 1970s, there was a significant shift in security policy. The new approach was known as 'Ulsterization', a term derived from 'Vietnamization', itself coined to describe American policy during the later phases of the Vietnam War, when an effort was made after 1969 to transfer responsibility from the American military to local South Vietnamese forces. As applied to British policy in Northern Ireland, the new approach entailed enhanced reliance on the (locally recruited) Royal Ulster Constabulary and Ulster Defence Regiment rather than on the British army (recruited from all of the United Kingdom), more vigorous covert security measures, and an attempt to redefine the conflict as terrorist rather than political. This found expression in 1976 in the phasing-out of 'special category' (in effect, political) status for newly convicted prisoners, resulting in a series of protests by republican prisoners. These culminated in a hunger strike in 1980, simultaneously undertaken by seven prisoners, that came to an end following a compromise.

When it became clear that the prisoners had not won political status, a second hunger strike began on a phased basis in March 1981, and resulted in the deaths of ten prisoners, with the Thatcher government resolutely refusing to yield to the prisoners' demands. The hunger strikes played a major role in encouraging Sinn Féin to follow a more political route. Bobby Sands, the first hunger striker to die, had been elected to the UK House of Commons as MP for Fermanagh and South Tyrone on 9 April 1981, and the eighth to die, Kieran Doherty, had been elected to the Dáil for Cavan–Monaghan at the general election on 11 June 1981. Indeed, the strong showing for 'H-block' candidates (those standing for political rights for republican prisoners in the 'H-blocks' of the Maze prison) at the 1981 Dáil general election contributed to Fianna Fáil's defeat, and showed that there was potentially significant electoral support for Sinn Féin.

3.1.3. British–Irish Context

On the Irish government side, there was a level of electoral instability at this time that did little to help policy continuity. Charles Haughey's Fianna Fáil government was replaced by a short-lived Fine Gael–Labour coalition headed by Garret FitzGerald on 30 June 1981; Haughey came back on 9 March 1982 at the head of a minority Fianna Fáil administration; but this was replaced in turn by a new Fine Gael–Labour coalition on 14 December 1982 that remained in office until 10 March 1987. British–Irish relations were also damaged by the political polarization resulting from the hunger strikes, and more specifically by the stance adopted by the Haughey government during the Falklands War (April–June 1982), when it withdrew Irish support for the British position (Dorr 2011; Kelly 2016b).

The effective British exclusion of the Irish government from any significant role in relation to Northern Ireland encouraged a new departure in the Republic, the creation of the New Ireland Forum. The brainchild of SDLP leader John Hume, this brought nationalist parties (other than Sinn Féin) together to explore long-term constitutional options. The Forum met from May 1983 to February 1984, and comprised representatives of the SDLP, Fianna Fáil, Fine Gael, and Labour. Its report, published on 2 May 1984, outlined three main options:

- a unitary state, which 'would embrace the island of Ireland governed as a single unit under one government and one parliament elected by all the people of the island';
- a federal or confederal state based on the two existing entities, which 'would entrench a measure of autonomy for both parts of Ireland within an all-Ireland framework'; and
- joint authority, under which 'the London and Dublin governments would have equal responsibility for all aspects of the government of Northern Ireland' (New Ireland Forum 1984).

Significantly, the report also stressed that the parties 'remain open to discuss other views which may contribute to political development', a provision of particular importance to Fine Gael, Labour, and the SDLP, who together made up a majority of the membership of the Forum. Under strong pressure from Charles Haughey, the Forum opted for the first of the options: 'a unitary state, achieved by agreement and consent, embracing the whole island of Ireland and providing irrevocable guarantees for the protection and preservation of both the unionist and nationalist identities.' However, the Forum's openness to 'other views' unlocked the door to negotiation with the British when the three main options proved unacceptable.

The British response to the Forum Report formed an important backdrop to the negotiation of the Anglo-Irish Agreement, and needs to be seen in the context of a series of British–Irish prime ministerial meetings (though continuity in these was disrupted by the Irish governmental instability of 1981–2). Several of these were independent bilateral meetings; others took place on the margins of European Council meetings in the period 1983–5 (for example, on 21 March 1983 a FitzGerald–Thatcher meeting in Brussels on the margins of the European summit symbolized an improvement in the relationship following the acrimony over Haughey's policy on the Falklands).

The important stand-alone meetings were as follows:

- 21 May 1980: a Haughey–Thatcher meeting in London, which committed the Irish and British governments to greater cooperation, and noted the 'unique relationship' between the two countries (at this meeting the Taoiseach famously presented the prime minister with a gift of an antique silver teapot);
- 8 December 1980: a Haughey–Thatcher meeting in Dublin, with other senior Irish and British ministers, which agreed to explore the relationship through joint studies, and referred to the 'totality of relationships' between the two countries, a phrase controversially used by the Irish side to indicate that all options were on the table;[4]
- 6 November 1981: a FitzGerald–Thatcher meeting in London, which agreed to establish the Anglo-Irish Intergovernmental Council as a mechanism to facilitate discussion between the two governments;
- 7 November 1983: a FitzGerald–Thatcher meeting in Chequers, which explored possible options for a settlement in Northern Ireland;
- 18–9 November 1984: a FitzGerald–Thatcher meeting in Chequers, after which Prime Minister Thatcher dismissed the three options outlined in the New Ireland Forum Report as being 'out';
- 15 November 1985: a FitzGerald–Thatcher meeting in Hillsborough, Co. Down, which approved the Anglo-Irish Agreement.

These meetings were supplemented by important meetings at ministerial and official levels, which, given their more specific focus, were able to bypass the tensions of the British–Irish relationship. These included, at political level, meetings over the 1982–5 period involving Peter Barry (Minister for Foreign Affairs), Dick Spring (Tánaiste and Minister for the Environment), and Michael Noonan (Minister for Justice) on the Irish side, and Geoffrey Howe (Foreign Secretary) and Douglas Hurd (Northern Ireland Secretary) on the British side.

At civil-service level, a much wider range of officials participated in these meetings, and officials themselves also engaged in important bilateral and sometimes personal meetings at which key outcomes were proposed. These included the officials who participated in the witness seminar presented here (including British Cabinet Secretary Robert Armstrong and his colleagues David Goodall and Ted Hallett, and Irish Government Secretary Dermot Nally and his colleagues from the Department of Foreign Affairs, Noel Dorr, Michael Lillis, and Seán Donlon). Other key officials from the departments mentioned, and members of other departments, played an important role. These included senior figures in the

---

[4] The joint studies, conducted by British and Irish civil servants, covered the areas of new institutional arrangements, citizenship rights, security matters, economic cooperation, and measures to encourage mutual understanding.

Northern Ireland Office and, on the Irish side, in the Department of Justice and the Office of the Attorney General.

3.1.4. The Witness Seminar

The witness seminar, which took place on 1 November 2006 in the Humanities Institute of Ireland, University College Dublin, included the following participants in the negotiations: Robert Armstrong, former Secretary of the Cabinet; Seán Donlon, former Secretary of the Department of Foreign Affairs; Noel Dorr, former Irish ambassador in London; Garret FitzGerald, former Taoiseach; David Goodall, formerly from the Cabinet Office; Ted Hallett formerly from the Foreign Office; Michael Lillis formerly from the Anglo-Irish division of the Department of Foreign Affairs; and Dermot Nally, former Secretary to the Government.

Academic questioners included John Coakley, Ronan Fanning, Christopher Farrington, and Susan McDermott.

3.2. Background to the Negotiations

3.2.1. Introductions

GARRET FITZGERALD: I was Taoiseach at the time and engaged in the whole process, about which I subsequently wrote.

MICHAEL LILLIS: I was Assistant Secretary in charge of the Anglo-Irish division of the Department of Foreign Affairs at the time, and was a participant in the negotiations.

TED HALLETT: At the time I was a research analyst in the Foreign Office in London dealing with Irish matters, and, although I wasn't involved in the meetings, I did see the papers and subsequently wrote an internal account of the negotiations.

DERMOT NALLY: I was secretary to the government when Robert Armstrong as Cabinet Secretary came to see me—and Seán Donlon—in the cabinet room in Government Buildings in March 1984 to explore the possibility of an agreement on the North; and, with the Taoiseach Dr FitzGerald's agreement, I stayed with the negotiation of the Agreement as Robert's counterpart, attending all meetings at official and prime-ministerial levels. I was thrown into this and many other things in 1973, and continued to be thrown in until 1993, so I was engaged in every negotiation between those two units for twenty years.

NOEL DORR: I was ambassador in London. I arrived there in September 1983 and was there until 1987, when I returned to be Secretary, now Secretary General as they call it, at the Department of Foreign Affairs from then until 1995.

DAVID GOODALL: I was in the Cabinet Office at the time, seconded from the Foreign Office. I was Robert Armstrong's sidekick in the negotiations.

ROBERT ARMSTRONG: I was the Secretary of the Cabinet at the time of the Anglo-Irish Agreement—and before and after. Mrs Thatcher asked me to lead the team which negotiated the Agreement with Dermot and his colleagues.

3.2.2. Context

Q: Why, in your view, was it necessary to arrive at an Agreement of this kind?

GARRET FITZGERALD: Well, I have recorded how it came about in my book.[5] The motivation arose from the obvious growth in support for Sinn Féin after the hunger strikes, to the point where they had about 40 per cent support from nationalists, and it was a feeling that I shared that if they went over 50 per cent they might be motivated to raise the level of violence to a civil-war level—which up to then they had always pulled back from—and that would be dangerous for the entire island. Therefore, although I had never wanted to, and had always opposed the idea of doing deals with Britain behind the backs of people in Northern Ireland, I felt that I couldn't allow scruples about that to continue to the point where there might be a crisis in the North. The time had come therefore to create conditions for a possible negotiation with Britain, and the implementation of British policy in a direction that hopefully would swing support back to the SDLP and lose support for Sinn Féin.

MICHAEL LILLIS: There was a discussion in government (i.e. the second coalition government) about the situation in Northern Ireland and there was a report to government which described the sense of both rising alarm and despondency following the events of the hunger strike, and the crisis, and the feeling that things were just drifting in a dangerous way.

DERMOT NALLY: Just to say some words in a very general way. First of all it is important to remember certain bits. Charlie Haughey came to power in December of 1979, Garret in June 1981, Charlie Haughey in March 1982, Garret in December 1982, Charlie in March 1987. That is the sequence, but the importance of those dates is that between December 1979 and December 1982 there were four changes of government and if you want a definition of instability that is it. On top of that there was the situation in Northern Ireland, which was always in danger of spilling over into the South, particularly in the aftermath of the hunger strikes.

On top of the frequent changes of government, and possibly as a consequence, there was huge financial instability. Anyway, the financial situation was dire, the political situation was dire, and the northern situation was even more

---

[5] See FitzGerald (1991: 460–575).

dire. That is the background of the breakdown in trust after the Dublin Castle meeting between Charles Haughey and Margaret Thatcher in December 1980.

MICHAEL LILLIS: I would add that Anglo-Irish relations were not in great shape. It was the aftermath of the events surrounding the Falklands.

DERMOT NALLY: There is one further point in [relation to] the instability. Something like 2.5 million in sterling was stolen in nearly 250 raids in 1979. That's in the South.

MICHAEL LILLIS: The Anglo-Irish relationship was still, I think rather—to use a good old term for it—'neuralgic' in the aftermath of those events. I renewed my regular discussions with John Hume in Derry and with others elsewhere in Northern Ireland. It is hard to describe how worried everybody was. Hume at that time was a very calm and, I think, wise observer of the scene on his own side of the sectarian or political divide, and he was more worried at that time about the future. He was looking at it obviously from the point of view of, shall we say, the nationalist community in Northern Ireland primarily, but he was also concerned about the state, because that group naturally looked to Dublin as being a mentor as well as a kind of a safety net for democratic politics. He was seriously concerned that the situation was no longer controllable, and not simply that the SDLP were losing ground to Sinn Féin, although obviously that was a major concern for him, but that we were, as Garret said, possibly heading for a kind of a very basic civil-war type of situation in the island.

In the South, in my recollection, and it goes back to the previous time that you were in government, Garret, but this had remained as a sort of residue around the place as you travelled around the country, there were still black flags in many villages from the time of the hunger strike. There is, as I think our British colleagues know, a sort of visceral thing on our side which has to be managed in a very positive way, and I suppose our feeling was that the British were not at that time contributing in a positive way to calming the situation or to managing it. So, the alarm was pretty general on our side. That is what I recollect as being the background to it.

GARRET FITZGERALD: Interesting. I recall you communicating to me and influencing my approach.

Q: Looking back on the statistics, we see that the earlier point in the troubles between 1970 and 1973 was really the worst peak in the number of deaths and the amount of violence, and then by the time we get to the late 1970s things began to calm down. Was there still a sense of urgency about the situation in Northern Ireland in 1983–4 more than there was in 1972–3 when you were going for Sunningdale?

GARRET FITZGERALD: There were three periods of deep concern. There was the initial outbreak of violence, the instability, and then government ministers resigning, which we came through successfully. In 1974 and late 1975 we feared British withdrawal and had reason—I think it was the thought of that which we now know from Wilson's memorandum—we have read it in Bernard Donoughue's book.[6] That was deeply disturbing, and in some ways almost more worrying than anything else. We feared that there would be a breakdown, and civil war would overflow down to us. We couldn't cope with it because we couldn't even strengthen our army to deal with the possible consequences, because of fear that if we did strengthen our army then all the unionists would see it as a threat. That was in some ways the worst crisis of all, in retrospect, but that is a personal judgement. The third was the hunger strike; the impact of that forced a rethink of policy, certainly on my part.

DERMOT NALLY: Just to illustrate the sense of instability in the North—there were strong rumours or strong views going around that it was deliberate IRA policy to kill or murder any Protestant within ten miles of the border, which produced a hell of a lot of disquiet in that particular area. The British embassy building in Ballsbridge came under threat from a mob at the time of the hunger strikes—smaller, thankfully, than the mob that attacked the Merrion Square building in 1972 after Bloody Sunday.

Q: To what extent was London at all aware of this, or reacting in any way?

DERMOT NALLY: Before Robert comes in: Jack Lynch met Margaret Thatcher in 1979. At the meeting there were a number of other [Irish] ministers. One of the ministers was a little bit forward with what he was saying. He said: 'Do you know, Prime Minister, you must understand that there are a lot of people in the South who believe in unity and really have some regard for what the IRA are doing.' The prime minister was furious; I have never seen anybody so angry in my life, and she stood up and nearly crossed the table. 'Are you condoning murder?', she roared. These were her words, and Jack Lynch's reaction in the end smoothed things over. 'We can't put a brake on this. We have to continue the discussion.' Fortunately things quietened down after, but a lot of damage had been done. It was in September 1979—immediately after the memorial ceremony for Mountbatten in Westminster Abbey. Towards the end of August 1979 I think was the time of the Mountbatten murder.[7]

NOEL DORR: We have got a very gloomy picture so far. I think that we need to look at the different efforts to solve the problem and see then also where the scene was in the early 1980s. My perception is something like this. When the problem broke out in its present form, or in its acute form, in Northern Ireland in the late 1960s, both governments reacted in an out-of-date way. The British view was that this was all settled in the 1920s and that Dublin was a foreign

---

[6] Donoughue (2006, esp. 132); see also Donoughue (1987: 128–37).

[7] Lord Louis Mountbatten, a relative of Queen Elizabeth II and uncle of Prince Philip, former Chief of the Defence Staff, and last Viceroy of India, was murdered, together with three others, in Mullaghmore, Co. Sligo, on 27 August 1979; on the same day, the British army suffered its largest ever number of casuaties (eighteen) in an IRA ambush at Warrenpoint.

government. The Irish government view fell back on the old shibboleth of partition as the real problem.

It took about four years of gradually growing realism to lead into Sunningdale, and Sunningdale was a serious and hopeful effort at the time. I have to say a good part of it was prepared by the Jack Lynch government, and then the new coalition government coming in March 1973 added more to it. Sunningdale was a really hopeful effort, building on the centre. Now, it fell apart for reasons which I won't go into. Then in the mid-1970s we had the murder of the British ambassador and, of course, the Mountbatten murder later on.[8] When Charlie Haughey came into office, he started something new, which shouldn't be forgotten here.

GARRET FITZGERALD: Yes, that's right.

NOEL DORR: Sunningdale involved essentially a benevolent British approach to the development of power-sharing institutions in Northern Ireland and a North–South link. The Irish government in the pre-Sunningdale period had been concerned to get across to the British side the idea that the form of government given to Stormont, when Stormont was created, was not suited to a divided community, and that it was important therefore to work towards power-sharing. That concept was accepted at Sunningdale—and also the role of Dublin as one of the sponsors, one of the two governments responsible for reaching a settlement, was accepted at that time.

When Charlie Haughey came to office in 1979, he set himself to woo Mrs Thatcher, and he had several preparatory meetings in May 1980—he had several lunches in Foreign Affairs, where he said, 'how do I approach this?' He had a meeting then in London with Mrs Thatcher on 21 May 1980. This was the famous 'teapot' session where he presented her with a silver teapot.

Anyway, after lunch he went into a one-to-one meeting with her—Dermot will remember this—and the delegations were outside, and he came out absolutely cock-a-hoop. He had the general sense that all kinds of possibilities were open, and he gave a press conference afterwards in the Irish embassy in London. The new theme that he was striking was building a new relationship between Dublin and London as distinct from the North–South relationship or even the power-sharing relationship within Northern Ireland. It was later called 'the totality of relationships'.

He had another meeting then in December in Dublin, where Mrs Thatcher brought over several members of her cabinet, and Dermot will describe that. I wasn't at that second meeting, but after that it was oversold by Brian Lenihan. Then you had the hunger strikes, and the Falklands issue, and all of that soured things very considerably.

---

[8] The British ambassador, Christopher Ewart-Biggs, was assassinated outside his residence in Dublin by the IRA on 21 July 1976.

But there was still a residual factor that became important afterwards in the Anglo-Irish Agreement. This was the setting-up of studies between the two governments to develop this wonderful perspective of a new relationship between Dublin and London, within which Northern Ireland could be addressed. Despite the sourness which had crept in at head-of-government level between the two sides, for the reasons I have mentioned, those studies did continue, and, indeed, it was on the margin of a meeting in connection with those studies, after Garret became Taoiseach, that Michael first passed on to David informal ideas that were eventually to lead on to the negotiation of the Anglo-Irish Agreement.

DERMOT NALLY: I was at the meeting in May 1980. What emerged from that meeting was a sentence which said that 'there would be no unity without the consent of a majority in Northern Ireland', and that is the first formal recognition [by Fianna Fáil] of the need of consent in Northern Ireland. Because there were a lot of problems, when the Taoiseach saw it he was disturbed, and he said 'How am I going to justify this?', and his answer was 'I can justify it on the grounds that it is a factual statement—not a constitutional statement, not a legal statement; it is a factual statement or a description of a position, and that is how I will justify it'.

He went along with the statement on that basis, which was exactly the same argument which was used in the Boland court case on Sunningdale. There were a large number of meetings on an official level that included Ken Bloomfield in the North and Ken Stowe.[9] Ken Stowe was the originator of the phrase 'the totality of relationships within these islands'. The phrase had been used before the December 1980 meeting at a large meeting in Belfast of civil servants from the South and the North to prepare for the December 1980 meeting—from which the 'joint studies' came about. There were to be studies by the two governments of a large range of fundamental issues, and there was to be a lot of cooperation, and so on. It was a wonderful opportunity, and Charles Haughey saw great prospects in it—too great, as it turned out.

As Noel says, Brian Lenihan then made a speech after the summit, which talked about constitutional change and possible Irish unity. Mrs Thatcher met the Taoiseach in March 1981 on the margins of a European Council in Maastricht. This time she was livid, nearly in flames. She spoke for twenty minutes, or half an hour, in what can only be described as the most vivid terms. 'I never mentioned Irish unity. What do you think my supporters think of me now? What have you done to me politically?' was the general theme. That was the end of the relationship between herself and Charlie Haughey; and that was the end of the possibility of change in the Northern Ireland scene

[9] Sir Kenneth Stowe was Principal Private Secretary to the Prime Minister, 1975–9, and Permanent Under-Secretary at the Northern Ireland Office, 1979–81.

involving those two individuals: that is my personal judgement. The Falklands added to the disagreements.[10]

TED HALLETT: Charlie sold the outcome as an agreement to go forward on the totality of relationships and he interpreted that as meaning that the British government would consult the Irish government on its Northern Ireland policies. Thatcher never accepted that interpretation.

DERMOT NALLY: She said, 'I never mentioned the word constitution, I never mentioned constitutional change. You use this word constitution, you bring it up all the time, it wasn't mentioned, what we talked about was institution.'

TED HALLETT: And one outcome of that was that when the British government launched the rolling devolution plan in 1982, they didn't consult the Irish government. Thatcher said in the House of Commons that there was no obligation on the British government to consult the Irish government on that approach, and that caused a major cooling in the relationship.

ROBERT ARMSTRONG: You are right in saying when Margaret Thatcher came in, following five years—two years of Harold Wilson, three of Jim Callaghan—she came in, if I may put it this way for short hand, with a lot of unionist baggage. She had been close to Airey Neave, who had been not only a friend but a very close political supporter. He had been killed in a car park in the House of Commons, and she was outraged by that.[11] So that, when she arrived in May 1979, I was still tucked away in the Home Office, but her natural instincts at that time, and I think one must say that Margaret's natural instincts are quite strong, were very much pro-unionist.

But she became, over the succeeding years, disenchanted with the perform-ance of the unionists in Northern Ireland, and the warmth of that relationship in her mind waned and cooled. She met Charlie Haughey—I think it must have been the 'teapot' meeting—I don't think I was at that meeting, but I remember her saying afterwards that we had all misunderstood Charlie Haughey, and that he was a romantic idealist. Some of us found that a bit rich.

GARRET FITZGERALD: He wooed well.

ROBERT ARMSTRONG: He wooed well, he undoubtedly wooed well, and she responded to that. The scales really fell from her eyes, and particularly over the Falklands, where she resented the attitude he took towards that very, very

---

[10] The Falklands War of April–June 1982 followed Argentinian occupation of the Falklands Islands, a British overseas territory in the South Atlantic. A British counter-attack on 2 April 1982 resulted in reassertion of British sovereignty there by 14 June 1982. Initial Irish government support for the British position was discontinued following the controversial sinking of the Argentinian cruiser *General Belgrano* on 2 May, resulting in a bitter breach between Charles Haughey and Margaret Thatcher. See Dorr (2011); Kelly (2016b).

[11] Airey Neave, MP, a close political supporter and confidant of Margaret Thatcher and her campaign manager in her bid for the leadership of the Conservative Party, was appointed Shadow Secretary for Northern Ireland after she became leader. He was assassinated by the Irish National Liberation Army on 30 March 1979.

strongly. I don't think she seriously considered making a negotiation with the Irish government in her first term. She had other preoccupations. Of course there was the Falklands affair, and the Irish reaction to that further alienated her, and, as was being said, she decided—they decided—to embark on the programme of rolling devolution in Northern Ireland. That would have been in January 1982; it was started under Jim Prior, and so in a sense the eggs were all in that basket at that time.[12]

We all understand that [Margaret Thatcher] was a conviction politician, and her views marked the whole thing strongly. But by the time she had her election in June 1983, it had become pretty clear that the rolling devolution programme was getting anywhere very slowly—if anywhere at all—and she was conscious that that really had failed. She was aware of political instability in the South of Ireland. I don't know how deeply or profoundly she was aware of the risks in the North. She took a very clear—if you like, a very hard—view on the hunger strike; she was not disposed at all to compromise on that. She took the view, to put it strongly, that that was a form of blackmail. So she stood fast on the matter of the hunger strike and allowed some people to die. She undoubtedly felt that that was a conviction, and she felt that was a threat to which her government must not give in.

But when [Margaret Thatcher] came back to government after the June 1983 election, I think she felt that she had come in with a large majority, but there were two outstanding problems. In her first term they had taken bold steps on the economy, and by June 1983 those were proving to be justified. She had done what she had done in Europe, and had held her position fast on that, and we had been threatened in the Falklands and that had come out right for her. She had won her victory in the Falklands and that undoubtedly trans-formed her political situation in Britain. She came in after the election in June 1983 with the sense that there were two major issues which had not been resolved in the first administration. One was Hong Kong, which we don't need to discuss any further, and the other was Northern Ireland.

She was conscious, as I say, that the programme of rolling devolution had not got anywhere. She was, I think, deeply conscious of the cost in terms of both lives and resources of what was happening in Northern Ireland, and felt that it was her duty to try to do something which would improve that situation—and that she would be criticized if she were not to do that.

As others before had seen, there were two aspects of the issue in Northern Ireland—what *we* did in Northern Ireland, and the relationship with the Irish government. 'Rolling devolution' having failed, she thought that she should approach the possibility of some kind of discussion or agreement with the Irish

---

[12] Jim Prior, Secretary of State for Northern Ireland, 1981–4, initiated the rolling devolution initiative; see Subsections 1.2.2 and 3.1.1.

government, and I have no doubt at all that the fact that Garret was the Taoiseach was an important factor in bringing her to this. Throughout, she trusted Garret in a way that she never trusted—or not after the outset—Charlie Haughey. In her own phrase about somebody else, she said that he was a man she could do business with—so that was an important element.

The other important element, I think, was that in July 1983, or thereabouts, with a large majority, she could look forward to being in office for four years. Garret had fairly recently come into power after an election which also looked as if it would give him a sustained term of office. So there was a period of three to four years open with Garret in Dublin and herself in London where there could be some attempt to reach some kind of agreement with the Irish government. And—David may know more about this—there was certainly a sense in London that the Irish government might be ready for this in a sense in which they might not have been ready earlier, so that there was readiness on both sides. She was not thrilled with the Forum and its three options, but nonetheless she felt that it was right to start talking.[13] I think one element of this may have been a conversation between David and Michael, almost an informal one, but where it became clear that there might be an opening which suggested that possibility. Was that in the autumn or the early autumn of 1983?

Anyway, that was an element in her; the fact that she knew that, and knew what David had reported about—that also was part of the process of her thinking. I think that that was really the motivation that was in her mind when she decided to authorize the opening of negotiations and to set up the team within government to do the negotiation.

I became involved rather exceptionally because she did not want the negotiation to be conducted either by the Foreign Office, which she never trusted, or by the Northern Ireland Office, which she trusted even less. She was very determined to keep a close watch on it herself, and so she asked me to lead the team that was conducting negotiations. I had some history in the issues, as you know, and I was glad to be able to take that on, and, as David has said—David was in the Cabinet Office at the time—we had the basis of the right team to do this job.

DAVID GOODALL: Well, just to add one or two things. First of all, an anecdote. In September, no, in late October 1982—in other words, after the Falklands—I had only recently come into the Cabinet Office and I had a long talk with Margaret Thatcher, the prime minister, after dinner one night, and the conversation turned to Northern Ireland. I said that I thought it was a scandal that the only place in the world where British lives were being lost in anger was

---

[13] A reference to the New Ireland Forum and the options of a unitary state, a federal or confederal one, and joint British–Irish authority in Northern Ireland.

actually within the United Kingdom. And so we had a long discussion about that, which I won't rehearse, but at the end of the discussion I remember her very vividly saying—and I sent a minute to Robert about it, I think—'if we get back again', she said, referring to the election the following year, 'I really would like to do something about Ireland'. So it was apparent from that conversation that, although people said she didn't know anything about Ireland, in fact she had learnt a lot about Ireland and she had read a lot about Ireland, but most of what she had got about it I think did come from Airey Neave, and I think that Enoch Powell also was...

ROBERT ARMSTRONG: And from Ian Gow, of course.[14]

DAVID GOODALL: From Ian Gow, of course. The second thing is, I don't know whether Robert would disagree, I think it is very hard to overestimate the impact on her personally of the whole Falklands affair. It was a tremendous risk that she took—she felt as if it was *her* war. She is tremendously grateful, I think, to the people who conducted the campaign under her leadership. She was tremendously grateful to the foreign leaders who stood by her. She said that Mitterrand rang her up and said 'we understand what you are about and we will back you'. She was correspondingly outraged, I think it would be true to say, by the action of the Irish government at that time. I came into it very late; I wasn't involved in the run-up or anything but I certainly saw that.

On the totality of relations, well, that happened before I was involved, but I do remember she was very angry. I remember her talking about it; she felt that she had been misled in using and endorsing the phrase 'the totality of relations' and that it had been used in a way which she had never intended. The other thing is—I think Robert has already said this—the fact that the 'rolling devolution' thing had obviously run out of steam. It wasn't getting anywhere. I had the feeling, coming into it, that she had the feeling that she would like to do something about it, but everybody—certainly the Northern Ireland Office, and this is no criticism of them—had simply run out of ideas. They just didn't know what to do. There was a sense of 'we have tried everything, and what are we going to do now?', so in that sense when the initiative came from Garret, and so on, there was a readiness to listen.

As far as Michael [Lillis] and I were concerned, it was a result of those conversations which set up the studies—would it have been in July 1983 after she came back into office; it certainly was in the summer? Dermot came over, and there was a proposal to build on the studies, which had been put absolutely on ice as a result of the Falklands, and to try and do something with them.

---

[14] Ian Gow, MP, served in several ministerial posts under Margaret Thatcher, and was assassinated by the IRA in 1990. Both Neave and Gow had a particular interest in Northern Ireland, and favoured a policy of integrating it in the UK; Gow resigned his government post in protest against the Anglo-Irish Agreement. Enoch Powell, MP, was a prominent right-wing Conservative, but resigned from the party and served as Ulster Unionist MP for South Down, 1974–87.

Dermot and Robert were nominated to conduct that study, and they delegated it in effect to an interdepartmental committee on both sides, which Michael and I led, responsible to our two principals. I think it was at the first meeting of that, which must have been in the summer, that you [Michael] took me for a walk along the canal and floated some of these ideas which were, of course, completely strange to me and were received in London with a good deal of scepticism, I think it's fair to say.

ROBERT ARMSTRONG: If I may just add one note to it, the fact that Dermot and I had worked together as fellow sherpas in economic summits when the Irish government were in the chair of the European Community, as it was then, and Dermot came to one—it was in Washington, wasn't it?[15]

DERMOT NALLY: Yes—Washington.

ROBERT ARMSTRONG: We came to know each other then, certainly on my side with a great deal of respect for Dermot, and that made it easier to start the ball rolling.

DERMOT NALLY: The first time I met Robert was before Sunningdale, and then we met on and off after that, and then you reappeared more or less formally with David in March 1984, when we said we would like to discuss the possibility of an agreement under three headings.

GARRET FITZGERALD: Can I go back over some things? Margaret Thatcher was elected leader of the Conservative Party. I met her in London ten days or so later. I was impressed by how extraordinarily pro-European she was. That didn't last, for some reason. But from then on, I saw her either in her room over in the Commons, or when I stayed late in the embassy over breakfast, whenever I could, you know, to brief her on Europe, which I thought would be helpful, because there might have been things she might not necessarily have picked up, and always, as I say, to have words about Northern Ireland towards the end. She wasn't that much interested. So, I thought it was essential to establish a good relationship with her. It seemed to me that she'd no difficulty about grasping things intellectually. There were problems with the emotional grasp because of her problems of empathy outside of southern England.

Once, while I was in opposition, I went to see Humphrey Atkins. Ken Stowe had just joined him from Downing Street, and within ten minutes, addressing me as leader of the opposition in Ireland, he was saying 'how do you think we can get around the prime minister on this?', and I was struck by the change in the British system. The whole system was reoriented to deal with the prime minister. Nonetheless, in January 1980, after Haughey came to power, I was in Washington with Seán Donlon. I was asked could I meet some officials who wanted to know what was Charlie Haughey going to do, and I replied that

---

[15] The Irish government chaired the rotating presidency of the Council of the European Communities in the first half of 1975, the second half of 1979, and the second half of 1984.

Charlie Haughey would seek to negotiate an agreement with Britain. Knowing the logic of his character and the Anglo-Irish situation, it seemed the logical thing to do, because it had the advantage that it would surprise everybody because he was seen as Anglophobe.

When it came to the negotiations, you [Robert Armstrong] were appointed on the British side, so the logical thing was Dermot on our side. I know from history the problems that can arise in the Prime Minister's Department and Foreign Affairs. It seemed to be important that we didn't get snarled up, and therefore I asked Dermot if he would lead a team of Foreign Affairs officials. That's how the team got constituted on our side, bringing in some from the Attorney General's Office and some from the Department of Justice—a very wise Secretary in the Department of Justice.

The idea of the New Ireland Forum was to create preconditions for possible negotiation, but there were two things I wanted from the Forum: one was a series of principles which the British government could accept and which could be incorporated, perhaps, in the preamble to an agreement; and, secondly, I wanted the concept of some kind of joint role in Northern Ireland to come out of it. If we could get that into this Forum Report, then when I came back with something other than a united Ireland, I would be safe-guarded against being attacked for having failed. I tried when I met Margaret Thatcher in 1983 to explain to her the thinking behind the work going on in the report, what I hoped to come out of it, but I think she was rather taken aback by the kind of language and saw the report negatively, even though I tried to explain to her this was a cover one had to have in order to get key things through.

When I met her in June 1983 for the first time in the second government, she was cooler than I had remembered when I met her in November 1981 during a meeting to set up the structure of the Anglo-Irish Council. We got on well at the time, despite the difficulties over the hunger strike.

3.3. The Negotiations

3.3.1. The First Informal Moves

NOEL DORR: To give some structure to it: in the late summer of 1983, Michael Lillis and David Goodall had exchanges that led to certain ideas. Michael Lillis put forward a role for the Irish government in Northern Ireland which would be 'Irish in' instead of 'Brits out'. It was focused particularly on the security area and the idea was that it would prove attractive to Mrs Thatcher. But it would also possibly be acceptable to the nationalist side because it had a security role for the Irish government within Northern Ireland, not just cooperation.

In any event, those ideas were floating around. In November 1983 there was a summit at Chequers from which the Irish side came away a little bit downcast because it didn't seem very hopeful. But what we didn't know was that after that summit Mrs Thatcher began to think about what might be done and consulted with David and Robert. Proposals began to emerge in early 1984 and then the whole thing began to gel into a negotiation.

MICHAEL LILLIS: I think there is a point that we omitted: that one of the really difficult issues that confronted democratic nationalists around that time was of course the relationship between the security forces and the minority community. It is so obvious and so enormous that we actually haven't mentioned it so far, but it was a huge issue in the relationship. I mean we have a phrase which is 'the politics of the latest outrage'; it is kind of the history of Anglo-Irish relations, if you like, but it certainly is a very prominent issue in Northern Ireland.

There had been a serious effort to pull the RUC around to a better attitude. The difficulty was that the RUC was recruited exclusively from one community—it wasn't the intention, but that was the fact. There was the UDR, which was a replacement for the B-Specials and which was simply seen by the nationalist community as the B-Specials, rightly or wrongly, I think largely rightly, actually.[16] That was the reality of daily life for Catholic people in Northern Ireland. They were held up at checkpoints routinely, and soldiers were obviously nervous about being shot; several of them were shot at checkpoints. These things impacted on the behaviour and attitude of everybody, and every single encounter in the lives of many Catholics was a minor disaster for everybody. There were also excesses; we all know about them. They were raised by the government at various stages with the British.

Now, the difficulty that we had, I am just going to turn this over, is how to engage Mrs Thatcher in a positive way with us in addressing the issue of Northern Ireland. Frankly, just speaking for myself, I was very pessimistic. I didn't know Mrs Thatcher; the Taoiseach knew her, Dermot knew her and obviously had heard her lively opinions as he has recounted. But everything that we had heard was along those lines that, you know, it was a terrible mess with [...] not alone the Falklands but the overselling of the 'totality of relations' and all that stuff. We had the hunger strike; she was obviously a hardliner. We felt she was too hard a liner, frankly. There is an old history of hunger strikes in this country; it goes back to the Brehon laws.[17]

ROBERT ARMSTRONG: She didn't know too much about Irish history.

---

[16] See Ch. 2, n. 50.

[17] The Brehon laws were a system of customary law administered by brehons (hereditary judges) in premodern Ireland. An aggrieved party could 'fast against' a debtor, a practice later ritualized into a symbolic fast. This, together with arguments relating to self-sacrifice, was used by hunger-strikers during the years of rebellion (e.g., by Terence MacSwiney, Lord Mayor of Cork, who died on hunger strike in 1920) to provide ideological justification for this practice; see Sweeney (1993: 421–37).

MICHAEL LILLIS: She didn't know too much about the Brehon laws—but how to get her to engage. The conundrum, therefore, was what was she interested in, and I think Garret has just said that the only thing that she was really focused on was security. What was actually the most disastrous area in Northern Ireland was the relationship between the security forces and the nationalist community. It was unfortunate, and nobody seemed to be addressing the fact that very frequently, in doing their job, they were actually making matters worse, whatever their intentions. In some cases their intentions were not the best, actually. However, the notion was to somehow or other get something started on an issue which was of intrinsic interest to us—fundamental interest to us.

We weren't playing a game, and so the canal conversation was actually addressed to precisely that issue. Happily, I think, David is of a literary turn of mind, and he somehow or other got wind of what I was trying to say to him, which is that you somehow or other have to transform that relationship between the security forces and the nationalist community or there is no hope of stability. Forget about a solution, or peace, or anything like that. That is where we should focus. Somehow or other, in order to transform that, there needs to be a significant Irish dimension.

Now, to be very frank with you, in the back of my mind, of course—I didn't say this to David but he certainly smelt this one, I am sure—is something with the elements of joint authority, because how else could you do it, unless we had some sort of a role there? I think that that was one of the things that helped to get the ball rolling, and then we went through all sorts of issues in the negotiations and came up with whatever each side thought was saleable and practical and the rest of it. It wasn't quite what our Taoiseach would have ideally wanted, which was something like joint authority, I believe, but it helped a bit.

GARRET FITZGERALD: But the credit for this goes to Michael, because it was Michael who suggested to me this novel approach, which I hadn't thought of. So, as a result, I authorized him to talk to David on a non-attributable basis— that he was acting on his own authority without any thought from me. Of course, I didn't tell the government that I had authorized it. It was done that way. When we met Margaret Thatcher she did ask me about the matter. I did point out Michael Lillis, but explained that he had acted without any authority.

TED HALLETT: There was a key incentive to the British to agree to this Irish role; it was an indication of willingness to amend the constitution.

GARRET FITZGERALD: To amend the constitution? No, that came later.

ROBERT ARMSTRONG: We certainly thought that something on that was possible quite early on.

NOEL DORR: I don't know how far to talk about these things even at this stage but when you talk about the actual security proposal—may I go on and say what it was?

GARRET FITZGERALD: Yes.

NOEL DORR: It was that the Irish army and police force would in fact police nationalist areas and there would be joint policing of certain other areas with the British forces within Northern Ireland. Now, I had shortly before this arrived in London from New York, and I believe that Michael thinks that my comments at the time took some of the steam out of the idea. What he had designed as a way of catching Mrs Thatcher's attention I took as overly ambitious, and I made this clear in the comments that I offered. In any event I think that Michael's idea was a very attractive bait to attract Mrs Thatcher, but on the other hand maybe I was too down to earth. I commented that this was not realistic and put forward certain other ideas connected with the proposal but in a wider context.

ROBERT ARMSTRONG: I simply want to say that, yes, security was in her thinking, but it stemmed from the sense of a loss of life, and, well, the resources too, but she was very conscious of the fact that people were dying and being injured in numbers—and particularly, of course, members of the security forces and the prison people. And in her [...] emotional thinking and her political thinking that was important, because I think she felt that she wanted to be seen as somebody who would tackle the matter. There were security dimensions to the way that things began; we will probably come to that later.

GARRET FITZGERALD: Can I just mention that I met her in March 1983, briefly, and in June I explained about the Forum. In November I had a private discussion with her and there was nobody else present. I think you felt that might be helpful. When I suggested that discussions might start with some of these issues, she replied 'Oh no, no, no, you can't do that because I have to answer questions in Parliament', and the opposition say 'how are negotiations going' so you forget about that.

So, in fact, we left the whole issue until further discussions, until the Forum Report was completed, and we brought it on that basis. To our great surprise, then, you arrived in Dublin in March with security proposals concerning a border band. Dermot came into my office to tell me this and he said 'something has happened; they have a band around the border; it means that they will have three borders rather than just one'. I sent him out rapidly to tell you 'no, no, no'—that wouldn't do at all.

ROBERT ARMSTRONG: I remember that!

DERMOT NALLY: These are just bits and scraps; I take it we haven't quite come to the 1985 Agreement yet? To go back to the hunger strikes, Charlie got on to her before the first strikes started.[18] He made three arguments. He said 'this will affect security in the South because there is a lot of sympathy, and what

---

[18] See Subsection 3.1.2.

will happen then is that the security situation will become worse; it will affect contributions in America, and the flow of money and the flow of arms will increase; and for these reasons, you and I must do everything we can to stop the strikes.' She said, 'yes, we are doing what we can, but if we give in no one in the world will be safe', and so the argument went on.

Then they met in Luxembourg on 1 December 1980. They talked about the hunger strikes again, and she said 'well, I can't do anything', and then, in the meeting of 8 December 1980, a lot of time was taken up with the hunger strikes and talk about the 'totality of relationships', and so on, but the hunger strikes were a predominant theme. Her stand on it was this: 'political status for the strikers—once it were conceded, no one in the world would be safe.' They are her own words; she said 'I will not concede', and that was it. On the defence aspect of that particular discussion, what C. J. Haughey offered, or what he said, was that 'we ensure that this country will never be used as a base to attack Britain', and that was about as far as it went.

NOEL DORR: But there is one point to remember about the hunger strikes. From Haughey's point of view he lost an election in June 1981 because of the hunger strikes, because he was losing seats in the border area. So, there was already bitterness present about the handling of the hunger strikes.

ROBERT ARMSTRONG: I really just wanted to say, and I hope that David will agree with this, I do think that the arrival of Geoffrey Howe in the Foreign Office and Douglas Hurd in the Northern Office was a very considerable help, because they were, I think I could say, wholeheartedly behind the idea of these sorts of negotiations.[19]

DAVID GOODALL: Well, Geoffrey was, more than Douglas, I think.

GARRET FITZGERALD: Yes, I agree with you.

ROBERT ARMSTRONG: Yes, Douglas was in favour but Geoffrey was very positive.

DAVID GOODALL: Could I add something—I am sorry—I just wanted to say in all the detail I think we are perhaps overlooking something that was important; that Mrs Thatcher had a deep distrust of Irish governments. A factor in her interest in security—I mean it is no good ignoring the fact that of course she thought that Irish governments successively (but not Garret's government) were conniving at the Republic being used as a safe haven for terrorists. That was a very important factor in her thinking. If you overlook that, you overlook something really very important indeed. That is why there was so much emphasis in her mind on security. She was eventually persuaded, but she did not trust—I mean she had a deep mistrust of Charlie Haughey after all of that. She couldn't believe that the Irish government couldn't do more to prevent

---

[19] Sir Geoffrey Howe, MP, was Foreign Secretary in Margaret Thatcher's government from June 1983 to July 1989. Douglas Hurd, MP, was Northern Ireland Secretary in the same government from September 1984 to September 1985.

cross-border terrorism, and so that coloured her whole view right from the beginning, I would say—I don't know if Robert would agree?

ROBERT ARMSTRONG: The other thing was that she felt doubly disenchanted by Charlie Haughey. She felt disenchanted way back in 1980 and the change from that. Then again in 1982 when initially the Irish government appeared to be supportive on the Falklands War and then he changed his tune.

DAVID GOODALL: Well, the other thing to add is that, in the event, I think she was very reluctantly persuaded that if you wanted to get better security cooperation with the South you had to pay a price in terms of giving the South some responsibility for it, and political responsibility in the North; I mean you couldn't have one without the other. Now, maybe that was wrong in the sense that the Republic was not in fact conniving. But I think it was a very powerful motivation in her way of looking at it.

Q: Why was the Agreement signed?

GARRET FITZGERALD: Well, it seems to me that the initial reaction to the Forum Report, and to our attempt to stimulate dialogue, was not as positive as I would have liked. I decided therefore I would have to play the articles 2 and 3 card.[20] I did not consult the government. In the second private talk with Margaret Thatcher in November 1984 I said to her: 'look, we are never going to solve this without resolving the issue of articles 2 and 3; we need something sufficient to enable us to go to the country with a reasonable chance of winning it because you will never placate unionist fears until this issue is resolved.'

But then she pulled back from that. Douglas Hurd was not happy about it, first of all because he felt it involved too high a price for it; it needed a ministerial rather than a civil-service representation in Belfast. Secondly, he might well have doubted our ability to carry it. He poured cold water on the idea and we had to abandon it, because if you didn't want articles 2 and 3, why should we get involved with it?

NOEL DORR: In May 1980 I was the political director in the Department of Foreign Affairs. Mr Haughey had two lunches with us in Foreign Affairs over the month of May, preparing for Mrs Thatcher. I was fairly exercised at the time about the articles 2 and 3 issue and I wrote a short paper, spontaneously—I wasn't asked to do it—proposing certain ideas in relation to the change in the articles and providing guarantees. I rather hesitantly passed it to him and he looked at it and was reasonably interested in it. He passed it to Pádraig Ó hAnnracháin, who was his political advisor, and said 'what do you

---

[20] This is a reference to articles 2 and 3 of the Irish constitution, which, as adopted in 1937, stated: '**Article 2:** The national territory consists of the whole island of Ireland, its islands and the territorial seas. **Article 3:** Pending the reintegration of the national territory, and without prejudice to the right of the parliament and government established by this constitution to exercise jurisdiction over the whole territory, the laws enacted by the parliament shall have the like area and extent of application as the laws of Saorstát Éireann and the like extraterritorial effect.'

think of that?'[21] I had the general impression that he was interested. Now, he may not ever have had the courage to do it, and maybe things weren't right, but it wasn't remote to his thinking. That paper proposed changing articles 2 and 3 in return for some sort of package.

GARRET FITZGERALD: George Colley had proposed that in a constitutional review in 1967.[22]

NOEL DORR: The Colley position is rather complex and I don't want to go into it. For the Anglo-Irish Agreement, it seemed to me that the situation was as follows. Previous efforts had been based on a three-step approach. Step one: you get some sort of political settlement which brings in the minority in the North. Step two: you have security forces created to defend that settlement. Step three: the procurement of minority acceptance of those security forces on the basis of step one. Michael's approach was to short circuit that into a two-step formula, where you involved the Irish government and security forces. In virtue of the degree of quasi-joint authority implicit in that arrangement, you therefore get minority support and you also deal with the security situation in Northern Ireland. I am saying this all subject to correction by Michael, but that is my sense of what was happening, and those ideas were offered to the British side.

DAVID GOODALL: That is it, plus the repeal of articles 2 and 3.

NOEL DORR: OK.

TED HALLETT: That was, as we understood it, part of the package from the beginning.

GARRET FITZGERALD: I should additionally state that during the election I had proposed an all-Ireland security and judicial system. So the idea was there. It was Michael who then gave it concrete form in order to interest the British in the possibility of an agreement.

NOEL DORR: It seemed unrealistic but it was intended to catch attention in the main.

3.3.2. The Negotiation Process

DERMOT NALLY: The actual negotiation started with a visit by Robert and David in March 1984. I had known Robert casually from Sunningdale, the 1979

---

[21] Pádraig Ó hAnnracháin was a long-standing press advisor in the Department of the Taoiseach and confidant of Charles Haughey.

[22] A cross-party committee chaired by George Colley, a Fianna Fáil minister, had recomended in 1967 that article 3 of the constitution be amended so that the territorial claim embodied in 'the right of the parliament and government established by this constitution to exercise jurisdiction' over the entire island be replaced by the aspiration that 'the Irish nation hereby proclaims its firm will that its territory be re-united in harmony and brotherly affection between all Irishmen'; see Ireland (1967: 5).

summit preparations in Washington, and the joint studies after the December 1980 meeting in Dublin [...] Robert proposed detailed contacts at official level on security issues, constitutional matters, government structures in Northern Ireland, human rights and identity, and so on. He also raised the question of security zones on both sides of the border that Garret has referred to. That was in March 1984.

ROBERT ARMSTRONG: I do think that Margaret Thatcher understood that an agreement might help to undermine the silent support for the IRA, particularly in Belfast—that there would be fewer safe houses and that kind of thing, if it was felt that the Irish government was in some sense representing the nationalist community.

GARRET FITZGERALD: So it was decided to change tack. Having said 'no' to the negotiations in the Forum, you arrived in Dublin in March. What precipitated that change of attitude on your side? A fundamental change, obviously.

DERMOT NALLY: The Forum Report wasn't published until after that meeting in the cabinet room—in May 1984.

GARRET FITZGERALD: Yes, the Forum Report was in May 1984. In March you arrived in Dublin with proposals for an agreement. I had been told the previous November there would be no discussion of any kind until the Forum Report came out.

NOEL DORR: I don't think that was fully taken on board by Mrs Thatcher. I mean the Forum was more important to the Irish side at that time.

DAVID GOODALL: The Cabinet approved the paper we took to Dublin in March and she had laryngitis at the time.[23]

NOEL DORR: To be honest, you [Garret] were a bit downcast after that summit in November 1983. I mean, we didn't feel that you were getting across terribly well to her.

GARRET FITZGERALD: No, although I thought that our own relationship had improved because I had supported Britain over the Falklands. Nonetheless, when I first met her in 1983 I didn't feel our relationship was as it had been in 1981, because the Falklands shadow seemed to hang over the whole of Ireland. By November things were better in that respect, but I had expected we might get preliminary talks underway while we were finalizing the Forum Report. I was a bit disappointed when I realized there were to be no negotiations at this

[23] The British proposal presented on 1 March 1984 (later known as the 'Armstrong Proposals') envisaged *inter alia* creating a 'security band' around the border; this would be policed by both states through a joint security commission, with a possible all-Ireland court and law commission; see Document 3.1. The Irish response on 11 May 1984, labelled the 'Nally Proposals' by the negotiators, proposed instead a system of joint authority in Northern Ireland; see Document 3.2. The latter proposals were viewed on the British side as 'fraught with difficulties' and as not offering 'an acceptable way forward'. See Annex A to report by Robert Armstrong to Prime Minister, 23 March 1984 TNA: PREM 19/1286.

stage. Contacts were thus temporarily broken off, and there was a little bit lost from that point of view. But I did think our overall relationship improved.

ROBERT ARMSTRONG: I think she was buying herself time to think it through first herself, and to talk to colleagues, because the decision to embark on it was, in British political terms, a very big one.

3.3.3. Security Cooperation

MICHAEL LILLIS: Let me say something here which is—I am going to step out of my role as being a member of the old team and just say something which I disagreed with, but I didn't say anything at the time. But anyway, when you came to Dublin with that proposal about the security forces on both sides of the border and it was—I think we were in the cabinet room where that meeting was?

DERMOT NALLY: Yes, that is where the original March 1984 meetings took place.

MICHAEL LILLIS: And the paper was handed around and I read it, and I have to say that I was immensely excited by that proposal, because I thought this was the beginning of a historic breakthrough. Frankly, I still believe that it was by far the most daring proposal which you ever brought to us—from our point of view as well as yours—and I don't think that has ever been said. Certainly I have never said it until this moment, because what you were going to do—big country, a lot of history—was inviting the security forces of another state to come into your territory.

GARRET FITZGERALD: And vice versa.

MICHAEL LILLIS: And vice versa, but we were going to negotiate that. We didn't even start to negotiate. Instead of which, everybody on our side jumped up and down and they said 'Oh my god, the RUC in Kerry', or somewhere, and we weren't going to . . .

ROBERT ARMSTRONG: More than five miles from the border . . .

GARRET FITZGERALD: It was because there would be two borders for the IRA to be chased across. It was a funny way of saying that. It wasn't a good reaction on my part.

MICHAEL LILLIS: It was the beginning of a negotiation. We missed the opportunity, it was the most fantastic proposal the British have ever made to us, and we kicked it out the door and I have always felt sorry that we did.

ROBERT ARMSTRONG: There is no doubt in my mind that Margaret was attracted by the proposal because there had been cases where—I don't know if they had been reported—but where the RUC were in hot pursuit and had to stop at the border. If they had been able to go on another couple of miles, that might have ended differently. I think we recognized that, if there was to be a border band, it couldn't be all on your side of the border.

MICHAEL LILLIS: I didn't see this as just about hot pursuit—I saw this as a tectonic plate.

DERMOT NALLY: It was a particularly sensitive issue, because I would say that Jack Lynch's government had fallen on a similar but even less fundamental proposal—about border overflights over, I think, five miles south of the border, and this became a huge issue, nothing to do with ground contact. It was air surveillance—about a reconnaissance zone for spotter aircraft. It became a huge issue politically for Jack Lynch. You might almost say he resigned as Taoiseach as a result of the resulting political flack—plus the Cork by-elections.[24]

MICHAEL LILLIS: Dermot, I saw it as the beginning of a serious negotiation about joint authority.

ROBERT ARMSTRONG: Where I would go along with that is that I thought that we thought the proposal had merit in itself, but we also thought that it was a way of unlocking the door or opening the door to negotiation.

DAVID GOODALL: Well, it was neuralgic both ways around, if I may say so, because the fact that it was so firmly rejected by you reinforced Mrs Thatcher's view that the Irish were not really serious about cross-border security—that when it came to actually doing cross-border security, that was out of court because of Irish national sensitivities. It was unfortunate both ways, really.

NOEL DORR: I think we should keep clear the distinction between two things. One, if I understand what Michael is saying, is that this could be the beginning of a real negotiation about something important that he wanted to achieve. On the other side of it, however, is the question of whether that proposal itself would have ever worked, or would have made things worse in the general area of security North and South. In other words, the proposal is one thing, but Michael's ambitions for what the proposal might ultimately be negotiated into are a very different matter, and I don't think we should confuse the two. I can't see, frankly, that it would have worked, for the reasons Garret has said; you would have a band on either side of the border and you would have a general mishmash. I think that would be more dangerous in some ways than maintenance of the status quo.

MICHAEL LILLIS: All of that would have been addressed in the negotiation, which we never let happen.

ROBERT ARMSTRONG: Well it was—when our negotiations began it was the Prime Minister, the Foreign Secretary, and the Secretary of State for Northern Ireland.

---

[24] Fine Gael comfortably defeated Fianna Fáil in two by-elections in Taoiseach Jack Lynch's home county on 7 November 1979: Cork City and Cork North-East, where Fianna Fáil had won 59% and 48%, respectively, of the first preference vote in the general election of June 1977. On 10 November 1979, the Irish Press reported that Lynch had agreed to military overflights across the border for limited distances.

GARRET FITZGERALD: Just the three.

ROBERT ARMSTRONG: Just the three, and I don't know if we ever called them a committee. It wasn't a formal committee.

GARRET FITZGERALD: I was told a Northern Ireland committee in theory existed, but this was not it.

ROBERT ARMSTRONG: There may have been a Northern Ireland committee but it wasn't dealing with this.

GARRET FITZGERALD: No, but I wondered why it was an ad hoc committee. Eventually I formed a view that maybe she didn't want the Lord Chancellor there, but then maybe that is just a thought of mine. It was just logical to have those three and nobody else?

NOEL DORR: There wasn't any love lost at the time, if I remember, between Margaret Thatcher and Jim Prior, who was the Northern Ireland Secretary.

ROBERT ARMSTRONG: That is quite true.

Q: There are two models of negotiation, one bargaining, where you give and take and compromise and all the rest, and one problem-solving. How do you describe the negotiation process?

ROBERT ARMSTRONG: Well, as we have already said, David and I came over here in March 1984, and I would say that for the first part of the process the discussions were in a sense exploratory—to find out what might be possible and what might not be possible. That phase went on for quite a bit of time.

But then there began to emerge a second stage, when the outlines of something possible were emerging. Then we were talking in detail about the various parts and various sections to be reviewed, and really drafting—I don't know how David would feel, but it certainly felt like that.

I suspect for both of us, but certainly for the British side, we were expected to report back to ministers, in particular to the Prime Minister, every time we had a meeting. We were expected, having reported back, to commission or receive instructions from this about the next meeting. So, we were not only negotiating, as it were, but we were reporting and getting our instructions and that could sometimes be quite difficult because Mrs Thatcher didn't keep the details in her mind necessarily, so there would be a certain amount of bringing her up to date with where we've got to and what happened before we've gone on to the next stage. At one or two stages that was quite laborious, but it went on working. I think that's the answer to your question. David, do you want to add to that?

DAVID GOODALL: Well, I think that is what happened. I've always thought the crucial thing about the negotiations was the establishment of confidence between the negotiators—I mean, at the very top between Garret and Margaret Thatcher, which was in a way a more precarious position. Quite early on, I think, we established—you [Robert] had already a relationship of confidence with Dermot—the fact, I think, that we really did actually trust one another, and it made the whole thing possible. I think there were various points in negotiations . . .

ROBERT ARMSTRONG: The point that I keep coming back to is that, although each side was negotiating in good faith for the interest of its government, we were all of one mind, wanting something to come out at the end.

DAVID GOODALL: We all wanted an agreement.

ROBERT ARMSTRONG: All wanted an agreement.

DAVID GOODALL: Yes, I think that's true. I think that's very important and that's part of the reason why there was confidence between us, I suppose, and there were various points where either one side or the other overestimated what their ministers would buy, so to speak. Things would seem to be going swimmingly, and then we would go back and Margaret Thatcher would say it was absolutely impossible, and there were certainly one or two moments when that happened on the Irish side. There was also an internal negotiation going on in London between the departments concerned, which at some moments was even more difficult than negotiating with the Irish. But yes, it started off as very exploratory didn't it—and then when we got going there were setbacks, weren't there? I can't now quite remember, there was one summit well before the 'out, out, out' business?[25]

3.3.4. The New Ireland Forum Report

GARRET FITZGERALD: The November 1984 summit was disappointing. She thought I was unhappy leaving and I said 'I was, yes'. I think it should be said, though, that she and I were both upset. I was upset because we moved backwards. We had gone quite a distance, and then Douglas Hurd came into the Northern Ireland Office, and he was much more cautious. My effort to play the articles 2 and 3 card had been rejected, and it looked as if we weren't going to get very much and, leaving, she said 'Are you happy Garret?', and I said I wasn't.

She then went to a press conference at five, and if you read the transcripts it was exceptionally helpful. She went out of her way to be helpful, saying things which she normally would not do, but she was concerned. The trouble was that the press, of course, didn't know what was happening in the negotiations. We had put forward our three alternatives, you had said 'no', and we moved on to do what we always knew was going to happen: the fourth one which was 'any other proposals?' [*laughter*].

---

[25] 'Out, out, out' refers to Margaret Thatcher's dismissal on 19 Novermber 1984 of three alternative models for the governance of Northern Ireland which had been put forward in the New Ireland Forum Report; see Subsection 3.1.3.

That was in July, I think. Things had gone well up until then. And when she was asked the question about the three points in the Forum, she perfectly correctly said 'out, out, out'—listen, they weren't even discussed, we were past that stage months ago—but her tone of voice was such that it was interpreted negatively.

Our man came up from that press conference and told us he wasn't there for that question in the end. So, he didn't hear it, and then I turned on the radio and couldn't hear what she said on BBC as it was blotted out. I therefore went in to the press conference knowing nothing about this, and all the journalists had come from her press conference. They all turned to me and I said 'I don't know what on earth they are talking about'. We gave several terrible interviews as we hadn't a clue what this was about. I went home a bit depressed but the next morning I woke up and realized there are advantages to this.

DERMOT NALLY: The Forum points had also been formally put to the British side at a meeting in London of the two official negotiating teams in June 1984, and just as formally rejected by them. So the three options had been off the table for a long time in November 1984. But nobody outside those directly involved knew it.

GARRET FITZGERALD: I could see that we now had an advantage, because I knew on your side people would be unhappy about the way this had emerged, that she'd come under pressure again from the civil servants to put things right. We were now in a position where, whatever setback there had been, there was a chance of moving on, because everybody was concerned with trying to make the best of the situation. So, I became quite positive at that stage, looking ahead strategically. But everybody misinterpreted the circumstances; she was not being negative, she was trying to be helpful. Only I understood this and no one else seemed to understand [*laughing*].

Then she arrived at a European Council meeting here, and we had to decide about the talks, and she had wonderful words. She said 'Garret, what did I do wrong?' It was my best moment of the entire negotiation. I told her what the problem had been, but she had difficulty in understanding. I could see why she was trying to be helpful and wondered why everybody should turn on her as if she behaved badly. It turned out well, because we then called in the United States, which put a bit of pressure on, and you guys sent your proposals back on 21 January and we were back on course again.[26]

DAVID GOODALL: But on a lower level—expectations on both sides had been, I think, realistically lowered as a result of that.

---

[26] For the text of the January draft, see Document 3.3; for a later British draft in March, see Document 3.4. The March draft shows a clear evolution in areas of agreement and marks an intermediate stage between the initial January draft and the final version agreed in November. It is rather longer and more detailed than the January draft, especially in respect of cultural and security issues, and stresses more strongly British commitment to devolved government in Northern Ireland.

GARRET FITZGERALD: Oh yes, we never quite got back to the point where we were in August or September, unfortunately.

DAVID GOODALL: I think in that sense it was more realistic afterwards than it was before. The other thing I would say about that, Garret—I don't know whether Robert would agree—is that the Forum thing was so much more important, as I think somebody said this morning, so much more politically important in Ireland than it was in Britain. I don't think British ministers ever really took the Forum Report terribly seriously. Maybe that's an exaggeration, but they weren't really terribly interested in the Forum Report. I think that's part of the reason why she sort of rather brushed it aside, but she didn't realize how.

MICHAEL LILLIS: No, no, I agree, and I think that all of the officials on the Irish side, starting with perhaps myself, were a bit guilty in that respect, because we didn't sufficiently emphasize [its importance]. I was looking at the Forum Report over the weekend, and if you look at the section which Garret mentioned, which is called 'Present Realities and Future Requirements', it is, you know I could quote it endlessly, it's all accepting the realities of unionism and their resentments and their doubts, and all the rest of it, and it is remarkable that a group of nationalist politicians representing the whole spectrum outside of Sinn Féin in those days could—including the SDLP, who represented a very sort of sensitive northern constituency of nationalism—could subscribe to these things. I think I underestimated it, to be honest with you, speaking for myself. I don't think that in our discussions we sufficiently emphasized what a big move this was from Irish nationalism.

NOEL DORR: I have three points. To go back to the first question that was asked about the nature of the negotiation: others have correctly said that it was exploratory at first, and Robert has said that it was an effort, while each side remained true to its instructions, at the same time to find ways through problems. I think that's something that needs very much to be emphasized, and it's a matter very much of personalities and abilities on each side. My perception was that we were dealing across the table with two people in particular, Robert and David here, who have an immense ability to draft.

But even more, whenever we came to a problem in another type of negotiation, it would be a big problem. Robert's approach was always 'how can we find a way around it?', and usually by drafting in his elegant hand we found a way around it, and David was equally good at drafting. So, I don't know if I can fit it exactly into the two types of negotiations that were raised, but certainly problem-solving sounds closer to it than the other one.

ROBERT ARMSTRONG: Well, no, Noel, let me say you were no mean draftsman yourself!

DERMOT NALLY: It should be mentioned that the negotiating teams on both sides had been strengthened, with the original team of Noel, Seán, Michael, and myself. There were Declan Quigley, the civil servant in charge of the Attorney

General's Office, to keep insight on the law, and Andy Ward, Secretary General of the Department of Justice, who was invaluable on security questions.

NOEL DORR: The second point on the 'out, out, out' issue—I was the Irish ambassador at the time, and the embassy was full of television cameras and media for the occasion of the summit. Garret came back after the summit to the embassy, and we instructed Justin Harmon, who was a colleague in the embassy, to go and listen to what Mrs Thatcher was saying at her press conference. But he was given an absolute instruction by the press side of the operation that he had to be back, as Garret's press conference was going to go live on the six o'clock television news in Ireland, and he had to be back in order to allow that to broadcast as the first item on the news. He therefore left Mrs Thatcher's press conference before the crucial thing; he came back and he gave a general picture of what had been said at the press conference.

Garret went down to the ballroom in the embassy, gave his press conference live on Irish television on the six o'clock news, and the first leading item went over to London. We had not been able to synchronize the feed, because at the time you couldn't receive Radio Éireann properly in the embassy. You couldn't, in other words, know what was happening in Ireland. I sat beside him at the press conference, and I have to say that it wasn't your best press conference—that is, apart from the fact that you didn't know what had been said by Mrs Thatcher. The result was that the Irish audience watching saw Mrs Thatcher saying 'That is out, that is out, that is out', aligned to the fact that on the other side—as I said, not your best press conference—that you were completely in ignorance of what the others probably knew at that time, that she had said this. That was very important.

Thirdly, on the Forum Report. When the Forum Report came out, I was instructed from Dublin to go and see Robert. I don't know if Robert remembers this, and he may not remember it as clearly as I do. I was to put to the British government, through Robert, the three options in the Forum Report. The key to the Forum Report is the two paragraphs—4.15 and 4.16—which talk about a settlement recognizing the legitimate rights of both sides. The final paragraph, which Garret has talked about already, is 5.10, which states that, after talking about federal, confederal, and joint authority, the parties in the Forum also remain open to discuss other views which may contribute to political development. That was the key that opened possibilities other than the federal and confederal options. But I was asked to go and formally put to the British government through Robert the federal and confederal options in the Forum Report.

Now, maybe it didn't leave much impression on Robert, but I did it honestly and with integrity. I didn't go in and say 'Ah, well, look, I'm just going through the motions'; I went in as instructed, authentically, to offer these three options, and Robert, in perhaps more pleasant language than Mrs Thatcher later used, more or less said 'no' to all three, and I reported that back. So that, if you like, opened the way for the Irish government to build on this other option—'other views that may contribute to political development'.

I think, finally, the summit of 1984 was probably about the time when both sides looked over the brink in the sense of considering the possibility of amending articles 2 and 3 of the constitution. Both sides drew back, not one side but both, because it was clear to both sides that that would have to be the basis for a very deep settlement in relation to Northern Ireland. The Irish side would be looking for a great deal more in order to be sure of getting a referendum through, and the British side was considering what would be needed also. So, if you like, both sides looked at the possibility around that time and then drew back, and maybe that gave, then, the more realistic tone to the negotiations thereafter.

DERMOT NALLY: The point was that we needed something like joint authority to balance a change in articles 2 and 3 of the constitution; and the British were saying that joint authority just was not on. So we had to work on other possibilities. During the negotiation—apart from the Chequers meeting in November 1984—there were brief meetings between the Taoiseach and the Prime Minister in the margins of the European Council in Brussels in March 1984 and 1985, in June 1984 in Fontainebleau—where the peacocks wandered about the lawns and the British EU contribution problem was settled—in December 1984, and on 29 June 1985 in Milan.

At the Milan meetings, the Taoiseach produced one of the most powerful and most telling arguments I have ever heard for re-enacting some form of political settlement on the North. He referred to the forced movement of population there, larger than anywhere in Europe since the end of the Second World War (and this in the United Kingdom!), and to the economic and social consequences of the continuing instability for the North, for the UK, and for the whole island of Ireland—and even, I think, for the place of Britain in the world. It was a most powerful oration.

ROBERT ARMSTRONG: When Noel came, I knew—well, I thought I knew—enough about Margaret Thatcher to know that federation and confederation, anything which might be described as joint authority, were not going to get past Margaret Thatcher, and that severely limited what we were able to do, of course, but it was part of the realism.

DERMOT NALLY: In March 1984, Robert phoned me to ask if he could come to Dublin to discuss certain aspects of the Northern problem. I agreed to the meeting and having mentioned it to the Taoiseach, met him and David in the cabinet room in Government Buildings. Seán Donlon and Brian McCarthy from my Department were also there. That was the beginning of the negotiations for us as far as I was concerned. It began formally in the cabinet room in Government Buildings on that March morning.

Robert suggested at the meeting that we negotiate under three headings. The first was security, the second was constitutional issues, and the third was the form of government for Northern Ireland, civil rights, and any other matters that come out of the negotiation. It was—is—a very big agenda, and having, of course, cleared it with the Taoiseach, we started in on it as two sides approaching the same questions from different principles and attitudes, and there was a certain element, not of suspicion, but of wariness, I think, on both sides.

There was a strong element that there were two sides to the negotiation, but, as the negotiation went on, those differences diminished and diminished and diminished, until finally they disappeared, well before the end of the process. I think everybody here who took part in it would agree that the two sides were negotiating as one, with a common purpose, and the common purpose was security, peace, good relations between the two countries, and all the rest of these good things.

I would say the net effect of the negotiation and of the Agreement was to bring Dublin and London much closer together. Now, I don't know—it's not for me to say what London thought or what London did—but we certainly had that impression. The second point about the 'out, out, out' speech: I still remember Mrs Thatcher when she came to the Dublin council and she said 'Garret'—or I think it was Gareth?

MICHAEL LILLIS: 'Gareth', she said 'Gareth', yes.

ROBERT ARMSTRONG: She always said 'Gareth'!

DERMOT NALLY: 'Gareth, I am doing everything possible for you. I'm going around here smiling all day' [*laughter*]. It was a fabulous team, including Andy Ward, Michael Lillis, and Seán Donlon in that encomium.

But just to show the complexity, we used the phrase—and you have mentioned this before, Garret—article 1 of the Agreement said that unity 'would come about' only with the consent of the majority in Northern Ireland. Now that was exactly the phrase used in the 1980 communiqué of the meeting between Margaret Thatcher and Mr Haughey, and it was that exact phrasing used by those two leaders. That was extremely important, but not only was that phrase important, and it was used to fantastic advantage on television when the initial attack on the Agreement came, the phrase itself 'could only come about' was wrong; 'could only come about' would be unconstitutional. The Agreement would run into trouble in the courts [*laughter*] because 'it could' would be unconstitutional, *à la* the Boland case after Sunningdale! It was recognition of a practical reality—a statement of fact.

I mention all this just to show the sort of verbal quagmire we were moving through. When you say 'would come about only' you're recognizing a factual position—that is, the factual position which every government had accepted—not the acceptance of the impossibility implied by 'could not'. And, true to form, the Agreement was, I think, challenged in the McGimpsey case in the Irish courts.[27]

ROBERT ARMSTRONG: Whether the word 'constitutional' was inserted before 'status' was the subject of quite a lot of argument.

MICHAEL LILLIS: I just want to say one other thing about article 1, because it's something I'm guilty of, Garret, and it actually appeared in the Good Friday Agreement and every subsequent agreement. But there is a little sub-paragraph (*b*) which said: 'The two governments [...] recognized that the present wish of a majority of the people of Northern Ireland is for no change in the status of Northern Ireland'—that had never appeared in the Haughey documents or in anything previously. And actually I suggested that, which was a bit subversive of me, but actually in the end sub-paragraph (*b*) is very helpful to the other side.

DAVID GOODALL: Yes, it was.

MICHAEL LILLIS: And what's interesting is that it's actually carried on in all subsequent agreements, including the Good Friday Agreement.

3.3.5. The Intergovernmental Conference

Q: The Intergovernmental Conference—the IGC. Where did the idea of it come from?

GARRET FITZGERALD: The word 'conference'—there was a lot of stress about what we would call it.

ROBERT ARMSTRONG: Yes, there was, wasn't there?

GARRET FITZGERALD: Did I suggest 'conference', or somebody else?

MICHAEL LILLIS: We had to rebut your 'committee', which we described as 'commit-tea' [*laughter*] do you remember that?

ROBERT ARMSTRONG: I do!

MICHAEL LILLIS: Because there was a popular programme at the time on Irish television which was about a local county council which would establish 'commit-teas' [*laughter*], and I persuaded myself, at least, that this gave us very strong grounds for it. It worked, to my surprise!

GARRET FITZGERALD: You must remember that the Anglo-Irish Intergovernmental Council was established in 1981. But in fact nobody took it very seriously, because the idea was that all meetings between the two governments would be called the Council. I think after a year or so we forgot about that, and I am not sure we ever used the phrase again.

---

[27] See Ch. 2, n. 32.

DERMOT NALLY: It was put into a draft of a communiqué from one of your meetings, Taoiseach, and the Prime Minister said: 'What's this about an "Anglo-Irish Intergovernmental Council"? I never agreed to a "Council"! Take it out.' I was surprised—because that happened to be an important part of the communiqué—when Robert said something like, 'Don't worry, Dermot, we'll fix it'. And he did. The Anglo-Irish Intergovernmental Council was agreed; the word appeared in the communiqué. There were three meetings of the Anglo-Irish Intergovernmental Council.[28]

GARRET FITZGERALD: That was in 1981.

NOEL DORR: It's worth focusing on, though, because it provided a safe haven for the conference. Just remember how it grew. It started with the Haughey–Thatcher meeting and the idea of setting up studies. By the time the studies came to be reported in 1981, Garret was in government and Haughey was out of office. One of the recommendations in the studies was that every meeting between the two governments would be called part of an Anglo-Irish Inter-governmental Council. But then, once there was an Intergovernmental Coun-cil, it was a safe cushion, so to speak, or thought to be one, within which to nestle the Anglo-Irish Intergovernmental Conference [AIIGC]. So it's quite important in that way—although it was actually not very much used as a title for the various intergovernmental meetings.

DAVID GOODALL: There was a moment at lunch when Dermot and Robert produced a draft communiqué and it started off 'There was a meeting of the Anglo-Irish Intergovernmental Council' and the Prime Minister read it out in total deep distaste and she said 'What is that?' and you [Garret] said 'You invented it, Margaret'. I remember that [laughter].

NOEL DORR: This was at Chequers in November 1984, and she was pretty scathing towards you, if I remember.

DERMOT NALLY: She said pointedly, staring at me: 'This fellow, he caused me all the trouble up to now; he is responsible for things going into the communiqué which got me in trouble' [laughter].

NOEL DORR: It was too wordy a communiqué to come from that—there were too many words in it for her!

DAVID GOODALL: She was so indignant, and Peter Barry said to me 'I'm not going to stay and listen to this', and he got up. I said sort of 'Remain calm'—he was going to walk out.

NOEL DORR: If I remember, the Irish side broke at the lunch and adjourned for a kind of council in another room. It resumed again after twenty minutes or so, and the eventual communiqué which came out of the November 1984 nego-tiations was rather shorter than the original draft.

---

[28] The Anglo-Irish Intergovernmental Council was agreed at the FitzGerald–Thatcher summit of 6 November 1981, see Coakley (2014: 78).

DAVID GOODALL: Don't say that!

Q: Wasn't this apparently cumbersome dual structure adopted though—a conference within a council, rather than simply redefining a council?

ROBERT ARMSTRONG: The Council is something that had been established and agreed, which therefore provided a framework.

DERMOT NALLY: There were twenty-three different titles considered for the conference.

NOEL DORR: It wasn't cumbersome.

DERMOT NALLY: There was a 'convocation', there was a 'consulate', there was a 'committee', there was a 'commission', there was a 'council'. I looked at the list the other day, and I said 'oh, my God! Did we ever do that?'

Q: Could the Council not have performed the duties of the Conference?

NOEL DORR: No, because the Council was simply an umbrella title that was to be put over all meetings of ministers at any level, and this included prime ministers and officials between the two governments. It was a worthy idea, but it didn't make any difference. It was a matter of calling all those meetings part of something intangible called the Anglo-Irish Intergovernmental Council, but in fact it had no other existence beyond those meetings, which would have been taking place anyway. But what it did do was provide a safer political framework within which to create the really active body, which was to be as a result of the Agreement.

MICHAEL LILLIS: The point about the Intergovernmental Conference—there were various reasons why we went through all these kinds of semantic issues—was that that would comprise at its highest level the Secretary of State of Northern Ireland, not the Prime Minister, and a minister that would be nominated by our side. We all knew it was going to be the Minister for Foreign Affairs, but he wasn't actually designated in the Agreement.

DAVID GOODALL: But you invented the word 'conference', didn't you, Robert?

ROBERT ARMSTRONG: I think so, yes. We'd gone around and around, hadn't we, as Dermot said?

DERMOT NALLY: Before the word 'conference' was accepted, there were tangled discussions about, I think, twenty-three different names. 'Commission' had too many implications of executive power; 'executive' was out for the same reason; 'council' was even worse because perhaps it implied not only executive functions but even legislative functions. Even the word 'conclave' came into the reckoning, but it was rejected as being too papal. And so on, until after great deliberation 'conference' was accepted.

DAVID GOODALL: Yes, I thought this metaphysical Irish objection to 'committee' was rather a pity, because I thought 'intergovernmental committee' was rather stronger than 'intergovernmental conference'. But Michael produced this thing about 'commit-teas' and that killed it dead.

NOEL DORR: It was the comic programme *Hall's Pictorial Weekly* which put us off.[29]

MICHAEL LILLIS: I think, and I don't know whether my Irish colleagues will agree with me, I think 'committee' on this side of the water still has somewhat weaker resonance.

SEÁN DONLON: It refers to the lowest form of life in the GAA![30]

ROBERT ARMSTRONG: Oh yes, I see!

3.3.6. The Judiciary and the Courts

Q: Was there a discussion on what would be included as part of the remit of the conference?

ROBERT ARMSTRONG: There was indeed.

MICHAEL LILLIS: But I think that the listing was a summary of what was discussed in detail, and then we went back and said this is what it is, that's my memory of it.

DAVID GOODALL: If I may say so, it started off because at the start Margaret Thatcher, the Prime Minister, was very strongly reluctant to see anything except security and related matters being made formally part of the remit of any Anglo-Irish structure. Cross-border cooperation was of course very important to us, but the extension to political matters, into making it really a body which could discuss anything, was in fact a considerable move forward in the negotiations from the British side. But there was, of course, a hiccough over the third item there—the administration of justice—the question of joint courts and all that, which was a subject in itself.

ROBERT ARMSTRONG: And that was kyboshed by Lord Hailsham.[31]

DAVID GOODALL: And Lord Hailsham kyboshed that, yes.

NOEL DORR: That was still alive as a possibility after the Agreement.

DAVID GOODALL: I know it was, but the Lord Chancellor killed it.

GARRET FITZGERALD: What exactly?

MICHAEL LILLIS: The mixed courts.

DAVID GOODALL: The joint courts.

ROBERT ARMSTRONG: Two Irish judges, was it two or one Irish judge in Northern Ireland, and one British judge in the South?

---

[29] *Hall's Pictorial Weekly* was a satirical programme, broadcast by RTÉ from 1971 to 1980, which often featured 'commit-teas' in such fictional rural locations as 'Ballymagash'.

[30] The Gaelic Athletic Association is a pan-Irish sporting organization with a hierarchical structure, of which the basic unit is the individual club, governed by an elected committee.

[31] Lord Hailsham (Quintin Hogg) was a senior Conservative politician who served as Lord Chancellor in the Thatcher government, 1979–87.

NOEL DORR: I was reporting from London about a fairly positive attitude on the part of some ministers towards this possibility. I went to see Hailsham, and he remembered his father's involvement and being in Northern Ireland in 1927. He was the one who killed it, but it was a live possibility as far as I was reporting home in 1986 after the Agreement. It's mentioned in the Agreement in a general way as a possibility, but, as Robert said, it would be some time before it was done—it wasn't ruled out.

DAVID GOODALL: Initially it had a very unfortunate history. I think this particular episode arose from the need to create the confidence of the minority in Northern Ireland in the institutions of the administration of justice. When it was first floated—I think by you in a conversation with the Prime Minister, but I can't now remember exactly—it was a proposal for a three-judge mixed court with one Irish judge.

GARRET FITZGERALD: And one Northern judge in the South.

DAVID GOODALL: Yes, one Northern judge, and she did not dismiss it out of hand. But of course she wasn't prepared for it either. But she didn't dismiss it out of hand, so the thing then acquired a run, and then we said obviously it would have to be cleared with the Lord Chief Justice of Northern Ireland, Lord Lowry. And Lord Lowry came to a rugby match at Lansdowne Road.[32]

GARRET FITZGERALD: I invited Lord Lowry to meet our new Chief Justice, and we had lunch together. In fact, our families had a close relationship—my mother would have been close friends with his wife, and indeed my father, when on the run, used to hide out in his father's house in Leeson Park.[33] You were safe in a unionist house when on the run. So we had a good relationship, and he seemed a very liberal man, and when I raised this with him after our Chief Justice had just left, he said 'yes, I want to say something to you; if you go ahead with this I shall ... '.

DAVID GOODALL: 'I will resign'.

GARRET FITZGERALD: ' ... I shall take it up with the Prime Minister, the Lord Chancellor, the Lord Secretary, and tell him our entire court will resign if you go ahead with this'. That was a bit disconcerting.

DAVID GOODALL: I always thought that was a prime example of the dangers of informal negotiation, because he didn't know—or at least he said he didn't know—that it was even discussed until you mentioned it to him, and then he came back and said it was absolute.

GARRET FITZGERALD: I thought it would help, but it didn't.

DAVID GOODALL: So, then, we fell back on the idea of three British judges.

---

[32] Lansdowne Road, Dublin, was the site of Ireland's main rugby ground, now the Aviva Stadium.
[33] Garret FitzGerald's mother, Mabel McConnell, was a close friend of Ena Lynd, who married Bill Lowry, QC (father of Lord Lowry), in whose house in Leeson Park, Dublin, Desmond FitzGerald occasionally took refuge while 'on the run' in 1919–21; see FitzGerald (1991: 3).

GARRET FITZGERALD: No, after the Agreement I suggested that issue of the three judges and that was knocked also on 2 October.

DAVID GOODALL: Hailsham knocked it.

GARRET FITZGERALD: He knocked it, and Whitelaw did not support it. I was disappointed, as I thought that he would support it.

NOEL DORR: It's in the Agreement in article 8. It mentions considering *inter alia* the 'possibility of mixed courts in both jurisdictions for the trial of certain offences'.

GARRET FITZGERALD: But we then thought that the court would not resign. At a meeting concerning the Single European Act in Milan in June 1985, I enquired whether Margaret Thatcher had received a letter, which I believe was sent, saying the court wouldn't all resign, and they would do what they were told and not object.

We had this most difficult meeting where she was conceding nothing on anything. So I launched out on a brief fifteen-minute account of recent Irish history, and I looked across at Dermot and I could see Dermot's facial expression; he thought I had wrecked everything. I went to town on it to try and make some impact, and eventually I am exhausted with this Anglo-Irish policy. She said, 'Oh, Garret, tell me more', which was most disconcerting for me, as I had nothing more to say [*laughter*]. It was deflating, it was a real anticlimax. But I mentioned in that discussion in Milan that she was going to get this letter from her judges, and she was not pleased at that, because I knew about the letter before she did.

DERMOT NALLY: You addressed her most fiercely in Milan. One of the things I remember about it was your statement that 'you, Prime Minister, are running a territory where there has been a greater movement of population, involuntary movement of population, than in any country in Europe'—this is the Belfast riots and so on, and that was the opening salvo.

GARRET FITZGERALD: Do you recall that meeting?

ROBERT ARMSTRONG: Yes, it was all killed by Lord Hailsham. His worries turned around the judicial oath, and he said judges in British courts were all to sign an oath of loyalty to the queen and an Irish judge would not be able to do that. But I think that was a cover for something deeper.

GARRET FITZGERALD: Antipathy in that family.

ROBERT ARMSTRONG: I think that Hailsham would have had a deep antipathy to the idea of mixed courts.

DAVID GOODALL: He recalled all that, he wrote in 1986—he wrote an absolutely killing minute. It would have been impossible for anybody to go ahead with the idea with the Lord Chancellor having put that on record. He was so absolutely opposed to it, but it was a pity because in the negotiation of the communiqué and of article 8 it had been quite a thorny subject. It was included in the Agreement on the understanding that it was something which the British would look at seriously. And also it played a part in the communiqué, and we did look at it seriously, but of course, we didn't do it, and so it looked in a sense like a breach of faith.

GARRET FITZGERALD: Were mixed courts still in play and shot down?

NOEL DORR: They were, yes.

MICHAEL LILLIS: I can confirm that from the point of view of the secretariat, because I recall we even advised some time in 1986 that this was not going to be a runner. And this was coming from Belfast.

GARRET FITZGERALD: Mixed courts?

MICHAEL LILLIS: Mixed courts. And the reason at that stage that we said we had better just back off for a while was that we had the unionist reaction to the Agreement, which was tumultuous; policemen were being burned out of their homes around various parts of Northern Ireland. It sustained very, very massive opposition, and Mrs Thatcher had told you that you got all the glory and she got nothing but the blame. I just didn't think—I mean there were other things that were of more immediate direct interest to the minority community which we could possibly have delivered without the thing going up to that level.

NOEL DORR: The prehistory—and I don't want to go back on it—was the fact that extradition was a sore point through the 1970s. After Sunningdale there was the law commission set-up, with judges from both sides, and they divided on the issue of whether extradition was possible or not. This wasn't just, as Michael implied, a matter for the minority, but it was also a way of handling this sore point of extradition for political offences.

DERMOT NALLY: Extradition was a sore point as long as I was in the job. Heath raised it with Cosgrave at their meeting in September 1973—referring as an example to a man responsible for a terrorist offence in Belfast who moved South, and was known to have committed other terrorist offences in the North from there, and he could not be extradited.[34]

MICHAEL LILLIS: The only document that I have retained from all of those years is a thing called the 'catechism'.[35] Do you remember that? [*general agreement*].

MICHAEL LILLIS: I have it right here, and if you don't mind, this was the answer Mrs Thatcher was supposed to give at the press conference had she been asked 'what is your position on joint courts?' She was supposed to have said—no doubt she had it off by heart—'we have not been able to see any easy or early way round the political and other difficulties involved, but we have in good faith and without commitment, provided in article 8 for the matter to be

[34] Irish courts normally rejected requests for the extradition of suspects if the latter could demonstrate that the alleged offences were politically motivated. See Subsection 2.3.4.

[35] The Anglo-Irish 'catechism' was drawn up by British and Irish officials as a briefing document for the prime ministers; for the text, see Document 3.5.

studied. We have not excluded the possibility of mixed courts in both jurisdictions for the trial of certain offences becoming feasible and acceptable at some future time.' I think it was actually a fair description of where we were.

DAVID GOODALL: That, of course, is when mixed courts were still being talked about—they were, really. It was Lord Lowry, above all, as well as the Lord Chancellor that finally gave the *coup de grâce* to three-judge courts. There was also a linkage, as I recall, in the drafting of the communiqué, which was another neuralgic issue, between the inclusion of a reference to mixed courts and the Irish signing-up to the European Convention on the Prevention of Terrorism. There was an element of *quid pro quo* in the inclusion of both in the communiqué. So there was then a feeling on her side—she felt a bit guilty about mixed courts, I think. But she also felt that you hadn't properly lived up to your undertaking either.

GARRET FITZGERALD: Well, we did. But our problem was that we really ceased to have a clear majority in parliament during 1986.[36] But we eventually got it through.

3.3.7. The US Dimension

Q: Seán Donlon, we invited everyone else around the table at the beginning of the day to introduce their own role in relation to the Agreement. You didn't get a chance to do so, and there is also an American dimension to this.

SEÁN DONLON: It's almost a separate chapter; it would take quite a bit of time. I went through papers over the weekend and they're voluminous—six volumes of fairly detailed stuff. In summary, we were keeping the Americans informed.

I was Secretary of the Department at the time. I had been ambassador in Washington. I had maintained contact with key people in Washington and had been briefing them on the progress of the negotiation, initially because we thought at some stage we would need American support to persuade Prime Minister Thatcher to do something, which turned out to be the case.

Then, as time went on, when we developed the concept of the International Fund for Ireland, we were also seeking, and we did get, a Congressional resolution, and a statement from President Reagan, and a statement from some other members of the House.[37] So, we were in constant contact with the Americans. Garret's book covers almost all of it. There is one crucial omission. After the 'out, out, out' summit and immediately after the Dublin summit,

---

[36] Following the general election of November 1982, Fine Gael had 70 seats and the Labour Party 16 out of a total of 166 in the Dáil, giving the coalition a total of 86. Following defections, especially after the foundation of the Progressive Democrats in 1985, the coalition's share of seats fell to 82 in late 1986, so that it no longer had an overall majority.

[37] For a detailed account of the American role at this period, see Wilson (1995: 226–50).

I went to Washington to see Tip O'Neill, and Tip wrote a letter to Reagan, during the late summer; it's in Tip's biography, written by Farrell.[38]

You see, there were two visits—the Prime Minister paid two visits to Washington, one in December to Camp David, and one more formal visit in February, when she addressed the joint session of Congress. But Tip O'Neill, in fact, Tip was taking a stronger line even than we were taking at home—Tip wanted the invitation cancelled, so that she would not address the joint session. Not for the first time, we found ourselves as Irish representatives in a position where we were persuading Irish Americans not to do the more extreme of the two things.

Q: Alistair McAlpine in his memoirs says that he asked Mrs Thatcher privately why she'd signed the Anglo-Irish Agreement, and he says she said: 'It was pressure from the Americans which made me sign *that* Agreement.'[39]

DAVID GOODALL: Well, I don't know what Robert would say to that; I read it and I thought, well, that's one piece of evidence, and of course I wasn't privy to what went on when she went to Washington and so on. I'd be interested to know what Robert thinks about this. I don't myself think that it was American pressure which caused her to sign the Agreement. But I do think American pressure played a considerable part in, so to speak, keeping her eye on the ball while the negotiations were going on. So I think that one comment is an exaggeration. This is purely impressionistic, but she and Reagan, after all, were very close. I mean it wasn't so much pressure as a sort of friendly thing, saying 'you know, it means a lot to us and it will mean a lot to you', and so on. So, she knew. And she did once say to me, ten years afterwards, when I asked her what she thought about the Agreement: 'Well, well, it did help with the Americans.' Obviously that was a factor. But I don't think that it was a decisive factor.

ROBERT ARMSTRONG: She wouldn't have signed an agreement which she was not going to sign because of the Americans.

GARRET FITZGERALD: But at the point where we had this 'out, out, out' business we were in contact with Tip O'Neill and Reagan. President Reagan did, I think, say that he'd like to hear when she came back in February as to how things were going. We were inclined to think that that request may have helped to speed up your reaction in sending new proposals.

NOEL DORR: When she addressed Congress at that time my memory is of the green character of her speech to Congress. It was almost like an Irish prime minister's speech in relation to what was lying ahead. In other words, she went quite far. But I come back to the point I made at the outset; I don't think Mrs Thatcher's subsequent pronouncements years afterwards as to why she did some things are wholly reliable.

---

[38] See Farrell (2011).   [39] See McAlpine (1998: 272).

ROBERT ARMSTRONG: Her instinctive feelings begin to prevail, whereas when she was in office those feelings were constrained by political reality. I think having started the process she wanted to reach an agreement. I don't think she wanted to go in front of the House of Commons, or any body, and say we tried but failed. She didn't like that.

DERMOT NALLY: Seán had done a magnificent job as ambassador in Washington, with access everywhere. When we went in there in 1990 as part of the Irish Presidency of that year we brought the Secretary General of the Council in Brussels with us—a Dane. He said at one of the meetings 'I have never seen such access for any country. You speak to the President. You meet the Vice-President. You are courted by the Speaker of the House. You meet the Chairwoman of the Senate. You can do this everywhere! We in Denmark have been looking for an official State visit for fifteen years—and we haven't succeeded.' That was Seán's legacy there, and that of his successors—with, of course, the importance of the Irish in the US and the International Fund for Ireland, that was worth then 100 or 200 million [euros].

GARRET FITZGERALD: More; 250 million.

SEÁN DONLON: Well, I mean Robert was involved in that.

DERMOT NALLY: Well, the two of you. The Fund, I think, is by now developed a lot more than the 200 million [euros]—maybe four times that figure.[40]

SEÁN DONLON: We did a joint trip. That was very near the end.

ROBERT ARMSTRONG: Mrs Thatcher was very conscious of the amount of money and resources that have gone into Northern Ireland.

DERMOT NALLY: As for the European Community contribution—she was saying that Britain contributes a huge proportion of the Community budget anyway.

NOEL DORR: The reference is in article 10 (a)—the possibility of securing international support for this work. I think it's brought in at least half a billion pounds into Northern Ireland and the border areas overall in the time since it was created.

DERMOT NALLY: I think it's even more—seven or eight hundred million.

SEÁN DONLON: The only general point I would make, having looked at papers in the last few days, is that, for students in ten years' time, I don't think any Anglo-Irish negotiation has as much detail recorded. There are volumes of stuff. You will be able to trace without too much difficulty the origin of specific phrases and sentences, because approximately, I think, there were six or eight Irish, what we call speaking notes. There were maybe four or five British

[40] The International Fund for Ireland was established by the British and Irish governments in 1986 following the Anglo-Irish Agreement. Funded by the British, Irish, American, Canadian, Australian, and New Zealand governments and the EU, it focuses on projects promoting reconciliation in Northern Ireland and the border counties, and had distributed almost one billion euros by 2018.

speaking notes, and that was before we came to an agreement, and then I think there are four.

DERMOT NALLY: And I made detailed notes of every official meeting between the Taoiseach and the Prime Minister during the negotiations. In addition, of course, there were, I think, about forty meetings at official level where I was Robert's counterpart on the Irish side.

GARRET FITZGERALD: And Noel's record, it is nearly 50,000 words of dialogue.

SEÁN DONLON: Much of our negotiation took place over meals, and you could see Noel writing on the back of a menu, and he would manage somehow or other to reconstruct in quite some detail. He also didn't go to bed at night. But I think the notes are, looking back on it, magnificent.

NOEL DORR: You had a prime minister who wanted to keep in close touch, and you wanted to brief her and keep her up to speed. We had a prime minister who wanted to be at the table in negotiations. Therefore it was necessary to give him the full flavour of what was happening. It was a matter of measuring and trying to report home as accurately as one could what exactly was possible—how far the British side were willing to go. It started accidentally, if I remember, at the first meeting. Michael did a note and I did a note. I have an inveterate habit of taking notes, so I just dictated them, usually at night. I was concerned to give Garret a flavour of what was happening.

GARRET FITZGERALD: I don't think any negotiations anywhere were as fully reported.

3.4. The Agreement

NOEL DORR: Perhaps it would be helpful just to clarify about the communiqué for those who may not know. In addition to the Anglo-Irish Agreement as published, there was a joint communiqué at the same time, and that was talked about in the negotiations. My memory is that we sort of used it as a device into which to project forward some of the issues that still remained hanging. So, if you like, you've got to read the two together, you've got to read the Agreement and the joint communiqué which goes with it, and included in that is the issue that Garret and David and Robert have been talking about—signing the European Convention on the suppression of terrorism, and so on. So there are a number of things in the communiqué that need to be read with the Agreement as the future programme of what would be done if some of the loose ends were left hanging.[41]

---

[41] For the text of the communiqué, see *Irish Times*, 16 November, 1985; for the text of the Agreement, see Document 3.6.

3.4.1. Article 2(b)

Q: The first two sentences of article 2(b) seem to represent an unbelievable concession by the British side.[42] What precisely do they mean? Are they a stick with which to beat unionism to the negotiating table?

DERMOT NALLY: There is a long-term theme in this—in 1973 all the political parties in the North with one exception were involved, plus the two governments. Then the political party who had been outside the Agreement wrecked the 1973 Agreement. It was wrecked by the Paisleyites, and action on the streets and in the power stations.

The 1985 Agreement was framed deliberately so that it could not be wrecked by that sort of action in the 1984–5 negotiations. It was an agreement between the two governments. We consulted with the SDLP and we brought them along with us, and I'm not sure what the arrangements on the other side were with the unionist people, but I don't think they were as close. There was a deep sense of hurt there. And that is reflected in the 100,000–200,000 protesters in the streets of Belfast after the 1985 Agreement—partly at the idea of the Anglo-Irish Intergovernmental Conference and the secretariat in Belfast.

But, if the unionist and nationalist parties had looked at the Agreement, they would have seen that they could have deprived the Conference of almost all of its functions by agreeing to work together in Stormont on Northern matters. It was exactly the same as the comment Peter Hain made before the recent establishment of the executive in the North: 'If you don't get together and administer the North by yourselves then London and Dublin will do it without you.'[43] But the message was not getting through in 1985. The war-weariness had not yet reached its peak, and the unionist reaction to the Agreement had not been analytical enough to see its advantage; it was far too emotional.

DAVID GOODALL: You could say that!

DERMOT NALLY: So the net effect of all this non-involvement was that you have an agreement between two governments to do certain things of extreme importance to the future of Northern Ireland, the future of Ireland, and the future of relations between the two countries, and that has been arrived at without telling the parties in the North and without consulting them over a period of five years or ten years. The message gets through gradually, and you

---

[42] The sentences are as follows: 'The United Kingdom Government accept that the Irish Government will put forward views and proposals on matters relating to Northern Ireland within the field of activity of the Conference in so far as those matters are not the responsibility of a devolved administration in Northern Ireland. In the interest of promoting peace and stability, determined efforts shall be made through the Conference to resolve any differences.'

[43] Peter Hain, MP, was Northern Ireland Secretary, 2005–7 (see Subsection 6.7.1).

find that both unionists and Sinn Féin and the IRA say 'well, really, we're not getting anywhere, thirty years of violence and nothing has happened; the only way we can do this is by negotiation of the type that involves the two governments'. That, I think, was a direct outcome of the way in which the 1985 Agreement was negotiated.

GARRET FITZGERALD: Yes, and the first sentence there is bridging a gap, a compromise between our joint authority and the British concern to avoid anything that would seem to impede their sovereignty. But our concern had to be not just consultation. We are used to consulting and being ignored—not just Britain—so we wanted to tie it down as best we could. That's as near as we could get to joint authority.

NOEL DORR: The second sentence particularly.

GARRET FITZGERALD: 'In the interest of promoting peace and stability, a determined effort shall be made'—that was as near as we could get to our objective.

DERMOT NALLY: You don't know, Garret, how many of the twenty-three different titles for this particular animal were dismissed, because 'that implies executive power, and this implies too much, this is too religious', and so on.

DAVID GOODALL: I think that is a formula which you, Robert, first of all invented and then sold to the Prime Minister.

ROBERT ARMSTRONG: 'To put forward views and proposals' was as far as we could get out of this, really.

DAVID GOODALL: Yes, but then 'determined': it was you that produced the phrase 'determined efforts shall be made through the conference', because the Irish side wanted it to be understood that agreement would have to be reached, which the Prime Minister rejected, and you came up with, I thought, that masterly phrase 'determined efforts shall be made to resolve any differences'.

NOEL DORR: The word 'shall' is important, and that whole sentence allowed us to say afterwards to critics that the role of the Irish government was more than consultative but less than executive—so that second sentence is a key sentence.

MICHAEL LILLIS: May I read from the 'catechism'? Because, as usual, catechisms are instructive [laughter]. The question: 'So the Irish role is intended to be only consultative?' This is the answer, now, and it comes from both the Taoiseach and the Prime Minister: 'The conference is a unique mechanism. There is no single word to describe its role. It will not have executive functions; article 2(b) of the Agreement makes it clear that there will be no derogation from sovereignty and that each government retains responsibility for the decisions and administration of government within its jurisdiction. But the conference will be more than just consultative in that the Irish side will put forward views and proposals on its own initiative as well as being invited to do so; and there is an obligation on both sides in the conference to make determined efforts to resolve any differences.'

And then there is an asterisk, and the asterisk says: 'the Taoiseach will add "in the interests of peace and stability"', not the Prime Minister. But actually 'in the interests of peace and stability' is in the Agreement, and I think that was our suggestion, and we persuaded ourselves, and I think we were right, that it is at least the intention, and perhaps an obligation, considerably more than consultative, and it's a very interesting and unique mechanism.

DERMOT NALLY: Before the press conference after the 1985 Agreement—just to prepare the ground for the forthcoming press conference—Robert was designated to put hard questions to the Taoiseach. And I was designated to question the Prime Minister.

ROBERT ARMSTRONG: Margaret said to you, didn't she: 'We've got a bit of time to spare; why don't we let Dermot ask me some questions, and Robert can ask you some questions, and see if we can answer them?'

NOEL DORR: Do our audience realize there are fifty pages of possible questions and answers that were worked out in the negotiations?

DERMOT NALLY: I still have the small cards with answers on them to the most critical questions—it was vital that both participated, and in each other's interests get the replies right.

Q: Did you discuss the negotiation of the 'catechism' as well?

GARRET FITZGERALD: That did take some time at the end, didn't it?

DERMOT NALLY: I have three cards here, one is extradition, one deals with mixed courts, and the other deals with the consultative [process . . .] and the fourth one—sorry, there are four cards—deals with status, so they were the main issues on which it was anticipated that there could be trouble. We have all these if anyone wants them?

NOEL DORR: There is another interesting sentence, the last sentence: 'There will be no derogation from sovereignty and each government retains responsibility for the decisions and administration of government within its own jurisdiction.' If you didn't have that last sentence it would be argued that what you were creating was a derogation from sovereignty. That sentence was asserting the opposite, so, whatever you deduced from the structure that has been created, you're being told flatly that this is not derogating from sovereignty. It's with a view to subsequent controversy that that was put in, and it probably did serve that purpose.

ROBERT ARMSTRONG: It was very important to her throughout that there should be no derogation from the issue of sovereignty; it seemed the best way to meet that was to say that.

MICHAEL LILLIS: By the way, just one interesting thing. The Good Friday Agreement has the entire Anglo-Irish Agreement in it, under the BIIGC section, word for word for the most part, but otherwise in substance, without any exception. There's one tiny exception; that is when they talk about 'determined efforts shall be made through the conference to resolve any differences'. That's in the BIIGC of the Good Friday Agreement, but the words 'to promote peace and stability' are not included. I'm told by some of those who were involved—and this may be news to you because maybe it was done at another level—that it was in order to reconcile Mr Trimble that those words were left out.

3.4.2. Constitutional Status

NOEL DORR: A constant factor in various efforts at a settlement has been to provide something on the status issue as a safety net for the unionists. Whatever else you put into the communiqué or the Agreement afterwards, they can therefore feel a reassurance that they're not going to be imperceptibly led into a united Ireland against their wishes.

In Sunningdale, that took the form of two parallel declarations. Here, the two are amalgamated in article 1 for the first time. Nevertheless, it did prove subsequently to be ambiguous for reasons which we've already talked about. But nevertheless, at the time, it looked as if we had now a common statement in relation to status, and that that would enable us to have a single text of the emerging agreement.

My memory is that, in the weeks before the Agreement finally emerged, it was suggested for once to try to have a common text. Each side deliberated with their respective Attorneys General and came back claiming that it isn't possible. So, the Irish side's text of the Anglo-Irish Agreement is described as an 'Agreement between the Government of Ireland and the Government of the United Kingdom'. The British text says 'Agreement between the Government of the United Kingdom of Great Britain and Northern Ireland and the Government of the Republic of Ireland'. Now the Irish heading 'Agreement between the government of Ireland and government of the United Kingdom' doesn't state 'the United Kingdom of Great Britain and Northern Ireland'. Similarly, on the British side, you have the full title, 'United Kingdom of Great Britain and Northern Ireland' stated, and you have 'Government of the Republic of Ireland'. That, if I'm right, was insisted upon by both legal sides at the time, and was still necessary, despite the apparent commonality of article 1.

GARRET FITZGERALD: I have no difficulty giving the proper names.

NOEL DORR: It was done at the time, on a legal basis. It wasn't just a casual thing. Each side went back and checked it out. On the Irish side, if you said 'the United Kingdom of Great Britain and Northern Ireland', there was a fear that even that might be challenged in the courts as unconstitutional, and, on the British side, no doubt you had similar issues about 'Ireland' and 'Republic of Ireland'.

DERMOT NALLY: We went back to the 1920 Government of Ireland Act, the Treaty of 1921, the 1926 Heads of Financial Settlement between the British Government and the Government of the Irish Free State, the 1938 Agreement between the Government of Ireland and the United Kingdom, the Free Trade Area Agreement, 1965, Sunningdale, 1973, and so on. I have the list of how the two entities were described here with me, in the various treaties, etc.[44]

ROBERT ARMSTRONG: It's partly a matter, if I remember rightly, of the way in which the Anglo-Irish Agreement was designated as a treaty in the British system, and it was introduced in the treaty series. I suspect it was the Foreign Office that insisted on this.

NOEL DORR: The Irish side wanted it registered at the UN, too, and therefore it was a treaty under article 102 of the UN Charter, which says that all treaties must be registered.

Q: Hume says this is a statement of British neutrality; that it's effectively accepting that Northern Ireland can secede from the union, unlike Scotland or Wales.

GARRET FITZGERALD: But in the 1920s and 1930s, Britain was positive; in those days there was no inhibition about saying they wished to see a united Ireland. After the war, that neutrality disappeared, and unfortunately there wasn't a willingness to express the same view, and this brought us back. The initial positivity retreated.

NOEL DORR: Remember, the Anglo-Irish Treaty in 1921 was between Great Britain and Ireland, with a provision in article 11 or 12 for an opt-out by the then parliament of Northern Ireland.[45]

DERMOT NALLY: And the introductory part of the Government of Ireland Act, 1920, and then the king's speech at the time, expressing hope for a coming-together of the two parts of Ireland.[46]

GARRET FITZGERALD: It created an all-Ireland state.

NOEL DORR: It was expressed as 'Articles of Agreement for a Treaty between Ireland and Great Britain'. But there was a consciousness even then of Northern Ireland as a separate entity which had the right to opt out.

GARRET FITZGERALD: The British formulation was positive in the 1920s and right up to the 1938 Agreement, in a way it hasn't been more recently. So, we were always anxious to get that. We were thinking about republicans in all of this. We wanted to get as far as we could towards Britain showing goodwill, not to persuade, but to be open.

---

[44] See Subsection 1.2.1.

[45] For the official text of the treaty, see Second Schedule to the Constitution of the Irish Free State (Saorstát Éireann) Act, 1922.

[46] For the king's speech, see *Parliamentary Debates, Northern Ireland: Senate*, vol. 1, cols 8–10, 22 June 1921.

ROBERT ARMSTRONG: I think, from our point of view, the important features in 1(c) were the words 'formally consent' and the words and the promise 'to introduce and support legislation'. We'd not seen anything as definite as that before.[47]

3.4.3. Devolution

Q: Which of the other articles in the Agreement are the most important ones?

MICHAEL LILLIS: Prisons? How about security—very important.

NOEL DORR: Devolution is an aspect that needs to be touched on. My memory is that at a certain point in the negotiation we were thinking it could be combined with devolution, and I think the British side more or less made it clear, 'look, you're not going to have devolution if you have this Agreement.' Now that's a very crude and simplistic way of putting it, but what I mean is that it became clear that it wasn't really compatible with devolution. Nevertheless, it was written into the Agreement that this role for the Irish government would diminish precisely to the extent that the parties in Northern Ireland could agree to work together and therefore have devolved government.

There are three relevant references to devolution. The first relates to the issue we have been discussing—that is, that the Irish government could put forward views and proposals on Northern Ireland matters insofar as those matters had not become the responsibility of a devolved administration there. The second is article 4, where the British government says it's their policy to secure devolution on a basis that would secure widespread acceptance throughout the community. And then both governments agree that it can only be done with the cooperation of the constitutional representatives. Then article 4(c) says that the conference shall be a framework within which the Irish government would put forward views and proposals on the modalities for bringing about devolution.

So, if you like, the Irish government has a role in business in relation to Northern Ireland, which will diminish to the extent that devolution takes place. But the Irish government also has a role in putting forward views about bringing about devolution.

MICHAEL LILLIS: Can you read out the last phrase of that paragraph?

NOEL DORR: 'In so far as they relate to the interests of the minority community.'

MICHAEL LILLIS: Because we had to be sensitive about the unionists.

NOEL DORR: And then, finally, in relation to article 10, where, if responsibility is devolved, machinery will need to be established by the responsible parties both North and South for practical cooperation. So, the three elements are: firstly, a

---

[47] See Document 3.6.

role for the Irish government until and unless devolution takes place, a role which will diminish to the extent that it does take place; secondly, a voice as far as the interests of the minority are concerned in bringing about devolution; and, thirdly, if devolution were to take place, some arrangements regarding North–South need to be negotiated, about how North–South would work in that situation.

DAVID GOODALL: Am I not right that the possible diminution in the Irish government's role was intended as an inducement to the Northern Ireland parties, and particularly the unionists, to, so to speak, go along with the Agreement with the promise that if they could agree to power-sharing the consequence would be to diminish the role of the government of Ireland? But at one point in the negotiations it was nearly the cause of a breakdown altogether, because, if I remember rightly, you—I mean you, the Irish side— at some stage argued that the British were making the achievement of devolution a precondition of any other elements in the Agreement coming into effect. As this was not going to happen, this was going to derail the whole process. But at that point we hadn't really focused very much on devolution.

MICHAEL LILLIS: I think the solution, which was an elegant one, and to which a chap called Tony Brennan made quite a contribution, was that our role in relation to any of the processes involving devolution—whether setting it up or sustaining it, and, more importantly even in the end, if it didn't survive—that our role would be confined to representing the interest of the minority.[48] We weren't in any sense to be seen to be representing the entire community in Northern Ireland. So, I mean, that survived, it actually did work.

3.5. Implementation

3.5.1. The Impact on Unionism and Nationalism

NOEL DORR: Could I raise a point of broader importance about the general nature of the Agreement? Until then, the British government view was that it had sole responsibility for the population of Northern Ireland, while the aspiration of the Irish government to unity was such that, in theory, it too ought to be concerned about all the people of Northern Ireland. But there is a sense in which this Agreement, for the first time, is a matter of choosing sides. The British government would look after the unionist interests, and the Irish government would measure what the minority needed in order to end the alienation; and the British government would measure how far the unionists could live with that.

---

[48] Tony Brennan was Deputy Under-Secretary in the Northern Ireland Office, 1982–7.

I remember Ken Whittaker coming to see me in the Department of Foreign Affairs afterwards, when I was at home, expressing great worry about this, and he made the very point which I'm trying to make—that, until then, Irish governments had always considered, at least in theory and in principle, that they had to be concerned about everybody in Northern Ireland, because of their general aspiration.

GARRET FITZGERALD: He didn't like this at all.

NOEL DORR: He didn't like this idea, that you look after the unionists' interests and we'll look after the interests of the minority. This, perhaps, is a weakness of the Agreement, but the Agreement succeeded brilliantly in improving the relationship between the two governments. It did not succeed in its other aim of improving the relationship of the communities in Northern Ireland, because the unionists rejected it.

But part of the problem was that we were measuring very carefully what the minority, particularly the SDLP, would need, and the British side, we assumed, were doing the same with the unionists. After all, Jim Molyneaux was a privy councillor, and there were other privy councillors.[49] Chris Patten, as a junior minister, had gone around the Northern Ireland parties in May 1985 to see if devolution could be agreed.[50]

So, we assumed all along that the British side were measuring what the unionists could accept. My memory, and others may not agree, was that even weeks before the Agreement was announced we were uncertain as to which side would rubbish it when it came out. It was trying to maintain a balance. A crucial factor was that Seamus Mallon was persuaded to endorse it for the minority.[51] I still think that if Paisley or someone had come out and waved it in the air and said this was a wonderful success, then the other side would have taken it amiss and would have said this was a failure.

GARRET FITZGERALD: We were worried about the SDLP. I remember, in February 1985, John Hume said 'you'll have to tell Seamus Mallon', and I said 'well, will you tell him?'—'no, no, you've got to tell him'. So we got Peter Barry to brief him on the Agreement. I was very nervous indeed, naturally. Mallon came over then to dinner in Government Buildings and sat down and didn't comment too much on it initially—'OK, I won't give a view on it now, but I'm

---

[49] James Molyneaux, MP for South Antrim and later for Lagan Valley, was leader of the Ulster Unionist Party, 1979–85. His appointment to the Privy Council in 1982 meant that he could be briefed on confidential political and security questions while being subject to the norm that privy councillors are bound to secrecy on such matters.

[50] Chris Patten, MP, Conservative politician, was Parliamentary Under-Secretary of State in the Northern Ireland Office, 1983–5; he later became Governor of Hong Kong, 1992–7, and chaired the Independent Commission on Policing for Northern Ireland, 1998–9.

[51] Seamus Mallon, MP for Newry and Armagh, 1986–2005, was a long-standing SDLP politician, deputy leader of the party, 1979–2001, and Deputy First Minister, 1999–2001.

not opposing it at this stage'. But we didn't get his clearance until the Monday, two days before the Agreement was signed.

Q: There seems to be an absence of symmetry on the two sides?

GARRET FITZGERALD: Well, we did try our own soundings. But I understood, or misunderstood, that the British had consulted Molyneaux, which was reassuring, and our own consultations with other people on the unionist side who were involved were reasonably assuring. But it transpired subsequently, we were told, that Molyneaux had refused the Privy Council briefing.

DAVID GOODALL: That's right, yes.

GARRET FITZGERALD: On the other hand, in January 1986 I received a fax from Unionist headquarters saying that they knew all along about this Agreement, and that a civil servant briefed them fully throughout, and they knew all about it. They had also been told at the same time that Tebbit had been busy telling Molyneaux that there would be no agreement on articles 2 and 3; that they couldn't both be true at the same time.[52] So, I remained totally confused as to what the unionists did know, and perhaps you can help us on that.

DAVID GOODALL: Well, I don't know what Robert would say, but my recollection is that our impression was that the SDLP were closely consulted at every stage by the Irish side [*chorus of disagreement*].

DAVID GOODALL: Well, all right: it was Hume who was closely consulted. But John Hume, after all, was the leader of the SDLP, whereas on our side it was the great unionist grievance after the Agreement was signed that you had the SDLP with you at every stage, while the unionists had been kept in the dark and they hadn't been consulted. It wasn't until very near the end of the process, either July or August—August, I think—1985, that Molyneaux was offered a Privy Council briefing, and, under the influence, I think, of Enoch Powell, declined it.

GARRET FITZGERALD: We didn't know that.

DAVID GOODALL: No, I dare say not. But in one sense it was the great weakness of the Agreement that it was concluded over the heads of the unionists. On the other hand, it was also the strength of the Agreement, because, unlike Sunningdale, as Dermot said, it was an agreement between the two governments, and therefore it couldn't be overturned by the political parties. But this also meant that the unionists, who could indeed have seized a flag and waved it and said this is a very good agreement, were totally outraged by it. The fact is that the unionists' attitude up to and during the negotiation was so hostile to any accommodation with the idea of an Irish dimension in the North that it simply wouldn't have been possible to consult them as the negotiations went along.

---

[52] Norman Tebbit, a Conservative MP from 1970 until 1992, was a senior British cabinet minister (1981–87) and a trusted advisor of Margaret Thatcher.

ROBERT ARMSTRONG: Yes, I think that is quite fair, and I think it was deliberate. If there was some informal process going on, I certainly wasn't aware of that, and I think throughout this we were thinking that the deliberate decision had been taken not to consult the unionists as we went along. But we and our political masters and mistress had to look at it to see if they thought that they would get away with it, or whether we would have a repeat of the Ulster workers' strike.[53] The calculation was that they would not like it at all, but they wouldn't go to the barricades about it.

GARRET FITZGERALD: We were getting the same sense from some unionists also, from June and July onwards. They didn't like it, but they would live with it. A major problem was that we couldn't get to Molyneaux. I twice tried to arrange to meet with Molyneaux, and, though he initially agreed, both attempts ended in failure.

ROBERT ARMSTRONG: What I don't know is how far the Prime Minister briefed Ian Gow. I think it is possible, because you know that Ian Gow resigned.[54]

GARRET FITZGERALD: Sure. But she didn't tell the unionists. But then, you see, the message I got from the unionists' headquarters was that they were informed by the civil service and knew everything that was in the Agreement.

DAVID GOODALL: There's a difference between the unionists being consulted, and what they learned through these unofficial contacts, and probably through Ian Gow and others. What stuck in their throats was that they were never officially informed about what was going on. So, they knew enough about it to know that they were going to greatly dislike it, but they weren't actually offered an official briefing on it until almost the whole thing was set in concrete.

ROBERT ARMSTRONG: Well, it was a deliberate decision.

Q: What did the Irish government expect the British government was going to deliver in terms of unionist support?

ROBERT ARMSTRONG: Throughout the process, and particularly towards the end of it, we were looking over our shoulders to see how this would go down with the unionists, and we had to make our own calculations about that, and we didn't try and push it further.

DAVID GOODALL: And Douglas Hurd said that now we really must, we really must, tell the unionists where the negotiations have got to.

DERMOT NALLY: The British attitude right to 1993—when I finally left Northern Ireland issues—was that they would not act as persuaders one way or the other.

NOEL DORR: I think our understanding was that they were measuring what they would get away with vis-à-vis the unionists. You've got to remember the background at the time. Unionists, and the unionist interest generally, had pulled down Sunningdale. The general idea of a Council of Ireland was

---

[53] See Subsections 2.1.3 and 2.4.1.   [54] See n. 14.

rejected; the Irish dimension was dismissed, so to speak. There was also the power-sharing issue, which didn't seem to be acceptable either. Chris Patten, as a junior minister, had been delegated in May 1985 to go around and make a last effort to get devolution in Northern Ireland on the basis of power-sharing, and he got nowhere on that.

So there was a feeling on the part of the British government, and presumably the Irish government, that we had better go ahead with this. This way the two governments will do it. We won't get the parties in Northern Ireland involved, but we will leave room and an incentive for them to eventually agree to devolution. They had their last chance, as they were already rejecting both power-sharing on the unionist side and an Irish dimension. Their last chance was the Patten effort. The British side was warning us, I think, that it'll be a long time before you get devolution. But we were seeing it as a built-in incentive here, and the justification for agreement.

MICHAEL LILLIS: Sorry, there's an argument, and this is mine—that the Agreement actually worked in terms of devolution and that is a surprising thing to say.

NOEL DORR: In the long run.

DERMOT NALLY: It was the same argument that Peter Hain used later with the unionists before the St Andrews Agreement to get the executive in the North into execution: 'If you don't get your act together and form an executive in the North, then the two governments will consult together about the administra-tion of the place.' It is one of the really important points in the 1985 Agree-ment, but the unionists were too busy reacting to take any notice of it then.

Q: Since the Irish government had a sponsorship role in relation to the national-ists, why then was the reciprocal idea not put in place, or the unionists given something to address this?

ROBERT ARMSTRONG: We were in direct rule.

NOEL DORR: The thinking of the Agreement was to redress an existing imbalance. Your question implies that you're approaching it on the basis of constructing a balance. But the thinking on the Irish side was always that there's been a terrible imbalance which needs to be redressed. Therefore, you talk about the interests of the minority community and how to bring them in to accept the reality of Northern Ireland, which is set out in article 1. The reality is that there will be no unity until a majority consents.

DAVID GOODALL: That is true, but that inevitably created a feeling in the unionist community that I amply understand, that it was all about redressing a balance in favour of the minority community. The minority community had their spokesmen and guarantors in the shape of the Irish government, and they had no such guarantor, because the British government took the position that, as there was direct rule in Northern Ireland, we had equal responsibility for both communities. So, who is left to speak for us, the unionists? It was very understandable.

NOEL DORR: We didn't expect the British side to act as persuaders. We were relying on them to measure what could be got away with, without putting the unionists to flight altogether, so to speak. It was up to them to measure what was just about tolerable. It was up to us to measure what was just about necessary from the viewpoint of the minority. Those two would come together. I would like to just ask my Irish colleagues, am I right in my memory that even a few weeks before the Agreement appeared in November 1985, we were unsure as to which side would greet it with pleasure and which side would reject it? Now maybe that's wrong.

SEÁN DONLON: Well, sorry, one footnote is important. I mean Garret has mentioned Seamus Mallon was not on board until the Monday evening. The other person was Eddie McGrady.[55] John Hume specifically asked us about two weeks beforehand would we brief Eddie McGrady. When McGrady was briefed, he indicated his approval. Seamus Mallon held out, and in fact I think it was Daithi Ó Ceallaigh who persuaded Seamus Mallon in a very, very lengthy conversation, over that particular weekend.[56] So, it wasn't simply a question of briefing John Hume and assuming because he was happy that the SDLP were on board.

MICHAEL LILLIS: I had a lot of talk with the SDLP at the time. When they saw this Agreement, they couldn't believe it. They could not believe that this was possible, and they were stunned with joy. That applied readily to Mallon all the way along as well—he pretended certain things, and he was in touch with the opposition, and all of that. But we weren't in the slightest doubt that this was going to be OK.

DAVID GOODALL: Once Douglas Hurd became Northern Ireland Secretary at some point along the road, he certainly raised the issue of consulting the unionists. The Prime Minister said 'no, this is not the time to reveal this, because it would be a wrecking move; it will wreck it'. I think it was the right judgement. I remember discussing this immediately afterwards with John Dunlop, the Presbyterian Moderator, who has always struck me as a most reasonable and wise man, and he was so hurt and angry: 'how could you do this without consulting us, without letting us know?' I said, 'well, because your community made it so clear from the very start that they wouldn't tolerate any kind of accommodation with the South, if we had consulted you there wouldn't have been a negotiation'. And he said 'well, I think perhaps that's true'.

---

[55] Eddie McGrady was a founding member of the SDLP and long-running candidate for South Down, a constituency he won in a close contest with the sitting MP, Enoch Powell, in 1987 and held until 2010. He was also a Member of the Legislative Assembly (MLA) for South Down, 1998–2003.
[56] Daithi Ó Ceallaigh was an official in the Department of Foreign Affairs, later head of the Anglo-Irish Division (2000–1), and ambassador to the United Kingdom (2001–7).

NOEL DORR: Apparently, Harold McCusker was another one who was deeply, deeply hurt by this.[57]

DERMOT NALLY: We just had the memory of Sunningdale and what had happened, and we were not going to leave ourselves open to the same things happening again.

NOEL DORR: Interestingly, we never mentioned the Brighton bomb or any bombs at this time.[58]

DERMOT NALLY: Oh, that was before Chequers, 1984.

DAVID GOODALL: Well, now that you have mentioned it, I don't know what Robert would say, but I thought it was one of the remarkable instances of Mrs Thatcher's courage and determination. I thought after the Brighton bomb, 'that's the end of this negotiation'. It hadn't got very far.

GARRET FITZGERALD: So did we.

DAVID GOODALL: But she carried on; whatever she felt, she carried on almost as though it hadn't happened.

DERMOT NALLY: Not only did she carry on as if nothing had happened, but she—Garret, I may be wrong in this—my recollection is that she said 'would you ever tell the people in Ireland that violence will not ever win; I want that message to be put across; the British people will never, never, never yield to violence, or threats of violence'. She put on one of the most vigorous and most admirable performances of courage and conviction that I have ever seen—this from a woman who a day or two before, by a simple event of fortune (Robin Butler told me about it), had escaped assassination or mutilation. This is on the morning after, when she had nearly been murdered.

3.5.2. Security

Q: On the question of implementation, how far do you think the full potential of the Agreement was realized, and if you think that it wasn't, why was this the case?

GARRET FITZGERALD: Well, there were four issues on security, which was our primary concern. We eventually got agreements in principle in Milan that were incorporated into the Agreement, though not as specifically as I had remembered in the communiqué. These issues included the possible release of

---

[57] Harold McCusker, Deputy Leader of the Ulster Unionist Party Assembly Group, 1982–6, and UUP MP for Upper Bann, 1983–90, resigned his seat in protest at the Anglo-Irish Agreement in 1985, along with all other sitting unionist MPs. He was re-elected in the 1986 Upper Bann by-election and retained the seat until his death in 1990.

[58] On 12 October 1984, during the Conservative Party's annual conference, an IRA bomb in the conference hotel in Brighton killed five people and injured many others, including Norman Tebbit and his wife; Mrs Thatcher narrowly escaped injury.

prisoners and a significant reduction in violence. We strengthened the provision about that significant reduction in violence. There was the police code of conduct; there was accompaniment of patrols; and there were the courts. They were the four issues, none of which emerged quite in the form that we had hoped. Now let's take each of these.

- The prisoners: we were approached, I think by your side. I had to say, look, we are not happy about the whole thing, but in the closing speech on the Agreement in the Commons there would be some mention of the possible release of prisoners and eventually the reduction in violence. We consented to that because we felt we understood your sensitivity to unionist feeling at the time. That was finally put in a year later by Nick Scott, I think, in a debate in the Commons, and it got no publicity whatsoever.[59] We had thought it would be important at the time. So, that was a bit of a disappointment, but we agreed to that.
- The courts: we've discussed [this] already.
- The conduct of the police: we got no value from it at all, as they subsequently didn't implement it, as I recall, although I'm open to correction on these things.
- And the other one, which was the most striking of all, was we had this provision that the Ulster Defence Regiment would 'operate only in support of the civil power, with the particular objective of ensuring, as rapidly as possible, that, save in the most exceptional circumstances, there is a police presence in all operations between the UDR patrols and the community'.

The last of these was vitally important, because there were all these patrols going around with the army arresting people, and we had always seen the role of the army anywhere as being to support the civil power—the police should do the arresting. If there's a danger of the police anywhere being shot, soldiers will protect them. We're all in favour of that, but we want to get to the stage where the police will do the arresting.

In the discussion on that issue, we understood that about one-third of patrols were not accompanied at that time. When we discussed the exceptional circumstances, what we were told, as I recall, was that, well, yes, if the police constable didn't turn up in time for the patrol, the patrol could go ahead. That's the exceptional circumstances. In the event, we understood that no significant change took place in this accompaniment, and I would never discover why this part of the Agreement, which we thought was extremely important, was not implemented, and I'm still puzzled about that.

[59] Nicholas Scott, MP, was Parliamentary Secretary at the Northern Ireland Office, 1981–6, and Minister of State there, 1986–7.

Q: Could we ask the British side if they have any comment to make on this?

DAVID GOODALL: I can't comment on it really, because I'm afraid my involvement really ended. I went to India, where there were other problems.

ROBERT ARMSTRONG: I think I'd probably retired, which I did at the end of 1987, and I don't remember, I'm afraid. I mean, I think the right things were said, but they didn't happen on the ground.

GARRET FITZGERALD: No, we found it puzzling that you had agreed so readily to accept in the exceptional circumstances the police were not turning up—in fact, no change took place at all.

TED HALLETT: I'm not sure it's correct to say that no change took place at all. There were efforts to ensure that UDR patrols were accompanied, but it took a very long time to register the difference.

NOEL DORR: You might just recall, it was a big issue at the time; it was taking the place of real police reform, so to speak. That was the substitute. That was the closest we got to that issue at that time, and, therefore, it was very important for the Irish side.

MICHAEL LILLIS: I was the Joint Secretary of the Anglo-Irish secretariat when this thing was launched, and we had an interesting group of people there, both on the British side certainly, excellent colleagues, and, on our side, my deputy was Daithi Ó Ceallaigh, whom you all know is the current ambassador in London. Daithi, on his own initiative, invented a very interesting mechanism which we called the log. This was literally implementing the Agreement in detail. The Irish side would make proposals, list the proposal, date it, and then there was a record of everything that happened. There was supposed to be a record of determined efforts where there was a difference to be resolved, and we had that. I'm told that this is continued today.[60]

We set about trying to make as many sensible proposals as we could from the word go, and get this thing to get a life of its own, so to speak. The record was very mixed. Now, let me just say, right up front, that the main event that took place, and which lasted for several months, was the unionist reaction to the Agreement. It was actually violent; police were attacked, and we were attacked in Maryfield all the time. It was a huge event, in that the RUC under Hermon—and I have a lot of criticism of Hermon and we'll come to that—I thought they were very firm and strong, and they did their job.[61] Tom King had just been appointed as Secretary of State. He and I got on very well on a personal basis, but he certainly didn't seem too happy with the Agreement, if I may say so.

---

[60] For a fascinating account of the operation of the Anglo-Irish secretariat in the form of a witness seminar, see Lillis (2016).

[61] Sir John Hermon rose through the ranks to be Chief Constable of the Royal Ulster Constabulary, 1980–9.

We met regularly, you know, we worked through a process and tried to get the thing moving on our various issues, and we did have some successes. Actually, we had quite a list. There were lots of things that were important to nationalists which were actually cleared up in the year that followed the Agreement. The reform of the police, that's actually more or less specified in one of the articles of the Agreement as being something that would be addressed, and we had several meetings with Sir John Hermon. So, when we reviewed the log at the end of the year, I would have to say that it was a disappointing product. There's no question about that. On the other hand, there was stuff that we didn't put in the log, which was that the overwhelming issue had been the unionist reaction, which proved that this Agreement involved a shifting of sectarian plates.

NOEL DORR: Once the Agreement is signed, its implementation becomes a matter for the Northern Ireland Office, and what was particularly important at that time was Tom King taking over. He may have got on well with you, but he and Peter Barry just grated off each other when we started meetings of the Anglo-Irish Intergovernmental Conference.

We, as officials on the Irish side, were so concerned at this that we tried to find a way where there would be less, if you like, asperity in their relationship. So, we suggested that they should meet for ten or fifteen minutes beforehand without officials, and then come out to the conference. It is fine for Robert and David and the rest of us to think up ideas, but the Northern Ireland Office people felt they had to carry this out, and it may have proved quite difficult on the ground.

GARRET FITZGERALD: We understand all the pressures, but nonetheless the British government formally agreed to this specific wording here and it didn't happen—virtually, hardly at all. We never got much beyond 65 per cent, never reached 70 per cent.[62] It's difficult because, you know, you sign an agreement, and it is specific in a point; you expect it to happen. It is not an agreement with the Northern Ireland Office or with Tom King; it is an agreement with Her Majesty's Government, and it is expected that will happen, and I kept raising this issue, and nothing happened. I have never understood how someone could sign their name and not have it implemented.

DAVID GOODALL: Well, Garret, there are two different things there, aren't there? One is whether what you say happened or not, and I think it did happen; and the other is why you can't understand why it happened. I think you have had the explanation, really. Once the Agreement—Robert will tell me if I am out of court—once the Agreement was signed and it had been achieved and, you know, there was a great sigh of relief from the Prime Minister and everybody,

---

[62] These figures refer to the percentages of UDR patrols that were accompanied by police.

and a feeling that now we can think about other things that are even more important, and so on. Now, they can all get on with it; and getting on with it was the business of the Northern Ireland Office.

Tom King—it is no secret he didn't like the Agreement. He came in at the very end; he hadn't taken part in any of the negotiations. He was dismayed by the whole thing; didn't like it; didn't think it was going to be operable; was strongly against having a joint secretariat in Belfast and was, I am exaggerating a bit, dragged into it. He didn't like it, and the Northern Ireland Office also had all the misgivings which Noel is talking about, because they were saying to themselves, to put it brutally, here are these bright chaps, the Cabinet Secretary and this renegade diplomat from the Foreign Office and others pushing us into this thing, leaving us to pick up the pieces, which is going to be bad news, which is going to enrage the unionist community—their bright ideas are going to lead to us having to deal with the mess.

That's it, you know, basically. So inevitably they didn't want to hurry, and the fact that the unionist community were up in arms made them even more reluctant to do things on the ground, which would then add to the fury of the unionist community. Now that may not be admirable, but that is the explanation.

DERMOT NALLY: For anyone that is interested in the details, I think if we had sufficient prescience we could have foreseen what would happen from an incident during the negotiation when the representative of the Northern Ireland Office was showing a great deal of reserve about a particular proposal for inclusion in the draft agreement. He was only moved to acceptance by some pretty strong words from Robert—the Northern Ireland Office were never, as far as I could see, enthusiastic supporters of what was happening. That feeling percolated to the workings of the joint secretariat, where they had a major role. In fact, they were required to implement things that they had huge reservations about.

A formal review of the Agreement took place in 1989. This is a list. 'Explicit confirmation of the policy pursued since 1984 that wherever possible patrols by the armed forces that were likely to be encountered by the public should be accompanied by a member of the RUC. Improvements in the procedure for handling complaints about the police. RUC has made considerable efforts to increase the level of recruitment from the minority community. The RUC Chief Constable has introduced a new code of conduct for RUC officers, placed in the House of Commons library on 15 March 1998. The Police Authority for Northern Ireland, Chief Constable have, etc. etc.' There is a whole string of 'improvements' listed.

GARRET FITZGERALD: Note that that is not the wording of what was agreed. It didn't say 'wherever possible'; it said 'save in the most exceptional circumstances' and 'as rapidly as possible', so that wording is not the wording agreed, and the issues about policing had nothing to do with the issue. Was that pursued as persistently as I was pursuing it when the government changed?

DERMOT NALLY: I doubt it. I tell you, when Mr Haughey came into government in 1987, the first parliamentary question to him was—would you please tell us Taoiseach, your attitude to the Anglo-Irish Agreement. The question comes around to me for an answer. So I put three or four words together and gave it to the Taoiseach—who had so stridently opposed the Agreement. It came back as a complete redraft, but the main point that came back was to the effect that 'this government abides by international agreements', and that was that. The Agreement was not going to be withdrawn or reneged on.

ROBERT ARMSTRONG: Do you remember, Dermot, when I came to visit you in Dublin after Haughey came in? It was one of the last things while I was Cabinet Secretary. I came over to see you and you took me in to see Charlie Haughey. It was quite soon after he had become Taoiseach again, and he said to me, 'You will know that I opposed the Anglo-Irish Agreement negotiations when I was in opposition; now I am in government I realize that we have never had such a good agreement out of the British before, and I should be out of my mind to reject it except in favour of something better.'

NOEL DORR: A few months after Mr Haughey came to office I recall a particular meeting around a table with him where he was expressing some exasperation at some British position. I then tried to explain what their position was, and he kind of turned on me and said: 'Dorr, if you think that I am going to give up the Anglo-Irish Agreement then you are very much mistaken.' I felt it was he who had negotiated it and I was coming in from outside.

SEÁN DONLON: The attitude of the Northern Ireland Office was unhelpful. I spent three or four days with Robert Andrew in September 1985 looking for premises for the joint secretariat.[63] I was astonished at how negative he was. He also brought in the point as to how could we possibly tell the British army what to do. That is a matter for the Secretary of State for Defence. No one in the Northern Ireland Office, no one in Downing Street, no one can tell the army what to do except MOD [the Ministry of Defence]. I don't think MOD had been consulted on this point.

ROBERT ARMSTRONG: They must have been consulted about the words they would use, I would think.

SEÁN DONLON: But their heart wasn't in it.

ROBERT ARMSTRONG: Their heart wasn't in it.

DAVID GOODALL: I think there were problems. The UDR was again a highly neuralgic thing—and I don't know why. We had a lot of complaints, not least from Seán, I remember, about the way the UDR behaved.

[63] Sir Robert Andrew was Permanent Under-Secretary at the Northern Ireland Office, 1984–8.

In August 1985 the UDR happened to be commanded by a man I was in the army with, we were subalterns together. He was a British regular officer, a Brigadier Preston. I wanted to see for myself what the UDR were like. We went and stayed a weekend with the Prestons, and he was an absolutely straight, regular British brigadier with a very strong sense of duty and all those things. He gave me an absolutely straight briefing with his chief of staff, and then he took me around to visit three UDR battalions—and I could tell you many stories about that.

Anyway, when I had finished, I thought that there were three things which could be done which would be painless. It doesn't bear directly on this question of the police, but I thought, first of all, that the establishment figure for the UDR, which was way above the actual establishment, could be reduced, that it would be clear that the UDR was not meant to be increased. I thought that the proportion of regular officers to local volunteer officers could be increased. And I thought that the areas over which the UDR operated could be somewhat reduced.

I put all those proposals to the Commander-in-Chief, Land Forces, in Northern Ireland, and he said 'well, I think those are worth doing'. I came back and I saw the Chief of Defence Staff in London, and he thought they were a good idea too. But I don't think any of them happened. I remember that when we discussed them at a meeting with the Prime Minister when Geoffrey Howe was away—Robert was there—and I tried to make a pitch for this, the Prime Minister said to me, 'I thought you were meant to be on our side', and Douglas Hurd was very, very [...] I mean he poured cold water over me. He did not want the UDR touched. But I don't quite know why that was.

NOEL DORR: The point is we talk about the UDR as part of the British army, and so on, but the reality on the ground was that the UDR was created in substitution for the B-Specials—it was a way of sanitizing the B-Specials and bringing them into the army. From the point of view of the minority, the UDR was your neighbours with guns and authority and a uniform at a barricade at night.

DAVID GOODALL: That's perfectly true. At the first UDR battalion I was introduced to, the commanding officer said, 'I would like you to meet my regimental sergeant major', and a huge man with a moustache in combat uniform came over to me and held out a great hand and said: 'Good morning, Mr Goodall, welcome to Northern Ireland—we hear you are from the Foreign Office; we hope you are not here to make a foreign country of us.'

MICHAEL LILLIS: We were extremely disappointed about this. It was an opportunity lost in many, many ways.

ROBERT ARMSTRONG: I don't know—I can't remember, even if I do—I certainly thought that this instruction had been given, and that they would be doing it, as they could get the policemen there, except in exceptional circumstances. I don't think I ever really found out whether that was happening.

GARRET FITZGERALD: I did raise it with you.

NOEL DORR: But when people are reluctant to implement, the exceptional circumstances will always prevail—there is an 'out' built into it. That is the simple explanation.

GARRET FITZGERALD: That was made very clear, but let me just say, I was pressed by Margaret Thatcher during 1986 to implement changes here in our police. There were sixteen different things she wanted done. There were two which were not to be implemented. One involved a splitting of authority in our system. We had a unified command; in a sense, there was one person in charge, and this proposed change seemed to me to weaken the system, and some other thing like that. Michael went home, saw the Minister for Justice, and saw the police, and we had the fourteen things done at once. That's the way you govern, and I found the British system a bit disappointing in this respect.

3.5.3. Politics after the Agreement

GARRET FITZGERALD: We must come to the unionist reaction, because first of all my recollection is that we were fearful of more violence on both sides. I think we took some steps to strengthen the army at that point, which we had not done previously.

DERMOT NALLY: Nothing very significant.

GARRET FITZGERALD: I think we did add some numbers, and we thought there could be quite a lot of violence, which didn't happen in that form. Unionist reaction was certainly more vigorous than we had anticipated, but I don't know what lay behind these things. It is possible, I suppose, that the two leaders, Paisley and Molyneaux, felt that in order to minimize the danger of violence, a public reaction was required.

NOEL DORR: I was at the first meeting of the Anglo-Irish Intergovernmental Conference in Stormont, and Michael was too. I think we sat in the government council chamber in Stormont. If you think from a unionist point of view, what that meant was that Dublin ministers were coming up and sitting—they were outside protesting—and Dublin ministers were sitting at the table in Stormont. It's not hard to understand their sense of violation or outrage at that, having resisted for forty, fifty years, whatever it was.

GARRET FITZGERALD: But the expression of it and the form it took may have helped to minimize violence; it had the exact effect that we intended in switching support back to the SDLP. It is odd, but I don't think unionists ever realized what a constructive move it was to protest the way they did, because, in fact, the security issues we had agreed, none of them happened quite the way we thought, or at the time we thought. We got a lot of things done under it. We were asked not to make an announcement of these achievements. We avoided claiming any results from the Agreement, not to aggravate the unionist side.

Eventually, later on, there was a swing back on the nationalist side. They didn't see the practical results on the security side. We had a conference here in the university some years ago. What emerged was that Sinn Féin were enormously impressed by the Agreement, that if I could get that far with Margaret Thatcher, then maybe they could get somewhere.[64]

SEÁN DONLON: I would regard one of the achievements of the Anglo-Irish Agreement, an unintended achievement, was that it facilitated Sinn Féin and the IRA to come in from the cold into the system.

MICHAEL LILLIS: I told David about this at the time. At the request of Mary Holland, whom many of us will remember, I had three meetings with Gerry Adams.[65] Two of them lasted a full day in her house here in Dublin, and I should stress very carefully, for people who are going to read this, the form of the discussions.

I had retired from the civil service for several months at this stage. She thought that it would be very useful for Adams to have an opportunity to talk to somebody about the whole situation, but, specifically, the Anglo-Irish Agreement. We had a meeting. We spent the first hour of the meeting—I just insisted on saying to him about how much I deplored the violence of the IRA and how shaming it was, etc., for me as an Irishman, and he took that patiently.

He questioned me for the rest of the time that we were together, and I did my best to give him the truth as far as I could represent it. His focus was on the Anglo-Irish Agreement quite a bit, on article 1, on British long-term intentions—that sort of stuff on how the British government works. He was very interested to know how to deal with the British government. He had already been in discussion with government officials.

He didn't, and I didn't ask him, say whether he thought the Agreement was a good thing or not because it was perfectly obvious that he thought it was; he even said that he thought it was an important move on the side of the British. I share Seán's view and that of the others that the Agreement certainly contributed, and I'm very glad that it did, to getting those people to move into politics—and away from violence.

---

[64] On 4 December 2000, Mitchel McLaughlin of Sinn Féin engaged in an exchange with Garret FtizGerald, from which this point emerged, in the course of an evening lecture series hosted by the Institute for British–Irish Studies, UCD; see McLaughlin (2001).

[65] Mary Holland (1935–2004) was a journalist working for the *Observer* and, later, the *Irish Times*.

3.6. The Significance of the Agreement

3.6.1. The Role of Civil Servants

Q: How important is continuity in the civil service in developing these Anglo-Irish relationships?

DERMOT NALLY: Well, I was there from 1973 to 1993, working directly with five different taoisigh, at different times, of course, as secretary to the government, or Cabinet Secretary in Robert's terms—from Sunningdale to the Downing Street Declaration. I tried to retire in January 1993, but I was hauled back in April by Albert Reynolds, and then in June finally immersed once again in the negotiations, this time of the Downing Street Declaration, mainly with Cabinet Secretary Robin Butler and Secretary to the Northern Ireland Office, John Chilcot. Seán Ó hUiginn and I worked on that project, including many visits to the Cabinet Office in London, with Martin Mansergh.[66] So, that's my record of continuity.

NOEL DORR: I was also there from 1973 to the 1990s, during the Downing Street Declaration, but I think that raises, without going into too much detail, another question, the advent of Mr Haughey to government, and the degree of continuity there. Dermot and I, I think, were the two; Michael and Seán left. I came back to Dublin as Secretary General, as they say now, in March 1987, just on the cusp of the transition between the two governments. Peter Barry was the minister as I came back, and within a week there was a new minister and a new government. I replaced Seán; Michael was still there; but there was a period of a few months of some suspicion and tension about Foreign Affairs and a belief that it had been too politicized. One of the things I like to think that we succeeded in doing is re-establishing a degree of confidence in the professional civil service. Dermot was very much handling that, I think, across the road in Merrion Street.[67] Within a few months, as I said, Mr Haughey more or less believed that he had negotiated the Agreement.

Q: Was the Anglo-Irish Agreement the result of a learning process that started at Sunningdale?

DERMOT NALLY: The negotiation and the parties to the Anglo-Irish Agreement— the way it was negotiated—were the result of the lessons of Sunningdale.

GARRET FITZGERALD: It started with the treaty in 1921.

DAVID GOODALL: I think you need people who have had a lot of experience and actually know what the whole problem is, but you also need one or two people who come to it new. Otherwise, you get so bogged down over the precedent of

---

[66] Dr Martin Mansergh was an advisor on Northern Ireland to successive taoisigh; see Subsection 1.4.1, Ch. 1, n. 28, and Appendix 1.1.
[67] A reference to the address of the Department of the Taoiseach.

what is possible, and you've been around it all before, and so on. If you have people who have no experience doing the whole thing, then that's a recipe for disaster, so I think, I don't know whether Robert would agree, I think you do need both.

ROBERT ARMSTRONG: Well, my own continuity really came from having my first close involvement in July or August 1971, when we were coming up to internment—then, of course, through that autumn and winter, and the Bloody Sunday events, and what followed that. Then I went off to the Home Office for a bit, and then came back. I felt that I'd had an involvement in Anglo-Irish business over quite a long time, and, as I said at the outset, I got to know Dermot, and there was an element of personal continuity in that.

I think I said elsewhere that you couldn't sit around the cabinet table in London and talk about Irish business without thinking of all the people who'd done that before you over the last 200 years. Here was our opportunity to add something to that story, and something better than had gone before. On the actual impact of the Anglo-Irish Agreement, I retired fairly soon afterwards, but my impression is that it actually was a turning point in relations between the two governments. It did establish this sense of trust, certainly at the official level, and to some extent at ministerial level. This has permeated things between the two governments more or less since that time; I personally think that without the Agreement Mr Blair and Mr Ahern wouldn't have got the Belfast Agreement, or even have started to get it. I think it was a turning point in the relations between the two governments. They had been rather distant, and certainly there had been too much megaphone diplomacy, and that changed, because of the process of the Agreement as much as what the Agreement itself contained.

DAVID GOODALL: It's difficult when you have been so involved with it to make a dispassionate judgement. Obviously, one of the big changes was that it actually for the first time admitted the Republic of Ireland into a real say in the affairs of Northern Ireland, hence all the unionists were unhappy. That was the big change, and that over time, although the unionists continued to hate it, they came to accept it. If that hadn't happened, there wouldn't have been a Belfast Agreement either, so in that sense I think that's true, and I think also that the fact that it brings the Irish government into it is important.

On whatever basis you like to define it, the business of running Northern Ireland greatly helped to promote understanding between ministers and officials, without which, again, the thing wouldn't have happened. So, although it didn't do what we hoped it would do—which as far as I'm concerned was bringing together the moderates on both sides, and isolating the extremists—it didn't do that, but it did create the conditions which made the subsequent progress possible, I think.

3.6.2. The Legacy of the Agreement

ROBERT ARMSTRONG: I'd just like to add, so long as she remained in government, Margaret Thatcher was resolute in her support of the Anglo-Irish
Agreement. You didn't see any sign of wavering from that, and she put
down any suggestion that came from other people that she should in some
way disown it or go away from it. It is only since she retired that she appears to
have suffered some sudden change of heart about it.

NOEL DORR: On the Anglo-Irish Agreement generally, I think, as I said earlier, it
did as others have said; it did make a huge difference to the relationship
between the two governments. Furthermore, there was an accepted channel,
which was the conference and the secretariat, for sorting out problems; that
was very good. It didn't succeed in its other aim of bringing reconciliation and
settlement between communities in Northern Ireland.

I see the Good Friday Agreement as constructed from a series of building
blocks stretching from Sunningdale, through the Anglo-Irish Agreement to
the Good Friday Agreement, and other things in between. If you indulge me
for a moment, at Sunningdale the things that emerged and became subsequently important were, first of all, the 'Irish dimension', which appeared in
the Green Paper in 1972, and which was given more worth, perhaps, than
might have been intended.[68] It meant that the problem was not finally settled
in 1920–1; it meant that it wasn't a claim by the South on the North; it meant
that intrinsic to the issue in Northern Ireland was an 'Irish dimension', and
that became the focus for Sunningdale, and it took further form in the Anglo-
Irish Agreement.

The second element that emerged was power-sharing, and that was very
important. Now, those two ideas have remained and carried forward. The
third one was a developing concept of 'consent', which took a rather poor form
there at Sunningdale, with the two parallel declarations, but it began to develop
further as we went on.

The Anglo-Irish Agreement then contributed a fleshing-out of the 'Irish
dimension' in a new way, which meant the Irish government had a role for the
first time in Northern Ireland, with a provision for devolution. That was a real
development of the Irish dimension. But both Sunningdale and the Anglo-
Irish Agreement were predicated on building from the centre outwards:
getting agreement with the centre moderate parties, thereby minimizing the
support for violence, and then acting firmly and resolutely against that violence. That was the concept then.[69]

---

[68] See the extended discussion in Subsection 2.2.3.
[69] See Subsections 2.4.1 and 4.3.5.

What has emerged newly since is that, on the basis of this Agreement, as Garret and others have said, people were weaned away from violence, and the Good Friday Agreement then, for the first time, tried to bring all concerned around the table, including those who had now turned, however half-heartedly at first, from violence. But the rest of the building blocks were very similar to what had gone before. In a sense, even though Sinn Féin and the former IRA and some others have come in, there's still a feeling of building on what is now the much wider centre ground and acting resolutely against the remaining dissidents.

DERMOT NALLY: Jack Lynch—I don't know where it was—was told that Northern Ireland is not your business. That was towards 1972. That situation has changed totally. It has always been part of the strategy of all the taoisigh that I have worked with that you can't get security unless you have support of the community. In order to get support of the community, you must end alienation. That has been a continuing thread throughout every negotiation. You can't get a solution; you cannot even get decent security when you don't have political and community support.

The other thread coming through every negotiation is that articles 2 and 3 are there, or were there, and, OK, we feel that they can be changed, but in order to change them we need something to show in exchange, and the question was—what is that something? And how big, or how small, can it be? That was the second question.

The third issue, certainly at the latter stages of the relationship, was: please do not be too insistent, or please do not create a situation where the British will get out of Northern Ireland, because that will be disaster. Total. If the British are to get out of Northern Ireland, it must be done by agreement. Following from that, I would like to thank Robert for what emerges from Bernard Donoughue's diaries.[70] It was something that all of us guessed, or we knew, when Harold Wilson was toying with the idea of something that was a 'known unknown'.[71] I think that there's a huge debt owed to him from this country for what he did at that time.

There was a fourth issue: David Goodall's part in the negotiations was also extraordinarily positive. He was the man who saw a trap in every place, and who, with the best will in the world, bowled innumerable googlies at us sitting on the other side of the table. Mrs Thatcher developed a great admiration for his perspicuity and his pertinacity; the Agreement is the better for his work.

[70] This is a reference to Robert Armstrong's resistance to the notion of a British withdrawal from Northern Ireland when this was being contemplated by Harold Wilson in May 1974; see Donoughue (2006: 129–33) and Subsection 2.4.2.

[71] A phrase popularized by US Defence Secretary Donald Rumsfeld in 2002 in making the case for invading Iraq.

SEÁN DONLON: Very briefly, I think the significance of the Agreement for Dublin was that it obviously gave us a role in Northern Ireland, but more important than that, I think, was the new relationship between Dublin and London. I came back into public service in Ireland when John Bruton became Taoiseach, and I was astonished at the ease of contact between the two governments, compared to what it had been ten years earlier—not just between Dermot's successors and Robert's successors, but between the two prime ministers. They were lifting up the phone almost to discuss football matches that neither knew anything about, and I believe that is probably its major contribution, because that has made an awful lot of things possible.

On the negative side, I think clearly it did, in the short term, deepen the split in Northern Ireland between nationalism and unionism. But eventually, I think, that is healing, and because it was influential in bringing the IRA inside the tent, I think it was a price worth paying.

DERMOT NALLY: The situation now is that Northern Ireland is welcome to join the South with agreement from the other island, and to join has tremendous advantages for North and South if the conditions are right, but that policy is a policy of invitation, it has nothing to do with agitation, it has nothing to do with violence.

TED HALLETT: The main benefit from my perspective is the greatly improved relationship between the two governments by providing this institutionalized framework for resolving differences. Over a period, after the initial difficulties of implementation, it did greatly improve relations between the two governments. In the longer term, after the painful unionist reaction, it did enable us to move to a situation in which unionists were prepared both to accept an institutionalized Irish dimension and power-sharing, which they probably wouldn't have done without the Agreement.

MICHAEL LILLIS: I agree with everything that's been said so far. I took the opportunity earlier to say how excited I had been by that proposal that you both brought to us in Dublin. What it showed to me was that the British side were thinking extremely seriously, and prepared to take, obviously, a major risk if it was going to work, and that was a huge encouragement, at least to me personally, because I hadn't seen anything like that before.

The other thing which I would just like to add to the observation that we made is that for a northern nationalist, in particular, there was a huge focus on what was called the 'unionist veto'. The Anglo-Irish Agreement unmistakeably and finally dealt with the issue of the 'unionist veto'. I think that was hugely important for the SDLP, and actually for people on the wilder side of nationalism in Northern Ireland, and helped us to get to where we are today. Having spent a bit of the weekend reading all of these documents which I haven't read for years, I was impressed to see how the 1985 Agreement is really very important in the Good Friday Agreement, textually as well as in terms of substance. We wouldn't have got it without the commitment of Garret FitzGerald.

ROBERT ARMSTRONG: I think that, having started the process, Mrs Thatcher was determined to see it through, if she could get a reasonably positive result. She was certainly very interested in the border band proposal, and wanted us to pursue that, but in a sense it drew her into the business of negotiating and talking.

The other thing to be said about her, you must forgive me if I put this wrongly, she was treating with the Irish government, truly, and without reservation, as the government of an independent, sovereign state. I think she was perhaps almost the first British prime minister—well, Ted Heath had done it to some extent at Sunningdale—to do so.

But I think the fact was that she was not burdened with the baggage of history in that sense, she was dealing with, as I say, the government of an independent sovereign state, and she undoubtedly felt it like that. Of course, Northern Ireland was a matter of common interest, but she clearly understood the importance of accepting the fact that Ireland was a separate, independent sovereign state, and she would deal with it on that basis. I think having that lead from the top made my task that much easier.

GARRET FITZGERALD: I must say I have a great sense of the continuity of that foreign policy. When the crisis came, we were totally unprepared; Noel has written about that. The Irish government hadn't thought of it at all. We had so cut ourselves off from the North, we just hadn't really given any serious thought to it, and in those years, 1969–72, it was pretty dreadful. But we came out the far end, and before that government ended Jack Lynch had turned things around, and he was out in America with O'Malley, just tackling the IRA there, trying to establish better relationships with Britain.[72]

I think, from 1972 on, with minor, not fundamental, discontinuities by Haughey, Irish policy has been consistent. Basically, we realized that the Northern Ireland thing had to be tackled quite differently, that it was to be resolved. There must be a sensitivity to the problems of the minority; this would have to be done with the cooperation of the British government, and if British policy, in security terms, was seen as negative, then we had to try and persuade the British government of that—persuade them to look at the minority problems which contributed to everything, and eventually the violence. I think all Irish governments, even the Haughey government (but there's some minor discontinuities there), saw that as their task.

---

[72] Desmond O'Malley was Minister for Justice in Jack Lynch's Fianna Fáil government, 1970–3.

We were fortunate in the personalities—Jim Callaghan had a positive role to play, and he helped block the idea of abandoning Northern Ireland.[73] For us to succeed, we needed a lot of things to happen, but we needed a better understanding in Britain, an empathy for the problems, and people with wisdom and a sense of history who could help tackle them. We were extraordinarily fortunate in you [Robert Armstrong and David Goodall], Geoffrey Howe, and, in a curious way, Margaret Thatcher.

When I met her first, she had seemed the most improbable person to do anything useful for Ireland, but, being an optimist by nature, I decided to woo her as best I could. I developed a good relationship with her in the hope that some day it would come in handy, and it did eventually.

Of course, the great thing about her was that, if she decided to do something, then that was that. Other prime ministers of other countries would be less good at carrying things through, but the combination of her commitment, once she became engaged, and the quality of the people who continued at that level, like Geoffrey Howe, made it possible to carry through the process that Irish foreign policy had been pursuing since about 1972, constructively trying to undo all the damage they'd done in earlier years—those negative, provocative policies. And so it came about.

At each stage here, everything is by action and reaction; the hunger strike and the errors made in it, and the huge gains that Sinn Féin claimed from that, led us, in particular, to shift policy. British policy changed. That led to the movement towards the Agreement; the Agreement itself precipitated changes in the North which made Sinn Féin then rethink. That was helped by constructive British government people like Peter Brooke and his sensitivity and determination.[74]

We were so fortunate in the people we had to deal with then, and since. Tony Blair had extraordinary commitment throughout the first year particularly, and thereafter has been important. Britain's interest in Ireland and ours don't necessarily totally coincide. It is concerned quite rightly with IRA violence in Britain; our concern is a different one—the matter of IRA criminality in Ireland. That has occasionally led to slight differences in our approach; we've perhaps been a bit tougher on the IRA in recent times than the British government, who have a slightly different agenda. But there is a common purpose there even, with slight differences in emphasis. So I would emphasize continuity in all of this.

ROBERT ARMSTRONG: Could I just add a tailpiece to what Garret said? I remind him of what he said to me at Chequers during these negotiations. I remember

[73] James Callaghan, MP, was responsible for Northern Ireland as Home Secretary (1967–70), and later served as Foreign Secretary (1974–6) and Prime Minister (1976–9).
[74] Peter Brooke was Secretary of State for Northern Ireland, 1989–92.

saying to him: 'Garret, the trouble is that the Irish are so very conscious of their history, it's very much alive with them.' And Garret said: 'you're quite wrong Robert, there is no Irish history, it's just that the present begins in 1169.'

NOEL DORR: Just one balancing footnote that needs to be said. We praised Robert and David so much, and others. A person listening, a unionist listening, might think this was all a huge conspiracy. But each side, and they in particular, represented with full integrity their government's position. And yet, we're able to overcome the obstacles; but that needs to be said.

GARRET FITZGERALD: Because there was a vital, common interest.

Documents

Document 3.1. 'Armstrong Proposals', 1 March 1984

THE ARMSTRONG PROPOSALS

(i) a solemn declaration of commitment by the Irish Government to respect the union, and to give expression to such a commitment *either* by seeking amendment of the territorial clauses in the Irish Constitution *or* by taking steps to ensure that the declaration would not be found unconstitutional by the Irish Supreme Court; the implementation of the other elements in the package to be dependent on the fulfilment of this commitment;

(ii) a commitment by the British Government to work towards the introduction of joint policing arrangements in areas on both sides of the Irish border, possibly extending to other areas of major terrorist activity in the North and for this purpose the establishment of a joint Anglo-Irish Security Commission tasked (a) to reach early agreement on the modalities (including unified arrangements for the administration of criminal justice in the area) and perhaps (b) to examine the possibilities for moving eventually towards the establishment of a joint police force operating throughout the same areas;

(iii) a commitment by the British Government to examine the possibilities for the progressive harmonisation of criminal law throughout Ireland and arrangements for associating Judges from each jurisdiction with criminal trials conducted in the other (ie steps towards an all-Ireland law-enforcement area); and, for this purpose, the establishment of a joint Anglo-Irish Law Commission (for which the post-Sunningdale Joint Commission would provide a precedent) tasked to investigate these matters;

(iv) the introduction by the British Government of measures to meet certain nationalist concerns in the North (eg repeal of the Flags and Emblems (Display) Act, Irish citizens to be allowed (subject to a residence qualification) to vote in local elections in Northern Ireland);

(v) enhanced responsibilities for local government in Northern Ireland, which could include a regional council based on the Assembly, with a committee system; and a new local authority structure with some councils having nationalist majorities.

Source: Annex B to report by Robert Armstrong to Prime Minister, 23 May 1984, TNA: PREM 19/1286.

Document 3.2. 'Nally Proposals', 11 May 1984

IRISH SPEAKING NOTE, 11 MAY 1984 (EXTRACT)

We would propose for consideration:
  (i) An *agreement* between our two countries embodying new arrangements.
 (ii) That each Government would solemnly undertake to guarantee specifically both to the unionists and to the nationalists of Northern Ireland the right to the political cultural and social expressions of their identities, and the protection of these identities regardless of any change that may occur in the constitutional position of Northern Ireland, as a result—and it could only be as a result—of the agreement of a majority of the people of Northern Ireland.
(iii) To this end the Agreement would establish a Joint Authority in Northern Ireland. The Joint Authority system should be durable but eventual Irish unity should not be excluded.
 (iv) The Joint Authority would be an Executive body from which the exercise of public authority in Northern Ireland would flow.
  (v) There would be a legislative assembly in Northern Ireland, and an Executive appointed by the Joint Authority in relation to which the assembly would have powers.
 (vi) Certain powers would be excepted to Westminster, until and unless they were transferred by a poll in Northern Ireland to Irish sovereignty, but there could be consultation within the Joint Authority about the exercise of these powers if requested by the Irish Government. These powers could include such matters as defence, foreign policy, and finance. But subject to agreement between the Governments and after consultation with the assembly, some functions, e.g. representation of Northern Ireland in the EEC, could be transferred to the Irish Government.
(vii) The excepted powers would, where appropriate be exercised through the Joint Authority with a view to securing consensus.
(viii) Certain powers would be *reserved* to the Joint Authority e.g. flags and emblems, languages, placenames, etc., broadcasting, post and telecommunications and security.
 (ix) The Joint Authority would comprise the two Governments, each of which would assign one Minister on a full-time basis to operate the system.
  (x) The assembly and Executive would together operate the full range of the remaining devolved powers subject to a series of checks and balances. Should these conditions not be fulfilled, the Joint Authority might for the time being, undertake the exercise of these powers.

(xi) Special arrangements would need to be agreed for decision making within the area of reserved powers of the Joint Authority, to provide for cases of possible differences of view between the two Governments in relation to such matters.

(xii) In the area of security there would be both for military and police in Northern Ireland a system of joint command with alternating command at the highest operational levels. It is understood that security responsibility could be shared by the Irish authorities only if an adequate political basis had been created along the lines set out herein.

(xiii) An all Ireland Court dealing with a range of matters would be established. There would also be a North–South Commission charged with the harmonisation of the criminal law in both areas.

(xiv) The people of Northern Ireland would be formally entitled to British and Irish citizenship.

Source: Extract from speaking notes for meeting on 11 May 1984, document in possession of authors; detailed summary available in memorandum from Robert Armstrong to Prime Minister, 23 May 1984, TNA: PREM 19/1286.

Document 3.3. Draft Agreement (British Version), 17 January 1985

SECRET AND PERSONAL
BRITISH PROPOSAL

There would be established within the framework of the Anglo-Irish Intergovernmental Council a joint body to consider on a regular basis and in relation to Northern Ireland;

a. legal matters;
b. relations between the police and the community;
c. prisons policy;
d. security co-ordination;
e. political and human rights questions.

Other topics might be added by agreement.

2. Unlike the existing AIIC machine this body would be primarily concerned with North/South rather than East/West relationships and would meet on a regular rather than an ad hoc basis. The British Government would accept the entitlement of the Government of the Republic of Ireland to put forward views on matters relating to Northern Ireland within the body's remit. In accordance with the general practice of the AIIC, every effort would be made to resolve any differences rather than simply reporting them to the two Governments. Attention at the highest level would thus be given to the matters in question; but there would be no derogation of sovereignty on the part of either the United Kingdom or the Republic. The focus of the body's work would be mainly in Northern Ireland; but some of

the matters under consideration would involve co-operative action in both parts of the island of Ireland, and possibly also in Great Britain. Some of the proposals considered in respect of Northern Ireland might also be found to have an application in the Republic.

3. The body would meet at Ministerial or official level, as required. There would be regular Ministerial meetings, say once every three months; and special meetings could be convened when necessary at the request of either side. Officials might meet in Sub-Committees more frequently. Membership would be small and flexible. There would be a small joint secretariat which could be located in Belfast. When the body met at Ministerial level the Secretary of State for Northern Ireland and the appropriate Minister from the Republic would be joint Chairmen. They would be accompanied by their Permanent Secretaries and by other officials and professional advisers.

4. The body (and its Sub-Committees of officials) could meet in separate modes for each of its main areas of interest, and additional members, appropriate to the subject matter, would attend; thus when it met in its legal mode the Attorneys General might attend.

Legal Matters

5. In this mode, the body would deal with issues of concern to both countries relating to the enforcement of the criminal law. A Sub-Committee could be established to examine whether there are areas of the criminal law applying in Northern Ireland and the Republic respectively which might be harmonised with advantage to both countries. Another Sub-Committee could consider whether there would be advantage in setting up any system of joint or mixed courts for terrorist crimes; and, if so, what form such a system might take. The body would also be concerned with the oversight and review of arrangements between the Republic and Northern Ireland for extradition and extra-territorial jurisdiction.

Relations between the Police and the Community

6. In this mode, the body would consider relations between *the police and the community*, with particular reference to the minority community in Northern Ireland. A programme of action might be put in hand which would include:

   i. the establishment of local consultative machinery;
   ii. training in community relations;
   iii. crime prevention schemes involving the community;
   iv. improvements in arrangements for handling complaints;
   v. action to increase the proportion of Catholics joining the RUC.

It would be accepted by both sides that these measures would be directed primarily towards Northern Ireland, with the object of making the police more readily accepted by the nationalist community there, but that some of them might be developed in ways which might also have an application in the Republic.

Prisons Policy

7. The body would also be able to discuss *policy issues in the prisons*. Individual cases could be raised as appropriate, so that explanations could be given or inquiries instituted.

Security Co-ordination

8. The body would consider at its regular meetings *the security situation*, with the Chief Constable and the Commissioner in attendance. This would provide an opportunity to discuss serious incidents, and forthcoming events (eg parades and processions), to identify policy issues, and to enhance co-operation between the security forces of the two Governments in the common fight against terrorism. The body would have no operational responsibilities; responsibility for police operations would remain with the heads of the respective police forces, and the Chief Constable of the RUC would maintain his existing links with the Secretary of State and the Commissioner of the Garda Síochána his accountability to the Minister of Justice.

9. The body would set in hand a programme of work to be undertaken by the Chief Constable and Commissioner and groups of officials in such areas as:

   i. the exchange of intelligence and the preparation of agreed threat assessments;
   ii. the establishment of effective liaison structures between the security forces of the two countries;
   iii. technical co-operation, eg in communications, forensic matters and control of explosives;
   iv. training and the exchange of personnel;
   v. cross-border co-operation and co-ordination of operational resources.

Political and Human Rights Questions

10. In this area the Committee, or a Sub-Committee, would concern itself with measures to recognise national identity, to protect human rights and to prevent discrimination. Here again, it would be accepted that the focus should be on Northern Ireland, but the possible application of any such measures to the Republic would not be excluded.

11. Measures to be considered in this area in respect of Northern Ireland include the use of the Irish language (eg in street names), changes in electoral arrangements, and the possibility of removing restrictions on the flying of flags. Consideration might be given to the benefits which could be expected from some form of Bill of Rights for Northern Ireland and the difficulties which this would present. If a Bill of Rights were judged to be desirable in Northern Ireland the Committee might also consider whether similar action should be taken in the Republic.

12. The Committee would provide opportunities to ensure that Irish views were taken into account by the Secretary of State for Northern Ireland in making the appointments to:

   Police Authority for Northern Ireland
   Police Complaints Board
   Fair Employment Agency
   Equal Opportunities Commission
   Standing Advisory Commission on Human Rights

Devolved Government

13. The arrangements described in this note would be largely unaffected by the creation of a devolved government in Northern Ireland. The exceptions are:

i. in paragraph 12, appointments to the Fair Employment Agency and the Equal Opportunities Commission (but not any of the other appointments) would fall to the devolved government, and the Secretary of State for Northern Ireland would be unable to offer to discuss them;

ii. some, but not most, of the issues arising under paragraph 10 would also be for the devolved government rather than the Secretary of State; but major issues such as electoral law, the law on discrimination and any Bill of Rights would remain within the Secretary of State's responsibilities, and available for discussion in the Standing Committee.

Source: TNA: PREM/19/1548.

Document 3.4. Draft Agreement (British Version), 15 March 1985

SECRET AND PERSONAL
DRAFT OF 15 MARCH 1985
BRITISH PROPOSAL OF MARCH

1. There would be established within the framework of the Anglo-Irish Intergovernmental Council a Standing Committee to deal on a regular basis and in relation to Northern Ireland with:

a. political matters;
b. security and related matters;
c. legal matters.

Other topics might be added by agreement.

2. Unlike the existing AIIC machinery this Committee would be primarily concerned with North/South rather than East/West relationships and would meet on a regular rather than an ad hoc basis. The British Government would accept that the Irish Government would put forward views and proposals on matters relating to Northern Ireland within the body's remit, which would thus receive attention at the highest level. There would be no derogation of sovereignty on the part of either the United Kingdom or the Republic, and the British Government would retain full responsibility for decisions; but, in the interest of promoting peace and stability, every effort would be made through the Standing Committee to take account of and so far as possible accommodate views and proposals put forward by the Irish Government before decisions were taken. The focus of the Committee's work would be mainly in Northern Ireland; but some of the matters under consideration would involve co-operative action in both parts of the island of Ireland, and possibly also in Great Britain. Some of the proposals considered in respect of Northern Ireland might also be found to have an application by the Irish authorities in the Republic.

3. The Standing Committee would meet at Ministerial or official level, as required. There would be regular and frequent Ministerial meetings; and special meetings could be convened when necessary at the request of either side. Officials might meet in Sub-Committees. Membership would be small and flexible. When the Standing Committee met at Ministerial

level the Secretary of State for Northern Ireland and an Irish Minister designated as the Permanent Irish Ministerial Representative would be joint Chairmen. Other British and Irish Ministers could attend meetings as appropriate: thus when legal matters were under consideration the Attorneys General might attend. Ministers would be accompanied by their officials and professional advisers: for example, when questions of security policy or security co-operation were being addressed they could be accompanied by the Chief Constable of the Royal Ulster Constabulary and the Commissioner of the Garda Síochána. There would be a small joint secretariat in Belfast, within which the Irish Government would maintain an office for the purpose of these arrangements.

4. In relation to matters coming within its remit, the Standing Committee would constitute a framework within which the Government of the United Kingdom and the Government of the Republic of Ireland could work together:

(i) for the accommodation of the rights and identities of the two traditions which exist in Northern Ireland; and
(ii) for peace, stability and prosperity throughout Ireland by promoting reconciliation, respect for human rights, co-operation against terrorism and the development of economic, social and cultural co-operation.

5. The Standing Committee would examine the scope for joint action to promote the social and economic reconstruction and improvement of those areas of both parts of Ireland which have suffered most severely from the consequences of the instability of recent years, including the possibility of securing wider international support to that end.

6. It is the declared policy of the British Government that responsibility in respect of certain matters within the remit of the Secretary of State for Northern Ireland should be devolved within Northern Ireland on a basis which would secure widespread acceptance throughout the community. The Irish Government support that policy. If a devolved Government were to be established, some of the arrangements described in this agreement would need to be reviewed.

7. Both Governments recognise that devolution can be achieved only with the co-operation of the constitutional representatives within Northern Ireland of both the traditions there. Nonetheless if full devolution had not taken place, the Standing Committee would consti-tute a framework within which the Irish Government could put forward views and proposals on the modalities of devolution in Northern Ireland, in so far as they bore on the interests of the minority community.

Political Matters

8. The Standing Committee would concern itself with measures to recognise and accom-modate the rights and identities of the two traditions in Northern Ireland, to protect human rights and to prevent discrimination. Measures to be considered in this area in respect of Northern Ireland include the use of the Irish language, changes in electoral arrangements, the avoidance of economic, social and cultural discrimination, and the advantages and disadvantages of some form of Bill of Rights in Northern Ireland.

9. The focus of discussion of these matters would be on Northern Ireland, but the possible application of any such measures by the Irish Authorities in the South would not be excluded.

10. The Standing Committee would provide opportunities for the expression of views and proposals by the Irish Government on appointments to be made by the Secretary of State for Northern Ireland to bodies including the:

Standing Advisory Commission on Human Rights
Fair Employment Agency
Equal Opportunities Commission
Police Authority of Northern Ireland
Police Complaints Board

Security and Related Matters
11. The Standing Committee would consider:

(a) security policy;
(b) relations between the security forces and the Community;
(c) security co-operation;
(d) prisons policy.

12. The Standing Committee would address the security situation at its regular meetings. This would provide an opportunity to address policy issues, serious incidents and forthcoming events (eg parades and processions).

13. The Standing Committee would have no operational responsibilities; responsibility for police operations would remain with the heads of the respective police forces, and the Chief Constable of the Royal Ulster Constabulary would maintain his existing links with the Secretary of State and the Commissioner of the Garda Síochána his accountability to the Minister of Justice.

14. With a view to enhancing co-operation between the security forces of the two Governments; the Standing Committee would set in hand a programme of work to be undertaken by the Chief Constable and the Commissioner and groups of officials in such areas as threat assessments, liaison structures, technical co-operation, training and exchange of personnel, and co-ordination of operational resources.

15. The Standing Committee would consider relations between the security forces and the community, with particular reference to the minority community in Northern Ireland. With a view to promoting greater confidence in the security system, a programme of action would be put in hand which might include: the establishment of local consultative machinery, training in community relations, crime prevention schemes involving the community, improvements in arrangements for handling complaints, and action to increase the proportion of Catholics in the RUC.

It would be accepted by both sides that these measures would be directed primarily towards Northern Ireland, with the object of making the security forces more readily accepted by the nationalist community there, but that some of them might be developed by the Irish authorities in ways which might also have an application in the South.

16. The Standing Committee would also be able to consider policy issues in the prisons. Individual cases could be raised as appropriate, so that explanations could be given or inquiries instituted.

Legal Matters

17. The Standing Committee would deal with issues of concern to both countries relating to the enforcement of the criminal law. In particular it would consider whether there are areas of the criminal law applying in the North and in the South respectively which might with benefit be harmonised. It could consider the case for establishing a system of joint courts for trying terrorist crimes and recommend what form such a system might take. It would also be concerned with the oversight and review of arrangements between North and South for extradition and extra-territorial jurisdiction.

Cross-border co-operation in economic, social and cultural matters

18. Unless and until it proved possible to achieve devolution on a basis which would secure widespread acceptance throughout the community, the Standing Committee would for the time being constitute a framework for the promotion of co-operation between North and South in Ireland in relation to cross-border aspects of economic, social and cultural matters in relation to which the Secretary of State continued to exercise responsibility.

19. If responsibility were devolved in respect of certain matters under this heading currently within the remit of the Secretary of State, there would need to be machinery for practical co-operation between the responsible authorities North and South in respect of cross-border aspects of those issues.

Interparliamentary relations

20. The two Governments agree that it would be for the Houses of Parliament at Westminster and the Oireachtas in Dublin to consider whether an Anglo-Irish Parliamentary Body of the kind adumbrated in the Anglo-Irish Studies Report of November 1981 could be established.

Source: TNA: PREM/19/1548.

Document 3.5. Anglo-Irish 'Catechism', 12 November 1985

QUESTION AND ANSWER PAPER
JOINT TEXT AS OF 12.11.85

Article I of the Agreement

PM 1   Q. Article 1 is ambiguous/imprecise about the status of Northern Ireland, says less than the Chequers communiqué etc. What does it mean?

A. Of course the two Governments approach this aspect of the matter from differing historical perceptions and from within differing constitutional frameworks. The Agreement does not change that. The position is clear. Northern Ireland is part of the United Kingdom.

What Article 1 does is to look to the future and set out—for the first time in a binding international agreement—what is common ground between us: that there will be no change in the present status of Northern Ireland without the freely given consent of the majority of its inhabitants; and that both Governments recognise that such consent does not at present exist.

[British Note 1: The foregoing could be used either as an answer to a question or as part of a freestanding statement about the Agreement and its significance.]

[British Note 2: The Taoiseach said in the Chequers communiqué of 19 November 1984 that 'any change in the constitutional status of Northern Ireland as part of the United Kingdom would only come about with the consent of a majority of the people of Northern Ireland'. But in order to maintain their ability to withstand the allegation that the Agreement is unconstitutional, the Irish would prefer HMG to use the points in the three answers above.]

T 2   Q. Taoiseach do you agree with the Prime Minister?

A. As the Prime Minister has said the two Governments approach this question from differing historical perceptions and from within differing constitutional frameworks. The Agreement does not change that.

It is of course a fact that Ireland is not united politically and that the British Government is responsible for the Government of Northern Ireland. What is important is what we have agreed about the future.

Note for Taoiseach: Following are additional items to be drawn on by the Taoiseach:— Successive Irish Governments have accepted the inescapable fact that Ireland is not united. Article l of the Agreement is consistent with this reality, and every other Article of the Agreement is based on it. This Agreement, in which the British Government accepts that the Irish Government has an important role in relation to Northern Ireland, would not be necessary were it not for the fact that, as a practical reality, Northern Ireland is within the United Kingdom. I believe that Article 1 of the Agreement provides a major reassurance to both sides in Northern Ireland and creates a basis for stability and progress.

Article 1 provides important reassurances both to unionists and to nationalists in the following ways: the Irish Government accept the fact that there does not now exist consent for any change in the status of Northern Ireland and that means that there does not now exist consent to establish Irish unity; the Irish Government accept that the principle of consent is central to the establishment of Irish unity. My Government is in fact saying that the reference in Article 3 of the Irish Constitution to the reintegration of the island of Ireland would only be given effect if a majority of the people of Northern Ireland consent to this, and we are moreover saying that that consent does not now exist.

Article 1 also contains an important reassurance to nationalists in Ireland: both Governments now agree that the only consideration which will be taken into account on the question of establishing Irish unity is the question of consent. That is of course what the Forum Report made clear as its approach. It means, for example, that the British Government in this international agreement commits itself to the view that other issues would not constitute obstacles to Irish unity if the principle of consent were satisfied.

Value of Agreement

PM 3   Q. Is this agreement not meaningless?

A. No single agreement is going to resolve the problems of Northern Ireland. This one is a useful step forward. It marks a change in the attitudes of the two Governments towards one another in relation to Northern Ireland. It incorporates formal Irish recognition that the status of Northern Ireland will remain as it is so long as a majority of the people there so wish, and that the present wish of a majority is for no change. It also incorporates formal British recognition that the Irish Government may advance views and proposals on aspects of Northern Ireland affairs and commits both Governments to make determined efforts to resolve any differences between them. It should be seen as promoting the development of closer and more systematic co-operation between the British and Irish Governments without affecting the position of Northern Ireland as part of the United Kingdom. The Agreement is also a useful step on the road to reconciliation between the two communities in Northern Ireland.

T 4   Q. This is all promises. It is full of commitments 'to study' and 'to consider' etc. but it is short of actual concrete measures to end alienation. After months of build-up to this summit aren't the results really an anti-climax?

A. No. This Agreement marks a new stage.in the development of the Anglo-Irish dialogue, giving the Irish Government for the first time a formal role in relation to Northern Ireland, involving systematic arrangements for resolving differences on the problems of Northern Ireland and a new level of cooperation between North and South. It will make a real difference to nationalists in Northern Ireland by providing new means for the expression of their identity and giving new scope for the expression of their aspirations. It would be selfish and irresponsible of us to withhold the progress involved here for the minority in Northern Ireland, merely for the sake of ideological concerns. As to alienation, the problems of nationalists in Northern Ireland have been focused on politics, security, human rights and the law. All of these problem areas have been provided for in this Agreement, and of course the very first meeting of the Conference will address all of these areas, notably the especially difficult area of relations between the minority community and the security system, on which some progress is already taking place.

Obviously this Agreement cannot resolve all the problems of Northern Ireland. But the Agreement is an important stage in the search for peace and stability. What it does is to provide within a new context the basic legal and institutional machinery through which the two Governments can fulfil their commitment of November 1984 to work together for the accommodation of the rights and identities of the two traditions in Northern Ireland. The new arrangements established today are, so far as I know, unique. This reflects the special nature of the Northern Ireland problem.

The Forum Report

PM 5 Q. The Agreement falls far short of even the least ambitious of the three options set out in the New Ireland Forum Report (i.e. joint authority).

A. Let us concentrate on what the two Governments *have* agreed. The Agreement represents the outcome of prolonged and serious negotiations. The arrangements it embodies are unique, reflecting both the closeness of the Anglo-Irish relationship and the special problems of Northern Ireland. The New Ireland Forum's meetings and reports helped to create the climate in which these negotiations became possible. The new Agreement accords with the spirit of conciliation which characterised much of the Forum Report.

PM 6   Q. Do you still reject the Forum Report?

A. The British Government has welcomed many positive elements of the Forum Report. We welcomed such principles as the clear and unambiguous acceptance that political change requires consent, the commitment to the politics of peaceful persuasion, and unqualified opposition to violence and those who support violence. We welcomed the recognition and respect which the Report gave, on the part of nationalists, to the distinctive identity of Northern Ireland unionists including their loyalty to the United Kingdom.

(If pressed again on the 'three illustrative models') I have said that I welcome many of the innovative features of the Report. But I do not think anyone would expect the British Government to endorse it in its entirety.

T 7   Q. Can you really say that this Agreement is based on the Forum Report? Does it not fall substantially short of joint authority, the least of the options proposed by the Forum?

A. The Irish side throughout these negotiations based their approach on the Forum Report. The necessary elements for progress proposed in Chapter 5 para. 2 of the Forum Report are all accommodated in today's Agreement. I believe above all that they are reflected in the commitment of the two Governments to work together for the accommodation of the rights and identities of the two traditions in Northern Ireland on the basis of the new arrangements and the shared priorities established by this Agreement. You will recall, moreover, that the Forum Report indicated the openness of the participants to discuss all other views which would contribute to political development i.e. views other than the three particular options set out in the Report. The purpose of any negotiation is to reach an accommodation of views and the British and Irish Governments have achieved that in this Agreement.

Role of Irish Government/British Sovereignty

PM 8   Q. By giving the Irish Government a role in relation to Northern Irish affairs, surely the Agreement infringes sovereignty?

A. No. There is no derogation from sovereignty and the Agreement makes this clear.

T&PM 9   Q. So is the Irish role intended to be only 'consultative'?

A. The Conference is a unique mechanism. There is no single word to describe its role. It will not have executive functions; Article 2(b) of the Agreement makes clear that there will be no derogation from sovereignty and that each Government retains responsibility for the decisions and administration of government within its jurisdiction.

But the Conference will be more than just consultative in that the Irish side will put forward views and proposals on its own initiative as well as being invited to do so; and there is an obligation on both sides in the Conference to make determined efforts to resolve any differences*; and one of the Conference's functions will be to promote cross-border co-operation between North and South in Ireland.

[N.B. It is accepted by both sides that the words 'consultative' and 'consultation' should not be used to describe the Agreement or the Arrangements provided for in it.]

[Note 2: *The Taoiseach will add 'in the interest of peace and stability'.]

PM 10   Q. So the Irish side will after all share in decision-making?

A. As Article 2(b) of the Agreement makes clear, each Government retains responsibility for the decisions and administration of government within its own jurisdiction. On matters covered by the Agreement, however, the British Government in taking its decisions will take full account of any views and proposals put forward by the Irish side, and also of the obligation on both sides to make determined efforts to resolve any differences.

PM 11   Q. Is it not setting Northern Ireland apart from the rest of the UK by giving another country a part of the government there?

A. There is a unique situation in Northern Ireland because of the division within the community there. The Agreement reaffirms the present status of Northern Ireland and makes clear that HMG remain responsible for the decisions and administration of government there.

PM&T 12   Q. What happens when differences cannot be resolved?

A. Article 2(b) makes it clear that each Government retains responsibility for the decisions and administration of government within its own jurisdiction. But a key point of the Agreement is that we are both committing ourselves to determined efforts to resolve differences [Taoiseach: in the interest of peace and stability].

Moreover, the Agreement reflects the careful consideration that the two Governments have given to minimising differences; it envisages for example a variety of levels at which matters can be considered and also provides for the convening of special meetings up to Ministerial level when required by either side.

PM 13   Q. The Agreement says in Article 2(b) that 'Determined efforts shall be made through the Committee to resolve any differences'. In the context, these are differences relating to views and proposals which the Irish Government have put forward on matters relating to Northern Ireland. What does this provision mean?

A. Let me start by emphasising the desire of both Governments to implement the Agreement in a spirit of co-operation and goodwill. That being so, we are not starting off in the belief that we shall confront many or substantial differences; the whole point of meeting together will be to find common ground, bearing in mind that the sentence you quote speaks of serving 'the interest of promoting peace and stability'. But if there *are* differences, both sides will work hard to resolve them, recognising that each Government retains responsibility for the decisions and administration of government within its jurisdiction.

Unionist Concerns on Irish Unity, Status and the Irish Government's Role

PM 14   Q. In November 1984 in the Communiqué issued after their Summit, the Prime Minister and the Taoiseach agreed 'that the identities of both the majority and minority communities in Northern Ireland should be recognised and respected, and reflected in the structures and processes of Northern Ireland in ways acceptable to both communities'. How will the Prime Minister and Taoiseach test the acceptability of the Agreement to the Unionist community?

A. The identity of the majority community is already recognised and respected in the way the majority desires by virtue of Northern Ireland being and remaining part of the United Kingdom. This Agreement provides means for the expression of the identity of the minority. The Agreement thus furthers the aim of making the structures and processes in Northern Ireland acceptable to *both* communities.

The elected representatives of the people of the United Kingdom as a whole will have the opportunity to express their views when Parliament debates the Agreement shortly.

PM 15   Q. Is the Agreement not the first step on the slippery slope to Irish unity?

A. No. The Agreement contains a formal and binding statement by the Irish and British Governments that the status of Northern Ireland remains unchanged. It commits the Irish Government to acknowledging the rights and identity of unionists. It commits the two Governments to the view that any change in this status would* only come about with the consent of a majority of the people of Northern Ireland; and that, if in the future a majority in Northern Ireland clearly wished for and formally consented to a united Ireland, the two Governments would introduce and support legislation in the respective Parliaments to give effect to this. This is the most formal commitment on this subject made by any Irish Government.

*(N.B. The Agreement says 'would' not 'could'.)

PM&T 16 Q. The Agreement establishes special channels for conveying the nationalist minority's views to the British Government. Why is nothing comparable proposed for the unionist majority?

A. The question is not comparing like with like. The unique arrangement we have made with the Irish Government reflects the position of a minority which looks to Dublin to express its aspirations. The unionists by definition identify with the United Kingdom; they have, and will continue to have, ready means of access to the British Government including unionist MPs in Westminster, and the Government pays close attention to their views.

PM 17   Q. Why has HMG failed to secure the abolition of Article 2 of the Irish Constitution?

A. The Agreement is the outcome of a thorough process of negotiation in which each side has had to take account of the constraints placed on the other. What is significant is that Article 1 formally commits the Irish Government, like the British I Government, to the position that the status of Northern Ireland will remain as it is so long as a majority there so wishes.

T 18   Q. Will you now hold a referendum on Articles 2 and 3 of the Constitution?

A. The changing of Articles 2 and 3 is not a part of this arrangement. I would again draw your attention to Article 1 of this Agreement. That provision involves a formal, solemn and joint reaffirmation by the two Governments of the principle of consent. It will be perfectly obvious that the overwhelming majority of Irish nationalists determinedly reject the use of force or threat of force in seeking to realise the aspiration of Irish unity. This was a basic principle of the Forum Report and a point strongly emphasised at the time. This Agreement puts the principle of consent beyond question and therefore gives a clear reassurance to unionists.

T 19   Q. Is this Agreement the first step on the road to British disengagement and a united Ireland?

[A.] Article 1 explains that any change in the status of Northern Ireland would only come about with the consent of a majority in Northern Ireland. It also recognises that that consent does not at present exist. If in the future a majority wished for and formally consented to a united Ireland, the two Governments would introduce and support legislation in their respective parliaments to give effect to this.

PM 20   Q. This Agreement seems to have something for everybody in Ireland except Ulster unionists. Is there any concession at all to fundamental unionist concerns in this Agreement?

A. The Agreement is designed to promote peace and stability to the benefit of *all* the people in North and South. There is also much in it which should be of especial value to unionists. For instance, Article 1 confirming the status of Northern Ireland; the intensified security cooperation provided for in the Agreement and already beginning to take place; and the Irish Government's acceptance of the validity of the unionist tradition in Ireland. The Taoiseach has also stated his Government's intention to accede to the European Convention on the Supression of Terrorism.

T 21   Q. Doesn't the Agreement maintain all the ambiguities in the Irish nationalist approach to Northern Ireland. Haven't you and Mrs Thatcher simply agreed to differ on this point so that there is no real concession to unionist concerns?

A. This Agreement involves a formal, solemn and joint reaffirnation by the two Governments of the principle of consent. That is something new—something special—and something which I am sure unionists will welcome. That principle is now clearly beyond question.

Furthermore, the Agreement makes clear the rejection by both Governments of any attempt to promote political objectives by violence or the threat of violence: this is a concern basic to constitutional nationalism in Ireland and it was a concern highlighted in the Report of the New Ireland Forum.

What both sides must do, and this is also explicitly recognised in the Agreement, is to continue their efforts to reconcile and to acknowledge the rights of the two major traditions that exist in Ireland. For our part we have made it clear that we have no designs on the rights of unionists. We accept and acknowledge their Britishness. While we shall by dialogue seek to persuade, we respect and will respect their reasons for opposing Irish unity.

Perhaps most important of all, this Agreement offers both communities in Northern Ireland a new opportunity to rebuild society—free from the tensions, the turmoil and animosities of the past—and to participate fully in the structures of government. I believe that unionists, no less than nationalists, fervently seek in Northern Ireland just such an opportunity.

PM 22   Q. Is the concession of a major role for Dublin not an admission of the failure of British and unionist policy in Northern Ireland over the past sixty years?

       A. No. I am concerned with the future, not the past. The Agreement shows that the two Governments are determined to work together in seeking peace and reconciliation in Ireland.

PM 23   Q. Twelve years ago, the loyalists in Northern Ireland defeated an Anglo-Irish Agreement based on power-sharing and a Council of Ireland. Won't they do the same this time?

       A. I believe that the great majority in Northern Ireland have a deep longing for peace. The Government have made a decision that action is necessary to support the democratic process in Northern Ireland and that it would be damaging and even dangerous to do nothing. Indeed, the two major unionist parties recognise in their policy documents that it is necessary to take action to accommodate the nationalist tradition. This Agreement tries to accommodate both traditions. I am determined that it should work, and work to the benefit of all.

Nationalist Concerns on Irish Unity, an 'Internal Solution' and the Application of Proposals in the South

PM&T 24   Q. The Agreement represents a betrayal of the nationalist cause and the abandonment of the goal of unity.

       A. This is more a question for the Irish Government. But as the Agreement makes clear, if at any time in the future a majority of the people of Northern Ireland formally consent to unity, then the two Governments will take the necessary steps to bring it about.

       (Additional points for the Taoiseach: This means that other considerations would not constitute obstacles to Irish unity if the principle of consent were satisfied. There is no abandonment of the aspiration to Irish unity to be achieved peacefully and by democratic means.)

T 25   Q. The Preamble speaks about diminishing the divisions in Northern Ireland? Isn't the real division the division of Ireland? What does this Agreement do to end partition?

       A. It is not the division of the territory of Ireland in my view which is the fundamental problem. Unity cannot be achieved and partition ended by erasing a line on a map. The basic division which we face is that arising from the competing identities and conflicting loyalties of nationalists and unionists in Ireland. That means that we can only proceed through persuasion and agreement as the Forum Report emphasises.

       The immediate priority must be to improve conditions on the ground for the nationalist minority in Northern Ireland; this has been a fundamental concern of my Government and it is a concern which is overriding in this Agreement.

       It is very important to note that this is the first formal agreement in which the British Government commit themselves to introduce and support legislation to give effect to their desire for Irish unity, if a majority of the people of Northern Ireland should formally consent to this.

T 26 Q. Is this not yet another effort to make Northern Ireland work on the basis of a purely internal solution?

A. No: this Agreement gives the Irish Government for the first time an important role in relation to Northern Ireland. In the Agreement, the British Government accepts that the Irish Government will put forward within the new Conference views and proposals on matters relating to Northern Ireland and, in the interest of peace and stability, undertakes with us to make determined efforts to resolve differences. By providing these practical arrangements through which the two Governments can work together for the accommodation of the rights and identities of the two traditions, the Agreement acknowledges the obvious reality that the Irish Government is involved in efforts to promote peace and stability in Northern Ireland.

T 27 Q. The leader of the Opposition in Dublin has called Northern Ireland a failed political entity. Is this Agreement not propping up this failed political entity?

A. So far as I am concerned we are talking about new political structures in Ireland: measures which accommodate the identity of Northern nationalists; measures which provide for the first time an important role for the Irish Government in the affairs of Northern Ireland; measures which put unionists and nationalists on an equal footing.

   I am interested in working for peace and stability. I am not interested in the question of whether Northern Ireland has or has not been a failure. So far as I am concerned these arrangements meet the requirement of the Forum: they transcend the context of Northern Ireland. They will benefit people in North and South.

T 28 Q. Why should the rights of unionists be placed on a par with those of nationalists given that nationalists represent the overwhelming majority of the people of the island of Ireland?

A. My immediate concern is to ensure that the rights of the nationalist minority in Northern Ireland are respected; this is an essential feature of the Agreement and of the Chequers Communiqué of last year. Article 1 reiterates the principle of consent in relation to unity. In this we have acknowledged a fundamental political reality; unity—true unity between all the people of Ireland—cannot be achieved by force, or coercion or subjection. Each of the two traditions must acknowledge and accommodate the concerns and the rights of the other; were the Irish nationalist tradition to seek supremacy or domination over unionists, the result would be even greater division and turmoil in Ireland.

T 29 Q. Some of the proposals under consideration by the Conference may have application in the Republic. What does this mean?

A. It simply means that certain measures taken in Northern Ireland—e.g. those designed to improve relations between local communities and the police force—may be found to have relevance and value outside the strict context of Northern Ireland.

   They might, for example, be seen to be of value in the South and indeed in Britain and be applied, as the case may be, in either jurisdiction.

Rights and Identities

PM 30   Q. How will the Agreement improve the human rights situation in Northern Ireland?

A. The Government have introduced many major improvements in recent years to ensure that human rights in Northern Ireland are protected as effectively as possible. The answer to your question is in the Agreement. Article 5 in particular provides that the Conference will discuss measures in this field.

PM 31   Q. Do you now propose to introduce legislation:
(a) giving the vote at local elections to Irish citizens resident in Northern Ireland;
(b) permitting the use of Irish as an official language;
(c) enabling the Irish tricolour to be flown from City Hall, Belfast and other public buildings in Northern Ireland.

A. All these matters are among those for consideration by the Conference. I should not anticipate that discussion.

Security in Northern Ireland

PM 32   Q. The Agreement means that the Irish Government will be able to interfere with the work of the security forces in Northern Ireland. This will greatly undermine their morale and efficiency.

A. There is no question of interference, and the Intergovernmental Conference will have no operational responsibilities. It will be to everyone's advantage to establish a systematic means of taking account of the Irish Government's views about security matters. I very much hope that this will reassure those in the minority community who have expressed a lack of confidence in the security forces. The co-operation foreseen in the Agreement will not be all one way. The Agreement will also intensify security co-operation between the authorities in both parts of Ireland and this should be greatly welcomed by all those who wish to defeat terrorism.

PM 33   Q. Are you not in Article 6 giving Dublin a right of veto on matters fundamentally affecting the security and well-being of the people of Ulster?

A. No. As Article 6 makes clear, the Irish Government may put forward views and proposals on the role and composition of certain bodies appointed by the Secretary of State for Northern Ireland or his Departments. It does not give the Irish Government a veto though every effort will be made by both sides to resolve any differences which may emerge.

T 34   Q. What concrete commitments have you got in relation to changes in RUC policy, practice and structure? What concrete changes do you believe are necessary to ensure minority confidence in the RUC?

A. This Agreement (Art. 7) indicates that the Conference will address matters relating to RUC policy issues as well as serious security incidents and forthcoming events. This would include, for example, parades and processions.

The two Governments see the need for a programme of special measures to improve relations between the security forces and the nationalist people. The Conference will also consider the composition and role of the Police Authority. The very first meeting of the Conference will consider measures which would underline respect for the rights and identity of nationalists as well as unionists on the part of the police.

T 35   Q. In the context of this Agreement, would you be free to criticise the RUC as you have done in the past or would you not be obliged to bear some of the blame in the event of another tragedy?

A. The commitment of the Irish Government and of the British Government is to make this Agreement work in relation to all matters within its scope and that very much includes the police.

PM 36   Q. Are the SDLP now expected to support the RUC and to encourage Catholics to join the force?

A. Everyone should support the security forces. It has long been the wish of the British Government to see more members of the minority community joining the RUC. We hope, following the Agreement, that this will happen more and that the SDLP will feel able to encourage Roman Catholics to join.

PM 37   Q. The clear implication of this Agreement is that the RUC has failed to discharge its duties fairly and even-handedly in the past. Are you not, therefore, accepting nationalist criticisms as valid?

A. We have always had full confidence in the RUC. I hope that following this Agreement the minority community will increasingly share that confidence.

T 38   Q. What concrete commitments have you got on the disbandment of the UDR? Is the regiment going to be phased out?

A. The UDR is a major concern to us and to the nationalist community in Northern Ireland who have often seen the force more as a focus of division than of harmony between themselves and unionists. At the same time, it has considerable importance to unionists, particularly in isolated rural areas. I recognise that there are many honourable men and women in the UDR and I condemn without reservation the campaign of murder against them.

Changes have already begun in relation to the UDR's contact with the public, which is where the problems have arisen. The first meeting of the Conference will review progress. In particular it will consider the application of the principle that the UDR operate only in support of the civil power, with the particular objective of ensuring as rapidly as possible that, save in the most exceptional circumstances, there is a police presence in all operations which involve direct contact with the community.

The first meeting will furthermore consider ways of underlining the policy that the UDR discharge their duties even-handedly and with equal respect for the unionist and nationalist identities and traditions.

PM 39   Q. The UDR are a particular reassurance to unionists in a minority position in border areas. Will you guarantee that the role of the UDR as a bulwark against IRA assassins will be maintained in these areas?

A. The UDR will not be disbanded. They are brave and dedicated people who have a major role in providing security in Northern Ireland. I recognise that there are difficulties in the UDR's relationship with the minority community. The Government keeps the role of the security forces, including the UDR, under review in the light of community relations as well as operational needs. Improvements will continue to be made.

PM 40   Q. Will you now move towards a general amnesty in Northern Ireland? Will prisoners with indeterminate sentences now be given a definite date for release?

A. Those possibilities do not arise from the Agreement itself. Any question of speeding up release from indeterminate sentences, if the Agreement led to a real reduction in violence, would be for the Secretary of State for Northern Ireland.

Judiciary

PM 41   Q. Article 8 represents an intolerable intrusion on the independence of the Northern Ireland judiciary.

A. This is nonsense. There is no threat to the independence of the judiciary anywhere in Ireland. The Agreement says in Article 8 that the two Governments agree on the importance of public confidence in the administration of justice and that the Conference will seek measures which would give substantial expression to this aim. Surely nobody can quarrel with that.

PM 42   Q. What is your position on joint courts?

A. [We have not been able to see any easy or early way round the political and other difficulties involved, but we have in good faith, and without commitment, provided in Article 8 for the matter to be studied. We have not excluded the possibility of mixed courts in both jurisdictions for the trial of certain offences becoming feasible and acceptable at some future time.]

[Note: This particular text was as far as officials could get on 12.11.85.]

PM 43   Q. Why are mixed courts highlighted in the Agreement?

A. Other ideas, such as extradition and the harmonisation of the criminal law, are also mentioned in the same Article of the Agreement.

Extradition

T 44   Q. Do you contemplate new legislation to facilitate extradition of IRA offenders? Will you accede to the European Convention?

A. I have said that it is the intention of the Irish Government to accede as soon as possible to the Convention on the Suppression of Terrorism.

The Communiqué has committed the two sides to work for early progress in

- relations between the security forces and the minority community in Northern Ireland;
- ways of improving security co-operation between the two Governments;
- and seeking measures which would give substantial expression to the aim that there is public confidence in the administration of justice.

It is against this background that the Irish Government has announced its intention to accede as soon as possible to the European Convention on the Suppression of Terrorism.

PM 45   Q. What guarantees have you got from Dr FitzGerald that the South will cease to provide a haven for IRA fugitive terrorists?

A. There are fugitive offenders in the North and in the South. On both sides of the border strenuous efforts are made to catch them. One of the main purposes of the Agreement will be to enhance the co-operation against Terrorism which already takes place between North and South. Article 8 of the Agreement foresees further consideration by the two Governments in the Intergovernmental Conference of the question of fugitive offenders. More-over the Taoiseach has announced his Government's intention to accede to the European Convention on the Suppression of Terrorism.

IRA Campaign

PM 46　Q. Will the Agreement not encourage the Provisional IRA in their murderous campaign?

A. One of the main effects of the Agreement will be that the British and Irish Governments will strengthen their co-operation in the fight against the men of violence. [The Provisionals have already denounced the Agreement, which hardly suggests that they feel encouraged by it.]

T&PM 47　Q. Will you now accept that the electoral success of Sinn Féin and the PIRA's campaign of violence including attacks on British cities, have brought both of you together in this Agreement today. Is this not confirmation of the success of the ballot box/armalite strategy?

A. Absolutely not. This Agreement is a rejection of terrorism. We are seeking to build up hope for the future where the IRA have sought only to destroy. We are seeking peace and reconciliation where the IRA have brought only strife, turmoil and tragedy. This Agreement will certainly reinforce the position of all who seek peace and stability by constitutional means.

Role of Irish Minister/Secretariat

PM 48　Q. Where will the permanent Secretariat be located and how will it be staffed?

A. The Secretariat will be very small. Its function will be to service meetings of the Intergovernmental Conference which will [normally] meet in Belfast and to act between meetings as a channel of communication.

(Note: the Irish would like to omit 'normally' and retain the final sentence.)

T&PM 49　Q. What will be the role of the Permanent Irish Ministerial Representative? Will he have direct contact on the ground with the nationalist community in Northern Ireland?

A. The role of the Permanent Irish Ministerial Representative will be to imple-ment the Agreement on behalf of the Irish Government as joint chairman of the Conference. This will not alter the Irish Government's freedom to maintain contact with people in Northern Ireland.

Public Bodies

T 50　Q. There are four vacancies still outstanding on the Police Authority? Are these to be your nominations? Is this marginal number of vacancies which has been set aside for your views an indication of what consultation will mean in practice?

A. The Irish Government will be putting forward views in relation to all present vacancies on the Police Authority for Northern Ireland as well as in relation to any vacancies which may arise in future. The precise number of vacancies which may happen to exist at the present time is less important than the Agreement's recognition of the principle that the Irish Government will put forward views and proposals on the role and composition of this body, and that there is a binding obligation on the two sides to resolve any differences [in the interest of peace and stability].

T 51   Q. You have a say in appointments to a number of bodies in Northern Ireland. Are Northern nationalists now expected to co-operate with these bodies as they are currently structured and to accept their legitimacy?

A. In presenting views on appointments and other matters relating to these bodies, the Irish Government will naturally be taking account of nationalist concerns and priorities. But my objective will be to ensure that all of these bodies adequately reflect the concerns of the entire community.

Devolution

PM 52   Q. Do you expect the SDLP to support this Agreement and to participate more in the political life of Northern Ireland?

A. We hope that the nationalist community as a whole will see this Agreement as evidence that progress can be made by constitutional means.

PM 53   Q. What proposals does the Northern Ireland Secretary have for encouraging a return to devolved government in Northern Ireland?

A. The Government remain committed to a return to devolved government in Northern Ireland as the best basis for political stability. We will do all we can to identify a scheme of administration acceptable to both sides of the community. We hope that the political parties in Northern Ireland will respond constructively to the opportunities this Agreement offers, and will help to work out satisfactory proposals for a newly devolved administration.

T&PM 54 Q. Do you now expect the SDLP to enter the Assembly?

A. The Agreement makes it clear that both Governments support a policy of devolution which would command widespread acceptance throughout Northern Ireland. The question of whether the SDLP should enter this or any future Assembly is a matter for that party to decide.

Fund

PM 55   Q. Reports that the United States Government will offer a large sum for expenditure in Ireland suggest that HMG entered into the Agreement in order to obtain US financial support.

A. The Agreement has been concluded on its merits. We naturally hope that friendly countries, including the United States, will welcome it.

Note for T and PM. [Article 10 (a) provides that the two Governments shall cooperate to promote the economic and social development of those parts of Ireland which have suffered most severely from the consequences of the instability of recent years and shall consider the possibility of securing international support for this work.]

T 56   Q. Is it possible that it is part of a package that the Irish Government will modify its policy on neutrality?

A. No.

NOTE: The following two questions are for answer after the US announcement

T 57   Q. Will contributions from America (and Europe) be matched by a contribution from the Dáil?

A. Any funds made available by the US and the member States of the European Community are intended to be specifically international expressions of support for the work of promoting reconstruction and reconcilation in Ireland. This is separate from the efforts of the Irish and British Governments so that the question therefore of my Government contributing to the Fund, as such, does not arise.

PM 58   Q. Why is the British Government not contributing to the Fund when the United States Government is forking out $.... million?

A. The British Government already makes a massive annual subvention contribution to the Province which is now running at around £1.5 billion per annum.

Review Clause/Requirement of Legislation

T 59   Q. Since the review provision applies only to the operations of the Conference and not to the declaration on status, have we not therefore recognised Northern Ireland without obtaining a corresponding guarantee that future British Governments will continue to accept that we have a policy role in Northern Ireland?

A. Article 1 of this Agreement incorporates the principle of consent enshrined in the Report of the Forum and accepted in Communiqués by successive Heads of Government in both countries. It also incorporates the agreement of the two Governments to support Irish unity in the event there is consent to that aim.

The two Governments have entered into this Agreement determined to make it work but experience may show that adjustments are desirable to the role and nature of the Conference's activities. The Review Clause will enable the two Governments to make such adjustments.

PM 60   Q. *Is such an Agreement possible without legislation?*

A. Yes. The Agreement is fully consistent with statute law relating to Northern Ireland.

Note: Square brackets in this document are reproduced from the original and do not represent editorial intervention, except in T 19 [A.]

Source: Document in possession of the authors.

Document 3.6. Anglo-Irish Agreement, 15 November 1985

AGREEMENT BETWEEN THE GOVERNMENT OF IRELAND AND THE GOVERNMENT OF THE UNITED KINGDOM

The Government of Ireland and the Government of the United Kingdom:

Wishing further to develop the unique relationship between their peoples and the close co-operation between their countries as friendly neighbours and as partners in the European Community;

Recognising the major interest of both their countries and, above all, of the people of Northern Ireland in diminishing the divisions there and achieving lasting peace and stability;

Recognising the need for continuing efforts to reconcile and to acknowledge the rights of the two major traditions that exist in Ireland, represented on the one hand by those who wish for no change in the present status of Northern Ireland and on the other hand by those who aspire to a sovereign united Ireland achieved by peaceful means and through agreement;

Reaffirming their total rejection of any attempt to promote political objectives by violence or the threat of violence and their determination to work together to ensure that those who adopt or support such methods do not succeed;

Recognising that a condition of genuine reconciliation and dialogue between unionists and nationalists is mutual recognition and acceptance of each other's rights;

Recognising and respecting the identities of the two communities in Northern Ireland, and the right of each to pursue its aspirations by peaceful and constitutional means;

Reaffirming their commitment to a society in Northern Ireland in which all may live in peace, free from discrimination and intolerance, and with the opportunity for both communities to participate fully in the structures and processes of government;

Have accordingly agreed as follows:

A. Status of Northern Ireland
Article 1
The two Governments

(a) affirm that any change in the status of Northern Ireland would only come about with the consent of a majority of the people of Northern Ireland;

(b) recognise that the present wish of a majority of the people of Northern Ireland is for no change in the status of Northern Ireland;

(c) declare that, if in the future a majority of the people of Northern Ireland clearly wish for and formally consent to the establishment of a united Ireland, they will introduce and support in the respective Parliaments legislation to give effect to that wish.

B. The Intergovernmental Conference
Article 2
(a) There is hereby established, within the framework of the Anglo-Irish Intergovernmental Council set up after the meeting between the two Heads of Government on 6 November 1981, an Intergovernmental Conference (hereinafter referred to as 'the Conference'), concerned with Northern Ireland and with relations between the two parts of the island of Ireland, to deal, as set out in this Agreement, on a regular basis with

  (i) political matters;
  (ii) security and related matters;
  (iii) legal matters, including the administration of justice;
  (iv) the promotion of cross-border co-operation.

(b) The United Kingdom Government accept that the Irish Government will put forward views and proposals on matters relating to Northern Ireland within the field of activity of the Conference in so far as those matters are not the responsibility of a devolved administration in Northern Ireland. In the interest of promoting peace and stability, determined efforts shall be made through the Conference to resolve any differences. The Conference will be mainly concerned with Northern Ireland; but some of the matters under consideration will involve cooperative action in both parts of the island of Ireland, and possibly also in Great Britain. Some of the proposals considered in respect of Northern Ireland may also be found to have application by the Irish Government. There is no derogation from the sovereignty of either the Irish Government or the United Kingdom Government, and each retains responsibility for the decisions and administration of government within its own jurisdiction.

Article 3

The Conference shall meet at Ministerial or official level, as required. The business of the Conference will thus receive attention at the highest level. Regular and frequent Ministerial meetings shall be held; and in particular special meetings shall be convened at the request of either side. Officials may meet in subordinate groups. Membership of the Conference and of sub-groups shall be small and flexible. When the Conference meets at Ministerial level an Irish Minister designated as the Permanent Irish Ministerial Representative and the Secretary of State for Northern Ireland shall be joint Chairmen. Within the framework of the Conference other Irish and British Ministers may hold or attend meetings as appropriate: when legal matters are under consideration the Attorneys General may attend. Ministers may be accompanied by their officials and their professional advisers: for example, when questions of security policy or security co-operation are being discussed, they may be accompanied by the Commissioner of the Garda Siochána and the Chief Constable of the Royal Ulster Constabulary; or when questions of economic or social policy, or co-operation are being discussed, they may be accompanied by officials of the relevant Departments. A Secretariat shall be established by the two Governments to service the Conference on a continuing basis in the discharge of its functions as set out in this Agreement.

Article 4

(a) In relation to matters coming within its field of activity, the Conference shall be a framework within which the Irish Government and the United Kingdom Government work together

- (i) for the accommodation of the rights and identities of the two traditions which exist in Northern Ireland; and
- (ii) for peace, stability and prosperity throughout the island of Ireland by promoting reconciliation, respect for human rights, co-operation against terrorism and the development of economic, social and cultural co-operation.

(b) It is the declared policy of the United Kingdom Government that responsibility in respect of certain matters within the powers of the Secretary of State for Northern Ireland should be devolved within Northern Ireland on a basis which would secure widespread acceptance throughout the community. The Irish Government support that policy.

(c) Both Governments recognise that devolution can be achieved only with the co-operation of constitutional representatives within Northern Ireland of both traditions there. The Conference shall be a framework within which the Irish Government may put forward views and proposals on the modalities of bringing about devolution in Northern Ireland, in so far as they relate to the interests of the minority community.

C. Political Matters
Article 5
(a) The Conference shall concern itself with measures to recognise and accommodate the rights and identities of the two traditions in Northern Ireland, to protect human rights and to prevent discrimination. Matters to be considered in this area include measures to foster the cultural heritage of both traditions, changes in electoral arrangements, the use of flags and emblems, the avoidance of economic and social discrimination and the advantages and disadvantages of a Bill of Rights in some form in Northern Ireland.

(b) The discussion of these matters shall be mainly concerned with Northern Ireland, but the possible application of any measures pursuant to this Article by the Irish Government in their jurisdiction shall not be excluded.

(c) If it should prove impossible to achieve and sustain devolution on a basis which secures widespread acceptance in Northern Ireland, the Conference shall be a framework within which the Irish Government may, where the interests of the minority community are significantly or especially affected, put forward views on proposals for major legislation and on major policy issues, which are within the purview of the Northern Ireland Departments and which remain the responsibility of the Secretary of State for Northern Ireland.

Article 6
The Conference shall be a framework within which the Irish Government may put forward views and proposals on the role and composition of bodies appointed by the Secretary of State for Northern Ireland or by Departments subject to his direction and control including

the Standing Advisory Commission on Human Rights;
the Fair Employment Agency;
the Equal Opportunities Commission;
the Police Authority for Northern Ireland;
the Police Complaints Board.

D. Security and Related Matters
Article 7
(a) The Conference shall consider

(i) security policy;
(ii) relations between the security forces and the community;
(iii) prisons policy.

(b) The Conference shall consider the security situation at its regular meetings and thus provide an opportunity to address policy issues, serious incidents and forthcoming events.

(c) The two Governments agree that there is a need for a programme of special measures in Northern Ireland to improve relations between the security forces and the community, with the object in particular of making the security forces more readily accepted by the nationalist community. Such a programme shall be developed, for the Conference's consideration, and may include the establishment of local consultative machinery, training in community relations, crime prevention schemes involving the community, improvements in arrangements for handling complaints, and action to increase the proportion of members of the minority in the Royal Ulster Constabulary. Elements of the programme may be considered by the Irish Government suitable for application within their jurisdiction.

(d) The Conference may consider policy issues relating to prisons. Individual cases may be raised as appropriate, so that information can be provided or inquiries instituted.

E. Legal Matters, Including the Administration of Justice
Article 8
The Conference shall deal with issues of concern to both countries relating to the enforcement of the criminal law. In particular it shall consider whether there are areas of the criminal law applying in the North and in the South respectively which might with benefit be harmonised. The two Governments agree on the importance of public confidence in the administration of justice. The Conference shall seek, with the help of advice from experts as appropriate, measures which would give substantial expression to this aim, considering inter alia the possibility of mixed courts in both jurisdictions for the trial of certain offences. The Conference shall also be concerned with policy aspects of extradition and extra-territorial jurisdiction as between North and South.

F. Cross-border Co-operation on Security, Economic, Social and Cultural Matters
Article 9
(a) With a view to enhancing cross-border co-operation on security matters, the Conference shall set in hand a programme of work to be undertaken by the Commissioner of the Garda Síochána and the Chief Constable of the Royal Ulster Constabulary and, where appropriate, groups of officials, in such areas as threat assessments, exchange of information, liaison structures, technical co-operation, training of personnel, and operational resources.

(b) The Conference shall have no operational responsibilities; responsibility for police operations shall remain with the heads of the respective police forces, the Commissioner of the Garda Síochána maintaining his links with the Minister for Justice and the Chief Constable of the Royal Ulster Constabulary his links with the Secretary of State for Northern Ireland.

Article 10
(a) The two Governments shall co-operate to promote the economic and social development of those areas of both parts of Ireland which have suffered most severely from the consequences of the instability of recent years, and shall consider the possibility of securing international support for this work.

(b) If it should prove impossible to achieve and sustain devolution on a basis which secures widespread acceptance in Northern Ireland, the Conference shall be a framework for the promotion of co-operation between the two parts of Ireland concerning cross-border aspects of economic, social and cultural matters in relation to which the Secretary of State for Northern Ireland continues to exercise authority.

(c) If responsibility is devolved in respect of certain matters in the economic, social or cultural areas currently within the responsibility of the Secretary of State for Northern Ireland, machinery will need to be established by the responsible authorities in the North and South for practical co-operation in respect of cross-border aspects of these issues.

G. Arrangements for Review
Article 11
At the end of three years from signature of this Agreement, or earlier if requested by either Government, the working of the Conference shall be reviewed by the two Governments to see whether any changes in the scope and nature of its activities are desirable.

H. Interparliamentary Relations
Article 12
It will be for Parliamentary decision in Dublin and in Westminster whether to establish an Anglo-Irish Parliamentary body of the kind adumbrated in the Anglo-Irish Studies Report of November 1981. The two Governments agree that they would give support as appropriate to such a body, if it were to be established.

I. Final Clauses
Article 13
This Agreement shall enter into force on the date on which the two Governments exchange notifications of their acceptance of this Agreement.

In witness whereof the undersigned, being duly authorised thereto by their respective Governments, have signed this Agreement.

Done in two originals at Hillsborough on the 15th day of November 1985

| For the Government of Ireland | For the Government of the United Kingdom |
| Gearóid Mac Gearailt | Margaret Thatcher |

Note: the second original text differed in the names of the contracting parties; it was an agreement between the Government of the United Kingdom of Great Britain and Northern Ireland and the Government of the Republic of Ireland.

Source: Ireland, 1985.

4

The Downing Street Declaration and Framework Documents, 1993–1995

4.1. Introduction

The Downing Street Declaration of 1993 and the Framework Documents of 1995 mark a new direction in British–Irish policy. Yet in important ways they follow from the Anglo-Irish Agreement of 1985, which had a double impact on political evolution in Northern Ireland. It directly affected the lives of Northern Ireland nationalists, since there now existed a mechanism that could be used systematically to bring their grievances in such areas as security policy to the attention of the British authorities. It also had a profound indirect effect, in encouraging two groups to reconsider their strategic approaches and policy goals. For unionists, there was now a strong incentive for compromise on the issue of power-sharing, since this offered a route to devolved government, and this would reduce the influence of the Irish government through the Anglo-Irish Intergovernmental Conference and its secretariat at Maryfield, outside Belfast.[1] For republicans, the political advances that the Agreement represented for their community demonstrated that progress could be achieved by peaceful means, that the party which used such means had been rewarded electorally for this (the SDLP share of the nationalist vote increased from 57 per cent in the 1983 House of Commons election to 65 per cent in 1987), and that a political strategy might be more effective than a military one. These shifts in perspective made it possible for the British and Irish governments to envisage a new path to a settlement. The way to this was paved by the Downing Street Declaration and the Framework Documents.

The Downing Street Declaration of 15 December 1993 was designed to outline the principles and parameters of future agreement, and the Framework Documents that followed on 22 February 1995 provided detail as to how these principles would be institutionalized. The Declaration was intended as a solemn statement that would indicate sufficient flexibility on the part of the British and Irish governments to allow all parties, including Sinn Féin, to engage in negotiations. Its particular significance lies in its role in preparing the ground for the IRA ceasefire of 31 August 1994 and, in the longer term, for the negotiations that

---

[1] On the unionist position, see Aughey (1989, 1999); Cochrane (1997); Farrington (2006).

Negotiating a Settlement in Northern Ireland, 1969–2019.
John Coakley and Jennifer Todd, Oxford University Press (2020). © John Coakley and Jennifer Todd.
DOI: 10.1093/oso/9780198841388.001.0001

followed, leading ultimately to the Good Friday Agreement. The joint British–Irish Framework Document outlined what the two governments believed a future settlement might look like in its North–South and British–Irish dimensions, while a second Framework Document, presented as one for which the British government was solely responsible, outlined the proposed structure of internal Northern Ireland institutions. While the British–Irish document was rejected by unionists, it remained an important backdrop to the later multi-party negotiations. Since most of the discussions that led to the Declaration and to the Framework Documents took place in secret, the perspectives of those involved have a particular significance.

While it is clear that the Downing Street Declaration and the Framework Documents marked a new turn in the efforts to resolve the Northern Ireland conflict, the character and direction of this change are much less clear. Some have taken the view that this shift constituted a new interpretation of constitutional principles on the part of the British and Irish governments.[2] For others, the shift was less radical, emphasizing the long-standing British commitment to what is called the 'principle of [majority] consent' in respect of constitutional change, and, within this, an attempt to bring in all of the parties to an agreement.[3] Meanwhile, the Irish government made more explicit its long-standing pragmatic acceptance of the 'principle of consent', and redefined national self-determination to refer not to the people of the whole island but to majorities in its two parts.[4] The British–Irish Framework Document provides some operationalization of the 'principle of consent', which for the first time is understood as operating at two levels: consent on the part of the two communities to internal arrangements in Northern Ireland, and an explicit reiteration of the requirement of consent on the part of majorities in the two jurisdictions to a united Ireland (a condition that had been accepted by the two governments since 1973). These principles were embedded within a complex structure of multilevelled governance, transcending the Irish border. Thus some have argued that it exemplifies a radical shift in modes of understanding of sovereignty, one which was taken forward into the negotiation of the Good Friday Agreement itself.[5]

The Downing Street Declaration was constructed as a message to republicans, to loyalists, and to unionists that the two governments were willing to take account of their interests and concerns, and to create political conditions where agreement would be possible. It was at the same time a statement of the principles followed by the governments, a statement further specified in the British–Irish

---

[2] See O'Duffy (2007); O'Leary (1995); Ruane and Todd (2014); Todd (2014).
[3] See the discussion in the witness seminar, and Ó Dochartaigh (2015); O'Kane (2007).
[4] On the changes in the Irish position, and the extent to which they maintained or changed nationalist principles, see Coakley (2017a, b).
[5] See discussions by Meehan (2014); Morison (2001); and the parallel discussions about sovereignty in the United Kingdom by Keating (2001, 2018).

Framework Document. This makes for a difficulty in interpreting the clauses of the documents: are they to be seen as codes addressing the concerns of the other political actors, as principles of future governance, or as both? The participants in the witness seminar and interviews treat them in both ways, and they also have subtly different interpretations of the principles at issue. The crucial 'principle of consent', for example, means that constitutional change to a united Ireland requires the consent of a majority in Northern Ireland (and in the Republic of Ireland). But this leaves unclear whether the status quo—British sovereignty—is indeed consistent with transborder institutions and a role for the Irish government. These are issues that were again to become of crucial importance after the Good Friday Agreement and in the 2010s.[6] It is thus particularly important to examine how the officials understood them in the 1990s—whether the ambiguities implied new forms of understanding, and/or a new flexibility, or simply an appeal to different constituencies. The witness seminar and interviews provide extended and frank discussion of the manner in which those who negotiated and drafted the Declaration and Frameworks understood the principles and the institutions that might embody them.

4.1.1. Political Background

The Downing Street Declaration emerged against a background of long-term Conservative government in Britain, stretching from 1979 to 1997 (see Table 4.1). A significant leadership change took place in November 1990, when Margaret Thatcher was ousted and replaced as party leader and prime minister by John Major. Although Major won a second term as prime minister at the general election of 9 April 1992, a small drop in Conservative support (from 42.2 per cent to 41.9 per cent) resulted in a big reduction in the size of the government's majority, which fell from fifty seats after the 1987 election to just twenty-one in 1992. This lead was progressively eroded as a result of by-election losses and defections, though it was not until the end of 1996 that the government became a minority one. As its majority fell, the Major government became increasingly vulnerable to backbench dissent and pressure from other parties, most significantly from the Ulster Unionist Party, with its block of nine MPs.

There was less continuity on the Irish side. The Fine Gael–Labour coalition headed by Garret FitzGerald that had taken office in December 1982 was replaced in March 1987 by a single-party Fianna Fáil government headed by Charles Haughey. In July 1989, Haughey led Fianna Fáil into its first-ever coalition, with the Progressive Democrats, following an indecisive general election. Albert Reynolds took over this government when Haughey was forced to resign in

---

[6] On the later disagreements, see Section 6.1 and Subsections 6.7.2, 7.2.4 and 7.3.1.

Table 4.1. Important political developments, 1985–1995

Date	Development
1 May 1987	Sinn Féin publishes *Scenario for Peace*, calling for political talks
11 January 1988	First meeting between John Hume and Gerry Adams, leaders of the SDLP and Sinn Féin, takes place; further meetings follow
9 November 1990	Northern Ireland Secretary Peter Brooke states Britain has 'no selfish economic or strategic interest' in Northern Ireland
17 June 1991	Inter-party talks brokered by Peter Brooke begin (suspended on 3 July; resumed under Sir Patrick Mayhew, 29 April 1992; end 10 November 1992)
9 April 1992	British general election; Major returned with very small majority
15 December 1993	Downing Street Declaration
29 January 1994	Sinn Féin leader Gerry Adams given visa to visit USA
31 August 1994	IRA announces ceasefire
13 October 1994	Loyalist paramilitary groups announce ceasefire
28 October 1994	Forum for Peace and Reconciliation opens in Dublin (work suspended 29 March 1996 due to ending of IRA ceasefire)
22 February 1995	Framework Documents published

February 1992, and, following the collapse of the coalition and another general election, he formed a new alliance with the Labour Party in January 1993. This coalition, too, broke apart, and Reynolds stood down as party leader and Taoiseach in December 1994. A 'rainbow coalition' of Fine Gael, Labour, and Democratic Left, led by John Bruton, took office instead.

While the Anglo-Irish Agreement recalibrated relations between the British and Irish governments and offered a more formal channel for cooperation between the two, it had no immediate effect on the level of violence; the IRA campaign continued. Neither did it do much to break the political stalemate; unionists continued to hold out against power-sharing, preventing the return of devolved government. Indeed, in the short term, unionist alienation was aggravated by the Agreement.

Nevertheless, subtle changes in approach were paving the way for a convergence in the positions of the parties to the conflict. First, there were signs of a significant strategic and ideological shift within the IRA and Sinn Féin. Second, this reorientation was reflected in efforts by Sinn Féin to participate in a political negotiation process, and in a willingness by other political leaders to encourage this. Third, the British government engaged in talks with the political parties and with the Irish government with a view to identifying the parameters of a settlement.[7]

---

[7] For background, see Bloomfield (1998, 2001); Coakley and Todd (2014a); English (2003); McLoughlin (2010); Ó Dochartaigh (2015).

Evidence of a fundamental shift within Sinn Féin began to emerge in the mid-1980s. The party leadership had, since the organization was founded in 1970, sought to defend traditional Sinn Féin orthodoxy.[8] This rested on three distinctive pillars. The best known was the attainment of Irish unity by reliance on the IRA, since it was believed that only military pressure on the British could achieve this. Sinn Féin also refused to contemplate attendance at the parliaments in Belfast, Dublin, and London, since they were seen as illegitimate, and the first two were presented as British-imposed institutions. To complete the package, the party elevated the results of the UK general election of 1918 to iconic status, since this was viewed as the last—and only—election at which the people of Ireland had been allowed to pass their collective verdict on the 'national question', voting for a thirty-two-county Irish republic separate from Great Britain.

Signs of dissatisfaction with this position crystallized after Sinn Féin's electoral successes in the early 1980s. A key component in the party's blueprint for Irish unity had been a federal Ireland with the four historic provinces as its component units. This was dropped in 1983. The following year Gerry Adams succeeded Ruairi Ó Brádaigh as party president, symbolizing a shift both towards a younger generation and towards the area where Sinn Féin was most active, Northern Ireland. In 1986, the party ended its policy of abstention from the Dáil, precipitating the withdrawal of a traditionalist faction led by Ó Brádaigh, who went on to form Republican Sinn Féin.[9] Evolution in the thinking of the party leadership was to be seen in a new 'discussion document', A Scenario for Peace, which, after restating the traditional republican interpretation of the right to national self-determination, proposed a British withdrawal and the transfer of power to 'an all-Ireland constitutional convention and national government'.[10] These strategic changes culminated in a formal offer by Gerry Adams to engage in a 'peace process', articulated in a letter to Prime Minister John Major on 20 August 1991 (see Document 4.2).[11]

The second broad change involved the gradual movement of Sinn Féin into the political mainstream, paving the way for the ending of its pariah status after the

---

[8] The 'Sinn Féin' label has been a contested one. The original Sinn Féin party broke up in 1922, with its two main wings now represented by Fine Gael and Fianna Fáil. The remnants retained the name Sinn Féin after the formation of Fianna Fáil in 1926, and, when an IRA campaign in Northern Ireland in 1956–62 proved ineffective in every respect, the party moved in the direction of social activism. More militant elements broke away in 1970, following a parallel split in the IRA, to form what is now known as Sinn Féin.

[9] See English (2003: 250–2).

[10] See Sinn Féin (1987); further evolution in republican thinking may be seen in a later policy document, Towards a Lasting Peace in Ireland (Sinn Féin 1992); see also Adams (2003: 41–114).

[11] Adams (2003: 99) stated later that the idea of writing to Major just after his installation as prime minister 'came to me after reading that Ho Chi Minh persisted in writing to heads of the various foreign governments involved in his country'. Although the letter was addressed to '10 Downing Street, Belfast' by one of Adams's 'geographically challenged colleagues', it reached the prime minister (Adams 2003: 99).

1994 ceasefire. The advent of a more pragmatic leadership in Sinn Féin opened up the potential for dialogue with other parties. Sinn Féin and IRA leaders had been in contact with the British government periodically since 1972, at different levels, including secret contacts between Martin McGuinness and a British intelligence official that continued episodically until the early 1990s. Leading Fianna Fáil politicians, such as Charles Haughey from the late 1980s onwards, sought to maintain similar (indirect) contacts. These were developed further by Albert Reynolds, who extended them also to contacts with loyalist paramilitary organizations.

The third major change was the emergence of a more purposeful position on the part of the British government, which also worked on several fronts to bring about a settlement. These included overtures to republicans, negotiations with the Northern Ireland parties, and talks with the Irish government. In a gesture towards the republican side, Northern Ireland Secretary Peter Brooke delivered a carefully crafted speech on 9 November 1990 in which he stated that the British government had 'no selfish strategic or economic interest' in Northern Ireland (see Document 4.1). The multiple meanings of this statement are discussed in the witness seminar that follows. Parallel to this, Brooke sought to launch multi-party talks, involving also the Irish government. These took shape in April 1991 and continued under Brooke's successor, Sir Patrick Mayhew, coming to an inconclusive end in November 1992.

The talks nevertheless broke new ground. They took place on the basis of the three 'strands' that ultimately formed the framework of the Good Friday Agreement (internal Northern Ireland matters, the North–South dimension, and the British–Irish relationship). They demonstrated how talks involving unionist parties could proceed while the Anglo-Irish Agreement remained in force, by making creative use of gaps between meetings of the Anglo-Irish Intergovernmental Conference, for unionists would negotiate only when they could claim the conference was dormant. The talks implied unionist acceptance of the principle of Irish government involvement in negotiations. They took place under an international chair. Finally, they introduced an important negotiating principle: that 'nothing is agreed until everything is agreed', such that any agreement would be a complex package where preferences in one field would be balanced against preferences in another.

4.1.2. The Pursuit of Agreement

Negotiations between the Sinn Féin leader, Gerry Adams, and the SDLP leader, John Hume, added a new dimension to the sequence of events that was to conclude in the Downing Street Declaration. Sinn Féin remained entirely excluded from the multi-party talks of 1991–2 because the IRA campaign was continuing. Bringing Sinn Féin 'in' became an increasing priority for the Irish government.

In addition to other contacts, a set of meetings between Sinn Féin and the SDLP took place during 1988. Talks continued intermittently between the two party leaders, Gerry Adams and John Hume, who by 1991 were working towards an agreed statement that—if accepted by the governments—would result in an IRA ceasefire and would open the door to talks on a settlement. Based on his discussions with the Sinn Féin leader, on 6 October 1991 John Hume prepared an early draft of a proposed British–Irish government statement that he hoped would be capable of bridging the gap between the IRA and the governments sufficiently to provide a momentum towards peace (Mallie and McKittrick 1996: 115–20; see Document 4.3). A few days later, Charles Haughey and his advisors worked to produce a revised version of this (Mallie and McKittrick 1996: 121–3; see Document 4.4.). This became the basis for preliminary—if reserved—analysis by the British side. The British also received an early Sinn Féin draft of the republican movement's preferred wording of a joint declaration in February 1992 (Document 4.5).[12]

Following this initial progress, the momentum towards the preparation of a joint declaration declined, and the negotiations were overshadowed by violent conflict in Northern Ireland. But the process resumed in earnest in early 1993, under the committed management of Taoiseach Albert Reynolds and Prime Minister John Major, with much of the work being carried out by a small group of officials led by their respective Cabinet Secretaries, Dermot Nally and Sir Robin Butler (later Lord Butler). A revised draft declaration prepared by Albert Reynolds and his advisors was given to the British in June 1993 (see Document 4.6), and subsequent developments of this sought to take account of the views of other parties to the conflict, as communicated to the Irish or British governments either directly or through intermediaries.[13] The witness seminar in this chapter focuses on the drafting that took place in 1993 and the extent to which the several drafts incorporated earlier texts.[14] The process was brought to a successful conclusion in December 1993, not helped by the leaking of a version of the British–Irish 'Framework Document' that the governments were simultaneously negotiating (see Document 4.7). The joint declaration by the two prime ministers in Downing Street on 15 December 1993 represented significant progress in efforts to marry conflicting versions of how the Irish problem could be resolved by peaceful democratic means (see Document 4.8).

The Declaration, together with other gestures by the British and Irish governments, was pivotal in persuading the IRA to declare a ceasefire on 31 August 1994. It at once affirmed and redefined self-determination, echoing and elaborating phrases already agreed at Sunningdale and in the Anglo-Irish Agreement. The declaration recorded the British government's statement of neutrality in respect of

---

[12] On the cool British reaction to the Irish government document, see Robin Butler to Stephen Wall, 30 January and 7 February 1992, TNA: PREM 19/3823.

[13] Dermot Nally's extensive notes from the process are deposited in UCD Archives (UCDA P254).

[14] See, in particular, Sections 4.4–4.5.

Irish unity and its commitment that 'it is for the people of the island of Ireland alone [...] to exercise their right of self-determination [...] to bring about a united Ireland, if that is their wish'. This appears to be an endorsement of the traditional republican demand for Irish self-determination; but it is qualified by the condition that the exercise of self-determination must be only 'by agreement between the two parts' of the island of Ireland, and then 'on the basis of consent, freely and concurrently given, North and South', thus giving each part of the island a veto on unity. Nevertheless, the statement was sufficient to allow the republican leadership to present it as a fundamental shift in the British position, though they stopped short of accepting it, instead posing a set of 'questions' to the British government (see Document 4.9). An IRA ceasefire was eventually announced on 31 August 1994. A subsequent ceasefire was announced on 13 October 1994 by the Combined Loyalist Military Command (an umbrella group that included the UDA and the UVF). At this stage, the path to comprehensive negotiations seemed open.

The ceasefires were followed by a series of discussions designed to pave the way for multi-party talks. Although Sinn Féin engaged in bilateral negotiations with the British and Irish governments, all-party talks remained somewhere in the distance, since the British government, but not the Irish government, insisted that IRA decommissioning was a condition of Sinn Féin entering multi-party talks. The Irish government, however, in line with its commitment in the Downing Street Declaration, convened a 'Forum for Peace and Reconciliation', comprising delegations from the main southern parties, the Alliance Party and both northern nationalist parties (including Sinn Féin). This first met in Dublin on 28 October 1994, but was adjourned on 29 March 1996, after the end of the IRA ceasefire, without producing a final report.[15]

Meanwhile, British and Irish government officials had continued their meetings in an effort to agree the detailed shape of a future settlement, resulting in the Framework Documents announced by Prime Minister John Major and Taoiseach John Bruton on 22 February 1995. One of the two documents (which we label the 'British–Irish' one; see Document 4.11) described 'a shared understanding between the British and Irish Governments to assist discussion and negotiation involving the Northern Ireland parties', and confirmed the three-strand approach (power-sharing devolution within Northern Ireland, the North–South dimension, and the British–Irish relationship) that had formed the basis of the Brooke–Mayhew talks in 1991–2. It outlined an architecture of cross-border and British–Irish institutions, and proposed constitutional guarantees that would provide a framework for settlement. The second document (which we label the 'Northern Ireland' one; see Document 4.10) was issued by the British government

[15] The Forum met briefly subsequently, in December 1997, and unsuccessful efforts were made to revive it in 2002–3 to fill the political vacuum caused by the suspension of the devolved institutions in Northern Ireland.

alone, and offered 'a framework for accountable government in Northern Ireland', articulating government thinking on the shape that devolved institutions might take, and the powers that would be transferred to them.

The Framework proposals were immediately rejected by unionist parties, while both the SDLP and Sinn Féin came to see them as outlining the minimal shape of an acceptable institutional agreement, with the latter interpreting the process as a stepping stone to Irish unity. Notwithstanding their negative reception by unionists, the Framework Documents remained important in the minds of the government negotiators who prepared the drafts of the Good Friday Agreement.

For ease of reference we include here a chronology—drawn from the witness seminar—of the negotiations that led to the Downing Street Declaration (see Table 4.2). The British had been given two different drafts of a proposed British–Irish declaration in 1991–2—one by the Irish government, the other, indirectly, by

Table 4.2. Stages in the British–Irish intergovernmental talks, 1991–1993

Date	Stage
20 August 1991	Letter from Gerry Adams to Prime Minister John Major proposing establishment of a 'peace process'
6 October 1991	Draft British–Irish government declaration produced by John Hume; later amended by Haughey and his advisors
21 February 1992	Prime Minister's office in possession of draft produced by Sinn Féin
1 February 1993	Letter to the British government purporting to come from the IRA stating: 'the conflict is over. Help us bring it to an end.'
29 March 1993	Reynolds works on draft of proposed joint declaration
19 June 1993	Draft Irish text; later handed to Robin Butler at Baldonnel aerodrome
4 August 1993	Robin Butler–Dermot Nally meeting [continues 5 August]
1 September 1993	John Major consults Jim Molyneaux, leader of UUP
10 September 1993	British and Irish officials meet
1 October 1993	Albert Reynolds consults Archbishop Eames and Revd Roy Magee
5 October 1993	Drafting meeting attended by British and Irish civil servants [continues 6 October]
29 October 1993	Brussels EC summit; Hume makes public existence of Hume–Adams document
1 November 1993	Letters exchanged between Major and Reynolds and messages exchanged between Lyne and Mansergh; British begin redraft of the Declaration
2 November 1993	Eames adds provisions to the declaration
10 November 1993	British and Irish officials meet; British uneasy about the draft document.
26 November 1993	British introduce new document
3 December 1993	British–Irish summit meeting; decision to return to the original draft
7 December 1993	Meeting between Dermot Nally and Robin Butler
14 December 1993	Final stages of negotiations
15 December 1993	London summit; Downing Street Declaration

Sinn Féin. Back-channel contact with the IRA was also ongoing until November 1993. The main British–Irish negotiations on the Downing Street Declaration, however, took place between June 1993 and 15 December 1993, and were particularly intense in their last two months. These negotiations overlapped in timing and personnel with ongoing British–Irish discussions among officials which resulted in the Framework Documents in February 1995.

4.1.3. The Witness Seminar and Interviews

The witness seminar, which took place on 2 June 2008 at the SAS Radisson Hotel, Stillorgan, Dublin, included the former Cabinet Secretary, Lord Butler; the former Secretary to the Government, Dermot Nally, who had been called back for the negotiations; his replacement as government secretary, Frank Murray; and Sir Quentin Thomas, formerly of the Northern Ireland Office (NIO).

The academic questioners included Michael Anderson, John Coakley, Christopher Farrington, Susan McDermott, Peter McLoughlin, Joseph Ruane, and Jennifer Todd.

Although the joint British-Irish Framework Document was mentioned in the witness seminar, it was not discussed in depth, so extracts are appended from separate interviews with Seán Ó hUiginn, formerly of the Department of Foreign Affairs, and Sir Quentin Thomas, formerly of the Northern Ireland Office, who led the Irish and British teams of officials who worked together on the drafting of the joint Framework Document. Both interviews were conducted by Jennifer Todd, respectively in Dublin on 23 October 2010 and in London on 21 September 2010.

4.2. Towards a New Initiative

DERMOT NALLY: As far as we are concerned, this project has been discussed with the previous Taoiseach, and he has said 'go ahead, we need an archive, we need to see the process for what it was in its completeness'. So, I have no problems, but let us see the text.

4.2.1. Participant Roles

Q: We invite the four participants to introduce themselves and to indicate the role they played during this period, beginning perhaps with you, Lord Butler.

ROBIN BUTLER: I am Robin Butler; I was involved in the Anglo-Irish and the Northern Ireland issue in two successive stages—when I was Private Secretary in 10 Downing Street, and then when I was Cabinet Secretary. The first stage was in 1972–5, when I was Edward Heath's Private Secretary, but not the

Principal Private Secretary (Robert Armstrong was the Principal Private Secretary), but I was dealing with Northern Ireland at the time of the Sunningdale Agreement and went to Sunningdale. That was my first introduction to this issue. Then I left Downing Street in 1975, and returned to the Treasury. I had nothing to do with Northern Ireland until I returned to Number 10 in 1982.

I was then Principal Private Secretary from 1982 to 1985, so it covered the period of the Anglo-Irish Agreement. But, really, I was not very closely involved in it. It was Robert Armstrong who led it, and somebody else was doing the job that I'd done in Number 10 as the junior Private Secretary dealing with Northern Ireland. So, although the negotiation of the Anglo-Irish Agreement went on under my nose, I was not really very directly involved in it myself.

I then left Downing Street again, in 1985, and returned as Cabinet Secretary in 1988, in succession to Robert Armstrong, and I was there for the next ten years. I was therefore involved, insofar as the Prime Minister was involved, over the development of the three-tiered, three-stranded initiative, and then the various things that happened in 1993, when there were three separate initiatives going on as far as the British government was concerned, one of which was the one that led to the Downing Street Declaration of 1993, and then after that the first ceasefire and the subsequent breakdown.

I left at the end of 1997, after eight months of Tony Blair, when he had first, as it were, got himself involved in the Northern Ireland situation, and in the lead-up to the Good Friday Agreement, but I was no longer in service by the time that the Good Friday Agreement took place in early 1998. So, I think that is an account of my involvement.

QUENTIN THOMAS: I am Quentin Thomas. Most of my career was in the Home Office. In 1988—November, I think—I was seconded to the Northern Ireland Office for two years, which turned out to be more like ten. I was the sort of Under-Secretary-level person in London concerned with political and constitutional matters until, I think, the summer of 1991, when I was promoted to be what was called the political director, in which position I remained until I left the Northern Ireland Office, very shortly after the Good Friday Agreement.

So, I was fairly closely involved from the Northern Ireland Office perspective in the development of the talks process. It was not called the talks process then, of course—we called it the 'nudge' initially. I was involved in the round-table talks of 1991, the round-table talks of 1992, and the three things that were going on in 1993 that Robin has referred to, including the one that culminated in the Downing Street Declaration, the clarification of the Downing Street Declaration.

I led the team of officials that met Sinn Féin three months after the ceasefire, in December 1994. We were also working on what became the Framework Documents, published in February 1995, and then on the launch of the talks process, following elections in spring of 1996 through until the Good Friday

Agreement on Good Friday of 1998.[16] So, that is my involvement. I am sorry
Seán Ó hUiginn is not here; he was my main sparring partner during this
period, though sadly not for the last year and a bit.

DERMOT NALLY: I was invited by the Taoiseach, Jack Lynch, to come to his office
in January 1973, and the Cabinet Secretary said to me 'Nally, you look after
Northern Ireland'. That was my introduction to the subject. Since then I have
worked on the Sunningdale Agreement; the summit between Charlie Haughey
and Mrs Thatcher of December 1980, which potentially was of considerable
importance but instead went totally the wrong way; the Anglo-Irish Agreement of 1985; and the Downing Street Declaration of 1993.

So, those twenty years were a small part of what occupied me, as I think
Frank will acknowledge, because I think Frank was working with me in a lot of
the stuff we were dealing with.

FRANK MURRAY: I came to the Department of the Taoiseach in January 1974, as
Private Secretary to Liam Cosgrave, who was then Taoiseach. I was not
primarily involved in relation to Anglo-Irish or Northern Ireland matters,
although I recall at that stage we got a lot of correspondence on Northern
Ireland issues, particularly from the United States. The theme of many of the
letters, indeed, would be that we weren't doing enough—we weren't standing
up for our people in Northern Ireland.

From 1977 until 1983, I worked on what might be called the Northern
Ireland desk in the Department of the Taoiseach.

From 1983 until the end of 1993, I was Assistant Secretary to the Government, dealing largely with normal cabinet office issues, the weekly government
business agenda, and so forth. I was not primarily dealing with anything to do
with Northern Ireland at that time, except perhaps in relation to some security
aspects. I filled in for Dermot while he was heavily engaged in the negotiations
for the Anglo-Irish Agreement in 1985. I got great exposure at that time to the
workings of cabinet government.

I replaced Dermot as Secretary to the Government and afterwards became
Secretary General to the government when he retired at the end—the very
end—of 1992, or the beginning of January 1993.

I am still involved with Northern Ireland. I am an independent commissioner for the location of victims' remains, something that was a side initiative
from the Good Friday Agreement itself, and, together with Sir Ken Bloomfield,
we have regular contacts, meetings with relatives, and we are still dealing with
or through our agents, representatives of the IRA and the INLA.[17] We are

---

[16] An election took place on 30 May 1996 to a Northern Ireland Forum; the election was used as a
mechanism for legitimizing the teams that took part in the later inter-party talks.

[17] The Independent Commission for the Location of Victims Remains was established on 27 April
1999 under the terms of the Good Friday Agreement; see <www.iclvr.ie> (accessed 21 May 2019). The
commissioners were Frank Murray and Sir Kenneth Bloomfield; see Appendix 1.1; Ch.2, n. 22.

trying to cope with all of the problems thrown up during the time we are talking of, and specifically finding the remains of about nine people at this stage, including Captain Nairac, which we are following up as assiduously as we can.[18]

4.2.2. Motivation for a New Initiative

Q: Why was a new initiative pursued so soon after the Anglo-Irish Agreement had been reached? Were there aspects of the agreement that the two governments found incomplete? Were there issues to do with the implementation of the Agreement with which one or other government had difficulties?

DERMOT NALLY: In 1985, Mrs Thatcher was happy with the agreement when she signed it, but she was unhappy with it afterwards, because it did not give what she thought she would get—in other words, far-improved security. As far as we were concerned, we were disappointed, because it was not built on. In other words, the amenities of the secretariat were used, but only to a very limited extent. The Anglo-Irish Intergovernmental Conference was supposed to build bridges between the two communities. People could work together, and by working together would become a little less inclined to shoot each other. But that was not working either, so things were simply ticking over.

Then somebody delivered a letter to Charlie Haughey in 1986, when he was in opposition. The letter purported to come from a senior republican and it said: 'If the British simply say that they will leave it to the people of Ireland to decide their own future, the IRA will be happy'. Now, Haughey never admitted to the existence of this letter, but it was part of the inspiration for his meetings with John Major, when John Major came back into power. Haughey's relations with Mrs Thatcher were such that I do not think they could speak seriously to each other, particularly after the Falklands.[19]

Now, that leads to the situation in or around 1990–3. Peter Brooke, the Northern Secretary, made a speech, the Whitbread speech, in which he used the phrase which is used in the joint declaration about the absence of 'selfish strategic or economic interest' in Northern Ireland.[20]

---

[18] Captain Robert Nairac, a British military intelligence officer, was abducted in South Armagh and murdered in May 1977. His body was not recovered. By early 2018, three bodies, including that of Captain Nairac, remained to be found.

[19] Haughey clashed with Thatcher when, as Taoiseach, he refused to support her military initiative to recapture the Falklands Islands; see Subsection 3.2.2.

[20] An advance copy of the speech was supplied to Sinn Féin, as confirmed by that party (see Sinn Féin 1994). The speech was so known because of the Whitbread restaurant in Brooke's London constituency in which it was delivered on 9 November 1990; for the text, see Document 4.1.

ROBIN BUTLER: November 1990.

DERMOT NALLY: November 1990. Now that was really the keystone. In one of his rare meetings with John Major, Haughey said we could build on that thought, we could build on that speech; Nally and Butler should get together and talk. They kept talking about this, that Nally and Butler should get together and solve the whole thing. But Haughey went out of office in January 1992, and Albert Reynolds came into office. There were many meetings; I have a list of them here.[21]

I have notes on the meetings between the two prime ministers, and in this I would just like to break the sequence a little and to say that on Northern Ireland there was no way that any solution could come other than by conversations between the two prime ministers—other than by interchanges between the prime ministers. It had to happen at prime-ministerial level because what was being discussed was sovereignty. You could have secretaries of state or ministers of state or ministers for foreign affairs or whoever, but, no matter who they were, the only serious discussions could be discussions between prime ministers.

Now, that brought us up to 1992. Albert came in after that and he started to say 'look, there is a chance for peace, I have a feeling that peace is on offer'—he had obviously been briefed by Haughey—'and we must grasp this chance'. A draft of the declaration was produced, and I have this original draft here. It is the Downing Street Declaration, an early draft.[22]

Incidentally, this heap of paper need not frighten you. It is simply that it is my own filing system. I retired in January 1993, and I was gone as Cabinet Secretary or Secretary to the Government from January 1993. But Albert kept coming back to me saying 'do this', or 'do that', or something else; and then he said: 'Will you come back and negotiate this with Robin Butler, or whoever comes up on the other side?' So I said 'yes, of course, I can't refuse a request from the Taoiseach'.

So that was how I came to be involved. But the involvement meant looking after myself in terms of paper. So I had the most peculiar collection of papers sitting around at home; all the drafts of the agreements, all the amendments that were made at each meeting, and more or less the progress on what happened, including the meetings between the two prime ministers, one on 3 December, which I thought was going to bring the whole thing down.[23]

---

[21] See n. 13.

[22] The first Irish government draft, based on the original Hume draft but revised by Haughey and his advisors, had reached the British by the end of January 1992 (see Document 4.4).

[23] See discussion at Subsection 4.4.5.

Q: So the initiative came from the Republicans? This influenced Haughey's thinking, and he decided to look for an alternative strategy to the Anglo-Irish Agreement?

DERMOT NALLY: The Anglo-Irish Agreement was based essentially on the thought that Sunningdale, which offered most promise of peace, had been collapsed because the streets had taken against it. So the Anglo-Irish Agreement was made in such a way that the streets could not collapse it. In other words, it was an agreement between the two governments, and if you wanted to shift the agreement you had to shift the two governments. I think that lesson got through at great cost. And, of course, the Anglo-Irish Agreement disappeared into the Good Friday Agreement, but that does not matter because it had served its purpose.

Q: Disappeared into the Good Friday Agreement or was written into the Good Friday Agreement in some respects?

DERMOT NALLY: The valuable parts of it were taken out and put into the Good Friday Agreement. But the Anglo-Irish Agreement was repealed because the unionists said: 'you know, we hate this document, 500,000 people have demonstrated on the streets, therefore part of our agreement to the Good Friday Agreement must depend on the abolition of the Anglo-Irish Agreement.'

Q: So, from the British perspective, then, what was the impetus for reconsidering? Perhaps, first, Lord Butler, what changes did you see in Anglo-Irish relations when you came back in 1988?

ROBIN BUTLER: Well that enables me just to say one thing, which I would like to say while I remember it. When I came back in 1988 as Cabinet Secretary, I inherited from Robert Armstrong something that he had set up with Dermot in the process of negotiating the Anglo Irish Agreement. When that process was finished, they agreed that a group of officials would continue to meet, about every three months, alternately in London and Dublin, to discuss whatever was about in Anglo-Irish relations.

Now, there was not an awful lot going on as regards Northern Ireland, but, of course, there were other issues—like issues that were coming up at EU councils and so on. We had a series of very nice dinners that took place either over here or in London. I remember on one occasion we combined it with the England–Ireland rugby match. The reason I want to emphasize this is that I think that the personal relations that were built up and maintained over the Anglo-Irish Agreement, and then maintained by that continuing process, which as I say I inherited and Dermot lived all the way through, were absolutely invaluable when it came to 1993, because there was a great trust between us on both sides.

Quentin will remember these because the Northern Ireland Office took part in them. I think what was important was that Dermot and I, the people who were closest to our respective heads of government, took part in them. So, I would just like that to be on record.

DERMOT NALLY: I second that part totally, the trust between the two sides.

ROBIN BUTLER: Now I am going to hand over to Quentin as to what happened after 1986, because I left Downing Street at the end of 1985. I think that what Dermot said about Margaret Thatcher's attitude was correct. I do not want to go back over the Anglo-Irish Agreement, but the pressure for the Anglo-Irish Agreement really came after 1983 with there being no forward impetus. That was the argument that really swayed Margaret Thatcher, and Willie Whitelaw cudgelled her into doing it.[24] Some of her closest friends were deeply opposed to it, as well as the unionists over here. Ian Gow famously resigned over it.[25] He had been parliamentary private secretary and meant a great deal to her.

So I think, as Dermot says, by the time I left Downing Street at the end of 1985, she was disenchanted with it; her relations with Charlie Haughey were very poor; she was not getting the security cooperation. When I came back in 1988, Margaret Thatcher was still Prime Minister, and Charlie Haughey was still the Taoiseach, and nothing was really going on at head-of-government level in Britain. Quentin will be able to say what was going on as far as the Northern Ireland Office was concerned, but, as I saw it, nothing really happened until John Major became Prime Minister in November 1990. That led very quickly to the Peter Brooke speech.

QUENTIN THOMAS: Interestingly, the formulation is a matter of moment—the formulation of 'a matter of no selfish strategic interest' had been used by the previous Secretary of State, Tom King.[26] But it had no resonance because he hadn't established the right sort of persona and profile, whereas by the time that speech came, it was 10–11 months after the speech in January 1990, when Peter Brooke had said, to universal scepticism, that he discerned that there was enough common ground for round-table talks to be meaningful, with some hope of success—a universal scepticism shared in Dublin, as I remember very well.[27]

DERMOT NALLY: I do not want to interrupt Quentin, but if you can get the note of the meeting between Charlie Haughey and Major in December 1991, you will find that Haughey is saying that we must build on Brooke's words, the Irish Convention.[28]

[24] Thatcher relied heavily on William Whitelaw's judgement as Home Secretary, and he played the role of Deputy Prime Minister until his resignation in December 1987.

[25] See Ch. 3, n. 14.

[26] At a speech to the Institute of Directors in Belfast on 26 September 1988, Tom King had asserted that the British government had 'no secret economic or strategic reason' for remaining in Northern Ireland; *Irish Times*, 5 October 1988.

[27] This speech was delivered by Peter Brooke in Bangor, Co. Down, on 9 January 1990.

[28] The significance of the phrase 'Irish convention' is discussed further in Subsections 4.3.4 and 4.4.4; see Documents 4.3–4.6.

QUENTIN THOMAS: In December 1991?

DERMOT NALLY: 1991, yes. 'We will build on an Irish Convention with wider representation than Brooke's three-stranded talks.'

QUENTIN THOMAS: Yes.

DERMOT NALLY: And there is the three-stranded talks [process] going on.

QUENTIN THOMAS: Yes, but we are a long way down the road. January 1990, March 1991, we've launched the three-stranded talks process, you are now a long way after that. The scepticism I am talking about is in January 1990, well before that.

ROBIN BUTLER: While Margaret Thatcher was still Prime Minister?

QUENTIN THOMAS: I think so. Shall I track back a bit? I was not there from 1985 to 1988. I was in the Home Office. When I came to the Northern Ireland Office, what I found on the Anglo-Irish Agreement was that people were working purposefully to have regular meetings of the conference, and to use Maryfield, and so on, and there was great determination by both governments to demonstrate that this agreement was a functioning entity and would not be seen off, despite unionist opposition.

But what I saw was shared frustration. The Irish government somehow felt that the British side had let them down. They were not using it purposely. It hadn't led to all the developments they had hoped for. The British side, particularly on the Prime Minister's part, had hoped for a much readier security cooperation. There were all sorts of haggles about cross-border pursuits and all the rest of it, and it was all pretty frustrating. I was not on the security side very much, but obviously I was interested in it. It was characterized mainly by bad temper and sheer frustration, I think.

The unionist alienation from the agreement and from the institutions of government was pretty total; unionist politicians wouldn't admit to talking to British ministers, and on the whole, did not. They would write to the permanent secretaries of departments in Northern Ireland of that period, not to British ministers, and if they bumped into them at funerals they might say a few words, that sort of thing. But there was pretty total shutdown. I think one of the first things was that it was not working very well; everybody was bad-tempered; everyone was determined to show that they wouldn't be seen off. And, as for the unionist nation, they had gone home, and that seemed deeply unsatisfactory. Although senior officials were meeting and having agreeable dinners, the main community in Northern Ireland were not even coming for breakfast, and that was a fundamental problem with the whole situation.

Tom King would have liked to have talks going. He tried quite hard. But the first obstacle in getting people together was the Anglo-Irish Agreement, and the unionists would not meet under the 'diktat', under the 'yoke', and so this led us into a period when we were almost wholly preoccupied with what we came to call 'gap theology'. We had to have a gap in between meetings during which talks could take place. And there was a question whether Maryfield should be suspended, and should the gap be long enough. The gap had to be long enough to be seen to be a special gap; but it mustn't be so long that we had in some way abrogated the Agreement.

So there were long and fairly difficult exchanges with our Irish colleagues to try and see whether we could indeed find a gap. The key thing that Peter Brooke said, in January 1990, was that, in the context of an overall negotiation, looking at everything under the sun, we might be able to replace the Agreement, which was a key signal to the unionists that the Agreement might not last forever.

That formulation, which was extremely cautious, and you know it was a very small gesture to the unionists actually, had been tried. Tom King had wanted to say it, but interestingly Margaret Thatcher wouldn't let him. But she did let Peter Brooke say it, and that, I think, was the key thing which enabled Peter Brooke to engage with Molyneaux and Paisley. It led to a very compli-cated minuet with all the players to concoct the text which became the basis for the round–table talks in 1991. This was issued in the form of a statement by Peter Brooke on 26 March 1991, but was in fact a shared document.[29] It was a document shared obviously with the Irish government, but also with the SDLP, the Alliance Party, and the two unionist parties.

What I would say about that new basis for talks was that it reflected an analysis. To get anywhere you had to have something distinct from Dermot's thesis that the two governments had to see off the street. I think the alternative analysis is that you can't see off the street; the street has to be co-opted, and there were two key features of the process, as I think we saw it.

The first was that there had to be a comprehensive cast list. That is to say, it had to involve all those players who had some significance but who were prepared to commit themselves to democratic means only, potentially includ-ing Sinn Féin, if they would make that step, but otherwise not including them.

And there should be a comprehensive agenda. You could not do one bit and, as it were, defer another, like article 4 of the Anglo-Irish Agreement, which kind of tells you how you ought to do devolution, but you will do it later. Or, like Sunningdale left the North–South machinery—it tells you something about it that was frightening, but it doesn't actually do it. It is so frightening that actually the thing collapses. So, you have got to do it all at once, and you have got to have everybody there. That was what we saw as the key building blocks, that are reflected in the March 1991 statement and carried into the 1991 talks, the 1992 talks, and eventually into the 1996–8 talks. That is my perspective on it.

---

[29] In a statement to the House of Commons on 26 March 1991, Brooke announced inter-party and intergovernmental agreement on 'intensive' three-stranded talks in an extended gap between meetings of the Anglo-Irish Intergovernmental Conference; *Hansard*, HC, vol. 188, cols 765–6, 26 March 1991.

4.3. Context of Negotiations

QUENTIN THOMAS: The Downing Street Declaration—obviously Dermot knows far more about the origins than I do. My memory is of a text coming from the South with different fingerprints on it—I think Gerry Adams's fingerprints on it; a Redemptorist priest's fingerprints on it; John Hume's fingerprints on it.[30] The key thing, and it remains to be seen if this is true—you have got the first text of it? My memory of the first text we saw is that it invited us to commit to a date for withdrawal, and that was its key feature. It was not that Gerry Adams said 'you have just got to say you will leave it to the Irish people to decide their own future; you have got to actually say you are pushing off'. Well, 'is it true?' is the first question.[31]

DERMOT NALLY: Yes.

4.3.1. Articles 2 and 3

ROBIN BUTLER: Well, I'd like to come back in due course to that and give an account of how I first saw it, but I think one thing to add was that another frustration during the period after the Anglo-Irish Agreement was articles 2 and 3 of the constitution.

QUENTIN THOMAS: The Anglo-Irish Agreement had been carefully drafted to avoid the need to amend articles 2 and 3 of the Irish constitution.

ROBIN BUTLER: But that was a frustration, was it not?

QUENTIN THOMAS: It was certainly a frustration for the unionists. Among other things, they took the view that articles 2 and 3 should be amended to reflect the principle that a united Ireland should be achieved only with the consent of a majority of the people of Northern Ireland. That boil had to be lanced (as eventually it was in the context of the Good Friday Agreement).

DERMOT NALLY: That was decided at Chequers, either Chequers 1 or 2, I am not sure which, in 1984–5, around November.[32] The original thought was that, if we get a big enough pile on one side, we can put that to the country, and that is the argument for revoking articles 2 and 3.

ROBIN BUTLER: That is what I remember, yes.

DERMOT NALLY: Now, as the negotiation went on, it became more and more realistic to say that the size of the concessions or the size of the institutions that would be established is not such as to enable the Irish government to put to the

---

[30] The Redemptorist priest was Fr Alec Reid of Clonard Monastery, Belfast, an important intermediary with Sinn Féin.

[31] For the text of the first Sinn Féin version of the proposed joint statement, see Document 4.5.

[32] The first two summit meetings between Garret FitzGerald and Margaret Thatcher under the framework of the Anglo-Irish Intergovernmental Council took place at the British Prime Minister's residence in Chequers, Buckinghamshire, on 7 November 1983 and 19 November 1984.

people a change in articles 2 and 3. Now our information, and we may be wrong on this, is that the British ambassador in Dublin was actually telling Mrs Thatcher and Robert that you cannot run a referendum on what is being offered in this agreement and win the referendum. You won't win it. In other words, there is an imbalance, and you cannot correct the imbalance. So, from that moment on, from the Chequers meeting, the idea of a constitutional change in exchange for what was happening on the other side just dropped out of the equation.

But you see another point in that, if you really want to have articles 2 and 3 taken out of the constitution, you have to have a Fianna Fáil government or something extremely strong for another government. Now that is a matter of local politics. The best arrangement would be Mrs Thatcher, a strong British prime minister on one side, upholding a very powerful set of institutions and arrangements on the Northern side, and then a Fianna Fáil government on the other. And I am not Fianna Fáil, just let me make that clear.

QUENTIN THOMAS: It is Nixon and China, isn't it?[33]

DERMOT NALLY: It is the Republican Party saying 'this is what we think should happen', and proposing the change in articles 2 and 3, which is what happened in 1998, and they got a 97 per cent majority for the change. But 1998 is very different from 1985 and 1973. You know, there were public opinion polls done in the late 1980s and they asked the populace at large, what do you regard as the most important subject? Northern Ireland was the most important subject for 3 per cent of the population.

4.3.2. The Status of Northern Ireland

Q: To get back to 'no selfish strategic or economic interest': could that have been said in 1972–3? At what point did it make sense from a British perspective to say that?

ROBIN BUTLER: Clearly it could have been said in 1972–3. Sunningdale, as I remember, said it introduced the principle of self-determination, did it not? And no change in the status of Northern Ireland without the consent of the people of Northern Ireland? Was that in Sunningdale?

DERMOT NALLY: Yes, it was. Sorry, not that there 'could', there 'would' be no change.

ROBIN BUTLER: As it was in the 1985 agreement.

DERMOT NALLY: There 'would' only be change.

---

[33] A reference to the surprise visit to China by US President Richard Nixon in 1972 that dramatically improved the relationship between the two countries. The fact that Nixon was a Republican (a party seen as more hard line on foreign policy than the Democrats) enhanced the significance of the gesture.

QUENTIN THOMAS: Weasel words that the unionists decoded in thirty seconds.

DERMOT NALLY: No, it was not the unionists; it was Boland who took a case in the High Court. And the High Court said that is not a promise of constitutional change.[34]

QUENTIN THOMAS: Exactly.

DERMOT NALLY: That is a political statement, and that finished Sunningdale, that particular judgment, because the High Court had said those words are simply a political promise. They're not in a treaty. They are in an agreement between two governments. It is a political agreement, a political document, not a legal document.

QUENTIN THOMAS: But I think I was talking about 1985, when the unionists decoded it in thirty seconds. There was a similar formulation used.

ROBIN BUTLER: I think in 1972 it was so built into the genes that Northern Ireland was an intrinsic part of the UK, that I do not think that thought had even occurred. To say that under certain circumstances the British would move out would have been very, very inflammatory.

Q: Did the 'no selfish strategic or economic interest' statement relate to the way Hume presented the Anglo-Irish Agreement? He suggested the Agreement was a statement of British neutrality.

ROBIN BUTLER: Can I make a comment on this? For reasons which Dermot has explained, the statements about the constitutional position from the Irish side in this period were carefully formulated to avoid the necessity for constitutional change. The statements from the British side were not so formulated. We do not have a constitution that had to be amended. So you do not have to decode what the British said. The British said, very clearly, and I do not know when they first said it, but they had been saying for a long time, not just in these documents, that if a majority of people in Northern Ireland wanted to join a united Ireland, fine, they would legislate, and that was not at all ambiguous in any of these documents. That was jolly good for Sinn Féin and nationalists, but that was not of course the concern for the unionists; they were concerned with the other bit.

Q: But it was a much stronger formulation that Brooke was using. It was something different to just talking about the whole idea of constitutional change?

ROBIN BUTLER: Well I think the selfish thing was deliberately a formulation that John Hume carried and was intended to send a signal to Sinn Féin, yes.

DERMOT NALLY: There is an even more important reason domestically for the phraseology that is used. The phraseology is that there would be no change in

---

[34] On the Boland case, see Subsections 2.1.3 and 2.3.3, and Ch. 2, n. 34.

the constitutional status of Northern Ireland. Now, if that word 'would' had been 'could', the court would have declared the statement unconstitutional.

ROBIN BUTLER: Absolutely.

DERMOT NALLY: Now there is a second reason for using 'would'. When Charlie Haughey met Mrs Thatcher in May 1980, this was their first meeting. The communiqué that was issued after that meeting said that there would be no change in the status of Northern Ireland without the consent of the people of Northern Ireland. And it is precisely that wording that is used in the Anglo-Irish Agreement. So, Haughey could not oppose the Agreement on any constitutional grounds, because he himself had used precisely the same words in the 1980 communiqué, after the meeting with Mrs Thatcher.

Now he seems to have overlooked, or forgotten, that fact, and he sent Lenihan to the United States to kick up a big row and say 'this is totally out'. Lenihan was told to come back—Lenihan was the Minister for Foreign Affairs—and was told by the 'four horsemen', 'you go back to Dublin and you tell Mr Haughey if he wants to spread that message, he need never set foot in the States again'.[35] That was while he was in opposition. But the whole purpose of the wording was to say, 'look, you have agreed this in government, you cannot now object to this particular formulation'.

ROBIN BUTLER: Can I just give you an analogy which I think may throw some light on the significance of this? In 1975 and on the full referendum on Britain's membership of the EU, Harold Wilson said—and I always admired this bit of fleet-footedness—'I will not recommend the people of Britain to vote yes to membership of the EU in the referendum, unless we get the following terms from the Dublin Council' (it just happened to be in Dublin; no significance about that). And a week later he said, 'if we get these terms from the Dublin Council, I will recommend the British people to vote yes'.[36]

This caught the Eurosceptics by surprise. They approved of the first statement; they were deeply concerned about the second statement. But Harold Wilson was able to say there is no significant difference between these two statements—they are logically the same thing. I think that was the nature of the shift between 'no change in the constitutional status of Northern Ireland without the consent of the people of Northern Ireland', and Peter Brooke's

[35] The 'four horsemen', Senators Ted Kennedy and Daniel Moynihan, New York Governor Hugh Carey, and House Speaker Tip O'Neill, acted as a powerful lobby arguing for a political strategy in Northern Ireland, in conjunction with John Hume. They strongly opposed the militant approach advocated by the IRA's American ally, NORAID.

[36] The Irish government held the presidency of the (rotating) Council of Ministers during the period January–June 1975. At the Dublin summit on 10–11 March 1975, sufficient concessions to the British were agreed to allow the Wilson government to support continued membership. In line with an election commitment, the British government then organized a referendum on 5 June 1975. In this, voters supported the UK's continuing EC membership by a majority of 67% to 33%.

statement 'no selfish and strategic interest', and also the statement, 'if the people of Northern Ireland so vote the British government will legislate'.

4.3.3. The Hume–Adams Draft

FRANK MURRAY: I recall having a private conversation with Albert Reynolds at one stage in relation to what ultimately became the Hume–Adams report about that, and what subsequently became the Downing Street Declaration. It is quite clear Albert wanted his own document, something very comprehensive, covering all of the issues on the record.

DERMOT NALLY: The simple fact was just as Frank has said. Albert had been working on the draft before Hume–Adams covered it anywhere, and his draft existed long before Hume–Adams was in any sort of a form that was comprehensible. This is the early draft, the one that Albert was working on, and I have it dated 29 March 1993. The one that was handed over was handed over in June.[37]

ROBIN BUTLER: Well that is very interesting. Can we just pursue this for a second, because Quentin will correct me—but Hume and Adams first started talking to each other, according to the notes I've got, in 1988. As these contacts went on, I think the British government was sceptical about whether anything would come out of it, but hopeful in the sense that, if Hume could affect Adams and could bring the Republican movement towards more constitutional ways, why should we oppose that? And the next note that I've got is that the first text of Hume–Adams reached us in 1992, and was an entirely unsatisfactory document. And then there was a revision which we received in 1993, which was still an unsatisfactory document.

When Albert first produced what we saw of his draft, the Downing Street Declaration, it was June 1993, that was the one that was delivered to me at Baldonnel. Having got the two documents, there were striking similarities between the two. I have never known—and it would be very interesting, I think this may be what Quentin was hinting at earlier—what the relationship between these two documents was; whether Hume–Adams, as it were, copied the draft that was being developed by Albert, or the other way around? Who the other players were in producing these separate bits of paper, I never knew. It would be a very interesting thing to hear something about that today if you were in a position to tell it.

---

[37] By February 1992 the British had both a Sinn Féin draft and an Irish government draft (the latter a revised version of the original Hume draft; Documents 4.4 and 4.5). In the discussion that follows, Butler and Thomas refer to these drafts, while Nally is speaking about a much later 1993 Irish government draft (Document 4.6).

DERMOT NALLY: I think John Major was furious when Hume intervened to say that he had given the document to the government, the Irish government.[38]

ROBIN BUTLER: He was.

DERMOT NALLY: This was in the middle of the negotiation. I think that John Major even went so far as to say the whole thing is off, or went close to saying it, because we cannot have the infection of Hume–Adams on it. Hume's relationship with Reynolds wasn't as great as it had been with other Taoisigh. Reynolds did not like this sort of sideshow going on. So, when John Major was talking to him, he was speaking to the converted. Now this did not become public for very good reasons, but that was the true situation. I was never involved in any negotiation where there were so many people with their fingers in the pie. Now, some of the fingers were very useful—the Revd Roy Magee, you had Archbishop Eames.[39]

QUENTIN THOMAS: Fr Alec Reid.

DERMOT NALLY: Alec Reid from the Clonard Monastery. And there is a letter from McGuinness also on the files somewhere. Now I have found that piece of the letter, which I think Alec Reid gave to Charlie Haughey in 1987—11 May 1987. Charlie Haughey was in opposition now. An extract from this letter refers to the right of the nationalist and unionist people of Ireland to decide their own constitutional and political future through dialogue among themselves and without dictation from the British authorities. Charlie was using it to back the Peter Brooke statement. He was so delighted by that and wanted to use it in some form, in some document. There was Alec Reid, Roy Magee, there was Molyneaux and there was somebody else, and they were all with their fingers somewhere or other in the pie—with justification, because the support of some of these people was very necessary if the agreement was to take off at all.

Q: Did you say Molyneaux?

DERMOT NALLY: Molyneaux, yes. I think Robin would probably be better able to talk about it.

ROBIN BUTLER: Yes, I will tell you about Molyneaux's part in it. But just to go back to the question, who was drafting Albert's statement? Do we know who?

DERMOT NALLY: We do not know. I was out. I had left on 15 January 1993. Now, this is very close to what was handed over in June, but it does have things that are objectionable. It assumes to, or it is assumed to, quote 'the British have no selfish strategic, political or economic interest'. You would object to political. It slipped in.

---

[38] In October 1993 John Hume made public the existence of a 'Hume–Adams' document.

[39] Revd Roy Magee, a Presbyterian minister with strong unionist views, acted as an intermediary with the Ulster Defence Association (UDA), with which he had close contacts. Robin Eames was Church of Ireland Archbishop of Armagh and Primate of All Ireland, 1986–2006, had close contacts with unionist politicians, and was an active facilitator of secret political dialogue (see also Subsection 5.2.1).

QUENTIN THOMAS: Does it have a date for withdrawal? Does it commit us to withdrawal?

DERMOT NALLY: It probably does, that is one of the things in the document.

ROBIN BUTLER: It committed us to being persuaders.[40]

QUENTIN THOMAS: Difficult to reconcile with the principle of consent, somehow. It always puzzled me how the Irish government were able to support it, since they were purportedly in favour of the principle of consent as well. But was what was handed to Robin an Irish government document by then or not?

DERMOT NALLY: It was.

QUENTIN THOMAS: But did that not have mention of withdrawal?

DERMOT NALLY: 'They affirm their readiness, in co-operation with the Irish government, to establish by legislation and procedure to reach agreement on how the right of self-determination could be exercised democratically and collectively allowing sufficient time for the building of consent and the building of a process of national reconciliation.' Now that is all-Ireland consent, and all-Ireland right of self-determination, and there is no reference, no specific reference, to consent in Northern Ireland. That is another feature of this particular document.

Q: By reference to British withdrawal you mean an explicit reference?

ROBIN BUTLER: Well that is my memory.

Q: Using those words?

ROBIN BUTLER: It certainly would have been more likely in the Hume–Adams, but my memory is that it was in the first one that we received from the Irish side. But Dermot would be able to confirm this, because he has all the documents, which we do not.

DERMOT NALLY: Well you'll really love this: 'the British government will use all their influence and energy to move forward the process of national reconciliation and to win the consent of a majority in Northern Ireland for agreement between all the people of Ireland on their political future, which recognises both the unity of Ireland and the special links and the unique relationship that exist between Ireland and Britain.'[41]

4.3.4. The Major–Reynolds Talks

ROBIN BUTLER: Now we committed ourselves to rigorous impartiality in what became the Framework Document. We wouldn't persuade the unionists to stay in the United Kingdom, and we weren't going to persuade the others to leave.

---

[40] The reference is to the republican demand that the British government become 'persuaders' in the sense of persuading the unionists to accept Irish unity.

[41] The quotation is from the June 1993 draft, para. 4 (see Document 4.6).

Would it be helpful if I just got on record the chronology as I remember it? I am going to leave out the parallel frame that was going on about then; what happened as a result was the 'conflict is over' message, which was going on at the same time.[42] At some point we ought to take account of that, and talk about how that influenced what the British government was doing.

My recollection is that we first had sight of Hume–Adams in 1992—it was very unhelpful—and a revision in 1993, which was also unhelpful. It did not seem to be offering any great way forward, except that Hume and Adams were talking to each other, which, as I say, we saw some advantage in.

What then happened was that, in June 1993, Albert sent this message asking to meet John Major, secretly. We felt that that was unrealistic, that prime ministers in this day and age couldn't meet each other secretly. It would get out, and then all hell would be let loose with the unionists and so on. But, on the other hand, John liked Albert Reynolds, and thought that he was trying to be helpful, and anyway he wouldn't rebuff an approach from another prime minister, so it was decided I should come over. That was when the Baldonnel meeting took place. At that meeting, Albert handed me this document, and said: 'If the British government can accept this, it will bring peace.' I remember looking at the document and seeing such similarities to Hume–Adams that I could see that it was not realistic, but it was not my job to be other than polite.

Q: Just to clarify, how had the British government seen Hume–Adams at that stage?

ROBIN BUTLER: Hume gave it to us. He was always coming up and getting bits of paper out of his pockets and giving them to us.

Q: To British officials as well as in Dublin, he was doing it that way?

ROBIN BUTLER: Yes, continuously. And so anyway, I took it back, and we looked at it, and said without a number of amendments there is nothing we can do with this, and anyway it is very like Hume–Adams. But we did suggest some amendments, which I took back to Albert, and I remember Albert saying: 'Oh amend it any way you like, you know this is the end of the thing'; but he said 'my goodness, you know if you miss this opportunity, do not think the IRA are defeated. They're not giving in. So do not, whatever you do, miss this opportunity for peace.' Anyway I took it back and we had some amendments, and I was sent over again with this. We were terribly worried about two things; we were terribly worried about what would be the reaction of unionists if they discovered that we were discussing a draft of this statement. We were also terribly worried about the world discovering what was going on in response to the 'conflict is over' message—and we were,

---

[42] As discussed in Subsection 4.3.6 and n. 46, this message purported to come from the IRA and a new phase of communication ensued between the British and the IRA.

as we thought, sending messages to the IRA. So, we were really living on tenterhooks.

In September, John Major decided that he would take Molyneaux into his confidence about the draft which Albert had given him and get his advice on what might make it acceptable. Molyneaux, I think to his eternal credit, first of all said: 'this document is far too green, you know. It is not going anywhere. I cannot see any way it can be made acceptable.' But he kept his own counsel. I mean he did not go off like a rocket and publish it, and denounce it, and so on. That was a terrific contribution to the whole thing, because we then had a link into the unionists. Molyneaux took on himself the risk that his colleagues would denounce him for not having told them that this thing was going on. But anyway he said this wouldn't go anywhere.

Then I was sent back to Albert with a very discouraging message saying that we really do not think we were going anywhere with this. Then Albert said: 'Well if they think this is too green a document, why don't I show it to Archbishop Eames and get his input?' So we said 'OK' to that. It was then given to Eames, who put in a whole lot of stuff. The draft looked absolutely ghastly by this time. But he put a whole lot of stuff on the unionist side to balance the document, and then Albert gave us back the document.

In November we said this document really is a dog's breakfast. Let's draft another document and offer it as acceptable from our point of view: keep the unionists' things, but also keep as much of the green stuff as we can live with. I was sent back to present this to Albert. That must have been at the latter part of November. Yes, it coincided with the exchanges about the 'conflict is over' message also being leaked.

I went back to Albert and said: 'Look, we can't go on with the draft that you have provided as amended by Archbishop Eames, but we have produced our own draft which we hope contains the green stuff and the unionist stuff, and we'd like you to have a look.' And Albert went off like a rocket and denounced it without even reading it, and said 'absolutely hopeless, no good', and sent me off with a flea in my ear. We then had to decide whether we would go back to negotiating on the draft with the Eames stuff in it, and we decided that we would do that, and then that happened, that meeting at Dublin Castle in the beginning of December.[43]

QUENTIN THOMAS: There was another leak at the same time wasn't there? Everything was leaked. There was a leak of what was supposed to have been the Irish government's draft response to our draft of what subsequently became the Framework Document. I do not think the Irish government

---

[43] A summit meeting between Albert Reynolds and John Major took place at Dublin Castle on 3 December 1993.

acknowledged that it was their draft.[44] That parallel negotiation about what became the Framework Document was, in my view, also a rather important matter, and another key building block towards the Good Friday Agreement, when it was published in February 1995.

Q: All of a sudden these documents come backwards and forwards, introducing talk of withdrawal, and persuaders, and these kinds of ideas, which hadn't really been on the British–Irish agenda at all. Did the British government see that as a kind of regression?

DERMOT NALLY: The documents do not come as government documents, because Albert was very, very strong on the point: 'if you put a time limit in, and say there must be Irish unity in fifteen years, or whatever time you say, you are contradicting yourself. It is a logical absurdity; we can't have that, throw it out. We can't ask them to be persuaders. They're not in the business of persuading. It is our business to persuade people if we want them to join us.' He was very, very strong on these points.

But just to go back to the document, the British alternative draft. The document came to us almost on the eve of the meeting of 3 December, and we (Robin and I) had been working on this since June, or maybe August or September, and working on the other document.

In the document that was submitted at the end of November [1993], the right to self-determination is expressed in terms of entirely separate rights north and south. The emphasis is on separation. We couldn't have that, it would have been unconstitutional if we'd tried to accept it. The emphasis on ending past divisions and working to build an agreed future is gone. The emphasis shifted away from the circumstances in which unity could be realized, to constitutional change in the South.

The British text, moreover, attempts to pre-empt the nature and scope of that constitutional change. The Convention is eliminated from the text; this is a convention of parties that support democratic processes and methods and so on. It was supposed to be held if the agreement was signed. It became the Forum for Peace and Reconciliation, as in the Downing Street Declaration. But the Convention is eliminated from the text, even though it would be an entirely Irish initiative. In other words, parties who support the democratic process and reject violence can meet together and talk about the future, but if you support violence you are out. In other words, it's an invitation to Sinn Féin to give up. All reference to common membership of the European Community is eliminated.

Now, with that coming, we simply cannot negotiate on the document that is being put forward to the summit. The result was one of the most aggressive

---

[44] A draft of the joint Framework Document was leaked to *The Times*, which published it on 1 February 1995.

summits between two prime ministers that I have ever attended; and I attended forty of them between Britain and Ireland over that period. Albert and Major were, I would say, almost grandstanding. They had asked us to come in and solve some of the things on the spot. But it was the worst possible outcome, that you have two heads of government negotiating on texts.

QUENTIN THOMAS: It's interesting that some of the faults that you identify in the text are in the Downing Street Declaration.

DERMOT NALLY: But in a different way.

QUENTIN THOMAS: Ah, in a different way? But it's interesting that you see them as fundamental problems. Yes, the commitment is a conditional commitment. It is precisely the commitment that we spent almost eighteen hours trying to extract in the 1992 talks in Dublin.[45] When we wanted, or particularly the unionists wanted, the Irish side to say that, in the context of an overall agreement—i.e. a condition which the Irish government controlled, because there could be no agreement without them—instead of saying you 'would', you said 'could'. But it wouldn't be said then, in September 1992.

Anyway, it is in paragraph 7 of the ultimate text, as is the proposition that it would be wrong for people to attempt to impose a united Ireland. Paragraph 5 'accepts, on behalf of the Irish government, that the democratic right [...] must be achieved and exercised with and subject to the agreement and consent of a majority of the people of Northern Ireland'. So, the key things we were seeking in that text, though the text may have been objectionable and its timing may have been unfortunate, were actually carried over into the ultimate text. Which is why I think—if the constitutional issue is the heart of the matter—the Downing Street Declaration is a key step from Sunningdale, from the Anglo-Irish Agreement, towards the Good Friday Agreement, when the acceptance of consent—meaning consent by a majority of people in the North—is absolutely unambiguous by both governments.

DERMOT NALLY: But the British government agreed that it is for the people of the island of Ireland alone; this is paragraph 4.

QUENTIN THOMAS: Self-determination? Yes that is there; that is correct.

DERMOT NALLY: That was in the original draft.

QUENTIN THOMAS: And that is great. It's always been my regret that, you know, as a junior official I failed the cowardice test—when Albert Reynolds, and all the breaking of pencils and things, said there is nothing in this text for us at all. It has always been my regret that I did not pipe up and say, 'Prime Minister, if

---

[45]   The Ulster Unionist Party leadership engaged in talks with the Irish government in Dublin Castle on 23 September 1992—talks that were of historic significance as the first such talks since the outbreak of the 'troubles'.

the Taoiseach thinks that there is nothing in this text for him, then I suggest that you remove that sentence because it may give you trouble'.

DERMOT NALLY: Albert came into office with two objectives, and, you might remember, he came into tea in the cabinet, in my room, while he was waiting for the debate, or waiting to be actually appointed as Taoiseach. One of the things he said was, I have two objectives, and one is Northern Ireland peace. Northern Ireland was very high on his list of priorities. Now you have Hume–Adams going on at the same time. Hume came in September when this whole process was well under way and said 'I have now presented my document to the government'. Albert was absolutely furious, and Major got up in the Commons and said 'the whole thing is off, we can't continue in this way'.

Q: Is it that both Hume and Reynolds thought that peace is now possible because republicans were beginning to shift? Why did either of them believe that what eventually transpired as a ceasefire was going to be possible?

DERMOT NALLY: First of all because of this letter, from a senior republican, that said: 'Leave us alone, we will work out our own future, and we are kind of tired of this.' Then there was also the one that Robin has referred to, the McGuinness message: 'The war is over. Will you please help us?' That is not the exact wording.[46]

ROBIN BUTLER: Yes: 'The conflict is over; you have to help us to bring it to an end.'

DERMOT NALLY: Now all these were floating in the air, and on top of that Albert was talking about his business contacts, and his knowledge of the North, and he said: 'I have a lot of kinds of contacts in the North, and they say that this is on at this time.'

Q: What was the British thinking at the same time?

ROBIN BUTLER: Well, our view of it was, of course, coloured by the fact that we had had this message in February, 'the conflict is over', to which we had sent a response. And so we were disposed to think that the IRA was prepared to stop if we could respond in a satisfactory way. And, secretly from the Irish government at that point, we had sent a response to the message we got in February. So yes, we were inclined to think that a satisfactory statement could lead to a cessation, and indeed, when the Downing Street Declaration was made, there was some talk that we would get a cessation, a statement from the IRA, within a week or two. Now that did not happen; it happened the following August.

QUENTIN THOMAS: It was meant to have both a positive and a negative effect. I mean the negative effect was that here was a key thing going on, and you as

---

[46] A letter from Gerry Adams to Prime Minister Major on 25 September 1991 stated that Sinn Féin was 'committed to establishing a peace process' and sought discussions; see Document 4.2. A message said to be from the IRA in early 1993 reportedly stated that 'the conflict is over but we need your advice on how to bring it to an end' (Powell 2008: 71–2). John Major (1999: 431) gives the date as February 1993.

Sinn Féin will be out of it unless you meet this prior condition of abandoning violence.

ROBIN BUTLER: You will not be part of it.

QUENTIN THOMAS: You will not be part of it. But the positive thing was to say, this is a comprehensive agenda, it is not us British who are the problem, we have no selfish strategic, etc. If consent is achieved, we will legislate for it, no problem. Come in. We thought we'd had this message. The Irish government, who we'd assumed had good reason to know, was saying that this formulation will be the trigger to bring violence to an end.

One of the puzzles, I think, for all of us, was: what was it about this declaration that was meant to have this effect? If it was about withdrawal, then that is not hard to understand. As we got closer to the final text, the confidence with which Irish government interlocutors were saying 'this declaration will bring peace' was diminished. I think it was being said with far less confidence by December than it had been said in June.

But what Dermot has read out going back to 1987 is effectively what is in paragraph 4 about recognizing the right of Irish self-determination, which we had to draft carefully among us. It is not essentially a problem for us, and if we'd known that was the key it would have been understandable. I think our worry was that the key was actually about withdrawal, which was obviously (*a*) nonsense, and (*b*) incompatible with both governments' positions on consent as we understood it.

DERMOT NALLY: You mention a very frightening word there—withdrawal. The consequence of withdrawal for us would have been horrific. I mean we had done paper, after paper, after paper, saying there will be civil war, the effect on your economy would be disastrous, you will have colossal unemployment, you will have a repeat of the 1920s. Do not even think of it, forget withdrawal. If it comes let it come, but do not start messing about with it. I think that message got through because we did say it very, very strongly and very frequently. No, please, no withdrawal, please stay.

Q: We did not get to the bottom of the recollection that one draft submitted to the British government came very close to looking for a British withdrawal.

DERMOT NALLY: I do not know where the passage is.

ROBIN BUTLER: No, and I have none of the documents, except the final one.

DERMOT NALLY: No, my recollection of that particular issue is that the statement in the final agreement is—this is at the end of paragraph 4, or in the middle of paragraph 4: 'The British government agree that it is for the people of the island of Ireland alone, by agreement between the two parts respectively, to exercise their right of self-determination, on the basis of consent, freely and concurrently given, North and South.' Incidentally we're very glad to see that we require our own consent.

ROBIN BUTLER: That requires the consent of the South as well as the North.

DERMOT NALLY: Which gives me a warm feeling, 'to bring about a united Ireland, if that is their wish'. Now, one of the changes made in the original of that is the change that Robin proposed one day, and that is that 'if that is their wish'—that phrase going in at the end, with which we can find no problem. And there was another small change somewhere. But otherwise, as far as I can remember, that is the original formulation.

ROBIN BUTLER: I do not think so, Dermot, no, I think another very important change was North and South. In other words I think the original formulation was a one-island referendum.

QUENTIN THOMAS: Oh, yes, that is right, this is the original.

ROBIN BUTLER: And it is because of that it has been separated, that there now is a reference also to amending the constitution. In your earlier exegesis you explain that the two issues were linked.

DERMOT NALLY: This is the original, this is the very early draft that I got in March: 'The British government accept the principle that the Irish people have the right to self-determination and that the exercise of this collective right democratically could take the form of agreed independent structures for the island as a whole. They affirm their readiness in cooperation with the Irish government to establish by legislation a procedure to reach agreement on how the right of self-determination could be exercised democratically and collect-ively, allowing sufficient time for the building of consent and the beginning of a process of national reconciliation.' We can see easily why you would not be too pleased with that sort of stuff, but that is the early draft—I'm not sure now if that is the June draft.

4.3.5. The Brooke–Mayhew Talks

Q: I have a question on the Brooke–Mayhew talks.[47] Did you expect them to succeed?

QUENTIN THOMAS: Well, we hoped they would succeed. We thought there was a reasonable chance, as Peter Brooke said in the speech in January 1990, if I remember rightly in Bangor: 'We think there is a sufficient common ground to make it reasonable to anticipate agreement.' Our analysis was that, properly considered in the right atmosphere, the different interests and objectives of the players could be reconciled, and that was a heroic assumption. But that is what we thought—in particular, that the whole issue of consent, which is central, could be resolved, as eventually it was; that everyone might be brought to accept that.

---

[47] This refers to the Brooke–Mayhew talks of 1991–2; see Subsection 4.1.1.

It seemed that Sinn Féin was proceeding—and this is where the Hume–Adams dialogue may have been very important indeed—was proceeding on a false analysis; that they were proceeding on a historical analysis that the British were the problem. They had to be driven into the sea. Whereas we thought that was wrong, and Dermot is confirming that he did not want to drive us into the sea anyway, because he was terrified that we would go away. But the problem was a group of fellow Irishmen, who called themselves unionists, who for perverse reasons of their own, and not just because of false consciousness, actually regard themselves as British, as much if not more than Irish. And many of them think they're Irish too, of course.

So yes, we did think that there was a prospect of an agreement and that there was a prospect of Sinn Féin coming in. I think that was more of a hope than an expectation. To speak for myself, although, as I said, our reasoning was that the process would bring both positive and negative pressure on the IRA and on Sinn Féin to come in, I myself was surprised that they did come in as soon as they did. I do not think that it was just because of the talks process. I think that was an important building block.

My own view would be that there were a whole lot of factors, and I think one of the key achievements of what Gerry Adams would call the 'securocrats'— the intelligence community, the army, the police—coupled with the robust position taken by all the major parties at Westminster, and indeed by the position of the main parties in Dublin, was that they could no longer sustain the belief that they could win by violence. I think to keep something like this going, you have to believe you can win, and I think that belief was denied them. So, I think the talks process was one of a number of factors, but that denial of belief in the possibility of their own victory was also extremely important.

In the literature, there is this dilemma that is sometimes posed, do you go for the moderates and cut out the extremes? Or do you pull in the extremes and forget the centre? Another point about the Anglo-Irish Agreement, incidentally, is that Dr Garret FitzGerald wanted quite explicitly to marginalize Sinn Féin and to reward the SDLP. I think subsequently both governments came to the view that that was a doomed project, and that you had to co-opt Sinn Féin.

But I have always thought that the dilemma between the centre and the extremes is a false dilemma. What you should try and do is proceed in a way which will bring in as many as possible—the extremes and the centre—because you are in trouble without either. Therefore, I think it is a false choice. But there were many in the process, I remember the Alliance Party often said 'you know, you should forget worrying about Sinn Féin; you should concentrate on people like us. We are in the middle of the road.'

So, I think some people did find it very difficult, yes. Obviously the unionists found it difficult to recognize that Sinn Féin might become a genuine player, and I think the Alliance Party did, and the SDLP wanted them to be in (with one-half of them) and another half saw that they were even more of a threat when they were in than when they were out.

Q: Could I just clarify, was one of the purposes of the process to put pressure on Sinn Féin to come in?

QUENTIN THOMAS: Yes, and that is explicit. You'll find speeches by both Brooke and Mayhew saying that 'on the right terms'—they should be co-opted 'on the right terms'—namely, on democratic terms. It was said again and again.

Q: Did the post-1989 developments, the fall of the Berlin wall and the new world order, have any impact on British thinking on Northern Ireland, or indeed Irish thinking on Northern Ireland? Were you aware of that as a changing context?

QUENTIN THOMAS: Not really, I think is the answer. In my case I do not know.

DERMOT NALLY: The articles in the Downing Street Declaration specifically designed to get Sinn Féin in are articles 10 and 11, which say if you give up your violence, we will have this forum for peace and reconciliation and we can talk about the future.

Q: That is the Downing Street Declaration, but I mean Brooke–Mayhew as a talks process.

QUENTIN THOMAS: From 1991 to 1992, yes it was.

DERMOT NALLY: The thing I do not really understand about the talks, this is the three-stranded talks—first Northern Ireland, everything within Northern Ireland, secondly relations within the island, and thirdly relations between the two islands—what stopped it going ahead? Was it relations in Northern Ireland?

QUENTIN THOMAS: What stopped it going ahead? We ran out of a gap. We pleaded with Dublin in November 1992, to extend the gap, and you wouldn't. That is what ended it. It did not end in a row, it did not break down. We ran out of gap.

ROBIN BUTLER: Sorry what do you mean by extend the gap?

QUENTIN THOMAS: Well, we had to have a gap between meetings of the inter-governmental conference under the Anglo-Irish Agreement because the unionists would not meet under that 'yoke'. So, we agreed an artificial short break in 1991. It ran out, the Irish government said quite properly we must meet again, so we did, we honoured our obligations. In 1992 we really made a lot of progress, particularly on strand one, that is true, but we got strand two and strand three to meet. We got the unionists to go to Dublin, the UUP, not the DUP, but we got the UUP to go to Dublin, and we pleaded to extend the gap. And your side, quite properly, said we won't. An election I think was in the offing. That is why it stopped; that is the only reason it stopped.

Q: But the UUP also said that they were bitterly disappointed at the response of Dublin.

QUENTIN THOMAS: Yes, why? Shall I tell you why? Because when we came to Dublin, unfortunately, the whole discussion was about articles 2 and 3. That was not our wish, but it was what the unionists made the discussion about. We wanted, as I think I alluded to earlier, to move from the position that you would change articles 2 and 3, that if you could you would, and although the formulation was entirely conditional, Irish ministers judged that it was wrong to make it, and so the unionists felt—the UUP felt—that they'd taken a political risk, they'd exposed their flank to the DUP, who hadn't come. They should have come because they'd committed themselves to coming. I think, you know, Paisley was very wrong not to have come; it was in all the scripts that we'd carefully negotiated that he *would* come. The UUP did come and took a risk, and they felt that they got nothing on that issue specifically, and they got nothing else, but that was the one they wanted.

Q: Was there anything else they looked for, can you recall?

QUENTIN THOMAS: Well that was all we really talked about. They felt they deserved a reward. Maybe they were wrong to think that, but they thought something should have come from that.

Q: What was the thinking on the Irish government side at the time? Was there a particular reason for deciding not to allow a bigger gap in meetings of the Anglo-Irish Intergovernmental Conference?

DERMOT NALLY: This was done by Foreign Affairs, by people running the secretariat. It did not come before me, on my desk, so what I am saying is assumption. I would say that this is a ploy to destroy the conference because, once it is deferred, once you get away from the habit, you can destroy it by not having another meeting, but having meetings outside the Anglo-Irish Inter-governmental Conference machinery.

QUENTIN THOMAS: I said the talks did not break down. The joint statement by the talks participants on 10 November 1992, I think, makes that clear—it's an agreed statement and sort of regretful, but they did not break down, they just ran out.

DERMOT NALLY: You would be handing the Anglo-Irish Agreement to the unionists.

QUENTIN THOMAS: Yes, I understand absolutely. But the fear was that the institutions would never be allowed to meet again. Now I understand that, and, given that the talks process dragged on until Good Friday 1998, that was a justifiable fear.

Q: But this did not, of course, bring the process to an end?

QUENTIN THOMAS: It does not bring the process to an end, because we would never admit that the process had ended. We maintained the fiction that the process was in being throughout the whole period. I think sometimes the only thing going was that no single player wanted to take responsibility for bringing it to an end. So others, in a sense, colluded in the fiction that it was still going.

We were always looking for a way of reconvening, and indeed one of the problems with Sinn Féin's entry was that we said, both governments said: 'If you abandon violence, you will be eligible to join the process.' So, when they did call their ceasefire, when they said 'OK', and I met them in Stormont in December 1994, they said 'OK, let's go, where are the talks?' The trouble is there aren't any at that moment, and you have to play your part in bringing about confidence among all the players, that they're all happy to go into the same room together, and the truth is we hadn't been able to get everyone in the room without you. With you, it is going to be even harder.

You know, it took a long time before we were able to get talks going with or without Sinn Féin; in fact, until 1996, after the elections, because the unionists had this brilliant perception that of course we can't talk to these people with blood on their hands. But up and down Northern Ireland we do business with them in district councils because they've been elected. So, why don't you have an election, then you can talk to them? And that is what happened.

4.3.6. Involvement of Sinn Féin

Q: To what extent were there differences in perspective within each side about the involvement of republicans?

QUENTIN THOMAS: I do not think there was a great difference on the statement of principle, that if they abandon violence they should join the process. It is formally there, as Dermot just reminded us, in paragraph 10, I think it is, of the Downing Street Declaration.

Where there did come a difference of view was on whether the condition had been met, because, when the IRA made their statement in August 1994, there were different views on whether they had meant that they really had abandoned violence. Irish colleagues urged us to take the view that yes, they had. British ministers said, well they could have used better language, they could have said 'permanent'—and that led to, well if they do not *say* 'permanent', they could *show* that they meant it to be permanent, if they started giving up arms.

So, then we get into decommissioning, which bedevils the process until, well, forever. But that is how we got into it. They do not say 'permanent', so we must have decommissioning as a proxy, and that is very difficult. So on that issue you could say that the British side were obviously right. It was not permanent because it broke down at Canary Wharf.[48]

---

[48] The IRA ceasefire announced on 31 August 1994 broke down on 9 February 1996 when an IRA spokesman announced that the ceasefire was over, and an IRA bomb in Canary Wharf in London's docklands killed two people.

My own view is that it doesn't show that the British were right, what I think is that it shows the difference between a sort of static analysis and a dynamic analysis. The static analysis says you have got to meet the condition, QED, you can come in. But what we were actually dealing with was a dynamic process of change, where the provisional movement were—with great difficulty—moving in, but they had to manage their movement so that they did not break up. We could have helped them, or we could have hindered them, and to some extent we were less helpful than we could have been.

ROBIN BUTLER: Yes, I mean on that, paragraph 10 of the Downing Street Declaration did use the word 'permanent', and that was why we subsequently thought that a statement by the IRA that does not use the word 'permanent' does not satisfy the condition. I think we had some subsequent difference with the Irish government over that.

One of the things that I felt at the time was that, when we were negotiating this, the Irish government made no difficulty about the word 'permanent'. I subsequently regret, actually, that this was not a point of more explicit negotiation between us.

DERMOT NALLY: Well, the wording of the ceasefire document is 'there will be a complete cessation of military operations, all our units have been instructed accordingly'. This was handed over to Charlie Bird, RTÉ, at 11.30 a.m. on 31 August 1994.

QUENTIN THOMAS: I took a view that it was pretty good, actually. The trouble is, it's sort of hopeless, because if you are worried about the absence of a word like 'permanent', you challenge people to use it, but the fact that you challenge people to use it means that they can never do it. That was true of decommissioning as well—that the worst condition for decommissioning was in response to a demand by the British.

DERMOT NALLY: Well, decommissioning was a futile argument, because if you decommission there is nothing to prevent you from buying more.

QUENTIN THOMAS: But, equally, if you have really given up, you do not need it anymore—and Canary Wharf showed they hadn't really given up. I think the real thing is it was all about management of change, and maybe we could all be more cunning, actually.

Q: You said that as you got closer to December the confidence of the Irish government that the statement would bring about this process of change diminished. How did the two governments see these interlinkages?

QUENTIN THOMAS: A key thing from our point of view was that we should say nothing privately that was inconsistent with what we were saying publicly. We were extremely anxious that the correspondence we were conducting with Sinn Féin was not only consistent with this, but actually everything we said, we said publicly. Indeed, the Taoiseach and the Prime Minister, I know Dermot will remember it well, issued a joint communiqué in which they confirmed publicly that there would be no private agreements with anybody.

DERMOT NALLY: That was always part of the understanding. The back channel, or whatever you like to call it, was stopped as far as the television tells us, sometime around 1992.

ROBIN BUTLER: It stopped when it became public; I think it was December 1993.

DERMOT NALLY: The person from MI6 quoted *forsan et haec olim meminisse iuvabit.*[49]

ROBIN BUTLER: Yes, that is right. That was not one of the authorized messages [*general laughter*].

DERMOT NALLY: But, strangely, when Charlie Haughey would be going to a European Council or a meeting of the great and the good, wherever it happened to be, he would always say, *forsan et haec olim meminisse iuvabit.* I thought it strange when I heard it coming across on the radio. 'Perhaps in times to come we will remember what we have done, with pleasure.'

ROBIN BUTLER: You have only left out the word *olim.*

Q: Did the revelation of that contact increase the dynamic?

QUENTIN THOMAS: No, I do not think it did, I think it was potentially damaging. I think everything was damaging about it. I think the fact that it became public reflected a loss of confidence in the correspondence, presumably by Sinn Féin.

The way it became public was potentially very damaging. I think the Secretary of State was fortunate that he carried it off without more political damage; without having to leave office, indeed. It was quite a tense parliamentary occasion. As it happened absolutely everything went right, including Paisley having a tantrum and getting thrown out.[50]

ROBIN BUTLER: Not everything went right actually. There were some mistakes in the documents.

QUENTIN THOMAS: There were some mistakes in the documents, and the version that Sinn Féin released was different in other respects too.[51] My conclusion from all of this is that, if you are ever in this position again, you should use the postal service. Then you know that, if it reaches the recipient—which it might not, but if it does—it will be what you put in the envelope.

ROBIN BUTLER: My recollection is a bit different. I feel that it was extraordinary that Paddy Mayhew did get away with it in the House of Commons. It was extraordinary, also, that it really did not interfere with the process very much—I mean the problem about the process leading up to the joint

[49] The quotation, from Virgil's *Aeneid*, bk 1, l. 203, may be translated as 'perhaps at some time it will help to remember these things'.

[50] See *Hansard*, HC, vol. 233, cols 789–91, 29 November (1993). This followed a disclosure in the newspaper the *Observer* on 28 November that secret talks had been taking place for many months between republicans and the British government, with the prime minister's approval.

[51] On 5 January 1994 Sinn Féin published its version of the communications between itself and the British government, *Setting the Record Straight*; see Sinn Féin (1994).

declaration was us producing a new draft, and it was not the leaking of the exchanges [with republicans] in response to the 'conflict is over' message.

QUENTIN THOMAS: It did partly demystify it all, did it not? I mean, it was never quite as mysterious and weird a thing to do again?

ROBIN BUTLER: I think it got across that we were seriously looking for opportunities to be helpful.

Q: It made it a turning point? Could that be so?

DERMOT NALLY: Well, Martin McGuinness at the time issued a two- or three-page, single-spaced statement that talked about these contacts, so there was just no point in trying to do anything other than 'well that is OK, then, that is it'.

ROBIN BUTLER: Except, of course, that he denied that he originated the first message, and that is still, as far as we are concerned, a mystery. Who did originate the 'conflict is over' message? It is suggested that it was a member of our security service that made it up. But if that is the case, you know the IRA must have been a bit puzzled to get our nine-paragraph reply. They did not indicate that they were puzzled about it.

QUENTIN THOMAS: Unless all the exchanges were made up.

ROBIN BUTLER: Whether they never got any further down the line in Curzon Street.[52]

QUENTIN THOMAS: Oh, dear, yes, the mind boggles.

4.3.7. British View of Conflict

Q: I am particularly interested in the British view, and the Irish view at the time. If you look at the Downing Street Declaration, there is reference to this long historical conflict that is now going to be resolved by mutual agreement and so on, and at the time as well there was a lot of reference to what took place in 1920–1, in terms of Michael Collins and so on. So, that is a kind of Irish nationalist understanding of what this process is. What was the British understanding of the process that you were engaged in? Was it solving the ancient Irish problem? Was it tidying up something left over from 1921? Is there an Empire relevance to any of this? What did you think? Or was it a day-to-day affair for you?

ROBIN BUTLER: Well, I am just going to give you one sentence and then ask Quentin Thomas. I think you know that principally we were standing up for the process of self-determination of the people of Northern Ireland. And you know we wanted to achieve peace on that basis; we were standing up for the process of self-determination and democratic methods of resolving differences.

---

[52] The headquarters of the British intelligence agency MI5 was located in Curzon Street, London.

QUENTIN THOMAS: I entirely agree, I think it is all about consent. I concede that the unit of determination of Northern Ireland is problematic—that it is a creation of a particular period, and that is disputed, but given the passage of time that was the only reality. You had to look at that unit, and the Irish side have in the Good Friday Agreement come to accept that as a valid unit. I think it was partly trying to show that democracy can work, that people can resolve differences, and that they do not have to bash each other over the head. They can find the right formulae to do this.

Another way of looking at it, which I think we often said to ourselves, and which I know Irish colleagues said to us as well, was that we were agreed about the future. To a large extent we were agreed about the present. What we had to do was to get the past off our backs, but on honourable terms. We had to help people to dispose of the past, without betraying.

Q: Your analysis of the problem appears very present centred—the application of a general principle to the problem?

ROBIN BUTLER: I think we should have one more thing and that was, and this is primarily what Quentin said, also: a fair deal for the minority in Ireland.

QUENTIN THOMAS: Oh yes, sure.

ROBIN BUTLER: You know that Ireland should be in the future instead of the past, and unlike the past have a civilized way of protecting the interests of the minority.

QUENTIN THOMAS: One thing that occurred to me, and it is not quite answering your point, but it is relevant to it: I think you could see the Downing Street Declaration as a sort of fulcrum between a nationalist–republican approach (which was hesitating on the brink of accepting Northern Ireland as a valid unit of determination), and a full-blown acceptance that it has to be like this (which you see in the most formal language in the Good Friday Agreement, which says—I mean in the mouth of Sinn Féin, the Irish government, everybody—that Northern Ireland is part of the United Kingdom and it is right that it should be, because that is what they want). I paraphrase.

But a key thing that happened immediately after this was that, I assume at Martin Mansergh's instigation and drafting, Albert Reynolds gave a series of speeches saying that—look at Korea, look at Germany, whenever you get a divided country it can only come together with the full-hearted consent of both parts. Never mind that they were torn apart in illegitimate ways or whatever, that is not the point, the point is you can only achieve unity in such circumstances. In other words what had seemed to us [...] a concession became full-hearted acceptance, and Mansergh, if you like, with Reynolds, made it a wholly respectable notion, when I think it may have been pussyfooted around before. I think this is the fulcrum, that is the point at which it shifts, and those speeches, I think, were very interesting and in many ways went further than the Downing Street Declaration.[53]

Q: I am intrigued again by the sense of history, because unionists must also have carried a deep historical sense into the process, while you simply had general principles which had to be respected.

QUENTIN THOMAS: We are all historically innocent.

FRANK MURRAY: Martin Mansergh, certainly I recall him drafting those speeches that you mentioned. He had a huge scholarly interest in self-determination as a concept, and went abroad, indeed, to increase his knowledge of this part.

QUENTIN THOMAS: I thought it was very significant.

4.4. The Negotiation Process

4.4.1. Sequence of Events

DERMOT NALLY: There is an article in the [Irish] *Sunday Press*, 19 December 1993, by Brendan O'Leary, and he heads the article: 'Every word of the Downing Street Declaration is carefully weighted and weighed, every sentence pieced together with exquisite care. The drafters of the second Downing Street Declaration went to extravagant lengths to produce a document to reassure everybody. Every paragraph bears the marks of the necessary ambiguities in constructing such a declaration; it is an exquisite diplomatic patchwork.' So take a bow Robin.

ROBIN BUTLER: I feel throughout this we were greatly helped by our dealing with these various strands that were going on. We were always absolutely clear about what our principles were, and in a sense that made it easy. The risk for John Major, and the risk we felt, was that we would be accused of being naive and buying a pig-in-a-poke. That was the danger.

DERMOT NALLY: Had Major got a majority in the Commons? Did he depend on the unionists? That was our impression at the time?

ROBIN BUTLER: Yes, that was another point.

Q: What did you think the republicans were doing at the time?

QUENTIN THOMAS: Well, we did not entirely know—always difficult to understand why people run around letting off bombs, isn't it? It is a strange way of proceeding. I think what we hoped, and thought was possible, was that they had come to the view our policies, among other things, were designed to bring

---

[53] Albert Reynolds drew an analogy with Germany, China, Korea, Yemen, and Cyprus in a speech during a Seanad debate on the Downing Street Declaration; *Seanad Debates*, vol. 138, cols 1902–3, 22 December 1993.

about change, and that, while they could not win by violence, they could find a decent way forward, and possibly of achieving their ultimate objective of Irish unity, by using peaceful and constitutional means.

I think, if you look at the extensive literature published under the name of G. Adams, you can see a very long-term attempt to shift the movement. It is problematic, and it is inconsistent with some of the actions that went on, like bombing people. But I think you can discern a very long-term attempt to shift the movement. One thing I do acknowledge is that, of all the players in this process, the party that moved by far the most was Sinn Féin. You could say they had furthest to go, and that would be true.

But, you know, the unionists did a bit, the SDLP did, the British, everyone had to adjust their position, or restate it or reformulate it. Sinn Féin were the people who really had to move, from saying that Northern Ireland was an illegitimate mini-state and 'blah, blah', to actually being ministers in the wretched thing, it was fantastic. To accept the principle of consent in the Good Friday Agreement, that was just extraordinary.

The other thing I think is extraordinary is, if you look at any political party, look at Blair and Brown to take an example, the tension between big players is very common indeed, and very difficult.[54] You can see it. Adams and McGuiness have been marching along, one in Belfast, one in Derry, difficult to communicate, because they're worried about communication, throughout this period, and no one's ever got a cigarette paper between them.

ROBIN BUTLER: As Quentin was saying, I agree entirely, we do not know, we could just see a little bit of light at the end of the tunnel, and we were prepared to go after it, on the basis of our principles, and to meet them every way we could, consistent with that. My interpretation is like his—not that republicans were defeated, but that they came to the conclusion that their objectives were more likely to be reached by participation than by terrorism, and I would say they did not change their objectives.

Q: Was Adams genuine, in attempting to bring in the rank and file? Or was this used as a political ploy to exact more concessions?

ROBIN BUTLER: The original drafts, the Hume–Adams document that we were presented with, were attempts to get more out of us than we were prepared to concede. That is what I mean by the risk of buying a pig-in-a-poke, and were we so desperate to get some sort of peace that we were prepared to make concessions?

The answer to that was: no concessions on principle. No secret agreements, and as I say there was never any sort of dispute about those principles within the British government. There were disputes about the modalities of communication, the risks we were taking, whether we were going to do great political

---

[54] This is a reference to the reputedly tense relationship Tony Blair had with his long-time colleague and successor as prime minister and party leader, Gordon Brown.

harm if these were revealed, those were the anxieties, but we knew all the time how far we could go in meeting them, and there were other things that in the original drafts of the declaration went too far.

Q: Was Adams taken as genuine?

QUENTIN THOMAS: Well, not from the outset. Nor were events consistent with being confident. They did go on using terrorism, and there is the famous phrase which is clearly a military one of 'They haven't gone away, you know', and that is why decommissioning, although in one sense it did not matter—and militarily it did not matter—but as a symbolic political matter it was hugely important.[55] Yes, you could exaggerate the extent of confidence.

Q: The last week of October 1993 is frequently cited as one of the darkest weeks of the Northern Ireland 'troubles', starting with the Shankill bombing and finishing with Greysteel.[56] How did that affect the negotiation process?

ROBIN BUTLER: John Major believed that was what caused the IRA to reopen the negotiations with us on what I call the 'conflict-is-over' strand. They came back at that point and restarted the dialogue that led to the November leak. Their 'conflict is over' message in February, our nine-paragraph reply, and a reply from them, immediately followed by Warrington.[57] This caused us to stop.

There was no further contact until after Shankill and Greysteel. Then the IRA suddenly resumed contact at the end of November, and we said: 'Well, we're prepared to enter dialogue in return for a permanent ceasefire, but we're not prepared to make any secret agreement.' John Major believed that it was consciousness of their excesses that brought them back into dialogue.

I think if we are going on to the causes of those various stages of the negotiation, I see there was a reference to a meeting in a letter that you showed me, a meeting between you and me on 4 August.

DERMOT NALLY: That's right, there was a meeting on 4 or 5 August and there was a meeting on 10 September.

ROBIN BUTLER: I think that meeting on 10 September must have been following Major showing the draft to Molyneaux and sending me back saying that we are not very optimistic about this.

---

[55] Gerry Adams, Sinn Féin leader, was reported as having said at a rally in Belfast on 13 August 1995 in respect of the IRA that 'They haven't gone away, you know'; *Irish Times*, 14 August 1995.

[56] These incidents refer to the IRA bombing of Frizzell's fish shop in the Shankill Road, Belfast, on 23 October 1993; one IRA member carrying the bomb and nine others were killed. On 30 October three UDA gunmen opened fire in a pub in a nationalist area in Greysteel, Co. Londonderry, killing eight people.

[57] An IRA bombing on 20 March 1993 in Warrington, a town between Liverpool and Manchester in England, took the lives of two children.

DERMOT NALLY: Yes, there was a meeting on 10 September, but that is you, me, Seán Ó hUiginn, and Quentin. This is a six-page note which I presume you do not want to read.

ROBIN BUTLER: The gist will do fine.

DERMOT NALLY: 'British Officials were at pains to signal that they saw this as complementing rather than substituting for the Butler–Nally discussion. The meeting made it very clear that the British are not ready to begin a drafting exercise in this forum. They were at pains, however, to avoid any negative connotation and convey a clear willingness to pursue the key issues in good faith in the context of the talks format.'

'It remains to be seen whether their concern is essentially procedural, i.e. a sequence for discussing these hypersensitive issues, or more substantive, in that they needed a second approach. Important to the discussion was a greater concern for the unionists' demands, for example on articles 2 and 3. If so, it may be difficult to square the circle of meeting such of the pro-unionist requirements and at the same time securing the basic requirements which have been highlighted as necessary for a cessation. This involves some degree of British tilt towards a pro-nationalist theory.'

'However, since it is clear that the talks context is the only option allowing for the further discussion of the key issues of the present text, and since the British officials are at pains to signal that they see this as complementing rather than substituting the Butler–Nally discussions, it would be difficult to justify our refusal to agree to their approach.'

QUENTIN THOMAS: Were we trying to push it into the discussions on what became the Framework Documents?

DERMOT NALLY: It looks as if we were trying to support the talks process rather than talk about something which had a Hume–Adams shadow on it.

ROBIN BUTLER: And then my notes suggest that Dick Spring's speech on the six principles played a very positive role.[58] That came about in September–October. Then there was the European Council, which I wasn't at, but you were Dermot?[59]

Then there were the events that we've described, of us trying to produce our own draft, my taking that over at the end of November, the Taoiseach saying, no, we couldn't go ahead with this, and then, on 3 December, the very direct-talking meeting, which I think we were all present at, where John Major and

---

[58] In a Dáil speech on 27 October 1993, Tánaiste Dick Spring outlined six 'democratic principles of peace'. Specifically, they were (1) that the people of Ireland, North and South, should freely determine their own future, (2) that this could be expressed in new structures arising out of the three-stranded relationship, (3) that there could be no change in Northern Ireland's status without freely given majority consent, (4) that this could be withheld, (5) that the consent principle could be written into the Irish constitution, and (6) that a place would be available at the conference table for Sinn Féin, once the IRA had renounced violence (*Dáil Debates*, vol. 435, cols 256–7, 27 October 1993).

[59] The European Council met in Brussels on 29 October and on 10–11 December 1993.

Reynolds had a session by themselves and where you and I were called in to try and bring some peace.

And then came what I regard as the crucial decision on our part, which was 'OK, we'll try and make the best of your text and not proceed on our text'. We had a meeting in London, in my room on the day of the University rugby match, which must have been the Tuesday. I remember it was on the day of the University rugby match because I had tickets and could not get to it. And then the final stages of negotiation were on the 14th, ending in the evening. You came over and signed the Agreement on the 15th, so I think that was the sequence of events.

DERMOT NALLY: Except I think it was the 13th.

ROBIN BUTLER: Was it? Yes.

Q: How far in the September–October period? Did I catch it rightly that drafting was going on on what was going to become the Framework Documents a year later? Was that going on simultaneously?

QUENTIN THOMAS: Well, it was, until that leak.[60] We had a regular gathering of the Liaison Group between the NIO and the DFA. There were other people on it, but that was essentially where we were meant to be talking about it. The idea was that one way of getting the talks back was for the two governments to table some sort of skeleton of what a settlement might look like. A number of the parties suggested this to us. In a way it was a trap, because you knew they would all denounce whatever you proposed.

Anyway, we willingly walked into this trap, and I think we had given our colleagues a draft, and for a number of meetings we'd had no response. Then the leak, which may or may not have been a step towards the response, effectively stopped all that. Does somebody know when that was?

Q: The leak occurred on 19 November.

QUENTIN THOMAS: It was not a good month.

DERMOT NALLY: I have a document here. This is the meeting on 6 October. Do you want to go through this in detail, or just 'the British government agrees'?

ROBIN BUTLER: Yes, I think it might be a good thing, actually. If you want to get to the points which we were discussing and were at stake, I think that is the only source of it we have.

4.4.2. Text: British Commitments

DERMOT NALLY: OK. Well in paragraph 3, about the third sentence, 'they therefore make a solemn commitment to promote cooperation at all levels

---

[60] A copy of the draft British–Irish Framework Document leaked to journalist Emily O'Reilly was published in the *Irish Press* on 19 November 1993; see Document 4.7.

on the basis of the fundamental principles, undertakings and obligations under an international agreement to which they have jointly committed themselves and guarantees which each government has given'.[61] 'Guarantees which each government has given' is inserted there. In paragraph 4, 'the Prime Minister reiterates on behalf of the British government that they have no selfish strategic or economic interest in Northern Ireland'. 'Political' comes out there.

This is fair enough, we have no problem with that. 'The British government': the original text was 'both governments agree that it is for the people of the island of Ireland alone to exercise their right of self-determination to bring about a united Ireland on the basis of consent freely and concurrently given, North and South'. [The changes are] 'to bring about a united Ireland', which is brought down from the middle of the sentence to the end, and that 'both governments' becomes 'the British government agrees that it is for the people of the island of Ireland.'

Q: Why was it decided that only the British government sign that, and not the two governments?

DERMOT NALLY: Well, because we already could argue that it is in the constitution that it is for the people of Ireland alone to exercise the right of self-determination. Now that argument stands anyway. We do not have to say it. It is only provoking people. If we say 'the British government agrees that it is for the people of the island of Ireland alone to exercise the right of self-determination on the basis of consent freely and concurrently given, North and South, to bring about a united Ireland', it is simply saying that the British government say 'if you can agree, we agree, to whatever you agree to'.

QUENTIN THOMAS: This whole paragraph by the end is a British paragraph; I mean the way it works in the end is paragraph 4 is for the British and paragraph 5 is for the Taoiseach and 6 and 7 go back to both governments.

DERMOT NALLY: 'They believe that the people'—this is the last sentence of paragraph 4—'they believe that the people of Britain would wish in friendship to all sides to encourage'—'encourage' comes out—'to enable the people of Ireland' goes in, which is fair enough. But that is one of the most important paragraphs in the text.

Q: Can I ask about the word 'political'? So 'no selfish strategic political or economic interests' was the original?

DERMOT NALLY: 'Political' was in the original document.

QUENTIN THOMAS: And 'political' was not in the Whitbread speech?

DERMOT NALLY: There is no 'political' in the Whitbread speech, there is no comma in the Whitbread speech.

---

[61] Paragraph 2 in the final version.

Q: Getting a comma in there would have meant that the British were declaring they had no strategic or economic interest—they may have a strategic interest in Northern Ireland, but not a selfish one.

DERMOT NALLY: On our side we were saying 'political' is a try-on. If people want to take it out, fine, I am not going to say anything about it. But for the same reason we couldn't argue about a comma going in there because we were trying to quote a speech which the British made and which they will stand over, or which they will support, and we cannot come along and say 'OK, we want you to support something you have not said'. So, the comma just disappeared into the distance, and we simply wanted to quote the Peter Brooke speech, and that is what that is.

Q: I am just wondering whether the people from the British side attached a great deal of significance to the absence of the comma?

ROBIN BUTLER: Yes.

Q: Can you just explain the significance?

ROBIN BUTLER: If you say 'no selfish *comma* strategic or economic' you are saying there are three possible interests and we do not have any of them. If there is no comma you are saying we do not have any strategic or economic interests of a selfish sort.

QUENTIN THOMAS: In other words, we are not occupying that bit of Ireland to protect ourselves from an attack by that route, as had been thought to be wise at certain points in the past when the French and Spanish landed things there.

Q: Well, what would be a non-selfish, strategic interest?

QUENTIN THOMAS: Personally I would not put great weight on it. It is just if someone introduces a comma you resist it.

It is a difference, sure. It is a transformation that one would resist. But, having said that, I do not know that I would be prepared to say what the difference between a 'selfish strategic' and a 'strategic' interest is.

ROBIN BUTLER: Quite, and I agree.

DERMOT NALLY: OK.

Q: What was the thinking behind cutting out the 'political' interest?

ROBIN BUTLER: What one is saying is that if you put in 'political' it means we do not care about the people in Northern Ireland.

Q: Except that, if 'political' is gone and the word 'selfish' stays, you do not have a selfish political interest in Northern Ireland, you have an unselfish political interest, so in a way once the comma is out the word 'political' becomes much less onerous than it would otherwise?

ROBIN BUTLER: I agree, but I think we then go back to Dermot's point that we were quoting a speech.

DERMOT NALLY: You have to take the context of the negotiation. We have a document which we worked on with a lot of sweat and effort. We wanted to reach agreement as far as it is possible, therefore we did not want to include in the document anything which is going to create more argument and possibly even slightly more antagonism. We want to get an agreement on this document, and for that reason we stick as closely as we can to what we can accept. We have accepted—everybody has accepted—the Whitbread speech, so why make an issue of it? That is the atmosphere of the talks, I think.

ROBIN BUTLER: I agree.

Q: The Irish government said it is for the Irish people North and South to define their own future. Is this not effectively saying that unionists are Irish? It doesn't give unionists the right of self-determination?

ROBIN BUTLER: I can't understand the point.

DERMOT NALLY: No, right through every negotiation the idea of an independent Northern Ireland is out, even if there's a suggestion or a hint of independence here.

QUENTIN THOMAS: I think you might be on a slightly different point. This recognizes the validity of a majority of the people of Northern Ireland to have a say; what it does not do is to recognize the unionist nation as an entity, even if it were to become a minority. Maybe it should, but it doesn't.

DERMOT NALLY: There is the further point in this, that one of the things that Hume always argued for was a plebiscite or referendum held on the same day in both parts of the island, which is what this is all about. So it is also a gesture towards undercutting the 1918 election.[62]

Q: When is the statement made about the rights of the people of Ireland, 'the British government accepts the rights ... '?

DERMOT NALLY: No, that's the original draft, not as it is there now. The original draft was changed quite a bit. That sentence, though, the thought behind it is in the original text, this is the 19 June text.

Q: When the British government recognizes the right of 'the people of Ireland, North and South', and so on, is that experienced as a concession, as a major break, or rupture, in British thinking about Northern Ireland?

QUENTIN THOMAS: No, I do not myself think it was. I think the key thing for us was that all subordinate clauses were there in this sentence about 'the British government agree that it is for the people of Ireland alone'. There are lots of subordinate clauses; what they are mainly to do is to make sure that Northern Ireland as a unit—or the majority of the people of Northern Ireland—have an arm-lock on it at each step. Once you've got that I do not think it is a great break for us to recognize the people of Ireland because, I think, it is not put this way here, but I think it is the case that there was virtually no British interest at

---

[62] Traditional republican ideology saw the 1918 general election as the last all-Ireland one and argued that the Sinn Féin victory then was an irreversible, democratic endorsement of a united Irish republic. John Hume argued that this legitimation of the militant campaign for Irish unity could be undermined if the existing constitutional position were to be recognized in an all-island referendum.

stake in this process greater than the interest of securing an agreement that everyone would underwrite.

The *reductio ad absurdum* is that, if in, not this document, but if in the talks process with all the players at the table they'd agreed that the moon was made of blue cheese, we would happily have agreed to it, because there is no British interest in denying that, greater than the interest in getting everybody to sign up to something. That is a *reductio ad absurdum*, but it reflects a sort of truth—that our greatest interest was for everyone to be happy, like the good Mummy.

Q: OK, the point I think was made this morning, though, that it would not have been possible to have said that in 1972 or 1973, I think that was your point—that it was still very much 'Northern Ireland is British'? Am I right?

DERMOT NALLY: No, you go back to the Government of Ireland Act and the first sentence, as far as I remember, says that we wish what we're doing now will develop in such a way that the people of all Ireland will do something or other.[63]

QUENTIN THOMAS: A lot of it is there, isn't it?

DERMOT NALLY: Yes, that is just there. That is a repetition of the Government of Ireland Act, not in the same language.

Q: Under the Crown, of course.

QUENTIN THOMAS: Yes, but the sentiment is there.

Q: Where did the actual phrase 'no selfish strategic or economic interest', at least from the British side, where did that come from?

QUENTIN THOMAS: I do not know, but it no doubt reflected advice that John Hume was giving us to the effect that look, these characters do not understand, they think you're the problem, they haven't grasped the point that you aren't the problem, the problem is the unionists and their views. Now, if you can just make it clear, says John Hume, it will all be much easier.

I think that Tom King, as I said earlier, was probably the first one to say this, and nothing happened, but I think that was the timing. I suspect we picked it up as a direct result of advice from John Hume—his analysis was that there was a fundamental misunderstanding on the part of the republicans, and that removing that misunderstanding could be a crucial step towards sorting this out, and that seemed to me to have been rather good advice.

ROBIN BUTLER: If I just go back to the comma, and say one thing more about that: now, as I said before, if you had a comma there, there are three types of interest, it would have been nonsense to say, for example, that we had no

---

[63] Clause 2 (1) of the Government of Ireland Act, 1920, proposed the establishment of a Council of Ireland 'with a view to the eventual establishment of a Parliament for the whole of Ireland, and to bringing about harmonious action between the parliaments and governments of Southern Ireland and Northern Ireland'.

economic interest in Northern Ireland because actually we obviously had, it was costing us a hell of a lot of money. So what we're saying is we've got no *selfish* economic or strategic interest in Northern Ireland, so, you know, we haven't got an interest where we want to keep Northern Ireland as part of the United Kingdom for reasons of our own self-interest. In fact, you could argue that our reasons of self-interest pointed the other way.

4.4.3. Text: Irish Commitments

Q: So, you were going through the sections, Dermot?

DERMOT NALLY: The only comment I can make on paragraph 5 is that the Revd Roy Magee came to us, and he said: 'Look, my people' (whoever they happen to be) 'would be very impressed to be included in the thoughts in the paragraph.' The thoughts are the ones that are set out beside their asterisks: the right of free political thought, the right of freedom of expression of religion, and so on. They went in at a very late stage in the draft—sorry, there are six not five, and these would be reflected in any future political and constitutional arrangements emerging from the new and more broadly based agreement.

We've no problem with signing off on the right of freedom of expression, of religion, and the right of free political thought, or the right to pursue democratically national and political aspirations, because that's what we've been talking about all the time. I'm not sure whether we just phoned you and said 'are these OK with you?'

ROBIN BUTLER: I do not remember any difficulty about this.

DERMOT NALLY: It was no problem anywhere.

ROBIN BUTLER: But I think one point to make about this is the point that Quentin just mentioned earlier, and I think it is an important point. An important stage of the negotiation of this was when we agreed we'd have one British paragraph and one Irish paragraph, so then I think you'll find in the original draft there wasn't something like that.

Q: I've always thought that paragraph was kind of the Irish government acting like persuaders or trying to take a step towards persuading the unionists?

ROBIN BUTLER: Yes.

DERMOT NALLY: Well, it was that, in fact.

Q: But that surely shouldn't have been in the original draft, then, because that would look too much like both governments saying this—that would look too much like the British government acting as persuaders?

DERMOT NALLY: I see your point. No—the origin of that is the contact that the Revd Roy Magee made. He said 'we would like these included', and I said 'fine, if you want them in'. The bonus that came from simply accepting what he was saying, with a very, very minor adjustment in the text somewhere, was a great bonus, because he went away saying 'well, they listened to us'; that was well worth having.

QUENTIN THOMAS: Was it here that we introduced the expression that the democratic right of self-determination by the people of Ireland as a whole must be achieved and exercised *with* and *subject to* the agreement and consent, which is paragraph 5. Consent refers to 'the majority of people in Northern Ireland'. I think the 'subject to' was introduced at our suggestion, so, although it is a Taoiseach's paragraph I do not think we refrained from making suggestions on it.

DERMOT NALLY: Yes, well I mean that is OK, all full of goodness and light, and right.

The only other suggestion on paragraph 5 at this stage, 5 October—this thing dated 7 October is an addendum at the very end of paragraph 5—I'm not sure how it reads in the final text, but this was the amendment being suggested at that time: 'Nothing inconsistent with justice and equity', 'respect the democratic dignity and the civil rights and the religious liberties of all of both communities which would be reflected in any future political and constitutional arrangements emerging from a new and more broadly based agreement'.

Q: In the first sentence of paragraph 5, where the Taoiseach considers the lessons of Irish history, etc., showing that 'stability and well-being will not be found under any political system which is refused allegiance or rejected on grounds of identity by a significant minority': as I recall those in terms of the principle of consent, there was a whole set of speeches, and one of them was Dick Spring's 'six principles', where he, I think, emphasized the need for the consent of the majority in Northern Ireland to constitutional change. Shortly thereafter both he and, I think, Albert Reynolds emphasized the need for consent of a minority in Northern Ireland to the situation there. So I always read that first sentence as needing widespread consent, and consent of the nationalist minority in Northern Ireland as well as the unionist majority in Northern Ireland, so it was somewhat broadening a notion of consent away from a majoritarian one.

DERMOT NALLY: Well, a significant minority, yes. If a significant minority do not give consent you're still in trouble.

QUENTIN THOMAS: But that also was conventional wisdom on the British side, with no hope of achieving stability without securing the consent of the nationalist minority as it was at the time within Northern Ireland.

DERMOT NALLY: Archbishop Eames had been conversing with the Taoiseach, or the Taoiseach was talking to Eames, I'm not sure which, but anyway Eames came back to the Taoiseach with these, and they said 'fine'. Now paragraph 6 in the final text, this has changed now completely.

QUENTIN THOMAS: But your paragraph 6 in that draft, how does that begin?

DERMOT NALLY: 'The Irish government accordingly commit themselves to working in the spirit and on the basis of the report of the New Ireland Forum.'[64]

ROBIN BUTLER: I think that was replaced by Eames.

DERMOT NALLY: It could have been. The New Ireland Forum was taken out because it's only a red flag.

QUENTIN THOMAS: Exactly.

DERMOT NALLY: You can say you want to achieve nationalist consensus, but you do not go back to the New Ireland Forum, which nearly split the national consensus, and when the Forum Report was printed or almost printed, Charlie Haughey came back and said 'No, that won't do, you haven't got a unitary state and because you haven't got a unitary state I'm never going to sign it'. So they had to redraft it and put in the option of a unitary state, so even from our point of view, even from the nationalist point of view, it would have been a provocation to include the New Ireland Forum. So, there's no change from the beginning of October in that paragraph, but then the final version is completely different.

4.4.4. Text: Constitutional Change

DERMOT NALLY: OK, then paragraph 7, my one begins 'in the light of their joint commitment'. I do not know how yours works, Quentin—this is paragraph 7 in my October draft.

QUENTIN THOMAS: Yes, well paragraph 7 on the final one begins differently, 'both governments accept that Irish unity will be achieved only by those who favour', and this is probably Eames.

ROBIN BUTLER: It was all Eames; paragraphs 6 and 7 are both Eames.

DERMOT NALLY: OK, well just if we stick with paragraph 7 as in this draft: 'it will be open to the convention to make recommendations and proposals on agreement as defined in the Forum Report and respect for the rights and identities [...]'. In other words this is a proposal for a convention to be established by the Irish government.

ROBIN BUTLER: And this becomes the Forum for Peace and Reconciliation in paragraph 11.

Q: Well, where did that idea come from?

DERMOT NALLY: That was in the original draft. It came from us, and the idea was that you must give up the violence; then you come in and talk, and this talk will

---

[64] On the New Ireland Forum, see Subsection 3.1.3.

be on an orderly basis, and the orderly basis is the forum, the convention here became a forum.

Q: Why would that forum be any different than, say, the inter-party talks that had gone before?

DERMOT NALLY: Well, let's say it would be talks between the nationalist parties including Sinn Féin, assuming Sinn Féin gave up violence, so in that sense it would be completely different from the original forum.

QUENTIN THOMAS: It was in your jurisdiction only?

DERMOT NALLY: Yes.

QUENTIN THOMAS: That was the key difference; it didn't involve the British government.

Q: What's the virtue of the Irish government doing this by themselves?

DERMOT NALLY: The basic purpose is to get Sinn Féin talking, because once a rebel talks it is the end of violence.

FRANK MURRAY: They're in the tent.

QUENTIN THOMAS: It was to give them somewhere to go, because there weren't any talks anywhere else. There were these notional virtual talks that we pretended were going on, but they weren't going on.

DERMOT NALLY: It was a mechanism to bring them in and to get them talking.

ROBIN BUTLER: And my recollection is that we tried hard to get this out because we didn't think it was helpful.

DERMOT NALLY: We didn't quite understand why.

ROBIN BUTLER: Well, because it was a diversion.

QUENTIN THOMAS: Well, I think you'll find in the original draft it wasn't just within your jurisdiction, it was going to be an all-Ireland convention.

DERMOT NALLY: The original draft was a convention: 'The Taoiseach has indicated to the British Prime Minister his intention of establishing a permanent Irish convention.'

QUENTIN THOMAS: Permanent, gosh?

DERMOT NALLY: 'A permanent Irish convention to consult and advise on the steps required to remove the barriers of distrust which at present divide the people of Ireland and which stand in the way of the exercise in common by them of self-determination on the basis of equality.'

QUENTIN THOMAS: But a draft even earlier than that may have made it all-Ireland?

ROBIN BUTLER: Well, I think that makes it all Ireland, it doesn't say within the jurisdiction. So I think we thought that the convention had tastes of the all-Ireland council and would be provocative to the unionists. We did our best to persuade you to drop it, and the concessions you made were to call it not a convention but a 'Forum for Peace and Reconciliation', and say it is going to be something you were going to do within your jurisdiction.

QUENTIN THOMAS: And it is no longer permanent. That must be a relief to everybody.

DERMOT NALLY: OK, well it hasn't gone away, you know. It is still there; the forum is there, the forum is OK. The suggestion was 'the convention will operate with full respect for the authority of the institutions as established by law in this state'. There was a change in the original draft, and it was intended to make Sinn Féin say 'well, OK, you're working under the Irish constitution'.[65]

QUENTIN THOMAS: But that doesn't seem to have survived to the final text?

DERMOT NALLY: After that we went to paragraph 8, where we took out the word 'all': 'The convention will be open to all democratically mandated political parties'; I do not know where we are now in the final version.

ROBIN BUTLER: The bit about the constitution; we would certainly have been very keen on it at the end of paragraph 7.

DERMOT NALLY: He [the Taoiseach] confirms, then, that in the event of an overall settlement the Irish government will reflect this in the constitution.

QUENTIN THOMAS: Yes, I mean that is what the Irish side did not want to say in the 1992 talks in Dublin. I think the change, what was said earlier by the Taoiseach about consent in this document, meant that at some point the Irish side were now recognizing this process was going to lead to amendment of articles 2 and 3.

DERMOT NALLY: Yes, it was never a problem, except the problem that it mightn't be accepted. Every person who approached the problem realistically said articles 2 and 3 must be changed, but they said 'we can't change them', or they said 'this is not the right time', or they said 'well, we need something to balance it in order to sell the idea'.

QUENTIN THOMAS: There's also the point you made earlier—that Albert Reynolds recognized that this was a horse which would be sold dearly and if possible several times over.

DERMOT NALLY: OK.

4.4.5. Towards Finalizing the Draft

ROBIN BUTLER: Now, do you want to go on to the next—what was the next stage of drafting? While Dermot is looking for this, let me just tell you an amusing anecdote which must have happened about this time. The one really serious problem we had with Molyneaux was when Molyneaux came to see John Major in a state of great fury, and said that he was being double-crossed by the British because he had a meeting with the Taoiseach and had seen an advice to the Taoiseach signed by me.

---

[65] See Document 4.6, para. 7.

Well of course this came as quite a surprise to me since I didn't remember signing any advice for the Taoiseach of any sort, and it turned out the explanation for this was that the Taoiseach's private secretary was called Butler, Colm Butler. It just shows what little things are in risk of throwing it. I remembered this and guessed that this must be what the document was, and so wrote to Molyneaux and said I think this must be the explanation. I got the most handsome and delightful apology from him: 'I quite understand, completely misunderstood.'

DERMOT NALLY: That was very nice of him.

ROBIN BUTLER: Very nice.

DERMOT NALLY: The next big event was the Brussels summit, 29 October, and the problem there was Hume–Adams; this is a joint statement by the Taoiseach and Prime Minister on 29 October.

QUENTIN THOMAS: And am I right in remembering that John Hume said publicly that he'd given a document, the outcome of this, and then he got on a plane to America and was incommunicado?

DERMOT NALLY: Yes.

QUENTIN THOMAS: And was it the case that there was no such document, or was there a document?

DERMOT NALLY: I never saw one.

QUENTIN THOMAS: No, I thought I understood that there wasn't in fact a document, that it was just a bluff.

FRANK MURRAY: Albert Reynolds told me there was no such document.

DERMOT NALLY: I'm sure, if there had been, he would have given it to me, given it to us.

ROBIN BUTLER: So what then happened?

DERMOT NALLY: This is the communiqué, part of the communiqué anyway. They acknowledged John Hume's 'courageous and imaginative efforts', and 'the Prime Minister and the Taoiseach agreed that any initiative can be taken only by the two governments, and there could be no question of their adopting or endorsing the report of the dialogue that was recently given to the Taoiseach and which he had not passed on to the British government'.

ROBIN BUTLER: Right, because it didn't exist.

DERMOT NALLY: Because it didn't exist. So that was the outcome of Brussels. It also said that 'there could be no secret agreements or understandings between governments and organizations supporting violence as a price for its cessation'.

Q: Can you just clarify the nature of the document that didn't exist? Because we spent some time earlier talking about earlier versions of the Hume–Adams document in 1992.

ROBIN BUTLER: Well I think it had been the case that John Hume had various texts which he'd variously given to people in Dublin and people in London or

Belfast, but when he made this great public demarche in the autumn of 1993 with a public product of this dialogue, no such document was handed over.

Q: A document presumably existed?

ROBIN BUTLER: Well lots of bits of paper existed.

QUENTIN THOMAS: There was no bit of paper specific to that date that was new and was now being formally handed over. It was a bluff designed to put us under pressure, I mean us—both governments.

DERMOT NALLY: But that's why the sentence is there quite plainly: 'the Prime Minister and the Taoiseach agreed that any initiative can be taken only by the two governments.'

FRANK MURRAY: Is there a possibility that John Hume had a document which Albert Reynolds didn't take from him—do not rule it out, that's all I say.[66]

DERMOT NALLY: Nobody that I have ever spoken to has seen the document.

Q: If it was being used for pressure, then, Hume must have given some indication of what it contained.

QUENTIN THOMAS: I think what's putting pressure on is a public statement by John Hume that there is an outcome and that it has been presented; it is that that puts pressure.

ROBIN BUTLER: Yes, so on we go. So, a good meeting at Brussels, but nothing that contributed specifically to this process apart from the two prime ministers at that stage being in harmony with each other.

DERMOT NALLY: Yes, now the next thing that I have is Eames on 2 November.[67]

ROBIN BUTLER: So this is Eames, this is where Eames comes in.

DERMOT NALLY: Yes, and it is fairly long, but it is more or less as it is in the final text.

ROBIN BUTLER: Yes, so that introduces paragraphs 6 and 7.

Q: Why was Eames approached?

ROBIN BUTLER: Because we'd said the document was hopelessly green, having shown it to Molyneaux, and it was the Taoiseach's idea: 'Well, look, let me show it to Eames', who is, you know, Protestant Archbishop, 'and see what his ideas are and what he can contribute', and he contributed this as a way of balancing the greenery.

Q: Why Eames and why not Molyneaux?

---

[66] Albert Reynolds recalled a 'tense' meeting with John Hume following his return from the USA, attended also by Dick Spring and Martin Mansergh, on the subject of the document. Dick Spring reacted negatively to a paper he was handed by Hume, commenting: 'What's this about? There's nothing in it.' Reynolds's own description of the document was that 'there were a few paragraphs that reiterated all the old aspirations that had formed the substance of a statement Hume and Adams had already published—nothing new whatsoever of any value or worth, no kind of "breakthrough" as had been intimated in the press'. Spring instructed Martin Mansergh to tear the paper up, but Mansergh quietly retained and filed the document. See Reynolds with Arlon (2009: 268).

[67] The reference is to additions to the draft suggested by the Church of Ireland Archbishop of Armagh, Robin Eames; see also n. 39.

ROBIN BUTLER: Because Molyneaux wasn't sufficiently enamoured with the document, so you couldn't ask him to do it.

Q: There doesn't seem to be much in paragraphs 6 and 7 other than good will?

ROBIN BUTLER: I do actually think these paragraphs in the end contributed a lot to getting the document acceptable, but part of my feeling anyway about this document, and what led to us offering a redraft, was that the thing had become too windy.

DERMOT NALLY: OK, now the next meeting, as far as I can make out, was sometime around 10 November, and my note is dated 10th. These are my notes of the meeting, then, actually taken at the meeting.

ROBIN BUTLER: And who was that meeting between?

DERMOT NALLY: You, me, Chilcot and Quentin, and it must have been Seán Ó hUiginn.

ROBIN BUTLER: Right, and what did we get up to there?

DERMOT NALLY: Well, we went through the Eames stuff and said 'fine'. In essence, the British said that their ministers, following several very agonized discussions, had concluded that they just could not get to the point where this is seriously on. That was November, things were looking fairly rough. They concluded that the Hume–Adams effect on unionist opinion made a joint statement in the text language impossible. The green language was just not a route they could take, because the unionists would not wear it. At the same time, Butler was at great pains to say that the process was not at an end. They see the desire for peace, about which they were working furiously on some other approach, about which they were totally vague.

ROBIN BUTLER: That's the 'conflict-is-over', yes.

DERMOT NALLY: They have just received the ecclesiastical language and would obviously be considering it carefully; they said the time was now so short that we should be available if necessary on a day's notice, or shorter, for further elaboration. The 2nd and 3rd of December were fast approaching; these things always approach very fast when you're coming up to a summit.

ROBIN BUTLER: That's right. Now what that hints at is that we were going to redraft the document.

Q: Was there any difference between the DFA and the Department of the Taoiseach's position with respect to these negotiations?

DERMOT NALLY: No, in fact the two of us worked very well together. The notes show Quentin Thomas questioning how much weight should be attached to Archbishop Eames's views or influence; he concluded by emphasizing again that the position was that the process had become tainted fatally. We stressed very strongly the emphasis in paragraph 6 and said that our information was that Molyneaux had indicated that, while he would not oppose, he could not support, he would passively accept the approach. After a very full and at times heated discussion, we concluded that the British should get in touch with us as soon as they had fully considered the completed text and had reached a conclusion.

ROBIN BUTLER: Yes, well, that all figures. That falls into place very well, and so it was after that we thought, well let's try and produce a text ourselves that the unionists will not think is so like Hume–Adams. What that reminds me is that that was part of the motivation for our providing our redraft. Now, although we had shown the text to Molyneaux, I'm sure we hadn't shown the text to Paisley. There may well have been some other meeting with Paisley at which John Major sort of tiptoed around what did he think of Hume–Adams and all that. Then we got our pens out and tried to produce a document that wouldn't look like Hume–Adams.

Q: Just to fill in the chronology, you've got Major's Guildhall speech on 15 November, where he says that if the IRA end violence for good then, after a sufficient interval to ensure the permanence of their intent, Sinn Féin can enter the political arena as a democratic party and join the dialogue; there can be no secret deals, no rewards for terrorism, no abandonment of the vital principle of majority consent; and you've got the Emily O'Reilly leak.

ROBIN BUTLER: That was very much what we had said to them in private, and that may be what triggered the leak, I do not know.

Q: Can I ask what impact your contacts with the IRA would have had on the drafting of the Downing Street Declaration?

ROBIN BUTLER: On the Downing Street Declaration, I do not think either of them had an impact on it. The Downing Street Declaration was going ahead on the process that we've been describing.

QUENTIN THOMAS: The correspondence we had through that channel did not involve anything like this text at all.

Q: And didn't influence the content of that text?

QUENTIN THOMAS: No.

ROBIN BUTLER: Except that we were saying the same things.

QUENTIN THOMAS: This says that, if they stopped, they can come into the talks process. We were saying that in other correspondence as well. I think in the correspondence we may have been more specific in saying three months, which period we more or less met to the day.

DERMOT NALLY: There was a period of three months mentioned at some time or another; there's a suggestion that it be included in the text, but it was taken out.

QUENTIN THOMAS: Right, but we'd said it anyway. We had a lot of internal argument about the length of that period.

DERMOT NALLY: The next thing that I have is this letter, which is unfortunately undated, from the Taoiseach to John Major, and it more or less says: 'You will understand that it is a politically untenable position for an Irish government to ignore what is widely felt to be the best opportunity for many years to bring about lasting peace, and for the two governments, and more especially the Irish government, to have refused even to explore the possibility. This has cast a shadow over the talks process and could give a disastrous new boost to Sinn Féin–IRA,' and so on.

ROBIN BUTLER: Yes, so that must have been after our 10 November meeting, but before the end of November row.

DERMOT NALLY: Yes, this is a letter from Major, a six-page letter to Reynolds on 12 November.

ROBIN BUTLER: 12 November, yes, so that will be presumably your reply?

DERMOT NALLY: He was of course very concerned at this suggestion that there is some kind of emerging rift between the two governments: 'he and I worked very closely together', and so on, 'only two weeks ago reached full agreement privately', and so on, 'we agreed in Brussels to aim at two complementary objectives, a complete cessation of violence and intensified efforts to find a basis for new talks. We did not suggest that one should proceed on condition upon the other. Both will be needed for a lasting settlement, and we should do all we can to take opportunities for progress.'

He referred to the upsurge in support for peace, and so on—'I cannot do and I know you won't ask me to endorse any course which instead of ending violence could increase it', and then referred to 'anxiety that a deal is being negotiated which would reward the years of terrorism; I've been intensely active since our meeting, as I promised to, but I need help and cooperation, as I need the cooperation of all the other participants, and seeing the leaders of all four constitutional parties—my talks with them, even my meeting with the DUP, have given grounds for encouragement. I've seen clear evidence that recent shocking events, pressure from both communities and the beneficial effect of the joint statement are acting on them.'

Michael Ancram has, meanwhile, completed the second round of exploratory meetings.[68] He has found some useful convergence between the parties on substantive issues, and also a sense that the governments must set the framework up for the next steps.

Q: Is there a sense that the process was entering flux?

DERMOT NALLY: There was a sense it was a kind of deep crisis. It looked as if it could be off completely. And then this is John Major's reply: 'There are a lot of reasons for things that are happening and I still want to preserve the context and still want to preserve the process.'

Then there's a letter to Martin Mansergh from Rod Lyne.[69] He says: 'Butler phoned me, he said he wanted to emphasize that although their position has not changed, that does not mean that they are not still in business. The present

---

[68] Michael Ancram, MP, was Undersecretary of State in the Northern Ireland Office, May 1993–January 1994; he later served as minister of state in the same office, January 1994–May 1997.

[69] See Ch. 1, n. 30.

word was not the final word. In fact, we are still very much in business and hope to be in a position to clarify things more on Thursday, end of this week, perhaps the middle of next week.' That's 16 November; time is running out.

Q: So you're in the process of redrafting the document?

QUENTIN THOMAS: That's right, correct.

DERMOT NALLY: 'Thank you for your letter. Your private secretary, Rod Lyne, has explained the background to it, and I'm sure that we've informed you in more detail of my position. I hasten to add that we have strongly urged the SDLP not to publish the proposals either now or in the future as obviously this would make it virtually impossible to make use of them in any form.'

Whatever the proposals were—I do not know what they were, but this is his letter to the Prime Minister dated 15 November: 'In conclusion I would urge you to consider with your colleagues the historic opportunity that exists when the cycle of violence in Ireland ends once and for all, and consider that a formula for it could save many lives over the next few years. I'm firmly convinced of that view and that we can make it work.' That's the gist of two pages.

Then on 14 November: 'Meeting with the SDLP, Sunday, 14 November. John Hume asked what exactly had come from the British in the June document; he wanted to know if it was true that neither government had accepted it.'

That is the document that was handed over in Baldonnel. At his meeting with Major he had stuck to the June document, which restated the principles set out by Brooke–Mayhew, self-determination simply, and so on. Albert said: while no text had been agreed, 'work was going on, on something or other', and that was it, that was the meeting with the SDLP. The Tánaiste made the point that Adams was anathema—this is the point he is making to Hume, that Adams was anathema and that the British feared a unionist backlash, which is plain enough. He had not given the Hume–Adams report to Major.

This is about the outline talks—'the Prime Minister recently had spent three times as much time on Northern Ireland as on any other question'. So, he is fairly deeply immersed in the whole thing. Then a conversation with Archbishop Eames: 'At a meeting in Downing Street he had fully backed the Taoiseach's initiative on the basis that it recognized the two traditions. He was, however, concerned about the hyping of the date 3 December. He said he had very frank discussions with the Prime Minister, which had gone beyond the document. The Prime Minister was concerned about in-fighting in his own party, though he genuinely wanted the peace initiative to go ahead. What was vitally important was that there was no give or change on the requirement of the need for the consent of a majority. I gave him an absolute reassurance on this that I felt Molyneaux might have been prepared to agree to at a direct meeting but for the leak.'

Q: Presumably that was the 19 November [1993] leak?[70]

DERMOT NALLY: Now this is 23 November, a fairly heavily amended draft. This is paragraph 4: 'The Prime Minister reiterates on behalf of the British government that while [acknowledging] the fundamental interests of Northern Ireland [...] its aim is to uphold with all legitimate means the democratic wishes of its people as to their constitutional status. They have no strategic etc.', and that's probably the final version of the text that is there in paragraph 4.

QUENTIN THOMAS: Yes, it has some interesting differences. Robin, I think this must have been your text?

DERMOT NALLY: 'The British government agree that it is for the people of the island of Ireland as a whole to exercise the right of self-determination on the basis of consent and to bring about a united Ireland if that is their wish'—and that's changed in the way that it is set out in detail here at the end.

Q: Different British–Irish perspectives?

DERMOT NALLY: I have a draft here, 26 November, John Major to Albert: 'the text would be seen as deriving from Hume-Adams [...] and thus would be assumed to be part of the negotiation with Sinn Féin. This is an impression which successive statements from Hume and Adams have done nothing to dispel. As we have agreed all along, association with Hume–Adams is the kiss of death. Robin will explain our thinking fully; he would see that the text incorporates much of the substance of the Joint Declaration.'

ROBIN BUTLER: So, this is our new text.

DERMOT NALLY: This is your new text, yes, and then that comes, that's the text attached here.

FRANK MURRAY: That is the 26th November, is it?

DERMOT NALLY: Yes.

FRANK MURRAY: Can I read you, just for the sake of completeness, the contemporaneous note in Seán Duignan's book? 'On that evening of 26 November I wrote: "Sir Robin Butler in from London. Produces alternative paper to Irish position paper, including proposals for unilateral changes to articles 2 and 3. Albert gives him hell. Tells him he hasn't a clue. He also tells him that his (Major's) alternative to the summit peace proposal, which involves the two leaders finding some kind of 'middle way', won't wash. He (Reynolds) will not buy some kind of 'sticking plaster' anodyne cover up. Why bother to have the summit at all? Who is trying to bluff who?"' For what it is worth, a contemporaneous note.[71]

ROBIN BUTLER: That seems a pretty mild account of it, really, to me.

DERMOT NALLY: The whole thrust and language of the revised document is firmly in the direction of further strengthening and reinforcing the Union,

---

[70] See n. 60.   [71] See Duignan (1995: 122).

and it is difficult to see how this is supposed to help elicit a cessation of violence from the Provisional IRA.

Q: Were there particular circumstances that got the Taoiseach so annoyed with you?

ROBIN BUTLER: Well, my recollection, to be frank, at the meeting is that he barely looked at it. He may have picked up on articles 2 and 3, but it was the fact that it was a completely new draft, I got the impression, that was the trouble. This had been something which he'd worked with, and as Dermot said much earlier, he'd been working for nine months on it and suddenly here with two or three days to go we produced an entirely new draft. And he just wasn't prepared to deal on that basis.

So, I do not think so much it was the content as the fact that it was throwing away, as he saw it, nine months of work and selling something they'd have to work on all over again. I think Dermot read out a little earlier an analysis of it, which must have been done after I got my bawling out, because it certainly wasn't analysed at the moment I handed it over.

Q: The purpose of the new draft was to try and get away from these statements Hume and Adams had been putting out.

ROBIN BUTLER: Yes, I mean it was to try to have something that the unionists would not see as founded on Hume–Adams.

It was designed to have everything in it that both sides attached importance to. I mean we worked very closely from the thing that we'd got, we cut out quite a lot of the Eames material, and it was a shorter, punchier document that was meant to contain the crucial things for both sides. It looked different; it looked fresh and more succinct.

QUENTIN THOMAS: And less green windiness I suspect, or what the unionists would regard as green windiness, and actually there was quite a lot of orange wind, as we've been saying, from Eames.

ROBIN BUTLER: Yes, it was meant to be a windless document.

Q: So, what was the British reaction when the Irish effectively threw the proposal out without even quite reading it?

ROBIN BUTLER: Well actually, that's interesting because I didn't realize, I thought that we didn't agree to go back to the old document until 3rd December. But it seems that Rod Lyne conceded that point much earlier in a phone call to Martin Mansergh. I do not know, really. We didn't want to have a breakdown with the Irish government is the truth of the matter.

QUENTIN THOMAS: We wanted to get an outcome if we could. It sounds as if the Prime Minister was particularly keen on that date.

ROBIN BUTLER: The 3rd December, well I think it had all been built up. It was known we were meeting on 3rd December, and we couldn't have cancelled the meeting on 3rd December without people interpreting it as being a breakdown.

DERMOT NALLY: For what it is worth, it is guaranteed to be a disaster to have heads of government drafting. I think that we were really asking for trouble if that is the way the thing ends. But on this particular occasion what struck me most forcibly was the size of the delegation on each side.

ROBIN BUTLER: Yes, Douglas Hurd came, I remember.

DERMOT NALLY: Yes, on our side was the Taoiseach accompanied by the Tánaiste and Minister of Foreign Affairs and Minister of Justice. That is four. Also present were Mr F[rank] Murray, Mr P[addy] Teahon, Mr D[ermot] Nally, Mr Martin Mansergh, Mr Noel Dorr, Mr [Joseph] Small, S[eán] Ó hUiginn, F[ergus] Finlay, D[eclan] O'Donovan, P[atrick] Hennessy, and T[im] Dalton. I do not know if anybody has counted that but it sounds like a football team, and it was crazy, utterly crazy, to have that number of people present at that type of a meeting.

So, right from the start, you could nearly write it off. They couldn't start it, and they argued, and in the middle of an argument Major broke the pencil, which of course is the part of the meeting that's remembered. This is a kind of verbatim note, this is the Taoiseach speaking: 'I have to say that my overall impression is that the balance of this text has been totally and absolutely offended. There is nothing in it on which the fellows can hang their hats; the balance of the document has been overwhelmingly disturbed.' I suppose the communiqué at the end of the meeting said that the meeting was constructive.

How it finished was they asked the two of us to go back and try and settle it or do something. I got a short typed summary of the conclusion of that meeting, and we had agreed on everything except three small points.

ROBIN BUTLER: At our meeting in my room, yes, I think that's true. I remember it. But then there was a phone call between John Major and Albert Reynolds which started with Albert Reynolds saying 'John, I'm absolutely so delighted that we've agreed the text', and this is referred to obliquely in John Major's book where he says 'Albert sometimes suggested you'd done a deal with him that you hadn't'; I think that is what he must be referring to. Anyway, I was with John Major in the flat and John said, 'Oh, I do not think so, Albert, I think there were just two or three things we've got to settle', and then actually they settled them without too much difficulty.

DERMOT NALLY: This is my note on paragraph 4: 'the retention of the word "assist" as a substitution for the word "help"', both of which the British object to.' I didn't hear any more about these; I do not know what that means because I haven't a paragraph 4 here. 'The phrase including "a united Ireland achieved by peaceful means and through agreement between North and South respectively": we think the underlying word should come out, since precisely the same thought occurs in the immediately following sentence.' I take it that's in paragraph 4.

ROBIN BUTLER: Yes.

DERMOT NALLY: And I'm not sure whether the words remained in it or came out, but anyway it is a minor point, and then paragraphs 10 to 12: 'the option appears to be either maintain paragraphs 10 and 11 as originally drafted with the words "Irish Forum for Peace and Reconciliation" substituted for "convention"'; that was accepted.

FRANK MURRAY: Yes, Forum for Peace and Reconciliation in 11.

DERMOT NALLY: 'Or perhaps substitute for the following three paragraphs two short paragraphs, one giving the British and Irish political dialogue, and the other the Irish line on the forum; a draft of these paragraphs is available. Obviously the option involving least risk is simply to retain paragraphs 10 and 11 as they are—but from conversations with Butler I expect the British will resist this strongly. I've given them your background on Molyneaux; they say there is some misunderstanding. Butler said that there were now some very agitated unionists about, because of a selective quotation, probably from the John Hume area, on self-determination. The Prime Minister is going to clear his diary for the rest of the afternoon so as to try to calm them. He is now suggesting tomorrow morning for his talk with you. I said that you might none the less wish to speak even briefly with the Prime Minister this afternoon, and Butler of course accepted this.' That is the end.

ROBIN BUTLER: Right, yes, that's interesting and obviously we did decide to retain 10, 11, 12, substituting 'Forum for Peace and Reconciliation'.

DERMOT NALLY: That's what came in the final version. So that is what, six or seven months?

Q: Just to go back to that crisis point, just how did you get over the crisis point?

DERMOT NALLY: Well, you heard Albert; he was climbing up the walls. Basically he was saying 'Look, you've been working on this bloody thing for the last three or four months, and this is what you come back with? It doesn't matter what's in it. Why don't you put these things into the draft that we've been talking about?' And then you go on to detail what is proposed, and his view on the detail—his view that I read out there—that it has changed the balance of the document totally and weakened it, that we can't understand it, we certainly couldn't sell it to Sinn Féin, so the whole thing was just fruitless.

ROBIN BUTLER: As I say, my recollection was it wasn't until the end of the meeting on 3 December that we agreed to go back to the original draft, and Dermot and I were instructed to meet and sort out any remaining difficulties on it.

DERMOT NALLY: Go and fix it. I have this; 7 December we met.

QUENTIN THOMAS: But I do not think we would accept, anyway, that the redraft was totally different in balance; that was obviously the perception of the Taoiseach before he read it, and he may have maintained that view after he did, if he ever did. I do not think we would accept that—but I haven't looked at that bit of paper for fifteen years, so I've no idea, but I'm sure it was intended to preserve the balance, but in a different language.

DERMOT NALLY: Yes, but it didn't. It had all sorts of stuff about the Irish constitution which would have blown the whole thing out of the water.

ROBIN BUTLER: Anyway, all I would say about that is that it was not meant to be a wrecking document; as, indeed, the subsequent events show, we were very, very keen to get an agreement. What it was meant to do was to reassure the unionists that this was not Hume–Adams.

DERMOT NALLY: There was nobody saying it was a wrecking document. I have the meeting on the 7th, I think it was—7th December.

ROBIN BUTLER: Actually, that would be a very interesting document. That would be what we agreed, and before the final three points that needed to be settled.

DERMOT NALLY: Yes, and Albert saw the three points, and he said: 'Lets agree to it—I am not going to spend time on that,' so he was happy.

4.5. Impact and Response

4.5.1. Responses to Declaration

ROBIN BUTLER: Again, my recollection is that we hoped there would be a much earlier response from Sinn Féin than there was.

FRANK MURRAY: Yes, that was shared on our side.

DERMOT NALLY: They kept putting it back. Adams was trying to convince his people that they should do this, and they had to go to this meeting, and that meeting, and that meeting. It was supposed to come before the end of the year, and then it was extended. Then it was supposed to come before the end of March. I think it was finally the end of August.

QUENTIN THOMAS: But he meanwhile demanded clarification, and, in what was no doubt unintentionally helpful, John Major refused to give any clarification. This is only one of the most dense and obscure bits of prose ever written. But we maintained the line that no clarification was needed or possible.

ROBIN BUTLER: He sent twenty questions.[72]

QUENTIN THOMAS: Well, in the end, we got around it with much help from Irish colleagues, particularly from Seán Ó hUiginn, who was to be very clear about what he thought would sell to the 'Shinners' and what would not. That sometimes made him look as if he was being tough on us, but I think what he was actually doing was being helpful and saying 'well, you know, you can say that if you want, but I do not think it will do the trick'. He did help on that question and answer; he helped very much.

---

[72] For the questions, see Document 4.9; for the British response on 19 May 1994 to a slightly different formulation of these questions, see Dunnigan (1995: 83–97).

ROBIN BUTLER: Again, my recollection is, I'm not quite sure it was twenty but I think it was, he sent twenty questions of which only one was for clarification of the talks.

Q: To whom did he send these twenty questions; did he send them to both prime ministers?

ROBIN BUTLER: I imagine so, formally, but effectively they wanted something from us, I think.

Q: If only one was a question, what were the other nineteen?

ROBIN BUTLER: They were all procedural, like how quickly can we end the talks, and that sort of thing.

Q: And so the ceasefire comes in August, and between December and August there's about a million things that happened. What was the role of the Declaration in that process?

ROBIN BUTLER: Quentin, do you want to answer this?

QUENTIN THOMAS: Well, I mean it is an interesting question. I do not know the answer. It was never us that said it would bring peace. It was what we were told by others, and we hoped that it was true, but wondered if it was, particularly after we'd finished and helpfully ruined the drafting of it.

I think it was probably one of the factors, but obviously there is a whole context this is about. If I'm right that they'd come to the view they couldn't secure their objectives by military means, that there was the talks process notionally if not actually, we'd shown we were prepared to have correspondence with them even if it had gone wrong in various ways. I think it probably was an important step on the way, but it is difficult to judge, to be honest.

DERMOT NALLY: I think that the reason for the delay was the political reality that Adams had to go around his different party branches and members. That takes quite a long time. He had to argue for the agreement in all the branches, which is quite a job. Without it there would have been nothing to argue about, and the violence could have continued, just gone on and on and on, because there was nothing there to hang their hat on, as Albert said.

So, the second thing is that parts of the agreement were echoes of the subterranean correspondence or subterranean knowledge, the message from Adams, the message from McGuinness. These echoes were kind of invitations to Sinn Féin to come in without, at the same time, rousing the unionists to the sort of fury that they had been provoked to before.

The third thing was that it was a sort of contradiction of what had happened in the Anglo-Irish Agreement. In other words, we're now consulting quietly and discreetly, with no publicity, and we want your views. Now I'd say without the Anglo-Irish Agreement they would never have broken in the way they did, but they had seen the two governments were prepared to go ahead and say 'well, we're going to do this; you come in or you stay out, do what you like, but we're doing it'. [Otherwise,] they would not have been quite so persuadable or quite so flexible.

ROBIN BUTLER: Yes, I agree with that.

Q: Did the unionists feel that they had been fully consulted in the preparation of the Downing Street Declaration?

ROBIN BUTLER: Well, they couldn't have done, because the UUP had never seen the text. Molyneaux had seen the text but had not shown it to his people. But I think Molyneaux, although I do not remember him saying anything publicly, I think moved pretty quickly to say that Eames had contributed to it, and it didn't seem too bad, it seemed balanced from his point of view.

QUENTIN THOMAS: Yes, I think one unionist judgement on it was that it was an orange text in green language. But I think the centrality of consent, and in the mouth of both the Prime Minister and the Taoiseach, in this document, and its much more forward position (maybe not more forward than you had always thought, but more forward than perhaps you had said) on constitutional reform, and on articles 2 and 3 and so on, must also have been noticed by people who had been screaming for it, as I said, in the talks process a year earlier.

I thought the unionist reaction to this was, for a grudging political culture, pretty good. Contrast this with the reaction to the Framework Document a little over a year later, in February 1995, which was not grudging acquiescence; it was much more hostile.

Q: One of the intentions was wanting to bring Sinn Féin into some kind of democratic process and talks process. So the question then is what kind of time horizons were you looking at?

QUENTIN THOMAS: I do not think we needed to answer that question at the time. The document as it came out had lots of plusses for us. If it could be done, and we thought it had been done, in a way which didn't put the unionists back. It firstly was a bit of joint work to which we attached importance, and the Irish government had attached importance. It certainly set out formally and publicly the conditions for bringing Sinn Féin in, it had things to say about the constitutional position which were helpful, and, in my view, they got even more helpful in the Framework Document. I think the answer is nobody had a view about the time, we didn't know—it might be next week, it might be next year, but it was all good, and there wasn't too much bad about it by the end.

DERMOT NALLY: And the best thing of it all, as far as the public was concerned, was that the two governments were producing this document, not one government, but two governments.

ROBIN BUTLER: I agree, I think that it is terribly important that, while the two governments were at odds with each other, the people who were in favour of violence could play them off, but when the two governments were shoulder to shoulder on the way forward, then the prospects for the terrorists were really very, very much reduced.

4.5.2. American Role and Perspective

The discussion moves on to the American role, questions about which had already been asked.

QUENTIN THOMAS: Well, I think in a way that's the answer to the American point. I remember one of these, I can't remember whether it was one of the four horsemen or whatever, I think it probably was, but one of those characters saying to me 'look, if you two governments do things you've got us, we'll support you, whatever you do, Anglo-Irish Agreement great—this is fine'; so, in a way, the more we could stick together the more that was the answer to the American question too.

Q: Is the fact that it is in a joint declaration which has been signed up to by the Irish government of value?

ROBIN BUTLER: Of course.

QUENTIN THOMAS: This is quite a formal bit of paper isn't it?

Q: What if the IRA's campaign had collapsed at the end of 1980s and the process then had to get under way to create some kind of political settlement, would it in any way have been an even more orange document?

QUENTIN THOMAS: Well, maybe we would not have needed this document. We would have been getting on with talks.

Q: Between?

QUENTIN THOMAS: When the talks, the 1991 talks, began, they didn't involve Sinn Féin. What I'm saying is that the fact that Sinn Féin weren't at the table didn't mean we, the British government and the Irish government, weren't very keen to reach a political settlement, and if Sinn Féin had laid down their arms earlier then, yes, a fortiori, we would have still been keen.

Terrorism is a huge issue, but the problem here was a disaffected minority within Northern Ireland, and a divided community within Northern Ireland, and divided communities on the island of Ireland. All those problems are there, whether there is a terrorist campaign or not, so I would have thought much of the attempted solutions would have been needed, even if you take terrorism out.

ROBIN BUTLER: There were some references earlier to the Americans, who of course in March gave Adams his visa, and John Major was very angry about that, because we were still waiting for the ceasefire and he felt that this was rewarding them. I remember I didn't actually share that view, not that it mattered. I thought that to give Adams a bit of a taste of being a world statesman, and so on, was all sort of fostering the pressure on him, and indeed when subsequently, a long way afterwards, the Americans refused to receive Adams after that murder in Belfast, I think that put a lot of pressure on Sinn Féin to join the administration.

DERMOT NALLY: Yes, I agree.

QUENTIN THOMAS: The fact that John Major was upset by it, I'm not suggesting for a moment this is why he did it, but he did increase the value of it to Adams, which was a good thing.

ROBIN BUTLER: No, I think he was genuine there.

QUENTIN THOMAS: I think he was, too, but I agree with you, I didn't think it mattered that much.

DERMOT NALLY: That is one of Garret FitzGerald's arguments about the Anglo-Irish Agreement. He said that when the nationalists saw the unionists getting themselves so worked up about it they thought it must be good news for the people of Ireland.

ROBIN BUTLER: Yes, when people left meetings smiling the other lot got terribly worried.

DERMOT NALLY: It is a strange world.

Q: Sir David Owen said that the British government was gradually opening itself to American influence in Northern Ireland in a way that was new, that made British sovereignty different than it had been understood in the past.[73] Do you think that is true?

QUENTIN THOMAS: No.

ROBIN BUTLER: No, I do not either.

QUENTIN THOMAS: I think the American role—books have been written, haven't they, like The Greening of America and how Clinton solved the Irish problems—I think it is all greatly exaggerated.[74] The Americans could be unhelpful, like giving lots of money to support terrorism, and they could be helpful in various ways, and one of the most helpful things they did was lending us George Mitchell—not to mediate, because he wasn't required to, and didn't want to, but just to be a very good professional chairman. But the notion that the American dimension was crucial in that way, I think, is a fallacy.

ROBIN BUTLER: I think we involved the Americans because we wanted their cooperation in preventing money going to the IRA and countering Noraid. We weren't very successful in that, but we were trying to, as it were, get them on our side.

DERMOT NALLY: One of the most successful advocates against Noraid and against that sort of subscription to the IRA was Seán Donlon, who was ambassador in the United States. He said 'you're not helping us, you're creating them'; these were his famous words. But, because he took that line, he was fired by Charlie Haughey, he was taken out of his job.[75]

---

[73] See Owen (2007).

[74] A reference to a book by Irish journalist Conor O'Clery (1996).

[75] This incident took place in June 1980, when Haughey planned to move Seán Donlon from Washington but was forced to back down by Irish American leaders.

FRANK MURRAY: Or an attempt to fire him was made.

DERMOT NALLY: Charlie called me into his office one day and said 'that will never happen again; the Americans have been on to me and told me if I do not leave Donlon where he is, I need not set my foot again in the States'. So, he gradually came to realize there were realities that we could do nothing with.

QUENTIN THOMAS: I mean, having said what I said, they could be helpful. The point when I remember the Americans being particularly helpful was after the 1997 election, when we knew what was keeping Sinn Féin out of the process and preventing a new ceasefire. With the help of our Irish colleagues, we wrote and met them, and they told us again what their problems were. We did an aide-memoire, which we thought answered these points and reflected Irish government comments. We then had another meeting and gave it to them and they said 'this isn't good enough', blah, blah, blah.

We had also drawn the Americans into this process and at that point we sort of said to colleagues in Dublin and through the embassy in London to Washington, 'look, these guys have asked these questions, we've answered them in ways you know, you've seen our answers and they're still moaning. This is the moment to press them.' And I think everybody did at that point row in behind, and the ceasefire of the summer 1997, when we were trying to revive it, occurred soon afterwards.

DERMOT NALLY: In addition to which they gave hundreds of millions of dollars to one fund.[76] That has probably reached a billion by now, which is not insignificant.

QUENTIN THOMAS: It is not insignificant!

ROBIN BUTLER: Was that Clinton or Bush?

QUENTIN THOMAS: This was Clinton.

4.5.3. Significance of the Declaration

Q: So what were the connections between the Downing Street Declaration and the Framework Documents, what was the intended connection?

QUENTIN THOMAS: Well, they're quite different in purpose, because the Framework Document was an attempt to sketch, do a draft, if you like, of the Good Friday Agreement. Then we had to wrestle with all the theology, so that the bit about the internal government of Northern Ireland had to be done by the

---

[76] A reference to the International Fund for Ireland, established in 1986 in the aftermath of the Anglo-Irish Agreement (see Subsection 3.3.7).

British government alone; obviously, other bits needed to be done by the two governments jointly.

And so it was not an attempt to answer the questions that this document answered and say what would happen—how to bring Sinn Féin in and set out certain constitutional points. It was a draft of what the institutional arrangements would be like. It was rubbished, and became one of these hate documents for the unionists in particular. My own assessment is that the Good Friday Agreement bears a very close resemblance to the Framework Document.

Q: How would you describe how the negotiations took place, or how the deals were made: was it bargaining, were you actually horse-trading, were you trying to get other things from the other side, or was it a kind of problem-solving approach?

ROBIN BUTLER: I think the whole story of the 'troubles' from 1970 onwards was that there were moments when you could make progress towards solving them, and there were moments when you couldn't, and what happened in the lead-up to the Downing Street Declaration was the resignation of Margaret Thatcher, and the arrival of John Major. With Albert Reynolds wanting to make this a priority, with John Major similarly wanting to do so, and the feeling that he'd got the sort of skills that could contribute to it, the messages that were coming from the IRA—that maybe they were ready for a better way of pursuing their objectives—this provided an opportunity.

Albert Reynolds, you know, took the lead in saying 'here is an opportunity you've got to take advantage of', and the negotiation was really how, in a way acceptable to both governments and to our constituents, we could take advantage of that. That was the nature of it, I think, it wasn't as it were horse-trading or anything, it was how you could edge an acceptable way forward without dropping off the pole on either side.

As I said earlier, and as Dermot endorsed, the personal relations that we'd established as officials from the time of the Anglo-Irish Agreement, and which through the set-up that Dermot and Robert [Armstrong] had put in place we continued, really stood us in hugely good stead in doing that, as did the affinity of the characters of Albert Reynolds and John Major. For all the differences they had, they were both deal-makers.

Q: In the negotiations, did you look after the unionists and the Irish look after the nationalists?

ROBIN BUTLER: No, not so much, but it was, if you like, a nationalist initiative, the Anglo-Irish Agreement in the first place, so the nationalists were being looked after because it was their initiative. I think, principally, we were making sure that we didn't produce something that was unacceptable, that the unionists couldn't acquiesce in or embrace. In a wider sense, John Major had to have in mind the Conservative Party. There was still—although it was no longer formally a Conservative and Unionist Party—that sort of historical connection. That is a reality.[77]

Q: Could you say a little bit more about that connection—is it an emotional connection, is it a political alliance?

ROBIN BUTLER: Well, it is a connection that some people actively represent, and Robert Salisbury, as he now is, Robert Cranborne, was very aggressively 'orange' in the British Cabinet.[78] And there were people like Michael Howard and Ken Clarke who were a mixture of unionist sympathizers and sceptical about the people we were dealing with—not the Irish government, but sceptical about the nationalists. These were very real considerations, as far as John Major was concerned.

QUENTIN THOMAS: Well, what I'd say, I agree with everything Robin has said, but this was the good bit. It wasn't horse-trading. It was problem-solving. I think, insofar as we had problems, they were often about the interrelationship between this rather agreeable exercise and the talks process, what we could do to revive it, keeping it going, working on the Framework Document, the correspondence that we were having with Sinn Féin, and all those things, and the interrelationship between them, to make up the whole picture. That was all difficult but this, although they managed to have a row in the end, this was quite agreeable stuff.

DERMOT NALLY: The character of the negotiation of the Anglo-Irish Agreement changed as the negotiation went on. You know that story that as we began we were trying to gain a maximum advantage, and probably the other side were trying to do exactly the same, but towards the end the argument became why do not you—that is, us, the Irish—represent the unionist point of view and we represent the nationalist point of view and we'll see what we can get from there.

It was a negotiation which changed in character totally, in that instead of being an antagonistic discussion, it became a discussion where each side was trying to help the other to produce a document which would be saleable and which would reach whatever the needs of the day happened to be. It was an extraordinary change of character.

I borrow the Belfast Agreement just to show the continuity of all this anyway. Paragraph 1 [contains] two small lines: 'recognise that it is for the people of the island of Ireland alone, by agreement between the two parts respectively, and without external impediment, to exercise their right of self-determination on the basis of consent, freely and concurrently given, North

---

[77] Although it retains the name Conservative and Unionist Party, its Ulster Unionist members resigned the party whip at Westminster after the suspension of Stormont in 1972, and the UUP formally ended its links with the Conservatives following the Anglo-Irish Agreement of 1985.

[78] A reference to a Conservative politician with strong unionist views, Robert Gascoyne-Cecil, Viscount Cranborne and, from 2003, Marquess of Salisbury.

and South, to bring about a united Ireland, if that is their wish; accepting that this right must be achieved and exercised with and subject to the agreement and consent of a majority of the people of Northern Ireland.' Why is there such a familiar ring about that?

ROBIN BUTLER: There is indeed.

DERMOT NALLY: So, the process of negotiation was continuous. The Anglo-Irish Agreement negotiation in the beginning was: what can we get which is big enough to justify changes in articles 2 and 3, which the government of that day can win at a referendum. That was always a very delicate political judgement. It wasn't for us to make, but we had it very much in mind. Changing articles 2 and 3 and changing the constitution was a difficult thing, as you know.

4.5.4. Irish Unity

Q: It seems to be the case that when there is no prospect of a united Ireland, Dublin governments do not hesitate to demand it, while if there is a real prospect of Irish unity Dublin governments have been historically much more circumspect?

DERMOT NALLY: Neutral.

QUENTIN THOMAS: I think this issue of a united Ireland is completely bogus if I may say so. The talks in 1992, as I said, were dominated by unionist worry about articles 2 and 3 and about constitutional formulations. Because of what is said in the Framework Document and in this Downing Street Declaration, the issue is hardly mentioned in the 1996–8 talks. If it is ever mentioned again, the answer endorsed by referendum North and South is very plainly put here, and it is a dog which isn't barking.

DERMOT NALLY: The other point is that you do not necessarily have to argue for unity in a way that could decompose this state. You can argue for unity as in the documents achieved by agreement over time, and as time goes by this place becomes more attractive, and the ideal solution is to find the unionists saying please let us have unity and the nationalists saying 'Oh, for God's sake, no, we do not want unity', which is making the unionists into a Fianna Fáil party and the nationalists into the Unionist Party, which is a transformation which could quite possibly happen.

FRANK MURRAY: Well, one former Unionist councillor has already joined Fianna Fáil.[79]

---

[79] A reference to Col. Harvey Bicker, elected to Down district council in 1997 and 2001 as an Ulster Unionist; he was appointed to the Council of State by President McAleese in 2004 and joined Fianna Fáil in 2008.

DERMOT NALLY: So it is something that can happen over time, and with agreement, but it certainly cannot happen suddenly, unless they want to ruin the whole island. This could possibly have repercussions on the other island, because if we were to assume the burdens that you at present bear, the financial burdens of Northern Ireland, it would wreck us. We'd have to devote the entire proceeds of that, the part that doesn't go to the European Community, to support the North, possibly two-thirds of income tax, or all of income tax.

The financial implications alone would be colossal, and they do not particularly want to have any more worries at the moment. But over time you can come to agreement, you can come to arrangements, and, thinking about it, one of the biggest contributions to unity could well be the M1 motorway to Belfast, and so on.

Q: Just a question about British perceptions of the Irish state. If we go back from the very beginning of the early 1970s to what they are now, have they changed quite fundamentally?

ROBIN BUTLER: Well, I would say that this is a function of the wealth of the Irish state, and as the economy of Ireland has grown and developed Ireland becomes a more important country, I mean not just to Britain, but within Europe and, indeed, the world. So that is the single, biggest change, as I see it, in the status of the Irish Republic during the last generation.

QUENTIN THOMAS: I think shared membership of the EU, which you mentioned, is pretty important too. There's a working relationship, no doubt, between all the members of the EU, but I suspect it is as close as any between two Anglophone countries.

DERMOT NALLY: It is the fourth or the fifth biggest customer of British exports; I'm not sure what the figure is at the moment, it used to be around fourth or fifth.

FRANK MURRAY: It is considerable, yes.

Q: The Downing Street Declaration, which we've mainly concerned ourselves with, was negotiated in a pre-Celtic Tiger period, when in fact it wasn't at all clear that we had really got out of the recession of the 1980s?

ROBIN BUTLER: No, there is no doubt that the Downing Street Declaration was directed towards the 'troubles'; there wasn't a change in economic status. It added nothing to that. It was directed towards the 'troubles'. But I ask you a question. I suspect, and it stems from something Dermot said but something I've long thought, as Ireland becomes a richer country, do you think it will strengthen not only the willingness but even the enthusiasm for a united Ireland in the South?

DERMOT NALLY: It might.

ROBIN BUTLER: Yes, it might.

DERMOT NALLY: I think it will, in that it is not only a question of wealth; it is a question of attitude, and if you look at when they were doing these things twenty or thirty years ago I would have found this country a most undesirable place to join. You had bans on contraceptives, you had book censorship, you had a kind of a church which was stupidly dominant, you had lots and lots of things that I would have said were totally undesirable. You had an economy that was crippled with peculiar forms of taxation; you had all the things that would not induce another country to join you.

FRANK MURRAY: A country that was very inward looking.

DERMOT NALLY: It was very inward looking. It is even now.

FRANK MURRAY: And that has changed.

QUENTIN THOMAS: These are excellent reasons why the North might want to join you, but what about the enthusiasm here for achieving Irish unity, which I think was your question.

ROBIN BUTLER: Yes, that was my point; it is something that becomes more desirable if you can afford it, if you see what I mean.

DERMOT NALLY: I would say that the enthusiasm is there, but it is sort of lukewarm, low key.

FRANK MURRAY: If that means that you have to give up the second BMW, well I might have to think about that. I'm being facetious.

ROBIN BUTLER: Good point. But you think of reunification of Germany.

FRANK MURRAY: There isn't the same driving urge.

ROBIN BUTLER: That was a very unattractive property to take possession of, but the West could afford to do it.

DERMOT NALLY: I was at a meeting with Chancellor Kohl and whoever happened to be Taoiseach at the time, which was Charlie Haughey. Kohl was talking about reunification; he said it was 'something that we had to do, there was no way we could have avoided it', because the East was collapsing. He said 'yesterday, fifteen thousand engineers crossed the border, chemists are coming across, the total economy there is in bits, the population is in revolt because the Stasi are being promised (I think it was two years) pay, just to go away'. He said 'imagine that sort of an offer being made to anybody', and we said 'what about costs?', and his answer was 'the cost doesn't worry West Germany, for the last ten or twenty years we have been growing, GNP has been growing and we can divert certain funds from border areas, we can divert certain funds from roads. We can take away the subsidy for that and the subsidy for this.'

He said the cost is not a problem; that was the greatest mistake he ever made in his life, because German unemployment never fell below, I think, about four or five million. We are twenty years after reunification, and the German economy nearly collapsed, because it had to introduce so much rigidity into its employment laws.

QUENTIN THOMAS: They paid a heavy cost, but actually in the long horizon of history that is a cost they managed to absorb.

ROBIN BUTLER: I was also thinking, you know, when you were asking your question, about Hong Kong, and our feeling about Hong Kong when we were negotiating with China. There was no real interest to us in retaining Hong Kong; on the other hand, there was a feeling of obligation to do our best for the people who we'd administered and not abandon them. I think that is very similar to what the feeling in the UK is now about Northern Ireland. The situation is quite different; we had no choice about Hong Kong in the end, but we did try, rather belatedly, to do good things for them.

Q: About the Good Friday Agreement, one thing that hasn't been discussed is that if the North wants to vote for a united Ireland, could the South possibly say 'no'—and presumably if the South says 'no' then Northern Ireland remains in the United Kingdom. This is the point, there isn't a third option?

DERMOT NALLY: A redraft has always been very, very careful to avoid a suggestion that there can be a possibility of an independent Northern Ireland, which is the third option.

QUENTIN THOMAS: Which has virtually no support from anyone.

Q: Is there a problem if the majority in the North wanted to leave the United Kingdom but the South refused to join up with them?

QUENTIN THOMAS: It would be a new one, wouldn't it?

Q: It would be a new one, yes. Is the agreement robust enough to withstand it? I do not recall—my recollection of the Agreement is it might not cover that possibility?

QUENTIN THOMAS: Well, it would just be in the United Kingdom, a united Ireland requires consent of all the people in both jurisdictions. So it would not be achieved, so [...] it is plain that Northern Ireland would remain in the United Kingdom.

ROBIN BUTLER: It would remain in the United Kingdom, unless at that point Northern Ireland said, as we have agreed there is no sign of it saying, 'we would prefer to be independent'. Then the situation would be very much like Scotland, and the question is whether, if Northern Ireland wished to be independent, whether we could hold them in the Union against their will, and I should think we'd be very unlikely to want to do that.

Q: You might have to become persuaders for Irish unity in another sense of the term!

4.5.5. Impact on Unionists

Q: Did you differentiate very much between what Molyneaux felt, or what Paisley felt, or did you think about the loyalists, or did you just tend to think, well, whatever Molyneaux says is enough, and everyone will follow him?

QUENTIN THOMAS: Well, no, not at all. It was helpful that for a period there was a leader of the UUP who seemed capable of delivering—there have been many periods when that has not been true. There was a brief period when, if Molyneaux said it, you could be pretty sure of the UUP. But the whole basis of the venture towards the Good Friday Agreement was to be inclusive, as I said—to have a comprehensive cast.

So, yes, we were at each step worried about whether you could get in or keep in the DUP. And it was with great regret, I think, to everyone that the DUP excluded themselves in the end. Now they've reincluded themselves, and Peter Robinson is to be elevated and so on—a great moment. I remember people saying the DUP would never deliver, and it couldn't deliver a milk bottle; well, I think they've had to eat their words.

I think the loyalists, yes, were a bit of a worry, but on a rather lower scale because of the view, although they were extremely dangerous, violent etc., and killed lots of people, I think there is a sense in which their campaign was reactive, and that if you took out IRA violence there was a reasonable expectation that loyalist violence would stop—maybe not immediately, and not that part of it which was wholly criminal, but there was a reasonable expectation that it would stop. I think the answer is that we worried about everybody.

Q: It is just that at this time the loyalist paramilitaries were much more active than they had been for a long time?

QUENTIN THOMAS: Yes, well I think we needed an agreement that would sell on the street. I think the moment at which the sensitivity about the loyalists was most obvious and overt was when we decided that—partly, I think, picking up the suggestion of the unionists, partly, I think, from George Mitchell in his decommissioning report—that there should be an election in 1996, a view which John Hume was deeply hostile to.

I think for a time it took a bit of effort to get the Irish side to agree with us in this analysis, but once we'd got there we then had to design an electoral system, the key feature of which had to be that nobody had proposed it, because then the other lot would say 'oh, you're doing it for that reason', so we had to invent something so crazy no one would ever suggest it, but we also needed to get the loyalists in, in a situation where they had low electoral support.[80]

---

[80] See Subsection 5.1.1 and Ch. 5, n.12.

So, as you know, we had disproportional representation from the list system, which meant that the top ten parties got in, and that's how we got the loyalists in, and that was a key consideration in designing that electoral system.

ROBIN BUTLER: Again, going back, one of the things that has always struck me when we were discussing the Anglo-Irish Agreement: there was a tendency on the part of the Irish government to say 'look, just tell the unionists you run Northern Ireland, please deliver the unionists'. Dermot, I would not accuse you, actually, or Frank, of saying it, but Seán certainly used to say it, I never quite knew whether that was naive or disingenuous. I think you'd acknowledged that the Irish government used to say that to us.

DERMOT NALLY: Yes, they used to say something like that.

ROBIN BUTLER: But the truth was that in the end, actually, we did topple Molyneaux, didn't we? We pushed him too far, not on this but on the marches.

QUENTIN THOMAS: And a sad fate happened to Trimble, but I didn't think it was our fault.

ROBIN BUTLER: No, but we had to worry all the time that if you had somebody reasonably sensible at the head of it you would not cause them to be outflanked by some lunatic. It is a miracle.

4.5.6. General Reflections

Q: What of the sensitivities in Northern Ireland?

QUENTIN THOMAS: Well, Sunningdale illustrated the dangers didn't it? People were co-opted, but they had no troops.

ROBIN BUTLER: And it was a miracle that, in the end, Paisley managed to bring his party across and survived. So one's always had to worry about something that's deliverable not just by the leader, but that the leader can bring the troops.

FRANK MURRAY: I suppose the Irish side always saw itself as the custodian and cultural guarantor of the nationalists, the SDLP; and, ergo, the British government had the same sort of role as regards the unionist side of the fence. Simplistic thinking perhaps, but...

QUENTIN THOMAS: Yes, it would have been a neat analysis, but we weren't able to do it.

Q: John Hume has been referred to at various stages, and I'm wondering what is the perception of John Hume's role?

QUENTIN THOMAS: Well, I thought he was an absolutely key player, and it can be said that he sacrificed his party for the process, and I think some of his colleagues said that to him as it was happening, and I suspect his answer would have been 'well, that's a reasonable sacrifice to make'. I think his role was pretty heroic, actually.

ROBIN BUTLER: I agree with that. He was always on the side of the angels.

FRANK MURRAY: He was, yes, he had a very difficult role and a party that was not an easy one to pull together.

Q: Thank you. I think we've come to the end of a very long day.

4.6. The Framework Documents

Even while the Downing Street Declaration was being prepared, negotiations were under way on the framework of institutions that could win widespread public agreement. Seán Ó hUiginn, Irish Department of Foreign Affairs, and Quentin Thomas, Northern Ireland Office, led, respectively, the Irish and British teams of officials who worked together to draft the joint British-Irish Framework Document, published on 22 February 1995.

4.6.1. An Irish View of the Negotiations

Q: What was your role at this time?

SEÁN Ó hUIGINN: The most important activity that I was involved in was, I think, taking forward the raw material from Hume–Adams into what became the Downing Street Declaration. Initially this involved drafting back and forth, mostly with Hume. I was not sitting for hours on end with him; he was not very good at the minutiae, even then. He was superb at the strategic overarching concepts, and he was good at reflecting on whether a draft did those justice or not.

After a while, we began to take the drafts to the British. Robin Butler, Dermot Nally, myself, and other senior British officials would have short, informal meetings in London and test out the different concepts. Initially we made a bid for the British to be persuaders for unity. I never expected that to be accepted, but the result was more or less where I had expected it to end up. They would be persuaders for agreement without prejudice to the content of agreement. That was still very valuable.

There was a 'liaison group' which brought together the Northern Ireland Office and ourselves under the chairmanship of Quentin Thomas, and I chaired the Irish side. There we did a fair amount of work that eventually merged into the Downing Street Declaration and also the [British–Irish] Framework Document. It functioned very well as a kind of a broad, informal intergovernmental forum. I hope it was congenial, but I think it was also actually very useful in terms of our getting to know the mindsets and the constraints under which the other side operated.

The Downing Street Declaration contained in embryonic form everything that was developed subsequently. I think it's best understood as the stall being set out for an IRA ceasefire.

Q: Was there a 'theological' side to the British perspective in the 1990s?[81]

SEÁN Ó hUIGINN: The British (barring any gross affront to their constitution) didn't really major on the theological side. They were obviously very alert to the principle of consent and made sure that the drafting was consistent with that. They resisted any idea that they would become persuaders for unity, but were then prepared to say: 'We would be persuaders for agreement.' We emphasized very much parity of esteem, and the need for a level playing field in negotiation. Left to itself, negotiation would have been very stacked against the nationalist side. Britain could have used its enormous weight, including the weight of benign inertia, to counter the development of the nationalist side of the negotiations. We had to have a proactive sense that, within the limits of the possible, we would sponsor a relatively level playing field.

Q: So, how do you do that?

SEÁN Ó hUIGINN: Well, you actively go out of your way to correct the bias. You don't say :'This is what we do in Britain, and so we can't have fair employment in Northern Ireland.' You say: 'This is an anomalous situation. We'll do something we don't do in Britain, we'll have fair employment in Northern Ireland,' and so on, and so on.

Q: At what point did the British become open to that?

SEÁN Ó hUIGINN: When they had tested to near destruction the easier options. It was very important for the Irish Government to have an extremely steady, an extremely consistent and an extremely realistic policy towards the British, and not to be blown around, since we were dealing with a [republican] constituency that was extraordinarily vulnerable to any mistake we made. There was also the recurring question for the republicans about what could be achieved: there was such a disproportion between Dublin and London that they said 'London will eat you for breakfast'.

I was very conscious that we were not looking for any huge concession from the British. We had convergent interests. We were trying to create stability in Ireland, for Northern Ireland could very easily destabilize the Republic. They had an interest in stability in Ireland, maybe not quite as much interest as we had, because Northern Ireland would never succeed in destabilizing Britain. Both states had an interest in stability, and what we were looking for was to a large extent subsumed in the word 'stability': that involved fairness, it meant sustainability of institutions, it meant a certain amount of mutual respect, all of

---

[81] In the negotiation processes, theories of sovereignty, constitutionality, and self-determination were sometimes referred to as 'theological'.

those things. So we were, to a very large extent, helping the British with objectives which were theirs also.

4.6.2. A British View of the Negotiations

QUENTIN THOMAS: The Liaison Group, in what I would regard as its creative period—when it did most of the negotiation for the Frameworks—was chaired by Seán on the Irish side and by me on ours, and it was a hugely useful process. I don't know what Irish colleagues would say they got out of it. But I do think I learnt a huge amount about nationalist preoccupations and the nationalist mindset, and it helped me to judge where the shoe would pinch and where we could push things. And I have said before, I think one of the things the Irish officials did for us was that they were kind of our unpaid consultants on nationalist sensibility and all of that—some of them rather aggressively and irritatingly, but that's what they were doing for us, and it was very helpful.

It was always amazing to me how very different these mindsets are. You could have an event—a bomb goes off, or somebody says something—and it's seen completely differently not only in London and Dublin but also in Belfast, actually. Even getting on the plane in between them, it felt very different witnessing such an event in Belfast from London. I thought it was a very creative relationship, and sometimes a very difficult one.

Q: I think from an Irish or perhaps nationalist perspective the power imbalance [between Ireland and Britain] was very high in consciousness?

QUENTIN THOMAS: Yes, I can see that; you need to counter that. That might be so, but in most things we weren't holding out. You tell us what will make everyone happy, and if it's in our power we'll be delighted to do it. That was, I think, genuinely our posture—not because we were magnanimous or hugely generous, but just because the main interest we had was in securing a settlement. We had no interest greater than that, no interest remotely compared with that. If we could stop people killing each other, and bombing each other, and bombing in what we're not allowed to call 'the mainland', that would be great, but that was really our interest.

4.6.3. The Significance of the British–Irish Framework Document

A British Perspective

QUENTIN THOMAS: I thought the Framework was more important than the joint Declaration. I've probably said that ad nauseam, but I think that's a much more fundamental piece of paper.

The Framework Document has quite a lot of stuff on the principle of consent, and it goes further than the joint Declaration, and the joint Declaration, as we know, had quite a bit on it. Some of the Framework is just repeating the joint Declaration. But there's this important stuff about us respecting the equal legitimacy and worth of the identity, sense of allegiance, aspiration, ethos, of both unionist and nationalist communities.

That was a step for the Irish government, you see, because, as I said earlier, they were sponsors of the nationalists. Now they're agreeing that both sides have a fair shot; the Irish government is going to introduce changes to the Irish constitution which will fully and demonstrably reflect the principle of consent, such that no territorial claim of right to jurisdiction over Northern Ireland contrary to the will of the majority of its people is asserted, while maintaining the birthright of everyone, etc.

Yes, respect the legitimacy of whatever choice is freely exercised by the majority of people in Northern Ireland with regard to its constitutional status, whether they prefer to continue to support the Union or not, thus acknowledging what they do so choose. So it's there; I don't know how far Sinn Féin fussed about these other words, but the deal is fundamentally around the consent principle in that sense—in the sense of the consent of this 'illegitimate' six-county unit.

Again, huge historical baggage has to be unloaded to accept that that is a legitimate entity for this purpose, but they did. My guess is that their essential brief in the Good Friday 1997–8 negotiations was: 'Keep them to the Frameworks. If they respect the Frameworks we'll be there.' That's my guess.

Q: The equality agenda was very important by that stage?

QUENTIN THOMAS: Well, this is in the Frameworks, of course. We committed ourselves, if I remember rightly, to administer Northern Ireland with rigorous impartiality so as not to influence or attempt to influence people to support the Union or not. We would not try to influence that by the way we conducted ourselves.

I remember in my early days in the Northern Ireland Office having very difficult discussions with Irish officials, and observing them and Irish ministers, and trying to get them to face up to the consent principle properly. Not just this stuff about: 'Well we know it would only happen if everyone consented.' We wanted to get them to accept, and say, that, as a matter of principle, not merely political reality, it would be wrong to have a united Ireland except with consent. And they wouldn't.

I think Martin Mansergh played a very significant role in that because he went further than the joint declaration and propounded the principle that, once a country has been divided, it can only be brought together by the consent of both sides. I think he completely changed the ideology of Fianna Fáil by sort of stealth, in a way.

I would think the republicans were pretty influenced by the Frameworks for agreement. They ought to have been; they were meant to have been. Everyone was meant to have been influenced by them. I believe that having a sketch plan of the outcome—the bits that were within the ambit of the Irish government—agreed with the Irish government was a hugely important thing.

I think there were wobbles during the [later peace and settlement] process when it seemed people were trying to play down the Framework. By the 1996–8 talks the constitutional issue did not bark. And why not? My answer is because it's in the Frameworks, and then the subsequent work done between Martin Mansergh and Seán Ó hUiginn on one side and John Chilcot and me on the other, when we were actually allowed to look at formulae for the reform of the Irish constitution—an amazing thing for British officials to be engaged in.

An Irish Perspective

Q: Were you negotiating at two levels at once from about 1994? On the one hand seeing what would be necessary to bring the republicans fully on board, and on the other hand finding a way to formulate this with the British to get a level playing field?

SEÁN Ó hUIGINN: Well, yes, there were manifestly many contradictory constituencies that all had to be roped in. I understand the scepticism about the peace process. Many people said this is an insane or a very quixotic enterprise. But at the same time, this was not an insoluble problem. The land theft that was at the origin of it, unlike in the Middle East, was 400 years ago in Ireland.[82] It was to some extent an ethnic conflict, but in a situation where many of the signifiers of ethnicity had long since evaporated—not all of them, but most of them. The cultural gap, as the unionists found to their chagrin, was pretty much invisible to outsiders.

Unionists regarded the near total ascendancy they enjoyed under Stormont as their birthright, and their opposition to anything that might dilute it in practice was logical rather than perverse, but it was an unsustainable strategy. I am afraid the only capacity the unionists had for political movement was a reactive one. They could move to defend themselves against the worst option downstream but they found it very hard to volunteer movement to the same point for its own sake, or for the sake of abstract principles like conciliation and so on.

So, it was necessary to pepper the Framework Document a little bit, in the knowledge that some, at least, marginal things could be sacrificed at a later stage to give the unionists a sense of having warded off the greater evil and, therefore, being able to sell the noxious movement to their followers. It sounds

---

[82] The reference is to the early seventeenth-century 'plantation' (colonization) of Ulster, which locked in economic, political, and cultural dominance of Protestants, and their dependence on British support.

a slightly cynical way of looking at it, but actually, I think, it's an accurate one. I think everything that happened from the Anglo-Irish Agreement on confirms the truth of that. So, clearly the Framework Document was seen as tilting a little bit in the nationalist direction.

The progress was fairly considerable in the early 1990s. You then got a situation where John Major was absolutely paralysed by his political context.[83] It meant that the whole game then was quite difficult, accepting that the train wouldn't move forward. The goal was to try to keep it on the rails so that the process didn't have to be reinvented when a new government came in, possibly even John Major, but at least with a new mandate and in a new capacity. As it turned out it was a Labour government. So, a lot of the latter part of my period there was essentially defensive—trying to make sure that the train stayed on the rails so as to avoid the enormous labour of having to get it back on the rails whenever a new government came in.

We tried to use the period essentially for educational purposes. Especially with the unionists, we tried to get home the idea—as Mo Mowlam put it—that 'the status quo is not an option'. She was regarded as the most diabolical heretic and enemy for having said this. So, we had to keep hammering the message that the status quo was not indeed an option, that something had to be thought [through], that flags had to be put downstream (even if we didn't think that unionists could or should be pushed that far), so that the unionists began to become a little bit conditioned to the idea that some movement would be necessary.

I think that was one aim, and we also tried to get home to the British officials that we were in the market for close cooperation on sustainable terms, but not for cooperation that either led nowhere or wasn't sustainable. I should, however, make the point that the British officials involved, notably Butler, Chilcot, and Thomas, were impressively able people, who generally used any flexibility allowed by the mandate from their ministers as constructively as they could. I had most dealings with Quentin Thomas, who made a key contribution to crafting language to accommodate the conflicting viewpoints, providing the foundation for the practical arrangements of the Good Friday Agreement and what flowed from that. Very often our dealings were more in the nature of a joint exploration to find the best outcome, rather than a confrontational negotiation.

Q: What was Sinn Féin thinking at this time?

SEÁN Ó HUIGINN: I'm not sure they knew themselves. It is self-evident that, if any of these agreements precluded a future option of Irish unity, they could never have touched it. There is a capacity of evolution in terms of either the

---

[83] This refers to the period 1996–7, when John Major gradually lost his parliamentary majority, leaving the Ulster Unionist Party in a pivotal position in the House of Commons.

demographics or the political inclinations of the population of Northern Ireland. So, it is not inconceivable that you could get an operational majority for a united Ireland. I think the scenario that's envisaged in the Agreement, and indeed in the Framework Document also, is that everything that was available to the nationalist community under the Anglo-Irish Agreement or subsequently in terms of an Irish dimension would at a minimum be available to the unionists in the event of a united Ireland.

Q: And the question of amending articles 2 and 3 of the Irish constitution?

SEÁN Ó hUIGINN: I think frankly it was common ground, indeed from the Anglo-Irish Agreement onwards, that the Irish constitution would have to be amended. There were two constraints. One was the legal one—that if you did it informally or in the wrong way it would probably be shot down in flames by the court.[84] And there was a negotiating one, that it was an asset that had more negative value in unionist eyes than it had positive value in ours. It was an extremely useful thing to have in a negotiating basket.

So, there was a determination not to throw it away before it could be validated as part of the wider package of agreement, which is indeed what happened. But I have to say that I saw very little agonizing about the principle of amending the constitution in this way, and certainly not at all on my part.

Q: What of the personalities?

SEÁN Ó hUIGINN: The successes of the peace process have led people to forget the great scepticism and often vehement hostility it met at the early stages. Albert Reynolds and Dick Spring have never been given sufficient credit for their political courage in embarking on the new policy, or for their skill in shaping it, in the absence of any pre-existing template, so that it vindicated democratic values rather than compromising them, as so many feared. I think Albert Reynolds's stewardship of the peace process was actually very decisive. I think people may criticize his wider character, and they don't give him credit for how good he was on this. He was so good partly because he was a good negotiator, partly because he understood the cultural background that the republicans were coming from, partly because he had a focus on the bottom line, which was part of his character, part of his business formation, and so on.

He really was very good at keeping things in focus and driving things forward. He had another gift which was fatal to him in terms of his premiership, which is a very great impatience with process. That turned out to be a great blessing, because one of the British 'arts' in terms of their statecraft is to drown you in process. By the time you wake up or struggle out of it, you're many miles downstream from where you started. Albert had the most utter

---

[84] The Irish Supreme Court is the ultimate arbiter as to the compatibility of legislation and public policy with the Irish constitution

and total and natural immunity to that, and it meant that he was actually a very good negotiator, also with John Major.

Q: And the long-term trends?

SEÁN Ó hUIGINN: I think the republican strategy is to establish considerable electoral success North and South and to use that (with tact and discretion and so on) to draw the objective of a united Ireland closer, and eventually to achieve it. I think the last election showed that that's not quite the linear progression that some of them believed it would be.[85] I think also if that happened that the electorate in the South would have the most decided views on Northern Ireland.

The scenario that's envisaged in the Agreement and indeed in the Framework Document also is that everything that was available to the nationalist community under the Anglo-Irish Agreement or subsequently in terms of an Irish dimension would at a minimum be available *mutatis mutandis* to the unionists in a united Ireland. I mean that's actually there, even if it's not much read or mentioned. If the time came, there is that theoretical protection against anything abrupt.

I think a much more solid protection for unionists would be the most decided resistance of the electorate of the South to anything that was coercive or turbulent in terms of a united Ireland. I believe that, if a united Ireland comes about, it will only happen when nobody minds much one way or the other, at least not to the point of violent resistance. That would be reinforced by both the theoretical commitment that is there, but much more by the likely temper within the Irish electorate in the South, which would be *festina lente* and a resolve not to repeat the mistakes that were made in reverse in regard to the creation of Northern Ireland.

Documents

Document 4.1. Brooke 'Whitbread' Speech, 9 November 1990

SPEECH MADE BY THE NORTHERN SECRETARY, MR BROOKE, IN HIS CONSTITUENCY

1. In Northern Ireland, two views about the ideal pattern of government have long confronted each other. There is the present reality—in fact and in international law—of the union—the union, that is, between Great Britain and Northern Ireland. That union is

---

[85] In the 2007 Dáil election Sinn Féin registered almost no improvement on its performance in the previous election in 2002; its share of the first preference vote increased from 6.5% to 6.9%, and it lost one of its five seats.

affirmed by the first section of the Northern Ireland Constitution Act of 1973, which declares that, in no event, will Northern Ireland or any part of it cease to be part of the United Kingdom without the consent of a majority of the people of Northern Ireland. We stand firmly by that most solemn declaration and assurance.

But in so doing, we acknowledge that there is another view—strongly held by the nationalist minority within Northern Ireland. That is the aspiration to a united Ireland—not simply to the Republic of Ireland which exists today but to a 32-county State covering all the territory of the island, and worthy in their view of the support of all Irish people.

2. It is possible to take either position with integrity. It is acceptable to uphold the one or advocate the other by all legitimate peaceful and democratic means. What is not acceptable, and what totally lacks integrity, is the promotion of either view by the crude and brutal methods of violence and coercion.

3. I believe, in particular, that a huge majority of those who would wish to see a united Ireland one day, both in the North and in the whole of Ireland, know in their hearts that a 32-county State in the terms I have used could never be created by force or advanced by putting a union of territories before a union of hearts and minds. A State brought into being by such corrupt methods could never live up to the vision of a united Ireland enjoying the loyalty and protecting the rights of Catholic, Protestant and dissenter. Ninety five percent of nationalists within the island of Ireland have chosen to assert their nationalism by casting their first preference votes for constitutional parties.

It is only a diminishing minority, whether in the Republic of Ireland or in Northern Ireland, who have deliberately chosen another path. It is their arrogant and wholly-mistaken belief that unity can be achieved by violence that is still causing death, injury and destruction, not only in Northern Ireland, but also here in Great Britain and, as recent events have shown, in Europe as well.

4. Many people have died over the last two decades because a minority will not accept that a unity of hearts and minds can never be achieved by such corrupt means as these. If this rate of killing applied across the United Kingdom as a whole, we should now be mourning something over 100,000 dead. To its enormous credit, and in spite of the appalling recurrence of 'tit-for-tat' killings, society in Northern Ireland has not disintegrated as, no doubt, the men of violence would like it to do.

On the contrary, I have been impressed and often greatly moved as I have met people, right across the province and in all walks of life, who remain determined to get on with their lives in peace, and to see the community in which they live becoming a better place for themselves and their children. But, while levels of violence have fallen far below their peak, there is no room for complacency. The grief and loss remain, and the appalling human waste.

Long after the names of victims are forgotten in the wider community, relatives still grieve for their dead and tend their wounded. In a hospital in Enniskillen, a loyal wife still sits regularly at the bedside of a husband who has never regained consciousness since that fatal Remembrance Day three years ago. We in the rest of the United Kingdom—indeed in its government and parliament—have suffered alongside the decent people of Northern Ireland. Nor have other countries, and other innocent lives, been spared the blight of violence. Men and women in uniform, going about their lawful duties, have been treated as so-called 'legitimate targets'. Assassins lurking in the shadows have usurped the name of soldier.

5. For what purpose does this killing continue? Why does the plea of the Pope himself, made so movingly on Irish soil, and recalled again by Bishop Cahal Daly, now designated Archbishop and Primate of All Ireland, at the Requiem Mass for Cardinal Ó Fiaich earlier this year, not received a positive answer? Why, in particular, has a desire for unity to be pursued in a way which can only deepen division?

6. At the heart of this matter, there is the question of the so-called 'British presence' in a part of Ireland. It is to remove that presence that republican terrorism is said to be dedicated. So let us examine, for a moment, just what the 'British presence' actually is.

7. It has four main aspects. The first, and perhaps the most high-profile aspect, is the visible presence and activity of British troops on the streets and in the countryside of Northern Ireland. There are two points to be made about this presence and activity. The first is that these troops are in reality United Kingdom troops, drawn from the whole of the United Kingdom and present in Northern Ireland because Northern Ireland is a part of the United Kingdom which needs them. The United Kingdom has, of course, no vested interest in maintaining these high force levels a day longer than is necessary.

8. And the second important point is that this kind of high military profile was made necessary by violence, will be maintained as long as there is violence, but will certainly be reduced when violence comes to an end. We have heard for so long about the 'security forces' because others have created a security situation.

What we want is a return as soon as possible to a situation in which the police service in Northern Ireland can, by itself, enforce the law and keep the peace for the benefit of its fellow citizens. But policemen are civilians drawn from the community they exist to serve. Today they are, and for many years have been, at risk from men and women prepared to kill and wound them in pursuit of political objectives. In such a situation, the police are entitled to have and will certainly get the additional support that the military can provide.

If the threat were no longer there, then the military support would no longer be necessary and Northern Ireland could have a police force with no need of army support or, indeed, for its own formidable arsenal of weapons.

9. The second aspect of the British presence is, of course, my own presence in Northern Ireland as Secretary of State, supported by a team of ministers and officials in the Northern Ireland Office and answerable to parliament at Westminster. But it is the clearly-stated policy of this government to seek to find ways of returning significant responsibilities for the affairs of Northern Ireland to locally-elected representatives in a way which would command widespread acceptance within Northern Ireland.

10. Thus it is that we have the extraordinary state of affairs in which a small group of people are mounting a terrorist campaign aimed at removal of 'the British presence', when it is the clear wish of the British Government to ask elected representatives of local people to assume as much responsibility as possible for their own affairs. It is interesting, is it not, that those who cry 'Brits out' are amongst the most nervous when they see any possibility of real movement towards giving real power and responsibility to the local people themselves.

11. The third main aspect of the 'British presence' is simply this: the transfer from the common exchequer every year of very large sums of money to enable programmes well beyond the capacity of locally-raised taxation to be carried out. This support is not given in

furtherance of some strategic interest or in the expectation of some corresponding gain to the people of Great Britain. It seeks no return other than the satisfaction of improving the conditions of life in Northern Ireland.

12. This brings me to the fourth and most significant aspect of the British presence. Every time I hear that call for 'Brits out', it brings home to me the paramount reality that the heart and core of the British presence is not the British army or British ministers, but the reality of nearly a million people living in a part of the island of Ireland who are, and who certainly regard themselves as, British.

This is not simply a debating point made by an English politician. It has been very specifically acknowledged by the democratically-elected representatives of all the parties of constitutional Irish nationalism through, for example, the New Ireland Forum Report of 1984. The report states that:

'Unionists generally regard themselves as being British, the inheritors of a specific communal loyalty to the British Crown. The traditional nationalist opposition to British rule is thus seen by unionists as incompatible with the survival of their own sense of identity...'.

This 'Britishness' (a word which the Forum report itself uses) is not only a legal status; it is also a fact of life and a product of history.

13. The Anglo-Irish Agreement, to which successive Irish governments have committed themselves, similarly acknowledges the reality that the people of Northern Ireland have different views about the status of Northern Ireland. The preamble to the agreement draws a distinction between 'those who wish for no change in the present status of Northern Ireland' and 'those who aspire to a sovereign united Ireland achieved by peaceful means and through agreement'.

Against that background, Article I of the agreement—registered at the United Nations as a binding international treaty—acknowledges that the status of Northern Ireland can only be determined by the people of Northern Ireland themselves, by affirming that any change in the present status would only come about with the consent of a majority of the people who live there. The article also recognised that the present wish of a majority of the people of Northern Ireland is for no change in the status of Northern Ireland.

14. The question which arises, therefore, is whether this sense of Britishness, deeply felt by one million people, and their desire for no change in the status of Northern Ireland, can be reconciled with an Irish identity which would embrace them and to which they would freely consent? At present, a great number of these people clearly do not feel or wish themselves to be Irish in the sense that nationalists would like them to do, although they may well feel Irish in other important respects; but the obstacle to the development of a new and more inclusive Irish identity if people want this for themselves is not to be sought in Great Britain.

Those who live here would not bar the way if, at some future time, that were to be the wish of the people of Northern Ireland themselves; indeed the government has made clear on several occasions, notably in signing the Anglo-Irish Agreement, that if, in the future, a majority of the people of Northern Ireland clearly wish for and formally consent to the establishment of a united Ireland, it would introduce and support in parliament legislation to give effect to that wish.

However, we will fully support our fellow-citizens while, by their own free and clearly-expressed wish, they remain our fellow-citizens. Partition is an acknowledgement of reality, not an assertion of national self-interest. The Border cannot simply be wished away.

15. There is, as we all know, some difference of emphasis between the Conservative and Labour Parties, in that the Labour Party have declared themselves to be in favour of unity. But neither party, I am sure, would tolerate a coerced unity brought about by force. It would not only be immoral; it would also be unworkable. Neither party stands in the way of constitutional and peaceful attempts by Irish nationalists to persuade unionists that a change in status could take place without prejudice to the interests of its community as reflected both in its Protestantism and in its 'Britishness'.

We continue to value the contribution which Northern Ireland and its people make to our union. As Remembrance Day draws near, and as plans are being made to commemorate next year the 75th anniversary of the Battle of the Somme, we do well to remember the form in which that contribution has often been made, though I should also pay tribute to those born in the Republic who laid down their lives in that same cause in both wars.

Both parties, indeed all the main parties in Great Britain and Irish Republic, not to mention the constitutional parties in Northern Ireland itself, cannot fail to see that continuing violence can only replenish old animosities and indefinitely postpone any real and lasting reconciliation between the traditions in Ireland, in whatever context that may be achieved.

16. Violence is futile. Violence can never be allowed to succeed. It is, and will remain, the first priority of the government to defeat terrorism, from whichever side of the community it comes. For this government, as for the vast majority of the people of Northern Ireland, there is no acceptable level of violence; and, for so long as violence continues, it will be met with a firm and resolute response.

It is, of course, in the interests of everyone that violence should end now. Just imagine what developments of positive benefit to all sections of the community and both parts of the island of Ireland would be bound to follow a permanent end to violence.

17. Military support for the police would in time no longer be required, and the police service would be able to play without diversion its proper role of helping the whole law-abiding community. An Irish republicanism seen to have finally renounced violence would be able, like other parties, to seek a role in the peaceful political life of the community. In Northern Ireland, it is not the aspiration to a sovereign, united Ireland, against which we set our face, but its violent expression.

I should hate to think that all those who have, in the past, voted for Sinn Féin political representatives were doing so without a care for the murder of their Protestant and Catholic neighbours. Or for the risk—which is a reality—that they themselves, a relative or a friend could become victims, either through retaliation or through the gross incompetence or brutal unconcern of the paramilitaries who purport to defend them.

18. Our unwillingness to do business with political representatives who support murder as a legitimate way of promoting a political goal does not indicate any unconcern with the real social and economic problems faced by those they represent or lack of respect for the Irish identity and culture of such people.

19. Only if violence is abandoned can a true reconciliation be achieved. There is a need for reconciliation at three levels—between the communities in Northern Ireland, within Ireland, and between the peoples of both these islands. The terrorists constitute a major

impediment on the road to peace and greater understanding and to new political institutions which adequately reflect everyone's interests.

The British Government has no selfish strategic or economic interest in Northern Ireland: our role is to help, enable and encourage. Britain's purpose, as I have sought to describe it, is not to occupy, oppress or exploit, but to ensure democratic debate and free democratic choice. That is our way.

Source: *Irish Times*, 10 November 1990.

Document 4.2. Letter from Gerry Adams to John Major, 20 August 1991

LETTER FROM GERRY ADAMS, MP, TO
JOHN MAJOR, MP, PRIME MINISTER, 20 AUGUST 1991

GERRY ADAMS MP
51/55 Bóthar na bhFál
Béal Feirste BT12 4PD

20 August 1991
Mr John Major MP
10 Downing Street
Belfast

A Chara

The present phase of the conflict in Ireland has now entered its 22nd year and there is no visible prospect of a resolution. The result is on going political violence and instability for both the Irish and the British people.

The central and most urgent issue facing us all must be how to resolve this crisis and bring the conflict to an end. This means creating the conditions of justice, equality and democracy through which a real and lasting peace can be achieved.

Such a process requires dialogue. The British government has a central responsibility to initiate such dialogue. For our part, Sinn Féin is prepared to face up to that task and to discharge our responsibilities in a positive and honourable way. We believe that peace can be achieved. We are prepared to take political risks. We are prepared to give and take. We are committed to establishing a peace process.

I am fully aware that such a path is fraught with difficulties. But I believe that we all have a responsibility to confront these difficulties and that with willingness a way can be found to initiate a process of real dialogue which would hopefully lead to the peaceful resolution of this conflict.

If you are genuinely interested in initiating such a process, you will find that Sinn Féin is willing to participate in a positive and flexible manner.

Is mise

GERRY ADAMS

Source: TNA: PREM 19/3409.

Document 4.3. Joint Declaration: First Hume Draft, 6 October 1991

AIM: A JOINT DECLARATION BY BOTH BRITISH AND IRISH PRIME MINISTERS

1. Leaving the past aside and regretting the pain and suffering caused by past failures to settle the relationships of the people of both islands satisfactorily.

2. Recognising that the implementation of the Single Market and the coming into being of European Union with the effective removal of all borders fundamentally changes the nature of British/Irish relationships. Further recognising that future developments which leave both parts of Ireland as the only part of the new Europe with no land links with the other regions, will intensify the common ground between both parts of Ireland and intensify the need for maximum co-operation to achieve maximum benefit from European Union.

3. Regret, however, that there remains a serious legacy of past relationships—a deeply divided people on the island of Ireland. This is a major concern of both governments and both deeply regret that these are the last remaining such divisions in the new European order.

4. Both governments recognise that these divisions can only end with the agreement of the people North and South in Ireland.

5. Both governments therefore commit themselves to using the maximum resources to create the atmosphere in which such agreement is made easier. Both governments find it unacceptable that these are the last remaining divisions in a Europe that has already ended many more deep and bitter quarrels. They will, therefore, promote intensive co-operation at all levels in order to strengthen the process of agreement.

6. The British Government reiterate yet again that they no longer have any selfish political or strategic interest in remaining in Ireland. Their sole interest is to see peace and agreement among the people who inhabit the island and will devote all their available resources to that end.

7. For its part the Irish Government recognises that the traditional objective of Irish nationalism—the exercise of self-determination by the people of Ireland as a whole— cannot be achieved without the agreement of the people of Northern Ireland. It would, therefore, commit itself to working for institutions of government North and South which would respect the diversity of the people of Ireland but allow them to work their substantial common ground together in order to build the necessary trust for an agreed future.

   In order to pursue that strategy the Irish Government would set up a permanent Irish Convention in order to plan and implement the steps and policies required to break down the barriers which divide the people of Ireland and which prevent the exercise of agreed self-determination. If the British Government refuse the joint declaration, the Irish Government would proceed to set up the Convention with the additional objective of planning and implementing the policies required to persuade the British Government to adopt our strategy and objectives. Membership of the Convention would consist of elected representatives of all parties in Ireland who share the objective of a united self-determined Ireland.

Source: Mallie and McKittrick (1996: 118–19). We gratefully acknowledge David McKittrick's permission to reproduce this.

Document 4.4. Joint Declaration: First Irish
Government Draft, *c.* December 1991

DRAFT 2. A STRATEGY FOR PEACE AND JUSTICE IN IRELAND:
A JOINT DECLARATION BY THE BRITISH PRIME MINISTER
AND THE TAOISEACH [C. DECEMBER 1991]

1. The British Prime Minister and the Taoiseach acknowledge that the most urgent and important challenge facing the people of Ireland, North and South, and the British and Irish Governments together, is finally to overcome the legacy of history and to heal past conflicts and differences, recognizing that past failures to settle relationships between the people of both islands satisfactorily has led to continuing tragedy and suffering.

2. They believe the development of closer European unity, which will result in the effective removal of borders, fundamentally changes the nature of British–Irish relationships and removes the basis of the historic conflict still taking place within the confines of Northern Ireland. These developments, and the fact that both parts of Ireland will in the future be the only considerable territory in the Community without land links to the other countries and regions, will intensify the need for both parts of Ireland to be united in their approach to all major issues, which affect the future of all the people of Ireland, North and South, in the context of the new Europe.

3. Both the British Prime Minister and the Taoiseach are convinced that the ending of conflict and healing of division can make a huge positive contribution to the future welfare and prosperity of both parts of Ireland, as well as bring to an end the last remaining divisions in a European Community that has already ended more deep and bitter quarrels. Both of them recognise that the ending of division can only come about with the agreement and co-operation of the people North and South. They therefore make a solemn commitment to use all their influence and resources to create an atmosphere which will foster agreement and reconciliation, and to promote intensive co-operation at all levels to strengthen the process of agreement and achieve closer unity of purpose.

4. The British Prime Minister reiterates on behalf of the British Government that they have no selfish, strategic, political or economic interest in Northern Ireland, and that their sole interest is to see peace, stability and reconciliation established by agreement among the people who inhabit the island. The British Government acknowledge it is the wish of the people of Britain to see the people of Ireland live together in unity and harmony, born of agreement with respect to their diverse traditions, and with full recognition of the special links and the unique relationship which exist between the peoples of Britain and Ireland.

5. The Taoiseach, on behalf of the Irish Government, accepts that the exercise of the democratic right of self-determination by the people of Ireland as a whole cannot in practice be achieved except with the agreement and the consent of the people of Northern Ireland and that it must consistent with justice and equity respect the democratic dignity and the civil rights of both communities, whether majority or minority. The Irish Government would, accordingly, commit themselves to working, in the spirit and on the basis of the Report of the New Ireland Forum, to create institutions and structures, which while respecting the diversity of the people of Ireland would enable them to work together in all

the areas where there is substantial common grounds. This would help to build the trust necessary for an agreed future leading to a closer form of unity by agreement. Such unity would, of course, require institutional recognition of the special links that exist between the peoples of Britain and Ireland as part of the totality of relationships, while taking account of the newly forged links with the rest of Europe.

6. In order to promote these aims the Taoiseach has indicated to the British Prime Minister his intention of establishing a permanent Irish Convention in order to consult and advise on the steps required to remove the barriers of distrust which divide the people of Ireland and which stand in the way of the exercise in common of self-determination on an equal basis. The Convention would be open to all democratic parties in Ireland, who share the objective of a united Ireland achieved peacefully through democratic self-determination, or who wish to share in dialogue about Ireland's political future and the welfare of all its people.

Note: If the British Government are unable to accept a Joint Declaration, the Irish Government will proceed to set up the Convention with the further objective of planning and implementing the policies required to persuade the British Government to adopt this strategy and these objectives.

Source: Annex to letter, Robin Butler to Stephen Wall, 30 January 1992, TNA: PREM/19/3823.

Document 4.5. Joint Declaration: Sinn Féin Draft, *c.* February 1992

DRAFT OF A DECLARATION WHICH SINN FEIN SUGGESTS SHOULD
BE MADE JOINTLY BY THE BRITISH AND DUBLIN GOVERNMENTS
[c. FEBRUARY 1992]

[1.] The British Prime Minister and the Taoiseach acknowledge that the most urgent and important issue facing the people of Ireland, north and south, and the British and Irish governments together, is to remove the causes of conflict, to overcome the legacy of history and to heal the divisions which have resulted, recognising that past failures to settle relationships between the people of both islands satisfactorily has led to continuing tragedy and suffering.

[2.] The development of closer European Unity will intensify the need for Ireland to be united in its approach to all major issues, in the context of Europe and beyond.

[3.] Both the British Prime Minister and the Taoiseach are convinced that the securing of a comprehensive political settlement, with the consequent ending of conflict and the healing of divisions, can make a huge positive contribution to the future welfare and prosperity of Ireland and its people, as well as bring to an end one of the last remaining divisions in Europe. Both of them recognise that the ending of division can only come about through the agreement and co-operation of the people, north and south, and that the present constitutional arrangements have inhibited the development of this process. They therefore make a solemn committment to create a new political framework, encompassing all the people of the island and, in this context, to use all their influence and resources to foster agreement and reconciliation among the people of Ireland and between the peoples of Ireland and Britain.

[4.] The British Prime Minister reiterates, on behalf of the British Government, that they have no selfish, strategic, political or economic interest in Northern Ireland, and that their sole interest is to see peace, stability and reconciliation established by agreement among the people who inhabit the island. The British Government acknowledges also that it is the wish of the people of Britain to see the people of Ireland live together in unity and harmony, with respect for their diverse traditions, independent, but with full recognition of the special links and the unique relationship which exists between the peoples of Britain and Ireland. The British Government, consequently, commits itself to such unity (within a period to be agreed) and to use all its influence and energy to win consent for this policy.

[5.] The Taoiseach, on behalf of the Irish Government, accepts that the exercise of the democratic right of self-determination by the people of Ireland as a whole would best be achieved with the agreement and the consent of the people of Northern Ireland and that it must, consistent with justice and equity, respect the democratic dignity and the civil rights of both communities. The Irish Government would, accordingly, commit itself to working in the spirit and on the basis of the Report of the New Ireland Forum, to create institutions and structures which, while respecting the diversity or the people of Ireland, would enable them to work together in all areas which affect them in common. This would help to build the trust necessary to end past divisions, leading to an agreed and peaceful future. Such structures would, of course, include institutional recognition of the special links that exist between the peoples of Britain and Ireland as part of the totality of relationships, while taking account of newly forged links with the rest of Europe.

[6.] Given the British Government's commitment to facilitate this process, by removing the constitutional barriers to peace and reconciliation, the Taoiseach has indicated to the British Prime Minister his intention of establishing a permanent Irish Convention in order to consult and advise on the steps required to realise the unity of the Irish people by removing the barriers of distrust which presently divide the people of Ireland and to develop adequate guarantees and safeguards for all sections of the Irish people, north and south. The convention would be open to all democratically mandated political parties in Ireland who share the objective of a United Ireland, or who wish to share in dialogue about Ireland's political future and the welfare of all its people.

Note: Numbering in square brackets was added in hand-writing.

Source: Annex to letter, W.R. Fittall to Stephen Wall, 21 February 1992, TNA: PREM/19/3823.

Document 4.6. Joint Declaration: Irish Government Draft, 19 June 1993

[DRAFT JOINT DECLARATION BY THE BRITISH
PRIME MINISTER AND THE TAOISEACH, 19 JUNE 1993]

1. The Taoiseach and the British Prime Minister acknowledge that the most urgent and important issue facing the people of Ireland, North and South, and the British and Irish Governments together, is to remove the causes of conflict, to overcome the legacy of history

and to heal the divisions which have resulted, recognising that past failures to settle relationships between the people of both islands satisfactorily has led to continuing tragedy and suffering.

2. They consider that the development of European Union fundamentally changes the nature and the context of British–Irish relationships and will progressively remove the basis of the conflict still taking place in Northern Ireland. The challenges and opportunities of European Union will, of themselves, require new approaches to serve interests common to both parts of Ireland.

3. The Taoiseach and the British Prime Minister are convinced of the inestimable value to both their peoples of healing divisions in Ireland and of ending a conflict which has been so manifestly to the detriment of all. Both recognise that the ending of divisions can come about only through the agreement and cooperation of the people, North and South, representing both traditions in Ireland. They therefore make a solemn commitment to promote cooperation at all levels. It is their aim to foster agreement and reconciliation, leading to a new political framework founded on consent and encompassing the whole island.

4. The British Prime Minister reiterates, on behalf of the British Government, that they have no selfish, strategic, political or economic interest in Northern Ireland, and that their sole interest is to see peace, stability and reconciliation established by agreement among the people who inhabit the island. The British Government accept the principle that the Irish people have the right to self-determination and that the exercise of this collective right democratically could take the form of agreed independent structures for the island as a whole. They affirm their readiness, in cooperation with the Irish Government, to establish by legislation a procedure to reach agreement on how the right of self-determination could be exercised democratically and collectively, allowing sufficient time for the building of consent and the beginning of a process of national reconciliation. The progress of this procedure will be reviewed within a specified time to be agreed and, as necessary, regularly thereafter. The British Government affirm their readiness to introduce the measures to give legislative effect to the exercise of the right of self-determination on that basis. The British Government will use all their influence and energy to move forward the process of national reconciliation and to win the consent of a majority in Northern Ireland for an agreement between all the people of Ireland on their political future, which recognises both the unity of Ireland and the special links and the unique relationship which exist between Ireland and Britain. They acknowledge that it is the wish of the people of Britain to see the people of Ireland live together in unity and harmony with respect for their diverse traditions, recognising that the whole island of Ireland has a right to independence based on agreement. For their part the Irish Government are committed to making substantial progress towards a new and agreed Ireland within a generation.

5. The Taoiseach, on behalf of the Irish Government, considers that the lessons of Irish history, and especially of Northern Ireland, show that stability and well-being will not be found under any political system which is refused allegiance or rejected on grounds of identity by a significant minority of those governed by it. He accepts, on behalf of the Irish Government, that the democratic right of self-determination by the people of Ireland as a whole must be achieved and exercised with the agreement and consent of the people of

Northern Ireland and must, consistent with justice and equity, respect the democratic dignity and the civil rights of both communities.

6. The Irish Government accordingly commit themselves to working in the spirit and on the basis of the Report of the New Ireland Forum, to create institutions and structures which, while respecting the diversity of the people of Ireland, would enable them to work together in all areas of common interest. This will help to build the trust necessary to end past divisions, leading to an agreed and peaceful future. Such structures would, of course, include institutional recognition of the special links that exist between the peoples of Britain and Ireland as part of the totality of relationships, while taking account of newly forged links with the rest of Europe.

7. In the light of their joint commitment to promote the foregoing objectives, the Taoiseach has indicated to the British Prime Minister his intention of establishing a permanent Irish Convention to consult and advise on the steps required to remove the barriers of distrust which at present divide the people of Ireland and which stand in the way of the exercise in common by them of self-determination on a basis of equality. It will be open to the Convention to make recommendations on ways in which agreement, as defined in the Forum Report, and respect for the rights and identities of both traditions in Ireland, can be promoted and established. The Convention will be governed by the authority of Bunreacht na hÉireann, and the institutions established under it. It will be a fundamental guiding principle of the Convention that all differences between the Irish people relating to the exercise in common of the right to self-determination will be resolved exclusively by peaceful, political means.

8. The Convention will be open to all democratically mandated political parties in Ireland which abide exclusively by the democratic process and wish to share in dialogue about Ireland's political future and the welfare of all its people.

Source: document in possession of the authors.

Document 4.7. Draft Framework Agreement:
Irish Press Leak, 19 November 1993

NORTH AND SOUTH: THE BLUEPRINT FOR PEACE
IRISH PRESS EXCLUSIVE BY EMILY O'REILLY, POLITICAL CORRESPONDENT
IRISH DRAFT: JOINT WORKING PAPER

Status of Paper
1. British and Irish officials were instructed at the meeting of the Anglo-Irish Intergovernmental Conference on September 10 to use their best endeavours to draft a joint illustrative working paper, without commitment on either side and ad referendum to ministers, whose object was to seek to identify, as a basis for discussion, aspects of a possible outcome, consistent with the agreed statement of 26 March 1991, likely to prove acceptable to all parties to talks. They were also instructed to submit their conclusions for discussions at the next meeting of the Inter-governmental Conference.

2. The Secretary of State informed the Conference that Michael Ancram would be continuing, within the same time frame, his bilateral discussions with the NI political parties.

3. The following joint paper represents the outcome of discussions within the Liaison Group for consideration by ministers in the Conference. It has been prepared without prejudice to the process agreed by the Taoiseach and the Prime Minister on 29 October, that their two governments must continue to work together in their own terms on a framework for peace, stability and reconciliation consistent with their international obligations and their wider responsibilities to both communities. It is accepted on both sides that this joint paper and the discussions related to it will not be the subject of discussion, still less negotiation with the Northern Ireland parties unless both governments agree beforehand whether and how this should be done.

General Considerations

4. The British and Irish governments are partners together in a unique relationship. Each is the other's closest neighbour. They are both members of the European Community.

5. Both governments are deeply affected by continuing conflict in Northern Ireland, and the legacy of their difficult historical relationship. They share a deep concern to find a solution to this tragic problem. They are committed to the search for a new beginning for relationships within Northern Ireland, within the island of Ireland and between the peoples of these islands. They accordingly look forward to further developing the partnership that already closely links both countries towards this end.

6. The two governments agreed in 1980 that the best prospect of achieving peace, reconciliation and stability and of improving relations between the peoples of their two countries was to address the totality of relationships within these islands. The Anglo-Irish Intergovernmental Council was established in 1981 with this purpose in view.

7. In the Anglo-Irish Agreement, signed in 1985, the two governments established.a structure, within the framework of the Anglo-Irish Intergovernmental Council, for dealing on a regular basis with a range of issues concerned with Northern Ireland and with relations between the two parts of the island of Ireland.

8. The Agreement reflects their common desire to work together to achieve the aims of promoting peace and stability in Northern Ireland; helping to reconcile the two major traditions in Ireland; creating a new climate of friendship and co-operation between the people of the two countries; and improving co-operation in combating terrorism.

9. The preamble to the Agreement sets out a number of principles which the two governments hold in common and on which the Agreement is based:

- recognition of the major interest of both countries and, above all, of the people of Northern Ireland in diminishing the divisions there and achieving lasting peace and stability;
- recognition of the need for continuing efforts to reconcile and to acknowledge the rights of the two major traditions that exist in Ireland, represented on the one hand by those who wish for no change in the present status of Northern Ireland, and on the other hand by those who aspire to a sovereign united Ireland achieved by peaceful means and through agreement;

- their total rejection of any attempt to promote political objectives by violence or the threat of violence and their determination to work together to ensure that those who adopt or support such methods do not succeed;
- recognition that a condition of genuine reconciliation and dialogue between unionists and nationalists is mutual recognition and acceptance of each other's rights;
- recognition of and respect for the identities of the two communities in Northern Ireland, and the right of each to pursue its aspirations by peaceful and constitutional means;
- their commitment to a society in Northern Ireland in which all may live in peace, free from discrimination and intolerance, and with the opportunity for both communities to participate fully in the structures and processes of government.

10. The Agreement established an Intergovernmental Conference in which the Irish Government puts forward views and proposals concerning stated aspects of Northern Ireland affairs; in which the promotion of cross-border co-operation is discussed; and in which determined efforts are made to resolve any difference between the two governments. Both governments agree that these elements of the present Agreement, and the institutional expression it provides for a legitimate concern and role for the Irish Government in relation to Northern Ireland, must be fully provided for in any new and more broadly based agreement.

11. Both governments re-affirm their full commitment to all the provisions of the Agreement and to its shared understandings and purposes set out in the preamble and in the Agreement itself as well as in the Hillsborough Communiqué of 15 November 1985. As its signatories, they are also prepared to consider a new and more broadly based agreement or structure if such an agreement can be arrived at through direct discussion and negotiation between all the parties concerned. They agree that any new agreement should enhance the structures of co-operation established between the two governments under the Agreement.

Principles for a New Approach

12. The search for agreement must build on a package of key principles, including the following, which are already encapsulated or implicit in the Anglo-Irish Agreement:

- The people living in Ireland, North and South, without coercion and without violence, should be free to determine their own future.
- That freedom can be expressed in the development of new structures for the governing of Northern Ireland, for relations between North and South and between the two islands, based on respect for the rights and identities of both traditions.
- No agreement can be reached in respect of any change in the present status of Northern Ireland without the freely expressed consent of a majority of the people of Northern Ireland.
- The foregoing principle implies also a clear recognition of the right of a majority of the people in Northern Ireland to withhold consent for any such change, unless and until they are persuaded by democratic political means only, free from coercion and violence.

- As an integral part of a democratic approach to peace, the Irish Government is prepared at the right time and in the right circumstances to seek to have the principle of consent, as defined in the Anglo-Irish Agreement, expressed in Irish fundamental law.
- Negotiations on a political settlement should take place only among those committed exclusively to constitutional methods and not with organisations who use, threaten or support violence for political ends. However, those who have demonstrably expressed their commitment to the democratic process by renouncing violence are entitled to a role in negotiations and both governments would wish to respond imaginatively and positively to the new situation which would arise in such circumstances.

13. The two governments will apply these principles in a joint approach based on the following elements and agreed policy considerations.

14. Northern Ireland is sui generis. Unlike the situation which prevails elsewhere through-out both islands, there is an absence of constitutional consensus among the people there. There are deep divisions between the members of the two main Irish traditions living in Northern Ireland in terms of their respective senses of identity and allegiance, their views on the present status of Northern Ireland and their vision of future relationships in Ireland and between the two islands.

15. Both governments accept that this unique and complex reality is not adequately reflected in their respective constitutional doctrines, at least in their strict consensus where there is none, whether in terms of membership of the United Kingdom or Irish unity. Both governments are open to change in this area, so as to reflect more accurately the realities of the situation and to encourage the process of agreement among all the people who inhabit the island.

16. Both governments agree to take as fundamental the equal respect for the legitimacy of the two major traditions that exist in Ireland, represented on the one hand by those who wish for no change in the present status of Northern Ireland and on the other hand by those who wish for a sovereign united Ireland achieved by peaceful means and by agreement. Their objective is to reconcile them, on a basis of mutual respect and in a manner which will contribute to the ending of divisions and can be accepted and endorsed by all the people living in Ireland.

17. Both governments will aim for a shared understanding of the constitutional issues so as to achieve a balanced accommodation of the differing positions of the two main traditions. A shared understanding should involve the fullest possible degree of endorsement by each government of the constitutional position of the other. It is accepted that such reciprocal endorsement would not be possible for an Irish constitutional position which failed to reflect without reservation the commitment subscribed to in article 1 of the Anglo-Irish Agreement. Neither would it be possible in respect of a British position which failed to acknowledge the full legitimacy and value of the goal of Irish unity by agreement, cherished by the greater number of people living in Ireland, and the consequential need for practical provisions to give that objective equally meaningful operational expression and opportunity, including in any future structures within Northern Ireland and between North and South.

18. Both governments accordingly commit themselves to create and sustain structures which will afford both the nationalist and unionist identities equally satisfactory, secure and

durable political administrative and symbolic expression and protection. They will co-operate to secure for them the necessary consent and allegiance of all the people of Ireland. They agree these structures must adequately reflect all the relationships involved.

Relationships within Northern Ireland

19. The governance and administration of Northern Ireland will be founded on full respect for, and equality of, human rights, as well as fundamental social, economic and cultural rights and on freedom from discrimination for all citizens and on parity of esteem and equality of treatment for the identity, ethos and allegiance of both communities. Both governments agree that these basic rights will be guaranteed and entrenched in a new Agreement.

20. Both governments wish to see new structures in Northern Ireland, which would assume executive and legislative responsibilities over a wide range of subjects. Such structures must provide for the equitable and effective participation in the discharge of these responsibilities by the elected representatives of both communities, and they must secure widespread acceptance throughout both communities. They should incorporate significant measures to promote consensual approaches and the mutual acceptance by representatives of both communities of each other's rights, identities and ethos.

Relationships between North and South

21. Both governments agree that new North–South institutions should be created in the context of a comprehensive new agreement. These will have clear institutional identity and purpose and will be mandated by legislation in both Parliaments to discharge or oversee a range of executive functions on matters which, by virtue of such legislation, the two governments decide will be administered uniformly throughout the island, or which the two administrations, North and South, subsequently agree are to be so administered.

22. These new structures will provide an institutional framework for practical and effective North–South co-operation and co-ordination for mutual benefit in the areas designated, and in particular will be the instrument for developing an integrated approach for the whole island in respect of the challenges and opportunities of the EC. They will operate on the basis of agreement between the two sides, appropriately mandated. The discharge of their mandates will be subject to regular parliamentary scrutiny, including in any inter-parliamentary forum which may be set up by agreement between elected representatives North and South.

23. Both governments furthermore agree that this North/South framework must operate in such a way so as to help heal divisions and promote reconciliation between the two traditions on the island of Ireland, provide a forum for acknowledging and accommodating their respective rights and identities and strengthening mutual respect between them, and have a mandate from the sovereign governments to promote co-operation, understanding and agreement among the institutions and people in both parts of the island.

Intergovernmental Relations

24. Both governments have made clear their readiness to consider a new and more broadly based agreement, if it can be arrived at through direct discussion and negotiation between all the parties concerned.

25. They envisage that under such a new Agreement a standing Intergovernmental Conference would be maintained involving, but not always attended only by, the Secretary of State for Northern Ireland and the designated representative of the Irish Government. It would continue to be supported by a permanent secretariat staffed by British and Irish civil servants.

26. Both governments envisage that representatives of agreed political institutions in Northern Ireland may be formally associated with the work of the Conference, in a manner to be agreed by both governments after consultation with them.

27. The two governments envisage that matters for which responsibility is transferred to new political institutions in Northern Ireland may be formally associated with the work of the Conference, in a manner to be agreed by both governments after consultation with them.

28. The Intergovernmental Conference will be the forum for both governments to jointly guarantee and monitor the commitment, to be enshrined in the mandate of any new local institutions and entrenched in a new Agreement, that such institutions will provide for the equitable and effective participation in power of representatives of both communities and will ensure full equality of rights and freedom from discrimination for all those governed by them, as well as parity of esteem for the identity, ethos and allegiance of the two communities. The Conference will have contingency powers of intervention and redress in the event that devolved institutions fail demonstrably to meet their obligations, or fail altogether to survive or to discharge their designated functions.

29. The Conference may also monitor and guarantee the effective discharge of its mandate by any new North–South body. Subject to the agreement of both Governments, such a body may also be associated in appropriate ways with the work of the Conference, where the wider role of the British Government is particularly relevant, for example in relation to developing an integrated North–South approach to the EC.

Endorsement

30. Both governments are agreed that any new agreement reflecting these principles would need to be acceptable to the people.

Source: *Irish Press* Exclusive by Emily O'Reilly, Political Correspondent, *Irish Press*, 19 November 1993.

Document 4.8. Downing Street Declaration, 15 December 1993

JOINT DECLARATION BY AN TAOISEACH, MR. ALBERT REYNOLDS,
T.D., AND THE BRITISH PRIME MINISTER, THE RT. HON. JOHN
MAJOR, M.P., 15 DECEMBER 1993

1. The Taoiseach, Mr Albert Reynolds, TD, and the Prime Minister, the Rt. Hon. John Major, MP, acknowledge that the most urgent and important issue facing the people of Ireland, North and South, and the British and Irish Governments together, is to remove the

causes of conflict, to overcome the legacy of history and to heal the divisions which have resulted, recognising the absence of a lasting and satisfactory settlement of relationships between the peoples of both islands has contributed to continuing tragedy and suffering. They believe that the development of an agreed framework for peace, which has been discussed between them since early last year, and which is based on a number of key principles articulated by the two Governments over the past 20 years, together with the adaptation of other widely accepted principles, provides the starting point of a peace process designed to culminate in a political settlement.

2. The Taoiseach and the Prime Minister are convinced of the inestimable value to both their peoples, and particularly for the next generation, of healing divisions in Ireland and of ending a conflict which has been so manifestly to the detriment of all. Both recognise that the ending of divisions can come about only through the agreement and co-operation of the people, North and South, representing both traditions in Ireland. They therefore make a solemn commitment to promote co-operation at all levels on the basis of the fundamental principles, undertakings, obligations under international agreements, to which they have jointly committed themselves, and the guarantees which each Government has given and now reaffirms, including Northern Ireland's statutory constitutional guarantee. It is their aim to foster agreement and reconciliation, leading to a new political framework founded on consent and encompassing arrangements within Northern Ireland, for the whole island, and between these islands.

3. They also consider that the development of Europe will, of itself, require new approaches to serve interests common to both parts of the island of Ireland, and to Ireland and the United Kingdom as partners in the European Union.

4. The Prime Minister, on behalf of the British Government, reaffirms that they will uphold the democratic wish of the greater number of the people of Northern Ireland on the issue of whether they prefer to support the Union or a sovereign united Ireland. On this basis, he reiterates, on the behalf of the British Government, that they have no selfish strategic or economic interest in Northern Ireland. Their primary interest is to see peace, stability and reconciliation established by agreement among all the people inhabit the island, and they will work together with the Irish Government to achieve such an agreement, which will embrace the totality of relationships. The role of the British Government will be to encourage, facilitate and enable the achievement of such agreement over a period through a process of dialogue and co-operation based on full respect for the rights and identities of both traditions in Ireland. They accept that such agreement may, as of right, take the form of agreed structures for the island as a whole, including a united Ireland achieved by peaceful means on the following basis. The British Government agree that it is for the people of the island of Ireland alone, by agreement between the two parts respectively, to exercise their right of self-determination on the basis of consent, freely and concurrently given, North and South, to bring about a united Ireland, if that is their wish. They reaffirm as a binding obligation that they will, for their part, introduce the necessary legislation to give effect to this, or equally to any measure of agreement on future relationships in Ireland which the people living in Ireland may themselves freely so determine without external impediment. They believe that the people of Britain would wish, in friendship to all sides, to enable the people of Ireland to reach agreement on how they may live together in harmony and in partnership, with respect for their diverse

traditions, and with full recognition of the special links and the unique relationship which exist between the peoples of Britain and Ireland.

5. The Taoiseach, on behalf of the Irish Government, considers that the lessons of Irish history, and especially of Northern Ireland, show that stability and well-being will not be found under any political system which is refused allegiance or rejected on grounds of identity by a significant minority of those governed by it. For this reason, it would be wrong to attempt to impose a united Ireland, in the absence of the freely given consent of the majority of the people of Northern Ireland. He accepts, on behalf of the Irish Government, that the democratic right of self-determination by the people of Ireland as a whole must be achieved and exercised with and subject to the agreement and consent of a majority of the people of Northern Ireland and must, consistent with justice and equity, respect the democratic dignity and the civil rights and religious liberties of both communities, including:

- the right of free political thought;
- the right of freedom and expression of religion;
- the right to pursue democratically national and political aspirations;
- the right to seek constitutional change by peaceful and legitimate means;
- the right to live wherever one chooses without hindrance;
- the right to equal opportunity in all social and economic activity, regardless of class, creed, sex or colour.

These would be reflected in any future political and constitutional arrangements emerging from a new and more broadly based agreement.

6. The Taoiseach however recognises the genuine difficulties and barriers to building relationships of trust either within or beyond Northern Ireland, from which both traditions suffer. He will work to create a new era of trust, in which suspicion of the motives and actions of others is removed on the part of either community. He considers that the future of the island depends on the nature of the relationship between the two main traditions that inhabit it. Every effort must be made to build a new sense of trust between those communities. In recognition of the fears of the Unionist community and as a token of his willingness to make a political contribution to the building up of that necessary trust, the Taoiseach will examine with his colleagues any elements in the democratic life and organisation of the Irish State that can be represented to the Irish Government in the course of political dialogue as a real and substantial threat to their way of life and ethos, or that can be represented as not being fully consistent with a modern democratic and pluralist society, and undertakes to examine any possible ways of removing such obstacles. Such an examination would of course have due regard to the desire to preserve those inherited values that are largely shared throughout the island or that belong to the cultural and historical roots of the people of this island in all their diversity. The Taoiseach hopes that over time a meeting of hearts and minds will develop, which will bring all the people of Ireland together, and will work towards that objective, but he pledges in the meantime that as a result of the efforts that will be made to build mutual confidence no Northern Unionist should ever have a fear in future that this ideal will be pursued either by threat or coercion.

7. Both Governments accept that Irish unity would be achieved only by those who favour this outcome persuading those who do not, peacefully and without coercion or violence, and that, if in the future a majority of the people of Northern Ireland are so persuaded, both

Governments will support and give legislative effect to their wish. But, notwithstanding the solemn affirmation by both Governments in the Anglo-Irish Agreement that any change in the status of Northern Ireland would only come about with the consent of a majority of the people of Northern Ireland, the Taoiseach also recognises the continuing uncertainties and misgivings which dominate so much of Northern Unionist attitudes towards the rest of Ireland. He believes that we stand at a stage of our history when the genuine feelings of all traditions in the North must be recognised and acknowledged. He appeals to both traditions at this time to grasp the opportunity for a fresh start and a new beginning, which could hold such promise for all our lives and the generations to come. He asks the people of Northern Ireland to look on the people of the Republic as friends, who share their grief and shame over all the suffering of the last quarter of a century, and who want to develop the best possible relationship with them, a relationship in which trust and new understanding can flourish and grow. The Taoiseach also acknowledges the presence in the Constitution of the Republic of elements which are deeply resented by Northern Unionists, but which at the same time reflect hopes and ideals which lie deep in the hearts of many Irish men and women North and South. But as we move towards a new era of understanding in which new relationships of trust may grow and bring peace to the island of Ireland, the Taoiseach believes that the time has come to consider together how best the hopes and identities of all can be expressed in more balanced ways, which no longer engender division and the lack of trust to which he has referred. He confirms that, in the event of an overall settlement, the Irish Government will, as part of a balanced constitutional accommodation, put forward and support proposals for change in the Irish Constitution which would fully reflect the principle of consent in Northern Ireland.

8. The Taoiseach recognises the need to engage in dialogue which would address with honesty and integrity the fears of all traditions. But that dialogue, both within the North and between the people and their representatives of both parts of Ireland, must be entered into with an acknowledgment that the future security and welfare of the people of the island will depend on an open, frank and balanced approach to all the problems which for too long have caused division.

9. The British and Irish Governments will seek, along with the Northern Ireland constitutional parties through a process of political dialogue, to create institutions and structures which, while respecting the diversity of the people of Ireland, would enable them to work together in all areas of common interest. This will help over a period to build the trust necessary to end past divisions, leading to an agreed and peaceful future. Such structures would, of course, include institutional recognition of the special links that exist between the peoples of Britain and Ireland as part of the totality of relationships, while taking account of newly forged links with the rest of Europe.

10. The British and Irish Governments reiterate that the achievement of peace must involve a permanent end to the use of, or support for, paramilitary violence. They confirm that, in these circumstances, democratically mandated parties which establish a commitment to exclusively peaceful methods and which have shown that they abide by the democratic process, are free to participate fully in democratic politics and to join in dialogue in due course between the Governments and the political parties on the way ahead.

11. The Irish Government would make their own arrangements within their jurisdiction to enable democratic parties to consult together and share in dialogue about the political future. The Taoiseach's intention is that these arrangements could include the establishment, in consultation with other parties, of a Forum for Peace and Reconciliation to make recommendations on ways in which agreement and trust between both traditions can be promoted and established.

12. The Taoiseach and the Prime Minister are determined to build on the fervent wish of both their peoples to see old fears and animosities replaced by a climate of peace. They believe the framework they have set out offers the people of Ireland, North and South, whatever their tradition, the basis to agree that from now on their differences can be negotiated and resolved exclusively by peaceful political means. They appeal to all concerned to grasp the opportunity for a new departure. That step would compromise no position or principle, nor prejudice the future of either community. On the contrary, it would be an incomparable gain for all. It would break decisively the cycle of violence and the intolerable suffering it entails for the people of these islands, particularly for both communities in Northern Ireland. It would allow the process of economic and social co-operation on the island to realise its full potential for prosperity and mutual understanding. It would transform the prospects for building on the progress already made in the Talks process, involving the two Governments and the constitutional parties in Northern Ireland. The Taoiseach and the Prime Minister believe that these arrangements offer an opportunity to lay the foundation for a more peaceful and harmonious future, devoid of the violence and bitter divisions which have scarred the past generation. They commit themselves and their Governments to continue to work together, unremittingly, towards that objective.

15 December 1993

Source: Ireland (1993).

Document 4.9. Sinn Féin Questions to British Government on Downing Street Declaration, 15 April 1994

[MATTERS RELATING TO THE DOWNING STREET DECLARATION WHICH REQUIRE CLARIFICATION]

The matters relating to the Downing Street Declaration which require clarification are:

a) Matters of text;
b) Its interpretation by the two governments and conflicting commentary on what it means;
c) The peace process which the two governments envisage developing from the declaration.

To avoid the problems which occurred in the recent past clarification by the British Government would of necessity be formal, in writing, properly authenticated and publicly acknowledged. Though it may not be necessary there needs to be a facility for supplementary questions to be answered, if these arise.

1. The long-term political objectives of the two Governments are of crucial importance if we are to move out of the present failed political structures. While accepting what he regards to be present political realities the Taoiseach has, nevertheless, clearly stated the long-term objectives of the Irish Government in the search for a lasting settlement. It is essential that the British Government displays the same honesty and frankness in outlining its long-term attitude towards the Irish people. What are the British Government's long-term interests and objectives in relation to Ireland?

2. The Taoiseach has made it clear that he sees no major difference of substance between the position put by him to you in June 1993 and the Downing Street Declaration of December 15.

   a) Do you share this view?
   b) On what basis did you reject the June position?
   c) If the difference is, as is claimed, minimal are you prepared to assist in closing this gap?

3. The British and Irish Governments have said that political structures cannot be predetermined, now, or in the future. How do you reconcile this with your adherence to the partition of Ireland and the maintenance of the union?

4. The British Government says, in the Downing Street Declaration, 'that they will uphold the democratic wishes of a greater number of the people of Northern Ireland'. What is the British Government's precise definition of 'a greater number of the people of Northern Ireland' and how would this be measured in practical terms?

5. The British Government has said that it has 'no selfish strategic or economic interest in Northern Ireland'. Would it not be more in accord with democratic principles for the British Government to base its Irish policy on the objective of ending the union?

6. On March 23, 1993, a representative of the British Government told representatives of Sinn Féin that: 'The final solution is union. It is going to happen anyway. The historical train—Europe—determines that. We are committed to Europe. Unionists will have to change. The island will be as one'. Is this the position of the British Government?

7. The British Government has said that its primary interest is to see agreement reached between all the Irish people.

   a) Given the continued intransigent attitude of the Unionist leaderships, how, in real terms is such agreement to be encouraged?
   b) What will be the response of the British Government if the Unionist parties refuse to engage in the search for agreement?
   c) What does the British Government consider to be a 'reasonable time-scale' for agreement to be reached.
   d) What is the framework which the British Government intends to create for the achievement of agreement?
   e) Does the British Government accept that, given the preponderance of the nationalist position and opposition to partition among the Irish people as a whole, that substantial movement on constitutional issues by the British Government and the Unionist Parties will be required if democratic agreement is to be reached?

f) How is agreement to be measured in practical terms and at what stage does the withholding or absence of agreement on the part of one section of the Irish people become a veto over change?

8. Given the British Government's agreement that it is for the Irish people to exercise our right to self-determination, what is the basis for the British Government's qualification of this right in Paragraph 4 of the Downing Street Declaration?

9. In the Downing Street Declaration the British Government gives a commitment to allow the Irish people to freely determine their future without external impediment or interference. Do you accept that the Government of Ireland Act, particularly Section 75, directly affects present political structures and that it can only be regarded as an external impediment and interference in the free determination by the Irish people of their future?

10. How does the British Government reconcile its stated objective of maintaining the union with its declared lack of strategic or economic interest in Ireland

11. Given the commitment by the two governments that everything will be on the table for negotiation:

a) Will the union between Ireland and Britain be on the agenda for negotiation
b) Will the Government of Ireland Act be on the agenda for negotiation?
c) Will you give a commitment to end the Government of Ireland Act as part of an overall settlement?

12. Given the statement by the British Government in the Downing Street Declaration that 'it is for the people of the island of Ireland alone, by agreement between the two parts respectively, to exercise their right of self-determination on the basis of consent';

a) Is the continued operation of the Government of Ireland Act subject to agreement on this basis?
b) Is the continued existence of the union subject to agreement on this basis?

13. Does the British Government accept that while the consent of a majority of the people of the 6 county state to constitutional change, as referred to in the Downing Street Declaration, may be desirable it is not a legal requirement in international law?

14. Given the commitment in the Downing Street Declaration to work towards a balanced constitutional accommodation does the British Government accept that the present structures and arrangements do not represent a balanced constitutional accommodation?

15. Given the commitment in the Downing Street Declaration to work towards a balanced constitutional accommodation, what constitutional options does the British government see as being consistent with this objective?

16. The Taoiseach has said that Unionists only possess a veto in regard to whether to belong to a sovereign United Ireland or the UK, that they do not possess a veto over the policy of the two governments or over interim measures which may be adopted. Is this also the position of the British Government?

17. The Taoiseach has said that political parties need not accept every phrase or word in the Downing Street Declaration. In fact the DUP have rejected the Declaration in total.

    a) Does absolute rejection of the Declaration by a political party exclude that party from involvement in talks on the development of new political arrangements.

    b) Do parties which are opposed to aspects of the Downing Street Declaration have the right to dissent from it and yet be engaged in talks on the development of new political arrangements.

18. Exploratory Dialogue. Sinn Fein, as a matter of policy, advocates inclusive dialogue without preconditions. We do not accept the imposition of preconditions on our party or on any other party. However, in the interests of clarity we wish to explore the British Government position on these matters as outlined in the Downing Street Declaration.

    a) The British Government has called upon Sinn Fein to renounce violence. What does this involve?

    b) Patrick Mayhew is reported as saying that a permanent cessation of violence 'is the way in which full recognition can be accorded to the mandate which Sinn Fein candidates are accorded at the polls' (*Irish Times*, Thursday, 14/4/94). How does the British Government reconcile its refusal to recognize our democratic mandate with its stated commitment to democratic principles?

    c) The British Prime Minister has referred to a period of decontamination for Sinn Fein. What does this mean?

    d) What would be the purpose of the exploratory dialogue between Sinn Fein and the British Government?

    e) How long would this exploratory dialogue last?

    f) Within this process, when would negotiations about the future constitutional and political shape of Ireland take place?

19. a) Given the declared opposition of both governments to coercion, how will the coercion of northern nationalists into the 6 county state be addressed in real terms?

    b) How will the denial of nationalist rights be redressed in real terms?

    c) When will repressive legislation be ended?

20. How would the process of demilitarisation be implemented in real terms.

21. An amnesty for political prisoners is an obvious element of a peace process. How will the British Government address this issue?

22. The Downing Street Declaration is described as 'the starting point of a peace process designed to culminate in a political settlement'. What are the subsequent steps which the British Government envisages in this suggested peace process?

Note: This document, with a covering letter from Sinn Féin President Gerry Adams dated 15 April 1994, was conveyed to the Irish Government and passed by an Irish official to his British counterpart. On 19 May 1994 a Northern Ireland Office statement replied to the questions, grouping them thematically. There are several discrepancies between the questions reproduced above and those in the British response. The latter are published in Dunnigan (1995: 83–97) and on the CAIN web site <cain.ulster.ac.uk/issues/politics/docs/nio/nio190594.htm> (accessed 9 May 2019).

Source: Annex to memorandum by Quentin Thomas, 19 April 1994, TNA: PREM 19 / 4778.

Document 4.10. Northern Ireland Framework Document, 22 February 1995

A FRAMEWORK FOR ACCOUNTABLE GOVERNMENT IN NORTHERN IRELAND, 22 FEBRUARY 1995

Introduction

1. This part sets out the Government's understanding of potentially acceptable elements for improving local accountability in Northern Ireland, as part of a comprehensive political settlement embracing relationships within Northern Ireland, between Northern Ireland and the Republic of Ireland, and between the two Governments.

2. The British and Irish Governments committed themselves in the Joint Declaration to seeking, along with the Northern Ireland constitutional parties through a process of political dialogue, to create institutions and structures which, while respecting the diversity of the people of Ireland, would enable them to work together in all areas of common interest. The two governments recognised that such structures would include institutional recognition of the special links that exist between the peoples of Britain and Ireland as part of the totality of relationships, while taking account of newly forged links with the rest of Europe.

3. It is the Government's aim to see the creation in Northern Ireland of local institutions of government that are directly accountable to the people—all the people—nd to which they can give their wholehearted commitment and support. With this in mind, and taking account of Northern Ireland's position as part of the United Kingdom and its relationship with the Republic of Ireland, it is possible to identify certain characteristics which should underlie any new political institutions in Northern Ireland. Such institutions should be:

- based on democratic principles and reflecting the wishes of the electorate;
- widely acceptable, in particular in the sense of providing an appropriate and equitable role for both sides of the community, such that both the main parts of the Northern Ireland community should be able to identify with them and feel their representatives had a meaningful function to perform;
- stable and durable in the sense of not being dependent on a particular election result or political deal. The system should, so far as possible, be self-sustaining;
- capable of development, in response to changing political realities, with the agreement of all concerned;
- workable, in the sense of being as straightforward to operate as possible;
- such as to avoid any entrenchment of the main community division and to encourage the development of a society in which both main traditions would be respected;
- such as to provide all the constitutional political parties with the opportunity to achieve a role at each level of responsibility, and to have a position proportional to their electoral strength in broad terms;
- able to function effectively, efficiently and decisively within clearly defined areas of responsibility;
- innovative, in the sense of learning from and not merely modelled on any previous arrangements;

- established within a defined relationship with UK institutions;
- competent to manage any relationship between Northern Ireland and the Republic of Ireland developed in political talks;
- capable of securing public endorsement;
- consistent with the maximum possible delegation of authority;
- such as to ensure the greatest possible degree of Parliamentary scrutiny of and public accountability for the exercise of powers of government within Northern Ireland.

4. The Government believe that there would also be strong support for the propositions that each individual and community in Northern Ireland has the right to define their own identity; that that right and identity should be respected; and that any new political institutions should be such as to give expression to the identity and validity of each main tradition.

Possible Arrangements: Outline

5. Based on its discussions with the Northern Ireland parties and bearing in mind the preferred characteristics mentioned above, the Government believe that there would be a broad measure of agreement for an outline framework for new political institutions in Northern Ireland to include:

- province-wide executive responsibilities;
- a single unicameral Assembly of about 90 members elected for a fixed 4 or 5 year term;
- elections to the Assembly by a form of proportional representation;
- a separate Panel, probably of 3 people elected within Northern Ireland, to complement the working of the Assembly. The Panel could be elected from a single Northern Ireland constituency by a system of proportional representation;
- a system of Assembly Committees, constituted broadly in proportion to party strengths in the Assembly, to oversee the work of the Northern Ireland Departments and other functions;
- legislative and executive responsibility over as wide a range of subjects as in 1973. If there were agreement it would be open to the Government to consider with the new institutions the scope for further transfers. Certain functions, including matters relating to the Crown, foreign affairs and defence, would remain at Westminster. It would be for consideration whether new institutions were given full legislative responsibility from day one or whether such responsibility would be assumed progressively;
- a system of detailed checks and balances intended to sustain confidence in the institutions. These might include powers for the Panel to nominate Assembly Committee Chairmen and Deputy Chairmen, to scrutinise and if necessary block legislation, and to arbitrate on public expenditure disputes; and a Code of Practice to specify the relationships between the Assembly, its Committees, Committee Chairmen and Departments;
- mechanisms to ensure adequate compliance with the UK's EU and other international obligations.

Possible Arrangements: Detail
Transferred Matters: Executive Responsibilities
6. Executive responsibilities in the transferred field would be discharged through Northern Ireland Departments, subject to the powers and roles of the Assembly and Panel. The chairman of the relevant Assembly departmental committee would be the Head of Department. These committees would be established from among the members of the Assembly on a basis providing an appropriate, fair and significant role for representatives of all main traditions in Northern Ireland. Departmental estimates, policies and actions would be subject to scrutiny by the relevant committee, which would have the power to compel attendance and call for papers. The Assembly would debate reports from, and call for the minutes of, each committee.

Assembly Committees: Appointment
7. The Chairmanships and Deputy Chairmanships of Assembly Committees would be allocated from among the members of the Assembly by the Assembly, acting by weighted majority, on the nomination of the Panel, acting by consensus. This procedure might operate as follows:

- the Panel, acting unanimously and after consultation with the Assembly party leaders, would draw up a list of nominations broadly reflecting proportional party strengths in the Assembly, and having regard to the likely ability of nominees to command the confidence of the Assembly;
- the Assembly would vote on the list of nominations as a whole, approval requiring a weighted majority of Assembly members;
- if the nominations were not approved, the Panel would draw up a revised list of nominations. The fact that a particular nomination had been rejected as part of a list would not prevent it being proposed again on a revised list;
- if a vacancy occurred during the life of the Assembly, this procedure would be repeated, with the Panel (after consultation with the Assembly party leaders) making a nomination for Assembly approval, by weighted majority, for each such vacancy;
- appointments would be held for the whole term of the Assembly, subject only to dismissal on the proposal of the Panel, acting unanimously, and with the approval, by weighted majority, of both the relevant Committee and the Assembly as a whole.

Transferred Matters: Legislation
8. The Northern Ireland Assembly would be the legislature in respect of transferred matters in Northern Ireland, subject to the powers and role of the Panel. All legislation would require the support of at least a majority of both the relevant Committee and the full Assembly. Legislation would be dealt with by majority decision unless a Business Committee (see paragraph 16) decided that the proposal was contentious, thus requiring weighted majority approval (at a level to be determined), or unless a petition to that effect secured a certain threshold support (at a level to be determined). Examples of measures which might be deemed contentious might include some financial measures or those with constitutional implications or significant implications for community relations.

Financial Arrangements

9. During future talks the participants would need to consider how the quantum of public expenditure would continue to be determined in the event of devolution, sources of funding, the role of the Secretary of State in any new arrangements, and the degree of discretion available to a local administration to allocate resources according to its own priorities. The Government would be ready to table ideas for consideration.

Non-Transferred Matters

10. The Secretary of State would remain accountable to the Westminster Parliament for matters not transferred. These might include matters relating to law and order, including firearms and explosives (but see paragraphs 13 and 14), as well as the criminal law. The Secretary of State would also have a continuing responsibility for securing public expenditure for Northern Ireland and would be Co-Chairman of the Intergovernmental Conference established under a new Agreement. The Talks participants would need to give further consideration to the relationship in the longer term between new political institutions and the Westminster Parliament, and the role of the Secretary of State. The Government would be prepared to table ideas to assist discussions.

11. Under its terms of reference the Northern Ireland Affairs Select Committee at Westminster would no longer be entitled to scrutinise any matters for which new political institutions became accountable.

Rights

12. Protection for specified civil, political, social and cultural rights would be reinforced in respect of a range of matters including those for which the new political institutions would have responsibility, on a basis arrived at in consultation with the parties. The means of such protection would accord with the constitutional arrangements of the United Kingdom, and could build on existing safeguards. The aim will be to ensure that under any political settlement legislation and executive action will operate fairly and impartially so as to ensure the protection of these agreed rights and to inspire the confidence of everyone in Northern Ireland

Law and Order

13. The Government wish to see the maintenance and development of a police service in Northern Ireland that is effective, operationally independent and accountable to the community which it serves. It must be capable of maintaining law and order, and of responding to any renewed terrorist threat should that prove necessary. Subject to these requirements, the Government are open to the consideration of proposals designed to enhance the extent to which the community at large in Northern Ireland can identify with and give full support to the police service.

14. The role of the new local institutions in policing and security matters will depend to a large extent on the level of the terrorist threat. So long as the threat is such that the active support of the armed services is necessary and emergency legislation is required, the Government's direct responsibility for these matters will continue, although there could be a consultative role for the local institutions. As that threat diminishes, so the likelihood increases that responsibility for policing matters, principally funding and the setting and monitoring of police objectives, could be transferred to the appropriate Assembly Committee.

Assembly

15. The Assembly would be presided over by a Speaker, elected by weighted majority.

16. Non-departmental committees of the Assembly would include a Business Committee to co-ordinate Assembly business; a General Purposes Committee (to include the Chairmen of Departmental Committees) to assist in co-ordinating the interests of the relevant committees on issues crossing departmental boundaries; a Public Accounts Committee; and other committees to act as a focus for the Assembly interest in particular areas such as non-transferred matters, cultural expression and diversity.

17. A Code of Practice would be drawn up to specify the respective roles, responsibilities and decision taking powers of Departments, Committee Chairmen, Assembly Committees and the Assembly at large. The Code would be reflected in the Standing Orders of the Assembly, which would be subject to weighted majority approval. The Code and Standing Orders would have particular regard to means of promoting cross-community consensus and securing an appropriate, fair and significant role for representatives of all main traditions.

The Panel

18. The Panel, whose role would complement the work of the Assembly, might undertake important consultative, monitoring, referral and representational functions. Decisions would be taken by consensus. Procedures would be devised for what, if anything, should happen were consensus not to be reached. The Panel could have a general duty to liaise, formally and informally, with the Assembly and the Secretary of State, and to give advice.

19. The Panel's role, powers, rights, duties and responsibilities would need to be carefully specified, including in legislation where appropriate, and could include:

- a role in the nomination of Chairmen and Deputy Chairmen of Assembly Committees (see paragraph 7);
- the consideration of proposed legislation specifically referred to it under Assembly procedures (with power to accept, reject, give an opinion or propose amendments);
- the ability to refer any proposed legislation for appropriate judicial consideration, eg, of whether it might be discriminatory or *ultra vires*;
- liaising with the Secretary of State on the overall level of public expenditure allocated to Northern Ireland Departments;
- arbitrating public expenditure allocation disputes between Departments, where these had not been resolved by the Finance Committee;
- the approval of designated public appointments in respect of transferred matters:
- advising the Secretary of State on appointments within his responsibility;
- the consideration of actions or proposals referred to it under Assembly procedures (with the power to give an opinion on or to make recommendations on such actions, and to refer them for any appropriate judicial consideration);
- preparation for the Assembly and the Secretary of State of regular (annual) reports on the activities of the Panel and their view of the operation of the new political institutions.

20. The Panel could have an important representational and promotional role, with a special commitment to the economic development of Northern Ireland through participation in joint promotional activities in collaboration with other interests.

21. The Panel would secure its share of resources from the Secretary of State independently from the rest of the transferred block, in order to ensure that it had financial independence and its resources were sufficient to carry out the full range of its statutory functions.

22. Arrangements for replacing Panel members who could not continue to discharge their duties would need to be considered.

Checks and Balances

23. The preceding paragraphs contain a number of checks and balances intended to give reassurance that new institutions would command the confidence of both main sections of the Northern Ireland community without prejudicing workability. In summary they are:

- elections to an Assembly by a system of proportional representation;
- separate elections to a Panel, also by a system of proportional representation;
- a balance of responsibility between the Assembly, Assembly Committees and the Panel (which could intervene on legislation or executive actions);
- Panel decisions to be unanimous;
- Assembly Committees established to give an appropriate, fair and significant role for all main traditions in Northern Ireland;
- Heads of Departments/Chairmen of Committees (and Deputy Chairmen) to be approved by joint action involving the Assembly and Panel and to require weighted majority approval in the Assembly;
- legislation to require majority support both in the relevant Committee and the Assembly, with provision for contentious legislation to require weighted majority approval.

24. The preceding paragraphs also contain ideas on the use of weighted majority voting in the Assembly as a means of ensuring cross-party support for;

- the appointment (or dismissal) of the Chairmen or Deputy Chairmen of Assembly Committees (paragraph 7);
- contentious legislation (paragraph 8);
- the election of the Assembly Speaker (paragraph 15);
- Assembly Standing Orders on the roles, responsibilities and decision-making powers of Departments, Committee Chairmen, Assembly Committees and the Assembly at large (paragraph 17).

25. Weighted majority voting might also be used in the Assembly Committees to ensure that minorities were not continually outvoted. The weighted majority required in these different circumstances would ultimately be for agreement by the parties in the Assembly but could be in the order of 65% to 75%.

26. Minimum threshold votes also offer a mechanism for protecting minority rights. Paragraph 8 suggests that if a petition in the Assembly secured a specified threshold of support it could require a particular piece of contentious legislation to be dealt with by weighted majority voting. The procedures in the Assembly might also be devised in such a

way as to allow draft legislation or other actions or proposals to be referred to the Panel if they secured a threshold vote (paragraph 19). Again, the precise quota required in each circumstance would be for determination by the parties in the Assembly but might be in the range of 25% to 35%.

Relationships with Other Institutions

27. The New Framework for Agreement envisages that relevant members of the Assembly would play a significant role in any new North/South institutions and could also have involvement in any new intergovernmental arrangements. Paragraphs 24 to 38 and 39 to 49 of that document refer. Annex B lists possible arrangements for co-ordination between institutions in Northern Ireland, between Northern Ireland and the Republic and between the two Governments.

Relationships with the European Union
European Union Aspects

28. New institutions in Northern Ireland would be responsible for implementing EC legislation and programmes in the transferred field. They would also be responsible for developing Northern Ireland's views on EU issues and representing them to the UK Government and in any new North/South Institutions. Further consideration would need to be given, with the British Government, to the arrangements which will be necessary for this purpose. These arrangements must respect the British Government's responsibility for the whole of the UK in the European Union and before the European Court of Justice.

Annex A: The Government's Approach to a Political Settlement

1. The Government's primary interest is to see peace, stability and reconciliation established by agreement among all the people who inhabit the island of Ireland and it has committed itself, in the Joint Declaration, to working with the Irish Government to achieve such an agreement, which will embrace the totality of relationships. The Government has defined its role as being to encourage, facilitate and enable the achievement of agreement over a period through a process of dialogue and co-operation based on full respect for the rights and identities of both traditions in Ireland.

2. The Government believe that if there is to be lasting peace, stability and reconciliation any new arrangements for the governance of Northern Ireland must take account of various political realities. These include:

- that any new arrangements for the governance of Northern Ireland must be acceptable to the people and give appropriate expression to the identity of each of the two main parts of the community. They should uphold and apply the principles of equality of opportunity, equity of treatment and parity of esteem already established by the Government;
- that any political agreement must address all the relevant relationships, not only those between the two main parts of the community within Northern Ireland, including the relationship between any new political institutions there and the Westminster Parliament, but also those between Northern Ireland and the Republic and between the United Kingdom and Irish Governments;

- the compelling need for the people of Northern Ireland to be given a greater say over their own affairs and for that to be reflected in greater political power, authority and responsibility being transferred to locally elected representatives within a framework of agreed relationships;
- that there can be no going back to a system of government in Northern Ireland which has the allegiance of, and is operated by, only one part of the community;
- the present reality, in fact and in international law, of the Union of Great Britain and Northern Ireland, affirmed in the Northern Ireland Constitution Act 1973. It is the clear position, as set out in the 1973 Act and the Anglo-Irish Agreement, that the current constitutional status of Northern Ireland as part of the United Kingdom will not change, save with the consent of a majority of the people of Northern Ireland, clearly expressed. This guarantee is reaffirmed in the Joint Declaration;
- the widespread acknowledgement that Northern Ireland's constitutional status as part of the United Kingdom is unlikely to change for the foreseeable future;
- that a significant minority of the people of Northern Ireland aspire to a sovereign united Ireland achieved by peaceful means and consent;
- that the right of a section of the Northern Ireland community to aspire to a sovereign united Ireland, achieved by peaceful means and through agreement, is no less legitimate than the wish of a present majority to retain Northern Ireland's status within the United Kingdom;
- that any change in Northern Ireland's constitutional status as part of the United Kingdom should come about only in accordance with the democratic wishes of the people of Northern Ireland, freely given and without coercion;
- that while any settlement is bound to require some compromise, success in obtaining an agreement should not in the Government's view require any of the participants to abandon their basic political principles or aspirations.

3. Bearing these realities in mind the Government is firmly of the view that the basis for a lasting settlement can only be achieved by dialogue between political representatives. It remains of the view, which has been supported by the main constitutional parties and the Irish Government since 1990, that the best chance of securing a comprehensive political accommodation lies through a process of dialogue involving the key political interests, is based on a comprehensive agenda, and addresses all three of the underlying relationships—those between the two main parts of the community in Northern Ireland, between the two parts of Ireland and between the two Sovereign States. The Government also remains of the view, which is accepted by the other participants, that agreements on one part of the process would in practice depend on agreement on the others.

4. The Government would therefore like to see further dialogue take place involving themselves, the Irish Government and all the main parties in Northern Ireland with a democratic mandate that have established a commitment to exclusively peaceful means. The fundamental interest of the British Government would be to secure an outcome broadly acceptable to the participants. Because it is essential that any outcome should attract widespread support the Government has undertaken to hold a referendum on any agreement that emerges from the Talks Process.

5. The ideas contained in Part I of this paper and the New Framework for Agreement represent an outline package which, in the Government's view, has the potential for securing

general agreement. For its part, the Government would accept an outcome from further Talks along the lines described in these papers. It would also, in principle, accept a range of other outcomes provided that any outcome was broadly acceptable to the other participants.

Annex B: An Outline of a Comprehensive Settlement

1. Drawing on the ideas on local accountability in Part I and on the New Framework for Agreement, it is possible to identify the main elements of where a possible settlement might be found. There might be public support for the following:

- *new political institutions in Northern Ireland* with a wide range of executive and legislative responsibilities. Such institutions would disperse executive responsibilities broadly in proportion to party strengths. There would be two main institutions, an elected Assembly and a separate, complementary body perhaps comprising 3 people—a Panel. There would be checks and balances within and between the Assembly and Panel, and a division of functions between them. There would be greater formal protection for civil rights;
- to cater for the North/South relationship there would be *a new North/South body or bodies*, an interparliamentary forum, an administrative support unit to service the body (or bodies) and the forum, and day-to-day North/South co-operation and communication between Departments, and between counterparts with relevant executive authority at the political level. The source of their authority would stem from the administrations in Belfast and Dublin. All decisions of the North/South body or bodies would be by agreement between the two sides. There would be appropriate political and financial accountability. The new North/South arrangements would be of sufficient strength and quality to further co-operation, mutual understanding and working together in the interests of both parts of the island;
- the Anglo-Irish Agreement would be replaced by a new *and more broadly-based agreement* between the two Governments reflecting the totality of relationships, and with provision for bilateral liaison, through an Intergovernmental Council. There would be a formal Intergovernmental Conference, with suitable rights of attendance and consultation for appropriate representatives of the new Northern Ireland political institutions. There would be a Secretariat to support the conference and provide a channel of communication. The new agreement would be arrived at through direct discussion between the two Governments and the other Talks participants, and Northern Ireland political representatives would play a greater part in it than at present;
- there would be a shared understanding of the constitutional issues, which achieved a balanced accommodation of the differing positions of the two main traditions;
- the overall outcome would be subject to popular endorsement in the form of a referendum in Northern Ireland and an appropriate test of opinion in the Republic.

Relationship between the Different Elements of an Overall Accommodation

2. If a settlement is achieved which addresses all the relevant relationships there would need to be co-ordination between the various structures. The Government envisage that any acceptable overall accommodation could include linkages of the following kinds:

- liaison between representatives of new Northern Ireland institutions such as the Assembly and the Panel and the British Government over transferred matters with implications for non-transferred responsibilities, and vice versa;
- liaison between new North/South institutions and the British Government over transferred matters with implications for the British Government's remaining responsibilities;
- ad hoc attendance by representatives of the British Government at new North/South institutions at their request (eg where the Northern Ireland side have raised matters of concern about non-transferred matters with their Republic of Ireland counterparts, which in turn have implications for the British Government);
- attendance by relevant Northern Ireland Heads of Department, and by Panel members, by invitation, at relevant parts of meetings of the successor to the Intergovernmental Conference;
- liaison outside the successor to the Intergovernmental Conference on non-transferred Northern Ireland matters between representatives of the new Northern Ireland institutions and members of the British and Irish Governments;
- attendance by representatives of the new Northern Ireland political institutions at meetings held under the Anglo-Irish Intergovernmental Council framework, where matters relevant to the new Northern Ireland institutions might arise.

3. This list is not exhaustive. The following possible further linking arrangements could be considered:

- permanent observer status for the British Government at meetings of the new North/South body, provided British Government representatives were not involved in decision taking;
- an umbrella institution for the new Strand 2 and Strand 3 institutions. These would normally meet separately, but could come together for periodic co-ordination or review sessions.

4. The Government, for its part, would be ready to consider linking arrangements of this sort provided the key distinctions between transferred and non-transferred matters, and between Northern Ireland and wider matters, were preserved. Any agreed overall accommodation is unlikely to be able to hold its shape if these distinctions are set aside

Source: United Kingdom (1995: 3–19).

Document 4.11. British-Irish Framework Document, 22 February 1995

A SHARED UNDERSTANDING BETWEEN THE BRITISH AND IRISH GOVERNMENTS TO ASSIST DISCUSSION AND NEGOTIATION INVOLVING THE NORTHERN IRELAND PARTIES

1. The Joint Declaration acknowledges that the most urgent and important issue facing the people of Ireland, North and South, and the British and Irish Governments together, is to remove the causes of conflict, to overcome the legacy of history and to heal the divisions which have resulted.

2. Both Governments recognise that there is much [cause] for deep regret on all sides in the long and often tragic history of Anglo-Irish relations, and of relations in Ireland. They believe it is now time to lay aside, with dignity and forbearance, the mistakes of the past. A collective effort is needed to create, through agreement and reconciliation, a new beginning founded on consent, for relationships within Northern Ireland, within the island of Ireland and between the peoples of these islands. The Joint Declaration itself represents an important step towards this goal, offering the people of Ireland, North and South, whatever their tradition, the basis to agree that from now on their differences can be negotiated and resolved exclusively by peaceful political means.

3. The announcements made by the Irish Republican Army on 31 August 1994 and the Combined Loyalist Military Command on 13 October 1994 are a welcome response to the profound desire of people throughout these islands for a permanent end to the violence which caused such immense suffering and waste and served only to reinforce the barriers of fear and hatred, impeding the search for agreement.

4. A climate of peace enables the process of healing to begin. It transforms the prospects for political progress, building on that already made in the Talks process. Everyone now has a role to play in moving irreversibly beyond the failures of the past and creating new relationships capable of perpetuating peace with freedom and justice.

5. In the Joint Declaration both Governments set themselves the aim of fostering agreement and reconciliation, leading to a new political framework founded on consent. A vital dimension of this three-stranded process is the search, through dialogue with the relevant Northern Ireland parties, for new institutions and structures to take account of the totality of relationships and to enable the people of Ireland to work together in all areas of common interest while fully respecting their diversity.

6. Both Governments are conscious of the widespread desire, throughout both islands and more widely, to see negotiations underway as soon as possible. They also acknowledge the many requests, from parties in Northern Ireland and elsewhere, for both Governments to set out their views on how agreement might be reached on relationships within the island of Ireland and between the peoples of these islands.

7. In this Framework Document both Governments therefore describe a shared understanding reached between them on the parameters of a possible outcome to the Talks process, consistent with the Joint Declaration and the statement of 26 March 1991. Through this they hope to give impetus and direction to the process and to show that a fair and honourable accommodation can be envisaged across all the relationships, which would enable people to work constructively for their mutual benefit, without compromising the essential principles or the long-term aspirations or interests of either tradition or of either community.

8. Both Governments are aware that the approach in this document presents challenges to strongly-held positions on all sides. However, a new beginning in relationships means addressing fundamental issues in a new way and inevitably requires significant movement from all sides. This document is not a rigid blueprint to be imposed but both Governments believe it sets out a realistic and balanced framework for agreement which could be achieved, with flexibility and goodwill on all sides, in comprehensive negotiations with

the relevant political parties in Northern Ireland. In this spirit, both Governments offer this document for consideration and accordingly strongly commend it to the parties, the people in the island of Ireland and more widely.

9. The primary objective of both Governments in their approach to Northern Ireland is to promote and establish agreement among the people of the island of Ireland, building on the Joint Declaration. To this end they will both deploy their political resources with the aim of securing a new and comprehensive agreement involving the relevant political parties in Northern Ireland and commanding the widest possible support.

10. They take as guiding principles for their co-operation in search of this agreement:

(i) the principle of self-determination, as set out in the Joint Declaration;
(ii) that the consent of the governed is an essential ingredient for stability in any political arrangement;
(iii) that agreement must be pursued and established by exclusively democratic, peaceful means, without resort to violence or coercion;
(iv) that any new political arrangements must be based on full respect for, and protection and expression of, the rights and identities of both traditions in Ireland and even-handedly afford both communities in Northern Ireland parity of esteem and treatment, including equality of opportunity and advantage.

11. They acknowledge that in Northern Ireland, unlike the situation which prevails elsewhere throughout both islands, there is a fundamental absence of consensus about constitutional issues. There are deep divisions between the members of the two main traditions living there over their respective senses of identity and allegiance, their views on the present status of Northern Ireland and their vision of future relationships in Ireland and between the two islands. However, the two Governments also recognise that the large majority of people, in both parts of Ireland, are at one in their commitment to the democratic process and in their desire to resolve political differences by peaceful means.

12. In their search for political agreement, based on consent, the two Governments are determined to address in a fresh way all of the relationships involved. Their aim is to overcome the legacy of division by reconciling the rights of both traditions in the fullest and most equitable manner. They will continue to work towards and encourage the achievement of agreement, so as to realise the goal set out in the statement of 26 March 1991 of 'a new beginning for relationships within Northern Ireland, within the island of Ireland and between the peoples of these islands'.

13. The two Governments will work together with the parties to achieve a comprehensive accommodation, the implementation of which would include interlocking and mutually supportive institutions across the three strands, including:

(a) structures within Northern Ireland (paragraphs 22 and 23)—to enable elected representatives in Northern Ireland to exercise shared administrative and legislative control over all those matters that can be agreed across both communities and which can most effectively and appropriately be dealt with at that level;

(b) North/South institutions (paragraphs 24–38)—with clear identity and purpose, to enable representatives of democratic institutions, North and South, to enter into new, co-operative and constructive relationships; to promote agreement among the people of the island of Ireland; to carry out on a democratically accountable basis delegated executive, harmonising and consultative functions over a range of designated matters to be agreed; and to serve to acknowledge and reconcile the rights, identities and aspirations of the two major traditions;

(c) East–West structures (paragraphs 39–49)—to enhance the existing basis for co-operation between the two Governments, and to promote, support and underwrite the fair and effective operation of the new arrangements.

Constitutional Issues

14. Both Governments accept that agreement on an overall settlement requires, inter alia, a balanced accommodation of the differing views of the two main traditions on the constitutional issues in relation to the special position of Northern Ireland.

15. Given the absence of consensus and depth of divisions between the two main traditions in Northern Ireland, the two Governments agree that such an accommodation will involve an agreed new approach to the traditional constitutional doctrines on both sides. This would be aimed at enhancing and codifying the fullest attainable measure of consent across both traditions in Ireland and fostering the growth of consensus between them.

16. In their approach to Northern Ireland they will apply the principle of self-determination by the people of Ireland on the basis set out in the Joint Declaration: the British Government recognise that it is for the people of Ireland alone, by agreement between the two parts respectively and without external impediment, to exercise their right of self-determination on the basis of consent, freely and concurrently given, North and South, to bring about a united Ireland, if that is their wish; the Irish Government accept that the democratic right of self-determination by the people of Ireland as a whole must be achieved and exercised with and subject to the agreement and consent of a majority of the people of Northern Ireland.

17. New arrangements should be in accordance with the commitments in the Anglo-Irish Agreement and in the Joint Declaration. They should acknowledge that it would be wrong to make any change in the status of Northern Ireland save with the consent of a majority of the people of Northern Ireland. If in future a majority of the people there wish for and formally consent to the establishment of a united Ireland, the two Governments will introduce and support legislation to give effect to that wish.

18. Both Governments recognise that Northern Ireland's current constitutional status reflects and relies upon the present wish of a majority of its people. They also acknowledge that at present a substantial minority of its people wish for a united Ireland. Reaffirming the commitment to encourage, facilitate and enable the achievement of agreement over a period among all the people who inhabit the island, they acknowledge that the option of a sovereign united Ireland does not command the consent of the unionist tradition, nor does the existing status of Northern Ireland command the consent of the nationalist tradition. Against this background, they acknowledge the need for new arrangements and

structures—to reflect the reality of diverse aspirations, to reconcile as fully as possible the rights of both traditions, and to promote co-operation between them, so as to foster the process of developing agreement and consensus between all the people of Ireland.

19. They agree that future arrangements relating to Northern Ireland, and Northern Ireland's wider relationships, should respect the full and equal legitimacy and worth of the identity, sense of allegiance, aspiration and ethos of both the unionist and nationalist communities there. Consequently, both Governments commit themselves to the principle that institutions and arrangements in Northern Ireland and North/South institutions should afford both communities secure and satisfactory political, administrative and symbolic expression and protection. In particular, they commit themselves to entrenched provisions guaranteeing equitable and effective political participation for whichever community finds itself in a minority position by reference to the Northern Ireland framework, or the wider Irish framework, as the case may be, consequent upon the operation of the principle of consent.

20. The British Government reaffirm that they will uphold the democratic wish of a greater number of the people of Northern Ireland on the issue of whether they prefer to support the Union or a sovereign united Ireland. On this basis, they reiterate that they have no selfish strategic or economic interest in Northern Ireland. For as long as the democratic wish of the people of Northern Ireland is for no change in its present status, the British Government pledge that their jurisdiction there will be exercised with rigorous impartiality on behalf of all the people of Northern Ireland in their diversity. It will be founded on the principles outlined in the previous paragraph with emphasis on full respect for, and equality of, civil, political, social and cultural rights and freedom from discrimination for all citizens, on parity of esteem, and on just and equal treatment for the identity, ethos and aspirations of both communities. The British Government will discharge their responsibilities in a way which does not prejudice the freedom of the people of Northern Ireland to determine, by peaceful and democratic means, its future constitutional status, whether in remaining a part of the United Kingdom or in forming part of a united Ireland. They will be equally cognizant of either option and open to its democratic realisation, and will not impede the latter option, their primary interest being to see peace, stability and reconciliation established by agreement among the people who inhabit the island. This new approach for Northern Ireland, based on the continuing willingness to accept the will of a majority of the people there, will be enshrined in British constitutional legislation embodying the principles and commitments in the Joint Declaration and this Framework Document, either by amendment of the Government of Ireland Act 1920 or by its replacement by appropriate new legislation, and appropriate new provisions entrenched by agreement.

21. As part of an agreement confirming the foregoing understanding between the two Governments on constitutional issues, the Irish Government will introduce and support proposals for change in the Irish Constitution to implement the commitments in the Joint Declaration. These changes in the Irish Constitution will fully reflect the principle of consent in Northern Ireland and demonstrably be such that no territorial claim of right to jurisdiction over Northern Ireland contrary to the will of a majority of its people is asserted, while maintaining the existing birthright of everyone born in either jurisdiction in

Ireland to be part, as of right, of the Irish nation. They will enable a new Agreement to be ratified which will include, as part of a new and equitable dispensation for Northern Ireland embodying the principles and commitments in the Joint Declaration and this Framework Document, recognition by both Governments of the legitimacy of whatever choice is freely exercised by a majority of the people of Northern Ireland with regard to its constitutional status, whether they prefer to continue to support the Union or a sovereign united Ireland.

Structures in Northern Ireland

22. Both Governments recognise that new political structures within Northern Ireland must depend on the co-operation of elected representatives there. They confirm that cross-community agreement is an essential requirement for the establishment and operation of such structures. They strongly favour and will support provision for cross-community consensus in relation to decisions affecting the basic rights, concerns and fundamental interests of both communities, for example on the lines adumbrated in Strand 1 discussions in the 1992 round-table talks.

23. While the principles and overall context for such new structures are a recognised concern of both Governments in the exercise of their respective responsibilities, they consider that the structures themselves would be most effectively negotiated, as part of a comprehensive three-stranded process, in direct dialogue involving the relevant political parties in Northern Ireland who would be called upon to operate them.

North/South Institutions

24. Both Governments consider that new institutions should be created to cater adequately for present and future political, social and economic inter-connections on the island of Ireland, enabling representatives of the main traditions, North and South, to enter agreed dynamic, new, co-operative and constructive relationships.

25. Both Governments agree that these institutions should include a North/South body involving Heads of Department on both sides and duly established and maintained by legislation in both sovereign Parliaments. This body would bring together these Heads of Department representing the Irish Government and new democratic institutions in Northern Ireland, to discharge or oversee delegated executive, harmonising or consultative functions, as appropriate, over a range of matters which the two Governments designate in the first instance in agreement with the parties or which the two administrations, North and South, subsequently agree to designate. It is envisaged that, in determining functions to be discharged or overseen by the North/South body, whether by executive action, harmonisation or consultation, account will be taken of:

(i) the common interest in a given matter on the part of both parts of the island; or

(ii) the mutual advantage of addressing a matter together; or

(iii) the mutual benefit which may derive from it being administered by the North/South body; or

(iv) the achievement of economies of scale and the avoidance of unnecessary duplication of effort.

In relevant posts in each of the two administrations participation in the North/South body would be a duty of service. Both Governments believe that the legislation should provide for a clear institutional identity and purpose for the North/South body. It would also establish the body's terms of reference, legal status and arrangements for political, legal, administrative and financial accountability. The North/South body could operate through, or oversee, a range of functionally-related subsidiary bodies or other entities established to administer designated functions on an all-island or cross-border basis.

26. Specific arrangements would need to be developed to apply to EU matters. Any EU matter relevant to the competence of either administration could be raised for consideration in the North/South body. Across all designated matters and in accordance with the delegated functions, both Governments agree that the body will have an important role, with their support and co-operation and in consultation with them, in developing on a continuing basis an agreed approach for the whole island in respect of the challenges and opportunities of the European Union. In respect of matters designated at the executive level, which would include all EC programmes and initiatives to be implemented on a cross-border or island-wide basis in Ireland, the body itself would be responsible, subject to the Treaty obligations of each Government, for the implementation and management of EC policies and programmes on a joint basis. This would include the preparation, in consultation with the two Governments, of joint submissions under EC programmes and initiatives and their joint monitoring and implementation, although individual projects could be implemented either jointly or separately.

27. Both Governments envisage regular and frequent meetings of the North/South body:

- to discharge the functions agreed for it in relation to a range of matters designated for treatment on an all-Ireland or cross-border basis;
- to oversee the work of subsidiary bodies.

28. The two Governments envisage that legislation in the sovereign Parliaments should designate those functions which should, from the outset, be discharged or overseen by the North/South body; and they will seek agreement on these, as on other features of North/South arrangements, in discussion with the relevant political parties in Northern Ireland. It would also be open to the North/South body to recommend to the respective administrations and legislatures for their consideration that new functions should be designated to be discharged or overseen by that body; and to recommend that matters already designated should be moved on the scale between consultation, harmonisation and executive action. Within those responsibilities transferred to new institutions in Northern Ireland, the British Government have no limits of their own to impose on the nature and extent of functions which could be agreed for designation at the outset or, subsequently, between the Irish Government and the Northern Ireland administration. Both Governments expect that significant responsibilities, including meaningful functions at executive level, will be a feature of such agreement. The British Government believe that, in principle, any function devolved to the institutions in Northern Ireland could be so designated, subject to any necessary savings in respect of the British Government's powers and duties, for example to ensure compliance with EU and international obligations. The Irish Government also expect to designate a comparable range of functions.

29. Although both Governments envisage that representatives of North and South in the body could raise for discussion any matter of interest to either side which falls within the competence of either administration, it is envisaged, as already mentioned, that its designated functions would fall into three broad categories:

consultative: the North/South body would be a forum where the two sides would consult on any aspect of designated matters on which either side wished to hold consultations. Both sides would share a duty to exchange information and to consult about existing and future policy, though there would be no formal requirement that agreement would be reached or that policy would be harmonised or implemented jointly, but the development of mutual understanding or common or agreed positions would be the general goal;

harmonising: in respect of these designated responsibilities there would be, in addition to the duty to exchange information and to consult on the formulation of policy, an obligation on both sides to use their best endeavours to reach agreement on a common policy and to make determined efforts to overcome any obstacles in the way of that objective, even though its implementation might be undertaken by the two administrations separately;

executive: in the case of these designated responsibilities the North/South body would itself be directly responsible for the establishment of an agreed policy and for its implementation on a joint basis. It would however be open to the body, where appropriate, to agree that the implementation of the agreed policy would be undertaken either by existing bodies, acting in an agency capacity, whether jointly or separately, North and South, or by new bodies specifically created and mandated for this purpose.

30. In this light, both Governments are continuing to give consideration to the range of functions that might, with the agreement of the parties, be designated at the outset and accordingly they will be ready to make proposals in that regard in future discussions with the relevant Northern Ireland parties.

31. By way of illustration, it is intended that these proposals would include at the executive level a range of functions, clearly defined in scope, from within the following broad categories:

- sectors involving a natural or physical all-Ireland framework;
- EC programmes and initiatives;
- marketing and promotion activities abroad; and
- culture and heritage.

32. Again, by way of illustration, the Governments would make proposals at the harmonising level for a broader range of functions, clearly defined in scope (including, as appropriate, relevant EU aspects), from within the following categories:

aspects of—

agriculture and fisheries;
industrial development;

consumer affairs;
transport;
energy;
trade;
health;
social welfare;
education; and
economic policy.

33. By way of example, the category of agriculture and fisheries might include agricultural and fisheries research, training and advisory services, and animal welfare; health might include co-operative ventures in medical, paramedical and nursing training, cross-border provision of hospital services and major emergency/accident planning; and education might include mutual recognition of teacher qualifications, co-operative ventures in higher education, in teacher training, in education for mutual understanding and in education for specialised needs.

34. The Governments also expect that a wide range of functions would be designated at the consultative level.

35. Both Governments envisage that all decisions within the body would be by agreement between the two sides. The Heads of Department on each side would operate within the overall terms of reference mandated by legislation in the two sovereign Parliaments. They would exercise their powers in accordance with the rules for democratic authority and accountability for this function in force in the Oireachtas and in new institutions in Northern Ireland. The operation of the North/South body's functions would be subject to regular scrutiny in agreed political institutions in Northern Ireland and the Oireachtas respectively.

36. Both Governments expect that there would be a Parliamentary Forum, with representatives from agreed political institutions in Northern Ireland and members of the Oireachtas, to consider a wide range of matters of mutual interest.

37. Both Governments envisage that the framework would include administrative support staffed jointly by members of the Northern Ireland Civil Service and the Irish Civil Service. They also envisage that both administrations will need to arrange finance for the North/South body and its agencies on the basis that these constitute a necessary public function.

38. Both Governments envisage that this new framework should serve to help heal the divisions among the communities on the island of Ireland; provide a forum for acknowledging the respective identities and requirements of the two major traditions; express and enlarge the mutual acceptance of the validity of those traditions; and promote understanding and agreement among the people and institutions in both parts of the island. The remit of the body should be dynamic, enabling progressive extension by agreement of its functions to new areas. Its role should develop to keep pace with the growth of harmonisation and with greater integration between the two economies.

East–West Structures

39. Both Governments envisage a new and more broadly-based Agreement, developing and extending their co-operation, reflecting the totality of relationships between the two islands, and dedicated to fostering co-operation, reconciliation and agreement in Ireland at all levels.

40. They intend that under such a new Agreement a standing Intergovernmental Conference will be maintained, chaired by the designated Irish Minister and by the Secretary of State for Northern Ireland. It would be supported by a Permanent Secretariat of civil servants from both Governments.

41. The Conference will be a forum through which the two Governments will work together in pursuance of their joint objectives of securing agreement and reconciliation amongst the people of the island of Ireland and of laying the foundations for a peaceful and harmonious future based on mutual trust and understanding between them.

42. The Conference will provide a continuing institutional expression for the Irish Government's recognised concern and role in relation to Northern Ireland. The Irish Government will put forward views and proposals on issues falling within the ambit of the new Conference or involving both Governments, and determined efforts will be made to resolve any differences between the two Governments. The Conference will be the principal instrument for an intensification of the co-operation and partnership between both Governments, with particular reference to the principles contained in the Joint Declaration, in this Framework Document and in the new Agreement, on a wide range of issues concerned with Northern Ireland and with the relations between the two parts of the island of Ireland. It will facilitate the promotion of lasting peace, stability, justice and reconciliation among the people of the island of Ireland and maintenance of effective security co-operation between the two Governments.

43. Both Governments believe that there should also be provision in the Agreement for developing co-operation between the two Governments and both islands on a range of 'East-West' issues and bilateral matters of mutual interest not covered by other specific arrangements, either through the Anglo-Irish Intergovernmental Council, the Conference or otherwise.

44. Both Governments accept that issues of law and order in Northern Ireland are closely intertwined with the issues of political consensus. For so long as these matters are not devolved, it will be for the Governments to consider ways in which a climate of peace, new institutions and the growth of political agreement may offer new possibilities and opportunities for enhancing community identification with policing in Northern Ireland, while maintaining the most effective possible deployment of the resources of each Government in their common determination to combat crime and prevent any possible recourse to the use or threat of violence for political ends, from any source whatsoever.

45. The Governments envisage that matters for which responsibility is transferred to new political institutions in Northern Ireland will be excluded from consideration in the Conference, except to the extent that the continuing responsibilities of the Secretary of

State for Northern Ireland are relevant, or that cross-border aspects of transferred issues are not otherwise provided for, or in the circumstances described in the following paragraph.

46. The Intergovernmental Conference will be a forum for the two Governments jointly to keep under review the workings of the Agreement and to promote, support and underwrite the fair and effective operation of all its provisions and the new arrangements established under it. Where either Government considers that any institution, established as part of the overall accommodation, is not properly functioning within the Agreement or that a breach of the Agreement has otherwise occurred, the Conference shall consider the matter on the basis of a shared commitment to arrive at a common position or, where that is not possible, to agree a procedure to resolve the difference between them. If the two Governments conclude that a breach has occurred in any of the above circumstances, either Government may make proposals for remedy and adequate measures to redress the situation shall be taken. However, each Government will be responsible for the implementation of such measures of redress within its own jurisdiction. There would be no derogation from the sovereignty of either Government; each will retain responsibility for the decisions and administration of government within its own jurisdiction.

47. In the event that devolved institutions in Northern Ireland ceased to operate, and direct rule from Westminster was reintroduced, the British Government agree that other arrangements would be made to implement the commitment to promote co-operation at all levels between the people, North and South, representing both traditions in Ireland, as agreed by the two Governments in the Joint Declaration, and to ensure that the co-operation that had been developed through the North/South body be maintained.

48. Both Governments envisage that representatives of agreed political institutions in Northern Ireland may be formally associated with the work of the Conference, in a manner and to an extent to be agreed by both Governments after consultation with them. This might involve giving them advance notice of what is to be discussed in the Conference, enabling them to express views to either Government and inviting them to participate in various aspects of the work of the Conference. Other more structured arrangements could be devised by agreement.

49. The Conference will also be a framework for consultation and coordination between both Governments and the new North/South institutions, where the wider role of the two Governments is particularly relevant to the work of those institutions, for example in a co-ordinated approach on EU issues. It would be for consideration by both Governments, in consultation with the relevant parties in the North, or with the institutions after they have been established, whether to achieve this through formal or ad hoc arrangements.

Protection of Rights

50. There is a large body of support, transcending the political divide, for the comprehensive protection and guarantee of fundamental human rights. Acknowledging this, both Governments envisage that the arrangements set out in this Framework Document will be complemented and underpinned by an explicit undertaking in the Agreement on the part

of each Government, equally, to ensure in its jurisdiction in the island of Ireland, in accordance with its constitutional arrangements, the systematic and effective protection of common specified civil, political, social and cultural rights. They will discuss and seek agreement with the relevant political parties in Northern Ireland as to what rights should be so specified and how they might best be further protected, having regard to each Government's overall responsibilities including its international obligations. Each Government will introduce appropriate legislation in its jurisdiction to give effect to any such measure of agreement.

51. In addition, both Governments would encourage democratic representatives from both jurisdictions in Ireland to adopt a Charter or Covenant, which might reflect and endorse agreed measures for the protection of the fundamental rights of everyone living in Ireland. It could also pledge a commitment to mutual respect and to the civil rights and religious liberties of both communities, including:

- the right of free political thought,
- the right to freedom and expression of religion,
- the right to pursue democratically national and political aspirations,
- the right to seek constitutional change by peaceful and legitimate means,
- the right to live wherever one chooses without hindrance,
- the right to equal opportunity in all social and economic activity, regardless of class, creed, gender or colour.

52. This Charter or Covenant might also contain a commitment to the principle of consent in the relationships between the two traditions in Ireland. It could incorporate also an enduring commitment on behalf of all the people of the island to guarantee and protect the rights, interests, ethos and dignity of the unionist community in any all-Ireland framework that might be developed with consent in the future, to at least the same extent as provided for the nationalist community in the context of Northern Ireland under the structures and provisions of the new Agreement.

53. The Covenant might also affirm on behalf of all traditions in Ireland a solemn commitment to the exclusively peaceful resolution of all differences between them including in relation to all issues of self-determination, and a solemn repudiation of all recourse to violence between them for any political end or purpose.

Conclusion

54. Both Governments agree that the issues set out in this Framework Document should be examined in the most comprehensive attainable negotiations with democratically mandated political parties in Northern Ireland which abide exclusively by peaceful means and wish to join in dialogue on the way ahead.

55. Both Governments intend that the outcome of these negotiations will be submitted for democratic ratification through referendums, North and South.

56. Both Governments believe that the present climate of peace, which owes much to the imagination, courage and steadfastness of all those who have suffered from violence, offers the best prospect for the Governments and the parties in Northern Ireland to work

to secure agreement and consent to a new political accommodation. To accomplish that would be an inestimable prize for all, and especially for people living in Northern Ireland, who have so much to gain from such an accommodation, in which the divisions of the past are laid aside for ever and differences are resolved by exclusively political means. Both Governments believe that a new political dispensation, such as they set out in this Framework Document, achieved through agreement and reconciliation and founded on the principle of consent, would achieve that objective and transform relationships in Northern Ireland, in the island of Ireland and between both islands.

57. With agreement, co-operation to the mutual benefit of all living in Ireland could develop without impediment, attaining its full potential for stimulating economic growth and prosperity. New arrangements could return power, authority and responsibility to locally-elected representatives in Northern Ireland on a basis acceptable to both sides of the community, enabling them to work together for the common welfare and interests of all the community. The diversity of identities and allegiances could be regarded by all as a source of mutual enrichment, rather than a threat to either side. The divisive issue of sovereignty might cease to be symbolic of the domination of one community over another. It would instead be for decision under agreed ground-rules, fair and balanced towards both aspirations, through a process of democratic persuasion governed by the principle of consent rather than by threat, fear or coercion. In such circumstances the Governments hope that the relationship between the traditions in Northern Ireland could become a positive bond of further understanding, co-operation and amity, rather than a source of contention, between the wider British and Irish democracies.

58. Accordingly the British and Irish Governments offer for consideration and strongly commend these proposals, trusting that, with generosity and goodwill, the peoples of these islands will build on them a new and lasting agreement.

Source: United Kingdom (1995: 23–37).

5

The Good Friday Agreement, 1998: Negotiation

5.1. Introduction

The Good Friday Agreement of 1998 marks the culmination of the intensive British–Irish negotiations of the 1990s. The Downing Street Declaration of 1993 had articulated clearly the principles that the British and Irish governments expected to underlie a constitutional settlement, and the Framework Documents of 1995 had outlined its probable institutional form. The Good Friday Agreement brought the Northern Ireland political parties directly into the negotiations. The eventual agreement—a full three years after the publication of the Framework Documents—was widely seen as a major advance in resolving the conflict.

The Good Friday Agreement of 10 April 1998 invites comparison with the Sunningdale Agreement of 1973, with which it shares certain structural features: power-sharing devolution, British–Irish involvement, and an Irish dimension. It was reached, however, in an utterly different political context in Britain and Ireland, and in Northern Ireland in particular. Strong and stable governments took office in 1997 in the United Kingdom and the Republic of Ireland, and there was new US interest and involvement in resolving the conflict. A changing political framework in the United Kingdom, with 'devolution all around', provided a favourable context for negotiations in Northern Ireland.

Within Northern Ireland itself, the 1994 ceasefires by the main loyalist and republican paramilitary organizations facilitated a change in strategic direction. The energies of loyalist and especially of republican activists were now channelled down a more political path (represented most dramatically in the electoral rise of Sinn Féin). Strong equality legislation in 1989 with effective machinery for implementing this, a changing socio-demographic balance, and greater cultural expression for nationalists provided a sense that the trajectory was moving towards greater communal equality This gave republicans some confidence that they could use negotiations and participation in agreed institutions to advance their long-term political aims. For precisely the same reasons—rooted in a perception that demographic and socio-economic change was likely to undermine the unionist position—unionists were under pressure to reach an accommodation before their resources weakened further. In addition, the Anglo-Irish Agreement of 1985, by strengthening the role of the Irish government in the absence of

Negotiating a Settlement in Northern Ireland, 1969–2019.
John Coakley and Jennifer Todd, Oxford University Press (2020). © John Coakley and Jennifer Todd.
DOI: 10.1093/oso/9780198841388.001.0001

devolution, gave unionists a powerful incentive to negotiate an alternative. The Good Friday Agreement was therefore the product of several strands of change that converged in 1997–8. The Downing Street Declaration and its principles for negotiation, and the Framework Documents with their institutional plan, provided the structure and impetus for a new round of inter-party talks that began in 1996, that would come in 1997 to include Sinn Féin, and that would result ultimately in the Good Friday Agreement.

The formal provisions of the Agreement, and the processes by which its key features were negotiated at political level, are relatively well known.[1] Specialized studies have provided a detailed analytical account of the institutions and processes of governance that emerged from the Agreement.[2] These works have clarified the ways in which the consociational provisions of the Good Friday Agreement differ from power-sharing in Sunningdale, and they have documented the much more elaborate reform provisions in the 1998 Agreement.

Debates continue on the rationale, meaning, and trajectory of the Good Friday Agreement. Did the parties enter agreement because new opportunities were opening for the main groups, or because the constitutional preconditions of nationalists had now been met (albeit in redefined form), or because the IRA was on the verge of defeat?[3] The meaning of the Agreement was contested from the start. Within days, Paul Bew published an article under the title 'The unionists have won, they just don't know it'.[4] The lowering of nationalist expectations has been emphasized by a range of scholars, with related judgements in respect of the role of Sinn Féin.[5] Others, however, have seen the constitutional arrangement less as a unionist victory than as a 'post-sovereigntist' squaring of the circle between nationalists and unionists, through a transformation in British and Irish interpretations of sovereignty and principles of territorial management with respect to Northern Ireland.[6] Some have emphasized the balance the Good Friday Agreement offered to the parties, although they have variously interpreted this by reference to its consociational provisions, its mechanisms designed to ensure

---

[1] On the institutional position, see McCrudden (1999) and McGarry and O'Leary (2004), and, on the negotiation process, see the several autobiographical or academic studies produced by some of the participants listed in Appendix 1.1. For other analyses, see Clancy (2010); Cox, Guelke, and Stephen (2006); De Bréadún (2008); Elliott (2007); Mallie and McKittrick (1996); Ruane and Todd (1999).

[2] On policing, see Doyle (2010); Mulcahy (2006); on power-sharing, Coakley (2009c, 2011); McEvoy (2015); McGarry and O'Leary (2004, 2008); Taylor (2009); on rights, Harvey (2001); Morison (2001); Ó Cinnéide (2013); on independent commissions, Walsh (2017); on North–South institutions, Coakley (2005, 2014); on elections, Garry (2016).

[3] For different views, see Bew, Frampton, and Gurruchaga (2009); O'Leary (2005); Ruane and Todd (2001).

[4] This was the title given by the newspaper editors, but it expresses the thrust of Bew's argument; see Bew (1998).

[5] For different views, see the contributors to Bric and Coakley (2004); see also McIntyre (1995); O'Leary (2005).

[6] Keating (2001); Meehan (2014); Morison (2001); Todd (2014, 2017).

inclusion, and its provisions in respect of cultural and socio-economic equality.[7] Finally, there are disagreements as to whether it is appropriate to see the Good Friday Agreement as a founding document—lodged internationally as the British–Irish Agreement—which acts as an informal constitution for Northern Ireland, or whether the relevant documents and principles are the British-enacted Northern Ireland Act, 1998, and its successors.[8]

The different party and government perspectives on the negotiations, the party decisions to accept the provisions of the Agreement in April 1998, and the rationale behind these decisions are of crucial importance when we consider these questions. They reveal the interpretations that were then invested in the Agreement and in its institutions, and that continue to be so invested. Institutions are more than buildings, as Jeffrey Donaldson says.[9] They are constituted by the people, parties, and politicians who work them, whose expectations, assumptions, and practices crucially shape institutional functioning.

From this perspective, the standpoint of the two governments is expressed not solely or primarily in law, but also in the various political judgements and informal encounters throughout the processes of negotiation and implementation. It is thus especially important to identify the interpretations and assumptions that each government (and its several agencies) brought to bear on the Agreement. This permits us to pinpoint those areas that have been particularly vulnerable to intergovernmental tensions, and to identify how they were, or were not, resolved.

The Agreement was deliberately designed to accommodate different interpretations. For example, the fact that the United Kingdom was legitimately in control of Northern Ireland was clear, but the implications of British sovereignty for cultural status, national expression, and cross-border links was not; neither did the Agreement define the ground of British state sovereignty in Northern Ireland. This 'constructive ambiguity' permitted agreement to be reached, but the difference in interpretations held open the prospect of future crises (see Chapters 6 and 7). It is important to see whether and how those interpretations were opposed from the start, and how far opposition hardened later.

The Agreement set in place not simply a set of institutions governed by formal provisions and laws, but also a set of expectations, incentives, and coordination practices responsive to the wider institutional matrix and underpinned by norms that were never fully articulated and that were in crucial respects ambiguous. To understand the politics of the time, and the politics that follows, it is essential to take into account the perceptions, expectations, and rationales of the actors involved. The interviews provide access to the parties' and the governments'

---

[7] See McGarry and O'Leary (2004); Ó Dochartaigh (2015); Ruane and Todd (2007, 2014); Tonge, Shirlow, and McAuley (2011); Wolff (2005).

[8] For the different implications of these respective stances, see Hadfield (1998) and McGarry and O'Leary (2004).

[9] See final paragraph of Subsection 5.3.2.

views. The party-political interviews conducted in 1998–9 provide important contemporary assessments before the provisions of the Agreement had again become politicized.

5.1.1. Political Context

The negotiation of the Agreement took place against a radically shifting political backdrop, with changes of government on both the British and the Irish sides. On the British side, the Conservative government of John Major was replaced in May 1997 by the Labour administration of Tony Blair, who was to remain in office until June 2007. The change was not merely one of political labels and party programmes: the Major government had an insecure position in the House of Commons, giving the Ulster Unionist Party considerable influence as a potential ally (or opponent) of the government. The new Labour government, however, came in with a huge majority, leaving it in a much more secure position. On the Irish side, the coalition headed by John Bruton was replaced after an election in June 1997 by a Fianna Fáil–Progressive Democrat coalition led by Bertie Ahern, who remained in office until May 2008.

As discussed in Chapter 4, the Downing Street Declaration had held out the promise of negotiations between 'democratically mandated parties which establish a commitment to exclusively peaceful methods and which have shown that they abide by the democratic process', and the Framework Documents were formally designed to define the broad parameters within which the British and Irish governments believed negotiations should take place. But other obstacles to negotiations presented themselves, notably a new British precondition for admission of Sinn Féin to the planned negotiation process (for important developments, see Table 5.1). The British government took the view that Sinn Féin's participation in negotiations depended on the 'decommissioning' of IRA weapons. By contrast, the Irish government's position was that sustained ceasefires were sufficient. At a conference organized by the State Department in Washington on 7 March 1995, Secretary of State Mayhew offered a three-point summary of a position that had been articulated by the British government for several months: before Sinn Féin could enter talks there would have to be (1) a willingness in principle to disarm progressively, (2) agreement on the modalities of achieving this, and (3) 'the actual decommissioning of some arms as a tangible confidence building measure and to signal the start of a process'.[10]

The third of these points, quickly labelled 'Washington Three', became a formidable obstacle to Sinn Féin's admission to the planned talks process.

---

[10] Mitchell (2000: 25); for political context, see also Cunningham (2001: 96–7).

Table 5.1. Important political developments, 1995–98

7 March 1995	Northern Ireland Secretary Mayhew announces conditions for entry to political talks (including decommissioning)
28 November 1995	British and Irish governments announce 'twin-track' approach: (1) inter-party talks; (2) creation of an international body on decommissioning
24 January 1996	International body on decommissioning issues its report (Mitchell report); recommends decommissioning alongside rather than as a prerequisite to talks
9 February 1996	IRA bomb in London signals end of ceasefire; ceasefire resumed 20 July 1997
30 May 1996	Election to Northern Ireland Forum; last meets 24 April 1998
10 June 1996	Beginning of multi-party talks in Belfast (excludes Sinn Féin)
1 May 1997	Election to UK House of Commons leads to Labour government led by Tony Blair; Mo Mowlam as Northern Ireland Secretary
26 August 1997	Governments establish an Independent International Commission on Decommissioning; chair, John de Chastelain); final report, 4 July 2011
15 September 1997	Multi-party talks resumed, now including Sinn Féin; DUP leave
12 January 1998	British and Irish governments present proposed heads of agreement
6 April 1998	'Mitchell draft' summarises possible shape of overall agreement
10 April 1998	Good Friday Agreement

An international body chaired by American Senator George Mitchell recommended on 24 January 1996 that the stalemate be resolved by means of a less absolute formula: the acceptance by all parties of exclusively democratic means to achieve political goals, and a commitment that weapons would be decommissioned in due course (the details were spelt out as six 'principles'; see Document 5.1, para. 20). The IRA, however, responded to the impasse by abandoning its ceasefire and engaging in a bombing attack in Canary Wharf, London, on 9 February 1996, stating that the British government had 'acted in bad faith with Mr Major and the Unionist leaders squandering this unprecedented opportunity to resolve the conflict'.[11]

Persisting in its efforts to start negotiations, the British government called an election to a Northern Ireland Forum for Political Dialogue on 30 May 1996. This was designed not just to provide a venue for discussion but also to give parties a fresh mandate to enter talks. It was, however, criticized by the SDLP and Sinn Féin, since it appeared to give priority to the 'internal' dimension of the conflict (strand one, as it became known). Special efforts were made to secure the representation of smaller parties with loyalist paramilitary links by using a special

---

[11] *Irish Times*, 10 February 1996.

Table 5.2. Results of election to Northern Ireland Forum, 1996

Party	votes	seats
Ulster Unionist Party	24.2	30
Democratic Unionist Party	18.8	24
UK Unionist Party	3.7	3
Progressive Unionist Party	3.5	2
Ulster Democratic Party	2.2	2
Other unionist	0.8	0
Alliance Party	6.5	7
NI Women's Coalition	1.0	2
Labour (NI)	0.9	2
Green Party	0.5	0
Other centre	1.1	0
SDLP	21.4	21
Sinn Féin	15.5	17
Other nationalist	0.0	0
Total.	100.0	110

Source: Computed from ARK (2019); Electoral Office for Northern Ireland (2019).

and unusual variant of the party-list system in the elections.[12] Although the Forum met periodically from 14 June 1996 to 24 April 1998, its deliberations were overshadowed by negotiations between parties and governments outside this framework. It did, however, provide a basis on which parties were invited to participate in all-party talks.

The composition of the Forum is summarized in Table 5.2. The five main parties were returned to the Forum (and, by extension, were represented in the talks process) following the same pattern as in local elections (with the Ulster Unionist Party as the largest party, followed by the DUP, and then by the two nationalist parties, the SDLP and Sinn Féin). Significantly, the Alliance Party was joined in the centre by two new groups: the Women's Coalition (formed just before the election, and strongly committed to an inclusive settlement) and a Labour coalition (made up of independent labour-leaning candidates). Of great importance was the inclusion of two unionist groups seen as reflecting the thinking of loyalist paramilitaries (the Progressive Unionist Party, close to the

[12] The electoral system provided for the return of ninety members of the 1996 Forum from eighteen five-member constituencies using a conventional closed-list system. A further twenty seats were allocated to the ten parties winning most votes (two to each). The Secretary of State was forced to intervene to designate the eligible parties to prevent the five largest parties from winning all twenty seats by resorting to tactical splits. The five additional parties that won two seats each were the UK Unionist Party (which would otherwise have won only one seat), and four parties which would not otherwise have won any: the Progressive Unionist Party, the Ulster Democratic Party, the Women's Coalition, and the Northern Ireland Labour Party.

Ulster Volunteer Force, and the Ulster Democratic Party, close to the Ulster Defence Association). A small party opposed to power-sharing, the UK Unionist Party, was also represented (one of its representatives was former Irish government minister Conor Cruise O'Brien).

5.1.2. Negotiations

The inter-party negotiations (excluding Sinn Féin) began in Stormont on 10 June 1996. They operated under guidelines agreed by the British and Irish governments, and, despite initial unionist objections, were chaired by Senator George Mitchell. The talks made little progress in their early months. The return of a new Labour government following the British general election of 1 May 1997 gave a fresh momentum to the process; unlike the outgoing Major government, it had a large parliamentary majority that gave it much greater freedom of action. Moreover, the Blair government quickly made clear its new stance on participation in the negotiations: Sinn Féin would be admitted to talks if the IRA reinstated its ceasefire and Sinn Féin accepted the democratic and peaceful path to political progress. Its new Northern Ireland Secretary, Mo Mowlam, also gave notice to unionists that 'the status quo is not an option', with the clear implication that if they did not negotiate their voice would not be heard in devising new arrangements for governance.

This new political environment led to a change in the republican position: the IRA reinstated its ceasefire on 20 July 1997. Sinn Féin accepted the Mitchell principles on 9 September and entered the talks process. Its presence, however, resulted in the permanent withdrawal of the DUP and of the small UK Unionist Party. All of the other parties that had secured representation in the Forum remained part of the negotiation process, and accepted the Agreement reached on 10 April 1998 under Mitchell's chairmanship.

Senator George Mitchell's role as chair of the multi-party negotiations received international support from co-chairs General John de Chastelain (a former head of the Canadian armed forces) and Harri Holkeri (a former Finnish prime minister). In their early stages (in 1996–7) the negotiations had involved Taoiseach John Bruton and Prime Minister John Major, as well as Northern Ireland Secretary Sir Patrick Mayhew and Tánaiste and Foreign Minister Dick Spring. Following the 1997 general elections in the Republic and the UK, the leading players were Taoiseach Bertie Ahern and Prime Minister Tony Blair, and Northern Ireland Secretary Mo Mowlam and Foreign Ministers Ray Burke and then David Andrews. The process was assisted by other politicians and by a large number of officials from the two jurisdictions.

The talks took place within ground rules that were agreed following prolonged negotiations between the parties, and were divided into three 'strands'—internal to Northern Ireland, North–South, and British–Irish. They followed the rule that 'nothing is agreed until everything is agreed', designed to maximize the acceptability of the final package, in that each party could be satisfied that compromise on one issue would not affect its overall interests. The chairpersons also introduced a new ground rule, that decommissioning would be discussed in a separate set of meetings (chaired by John de Chastelain) so that it did not intrude on the political discussions. The first stage of the talks involved plenary sessions, described by one participant as akin to the horse riders at the Dublin Horse Show walking around the ring and looking at the jumps before beginning the competition. They nevertheless helped the parties to develop a shared language.[13] The effective negotiations were bilateral (between representatives of one or sometimes two governments and one party) and sequential (with the talks moving along from party to party), rather than multilateral and simultaneous. The larger parties had a greater degree of access and input.

The urgency of discussions increased after Christmas 1997, when a series of loyalist murders threatened to derail the process. The negotiations were pushed ahead vigorously by the British and Irish governments, which published their own brief document, a proposed 'heads of agreement', on 12 January 1998 (see Document 5.2), following up with documents outlining options for strands two and three on 27 January. On 26 March, George Mitchell declared a deadline of Easter (or, more specifically, Thursday, 9 April) for the conclusion of the talks. Just before this expired, on 6 April 1998, he circulated a draft of a potential agreement (see Document 5.3). Though labelled the 'Mitchell Draft', this had in fact been put together by the two governments on the basis of their exchanges with the parties.

The governments were also responsible for drafting the final agreement, based on horse-trading with the parties. On the final days and nights, negotiations were non-stop, and it looked as if Mitchell's deadline would be missed. They indeed spilled over into Good Friday, and not until the very last moment was it clear that an agreement had been reached. In the final hours, agreement rested on informal undertakings as well as on a formally agreed document.[14] The best-known example is a letter on Good Friday from Tony Blair to Ulster Unionist leader David Trimble indicating that it was the British government intent that, without decommissioning, republicans would not sit in the executive. Although this was not spelt out in the Agreement itself, it was critical in securing Ulster Unionist acceptance of the deal.

---

[13] See Subsection 5.4.2.
[14] For the text of the Agreement, see Document 5.4.

5.1.3. Provisions of the Good Friday Agreement

The core institutional aspects of the Agreement revolved around the three 'strands' that had been central to the negotiation process since 1991, as already discussed. First, it was agreed that the existing bicommunal division would be reflected in a new assembly in which each member would self-designate as either 'nationalist', or 'unionist', or 'other'. This was designed to facilitate a system of mutual veto over communally sensitive matters through mechanisms of parallel consent and weighted majority voting. The executive would be composed in proportion to the balance of parties in the Assembly, and would be headed by a dual prime ministerial arrangement, with a First Minister and a Deputy First Minister with equal powers elected by the Assembly voting on a cross-community basis, thus in effect guaranteeing one from the unionist and one from the nationalist designation.

Second, there would be a North/South Ministerial Council (NSMC), certain specific 'areas of cooperation', and a set of North–South 'implementation bodies' to promote cooperation between the two parts of Ireland. In order to reassure nationalists that unionists could not later undermine the Council (as they had done after Sunningdale in 1974), the Council and the Assembly were defined as 'so closely inter-related that the success of each depends on that of the other'. In order to reassure unionists that the Council would not acquire excessive powers, it was made accountable to the Dáil and the Northern Ireland Assembly. With a view to ensuring that the Council was effective, it was to have a standing secretariat and it was required to institute 'implementation bodies', which would have a certain independent momentum in taking forward their defined remit.[15]

Third, a British–Irish Council would promote cooperation between eight governments: those of Ireland and the United Kingdom, the three UK devolved administrations, and the three crown dependencies of Guernsey, Jersey, and the Isle of Man. There would also be a British–Irish Intergovernmental Conference that would continue to oversee matters of bilateral interest, and that—in its ground rules—repeated many of the provisions of the Anglo-Irish Intergovernmental Conference set up in 1985, except that now its remit was smaller so long as a devolved Northern Ireland government was responsible for internal Northern Irish affairs. Again, the unionist desire to replace the Anglo-Irish Agreement was met, as was the nationalist interest in retaining strong British–Irish oversight of the process and principles of agreement.

The Agreement extended much more widely than over institutional matters. It explicitly affirmed the 'principle of consent', in that the constitutional status of Northern Ireland as part of the United Kingdom would depend on the will of a

---

[15] In the event, these implementation bodies have kept functioning through recurrent suspensions of the Assembly.

majority of the population there, and it acknowledged that a majority of the population of Northern Ireland currently wished to remain in the United Kingdom. It provided a route to Irish unity, through the will of a majority in each part of the island. The Irish government agreed to support a constitutional amendment to underwrite this.

In what was sometimes called the 'confidence-building agenda', the Agreement provided very strong statements of principle and institutional provisions to secure equality and human rights, with equality legislation further strengthened in the Northern Ireland Act (1998). It sought to promote equality in the domains of cultural relations and symbols, in economic and social status, and in citizenship rights. It provided for the guarantee of human rights. It instituted a new Equality Commission, and a Northern Ireland Human Rights Commission. It proposed an overhaul of the criminal justice system, a reconstitution of the police service, and a reduction in the British military presence, while Sinn Féin agreed to encourage the disarmament of the IRA. The reconstitution of policing was to be taken forward by an independent commission, tasked with a strong equality mandate. Arrangements were to be made for the early release of political prisoners and for assistance for the victims of the violence.

Some principles were clear and recurrent throughout the final document: equality, democracy, exclusively peaceful forms of political action, and mutual respect, for example. But this was an agreement brokered at the last minute, the product of repeated redrafting. Full consistency was not achieved, sometimes by mistake and sometimes by intent to satisfy different parties and interests. It is, therefore, all the more important to examine how the parties and governments understood the provisions.

5.1.4. The Interviews

This chapter begins with interviews with Sir John Major, British Prime Minister between 1990 and 1997, and Bertie Ahern, Taoiseach between 1997 and 2008. It continues with interviews with two unionist negotiators in the multi-party talks, Antony Alcock and Sir Jeffrey Donaldson, and with two SDLP negotiators, Seán Farren and Mark Durkan. The discussion that follows is drawn from separate interviews with each, with excerpts approved and amended for this book.[16]

---

[16] The interviews took place as follows. Jennifer Todd interviewed John Major in September 2010 and Bertie Ahern in November 2017. Mark Crystall interviewed Antony Alcock in March 1999 and again some weeks later. Claire Mitchell interviewed Jeffrey Donaldson in December 1998. Muiris MacCarthaigh interviewed Seán Farren in December 1998, and Mark Durkan on two separate occasions early in 1999, and Jennifer Todd conducted a follow-up clarificatory interview with Mark Durkan in December 2017.

5.2. Government Perspectives

5.2.1. Sir John Major

Early Role

Q: What was your view of the Anglo-Irish Agreement, before you took up your premiership?

JOHN MAJOR: Before becoming prime minister I hadn't been involved in the Anglo-Irish Agreement, and my level of understanding about Northern Ireland, its problems, and the relationship with the South, was therefore limited. I remember the efforts of the Anglo-Irish Agreement and the political pain it caused. Ian Gow resigned. No one was closer to Margaret Thatcher than Ian, yet the Agreement exposed such sores between them that he resigned. It was an early indication to me of the quagmire that existed in the search for a solution for the Northern Ireland problem.

I remember that the tea-room gossip at the time in the House of Commons was that a solution was impossible. The problems were so severe that there would never be a solution; there was no real, genuine desire for a solution on either side, because it meant making compromises, and we should leave it to the security teams—'park it to one side' was the general political opinion. The other thing that struck me very much about it was, whenever there was an atrocity by the IRA, there was a response from the British government which, by and large, amounted to 'come out with your weapons thrown away and your hands up and we'll talk to you'. This seemed to be as certain to achieve nothing as you could possibly imagine. Given that I had no direct relationship with the Anglo-Irish Agreement, I simply observed that it didn't make very much progress and, for me, it highlighted the problems that existed over Northern Ireland.

Q: Did it bring changes in the British–Irish relationship?

JOHN MAJOR: No, I don't think so. There were contacts, of course, between the two governments after the Anglo-Irish Agreement. But I remember being shocked when I became prime minister and met Charlie Haughey, who was Taoiseach, and learned that Charlie and the prime minister hardly met at all. They might have brushed up against one another at European summits, but that was all. There was no real relationship. There might have been contacts below the level of prime minister, but, if there was ever to be a solution to the Northern Ireland dispute, it could not happen without the involvement of the two prime ministers. So, I was surprised and shocked that no such relationship existed, and I agreed with Charlie Haughey that, as a preliminary, we would meet for two summits a year. I believed that we could do more on Northern Ireland. At the time, the relationship was one of mutual suspicion, which has bedevilled Irish relationships in so many ways—and it was a distant relationship.

Q: What did you talk about with Charlie Haughey when you met him?

JOHN MAJOR: Our mutual interest in the European Union. Also, the Northern Ireland problem in broad outline—but we made no progress on it at all.

Q: When Albert Reynolds came into office?

JOHN MAJOR: We saw one another much more frequently. The idea of two summits a year fell by the board because we were talking all the time.

Q: How did that come about?

JOHN MAJOR: Albert came to Downing Street for a meeting; it may have been one of the regular summits. After formal talks in the Cabinet Room, we went upstairs to the White Room—just the two of us—and started talking on our own. Our subject was Northern Ireland. There was an openness that there had never been with Charlie Haughey, and, I think, an openness Albert hadn't expected either. We started talking about what it meant for the next generation. Albert felt we couldn't ignore the problem, as did I. I felt that, if people had been putting bombs in Surrey or Sussex, it would have been at the top of the British government's agenda. And, since they were putting bombs in Northern Ireland, which was also part of Great Britain and Northern Ireland, it was equally unacceptable. We agreed at that very first meeting, very quickly, within half an hour, just the two of us, that we would do all we could to go where no one had gone before in terms of trying to reach an agreement over Northern Ireland. It was very easy to come to that agreement with Albert. There was no problem about it; there was a meeting of minds. Both of us, in a sense, were political outsiders—that may have helped. Certainly, there was an empathy. I knew when I met Albert that he was a man I could do business with. And I knew he was a man that I would remain friendly with whatever else happened. That judgement turned out to be correct.

Background to the Agreement

Q: Did you have a picture of what a settlement would be?

JOHN MAJOR: Did I have an idea of what an agreement would look like? In a sense, yes, I did, simply by excluding what was impossible. Was it possible, I asked myself, to agree to a united Ireland? No, it wasn't, it was neither possible nor desirable. We had obligations to the Protestants in the North, and a united Ireland would have been a violent and unpleasant business. It wasn't politically practicable. Nor would it have been fair. So we couldn't agree to a united Ireland.

Was it possible to maintain the status quo in Northern Ireland equally? No, it wasn't. The Catholics in Northern Ireland were discriminated against, very badly, and that wasn't tolerable. The quality of life in Northern Ireland was very bad. Was it acceptable that people never knew from one day to the next whether they were going to be the subject of some sort of violence? No, it wasn't.

So the extremes—the status quo and integration—were non-starters. That being so, we had to find a middle way. But what was there that would satisfy both aspirations? One option was some form of condominium settlement, in which we built on some of the ideas in the Anglo-Irish Agreement and produced a government that would not discriminate against Catholics. Such a body might attract their involvement in it, but would retain its allegiance to the United Kingdom until, or unless, the people of Northern Ireland wanted something separate.

By this time Peter Brooke had made his famous speech about 'no selfish strategic or economic interest'.[17] Indeed, he said that a few days before I became prime minister, so that was always there in the background. We were always trying to make clear that we had an obligation to the North that we couldn't duck, but that we were not willing to hang on to it as though it was a colonial possession. We were willing to reach a settlement that would make the lives of the people who lived in Northern Ireland tolerable. So, when you strip away all the things that were impossible, you came to what was possible. And the only thing that was possible was some form of devolution of power to Northern Ireland, in which both communities had a share in government. Now, that was clear to me simply because I excluded possibilities. But how to get to it was a different matter. And putting it together was like dealing with a multidimensional Rubik's cube.

Q: That famous speech about 'no selfish strategic or economic interest', when you heard that did that strike you as a departure from British policy or was it commonsensical?

JOHN MAJOR: It struck me as common sense. I was not involved, but I did not agree with the old position which seemed to guarantee a continuation in hostilities. What the IRA were doing was terrible. The desired outcome was to stop that. Were you likely to stop that simply by saying 'we denounce terror and we will never have anything to do with you until you come out with your hands up?' The answer is no. That pretended to be very strong government. In fact, it was largely ducking the problem.

To get a Northern Ireland settlement, you had to have contact with the IRA. You had to try and find a way through. And what I did regularly, from a very early stage, was just to sit there on my own, and try and think myself into the mind of the IRA—and particularly Adams and McGuinness. I tried to think as a republican and see what they could see, understand the suspicions they had, try and work out how they would react to anything that we did. I spent a good deal more time than Mr Adams might ever imagine thinking myself into his position—trying to imagine what he would do, what could

---

[17] See Ch. 4, n. 20, and Document 4.1.

reassure him, what could persuade him to move away from the position he was holding without creating merry mayhem elsewhere. So it took a lot of time.

The conclusions I reached were quite wide ranging. The first was that the IRA had spent a quarter of a century indulging in violence and nothing had changed. The British government hadn't changed. They had not moved one inch towards the IRA's objective. And IRA activists had spent—a whole generation had spent—the cream of their life engaged in this struggle, and nothing had happened. And I thought: 'Their children could do exactly the same. We could go on exactly this way.'

We had been getting very preliminary signs from the late 1980s that the IRA might be thinking of an alternative approach. I believed that we should try and make it possible for them to make an alternative approach: to look at a way in which we could bring republican views—not necessarily Mr McGuinness and Mr Adams—but republican views into respectable politics and give them a voice. I thought we had to try and make it possible for that to happen, because we would make it more difficult for them to continue violence. But the key conclusion I reached was that they might be getting war weary. They'd spent a whole generation pursuing violence and the net result was nothing.

Q: So, from the beginning you were thinking of settlement and peace processes intertwined?

JOHN MAJOR: They had to be. No point in having a peace process without a settlement. It would be like walking over a half-finished bridge over a chasm. It wouldn't have survived. You'd have got to the end of the bridge and stayed there forever or fallen off the edge. So, yes, they had to be intertwined. That was the purpose of the Downing Street Declaration followed by the Framework agreement.

Q: Were the Unionists speaking to the British government by this stage?

JOHN MAJOR: They were always speaking to the British government. Usually to tell us that we had to stand firm and do absolutely nothing.

Q: Some within the Conservative Party were worried that sovereignty in Northern Ireland had changed?

JOHN MAJOR: Yes, they certainly were. There was a section of the Conservative Party that was hostile to the whole process from the start. If we had had a free vote in the party on my policy, I'm not at all sure the policy would have been carried. I'm not even sure there was a clear majority for it in cabinet. People acquiesced. One or two very big beasts in that cabinet thought I was just being led by the nose and it would be bound to end in tears.

Q: And yet the Downing Street Declaration got wide agreement?

JOHN MAJOR: It did. It got huge agreement around the world. It got a 97 per cent approval in Ireland. And it boxed Gerry Adams in, which is why he didn't know what to do and asked for clarification of what the document meant. I had some sympathy for that so I said 'pose us your questions', which, after an interval, he did. And the questions were pathetic, really. His argument for clarification was to buy him time. I was perfectly happy to give him time, because he was caught in a box. The British and Irish governments had got an agreement. The public overwhelmingly backed that agreement. The media had been unable to unpick that agreement. And—crucially—the United States government was wholly in favour of the agreement. Nobody opposed it. So, Adams and McGuiness were locked in, and they asked for clarification in order to buy time before eventually accepting that things couldn't continue as they had before.

Q: Did you actually think they were going to declare a ceasefire?

JOHN MAJOR: I thought it was very likely, yes. They were very much on the back foot. The only way I could see they could get the initiative back was to declare a ceasefire, so I wasn't a bit surprised when they did that. When they did it, they did so with great aplomb, people out on the streets making a great fuss, which upset the unionists no end, because they feared there was something in the agreement that they hadn't spotted. So, it was a very smart piece of work by Adams and McGuinness, but I wasn't surprised. I thought they had no choice.

Q: What was Albert Reynolds's role in the process?

JOHN MAJOR: He was the facilitator. It couldn't have happened without Albert. I had my difficulties in the House of Commons and took risks, but so did Albert. Albert took risks in parliament. He took risks with upsetting the IRA, although he was quite close to their leaders which was quite useful. I knew, of course, he was close to them.

Q: The Framework Documents got less support?[18]

JOHN MAJOR: Yes. I think there was an inevitability about that because the Downing Street Declaration was seen as a breakthrough. Seamus Mallon said it was the most important document in 150 years. But the Framework Document began to touch very sensitive issues. It began to outline what an agreement might actually look like, not just the principles of an agreement, not just desirable consensus between the British and Irish governments, but details of the government of Northern Ireland, the relationship between Northern Ireland and the Republic, and between Dublin and London.

So, clearly, it was going to be more difficult. And there were many hardline unionists opposed to it. The *Times* ran an article that was quite disgraceful.[19] They had a leak; the Framework Document was leaked to them from a hostile Protestant source within a hostile Protestant community. And they nearly

---

[18] See Subsection 4.1.2 and Documents 4.10 and 4.11.
[19] In a front-page article, journalist Matthew d'Ancona reported that the draft British–Irish Framework Document 'brings the prospect of a united Ireland closer than it has been at any time since partition in 1920'; there would be 'a joint North–South Irish authority with radical executive powers' so sweeping that many would see it as 'the engine for the reunification of Ireland'; see *The Times*, 1 February 1995; for background, Godson (2004: 122–3).

wrecked the peace process by printing it. They told us they'd got it; they told us what they were going to write. We told them that they were wrong, that what they were printing was damaging, that we didn't wish them to print it because it would harm the peace process and that it had come from a prejudiced source. They still printed it. It caused absolute mayhem in parliament.

Q: Around this time there was a change of government and John Bruton came into power.

JOHN MAJOR: That was before the Framework agreement. We negotiated the Frameworks with John, if I remember rightly. It was different from dealing with Albert, not least because John faced different pressures. Albert was able to be close to the Provisionals, John Bruton plainly wasn't. And so he had more political difficulties in carrying through the negotiations on the Framework agreement. And more suspicion was aroused in Ireland because it was John Bruton that negotiated it rather than Albert Reynolds. But he was a good interlocutor and he did what he thought was right. And he, too, had the same objective as Albert.

The Unionist Position

Q: When unionists reacted against the Frameworks, how did you respond?

JOHN MAJOR: We had to try and persuade them that they were wrong. I had innumerable meetings in Downing Street separately with the Unionists and the Democratic Unionists, privately with Jim Molyneaux and Ian Paisley. Time and time again we went over things and I gave my word. Occasionally I brought in church leaders. I kept in close touch with church leaders all the time, Robin Eames[20] particularly, but not only Robin. Once or twice, I gave them my word as to what was happening and they gave their word to the unionists or the nationalists as the case may be, and they were able to accept their word rather than mine. It happened because the churchmen, especially Robin, accepted my word. It was a slightly convoluted way of doing business but it worked.

Q: And David Trimble? He would have taken over in your time as prime minister?

JOHN MAJOR: He did, yes, absolutely he did, and he changed the moment he became leader. It was as though he'd flipped a switch and the David Trimble who was one of the great 'Mr Nos' became a 'Mr Maybe' and then eventually a 'Mr Yes'.

Q: How do you interpret that?

JOHN MAJOR: The internal struggles of politics. Internal ambitions, the reality of actually being the leader and having to explain what you do. There is a world of difference between being the man ultimately responsible and someone who is

---

[20] See Ch. 4, n. 39.

close to the top but not ultimately responsible. It's very, very different. And the moment David became leader he saw that very quickly. And he became a very positive force.

The IRA Position

Q: Can you say something about the decommissioning issue?

JOHN MAJOR: It was always a false issue. But it was real because of the reaction of the parties to decommissioning. If you look at it, even if the IRA had decommissioned on day one, they could have recommissioned later. Of course they could. So, why did it matter? It mattered because, if they didn't show good faith on decommissioning, the unionists were never going to sit at the table in joint government.

Q: Did you anticipate the breach of the IRA ceasefire in 1996?

JOHN MAJOR: No, not really. I feared it but didn't anticipate it. Why did they do it? I'll tell you why I think they did it. We had spent a lot of time on decommissioning and had run into a temporary road block. It was only temporary, but it was a road block. And they saw the likelihood that the Conservative government was going to lose an election which might well have come in 1996; many people expected it in October of that year. I think the IRA were setting up a negotiating position with an incoming government. If we had had a big majority in the 1990s—and if we had been ahead in the opinion polls and expected to win in 1997—then I don't think the IRA would have returned to violence, and the whole peace process would have been accelerated.

There's a secondary reason, too, and that's their volunteers. There was one bit of psychology with the IRA that I came to realize. I had difficult backbenchers; so did they. But their backbenchers were more violent than mine, and every time they let off a bomb they showed their backbenchers that they were not negotiating from weakness, they were negotiating from strength, and they still had the power to disrupt. I think that was a significant part of keeping the volunteers in the IRA movement together.

Q: On your reading, then, they were highly strategic actors?

JOHN MAJOR: They were smart. McGuinness and Adams were smart. I think the bomb had two purposes, keeping the volunteers happy—they were getting very frustrated—and setting out a position from which they could say to the incoming government: 'well, these are the people we are unable to make any more progress with, we can and will stop violence if ...'.

Q: Is there anything that I have missed?

JOHN MAJOR: The only really important thing to say is to emphasize something I touched on. All the time you were dealing with fear on both sides that they were going to be betrayed. The unionists were always afraid someone would betray them, and the nationalists were afraid that the British government would roll over the Irish government. Both sides were suspicious of everything. They sniffed at every document as if a cobra were about to rise out of it and strike them. Such mutual suspicion and historical loathing were a reality you had to deal with at every step along the way.

Q: Did you deal with that personally?

JOHN MAJOR: Yes. So did Paddy Mayhew on another level. But I did a lot of it, yes. Some of the things we did were very controversial in the UK—for example, when I changed the rules that had forbidden the IRA to appear on television. I went to Belfast and made a speech that removed all those restrictions. That caused a lot of agony and soul searching. I thought it was inevitable and had no hesitation in doing it.

Q: You were the first British prime minister to actually become very involved in the Northern Ireland process?

JOHN MAJOR: Well, after Gladstone and Lloyd George, probably. Yes.[21] But no single person or handful of people is responsible for the peace process coming to a successful conclusion. It was a very large cast list. Some of them were completely anonymous, that others will never know about. Others, like Robin Eames, weren't anonymous. And, although I disliked everything they stood for, the leadership of the IRA were very courageous in standing down those who wanted violence to continue. We had people who opposed it; they had people who would kill in opposition to it. So, they took their own risks and we tried, in thinking about their position, to try and make it as easy for them to carry their volunteers as we possibly could. They probably never saw it that way. But we did.

5.2.2. Bertie Ahern

Early Role

Q: When you entered the cabinet, what was your understanding of the Northern Ireland conflict, and what was needed for a settlement?

BERTIE AHERN: I joined the cabinet in 1987. It had been almost twenty years since I left school and the conflict had gone on, year in, year out, since then. I entered the Dáil in 1977, and every year the conflict was non-stop. The Sunningdale Agreement had taken place in the 1970s while I was studying accountancy, and the Anglo-Irish Agreement took place in 1985. They made a big contribution, but—and I always felt strongly about this—they excluded

---

[21] William Ewart Gladstone, prime minister intermittently 1868–94, developed a particular interest in the 'Irish question', which he tried to resolve by economic measures (including the Land Act Of 1881) and by granting 'home rule' to Ireland (though his home rule bills of 1886 and 1893 were defeated in parliament). David Lloyd George, prime minister 1916–22, sought to bring the Irish armed conflict to an end through the Anglo-Irish Treaty of 1921.

people. I was involved in industrial-relations negotiations, and I used to think that if you were trying to resolve a strike in CIÉ and you only spoke to the employers and didn't speak to the unions, how could you ever resolve the strike?[22]

The difficulty with Sunningdale, and to a greater extent with the Anglo-Irish Agreement, was that they didn't bring in the parties that were involved in conflict. That was a deep failure, in my view. I don't subscribe to the view that the Anglo-Irish Agreement was a great landmark for the future. It did give the Irish government the opportunity of having an involvement in the North— they were up in Maryfield, and being helicoptered in and helicoptered out.[23] I think that the significance of the Anglo-Irish Agreement has been overplayed.

When I came into the cabinet in 1987, Charlie Haughey started very low-level contacts between Fianna Fáil and the northern parties through the Redemptorist Order. Dermot Ahern attended those meetings on behalf of Fianna Fáil.[24] Not a lot happened, but it was the start of a process that the Redemptorists were trying to bring together.

Then the multi-party talks took place in 1991–2.[25] Our side was led by John Wilson.[26] I was very *au fait* with what was going on at that time. Because I was minister of finance, I wasn't involved in the day-to-day talks, but I was getting all the papers. I knew the insights and the arguments and I regularly spoke to John Wilson—almost every week—about it. It seemed to me at that stage that there was an opportunity here, because it was the first really meaningful dialogue the parties were involved in.

I think that the very good thing about the 1991–2 talks was that all the parties started drawing up position papers. They started saying what it was they wanted, rather than just saying we're against this or that. I think that was very useful. I remember reading those papers at the time and afterwards. It was useful because you could see what the unionists were saying, and what the nationalists were saying. That was a very useful contribution.

---

[22] CIÉ (Córas Iompair Éireann, the transport corporation of Ireland) is a holding company for the state bus and rail services. Bertie Ahern gained a reputation as a skilful negotiator during his time as Minister for Labour, 1987–91.

[23] Maryfield, just outside Belfast in Hollywood, Co. Down, was the location of the Anglo-Irish Secretariat.

[24] Dermot Ahern, Fianna Fáil TD for Louth, 1987–2011 and government minister 1997–2011, was government chief whip and Minister for State (junior minister) at the Department of Defence, 1991–2.

[25] Later dubbed the Brooke–Mayhew talks, exploratory discussions between the main Northern Ireland parties (excluding Sinn Féin) began on 30 April 1991, moved to a more formal level on 17 June, extended to include the Irish government on 8 July 1992, and came to an end on 10 November 1992 (see Subsections 4.1.1 and 4.3.5).

[26] John Wilson, Fianna Fáil TD for Cavan, 1973–7, and for Cavan–Monaghan, 1977–92, was Tánaiste (deputy prime minister) at this time.

Albert Reynolds then took over, and a lot of that work became very useful in drafting the Downing Street Declaration. It was important because it was the two governments, led by John Major and Albert Reynolds, setting down where and what were the causes of the conflict. It was Albert who was leading that, of course, as Taoiseach, and I was involved in some of the discussions with a man who did great work in helping to draft the Declaration, Archbishop Eames. I went to his house and I met him, and he was very, very helpful. Because he was close to David Trimble, it was a very helpful exercise.

The Downing Street Declaration then became the document for us to work with. Albert continued working, holding his hand out to republicans—some private talks went on, not with him, but with others, tick-tacking back and forth. That led to the republican ceasefire in August 1994 and the loyalist ceasefire in October 1994, and Gusty Spence apologizing for the 'troubles'. All of that work was good.

I was very involved in the next stage as part of Albert Reynolds's government, as we reached our final days, in those very odd circumstances.[27] We then prepared the Framework Document, which was published in February 1995. All of the work for that on the Irish side was done by the Reynolds government. The Framework Documents—that was how we were going to make the Downing Street Declaration work.

That should have had effect in 1995, but then Patrick Mayhew[28] got up on his high horse and asked if the IRA's ceasefire was permanent, and he started to ask when decommissioning was going to happen, and to say that there couldn't be progress without it. That was a disaster, really; I told the British this at the time. I was leader of the opposition.[29]

Then the British introduced this 'Washington Three' criterion,[30] and they sucked the Irish government into that. I don't want to criticize anyone these long years later, but that was a disaster. Then—totally wrongly—the IRA broke the ceasefire in January 1996. Humpty Dumpty fell off the wall, the process was on the ground again, and we had to pick it up again.

The Forum for Peace and Reconciliation had been going on.[31] That collapsed because the ceasefire had broken down, and that good dialogue that we

---

[27] In one of the most unusual circumstances to bring down a government, the Fianna Fáil–Labour coalition headed by Albert Reynolds collapsed on 16 November 1994 following Reynolds's decision to appoint as President of the High Court someone whose suitability for the post had been rejected by the Labour Party.

[28] Patrick Mayhew, a Conservative politician of Anglo-Irish background, was Secretary of State for Northern Ireland, 1992–7, and played a central role in insisting on the need for decommissioning of paramilitary weapons. See also Subsections 4.3.6 and 5.2.1.

[29] Following the collapse of his government, Albert Reynolds resigned as leader of Fianna Fáil, which now went into opposition; he was succeeded as party leader by Bertie Ahern on 19 November 1994.

[30] See Subsection 5.1.1.

[31] The Forum brought together most significant non-unionist political parties, including Sinn Féin, the SDLP, and the Alliance Party, for a series of talks in 1994–6. See Subsections 4.1.2 and 4.4.4.

were engaging in at the Forum, that stopped as well. So, really, 1996 and the first half of 1997 were just written off.

Negotiating the Agreement

BERTIE AHERN: To take it from there, Tony Blair and I were both leaders in opposition, both of us were young in those days. Both of us started communicating with each other on a regular basis. We had meetings here, including one in the Gresham Hotel—that was a secret meeting. I think then we met in Government Buildings. I went over to meetings in the House of Commons, and Mo Mowlam then came on board. Ray Burke was on board with me at that stage, in opposition. Then I went up to meet the Unionists in Glengall Street, the first time ever.[32] I met Sinn Féin in Conway Mill.[33] So, while in opposition, we got deeply engaged in trying to find a way of moving forward.

To go back to your first question, I always thought, if we could stop the violence, maybe you could have dialogue. It was not easy: Sunningdale had failed; the Anglo-Irish Agreement had failed; nothing came of the 1991–2 talks; there were other efforts, all well-meaning efforts, all constructive efforts. But the difficulty was that they weren't inclusive, and as long as they weren't inclusive you were going to get nowhere.

So, my idea all along was, first, to try to get a ceasefire and, second, to try to get an inclusive process. I didn't think beyond that. I thought that, if you could do those two things, you might get somewhere. I was elected Taoiseach, and Tony Blair and I both agreed that was the issue: could we stop the violence and get an inclusive process, and then see where we go from there?

Q: What did you see as the bottom line for the nationalists and the republicans at that stage?

BERTIE AHERN: The Mitchell Principles had been drafted in 1995 and were very helpful. It was my job to try to get the republicans on board; Tony was keeping the unionists and the loyalists on board. My line to them—my view—was that, if you are on ceasefire, if there's peace, if you stop trying to achieve your political ends through violence or a combination of violence and a ballot box, then we can start addressing the causes of conflict. Then we can start looking for equality, parity of esteem, fairness of the system, reviewing the police force, ultimately turning to change it totally, dealing with the prisoners issue, trying to get normality and fairness for nationalist people.

---

[32] The administrative office of the Ulster Unionist Party was located at 3 Glengall Street in central Belfast for several decades before moving to East Belfast in 2001. This was the first occasion on which the leader of a major southern party had visited the party's headquarters.

[33] Conway Mill is a former linen mill off the Falls Road, Belfast, that was converted in the 1980s to serve as a community cultural centre.

I made it clear to them all along that, if we don't get peace, if we don't stop the violence, if we don't stop the efforts to achieve aims through violence, then we can do nothing. So, I think the big success was in June 1997, when we managed to get the ceasefire restored. It wasn't without its ups and downs, but we got it. Tony Blair and I had promised that, if that happened, we wouldn't have a long gap as happened before, we would move quickly, if the violence stopped, to talks on 1 September 1997. That's where the multi-party talks started, with George Mitchell chairing.

Q: Today you hear people saying, well, equality had been sorted out in 1972, even in 1970?

BERTIE AHERN: The Good Friday Agreement set out the principles, all the principles, in all the areas. We had decommissioning, which didn't work out so easily, that was a nightmare; the reform of policing; a new criminal justice system; a new oversight commissioner; a new ombudsperson. There was huge international involvement. It was an enormous change, a huge change from what was there in the old system: to change the legislation, to set up an equality act, to pass the criminal justice act, to reform policing with Chris Patten, to release the prisoners on licence. So much happened in those few years.

5.3. Ulster Unionist Perspectives

5.3.1. Antony Alcock

Background to the Talks

Q: What was the role of the Irish and British governments before the talks process began?

ANTONY ALCOCK: It was quite clear that both governments had really had enough. I mean, this Northern Ireland question has been going on basically since 1969, so that's very, very nearly thirty years, and no progress had been made whatsoever. For a long time, certainly for the first twenty-five years of this, the idea had been to try and conciliate nationalists and snub unionists; the 1985 Anglo-Irish Agreement, which involved no consultation with the unionists, was seen as continual slapping in the face, and, eventually, it got down to the fact that this was getting people nowhere. Now, the Irish government themselves, I think, were also very concerned that things weren't getting anywhere, and there was continued violence and the fear that the violence would spill over into the Republic—quite apart from the fact that this whole atmosphere of violence was aiding crime of all sorts, like drugs and things like that, by paramilitary organizations. In other words, as the national conflict escalated, so did crime by paramilitaries, and I would say the British and Irish governments eventually felt that they'd had enough: how are they going to advance things?

Of course, the Irish government themselves had various weaknesses because of the nature of the coalition and various scandals that had occurred, but I think that the Irish government's attitude, certainly since Reynolds became Taoiseach, was very much a change for the better in that there was recognition of the unionist position; there was recognition the problem had to be solved and the sooner they got on with it the better.

Q: What was the UUP's reaction to the Blair government and their programme for devolution?

ANTONY ALCOCK: There were mixed feelings about this. One, they were pleased because talks were going to start, and it was, after all, the policy of the UUP that we should try and get an assembly and a devolved government in Northern Ireland. The other point, though, for which we were fiercely attacked of course, was that we had given manifesto promises that we wouldn't sit down with Sinn Féin unless they actually had decommissioned.

Now, the Blair government was playing its usual tricks by saying 'well, they will probably start disarmament during the talks', and we said 'OK, if you promise to start disarming during the talks, we can run with it'. Of course, as you know, that didn't happen and a lot of the problems that we face now [March 1999] arise precisely because of this slippery way of doing things where we give up manifesto pledges to try and keep the talks going, but we get nothing in return. And at the same time we just get abused by unionists like the Paisleyites and McCartneyites, as well as large numbers of people within the Unionist Party itself.

Q: What about Scottish and Welsh devolution?

ANTONY ALCOCK: Yes, this was definitely a plus, and where it was particularly a plus was because it ended a long-running debate in the Unionist Party as to whether we should go for complete integration into Britain and be as much part of Britain as Cheshire or Surrey or whether we should have devolved government. Now, the question of devolved government had been an issue ever since the foundation of the Northern Ireland state, because, even at that time, Carson was pointing out that, by having a separate government for Northern Ireland, that made us different from the rest of the United Kingdom. Well, now that Wales and Scotland were getting devolution, this distinction no longer applied, and therefore, in that sense, the debate ended. For example, the former leader Sir James Molyneaux was very much an integrationist; Trimble and others are much more—'regionalists', I'd call them.

Q: What was the general UUP feeling in summer 1997 after the IRA ceasefire and as it appeared that Sinn Féin would join the talks process?

ANTONY ALCOCK: A kind of guarded optimism.

Q: Was there more unity in the party at that stage?

ANTONY ALCOCK: Oh, yes. There was much more unity. All the people who became known as the baby barristers,[34] they were always very eager to get going, you know, and to show up Irish nationalism and Sinn Féin and things like this. I remember that they would—in the debates and the Northern Ireland Forum[35]—they would stand up for being in the talks process, as opposed to the DUP, who were outside it. So, there was no doubting their enthusiasm.

The Form of the Talks Process

Q: How was the UUP team organized for the talks process?

ANTONY ALCOCK: You were divided up into teams. There were twelve negotiators altogether. You see, there were about thirty UUP members in the Forum, but twelve people were negotiators. Now, this is, I think, an important point. Trimble had been very clever in that, when he prepared his team, he prepared a team which didn't merely reflect rural and Orange values. He knew what the battleground was going to be, and where you wanted things, and there were going to be cross-border things, and articles 2 and 3, and all these things like the police and reform, and therefore twelve negotiators were deliberately chosen. Most of them were lawyers, because most of the issues were legal ones, like articles 2 and 3. When it came to the question of the language and when it came to cross-border cooperation, then he would call upon me; he wanted me in because of my expertise on Europe, and therefore, when I failed to get elected to the Forum, each party could appoint two [additional] people to the Forum, and I was one of the two people who were appointed, the other one being now Sir John Gorman, who, again, Trimble chose to be the speaker.[36] He was Catholic. So, he was chosen deliberately; he got his team together very, very deliberately.

Q: So, you felt that the UUP were in a strong position?

ANTONY ALCOCK: A very strong position, you see, and this certainly came out when we discussed human rights with the Irish Republic and found that they'd hardly ratified a single human-rights agreement passed by an international organization, ever. When Dermot Nesbitt[37] and I tackled them about this, we were told to stop preaching at them. We used the expertise that we had in a very good way, and we were able to quote them things from the Charter of Minority Languages, the Framework Convention on the Protection of

---

[34] A group of young, activist law graduates, several of whom, including Arlene Foster, later joined the DUP.

[35] The Northern Ireland Forum for Political Dialogue, the election to which was used to determine participation in the talks process, continued in existence alongside the talks; see Subsection 5.1.1.

[36] Ninety members of the Forum were elected on the party-list system, but each of the ten largest parties could nominate two additional members.

[37] Dermot Nesbitt was a prominent member of the Ulster Unionist talks team and an academic in Queen's University Belfast.

Minorities, and a whole lot of examples of how cross-border operations had operated elsewhere in Europe, and this really rather left the Irish baffled.[38] Now, nevertheless, there's a point behind this, and I think this is an important issue. What we did not like about the Northern Ireland Office was that it went along with the Irish government and Irish nationalism in saying the Northern Ireland question is unique and, therefore, requires unique solutions, whereas we said the Northern Ireland situation is not unique. There are all sorts of places like it in Europe and all sorts of arrangements have been tried to solve these, and this is the distilled wisdom from it; therefore, don't go and do something stupid which has already failed elsewhere.

Principles and Objectives

ANTONY ALCOCK: We were very strong on the Mitchell Principles and I think we accepted that nothing was agreed until everything is agreed, but I don't think we were aware of the size of the package when we started out. The UUP certainly hoped to have articles 2 and 3 of the Irish constitution changed. That was a paramount objective. Obviously, decommissioning or an end to the violence, but it was considered that all these things would come together.

We'd always known that this would be particularly difficult because it was thought that articles 2 and 3 were such an integral part of the Irish psyche that to have them removed would be a tremendous and difficult achievement for unionism. I think it was probably good that Ahern became Taoiseach, but we had to find these things out through sort of probing, because one of the things which rather surprised me was that the Irish government would change its position quite frequently, saying 'on no account would we get rid of the articles' and then saying 'oh, well, it depends what we get in return'.

Now, I have to say that the Ulster Unionist Party had the gravest suspicions about the Northern Ireland Office and they always have. That is simply because they believe, and have believed for a long time, that the ultimate aim of the British government is to get rid of Northern Ireland, and we do know of cases—and I put them in my diary, but I haven't got them now—where we know that several members of the Northern Ireland Office had declared that they hoped and believed that a united Ireland would be the correct final solution. So, as far as the Northern Ireland Office was concerned, there were very few people in it, very few people in it with whom unionists had any confidence whatsoever, either the ministers or the actual staff on the ground.

Q: What were the crunch issues for the UUP at this time?

---

[38] The European Charter for Regional or Minority Languages and the Framework Convention for the Protection of National Minorities were adopted by the Council of Europe in 1992 and 1994 respectively as mechanisms for the protection of minority languages and national minorities.

ANTONY ALCOCK: Articles 2 and 3; cross-border bodies, yes, but with ratification of decisions by the respective jurisdictions, Assembly and Dáil. I should have said that these were the particular problems that I was associated with. Obviously, I think maintenance of the police, you know, the RUC, decommissioning. But, the number of cross-border bodies, I think, was also an issue.

Q: The British Irish Council?

ANTONY ALCOCK: The British Irish Council? Yes, that was very important because we wanted, if you like, to restore the political unity of the British Isles, and, of course, we have to remember that in the middle of these talks the Labour Party came to power with its devolutionary programme. I personally welcomed this because it ended a long-running discussion in the Unionist Party as to whether we wanted to be integrated entirely into Britain, or whether we should have devolution.

In political science terms, it's always a very important point: is devolution the first step on the slippery slope to secession and dissolution? Or is it, in fact, a means of strengthening the unity of the state? And, really, the jury in Europe is out. In some cases it works, like in South Tyrol. Really, I think, in the Basque Country probably as well. In other countries, like Czechoslovakia, it hasn't worked, and in Belgium, Heaven knows what's going to happen. However, we did want this Council of the British Isles to balance things and we wanted ourselves to be brought in.[39]

What I haven't stressed so much was the feeling in the Ulster Unionist Party that we were very much second cousins, sort of out on a limb. We wanted recognition, hence the importance of the change of articles 2 and 3, but Northern Ireland needed recognition in its own right, and therefore, being part of a group of players—Scotland, Wales, the Republic, and England, no matter what form England eventually takes—was, I think, important for us. It was also important as a selling point to the unionist political community.

Q: How far apart were unionism and nationalism and republicanism in September 1997?

ANTONY ALCOCK: Well, probably quite far. There's no doubt that some conversations were held between the leadership of the UUP and the leadership of the SDLP, but it was always seen as a very bad sign, for example, that the SDLP did not want the Forum for starters. And immediately, you had the Drumcree of 1996.[40] They took that as a swift opportunity to leave.

So, our view was: here was the Forum, which had lots of committees. Committees were set up to examine lots of sectoral things like health,

---

[39] Initially proposed by David Trimble as a Council of the Isles, this eventually took shape as the British–Irish Council. It was seen by unionists as a counter-balance to the North/South Ministerial Council.

[40] The RUC had prevented a controversial Orange march from proceeding from Drumcree church to the centre of Portadown through the mainly Catholic Garvaghy Road in July 1995, but in July 1996 reversed this position; in response, the SDLP announced a policy of non-participation in the Forum.

education, agriculture, you know, and what do the SDLP do? They walk out. And we have exactly the same situation now [March 1999]. Now, maybe I'm breaking ahead here, but, you know, one of the issues involved right now is will the SDLP guarantee to throw out Sinn Féin if there's no disarmament?

Well, for the reform of the Northern Ireland state, I think there was general acceptance that there would have to be some change. The one thing I think was a sticking point had to do with the reform of the RUC. What do you mean by reform, especially when we know that Sinn Féin were demanding the abolition of the RUC and its replacement by a completely new body which might even include ex-terrorists? So, there, with those sorts of demands there was not much ground for compromise. The Irish language? I'm afraid unionists don't think very much of the Irish language or don't think much of its future. I myself have a more liberal view on this, since I'm an expert on the question of minorities. But there was certainly a fear that Northern Ireland would be gaelicized. As for an assembly and how it would work, I don't suppose there was very much discussion about that.

The Negotiation Process

Q: When did the UUP see a breakthrough towards agreement?

ANTONY ALCOCK: It's rather a difficult question to answer because, in a negotiating situation where nothing was agreed until everything was agreed, everybody was really hanging on until the last moment. Also, the fact of the matter was that there was the Irish government and there was the Irish civil service and the Irish Ministry of Foreign Affairs. And on the English side, there was the Northern Ireland Office and the Prime Minister's Office.

So there was a problem that sometimes we didn't know to whom we were talking. Sometimes you would get an assurance, 'yes the articles are going to be changed', and then a draft paper would come which shows this quite clearly was not part of the thinking. So, really, it was only quite at the end, when everything had to be done. You have to try and realize that when Mitchell said 'I want this wound up in three weeks', by Good Friday, nothing at that time had been resolved. Everybody knew very vaguely what might happen, but clearly the Irish government was not going to bargain away the articles for nothing.

Q: What of the expulsion of Sinn Féin from the talks, and then their reinstatement? Did you feel, then, that Sinn Féin and the SDLP were locked in?

ANTONY ALCOCK: We always knew that the British and Irish governments wanted Sinn Féin in. I mean, all this business about expelling them for a week was just a show, it was just fatuous, sort of play acting, presumably to soothe the dinosaur elements of the Unionist Party, but nobody was deceived. They were absolutely in the process. The only people at the edge of the process were us, because we were the ones who were actually teetering on the window ledge.[41]

Q: Was that a feeling that ran right through this whole period?

ANTONY ALCOCK: Oh yes. There's one particular detail [in the final weeks of the talks] on one of the cross-border bodies about the promotion of the Irish language, and I think I am right in saying that when Trimble was talking to Liz O'Donnell about this, he actually tore a pencil out of her hand and crossed it out and said 'we're not having this'.[42] I'd have to look and see which the bodies were which we objected to. I mean, you could probably see it from their elimination from the final list, but this was a matter of great concern.

I think we were put in the position that, first of all, we had to come up with an agreement because we couldn't allow this thing to drag on; you'd have a referendum on this and you wanted the referendum before the marching season. That was one aspect. Second, if the place collapsed, if the talks collapsed, then probably there would be a resumption of violence, and we were under such pressure that I seem to remember David Trimble saying to the team 'well, we've got time to concentrate on one issue and get our way on that. Which should it be?' and he said—I remember him saying this—'we'll have to ditch the prisoners', so that was the question of prisoner releases, and as we know, prisoner releases have caused great dismay in the unionist community.[43]

Q: What about human rights and equality? How much negotiation took place on that?

ANTONY ALCOCK: Well, not all that much. We disliked the human rights set-up in Northern Ireland because all these bodies which had been set up were quite clearly weighted in favour of the nationalist community, and, therefore, what we were concerned about was not so much that there should be a human-rights commission—we were quite happy about that—but really its composition. We really did hope that when this Human Rights Commission was established after the negotiations that it would be fairer than the one that existed before. On the Standing Advisory Committee on Human Rights,[44] my Queen's opposite number, Dermot Nesbitt of the Ulster Unionist Party, was

[41] The reference is to the phrase 'on the window ledge of the union', used frequently by unionists to describe their position after the Anglo-Irish Agreement of 1985.

[42] The reference is to the negotiations on the cross-border bodies listed in the Mitchell draft, which was given to the parties on 6 April 1998. Liz O'Donnell, a member of the small Progressive Democrat party in the Republic, was at the time Minister of State at the Department of Foreign Affairs and an Irish government participant in the multi-party talks.

[43] In the last days of the talks, Sinn Féin and the small loyalist parties agreed with the government that all qualifying paramilitary prisoners would be released within two years.

[44] Set up in 1973, the Standing Advisory Committee on Human Rights (SACHR) was responsible for some important interventions in the area of equality, and also had a role in the equality agenda in the Good Friday Agreement.

the only unionist representative, and on several occasions had had to present minority reports in regard to various aspects of human rights.

Certainly the Ulster Unionist Party saw this Standing Committee on Human Rights as packed with people who might have been Protestants but were nevertheless pro-nationalist, and certainly hostile to the unionist community, and I have to say that now [March 1999] I don't think the unionist community is happy with the present composition of the human-rights commission, so, I think that there, once again, we have been let down.[45]

Q: And the Irish government's role here, and their record on human rights?

ANTONY ALCOCK: Yes, this gave us a good opportunity to counter-attack, when we soon found out just how many human-rights conventions the Irish Republic had actually ratified, and this gave us an opportunity to counter-attack, and in fact the Irish government also agreed in the Agreement to take on board the European Convention on Human Rights. The British government said, of course, that they would put this into British domestic law. This may be more difficult for the Irish Republic, but, from what I remember of the Agreement, the Irish Republic is also bound to implement large parts of it.[46]

Q: Was there a feeling that the IRA would decommission? In hindsight, was that not a mistake?

ANTONY ALCOCK: Oh, yes, I think it was, yes. People suddenly realized that the IRA were not going to do this. But all the negotiators negotiated in good faith, and there was the overwhelming support by the people, after a thirty-year conflict, thirty years of violent conflict. For Heaven's sake, let us now bring an end to this. This is what the governments had gone for. This is what the Unionist Party wanted: an end to the bombings. I say the people of Ireland, north and south, have spoken.

You know, here is an opportunity for all sorts of gunmen, if they disarm they are going to get all sorts of money, certainly north of the border. The paramilitaries were going to get released from prison, were going to have money to be re-educated and reintegrated into society. What more do they want? So perhaps it was naive, but I would say that that was a fundamental failing—particularly by the British and Irish governments—that they did not

---

[45] The Northern Ireland Human Rights Commission (NIHRC) was established in 1999 as an independent agency for the protection of human rights. It is headed by a chief commissioner (in succession Brice Dickson, 1999–2005, Monica McWilliams, 2005–11, Michael O'Flaherty, 2011–13, and Les Allenby, since 2014), several part-time commissioners, and a permanent administrative staff. The first commission included several prominent non-unionist human-rights activists.

[46] The Irish government had ratified the European Convention on Human Rights in 1953, but now agreed to 'bring forward measures to strengthen and underpin the constitutional protection of human rights', drawing *inter alia* on the European Convention on Human Rights. Among other commitments, it also agreed to establish a Human Rights Commission and to ratify the Council of Europe Framework Convention on National Minorities. The British government agreed to incorporate the Convention into Northern Ireland law.

make it clear that, if there was no disarmament, they would take the sternest measures.

If you look in the Agreement, decommissioning has got to be within two years of the Agreement, and what one didn't see was this time lag between the establishment of the Assembly and the putative surrendering of the last ounce of semtex.[47] Now, normally that Assembly should have come into being in October 1998 and had powers transferred to it in February 1999. That would still have left fourteen months for the final decommissioning to take place in which, in theory, Sinn Féin would be in government and the IRA would not have been disarmed. Well, obviously, the UUP or Trimble has to be responsible for accepting such a situation, but I think he did it in good faith. I think the governments did it in good faith, knowing this would happen, in the belief that everybody would be so relieved that at last this problem was over, and there would be no need to have these arms. Everybody has been bitterly disappointed, and so bitterly disappointed that, indeed, it risks the whole Agreement being scuppered.

Q: Why do you think that such differences emerged in the Unionist delegation in the final period of talks?

ANTONY ALCOCK: Well, part of the problem was that David Trimble's control of his party was very very weak. He had been elected two or three years before, unexpectedly. Not one of his MPs voted for him; not one of his party officers voted for him. So, he found himself really alone, and yet, suddenly, he was a key player in Northern Ireland politics. There had been many attempts to try and subvert his authority, and a focus for this was the parliamentary group. I think it was six MPs. Of the nine MPs, the only ones who were loyal to him during the negotiations were Ken Maginnis and John Taylor.[48] Jeffrey Donaldson, I might add, was a loyal and a very very hard worker, and didn't kick up any trouble until right at the very end, when he said very quietly 'I'm sorry. I personally can't accept this [...] Agreement', but he really didn't cause, as far as I know, much trouble before then. The real source of the trouble was not only those six MPs, but, through their influence, they were influencing a whole lot of backwoodsmen, I mean Willie Ross in the East Londonderry constituency, Thompson in [West] Tyrone. You know, afterwards, when we went around trying to convince people to support the Agreement in the referendum and things like that, we were getting very hostile receptions.

Q: You were pro-Agreement?

---

[47] Unionist critics complained that 'not a single bullet or an ounce of semtex' (plastic explosive) had been surrendered by the IRA at this stage; see, e.g., Robert McCartney, *Northern Ireland Assembly Debates*, 15 December 1998.

[48] Apart from Trimble himself, there were nine UUP MPs, of whom six were critical of his leadership.

ANTONY ALCOCK: Yes. I still am, for the reason that we gave nationalism an opportunity to get off the hook. We will swallow the line that the IRA and Sinn Féin are different as long as the IRA decommission. They didn't do so.

Can I go back and say that this seemed to be justified when we had the referendum, when so many people believed, not so much the fine print of the Agreement, but that things henceforward are going to change completely. We're going to have a new start. And when the IRA refused to decommission, then, you know, suddenly people started to realize that nothing would change, and nothing has changed now.

So, you see, throughout the whole unionist community, we'd done our very best to try to get an agreement, and I thought, well, my God, the prisoners are going to be free, everybody wants the war to be over except for these bloody people who have their loyalties in the 1918 Dáil or something like that; half a dozen idiots.[49] It just hasn't turned out that way and, for me, I always felt, why did I come to Northern Ireland at all? The answer seemed to me that I could use my expertise in a situation like this one. We did use it, and I believe we got a good agreement, which, if it had been respected, would indeed have brought about a lasting peace on this island, and I would have felt my own existence in this world would have been justified.

Well, should decommissioning occur, then we will win a smashing victory. I wrote the communiqué which David Trimble read out at the time that he actually accepted the deal, with the proviso that it would have to be accepted again by his party officers and things. I said, this is a good day for unionism. I read this Agreement as a victory. We can start afresh, we've got the articles changed, we've got the cross-border bodies which exist anyway all over Europe. I had a tremendous row with Willie Ross in the party executive on that. As I was saying, I thought we'd won a smashing victory. We actually had taken an axe to the roots of Irish nationalism.

Q: How do you feel now, a year after the Agreement? How would you assess the strength of unionism, especially the UUP?

ANTONY ALCOCK: I don't think they know where they're going. Well, let's say they vote down the Agreement; the Agreement will be suspended. What will happen? Nobody knows. Will the violence recommence? Let's be honest about this. The IRA can say, as long as the Ulster or the Orange Defenders and [such] people go around throwing bombs and killing Catholics, why should they disarm? History is about transition. What is there to transition to? The only thing that unionists can think of, the only transition possible, is to a united Ireland. That is their nightmare.

---

[49] A reference to those republicans who used the Sinn Féin victory in the 1918 general election to justify the IRA campaign; see Ch. 4, n. 62.

Now, one thing which might well happen is, you know, the federalization of Britain. We can see what's happening in Europe. It is not impossible that, in fifty years time, Northern Ireland will be a region in a United Europe, but nobody wants to think about that, and that's because, basically, no one has ever thought in terms of Europe, as evidenced, of course, by the European elections, where the question is, is this a referendum on the Good Friday Agreement? European issues never appear, and even though we've got enough of them with the BSE, the fish, the environment, there are hundreds of European issues, but they're just not interested in it.[50]

5.3.2. Jeffrey Donaldson

The Talks Process

Q: What was your perception of the talks process in 1997, once it became clear that Sinn Féin would be involved?

JEFFREY DONALDSON: When it became clear after the IRA declared the reinstatement of its ceasefire that the government were going to invite them into the talks process, the Ulster Unionist Party had a very difficult decision to make. The DUP and the UK Unionist Party made it clear that they were withdrawing from the talks. We had to decide whether we should also withdraw from the talks, given that Sinn Féin/IRA had not delivered on decommissioning in advance of their entry to the talks. That had been one of the conditions which we had previously set forward, and which was given a lot of consideration.

In the end we decided that we should stay in the talks rather than pull out on Sinn Féin's entry. But we decided that we should press very hard for the Mitchell compromise, which was that decommissioning would take place alongside the talks, so when Sinn Féin gained entry we stayed in the talks. But we stayed in on the basis that we would argue very strongly that, as part of their signing-up to the Mitchell principles, one of those principles required them to pursue the decommissioning of terrorist weapons and that George Mitchell himself had proposed in his report, prior to the talks beginning, that the best way to deal with decommissioning was to see it happen alongside the talks process.

And so, with considerable reluctance, we decided that it was in the best interest of the people that we represented to stay in the talks, because we were concerned that, if the talks process collapsed at that stage, because of our withdrawal, the government, along with the Irish government, would simply

---

[50] Bovine spongiform encephalopathy (BSE), often referred to as 'mad cow disease', is a disease of cattle that spread from a single British case in the mid-1980s to become a Europe-wide public-health issue. Among the consequences of the BSE outbreak was the banning of beef exports from the UK to the remainder of the EU between March 1996 and May 2006.

continue some kind of other process which we would have much less influence over.

We certainly thought that agreement was possible, but improbable, given the gulf that existed between, on the one hand, Sinn Féin, holding a very strong republican viewpoint, and ourselves and the loyalist parties, holding a very strong pro-unionist viewpoint. We felt that it was important to try and get back to Northern Ireland some sort of government in the form of an assembly. We were quite willing to discuss the basis of cooperation between Northern Ireland and the Irish Republic. We very strongly wanted to see the third dimension (of British–Irish relations) being given more prominence: institutions would be established which would facilitate cooperation throughout the islands and would provide a framework through which cooperation would take place on a multidimensional basis.

Those were our objectives. We also had a key objective, the removal of the Republic's territorial claim over Northern Ireland. We felt that was very important. So, alongside decommissioning, there were the constitutional objectives, and the objective of having new institutions of government created which would facilitate a reconciliation between the various traditions that exist on these islands.

Q: Did you find that you had any friends or allies within the talks?

JEFFREY DONALDSON: That varied depending on the issue. On decommissioning we operated very much on our own. The loyalist parties obviously supported the loyalist terrorist organizations and were not pushing for decommissioning. Prisoner releases were quite a high priority for them. We would, however, have had support from the loyalist parties on the constitutional issues. We were at odds with the SDLP and the Irish government, particularly on some of the constitutional issues. The British government tended to take a fairly neutral view on just about everything. They pretended at times to be the facilitator holding the ring, rather than putting forward specific views. But towards the latter end of the talks process it became clear that they were far from being facilitators. They were actually pushing certain options.

Q: What role did the British government and its officials have in the early stages of negotiations?

JEFFREY DONALDSON: In the early stages of the negotiations they were very much involved in the decision to bring Sinn Féin into the talks following the reinstatement of the IRA ceasefire. In the early stages of the talks they tended to sort of step back a little bit and allow people to put forward views and so on. The prime minister would have been involved to a certain extent in trying to encourage parties to make progress, particularly on the North–South issues. But it was only really in the latter part that the British government became very, very proactive and really took a lead on many of the issues—not least the whole issue of the Assembly and the North–South institutions.

Q: And what about the Irish government?

JEFFREY DONALDSON: We could never really pin them down on articles 2 and 3. Right up until the final days of the negotiations, they talked in broad generalisms but didn't really get down to the specific wording. So, we could never get a text out of them on what kind of formal words they would envisage in amending their constitution. They were also quite defensive on the whole issue of North–South cooperation, defending the ideas they had put forward in the Framework Documents. It took some time to move them away from the very fixed ideas they had set out in the Framework Documents. So, I would say that there was a difficult relationship between ourselves and the Irish government in the negotiations.

Q: What kind of a role did the PUP and maybe to a lesser extent the UDP play in negotiations?

JEFFREY DONALDSON: I don't think that they made a huge difference. In terms of the mechanisms of the talks process and how the voting procedure worked, the Ulster Unionist Party on their own did not represent a majority of unionists, as was required within the talks process. So, they needed the votes; in the absence of the DUP and the UK Unionist Party, they needed the votes of at least one of the loyalist parties to secure unionist consensus to agree to anything that was in the talks. So, at a practical level, you know, the Ulster Unionist Party was quite dependent upon one or other of the loyalist parties to get anything through the talks. But, in terms of the negotiations, the real negotiations took place between the two governments, the SDLP and the Ulster Unionist Party.

Their presence facilitated a plurality of voices because they got their say whenever we were in plenary sessions. But the real negotiations didn't take place in the plenary sessions. They took place on a bilateral basis, and the main players were the British government, the Irish government, the SDLP, and the Ulster Unionist Party. Of the smaller parties, inevitably Sinn Féin had the most influence. But even their influence within the final outcome on the constitutional issues was not strong. Like the loyalist parties, their influence was focused more on the prisoner release, decommissioning aspects, and what they called the equality agenda, and their attacks on the RUC. They tended to focus on those kinds of issues. So I would say that when you get into the minutiae of the detail of the negotiations, the smaller parties had very little input.

In that sense the loyalists were pretty peripheral on the main constitutional issues. They tended to focus much more on the confidence-building aspects: prisoner releases, decommissioning, and so on. So, it was a difficult relationship. The Ulster Unionist Party knew that it needed to take at least one of the loyalist parties with it in terms of getting anything through the talks, and that turned out to be quite important in the final analysis, because the loyalists had us over a barrel on decommissioning and the release of prisoners. They knew that the Unionist Party on its own couldn't deliver the Agreement. In the absence of the DUP and the UK Unionist Party, on the prisoner release issue and the decommissioning issue, although we argued very strongly on those aspects, our hands were tied to a certain extent, because of our dependence on the support of a least one of the loyalist parties.

Q: How concerned were you about the non-participation of the DUP and the UK Unionist Party?

JEFFREY DONALDSON: Very concerned, because they represented a significant proportion—between them, up to a quarter of the electorate of Northern Ireland. It seriously impaired the unionist position in the talks and undermined our negotiating strength not to have the DUP and the UK Unionist Party in the talks process.

Perspectives on the Agreement

Q: How do you see the Agreement on the Assembly? Is it a form of power-sharing? Or do you perceive it differently from that?

JEFFREY DONALDSON: We call it responsibility sharing, that is how we see it. Ironically on the D'Hondt system nationalists secured about 40 percent of the votes. In the Assembly elections it's working out that they'll actually get half of the seats in the executive. So, the system has actually been very, very generous to the nationalist community.[51]

Q: What of the constitutional issues?

JEFFREY DONALDSON: Given the noises that we had been hearing from the Irish government, we were fairly confident that the constitutional changes that we wanted to see in terms of articles 2 and 3 would actually come. And we had tasked some constitutional lawyers to look also at the whole question of what the Irish government talked about as their *quid pro quo*: the repeal of the Government of Ireland Act, section 75.[52]

We looked at that. We looked at the constitutional implications of that. We got lawyers to look at the constitutional implications of that. The advice that we were getting from people regarded as very well-informed constitutional lawyers was that it doesn't really make any difference in terms of Northern Ireland's constitutional position to have section 75 of the

---

[51] The D'Hondt system was devised by the Belgian mathematician Victor D'Hondt in the late nineteenth century. It is widely used in parliamentary elections in continental Europe, and is designed to ensure that each party gets its 'proportionate' number of seats. Using a division table, seats are allocated in succession to parties to ensure that the ratio of seats to votes for each party is as close as possible to the 'average'. Because of its bias in favour of larger parties and the much greater fragmentation on the unionist side than on the nationalist side following the 1998 Assembly election, nationalists and unionists were each entitled to five ministerial posts.

[52] Section 75 of the Government of Ireland Act, 1920, provided that, notwithstanding the creation of new parliaments in Ireland, 'the supreme authority of the Parliament of the United Kingdom shall remain unaffected and undiminished over all persons, matters, and things in Ireland and every part thereof'.

Government of Ireland Act repealed. In fact, there will be a provision in the new Northern Ireland Act, 1998, as there was in the 1973 Northern Ireland Constitution Act, which would provide for the whole question of the sovereignty of Parliament.

So we weren't going to, as it were, freak out and go AWOL on the whole question of section 75 of the Government of Ireland Act, because at the end of the day the principle of consent was enshrined in the constitutional arrangements. So, it was clear that Northern Ireland's position as part of the United Kingdom would only and could only be determined by the exercise of the will of the people. In other words, a constitutional change would only come about if that's what the people of Northern Ireland wanted, and the Irish government accepted that. I think that the consent principle underpins that constitutional arrangement and that is very important.

Q: And strand three, the British–Irish dimension, did you have to really fight your corner for that?

JEFFREY DONALDSON: We did initially. But eventually it became accepted, and in the final parts of the negotiations it was taken as read. The real negotiations and the trade-off took place between strand one and strand two. Strand three was more or less accepted; that was going to happen.

Q: What about the equality agenda?

JEFFREY DONALDSON: The equality agenda was rarely discussed within the negotiations. There was a subcommittee of the talks process which dealt with confidence-building issues. There was also a subcommittee which dealt with decommissioning. The confidence-building subcommittee had discussions about equality issues. Sinn Féin would raise these matters. But that subcommittee never really brought forward any substantial report, and the equality issues really only emerged in the final draft.

So, I think this is where the British government and the Irish government had been doing a lot of work behind the scenes, and obviously they had been discussing privately with Sinn Féin about some of these issues. They didn't get an airing of any substance in the plenary negotiations. You'd get these very bland reports coming back from the subcommittee just to say that discussions were continuing. So, you know, I would have to say that we didn't have a big input into the whole question of the equality agenda, as Sinn Féin call it. It emerged at the final hour.

Q: What did you make of it when it was sprung?

JEFFREY DONALDSON: Well, to be honest, we were very much focused on the constitutional questions and on strand two and strand one. I would have to say that in my opinion the Ulster Unionist Party didn't give enough attention to these issues, and they got slipped in. Our focus was elsewhere: on decommissioning, on the nature and scope of the Assembly, the nature and scope of the

North–South bodies. I think that, in hindsight, we ought to have deployed some of our negotiators to look more closely at these issues, because they are part of the Agreement which we didn't give enough attention to, and I just wonder if somewhere along the way they're not going to jump up and bite us.

I'm not in any way against the idea of equality. But I worry at times that we—as a society—we are becoming too much of a grievance society.

The Decommissioning Issue

Q: What were your hopes and fears of decommissioning at the time of the negotiations?

JEFFREY DONALDSON: My fears were that it would be fudged as it had been fudged right down the line. Now, if confidence-building is a process that is to work, it has to be a two-way process. If those who have been engaged in violence, and used violence, and supported violence in the past to pursue their political agenda, are to be rehabilitated into society, then society is having to build confidence in those people. But, equally, if society is to have confidence in those people, then they've got to demonstrate that they're prepared to play by the normal rules. When you look at the enormous amount of concessions that have been made to the terrorist groupings, not least on the question of prisoner releases, I certainly felt, and still feel, that decommissioning is important in terms of demonstrating in a tangible way that people are moving beyond violence and into the democratic process.

I had great difficulties, and still do, with the idea of the early release of terrorist prisoners—purely from the point of view of justice. What I wanted to see was [when] people say that they are committed to exclusively peaceful means, that they actually demonstrated that in tangible terms, that it wasn't just lip service, some sort of paper commitment.

For me the Agreement fell far short in that nothing happens on decommissioning, and the confidence that needs to be built to make this thing work is absent. If David Trimble and Gerry Adams are going to sit together in government and work together in government, and there is an absence of trust and confidence, then it won't work. It's as simple as that. Therefore decommissioning, in my opinion, should have been dealt with more adequately within the Agreement. It wasn't, and we now live with the consequences of that.

Concluding the Agreement

Q: Can you tell me about the final hours of the negotiations

JEFFREY DONALDSON: I was determined to stay in until the end, and I did. I only left the talks whenever the final decisions had been taken. In the early hours of Good Friday morning, Gerry Adams and Martin McGuiness walked into a room and held a crisis meeting with Bertie Ahern and Tony Blair and

George Mitchell. They basically told the two prime ministers and the talks chairman, 'we're packing and we're leaving unless you give us an undertaking that the prisoners will all be released within two years and you remove the linkage between decommissioning, the release of prisoners and the holding of ministerial office'. In effect, in my opinion, Sinn Féin/IRA put a gun to their head metaphorically, and said we're out of here.

We all know the consequences of what they meant by that. So that was discussed and debated within the Unionist Party's negotiating team. There were five of us within the negotiating team who felt that we could not support the final draft of the Agreement because of major deficiencies in these kinds of areas.

Remember, the prime minister asked us in the final hours, if there is one thing here that you want changed what is it? Of all the things—I mean, we had about a dozen points that we were unhappy about. I was clear that the one issue that we needed was the question of the linkage between decommissioning and the holding of ministerial office. The prime minister couldn't deliver that. And so, David Trimble, John Taylor, and the majority of the negotiating team decided to go with the Agreement. And myself and some other colleagues felt that we couldn't.

There was enormous pressure put on David Trimble. What happened was that after the Sinn Féin threat during the night the government agreed to these key changes in the final text. At that stage, about seven or eight o'clock in the morning, the government spin doctors started spinning to the media that there was likely to be an agreement and that an announcement would be made shortly, and that news went out right across the world. So CNN, you know, BBC—everywhere there was an expectation created that an agreement was imminent. So David Trimble was put under enormous pressure.

We met for about three hours that afternoon, and about every half hour the door knocks and it's Tony Blair's chief of staff, Jonathon Powell: 'What's happening?', you know... 'Have you decided what you're going to do?' And we reached a stage where we just locked the door. We kept on discussing, and the notes started coming in under the door. Then Bill Clinton rang, and so on. So, a lot of pressure was put on David Trimble. In my opinion David Trimble in the end was pressurized through the expectation that had been created out there in the media. If he had walked out there and said; 'No, I cannot accept this final draft', he would have been portrayed as the man who wrecked the chance of agreement. Because David Trimble wasn't the person who went in and said 'If I walk out of here, the ceasefire is over', that put Gerry Adams in a much more powerful position.

So, yes, in those final hours, and particularly in the final twelve hours, there was enormous pressure specifically placed on David Trimble to sign up to the Agreement.

Q: In retrospect, if you had to draw up a balance sheet of gains and losses, how do you think you managed in getting your core interests protected?

JEFFREY DONALDSON: Setting aside decommissioning and prisoner releases and the confidence-building issues, setting those aspects aside for the moment, and looking at the three strands, on balance I don't think that one side got more than the other.

What we've got is a compromise, and in many ways it's a complex compromise. It's a very difficult compromise. In practice it's going to be very difficult to work, because of the weighted majority voting system, you know, the need for consensus.[53]

In a sense, Good Friday did not conclude the negotiations. The negotiations continue. In a sense Good Friday created a further embellishment of the framework. It—the Good Friday Agreement, the Belfast Agreement—created structures. But it's like a building: a building can only function properly if you put people into it. Otherwise it's just a monument. It's just a structure. It's people who make things work, and people can make things work if they trust each other. But if they don't trust each other, then, such is human nature, it is very difficult for those institutions and those structures to work. So, I think what we have is a very, very delicate balance, and that balance, if it tips one way or the other, could up-end the whole thing. I think there is a danger that that could happen.

5.4. SDLP Perspectives

5.4.1. Seán Farren

The Talks Process

Q: What was the SDLP's view of the talks process when it became clear that Sinn Féin would be involved?

SEÁN FARREN: Sinn Féin's entry was no longer problematic once the conditions had been deemed to have been met by the two governments. The question was, then, would the Ulster Unionists remain in the talks? Certainly, the DUP and the UK Unionist Party had made it clear that they would withdraw, but during the summer the Ulster Unionist Party leader, David Trimble, had indicated that he was going to take soundings within his own community as to what the Ulster Unionist Party should do. It was quite clear from the way in which he

---

[53] The Agreement provided for cross-community decision-making in the Assembly in key areas by 'parallel consent' (support from an overall majority, including a majority of unionists and nationalists), or by 'weighted majority' (support from 60% of all members and from at least 40% of unionists and nationalists), with additional provision allowing 'a significant minority of Assembly members' (30 out of 108) to trigger a petition of concern that would require such a qualified majority.

was reacting over the summer that he was seeking the kind of reassurances necessary from his own community to enable him to stay there. He obviously got these, and the Ulster Unionist Party declared that they were going to continue to take part in the talks, and so they did, and in a sense, almost from that decision onwards, it was increasingly clear that there was going to be a positive outcome of some kind to the talks, because all of the key players were now participating, and there was no question of the SDLP not participating.

Q: What were the vital interests the SDLP wanted to protect during the talks?

SEÁN FARREN: The vital interests the SDLP wanted to protect had been signalled for a very long time. In fact, you know, you can go right back to the New Ireland Forum, I suppose, and, indeed, prior to that, when the SDLP articulated its requirements.[54] These were threefold: that relationships within the North between the two communities would be satisfactorily addressed in a political and constitutional way; likewise, relationships between North and South; and likewise, relationships between Ireland as a whole and Britain.

So, the vital interests were within that framework of relationships, and primarily involved the identity and political affiliations and allegiances of the nationalist community. Those vital interests could only be protected, as we saw it, within the wider framework of those three relationships. So our key objectives were to convince the other parties that those relationships were essential, the essential bedrock, if you like, to any new arrangement, and that the need was to provide political institutions which would express those relationships and guarantee the identities of the various sections of the community.

Strand one was the strand in which to guarantee that there would be equality, justice, fairness, parity of esteem. If you like, all those terms sum up the SDLP's philosophy and indeed its political objectives, as far as any new arrangements for the North itself were concerned.

Strand Two

SEÁN FARREN: Strand two was the North–South relationship. If you go back to the 1991–2 Brooke–Mayhew talks[55] and if you read the submissions made by the Ulster Unionist Party at that stage, they virtually dismiss the North–South relationship and see it as something which was, you know, a purely nationalist requirement, not one that impinged on them except insofar as cooperation on practical matters might be deemed worthy and maybe necessary in some instances, as between two neighbouring foreign states. They always liked to

---

[54] The SDLP position had been articulated in several documents going back to *Towards a New Ireland* (Social Democratic and Labour Party 1972), and was presented again at the New Ireland Forum (1983–4).

[55] See Subsections 4.1.1 and 4.3.5.

insinuate that the South was a foreign state. But if you look at their submission in the recent (1996–8) talks, you'll see a sea change; you'll see an acknowledgement of the relationships thesis. I would credit the SDLP's articulation of our views in 1991–2 and their [the UUP's] reflection on what we said then as strongly influencing their submissions in the 1996–8 talks. The other party, of course, that needed significant convincing was Sinn Féin.

Sinn Féin, without openly acknowledging it, had begun to change, and some of the changes were signalled in the statements made jointly by John Hume and Gerry Adams.[56] In particular, you'd hear Adams acknowledging that there could be no agreement, no settlement, which did not have the full allegiance of both unionist and nationalist traditions. So, here you were seeing the beginning of a movement away from the very, very traditional republican position.

Unionists conceived the situation as one where they had had control, and in which any change meant that they had less, and, therefore, they were the ones that had most fears, most concerns. They had concerns about the degree of power and influence that would be distributed to the nationalist community within the North, but most particularly, of course, they had concerns about the North/South Ministerial Council—if this was an even greater toehold for the southern government in the affairs of Northern Ireland, given that the Anglo-Irish Agreement had provided the Irish government with its first toehold in the affairs of the North.

One of the things that they claimed they had achieved was to diminish the southern government's role, but I think that's more rhetorical and a kind of attempt at face-saving than anything else. The talks took so long because of all these fears, because of the issue of decommissioning, because of matters which had to do with what was called the confidence-building agenda, which was an aspect of the talks that was novel for these negotiations.[57]

In previous negotiations, there was not a part of the agenda which was anything like the confidence-building part of the agenda that we had this time. Yes, on previous occasions the question of prisoners was always one that people recognized would have to be addressed, but when you look at the confidence-building measures, taking in decommissioning, taking in the prisoners issue, taking in the victims issue, taking in economic issues, taking in equality issues, taking in language issues, you have a much wider agenda.

Unionists, as I said earlier, wanted to ensure that there was very little flexibility, very little by way of independent authority, which the ministerial council could exercise, and Sinn Féin, as I said, wanted to see the ministerial council as something that could operate virtually autonomously. Now, we felt there was a need to strike a middle road there, that, while there was

---

[56] See discussion in Subsection 4.1.2.
[57] See Subsection 5.1.3.

accountability back to Belfast and back to Dublin, nonetheless, some degree of—I don't want to use the word 'autonomy'—some degree of independent action (but one which did carry with it both the authority of Belfast and Dublin) could be allowed to the North/South Ministerial Council.

That's why we put forward the idea, along with the Irish government, of implementation bodies being established by the council. These would have an executive authority under the council to take forward the council's policy. The previous word that was used was 'executive authority', for example in the Framework Documents and, indeed, going back to our own ideas in the 1991–2 talks. The word 'implementation' replaced 'executive authority', because unionists strongly objected to 'executive', which they said smelt too much of independence [for this all-Ireland body].

So, we were then trying to argue for a council that had a degree of executive independence, but, nonetheless, that independence would be constrained by accountability back to Belfast, on the one hand, [and] accountability back to Dublin, on the other. Given the financial constraints that could be operated from either of these two outside sources, the Ministerial Council would not be an autonomous body or an embryonic all-Ireland institution, floating away from any lines of accountability to Belfast and Dublin.

Q: On strand one, when did you reach agreement with the unionists?

SEÁN FARREN: We had argued very strongly for a cabinet system of government, as opposed to the committee system proposed by the UUP. I think myself that they had begun to see merit in our ideas anyway, but it took until the last minute.

They abandoned the committee system in the very last two meetings that we held with them. They were the meetings at midnight and at one o'clock in the morning of Good Friday. It didn't take a great deal of persuasion at that particular point because they simply said 'alright, we'll have that'. We had proposed executive heads of each department, I think we had [called] them HODs, heads of department, or something like that, and they said 'oh well, no, let's call them ministers'. I remember David Trimble saying 'let's have them, let's give them the title and, in a sense, the dignity of being what everybody recognizes them to be'. We were happy enough with that, but that didn't come until the last minute.

Q: Did the SDLP support the Mitchell draft proposals on the North/South Ministerial Council and, if so, what did it take for the SDLP to accept the final proposals in the Agreement?[58]

SEÁN FARREN: Much of the North–South negotiation was being conducted by Dublin and therefore, on the detail of the North/South Ministerial Council,

---

[58] For the text of the Mitchell draft, see Document 5.3.

how it would operate, we would have to be guided by what Dublin felt they could operate. I mean [...] the North/South Ministerial Council would put nationalists on the same side as unionists and Dublin would be on the other side of the table, figuratively, and we had to be guided by the way in which Dublin saw the North–South Council working. It required the wholesale rewriting of the areas of North–South cooperation. That annex in the Mitchell draft which contained the areas for North–South cooperation and implementation bodies was closer to the kind of thinking that you find in the Framework Documents than in what you find in the Good Friday Agreement document.

Q: Who proposed the number of areas for cooperation?

SEÁN FARREN: Well, remember that a number of these had their origin in the Framework Documents, and the Ulster Unionists took fright at a number of areas like trade and business development and inward investment. I mean, they claimed last week in the run-up to last week's agreement[59] that they couldn't accept our suggestions because they had deliberately got them out of the list for the Good Friday Agreement, and even though the list in the Good Friday Agreement is permissive, they felt that they couldn't let in what they had already got out. They had also got out the reference to the Irish language, and both are back, notwithstanding their objections.[60]

Many of the details on the North–South strand were negotiated from within the Taoiseach's group and the Irish delegation, and then by the Taoiseach himself when he came up [to join the talks]. We were brought in from time to time, but really to be advised as to what changes they were making, and on a few occasions we were able to offer additional advice and to get some changes into the text. But the texts at that stage were the property of the Irish and the British governments. The British were keeping the unionists on board, and the Irish, if you like, were keeping ourselves and Sinn Féin on board.

So, we were playing a subsidiary role with respect to strand two. We weren't unhappy with that because we recognized the Irish government had [...] authority and obviously, we wanted to make sure that they wouldn't compromise below a certain point, but at the same time, if they decided to, there wasn't an awful lot we could do about it. You know, we'd then have to live with the question as to whether or not we sacrificed the whole thing because the North–South agreement didn't go far enough for us.

[59] Agreement on the North–South implementation bodies and new government departments was reached on 18 December 1998.

[60] The implementation bodies agreed in December 1998 included three proposed by nationalists (in the areas of trade and business development, Special EU Programmes, and the Irish language) and three proposed by unionists (Irish Lights, the Food Safety Authority, and Waterways Ireland).

Strand One

Q: To go back to strand one, what about the technicalities, such as the rule of parallel consent and weighted majority voting and the D'Hondt method of allocation of ministries? Do they protect the SDLP's interests?

SEÁN FARREN: Well, we debated long and hard over the parallel consent clause.[61] We knew that there had to be some weighted majority system and at one stage we had a big board out on which we worked out and demonstrated to each other the consequences of various weightings with respect to the vote. There were some people who felt that we had to have a very high threshold, and we worked out in various scenarios what the consequences of a high threshold would be, and what the consequences of various other thresholds would be.

The actual mechanisms were something, as I say, we debated long and hard over, and, as you know, the Agreement contains provision for two forms of weighted majority—the stronger form and a slightly weaker form. Both, I think, will not be required to be invoked very often. There will be certain key decisions that will always require a weighted majority, but these will be few and far between. There is provision for other opportunities to use weighted voting, but they are essentially safety nets for both communities, for the Ulster Unionists as well as for us.

The D'Hondt system, to be honest, I can't remember who proposed that initially.[62] I remember it surfaced during the Brooke–Mayhew talks as a mechanism that could be used—because at that stage people were talking about the allocation of committee chairmanships and the parties that had proposed that, perhaps it was from them that it came. So D'Hondt has been in my consciousness since 1991–2.

On the allocation of ministerial office, it will give a reasonably fair representation to the SDLP, where the SDLP will have three out of ten, the Ulster Unionists the same, the DUP two, and Sinn Féin two. So, there will be a reasonably fair representation for both communities, if you take it in the aggregate, on both sides, five and five, and together with the First and Deputy First Minister, then there will be six and six, and on a party basis, the SDLP will have four and the Ulster Unionists will have four. So, there is a considerable form of protection, and the mechanism removes the obvious kind of unseemly squabble that there could be with respect to the allocation of posts. Across four parties, I think some kind of mechanism like that is highly desirable in our situation.

Q: Do you see the Agreement as an interim or a permanent settlement?

SEÁN FARREN: I see the Agreement, like all political agreements, as something which is capable of evolution. It will change but—and this is the strength of

---

[61] See Subsection 5.4.2 and Ch.5, n. 53.
[62] See n. 51.

it—if it succeeds, it will change by consent. I would not use the language of transition, because transition means that you have some sense of where you're going. The process can only grow, develop, change by agreement of the significant participants, and that's how I see it.

I don't believe that political institutions stand still; otherwise they atrophy. Sometimes, they change and evolve very slowly, but change and evolve they do, and must, and will, and so will the institutions that we have created. I think we're probably moving constitutionally into uncharted waters if we're going to move at all from the base, and the constitutional aspects will probably be the ones that will change most slowly, because you don't change constitutions very often. Constitutional changes leave open the question, for example, of Irish unity, to the will and determination of the majority of people in the North. I think as people work out this Agreement bonds may be created on a North–South basis that weren't there before, but so also will they be created on an East–West basis.

Q: To what extent is a culture of negotiation and compromise building up?

SEÁN FARREN: Well, perhaps that's one of the things that we're now witnessing. We have been in constant negotiations since the Good Friday Agreement—I suppose, most particularly since the establishment of the Assembly—working out the details of the Good Friday Agreement. I see the next four years [1999–2003] as almost being an extension of the negotiations because we will be working out and testing and monitoring whether what we decide now in terms of the institutions and the organization and logistics for those institutions, whether it is going to be in the best long-term interest, or whether at the end of this period we change. The Agreement does make clear provision for an overall review of the Agreement after four years, so we will have a review and that review could be fairly extensive—but it may not be, depending on what the experience is between now and then.

5.4.2. Mark Durkan

The Talks Process

Q: what was the SDLP's view when it became clear in the summer of 1997 that Sinn Féin were about to enter the talks?

MARK DURKAN: We were glad that things were moving. From the start of the new talks [10 June 1996] through to the summer of 1997, we had tried to prevent the process from stalling completely. We had to protect the talks ground rules, so as to preserve the prospect for inclusive talks.

In the autumn of 1996, John Hume had put proposals to John Major on how—in the event of a restored IRA ceasefire—Sinn Féin might enter the talks. These proposals were brokered through Fr Alec Reid and Gerry Adams. Major rejected them. Instead, he announced a series of sequenced tests of any ceasefire, and it all sounded very open-ended. Fr Reid was dejected and John Hume frustrated. I suggested that they propose that all the tests could be assessed and verified within a defined period.

Prior to the 1997 election, Paul Murphy was sounding out the Northern parties on the state of the talks.[63] We suggested that Tony Blair, who had supported Major's response in November 1996, should clarify that the tests did not have to be sequential or open-ended. This in effect became the new policy and it gave clear terms of entry for Sinn Féin to the talks.

We believed that the Ulster Unionists would stay in the talks, even with Sinn Féin inside. We had come to that conclusion partly because David Trimble had clearly differentiated between the terms of entry for Sinn Féin to the talks and the issue of decommissioning. Up to that point these issues had always been treated as though they were one and the same thing. Trimble indicated to us that he wanted to deal with these as two separate issues so that when he lost on the one, he could still have his position on the other.

Q: How did the SDLP see its role?

MARK DURKAN: In many ways we were the guardians of the process, for it was structured on our analysis of the three strands. The party faced a particular difficulty in that the Irish government wasn't involved in strand-one negotiations and wasn't likely to be involved. Sinn Féin were opting out of making strand-one proposals and heckling our contributions in the plenaries, so we were on our own. Obviously we had to get strand one right, but when you're in there as the only nationalist voice, and coming in with quite new ideas that we hadn't put forward in previous talks, it's hard. Yet in the end we got most of our proposals into the Agreement—more so than any other party did.

Q: What were the key issues?

MARK DURKAN: The potential deal-breakers from our point of view were that the strand-two arrangements should be self-standing, not just a subset of strand three. We actually took a very positive and proactive approach to strand three, although a lot of people think the whole question of the British–Irish Council is very much a unionist concept. If people actually care to check back, our response in the Forum for Peace and Reconciliation in June 1995 was that the British–Irish Framework Document was very limited in its strand-three prospectus.

We wanted a positive role for a British–Irish Council. We were very clear that it could not in some way be used as an outer casing overarching strand two. We wanted strand two to have a standing of its own. We had to make sure

[63] Paul Murphy, Labour MP for Torfaen, Wales, 1987–2015, was a close ally of Tony Blair, later Minister of State for political development in the Northern Ireland Office, 1997–9, and Secretary of State for Northern Ireland, 2002–5.

that the necessary features and elements of strand two would be there from day one. We were saying the people are going to have to vote on this Agreement in a referendum North and South, and they have to be able to look at *all* the elements together and measure them side by side. They have to know that whenever power is transferred to the new institutions there isn't just power being transferred to new northern institutions, but that at the same time the other North–South arrangements will also be established.

In relation to strand one, we had a series of key requirements. We had come into the negotiations calling for ministers and a proper executive—not just separate ministerial responsibilities, but also a collective executive entity allocated on the D'Hondt system or other such inclusive formula.[64] It was very important to us that we got that into the Agreement. It was only in the final weeks of the talks that we formalized the concept of the office of joint first ministers.

Strand One

Q: What was at stake in strand one?

MARK DURKAN: Our proposals for ministers to be appointed according to D'Hondt, or a variant, surprised all the other parties and drew a lot of fire from the UUP. They used the prospect of Sinn Féin ministers like a visual aid to reinforce their antipathy to ministers per se. Instead the UUP offered committee chairs or secretaries apportioned by D'Hondt, but decision-making remained by majority rule, with only vague qualifications. We sensed the shadow of Sunningdale: the UUP wanted to claim there was 'no executive power-sharing' and to prevent any ministerial 'Council of Ireland'. Meanwhile Alliance were pushing a voluntary coalition model.

We wanted to avoid a system that could be undermined electorally, if voters switched allegiance: every party had to be included, depending on electoral support. This was also a way of keeping public support and confidence in the process: we had to show that this wasn't just an arrangement by parties who wanted themselves to be in government and to keep out others. In fact—and I pointed this out to the other parties—this was a variation of our proposal in the Mayhew talks to elect three commissioners regionally by STV who could then appoint ministers.[65]

Q: Was strand one based on a concept of 'group rights'?

---

[64] On the party's early position on power sharing, see Social Democratic and Labour Party (1972).

[65] During the Mayhew talks in 1992 the SDLP had proposed the creation of a six-member Executive Commission (alongside a Parliamentary Assembly) made up of three members elected by STV from the territory of Northern Ireland (in effect, in the same way as Northern Ireland's European Parliament representatives) and one member each nominated by the British government, the Irish government, and the European Community; the elected member with the largest number of first preference votes would preside over the Commission; *Irish Times*, 13 May 1992.

MARK DURKAN: The UUP resisted any detailed development of rights and equality protections within strand one, and Sinn Féin didn't want to talk about strand one at all. This is why equality and rights are addressed in a separate section of the Agreement. But there was still the need to cross-reference rights and equality considerations in the strand-one provisions.

A key issue for us was to equality-proof and rights-proof Assembly procedures and to do so without dead-end, tit-for-tat vetoes. We asked how the principle of 'sufficient consensus' from the talks could be carried over into the new institutions. How could ministers be challenged if their policies breached equality guidelines? This led to the idea of a 'petition of concern' that would trigger the formation of an ad hoc special committee that would assess the evidence. This would also give a role to the Human Rights and Equality Commissions. We deliberately provided for such a special committee as a way of acknowledging sensitivities, so that policies could be modified according to evidence and argument. These paragraphs of the Agreement were not included in the Northern Ireland Act, 1998.[66] When we raised this, the UK government provided an amendment simply saying that the Assembly's standing orders would make provision for the special procedure outlined in those paragraphs, but this was never properly done.[67] So there were complicated interlinking issues. Our challenge was to get the detail and balance right in circumstances where the other parties were very sceptical of our ideas.

In fact, we came to convergence with the UUP first on the proposal for an elected office of joint first ministers. We suggested the concept of joint first ministers in part because the unionists didn't want a pure cabinet-style model, so we saw the joint office as a way of ensuring that there could be coherence in the executive, short of a standard cabinet-style model. It was partly done so that people would have a sense that there is balance in this Agreement and that it is not like the old Stormont model. We were also strongly holding out for the principle of parallel consent, a cross-community support requirement, and we were the only party doing this. Even George Mitchell was pleading with us on the weekend before Good Friday not to be unreasonable. He just couldn't understand why we were prepared to make this a deal-breaker.

We had difficulty in selling the concept of joint First Ministers, and it was only on the Friday before Good Friday [3 April 1998] that Seamus Mallon and I sat down with Reg Empey and David Trimble to put forward this idea.

---

[66] Good Friday Agreement, Strand One, paras 11–13.

[67] The petition of concern was later (after 2007) taken up by some parties (and especially the DUP) as a device to stall or stop changes of which it disapproved. For example, legalization of same-sex marriage, which was supported by a majority of the Assembly in 2015, was prevented when a DUP petition of concern triggered a weighted majority requirement, giving the party a veto on this.

They said: 'Well if we give you the First and Deputy First Minister, we have to agree that that is in lieu of the formal parallel consent requirement.' We said: 'No, we actually see strength in both.'

What wasn't agreed at that stage was the precise formula for appointing the First and Deputy First Minister. People said, 'Well, maybe it would be the two largest parties' and then when we were putting some of these concepts to the Alliance Party, in bilateral talks with them, they came up with a formula and said, 'Well it could be somebody from the largest designation who would be First Minister and somebody from the second largest designation who would be Deputy First Minister and then somebody from the third largest designation who would be speaker', and they added, 'that would mean we could say to our people it's not a matter of just unionists and nationalists, if the non-unionists or non-nationalists in the "other" group grows then maybe they could be Deputy First Minister'.

Effectively we suggested 'Well, what about saying First and Deputy First Minister should be elected jointly on the basis of parallel consent', because parallel consent solved that particular conundrum and seemed very appropriate to the appointment of First and Deputy First Minister. When they accepted it, we were able to say: 'Well if you admit the concept here, let it apply elsewhere.'

Q: How did agreement on your ministerial model happen?

MARK DURKAN: We had already had a meeting with the UUP, a little more than a week out from the deadline. Seamus Mallon suggested we take an overview, to look at what is in the unionist ideas that is also in ours, and vice versa. That was a useful exercise. We were able to identify more than a dozen different features that were common in our respective positions. Seamus went through six or seven points, saying that in our arrangements the key political people would be appointed by a formula such as D'Hondt or some other proportionate means (because at that stage we hadn't even agreed if they would be ministers, secretaries, or whatever). Our assumption was that they would say 'well, yes, we can agree that', so we were looking for those sorts of propositions on which agreement was potentially possible.

Seamus was able to establish six points like that and then Reg Empey had a go at six or seven. That was a good meeting. For the first time we got a sense that people were actually thinking themselves into these political scenarios, and at times when they were talking about what 'we' might do, it was a collective 'we' as opposed to just them as a party.

The following Friday [3 April)], Seamus and I went down to the Ulster Unionists' room and met David Trimble and Reg Empey. It was an attempt by us to say 'if we agree these points, is there more we could do?' We listened to a lot of problems that they had. They had a whole load of concerns about the concept of an executive and a cabinet-style arrangement. They acknowledged that their proposed system of committees—a council-style model of a whole series of committees without ministers but with chairs or secretaries—didn't allow for the sort of executive coherence that we were saying good government needed, nor the sort of collective planning and resource allocation that would be needed on an ongoing basis. So, they had sort of conceded that there was something wanting in their model, but they were 'iffy' about ours, and they went through their observations and anxieties. It was at that meeting that we first outlined to them the concept that we had developed only in the preceding weeks: a joint office of first ministers.

Q: Did the Mitchell draft reflect your views?[68]

MARK DURKAN: In the Mitchell draft [7–8 April 1998], a lot of things were left open and optional in strand one, so it was very weak from our point of view, and it was giving us very serious problems. I think people didn't realize just how worried and concerned we were about strand one. The whole headline interest was about strand two: you got very heavy reactions to the draft of strand two from the unionists, and meanwhile Sinn Féin were out posing for the cameras. I don't think they realized just how bad strand one was, particularly in the context of likely slippage from the strand-two text.

Then suddenly Sinn Féin took a position on strand one. They were now saying, 'ministers, not secretaries'. They were suddenly saying to the governments and to George Mitchell that they wanted parallel consent, whereas up to that point they had been silent on the issue. They similarly started arguing for another safeguard that we had proposed, that people could raise a petition of concern.[69] So essentially they were taking bits from our position and simply adding their own signature. George Mitchell joked with some of us on the corridor that he asked them how come they got religion so fast but so late.

Our concern on strand one was to tighten up our own proposals. We were continually drafting and redrafting, Seán [Farren] and myself in particular, and we were trying to get contact with other parties, where we could, to try to lock some of these ideas into other people's thinking, because we knew we were going to be asking people to go for quite a significant departure from the Mitchell draft in terms of strand one. The Ulster Unionists wouldn't talk to us for a couple of days; they were concentrating solely on the governments in relation to strand two. It was even hard to get Alliance to engage at that time. People were saying that we were talking out of turn, did we not realize the negotiations were in crisis and were probably going to break over strand two, and why were we talking to them about strand one?

It was only on the Thursday evening [9 April] that we got into the strand-one discussions with the unionists after Bertie and Blair had more or less

---

[68] See subsection 5.1.2 and, for the text, Document 5.3.
[69] See n. 53.

settled the compromises and commitments they were going for in strand two. This had some implications in terms of strand one. Right up to the Thursday, Mitchell was still telling us we weren't going to get agreement on parallel consent, joint first ministers, and a full-blown executive. That was his 'read' of it, and he couldn't see why other parties would be going for it. We wouldn't have been in a very comfortable position if we hadn't already made an effort to convince the smaller parties.

There were some difficult issues. Seán and I were making the point that we would need a fall back from parallel consent, because parallel consent could be frustrated: Paisley might get enough numbers with it, or Trimble's margins might be so narrow that it wouldn't work. Now we had real difficulty in persuading colleagues that such a scenario could arise because people were very fixed on parallel consent and only parallel consent, and we were saying 'yeah, but there would be a case for some sort of qualified weighted majority mechanism as well'.[70]

Now, the Mitchell draft suggested a weighted majority, and favoured simply a 60 per cent majority that didn't require any degree of nationalist or unionist support, rather than the parallel consent model that we argued for. In a discussion between ourselves and some of the Dublin government representatives the idea came up that it would be a two-thirds majority including at least a third of unionists and a third of nationalists; the idea of a third, I suppose, was to try to keep the notional symmetry that was there in the parallel-consent mechanism. I just found myself looking all the time, saying that's still not right, and we went through it ourselves on flip charts, going through the numbers and the scenarios.

It would be the second meeting on that Holy Thursday–Good Friday night [9–10 April] that we would get agreement from the Unionists. The meeting ran after midnight, until about 2 a.m. We didn't expect to get total closure with the Unionists then, and we didn't agree everything, but we did agree key issues, including the executive, parallel consent, and a weighted majority measure of 60 per cent overall and 40 per cent from each designation.[71]

Strand Two

Q: And strand two? How was agreement reached?

MARK DURKAN: In late 1996 and early 1997 the SDLP and UUP talks team members had conducted a series of language-proofing exchanges with a flip chart in a room in Castle Buildings. This was the period when the UUP would not commence actual negotiations on the already agreed agenda until they were satisfied about decommissioning. A few of us from each party met a

---

[70] See Subsection 5.4.1 and n. 53.
[71] The reference is to self-designated 'unionists' and self-designated 'nationalists' in the Assembly.

number of times to explore verbal sensitivities and test for mutually acceptable terminology.

These exchanges anticipated the negotiations to follow, but they were not shadow negotiations. They were talks about the language that might be used in negotiations to minimize contention. The UUP told us that a term like 'Council of Ireland' or even 'All-Ireland' or 'All-Island Council of Ministers' would be a non-starter: they would not be proposing to have 'ministers' in the North. So, if meetings could not be 'All-Ireland', they might be called 'North–South'. They didn't like the idea of such meetings being able to 'decide' but they might accept 'agree'. Whatever was 'agreed' was not to be 'executed', as they would not broach the idea of cross-border executive capacity. They were adamant about refusing any proposals with terms like 'executive agencies'. We were practically thesaurus testing as we worked through options, to find that they would concur that whatever was 'agreed' 'North–South' could be 'implemented' not by 'agencies' but perhaps by some 'body'. This explains why we ended up with clunky nomenclature like 'North/South Ministerial Council' and 'North–South implementation bodies'.

When the talks moved onto the actual negotiating agenda (that the UUP had already agreed and tabled jointly with us), we were frustrated at what we saw as their evasion and diversion on strand two. They argued that any necessary North–South engagement could be politician-free and conducted at technocratic level. For a period they were saying that coordination was only really relevant on EU-related matters and that it should be at member-state level. They even argued that we did not need a distinct North–South strand; this should instead be a subset of strand three, East–West. They were quite capricious about their defaulting: they alluded to the 'nothing is agreed until everything is agreed' rubric, pointing out that they were not yet agreeing to having ministers in Northern Ireland. Conversely, they were resistant to any suggestions that EU programmes might be framed on an all-island basis, or that directives (in such areas as the environment) be transposed island-wide.

This was difficult for the Irish government and ourselves. Meanwhile, Sinn Féin were pointedly only positing a united Ireland scenario and using the UUP's dismissive truculence to criticize us and the Irish government. This continued into 1998.

Q: What did you do?

MARK DURKAN: Given this lack of real engagement on strand two, the Irish government was keen to ensure that there was more shape and substance on the table once the Easter deadline for agreement was set. The Irish government was concerned to avoid a thin text on strand two that did no more than summarize the lowest common denominator between the parties.

The so-called Mitchell Draft had much fuller strand-two provisions than the final Agreement. George Mitchell himself had no editorial say in the document, which was negotiated between the two governments. He thought it was a mistake by the Irish government to have no square brackets or italics in the strand-two text to indicate points open to negotiation. Tony Blair told us: 'I allowed the Irish to over-negotiate this paper as it was always going to come down to them and yourselves having to compromise with the Unionists, who are not going to agree to this much.'

The UUP and John Alderdice went ape at the 'Mitchell document' on strand two, and the two loyalist parties were disgruntled as well. This eclipsed their consideration of other dimensions like strand one, rights and equality, or policing for a couple of days. It was deal-breaker stuff as far as the UUP and Alderdice were concerned.

As Blair and Mitchell had predicted, the Irish government conceded slippage in the text so that it became less definitive, more conditional, with a more selective prospectus and a narrower technocratic tone. By this stage there was serious risk of the talks failing: strand two was being diminished, and strand one was still inadequate. We were trying to shore up the Irish government's position during this time. We were worried about the loss of scope, scale, and specifics, and this was the focus of our bilaterals with both governments, especially the Irish government.

The Irish government agreed that the institutional framework of strand two had to be substantive enough to balance and complement the constitutional change to articles 2 and 3. When we made that point in a corridor meeting with David Trimble, he was dismissive and critical about the constitutional change and complained about Dublin's high-handedness.

In the end, the Irish government found itself whittling down more of the strand-two text. We had misgivings about the tentative and loose state of the text. They stressed that they had fixed a backstop with the British government—a deadline of 31 October 1998 for having the institutions in place. Seamus Mallon questioned the reliability of this deadline, and both governments argued that they had insisted on it despite Trimble's reluctance. The Taoiseach said he believed that the UUP knew that both governments were serious about this deadline and that they would be prepared to leverage it. Having got textual changes, he believed the unionists could be cooperative in agreeing the particular sectoral formats and implementation bodies. When we asked how the backstop would be leveraged in the event of difficulty, the Taoiseach told us that he and Blair had agreed on this but shared no detail. Similarly, in answer to our concerns the prime minister emphasized the political guarantee of the October deadline but provided no further detail.

It was left to us to test the UUP's intent on strand two in the context of the remaining strand-one negotiations. The arrangements for joint first ministers and the executive would touch on strand two—for example, in the assignment of ministers to the North–South council meetings. Signals were mixed, but John Hume accepted unionists' concern to avoid any scenario where the first ministers would have to make a martyr of a minister who declined to participate in any given strand-two or [strand-]three business. The fact that we had the UUP now agreeing to ministers in the North, even an executive committee, which they had resisted, and a North/South Ministerial Council, marked progress that even George Mitchell had doubted was possible.

Q: How did it work out?

MARK DURKAN: The backstop of 31 October 1998 passed without progress on strand two and without any really active intervention by either government. The process was gridlocked again. The UUP insisted that satisfactory progress on decommissioning was a precondition for appointing the executive. This in turn blocked the establishment of the North/South Ministerial Council. This was contrary to the Agreement itself. Tony Blair's personal assurances (his 'blackboard pledge' during the May referendum campaign) had encouraged Trimble in this stance, and he also claimed a manifesto mandate for it.[72] We were paying a price for the Irish government's unnecessary drafting of a cross-reference to the strand-one provisions for exclusion from ministerial office in the Agreement's text on decommissioning. Meanwhile Sinn Féin were saying that decommissioning was not a requirement or obligation of the Agreement at any stage.

We tried to engage with the UUP on possible defined areas of cooperation, sectoral formats, and implementation bodies under the North/South Ministerial Council. There was no real urgency from the UUP. When we did get into discussions, their line of argument changed depending on who we were talking to. They stressed that they were under pressure internally as well as from the DUP, and that strand-two details would be very sensitive. As the only unionists to participate, they said they would have an undue attendance burden due to the 'sufficient inclusion' rule for unionist/nationalist accompanying ministers.[73]

---

[72] The personal pledge which the Prime Minister, Mr Tony Blair, made to the people of Northern Ireland on the evening of Wednesday, 20 May 1998 (two days prior to the Referendum), at the University of Ulster at Coleraine was as follows: 'I pledge to the people of Northern Ireland:

- No change in the status of Northern Ireland without the express consent of the people of Northern Ireland.
- Power to take decisions returned to a Northern Ireland Assembly, with accountable North/South co-operation.
- Fairness and equality guaranteed for all.
- Those who use or threaten violence excluded from the Government of Northern Ireland.
- Prisoners kept in unless violence is given up for good. Whatever the referendum result, as Prime Minister of the United Kingdom I will continue to work for stability and prosperity for all the people of Northern Ireland' (Gay 1998: 9).

[73] The agreement required that sectoral meetings of the NSMC be attended not just by the relevant northern and southern ministers, but also by a second northern minister of the opposite designation; thus, UUP ministers would have to service not just sectors where they held the ministry, but also ones where a nationalist minister was responsible.

They didn't want anything expansive, and some argued that the more the sectors or bodies could be presented as technocratic and/or with a concentration on EU-related cross-border issues, the more they could defend them.

Q: How was this resolved?

MARK DURKAN: Given the decommissioning stand-off, negotiations were difficult.[74] They were also complicated by our work on the departmental structures, which would define ministers' remits. The UUP were defensive. They worried not simply about the status and scope of the bodies, but also about the broader areas of cooperation and sectoral formats under the North/South Ministerial Council. They worried about the risk of 'solo runs' by departmental ministers; they feared creeping expansion of the bodies. We had to develop processes of advance transparency, executive approval, and accompanying ministers for all NSMC meetings.

The Agreement had provided for 'at least' twelve bodies and areas of cooperation. We took this as a minimum, while the UUP held it as a maximum. Their emphasis was solely on 'cross-border' bodies, whereas we stood by the language of 'all-island and cross-border' bodies. We proposed trade, business development, and inward investment as a sector with an implementation body, and we liaised with the Irish government. This was not one of the 'at least twelve' areas listed as examples in the Agreement text. The UUP was resistant. We were not proposing a straight merger of IDA and IDB but that's what they argued.[75] As it happens, it was the Irish government that definitively took 'inward investment' out of the picture. DFA officials told us that Mary Harney was ruling out inward investment.[76] We had to go instead for 'trade and business development'. We also suggested a 'company' to market the island for tourism in addition to the six 'bodies'. Meanwhile the UUP argued that much of the cooperation was really just technocratic coordination in relation to EU directives or funding.

Q: So then, in 1999, do you remain optimistic now?

MARK DURKAN: Purposeful!

---

[74] Absence of IRA decommissioning was a continuing grievance of the UUP, obstructing the negotiations.

[75] IDA (Industrial Development Authority) Ireland is the agency responsible for industrial development in the Republic; IDB (Industrial Development Board for Northern Ireland) is its northern counterpart.

[76] Mary Harney, leader of the Progressive Democrats in the Republic of Ireland, was Tánaiste, 1997–2006, and Minister for Enterprise, Trade and Employment, 1997–2004, with responsibility for the IDA and inward investment policy in the Republic.

Documents

Document 5.1. Mitchell Report, 22 January 1996

REPORT OF THE INTERNATIONAL BODY ON ARMS DECOMMISSIONING, 22 JANUARY 1996

I. Introduction

1. On 28 November, 1995, the British and Irish Governments issued a Communiqué which announced the launching in Northern Ireland of a '"twin track" process to make progress in parallel on the decommissioning issue and on all-party negotiations'.

2. One track was 'to invite the parties to intensive preparatory talks with a remit to reach widespread agreement on the basis, participation, structure, format and agenda to bring all parties together for substantive negotiations aimed at a political settlement based on consent'. This has become known as the political track.

3. The other track concerned the decommissioning of arms and was set forth as follows in the Communiqué:

'5. In parallel, the two Governments have agreed to establish an International Body to provide an independent assessment of the decommissioning issue.

6. Recognising the widely expressed desire to see all arms removed from Irish politics, the two Governments will ask the International Body to report on the arrangements necessary for the removal from the political equation of arms silenced by virtue of the welcome decisions taken last Summer and Autumn by those organisations that previously supported the use of arms for political purposes.

7. In particular, the two Governments will ask the Body to:

—identify and advise on a suitable and acceptable method for full and verifiable decommissioning; and

—report whether there is a clear commitment on the part of those in possession of such arms to work constructively to achieve that.

8. It will be for the International Body to determine its own procedures. The two Governments expect it to consult widely, to invite relevant parties to submit their analysis of matters relevant to the decommissioning issue and, in reaching its conclusions within its remit, to consider such evidence on its merits.'

4. We are that Body. This is our report. We have no stake in Northern Ireland other than an interest in seeing an end to the conflict and in the ability of its people to live in peace. Our role is to bring an independent perspective to the issue. We are motivated solely by our wish to help. This assessment represents our best and our independent judgement. We are unanimous in our views. There are no differences of opinion among us.

5. To provide us with sufficient information to meet our remit, we held two series of meetings in Belfast, Dublin and London: the first, 15 through 18 December, 1995; the second, 11 through 22 January, 1996. In addition, we held an organisational meeting in New York on December 9, 1995.

6. In the course of our meetings we heard orally and in writing from dozens of government officials, political leaders, church officials and representatives of other organisations and institutions. We received hundreds of letters and telephone calls from members of the public and met with many others. We thank all for their submissions. Contributions from those who suffered losses during the time of troubles but are strongly committed to the peace process were especially moving. All the submissions have been carefully reviewed and considered.

II. Discussion

7. Our examination of the issues and of the facts, and the perspectives brought to us by those who briefed us or who made written representations to us, convince us that while there is no simple solution to the conflict in Northern Ireland, the factors on which a process for peace must be based are already known. We can indicate the way we believe these factors should be addressed so that decommissioning of arms and all-party negoti-ations can proceed, but only resolute action by the parties themselves will produce progress.

8. That noted, we are aware of the enormous contribution already made by individuals and groups in advancing the process of peace in Northern Ireland to its current stage. The tireless and courageous efforts of Prime Minister John Major and Taoiseach John Bruton (and before him Albert Reynolds) have been essential to the peace process. They have been joined by other political leaders, institutions, organisations and individuals in the promo-tion of peace.

9. We considered our task in the light of our responsibility to all of the people of Northern Ireland; the need for the people to be reassured that their democratic and moral expect-ations can be realised; and in the spirit of serious efforts made by the British and Irish Governments to advance the peace process.

10. For nearly a year and a half the guns have been silent in Northern Ireland. The people want that silence to continue. They want lasting peace in a just society in which paramilitary violence plays no part. That was the dominant theme expressed in the many letters and calls we received from those in the North and South, Unionist and Nationalist, Catholic and Protestant, Loyalist and Republican.

11. Notwithstanding reprehensible 'punishment' killings and beatings, the sustained obser-vance of the ceasefires should not be devalued. It is a significant factor which must be given due weight in assessing the commitment of the paramilitaries to 'work constructively to achieve' full and verifiable decommissioning.

12. Since the ceasefires, the political debate has focused largely on the differences that have prevented the commencement of all-party negotiations intended to achieve an agreed political settlement. This circumstance has obscured the widespread agreement that exists—so widespread that it tends to be taken for granted. In fact, members of both traditions may be less far apart on the resolution of their differences than they believe.

13. No one should underestimate the value of the consensus for peace, and the fact that no significant group is actively seeking to end it.

14. In paragraph five of the Communiqué we were asked 'to provide an independent assessment of the decommissioning issue'. It is a serious issue. It is also a symptom of a larger problem: the absence of trust. Common to many of our meetings were arguments,

steeped in history, as to why the other side cannot be trusted. As a consequence, even well-intentioned acts are often viewed with suspicion and hostility.

15. But a resolution of the decommissioning issue—or any other issue—will not be found if the parties resort to their vast inventories of historical recrimination. Or, as it was put to us several times, what is really needed is the decommissioning of mind-sets in Northern Ireland.

16. We have asked ourselves how those who have suffered during the many years of internal strife can accept the fact that the establishment of a lasting peace will call for reconciliation with those they hold responsible for their loss and pain. Surely the continued suffering and bereavement of individuals and of families should never be forgotten. But if the focus remains on the past, the past will become the future, and that is something no one can desire.

17. Everyone with whom we spoke agrees in principle with the need to decommission. There are differences on the timing and context—indeed, those differences led to the creation of this Body—but they should not obscure the nearly universal support which exists for the total and verifiable disarmament of all paramilitary organisations. That must continue to be a principal objective.

18. However the issue of decommissioning is resolved, that alone will not lead directly to all-party negotiations. Much work remains on the many issues involved in the political track. The parties should address those issues with urgency.

III. Recommendations: Principles of Democracy and non-violence

19. To reach an agreed political settlement and to take the gun out of Irish politics, there must be commitment and adherence to fundamental principles of democracy and non-violence. Participants in all-party negotiations should affirm their commitment to such principles.

20. Accordingly, we recommend that the parties to such negotiations affirm their total and absolute commitment:

   a. *To democratic and exclusively peaceful means of resolving political issues;*
   b. *To the total disarmament of all paramilitary organisations;*
   c. *To agree that such disarmament must be verifiable to the satisfaction of an independent commission;*
   d. *To renounce for themselves, and to oppose any effort by others, to use force, or threaten to use force, to influence the course or the outcome of all-party negotiations;*
   e. *To agree to abide by the terms of any agreement reached in all-party negotiations and to resort to democratic and exclusively peaceful methods in trying to alter any aspect of that outcome with which they may disagree; and,*
   f. *To urge that 'punishment' killings and beatings stop and to take effective steps to prevent such actions.*

21. We join the Governments, religious leaders and many others in condemning 'punishment' killings and beatings. They contribute to the fear that those who have used violence to pursue political objectives in the past will do so again in the future. Such actions have no place in a lawful society.

22. Those who demand decommissioning prior to all-party negotiations do so out of concern that the paramilitaries will use force, or threaten to use force, to influence the

negotiations, or to change any aspect of the outcome of negotiations with which they disagree. Given the history of Northern Ireland, this is not an unreasonable concern. The principles we recommend address those concerns directly.

23. These commitments, when made and honoured, would remove the threat of force before, during and after all-party negotiations. They would focus all concerned on what is ultimately essential if the gun is to be taken out of Irish politics: an agreed political settlement and the total and verifiable disarmament of all paramilitary organisations. That should encourage the belief that the peace process will truly be an exercise in democracy, not one influenced by the threat of violence.

IV. Commitment to Decommissioning

24. The second of the specific questions in paragraph seven of the Communiqué asks us 'to report whether there is a clear commitment on the part of those in possession of such arms to work constructively to achieve' full and verifiable decommissioning.

25. We have concluded that there is a clear commitment on the part of those in possession of such arms to work constructively to achieve full and verifiable decommissioning as part of the process of all-party negotiations; but that commitment does not include decommissioning prior to such negotiations.

26. After careful consideration, on the basis of intensive discussions with the Governments, the political parties, religious leaders, the security forces, and many others, we have concluded that the paramilitary organisations will not decommission any arms prior to all-party negotiations. That was the unanimous and emphatically expressed view of the representatives of the political parties close to paramilitary organisations on both sides. It was also the view of the vast majority of the organisations and individuals who made oral and written submissions. It is not that they are all opposed to prior decommissioning. To the contrary, many favour it. But they are convinced that it will not happen. That is the reality with which all concerned must deal.

27. Competing views were advanced on prior decommissioning. One was that decommissioning of arms must occur prior to all-party negotiations. We were told that the clearest demonstration of adherence to democratic principles, and of a permanent end to the use of violence, is the safe removal and disposal of paramilitary arms, and that at this time only a start to decommissioning will provide the confidence necessary for all-party negotiations to commence. In this view, all parties were aware of the need for prior decommissioning before the ceasefires were announced and should not now be able to avoid that requirement.

28. In the competing view we were told that decommissioning of arms prior to all-party negotiations was not requested before the announcement of the cease-fires, and that had it been, there would have been no cease-fires; that those who entered into cease-fires did so in the belief they would lead immediately to all-party negotiations; and that the request for prior decommissioning, seriously pursued for the first time months after the cease-fires were declared, is merely a tactic to delay or deny such negotiations. In this view, the cease-fires having been maintained for nearly a year and a half, all-party negotiations should begin immediately with no further requirements.

29. We believe that each side of this argument reflects a core of reasonable concern which deserves to be understood and addressed by the other side.

30. Those who insist on prior decommissioning need to be reassured that the commitment to peaceful and democratic means by those formerly supportive of politically motivated violence is genuine and irreversible, and that the threat or use of such violence will not be invoked to influence the process of negotiations or to change any agreed settlement.

31. Those who have been persuaded to abandon violence for the peaceful political path need to be reassured that a meaningful and inclusive process of negotiation is genuinely being offered to address the legitimate concerns of their traditions and the need for new political arrangements with which all can identify.

32. Clearly, new approaches must be explored to overcome this impasse. That is the purpose of the six principles we recommend. They invoke a comprehensive commitment to democracy and non-violence that is intended to reassure all parties to the negotiations.

V. Decommissioning During All-Party Negotiations
33. One side has insisted that some decommissioning of arms must take place before all-party negotiations can begin. The other side has insisted that no decommissioning can take place until the end of the process, after an agreed settlement has been reached. This has resulted in the current impasse.

34. The parties should consider an approach under which some decommissioning would take place during the process of all-party negotiations, rather than before or after as the parties now urge. Such an approach represents a compromise. If the peace process is to move forward, the current impasse must be overcome. While both sides have been adamant in their positions, both have repeatedly expressed the desire to move forward. This approach provides them that opportunity.

35. In addition, it offers the parties an opportunity to use the process of decommissioning to build confidence one step at a time during negotiations. As progress is made on political issues, even modest mutual steps on decommissioning could help create the atmosphere needed for further steps in a progressive pattern of mounting trust and confidence.

VI. Recommendations: Guidelines on the Modalities of Decommissioning
36. The first of the specific questions in paragraph seven of the Communiqué asks us 'to identify and advise on a suitable and acceptable method for full and verifiable decommissioning'.

37. We recommend the following guidelines on the modalities of decommissioning. These recommendations are realistic in light of the nature and scale of the arsenals in question, estimates of which were provided to us by the Governments and their security forces. We believe these estimates to be accurate.

38. Decommissioning should receive a high priority in all-party negotiations. The details of decommissioning, including supporting confidence-building measures, timing and sequencing, have to be determined by the parties themselves.

The decommissioning process should suggest neither victory nor defeat.
39. The cease-fires and the peace process are products not of surrender but rather of a willingness to address differences through political means. This essential fact should be

reflected clearly in the modalities of the decommissioning process, which should not require that any party be seen to surrender.

The decommissioning process should take place to the satisfaction of an independent commission.
40. The decommissioning process should take place to the satisfaction of an independent commission acceptable to all parties. The commission would be appointed by the British and Irish Governments on the basis of consultations with the other parties to the negotiating process.

41. The commission should be able to operate independently in both jurisdictions, and should enjoy appropriate legal status and immunity.

42. In addition to having available to it independent sources of legal and technical advice and adequate field resources to receive and audit armaments and to observe and verify the decommissioning process, the commission should be able to call upon the resources and the relevant technical expertise of the British and Irish Armies, when it is appropriate.

The decommissioning process should result in the complete destruction of armaments in a manner that contributes to public safety.
43. The decommissioning process should result in the complete destruction of the armaments. Procedures for destruction would include the cutting up or chipping of small arms and other weapons, the controlled explosion of ammunition and explosives, and other forms of conventional munitions disposal.

44. The decommissioning process could encompass a variety of methods, subject to negotiation, including:

- the transfer of armaments to the commission or to the designated representatives of either Government, for subsequent destruction;
- the provision of information to the commission or to designated representatives of either Government, leading to the discovery of armaments for subsequent destruction; and,
- the depositing of armaments for collection and subsequent destruction, by the commission or by representatives of either Government.

Parties should also have the option of destroying their weapons themselves.

45. Priority should be accorded throughout to ensuring that armaments are safely handled and stored, and are not misappropriated.

The decommissioning process should be fully verifiable.
46. Whatever the options chosen for the destruction of armaments, including the destruction of weapons by the parties themselves, verification must occur to the satisfaction of the commission.

47. The commission would record information required to monitor the process effectively. The commission should have available to it the relevant data of the *Garda Síochána* and the Royal Ulster Constabulary. It would report periodically to relevant parties on progress achieved in the decommissioning process.

The decommissioning process should not expose individuals to prosecution.
48. Individuals involved in the decommissioning process should not be prosecuted for the possession of those armaments; amnesties should be established in law in both jurisdictions. Armaments made available for decommissioning, whether directly or indirectly, should be exempt under law from forensic examination, and information obtained as a result of the decommissioning process should be inadmissible as evidence in courts of law in either jurisdiction.

49. Groups in possession of illegal armaments should be free to organise their participation in the decommissioning process as they judge appropriate, e.g. groups may designate particular individuals to deposit armaments on their behalf.

The decommissioning process should be mutual.
50. Decommissioning would take place on the basis of the mutual commitment and participation of the paramilitary organisations.

This offers the parties another opportunity to use the process of decommissioning to build confidence one step at a time during negotiations.

VII. Further Confidence-building

51. It is important for all participants to take steps to build confidence throughout the peace process. In the course of our discussions, many urged that certain actions other than decommissioning be taken to build confidence. We make no recommendations on them since they are outside our remit, but we believe it appropriate to comment on some since success in the peace process cannot be achieved solely by reference to the decommissioning of arms.

52. Support for the use of violence is incompatible with participation in the democratic process. The early termination of paramilitary activities, including surveillance and targeting, would demonstrate a commitment to peaceful methods and so build trust among other parties and alleviate the fears and anxieties of the general population. So, too, would the provision of information on the status of missing persons, and the return of those who have been forced to leave their communities under threat.

53. Continued action by the Governments on prisoners would bolster trust. So would early implementation of the proposed review of emergency legislation, consistent with the evolving security situation.

54. Different views were expressed as to the weapons to be decommissioned. In the Communiqué, the Governments made clear their view that our remit is limited to those weapons held by paramilitary organisations. We accept and share that view. There is no equivalence between such weapons and those held by security forces. However, in the context of building mutual confidence, we welcome the commitment of the Governments, as stated in paragraph nine of the Communiqué, 'to continue to take responsive measures, advised by their respective security authorities, as the threat reduces'.

55. We share the hope, expressed by many on all sides, that policing in Northern Ireland can be normalised as soon as the security situation permits. A review of the situation with respect to legally registered weapons and the use of plastic bullets, and continued progress toward more balanced representation in the police force would contribute to the building of trust.

56. Several oral and written submissions raised the idea of an elected body. We note the reference in paragraph three of the Communiqué to 'whether and how an elected body could play a part'. Elections held in accordance with democratic principles express and reflect the popular will. If it were broadly acceptable, with an appropriate mandate, and within the three-strand structure, an elective process could contribute to the building of confidence.

57. Finally, the importance of further progress in the social and economic development of Northern Ireland and its communities was emphasised time and again in our meetings, in the context of building confidence and establishing a lasting peace.

VIII. Concluding Remarks

58. Last week we stood in Belfast and looked at a thirty foot high wall and at barriers topped with iron and barbed wire. The wall, which has ironically come to be known as the 'peace line', is a tangible symbol of the division of the people of Northern Ireland into two hostile communities. To the outsider both are warm and generous. Between themselves they are fearful and antagonistic.

59. Yet, it is now clear beyond doubt that the vast majority of the people of both traditions want to turn away from the bitter past. There is a powerful desire for peace in Northern Ireland. It is that desire which creates the present opportunity.

60. This is a critical time in the history of Northern Ireland. The peace process will move forward or this society could slip back to the horror of the past quarter century.

61. Rigid adherence by the parties to their past positions will simply continue the stalemate which has already lasted too long. In a society as deeply divided as Northern Ireland, reaching across the 'peace line' requires a willingness to take risks for peace.

62. The risk may seem high but the reward is great: a future of peace, equality and prosperity for all the people of Northern Ireland.

George J. Mitchell; John de Chastelain; Harri Holkeri.
22 January 1996

Source: International Body (1996).

Document 5.2. Heads of Agreement, 12 January 1998

PROPOSITIONS ON HEADS OF AGREEMENT, ISSUED BY THE BRITISH AND IRISH GOVERNMENTS, 12 JANUARY 1998

Balanced constitutional change, based on commitment to the principle of consent in all its aspects by both British and Irish governments, to include both changes to the Irish Constitution and to British constitutional legislation.

Democratically-elected institutions in Northern Ireland, to include a Northern Ireland Assembly, elected by a system of proportional representation, exercising devolved executive and legislative responsibility over at least the responsibilities of the six Northern Ireland Departments and with provisions to ensure that all sections of the community can participate and work together successfully in the operation of these institutions and that all sections of the community are protected.

A new British–Irish Agreement to replace the existing Anglo-Irish Agreement and help establish close co-operation and enhance relationships, embracing:

- An intergovernmental Council to deal with the totality of relationships, to include representatives of the British and Irish Governments, the Northern Ireland Administration and the devolved institutions in Scotland and Wales, with meetings twice a year at Summit level.
- A North/South ministerial council to bring together those with executive responsibilities in Northern Ireland and the Irish Government in particular areas. Each side will consult, co-operate and take decisions on matters of mutual interest within the mandate of, and accountable to, the Northern Ireland Assembly and the Oireachtas respectively. All decisions will be by agreement between the two sides, North and South.
- Suitable implementation bodies and mechanisms for policies agreed by the North/South council in meaningful areas and at an all-island level.
- Standing intergovernmental machinery between the Irish and British Governments, covering issues of mutual interest, including non-devolved issues for Northern Ireland, when representatives of the Northern Ireland Administration would be involved.

Provision to safeguard the rights of both communities in Northern Ireland, through arrangements for the comprehensive protection of fundamental human, civil, political, social, economic and cultural rights, including a Bill of Rights for Northern Ireland supplementing the provisions of the European Convention and to achieve full respect for the principles of equity of treatment and freedom from discrimination, and the cultural identity and ethos of both communities. Appropriate steps to ensure an equivalent level of protection in the Republic.

Effective and practical measures to establish and consolidate an acceptable peaceful society, dealing with issues such as prisoners, security in all its aspects, policing and decommissioning of weapons.

Source: Gay and Morgan (1998: 61).

Document 5.3. Mitchell Draft Agreement, 6 April 1998

THE INDEPENDENT CHAIRMEN: DRAFT PAPER FOR DISCUSSION

Table of Contents
1. Declaration of Support
2. Constitutional Issues
   Annex A: Draft Clauses/Schedules for Incorporation in British Legislation
   Annex B: Irish Government Draft Legislation
3. Strand One: Democratic Institutions in Northern Ireland
4. Strand Two: North/South Ministerial Council
   Annex A: List of specified areas where the Council to use best endeavours to reach agreement on the adoption of common policies.

Annex B: List of specified areas in which Council is to take decisions on action for implementation separately in each jurisdiction.

Annex C: List of Implementation Bodies in specified areas in which the Council is to take decisions on action at an all-Island and cross-border level.

5. Strand Three:
   British–Irish Council
   British–Irish Intergovernmental Conference
6. Rights, Safeguards and Equality of Opportunity
   Human Rights
      United Kingdom Legislation
      New Institutions in Northern Ireland
      Comparable Steps by the Irish Government
      A Joint Committee
      Victims of Violence and Reconciliation
   Economic, Social and Cultural Issues
7. Decommissioning
8. Security
9. Policing and Justice
      Annex A: Commission on Policing for Northern Ireland
      Annex B: Review of the Criminal Justice System
10. Prisoners
11. Validation, Implementation and Review
    Validation and Implementation
    Review Procedures Following Implementation

Declaration of Support

1. We, the participants in the multi-party negotiations, believe that the agreement we have negotiated offers a truly historic opportunity for a new beginning.

2. The failures of the past have left a deep and profoundly regrettable legacy of suffering. We must never forget those who have been injured or who have died, and their families. But we can best honour them through a fresh start, in which we firmly dedicate ourselves to the achievement of reconciliation, tolerance, and mutual trust, and to the protection and vindication of the human rights of all.

3. We are committed to partnership, equality and mutual respect as the basis of relationships within Northern Ireland, between North and South, and between these islands.

4. We reaffirm our total and absolute commitment to exclusively democratic and peaceful means of resolving differences on political issues, and our opposition to any use or threat of force by others for any political purpose, whether in regard to this agreement or otherwise.

5. We acknowledge the substantial differences between our continuing, and equally legitimate, political aspirations. However, we pledge that we will, in good faith, work to ensure the success of each and every one of the arrangements to be established under this agreement. It is accepted that all of the institutional arrangements—an Assembly in Northern Ireland, a North/South Ministerial Council, implementation bodies, a British–Irish Council, and a

British–Irish Intergovernmental Conference—are interlocking and mutually supportive and that all will enter into force at or around the same time.

6. Accordingly, in a spirit of concord, we strongly commend this agreement to the people, North and South, for their approval.

Constitutional Issues

1. The participants endorse the commitment made by the British and Irish Governments that, in a new British–Irish Agreement replacing the Anglo-Irish Agreement, they will:

 (i) recognise the legitimacy of whatever choice is freely exercised by a majority of the people of Northern Ireland with regard to its status, whether they prefer to continue to support the Union with Great Britain or a sovereign united Ireland;

 (ii) recognise that it is for the people of the island of Ireland alone, by agreement between the two parts respectively and without external impediment, to exercise their right of self-determination on the basis of consent, freely and concurrently given, North and South, to bring about a united Ireland, if that is their wish; accepting that this right must be achieved and exercised with and subject to the agreement and consent of a majority of the people of Northern Ireland;

 (iii) acknowledge that while a substantial section of the people in Northern Ireland share the legitimate wish of a majority of the people of the island of Ireland for a united Ireland, the present wish of a majority of the people of Northern Ireland, freely exercised and legitimate, is to maintain the Union and, accordingly, that Northern Ireland's status as part of the United Kingdom reflects and relies upon that wish; and that it would be wrong to make any change in the status of Northern Ireland save with the consent of a majority of its people;

 (iv) affirm that if, in the future, the people of the island of Ireland exercise their right of self-determination on the basis set out in sections (i) and (ii) above to bring about a united Ireland, it will be a binding obligation on both Governments to introduce and support in the respective Parliaments legislation to give effect to that wish;

 (v) affirm that whatever choice is freely exercised by a majority of the people of Northern Ireland, the power of the sovereign government with jurisdiction there shall be exercised with rigorous impartiality on behalf of all the people in the diversity of their identities and traditions and shall be founded on the principles of full respect for, and equality of, civil, political, social and cultural rights, of freedom from discrimination for all citizens, and of parity of esteem and of just and equal treatment for the identity, ethos, and aspirations of both communities;

 (vi) recognise the birthright of all the people of Northern Ireland to identify themselves and be accepted as Irish or British, or both, as they may so choose, and accordingly confirm that their right to hold both British and Irish citizenship is accepted by both Governments and would not be affected by any future change in the status of Northern Ireland.

2. The participants also note that the two Governments have accordingly undertaken in the context of this comprehensive political agreement, to propose and support changes in, respectively, the Irish Constitution and in British legislation relating to the constitutional status of Northern Ireland.

Annex A: Draft Clauses/Schedules for Incorporation in British Legislation

1. (1) It is hereby declared that Northern Ireland in its entirety remains part of the United Kingdom and shall not cease to be so without the consent of a majority of the people of Northern Ireland voting in a poll held for the purposes of this section in accordance with Schedule 1.

   (2) But if the wish expressed by a majority in such a poll is that Northern Ireland should cease to be part of the United Kingdom and form part of a united Ireland, the Secretary of State shall lay before Parliament such proposals to give effect to that wish as may be agreed between Her Majesty's Government in the United Kingdom and the Government of Ireland.

2. The Government of Ireland Act 1920 shall cease to have effect; and this Act shall have effect notwithstanding any other previous enactment.

Schedule 1. Polls for the Purpose of Section 1

1. The Secretary of State may by order direct the holding of a poll for the purposes of section 1 on a date specified in the order.

2. Subject to paragraph 3, the Secretary of State shall exercise the power under paragraph 1 if at any time it appears likely to him that a majority of those voting would express a wish that Northern Ireland should cease to be part of the United Kingdom and form part of a united Ireland.

3. The Secretary of State shall not make an order under paragraph 1 earlier than five years after the holding of a previous poll under this Schedule.

4. [Remaining paragraphs along the lines of paragraphs 2 and 3 of existing Schedule 1 to 1973 Act.]

Annex B. Irish Government Draft Legislation

Add to Article 29 the following sections:

7. 1. In this section and in section 8 of this Article 'the Agreement' means the British–Irish Agreement done at Belfast on the ___ day of ___1998.

   2. The State may ratify the Agreement.

   3. Any institution established by or under the Agreement may exercise the powers and functions thereby conferred on it in respect of all or any part of the island of Ireland notwithstanding any other provision of this Constitution conferring the exercise of a like power or function on another person or organ of State appointed under or established by this Constitution. Any power or function conferred on such an institution in relation to the settlement of disputes may be in lieu of any like power or function conferred by this Constitution on any such other person or organ of State as aforesaid.

8. 1. If the Government declare that the State has become obliged, pursuant to the Agreement, to give effect to the amendment of this Constitution referred to therein, then, notwithstanding Article 46 hereof, this Constitution shall be amended.

   i. by the substitution of the following Articles for Articles 2 and 3:

   'Article 2

   It is the entitlement and birthright of every person born in the island of Ireland, which includes its islands and seas, to be part of the Irish nation. That is also the entitlement of all persons qualified in accordance with law to be citizens of Ireland. Furthermore, the Irish nation cherishes its special affinity with people of Irish ancestry living abroad who share its cultural identity and heritage.

Article 3

1. It is the firm will of the Irish nation, in harmony and friendship, to unite all the people who share the territory of the island of Ireland, in all the diversity of their identities and traditions, recognising that a united Ireland shall be brought about only by peaceful means with the consent of a majority of the people, democratically expressed, in both jurisdictions in the island. Until then, the laws enacted by the Parliament established by this Constitution shall have the like area and extent of application as the laws enacted by the Parliament that existed immediately before the coming into operation of this Constitution.

2. Institutions with executive powers and functions that are shared between those jurisdictions may be established by their respective responsible authorities for stated purposes and may exercise powers and functions in respect of all or any part of the island.'

and

ii. by the addition of the following section to this Article:

'8. The State may exercise extra-territorial jurisdiction in accordance with the generally recognised principles of international law.'

2. If a declaration under this section is not made within twelve months of this section being added to this Constitution or such longer period as may be determined by law, section 7 of this Article and this section shall cease to have effect and shall be omitted from every official text of this Constitution published thereafter.

3. If such a declaration is made, this section, other than the amendment effected thereby, shall be omitted from every official text of this Constitution published thereafter, but notwithstanding such omission this section shall continue to have the force of law.

Strand One Democratic Institutions in Northern Ireland

1. The following is intended to provide for a democratically elected Assembly in Northern Ireland which is *inclusive* in its membership, capable of exercising *executive and legislative authority*, and subject to *safeguards* to protect the rights and interests of all sides of the community.

The Assembly

2. An Assembly will be elected by PR(STV) from existing Westminster constituencies. *[Note from the Independent Chairmen: There is disagreement among participants as to the size of the Assembly and as to whether the election system should provide greater opportunity to small parties to be represented in the Assembly. We believe that it should.*

Options for your consideration include, but are not limited to:

(a) increasing the number of seats per constituency from 5 to 6; and/or

(b) providing a top-up of 10 or 20 additional seats.]

3. The Assembly will exercise full legislative and executive authority in respect of those matters currently within the responsibility of the six Northern Ireland Government Departments, with the possibility of taking on responsibility for other matters as detailed elsewhere in this agreement.

4. The Assembly—operating where appropriate on a cross-community basis—will be the prime source of authority in respect of all devolved responsibilities.

Safeguards

5. There will be safeguards to ensure that all sections of the community can participate and work together successfully in the operation of these institutions and that all sections of the community are protected, including:

[Note from the Chairmen: There is disagreement among participants as to whether the executive heads of departments should be titled 'Assembly Secretaries' or 'Ministers'. Throughout this text the position will be titled 'Assembly Secretary/Minister'.]

  (a) allocations of Committee Chairs, Assembly Secretaries/Ministers and Committee membership in proportion to party strengths;
  (b) the European Convention on Human Rights (ECHR) and any Bill of Rights for Northern Ireland supplementing it which neither the Assembly nor public bodies can infringe, together with a Human Rights Commission;
  (c) arrangements to provide that key decisions and legislation are proofed to ensure that they do not infringe the ECHR and any Bill of Rights for Northern Ireland;
  (d) arrangements to ensure key decisions are taken on a cross community basis;

[Note from the Chairmen: There is disagreement among the participants as to the nature of such arrangements. Options for your consideration include, but are not limited, to the following:

  (a) That this might require that any key decision would only pass if it is supported by:

  either a majority of those members present and voting which includes majorities of those who identify themselves (at the outset) as Nationalist and Unionist respectively or a weighted majority (two thirds) of those members present and voting.
In this alternative key decisions requiring cross-community support would be designated in advance (eg election of presiding officer, standing orders, budget allocations, employment equality, cultural issues) and/or be triggered by a right of petition exercised by a significant minority of Assembly members, (—%); or

  (b) Some combination of parallel consent and a weighted majority; or
  (c) Another alternative would be to give to the Chair and Deputy Chair of the Executive/ Liaison Committee (see paragraph 17 below) joint authority over key decisions; this would insure cross-community support. Obviously, its effectiveness would depend on the definition of what are key decisions.]

  (e) an Equality Commission to monitor a statutory obligation to promote equality of opportunity in specified areas and parity of esteem between the two main communities, and to investigate individual complaints against public bodies.

Operation of the Assembly

6. *[Note from the Chairmen: The parties are in disagreement as to the allocation of the position of Chair of the Assembly and as to whether there should be a Deputy Chair. Options for your consideration include, but are nor limited to, the following:*

    (a) *The Chair and Deputy Chair of the Assembly will be elected on a cross-community basis, as set out in paragraph 5(d) above.*

    (b) *There will be a Chair of the Assembly, elected from among those who are not aligned with either of the two major communities.]*

7. There will be a Committee for each of the main executive functions of the Northern Ireland Administration. The Chairs and Deputy Chairs of the Assembly Committees will be allocated proportionally, using the d'Hondt system. Membership of the Committees will be in broad proportion to party strengths in the Assembly to ensure that the opportunity of Committee places is available to all members.

8. The Committees will have a scrutiny, policy development and consultation role with respect to the Department with which each is associated, and will have a role in initiation of legislation. They should have the power to:

- agree Departmental budgets and Annual Plans
- approve relevant secondary legislation and take the Committee stage of relevant primary legislation
- call for persons and papers
- initiate enquiries and make reports.

9. Standing Committees other than Departmental Committees may be established as may be required from time to time.

Executive Authority

[Note from the Chairmen: There is disagreement among the participants as to whether executive authority should be vested in an Executive Committee or a Liaison committee. Throughout this text the Committee will be titled 'Executive/Liaison Committee'.]

10. Executive authority to be discharged on behalf of the Assembly by up to [ten) Assembly Secretaries/Ministers, with posts allocated to parties on the basis of the d'Hondt system by reference to the number of seats each party has in the Assembly.

11. A party may decline the opportunity to nominate a person to serve as an Assembly Secretary/Minister or may subsequently change its nominee.

12. An individual may be excluded or removed from office by a decision of the Assembly taken on a cross-community basis, when he loses the confidence of the Assembly, voting on a cross-community basis either for failure to meet his responsibilities or because the Assembly believes, on a cross-community basis, that his retention of office is incompatible with democratic expectations and constraints.

13. Assembly Secretaries/Ministers will be political Heads of the Northern Ireland Departments, and will liaise regularly with their respective Committee.

14. As a condition of appointment, Assembly Secretaries/Ministers will affirm their readiness to discharge effectively and in good faith all the responsibilities attaching to their posts, provided, however, that refusal to serve as an Assembly Secretary/Minister will not be grounds for removal from the Assembly.

15. Assembly Secretaries/Ministers will have full executive authority in their respective areas of responsibility, within any broad programme agreed by the Executive/Liaison Committee (see below) and endorsed by the Assembly as a whole on a cross-community basis; or in accordance with budgetary policy or legislative proposals approved, on a cross-community basis, after scrutiny by the Departmental Committee and by the Assembly. In the event of any dispute between an Assembly Secretary/Minister and the Committee, the Assembly as a whole to have the power of decision exercised on a cross-community basis.

Executive Liaison Committee

16. The Assembly Secretaries/Ministers will constitute an Executive/Liaison Committee.

17. Two Assembly Secretaries/Ministers will be selected as chair and deputy chair respectively, on a basis which ensures that between them they represent both main parts of the community in Northern Ireland.

[Note from the Chairmen: There is disagreement among the participants as to the nature of such arrangements. An option for your consideration is that this could be achieved by requiring the Committee's nominations to be endorsed by the Assembly on a cross-community basis.]

The Chair and Deputy Chair will be given ex-officio titles of First Secretary/Minister and Deputy First Secretary/Minister. Duties would, inter alia, include dealing with, and co-ordinating, the response of the Northern Ireland Administration to external relationships.

18. The Executive/Liaison Committee will provide a forum for the discussion of and agreement on issues which cut across the responsibilities of two or more Assembly Secretaries/Ministers, for prioritising executive and legislative proposals and recommending a common position where necessary (eg in dealing with external relationships).

19. The Executive/Liaison Committee will seek to agree each year, and review as necessary, a programme incorporating an agreed budget linked to policies and programmes, subject to approval by the Assembly, after scrutiny in Assembly Committees, on a cross-community basis.

Code of Practice

20. A Code of Practice will be drawn up by the Assembly on the basis of a cross-community vote. Any amendments to the Code will be made on a cross-community basis. The Code would codify and build upon the provisions of this agreement.

Legislation

21. The Assembly will have authority to pass primary legislation for Northern Ireland in devolved areas, subject to:

   (a) the ECHR and any Bill of Rights for Northern Ireland supplementing it which, if the courts found to be breached, would render the relevant legislation null and void;

(b) decisions by simple majority of members voting except when decision on a cross-community basis is required;

(c) detailed scrutiny and approval in the relevant departmental committee;

(d) mechanisms, based on arrangements proposed for the Scottish Parliament, to ensure suitable co-ordination, and avoid disputes, between the Assembly and the Westminster Parliament;

(e) option of the Assembly seeking to include Northern Ireland provisions in United Kingdom-wide legislation in Westminster Parliament especially on devolved issues where parity normally maintained (eg social security, company law).

22. The Assembly will have authority to legislate in reserved areas with the approval of the Secretary of State and subject to Parliamentary control.

23. Disputes over legislative competence will be decided by the Courts.

24. Legislation could be initiated by an individual, a Committee or an Assembly Secretary/Minister.

Relations with Other Institutions

25. Arrangements to represent the Assembly as a whole, at Summit level and in dealings with other institutions, will be in accordance with paragraph 17. Otherwise, representation to be by the Assembly Secretary/Minister of the relevant departmental committee.

26. Terms will be agreed between appropriate Assembly representatives and the Government of the United Kingdom to ensure effective co-ordination and input by Assembly Secretaries to national policy making, including on EU issues.

27. Role of Secretary of State:

(a) to remain responsible for NIO matters not devolved to the Assembly, subject to regular consultation with the Assembly and Assembly Secretaries/Ministers;

(b) to approve and lay before the Westminster Parliament any Assembly legislation on reserved matters;

(c) to represent Northern Ireland interests in the United Kingdom Cabinet;

(d) to have the right to attend the Assembly at their invitation.

28. The Westminster Parliament (whose power to make legislation for Northern Ireland would remain unaffected) will:

(a) legislate for non-devolved issues, other than where the Assembly legislates with approval of Secretary of State and subject to control of Parliament;

(b) to legislate as necessary to ensure United Kingdom's international obligations are met in respect of Northern Ireland;

(c) scrutinise, including through the Northern Ireland Grand and Select Committees, the responsibilities of the Secretary of State.

29. A consultative Civic Forum will be established. It will be comprised of representatives of the business, trade union and voluntary sectors, and such other sectors as agreed by the First Secretary/Minister and the Deputy First Secretary/Minister. It will act as a consultative mechanism on social, economic and cultural issues. The First Secretary/Minister and the

Deputy First Secretary/Minister will by agreement provide administrative support for the Civic Forum and establish guidelines for the selection of representatives to the Civic Forum.

Transitional Arrangements

30. The Assembly will meet first for the purpose of organisation, without legislative or executive powers, to resolve its standing orders and working practices and make preparations for the effective functioning of the Assembly, the British–Irish Council and the North/South Ministerial Council and associated implementation bodies.

Review

31. After a specified period there will be a review of these arrangements, including the details of electoral arrangements and of the Assembly's procedures, with a view to agreeing any adjustments necessary in the interests of efficiency and fairness.

Strand Two

North/South Ministerial Council

1. Under a new British/Irish Agreement dealing with the totality of relationships, and related legislation at Westminster and in the Oireachtas, a North/South Ministerial Council to be established to bring together those with executive responsibilities in Northern Ireland and the Irish Government, to develop consultation, co-operation and action within the island of Ireland—including through implementation on an all-island basis—on matters of mutual interest within the competence of the administrations, North and South.

2. All Council decisions to be by agreement between the two sides. Northern Ireland to be represented by [executive members of the Northern Ireland Administration], the Irish Government by the Taoiseach and relevant Ministers, all operating in accordance with the rules for democratic authority and accountability in force in the Northern Ireland Assembly and the Oireachtas respectively. Participation in the Council to be one of the essential responsibilities attaching to relevant posts in the two Administrations.

3. The Council to meet in different formats:

    (i) in plenary format twice a year, with Northern Ireland representation [led by the First Secretary and Deputy Secretary] and the Irish Government led by the Taoiseach;

    (ii) in specific sectoral formats on a regular and frequent basis with each side represented by the appropriate Minister [Assembly Secretary];

    (iii) in an appropriate format to consider institutional or cross sectoral matters (including in relation to the EU) and to resolve disagreement.

4. Agendas for all meetings to be settled by prior agreement between the two sides, but open to either to propose any matter for consideration or action.

5. The Council:

    (i) to exchange information, discuss and consult with a view to co-operating on matters of mutual interest within the competence of both administrations;

    (ii) to use best endeavours to reach agreement on the adoption of common policies in the areas listed in Annex A, making determined efforts to overcome any disagreements;

(iii) in specified areas set out in Annex B to take decisions on action for implementation separately in each jurisdiction;

(iv) in other specified meaningful areas set out in Annex C to take decisions on action at an all-island and cross-border level through implementation bodies to be established as set out in paragraphs 7 and 8 below.

6. Each side to be in a position to take decisions in the Council within the defined authority of those attending, through the arrangements in place for co-ordination of executive functions within each jurisdiction. Each side to remain accountable to the Assembly and Oireachtas respectively, whose approval, through the arrangements in place on either side, would be required for decisions beyond the defined authority of those attending.

7. For the areas listed in Annex C, where it is agreed that new implementation bodies are to be established, the two Governments to make all necessary legislative and other preparations to ensure the establishment of these bodies at the inception of the British/Irish Agreement or as soon as feasible thereafter, such that these bodies function effectively as rapidly as possible. The bodies to have a clear operational remit. To implement, on an all-island and cross-border basis, policies agreed in the Council. To report to the Council while remaining subject to normal accountability to the Northern Ireland Assembly and the Oireachtas, through the Council.

8. Any further bodies in addition to those specified in the Annexes, and other developments of these arrangements, to be by agreement in the Council and with the specific endorsement of the Northern Ireland Assembly and the Oireachtas, subject to the extent of the competences and responsibility of the two administrations.

9. Disagreements within the Council to be addressed in the format described at paragraph 3 (iii) above or in the plenary format. By agreement between the two sides, experts could be appointed to consider a particular matter and report.

10. The necessary costs of the Council and the funding of implementation bodes to be agreed within the Council, subject to normal procedures in the Oireachtas and the Northern Ireland Assembly. Funds to be provided by the two Administrations on the basis that the Council and the implementation bodies constitute a necessary public function.

11. The Council's expenditure to be audited jointly by the Comptroller and the Auditor-General's Office and by the Northern Ireland Audit Office. Their joint report to be submitted simultaneously to the Oireachtas and to the Assembly.

12. The Council to be supported by a standing joint Secretariat, staffed by members of the Northern Ireland Civil Service and the Irish Civil Service.

13. The Council to consider the European Union dimension of relevant matters, including the implementation of EU policies and programmes and proposals under consideration in the EU framework. Arrangements to be made to ensure that the views of the Council are taken into account and represented appropriately at relevant EU meetings.

14. The Northern Ireland Assembly arid the Oireachtas to be encouraged to develop a joint parliamentary forum, bringing together equal numbers from both institutions for discussion of matters of mutual interest and concern.

15. Consideration to be given to the establishment of an independent consultative forum appointed by the two administrations, representative of civil society, comprising the social partners and other members with expertise in social, cultural, economic and other issues.

Annex A
List of specified areas where the Council to use best endeavours to reach agreement on the adoption of common policies [para 5 (ii)]

Agriculture

- research, training and advisory services
- development of the blood stock and greyhound industries
- rural development

Education and Training

- tourism training
- education for students with special needs
- education for mutual understanding
- teacher qualifications and exchanges
- higher and further education
- combating educational disadvantage

Health

- general hospital services and accident/emergency planning
- food safety

Industrial and Trade Matters

- management development services to industry
- trading standards
- public purchasing
- supervision of credit unions
- occupational health and safety

Marine and Waterways

- inland fisheries
- approaches to the Common Fisheries Policy
- fish health
- fisheries education, research and training

Energy and Transport

- geological survey
- energy projects
- road and rail issues

Environment

- physical planning and development strategy
- road safety

Annex B
List of specified areas in which Council is to take decisions on action for implementation separately in each jurisdiction [para 5 (iii)] [*Items in brackets are not agreed*].

Agriculture

- Animal and plant health
- [Approaches to Common Agricultural Policy]

Education and Youth

- Education and training programmes

Social Welfare/Community Activity

- entitlements of cross-border workers and fraud control
- support for voluntary community activity

The Environment

- environmental protection, waste management and pollution control
- mapping
- wildlife conservation

Culture Heritage and the Arts

- heritage protection and restoration
- cultural promotion abroad

Health

- disease registries, clinical trials and high cost, high technology areas
- post-graduate medical teaching and training
- health promotion strategies

Marine and Waterways

- aquaculture and marine matters [including research?] and drainage

Sport

- promotion and support of joint activities and strategic planning of facilities

Science and Technology

- promotion of scientific and technological research and its application

Annex C

List of Implementation Bodies in specified areas in which the Council is to take decisions on action at an all-island and cross-border level (paras 5 (iv) and 7). [*Items through Inland Waterways Body are agreed; all items thereafter are not agreed.*]

- a Tourism Body, covering promotion, marketing, research and product development for the island as a whole;
- an Environmental Protection Body, covering co-operation on environmental protection, pollution, water quality and waste management and related matters in cross-border areas, as well as the development of a strategic approach for the island as a whole.
- an EU Programmes Implementation Body covering work on the North/South INTERREG programme, the Special Programme for Peace and Reconciliation and LEADER II (or its successor)
- a Transport Planning Body covering the co-ordination and development of the major transport services in Ireland, consideration of strategic issues in relation to road and rail networks and ports.

- an Inland Waterways Body covering the joint development and management of inland waterways.
- an Irish Language Promotion Body, promoting the use of the Irish Language to include an element of advice and support for Irish-medium education, supplementing and supporting the efforts of the voluntary support and co-ordination agencies in this latter sphere.
- a Trade Promotion and Indigenous Company Development Body, supporting the development of indigenous enterprise and companies in the industrial and services sectors, including industrial training and the promotion of exports and of innovation and scientific and technological research and development. [*It would be the objective to retain the facilities which Northern Ireland exporters can avail of through the IDB and the Foreign and Commonwealth Office, acting as agents for the UK Department of Trade and Industry.*]
- an Arts Body, with functions in regard to promotion of the arts discharged in the Republic by An Chomhairle Ealaíon (The Arts Council) and in Northern Ireland by the Arts Council of Northern Ireland.

Strand Three
British–Irish Council

1. A British–Irish Council (BIC) will be established under a new British-Irish Agreement to promote the harmonious and mutually beneficial development of the totality of relationships among the peoples of these islands.

2. Membership of the BIC will comprise representatives of the British and Irish Governments, devolved institutions in Northern Ireland, Scotland and Wales, when established, and, if appropriate, elsewhere in the United Kingdom, together with representatives of the Isle of Man and the Channel Islands.

3. The BIC will meet twice a year at Summit level, with other meetings on sectoral issues comprising appropriate representatives of the relevant members to be convened as necessary.

4. Representatives of members will operate in accordance with whatever procedures for democratic authority and accountability are in force in their respective elected institutions.

5. The BIC will consider, and will promote, consultation and co-operation on matters of common interest falling within the competence of its members. Suitable issues for early discussion in the BIC could include: transport links; environmental issues; cultural issues; minority languages; approaches to European Union (EU) issues.

6. It will be open to the BIC to agree common policies or common actions. Individual members may opt not to participate in such common policies and common action.

7. The BIC normally will operate by consensus. In relation to decisions on common policies or common actions, including their means of implementation, it will operate by agreement of all members participating in such policies or actions.

8. The members of the BIC, on a basis to be agreed between them, will provide such financial support as it may require.

9. A secretariat for the BIC will be provided by the British and Irish Governments in co-ordination with officials of each of the other members.

10. In addition to the structures provided for under this agreement, it will be open to two or more members to develop bilateral or multilateral arrangements between them. Such

arrangements could include, subject to the agreement of the members concerned, mechanisms to enable consultation, co-operation and joint decision-making on matters of mutual interest; and mechanisms to implement any joint decisions they may reach. These arrangements will not require the prior approval of the BIC as a whole and will operate independently of it.

11. The elected institutions of the members will be encouraged to develop interparliamentary links perhaps building on the British–Irish Interparliamentary Body.

12. The full membership of the BIC will keep under review the workings of the Council including a formal published review at an appropriate time after the Agreement comes into effect and will contribute as appropriate to any review of the overall political agreement arising from the multi-party negotiations.

British–Irish Intergovernmental Conference

1. There will be a new British–Irish Agreement dealing with the totality of relationships. It will establish a standing *British–Irish intergovernmental Conference*, which will subsume both the Anglo-Irish Intergovernmental Council and the Intergovernmental Conference established under the 1985 Agreement.

2. The Conference will bring together the British and Irish Governments to promote bilateral co-operation at all levels on all matters of mutual interest within the competence of both Governments.

3. The Conference will meet as required at Summit level (Prime Minister and Taoiseach). Otherwise, Governments will be represented by appropriate Ministers. Advisers, including police and security advisers, will attend as appropriate.

4. All decisions will be by agreement between both Governments. The Governments will make determined efforts to resolve disagreements between them. There will be no derogation from sovereignty of either Government.

5. In recognition of the Irish Government's special interest in Northern Ireland and of the extent to which issues of mutual concern arise in relation to Northern Ireland, there will be regular and frequent meetings of the Conference concerned with non-devolved Northern Ireland matters, on which the Irish Government may put forward views and proposals. These meetings, to be co-chaired by the Minister for Foreign Affairs and the Secretary of State for Northern Ireland, would also deal with all-island and cross-border co-operation on non-devolved issues.

6. Co-operation within the framework of the Conference will include facilitation of co-operation in security matters. The Conference also will address, in particular, the areas of rights, justice, prisons and policing in Northern Ireland (unless and until responsibility is devolved to a Northern Ireland administration) and will intensify co-operation between the two Governments on the all-island or cross border aspects of these matters.

7. Relevant executive members of the Northern Ireland Administration will be involved in meetings of the Conference, and in the reviews referred to in paragraph 9 below to discuss non-devolved Northern Ireland matters. The Northern Ireland Administration will be given advance notice of what is to be discussed at such meetings of the Conference, and will be invited to express views to both Governments in advance. Representatives of the

Northern Ireland Administration will attend meetings of the Conference as and when appropriate. The two Governments will meet on their own as and when necessary.

8. The Conference will be supported by officials of the British and Irish Governments, including by a standing joint secretariat of officials dealing with non-devolved Northern Ireland matters.

9. The Conference will keep under review the workings of the new British–Irish Agreement and the machinery arid institutions established under it, including a formal published review three years after the Agreement comes into effect. Representatives of the Northern Ireland Administration will be invited to express views to the Conference in this context. The Conference will contribute as appropriate to any review of the overall political agreement arising from the multi-party negotiations.

Rights, Safeguards and Equality of Opportunity
Human Rights
1. The parties affirm their commitment to the mutual respect, the civil rights and the religious liberties of everyone in the community. Against the background of the recent history of communal conflict, the parties affirm in particular:

- the right of free political thought;
- the right to freedom and expression of religion;
- the right to pursue democratically national and political aspirations;
- the right to seek constitutional change by peaceful and legitimate means;
- the right to freely choose one's place of residence;
- the right to equal opportunity in all social and economic activity, regardless of class, creed, gender or colour; and
- the right to freedom from sectarian harassment.

United Kingdom Legislation
2. The British Government will complete incorporation into Northern Ireland law of the European Convention on Human Rights (ECHR), with direct access to the courts, and remedies for breach of the Convention, including power for the courts to overrule Assembly legislation on grounds of inconsistency.

3. The British Government has proposed as a particular priority the creation of a statutory obligation on public authorities in Northern Ireland to carry out all their functions with due regard to the need to promote equality of opportunity in relation to religion and political opinion; gender; race; disability; age; marital status; dependants; and sexual orientation. Public bodies would be required to draw up statutory schemes showing how they would implement this obligation. Such schemes would cover arrangements for policy appraisal, public consultation, public access to services, monitoring and timetables.

4. The new Northern Ireland Human Rights Commission (see paragraph 5 below) will be invited to advise on the scope for defining, in Westminster legislation, rights supplementary to those in the European Convention on Human Rights, to reflect the particular circumstances of Northern Ireland. These additional rights to reflect the principles of mutual respect for the identity and ethos of both communities and parity of esteem, and—taken

together with the ECHR—to constitute a Bill of Rights for Northern Ireland. Among the issues for consideration by the Commission will be:

- the formulation of a general obligation on government and public bodies fully to respect, on the basis of equality of treatment, the identity and ethos of both communities in Northern Ireland;
- a clear formulation of the rights not to be discriminated against and to equality of opportunity in both the public and private sectors.

New Institutions in Northern Ireland

5. A new Northern Ireland Human Rights Commission will be established by Westminster legislation, independent of Government, with an extended and enhanced role beyond that currently exercised by the Standing Advisory Commission on Human Rights, to include keeping under review the adequacy and effectiveness of laws and practices, making recommendations to Government as necessary; providing information and promoting awareness of human rights; considering draft legislation referred to them by the new Assembly; and, in appropriate cases, bringing court proceedings or providing assistance to individuals doing so.

6. The British Government has proposed a new statutory Equality Commission to replace the Fair Employment Commission, the Equal Opportunities Commission (NI), the Commission for Racial Equality (NI) and the Disability Council—such a unified Commission will advise on, validate and monitor the statutory obligation and will investigate complaints of default.

7. These improvements will build on existing protections in Westminster legislation in respect of the judiciary, the system of justice and policing.

Comparable Steps by the Irish Government

8. The Irish Government will also take steps to further strengthen the protection of human rights in its jurisdiction. The Government will, taking account of the work of the All-Party Oireachtas Committee on the Constitution and the Report of the Constitution Review Group, bring forward measures to strengthen and underpin the constitutional protection of human rights. These proposals will draw on the European Convention on Human Rights and other international legal instruments in the field of human rights and will ensure at least an equivalent level of protection of human rights as will pertain in Northern Ireland. In addition, the Irish Government will

- establish a Human Rights Commission with a mandate and remit equivalent to that within Northern Ireland;
- proceed with arrangements to ratify the Council of Europe Framework Convention on National Minorities (already ratified by the UK);
- implement enhanced employment equality legislation; and
- introduce equal status legislation.

A Joint Committee

9. It is envisaged that there would be a joint committee of representatives of the two Human Rights Commissions, North and South, as a forum for consideration of human rights issues in the island of Ireland. The joint committee will consider among other matters the possibility of establishing a charter, open to signature by all democratic political parties,

reflecting and endorsing agreed measures for the protection of the fundamental rights of everyone living in the island of Ireland.

Victims of Violence and Reconciliation

10. The participants believe it is essential to acknowledge and address the suffering of the victims of violence as a necessary element of reconciliation. Sufficient resources, including statutory funding as necessary, should be allocated to victims' treatment and support programmes.

11. The participants recognise and value the work being done by many organisations to develop reconciliation and mutual understanding and respect between communities and traditions, in Northern Ireland and between North and South, and they see such work as having a vital role in consolidating peace and political agreement. Accordingly they pledge their continuing support to such organisations and will positively examine the case for enhanced financial assistance for the work of reconciliation.

Economic, Social and Cultural Issues

1. The British Government will pursue broad policies for sustained economic growth and stability in Northern Ireland, and will reduce social exclusion, pending devolution of powers to a new Northern Ireland Assembly.

2. In the light of reactions to public consultation currently under way, the British Government will make rapid progress with:

   (i) a new regional development strategy for Northern Ireland, for consideration in due course by a new Northern Ireland Assembly, which would go beyond conventional land use and planning issues to include:

   - tackling the problems of a divided society and social cohesion;
   - generating a dynamic region and promoting sustainable developments;
   - protecting and enhancing the environment;
   - deciding on major new development;
   - producing new approaches to transport issues;
   - strengthening the physical infrastructure of the region;
   - developing the advantages and resources of rural areas; and
   - rejuvenating major urban centres;

   (ii) a new economic development strategy for Northern Ireland, for consideration in due course by a new Northern Ireland Assembly, which would provide for short and medium term economic planning linked as appropriate to the regional development strategy;

   (iii) measures on employment equality, including:

   - the extension of anti-discrimination legislation to the supply of goods, facilities and services;
   - the strengthening of other aspects of existing fair employment laws;
   - at the earliest possible time, a review of the national security aspects of the present fair employment legislation;
   - a new more focused Targeting Social Need initiative to combat deprivation defined objectively; and

- a range of measures aimed at combating unemployment, in particular youth and long-term unemployment, and at progressively eliminating the differential in employment rates between the two communities by targeting objective need.

3. All participants recognise the importance of respect, understanding and tolerance in relation to linguistic diversity, which is part of the cultural wealth of the people of the island of Ireland.

The British Government will in particular, in relation to the Irish language, pending the transfer of responsibility to a new Northern Ireland Assembly:

- take resolute action to promote the language;
- facilitate the use of the language in speech and writing in public and private life, where there is appropriate demand;
- seek to remove, where possible, restrictions which would discourage or work against the maintenance or development of the language;
- continue to take into consideration the needs and wishes expressed by users of the language in determining policy;
- impose a statutory duty on the Department of Education for Northern Ireland to encourage and facilitate Irish medium education; and
- explore urgently with the relevant British authorities, and in co-operation with the Irish broadcasting authorities, the scope for achieving more widespread availability of Teilifís na Gaeilge in Northern Ireland.

The parties will seek to secure agreement that this commitment will be sustained by a new Northern Ireland Assembly.

4. All participants acknowledge the sensitivity of the use of symbols and emblems for public purposes, and the need in particular in creating the new institutions to ensure that such symbols and emblems are used in a manner which promotes mutual respect rather than division. Arrangements will be made to monitor this issue and consider what action might be required.

Decommissioning

1. The participants agreed, in the Procedural Motion adopted on 24 September 1997, 'that the resolution of the Decommissioning issue is an indispensable part of the process of negotiation.' It is, therefore, an indispensable part of this agreement.

2. The Participants note the progress made by the Independent International Commission on Decommissioning and the Governments in developing schemes which represent a workable basis for achieving the decommissioning of illegally-held arms in the possession of paramilitary groups.

3. All participants reaffirm their commitment to the total disarmament of all paramilitary organisations and their intention to continue to work constructively with the Independent Commission on Decommissioning to achieve this.

4. All participants undertake to work constructively and in good faith with the Independent Commission to achieve the decommissioning of all paramilitary arms within a fixed and limited period of [X years following endorsement in referendums North and South of the overall settlement] in the context of the implementation of the overall settlement.

5. The Independent Commission will monitor, review and verify progress on decommissioning of illegal arms, and will report to both Governments at regular intervals.

6. Both Governments will take all necessary steps to facilitate the decommissioning process.

[Note from the Independent Chairmen: Remaining to be resolved is the time frame for decommissioning (paragraph 3 above).]

Security

1. The Participants note that the development of a peaceful environment on the basis of this Agreement can and should mean a normalisation of security arrangements and practices.

2. The British Government will make progress towards the objective of as early a return as possible to normal security arrangements in Northern Ireland, consistent with the level of threat and with a published overall strategy, dealing with:

(i) the reduction of the numbers and role of the Armed Forces deployed in Northern Ireland to levels compatible with a normal peaceful society;
(ii) the removal of security installations;
(iii) the removal of emergency powers in Northern Ireland;
(iv) other appropriate measures consistent with a move to normalisation.

3. The Secretary of State will consult regularly on progress, and the response to any continuing paramilitary activity, with the Irish Government and the political parties, as appropriate.

4. The British Government will continue its consultation on firearms regulation on the basis of the document published on 2 April 1998, and will review progress with the Irish Government and the political parties as appropriate.

5. The Irish Government will initiate a wide-ranging review of the Offences Against the State Acts 1939–85 with a view to both reform and dispensing with those elements no longer required as circumstances permit.

Policing and Justice

1. The Participants recognise that policing is a central issue in any society. They equally recognise that Northern Ireland's history of deep divisions have made it highly emotive, with great hurt suffered and sacrifices made by many individuals. They believe that this Agreement offers a unique opportunity to bring about a new political dispensation which will recognise the full and equal legitimacy and worth of the identities, senses of allegiance and ethos of all sections of the community in Northern Ireland. They consider that this opportunity should inform and underpin the development of a police service representative in terms of the make-up of the community as a whole and which, in the absence of threats which require otherwise, should be routinely unarmed.

2. The Participants believe it essential that policing structures and arrangements are such that the police service is professional, effective and efficient, fair and impartial, free from partisan political control; accountable, both under the law for its actions and to the community it serves; representative of the society it polices, and operates within a coherent and co-operative criminal justice system. The Participants also believe that those structures

and arrangements must be capable of maintaining law and order including responding effectively to crime and to any terrorist threat and to public order problems, as a police service which cannot do so will fail to win public confidence and acceptance. They believe that any such structures and arrangements should be capable of delivering a policing service, in constructive and inclusive partnerships with the community at all levels, and with authority and responsibility exercised at the lowest level possible, consistent with the foregoing principles. These arrangements should be based on principles of protection of human rights and professional integrity and should be unambiguously accepted and actively supported by the entire community.

3. An Independent Commission will be established to make recommendations for future policing arrangements in Northern Ireland within the agreed framework of principles reflected in the paragraphs above and in accordance with the terms of reference at Annex A. The Commission will be broadly representative with expert and international representation among its membership and will be asked to consult widely and to report no later than Summer 1999.

4. The Participants believe that the criminal justice system should be designed to:

- deliver a fair and impartial system of justice to the community;
- be responsive to the community's concerns, and encouraging community involvement where appropriate;
- have the confidence of all parts of the community;
- deliver justice efficiently and effectively.

5. There will be a parallel wide-ranging review of those aspects of criminal justice other than policing and those aspects of the system relating to the emergency legislation to be carried out by the British Government through a mechanism with an independent element, in consultation with the political parties and others. The review will commence as soon as possible, will include wide consultation, and a report will be made to the Secretary of State no later than Autumn 1999. Terms of Reference are attached at Annex B.

6. Implementation of the recommendations arising from both reviews will be discussed with the political parties and with the Irish Government.

7. The Participants also to note that the British Government remains ready in principle, with the broad support of the political parties, and after consultation, as appropriate, with the Irish Government, in the context of ongoing implementation of the relevant recommendations, to devolve responsibility for policing and justice issues.

Annex A. Commission on Policing for Northern Ireland
Relevant Principles

Policing structures and arrangements should be such that:

- the police service is professional, effective and efficient, fair and impartial, free from partisan political control; accountable, both under the law for its actions and to the community it serves; representative of the society it polices and operates within a coherent and co-operative criminal justice system;

- they are capable of maintaining law and order including responding effectively to crime and to any terrorist threat, and to public order problems, as a police service which cannot do so will fail to win public confidence and acceptance;
- they are capable of delivering a policing service, in constructive and inclusive partnerships with the community at all levels, and with authority and responsibility to be exercised at the lowest level consistent with the foregoing principles; and
- these arrangements should be based on principles of protection of human rights and professional integrity, and should be unambiguously accepted and actively supported by the entire community.

Terms of Reference

Taking account of these principles the Commission will inquire into policing in Northern Ireland and, on the basis of its findings, bring forward proposals for future policing structures and arrangements.

Its proposals on policing should be designed to ensure that policing arrangements, including composition, recruitment, training, culture, ethos and symbols, are such that in a new approach Northern Ireland has a police service that can enjoy widespread support from and is seen as an integral part of the community as a whole.

Its proposals should include recommendations covering any issues (such as training and severance arrangements) required in the transition to policing in a peaceful society.

Its proposals should also be designed to ensure that:

- the police service is structured, managed and resourced so that it can be effective in discharging its full range of function (including proposals on any necessary arrangements for the transition to policing a normal peaceful society);
- that the legislative and constitutional framework requires the impartial discharge of policing functions and conforms with internationally accepted norms in relation to policing standards;
- the police operate within a clear framework of accountability to the law and the community they serve, so:
- they are constrained by, accountable to and act only within the law;
- their powers and procedures, like the law they enforce, are clearly established and publicly available;
- there are open, accessible and independent means of investigating and adjudicating upon complaints against the police;
- there are clear arrangements enabling local people, and their political representatives, to articulate concerns about policing (subject to safeguards to ensure police impartiality and freedom from partisan political control) and to establish publicly policing priorities and influence policing policies;
- there are arrangements for accountability and for the effective, efficient and economic use of resources in achieving policing objectives;
- there are means to ensure independent professional scrutiny and inspection of the police service to ensure that proper professional standards are maintained;
- the scope for structured co-operation with the Garda Síochána and other police forces is addressed; and

- the management of public order events which can impose exceptional demands on policing resources is also addressed.

The Commission should focus on policing issues, but if it identifies other aspects of the criminal justice system relevant to its work on policing, including the role of the police in prosecution, then it should draw the attention of the Government to those matters.

The Commission should consult widely, including with non-governmental expert organisations, and through such focus groups as they consider it appropriate to establish.

The Government proposes to establish the Commission as soon as possible, with the aim of it starting work as soon as possible and publishing its final report by Summer 1999.

Annex B. Review of The Criminal Justice System
Overview and Relevant Principles

The criminal justice system in Northern Ireland exists to uphold the rule of law. It is concerned with crime in all its elements and the process which brings offenders to account, but constitutes only a part of society's response to crime. It involves a number of publicly funded bodies, as well as professions, defendants, witnesses and victims. The criminal justice system should be such as to:

- deliver a fair and impartial system of justice to the community;
- be responsive to the community's concerns, and encourage community involvement where appropriate;
- have the confidence of all parts of the community;
- deliver justice efficiently and effectively.

Terms of Reference

Taking account of these points, the review will address the structure, management and resourcing of publicly funded elements of the criminal justice system and will bring forward proposals for future criminal justice arrangements (other than policing and those aspects of the system relating to emergency legislation, which the Government is considering separately) covering such issues as:

- the arrangements for making appointments to the judiciary and magistracy, and safeguards for protecting their independence;
- the arrangements for the organisation and supervision of the prosecution process, and for safeguarding its independence;
- measures to improve the responsiveness and accountability of, and any lay participation in the criminal justice system;
- mechanisms for addressing law reform;
- the scope for structured co-operation between the criminal justice agencies on both parts of the island; and
- the structure and organisation of criminal justice functions that might be devolved to an Assembly, including the possibility of establishing a Department of Justice, while safeguarding the essential independence of many of the key functions in this area.

The Government proposes to commence the review as soon as possible, consulting with the political parties and others, including non-governmental expert organisations. The review will be completed by Autumn 1999.

Prisoners

1. Both Governments will put in place mechanisms to provide for an accelerated programme for the release of prisoners, including transferred prisoners, convicted of scheduled offences in Northern Ireland or, in the case of those sentenced outside Northern Ireland, similar offences (referred to hereafter as qualifying prisoners). Any such arrangements will protect the rights of individual prisoners under national and international law.

2. Prisoners affiliated to organisations which have not established or are not maintaining a complete and unequivocal ceasefire will not benefit from the arrangements. The situation in this regard will be kept under review.

3. Both Governments will complete a review process within a fixed time frame and set prospective release dates for all qualifying prisoners. The intention will be to provide for the advance of the release dates of qualifying prisoners while allowing account to be taken of the seriousness of the offences for which the person was convicted and the need to protect the community.

4. The Governments will introduce the appropriate legislation to give effect to these arrangements by the end of June 1998.

5. The Governments continue to recognise the importance of measures to facilitate the reintegration of prisoners into the community by providing support both prior to and after release, including assistance directed towards availing of employment opportunities, retraining and/or reskilling, and further education.

Validation, Implementation and Review

Validation and Implementation

1. The two Governments will as soon as possible sign a new British–Irish Agreement replacing the 1985 Anglo-Irish Agreement, embodying understandings on constitutional issues and affirming their solemn commitment to support and, where appropriate, implement the agreement reached by the participants in the negotiations which shall be annexed to the Agreement.

2. Each Government wilt organise a referendum on 22 May 1998. Subject to Parliamentary approval, a consultative referendum in Northern Ireland, organised under the terms of the Northern Ireland (Entry to Negotiations, etc.) Act 1996, will address the question: 'Do you support the agreement reached in the multi-party talks on Northern Ireland and set out in Command Paper 3883?'. The Irish Government will introduce and support in the Oireachtas a Bill to amend the Constitution as described in paragraph 2 of the section 'Constitutional Issues' and in Annex B, as follows: (a) to amend Articles 2 and 3 as described in paragraph 8.1 in Annex B above and (b) to amend Article 29 to permit the Government to ratify the new British–Irish Agreement. On passage by the Oireachtas, the Bill will be put to referendum.

3. If majorities of those voting in each of the referendums support this agreement, the Governments will then introduce and support, in their respective Parliaments, such legislation as may be necessary to give effect to all aspects of this agreement, and will take whatever ancillary steps as may be required including the holding of elections on 25 June, subject to Parliamentary approval, to the Assembly, which would meet initially in a 'shadow' mode. When all arrangements are in place for the new institutions to assume their functions as set

out in this agreement, the Governments will ratify the British–Irish Agreement. It is the intention of the Governments that this be achieved by no later than February 1999.

4. In the interim, aspects of the implementation of the agreement will be reviewed at meetings of those parties relevant in the particular case (taking into account, once Assembly elections have been held, of the results of those elections) in the particular case, under the Chairmanship of the British Government or the two Governments, as may be appropriate; and representatives of the two Governments and all relevant parties may meet under [Independent Chairmanship] to review implementation of the agreement as a whole.

Review Procedures Following Implementation

5. Each institution may, at any time, review any problems that may arise in its operation and, where no other institution is affected, take remedial action in consultation as necessary with the relevant Government or Governments. It will be for each institution to determine its own procedures for review.

6. If there are difficulties in the operation of a particular institution, which have implications for another institution, they may review their operations separately and jointly and agree on remedial action to be taken under their respective authorities.

7. If difficulties arise which require remedial action across the range of Institutions, or otherwise required amendment of the British–Irish Agreement or relevant legislation, the process of review will fall to the two Governments in consultation with the parties in the Northern Ireland Assembly. Each Government will be responsible for action in its own jurisdiction.

8. Notwithstanding the above, each institution will publish an annual report on its operations. In addition the two Governments and the parties in the Assembly will convene a conference 4 years after the agreement comes into effect, to review and report on its operation.

Source: Linenhall Library, P8642.

Document 5.4. Good Friday Agreement, 10 April 1998

THE AGREEMENT:
AGREEMENT REACHED IN THE MULTI-PARTY NEGOTIATIONS

Table of Contents
Declaration of Support
Constitutional Issues
    Annex A: Draft Clauses/Schedules for Incorporation in British Legislation
    Annex B: Irish Government Draft Legislation
Strand One:
    Democratic Institutions in Northern Ireland
Strand Two:
    North/South Ministerial Council
Strand Three:
    British–Irish Council
    British–Irish Intergovernmental Conference

Declaration of Support

1. We, the participants in the multi-party negotiations, believe that the agreement we have negotiated offers a truly historic opportunity for a new beginning.

2. The tragedies of the past have left a deep and profoundly regrettable legacy of suffering. We must never forget those who have died or been injured, and their families. But we can best honour them through a fresh start, in which we firmly dedicate ourselves to the achievement of reconciliation, tolerance, and mutual trust, and to the protection and vindication of the human rights of all.

3. We are committed to partnership, equality and mutual respect as the basis of relationships within Northern Ireland, between North and South, and between these islands.

4. We reaffirm our total and absolute commitment to exclusively democratic and peaceful means of resolving differences on political issues, and our opposition to any use or threat of force by others for any political purpose, whether in regard to this agreement or otherwise.

5. We acknowledge the substantial differences between our continuing, and equally legitimate, political aspirations. However, we will endeavour to strive in every practical way towards reconciliation and rapprochement within the framework of democratic and agreed arrangements. We pledge that we will, in good faith, work to ensure the success of each and every one of the arrangements to be established under this agreement. It is accepted that all of the institutional and constitutional arrangements—an Assembly in Northern Ireland, a North/South Ministerial Council, implementation bodies, a British–Irish Council and a British–Irish Intergovernmental Conference and any amendments to British Acts of Parliament and the Constitution of Ireland—are interlocking and interdependent and that in

particular the functioning of the Assembly and the North/South Council are so closely inter-related that the success of each depends on that of the other.

6. Accordingly, in a spirit of concord, we strongly commend this agreement to the people, North and South, for their approval.

Constitutional Issues

1. The participants endorse the commitment made by the British and Irish Governments that, in a new British–Irish Agreement replacing the Anglo-Irish Agreement, they will:

   (i) recognise the legitimacy of whatever choice is freely exercised by a majority of the people of Northern Ireland with regard to its status, whether they prefer to continue to support the Union with Great Britain or a sovereign united Ireland;

   (ii) recognise that it is for the people of the island of Ireland alone, by agreement between the two parts respectively and without external impediment, to exercise their right of self-determination on the basis of consent, freely and concurrently given, North and South, to bring about a united Ireland, if that is their wish, accepting that this right must be achieved and exercised with and subject to the agreement and consent of a majority of the people of Northern Ireland;

   (iii) acknowledge that while a substantial section of the people in Northern Ireland share the legitimate wish of a majority of the people of the island of Ireland for a united Ireland, the present wish of a majority of the people of Northern Ireland, freely exercised and legitimate, is to maintain the Union and, accordingly, that Northern Ireland's status as part of the United Kingdom reflects and relies upon that wish; and that it would be wrong to make any change in the status of Northern Ireland save with the consent of a majority of its people;

   (iv) affirm that if, in the future, the people of the island of Ireland exercise their right of self-determination on the basis set out in sections (i) and (ii) above to bring about a united Ireland, it will be a binding obligation on both Governments to introduce and support in the respective Parliaments legislation to give effect to that wish;

   (v) affirm that whatever choice is freely exercised by a majority of the people of Northern Ireland, the power of the sovereign government with jurisdiction there shall be exercised with rigorous impartiality on behalf of all the people in the diversity of their identities and traditions and shall be founded on the principles of full respect for, and equality of, civil, political, social and cultural rights, of freedom from discrimination for all citizens, and of parity of esteem and of just and equal treatment for the identity, ethos, and aspirations of both communities;

   (vi) recognise the birthright of all the people of Northern Ireland to identify themselves and be accepted as Irish or British, or both, as they may so choose, and accordingly confirm that their right to hold both British and Irish citizenship is accepted by both Governments and would not be affected by any future change in the status of Northern Ireland.

2. The participants also note that the two Governments have accordingly undertaken in the context of this comprehensive political agreement, to propose and support changes in, respectively, the Irish Constitution and in British legislation relating to the constitutional status of Northern Ireland.

Annex A. Draft Clauses/Schedules for Incorporation in British Legislation

1. (1) It is hereby declared that Northern Ireland in its entirety remains part of the United Kingdom and shall not cease to be so without the consent of a majority of the people of Northern Ireland voting in a poll held for the purposes of this section in accordance with Schedule 1.

   (2) But if the wish expressed by a majority in such a poll is that Northern Ireland should cease to be part of the United Kingdom and form part of a united Ireland, the Secretary of State shall lay before Parliament such proposals to give effect to that wish as may be agreed between Her Majesty's Government in the United Kingdom and the Government of Ireland.

2. The Government of Ireland Act 1920 is repealed; and this Act shall have effect notwithstanding any other previous enactment.

Schedule 1. Polls For The Purpose of Section 1

1. The Secretary of State may by order direct the holding of a poll for the purposes of section 1 on a date specified in the order.

2. Subject to paragraph 3, the Secretary of State shall exercise the power under paragraph 1 if at any time it appears likely to him that a majority of those voting would express a wish that Northern Ireland should cease to be part of the United Kingdom and form part of a united Ireland.

3. The Secretary of State shall not make an order under paragraph 1 earlier than seven years after the holding of a previous poll under this Schedule.

4. (Remaining paragraphs along the lines of paragraphs 2 and 3 of existing Schedule 1 to 1973 Act.)

Annex B

Irish Government Draft Legislation to Amend the Constitution
Add to Article 29 the following sections:

7. 1. The State may consent to be bound by the British–Irish Agreement done at Belfast on the __ day of __ 1998, hereinafter called the Agreement.

   2. Any institution established by or under the Agreement may exercise the powers and functions thereby conferred on it in respect of all or any part of the island of Ireland notwithstanding any other provision of this Constitution conferring a like power or function on any person or any organ of State appointed under or created or established by or under this Constitution. Any power or function conferred on such an institution in relation to the settlement or resolution of disputes or controversies may be in addition to or in substitution for any like power or function conferred by this Constitution on any such other person or organ of State as aforesaid.

   3. If the Government declare that the State has become obliged, pursuant to the Agreement, to give effect to the amendment of this Constitution referred to therein, then, notwithstanding Article 46 hereof, this Constitution shall be amended as follows.

      i. the following Articles shall be substituted for Articles 2 and 3 of the Irish text:
         2. [Irish text to be inserted here]
         3. [Irish text to be inserted here]'

ii. the following Articles shall be substituted for Articles 2 and 3 of the English text:

'Article 2

It is the entitlement and birthright of every person born in the island of Ireland, which includes its islands and seas, to be part of the Irish nation. That is also the entitlement of all persons qualified in accordance with law to be citizens of Ireland. Furthermore, the Irish nation cherishes its special affinity with people of Irish ancestry living abroad who share its cultural identity and heritage.

Article 3

1. It is the firm will of the Irish nation, in harmony and friendship, to unite all the people who share the territory of the island of Ireland, in all the diversity of their identities and traditions, recognising that a united Ireland shall be brought about only by peaceful means with the consent of a majority of the people, democratically expressed, in both jurisdictions in the island. Until then, the laws enacted by the Parliament established by this Constitution shall have the like area and extent of application as the laws enacted by the Parliament that existed immediately before the coming into operation of this Constitution.

2. Institutions with executive powers and functions that are shared between those jurisdictions may be established by their respective responsible authorities for stated purposes and may exercise powers and functions in respect of all or any part of the island.'

iii. the following section shall be added to the Irish text of this Article:

'8. [Irish text to be inserted here]'
and

iv. the following section shall be added to the English text of this Article:

'8. The State may exercise extra-territorial jurisdiction in accordance with the generally recognised principles of international law.'

4. If a declaration under this section is made, this subsection and subsection 3, other than the amendment of this Constitution effected thereby, and subsection 5 of this section shall be omitted from every official text of this Constitution published thereafter, but notwithstanding such omission this section shall continue to have the force of law.

5. If such a declaration is not made within twelve months of this section being added to this Constitution or such longer period as may be provided for by law, this section shall cease to have effect and shall be omitted from every official text of this Constitution published thereafter.

Strand One

Democratic Institutions in Northern Ireland

1. This agreement provides for a democratically elected Assembly in Northern Ireland which is inclusive in its membership, capable of exercising executive and legislative authority, and subject to safeguards to protect the rights and interests of all sides of the community.

The Assembly

2. A 108-member Assembly will be elected by PR(STV) from existing Westminster constituencies.

3. The Assembly will exercise full legislative and executive authority in respect of those matters currently within the responsibility of the six Northern Ireland Government Departments, with the possibility of taking on responsibility for other matters as detailed elsewhere in this agreement.

4. The Assembly—operating where appropriate on a cross-community basis —will be the prime source of authority in respect of all devolved responsibilities.

Safeguards

5. There will be safeguards to ensure that all sections of the community can participate and work together successfully in the operation of these institutions and that all sections of the community are protected, including:

  (a) allocations of Committee Chairs, Ministers and Committee membership in proportion to party strengths;
  (b) the European Convention on Human Rights (ECHR) and any Bill of Rights for Northern Ireland supplementing it, which neither the Assembly nor public bodies can infringe, together with a Human Rights Commission;
  (c) arrangements to provide that key decisions and legislation are proofed to ensure that they do not infringe the ECHR and any Bill of Rights for Northern Ireland;
  (d) arrangements to ensure key decisions are taken on a cross-community basis;
    (i) *either* parallel consent, i.e. a majority of those members present and voting, including a majority of the unionist and nationalist designations present and voting;
    (ii) *or* a weighted majority (60%) of members present and voting, including at least 40% of each of the nationalist and unionist designations present and voting.

      Key decisions requiring cross-community support will be designated in advance, including election of the Chair of the Assembly, the First Minister and Deputy First Minister, standing orders and budget allocations. In other cases such decisions could be triggered by a petition of concern brought by a significant minority of Assembly members (30/108).

  (e) an Equality Commission to monitor a statutory obligation to promote equality of opportunity in specified areas and parity of esteem between the two main communities, and to investigate individual complaints against public bodies.

Operation of the Assembly

6. At their first meeting, members of the Assembly will register a designation of identity—nationalist, unionist or other—for the purposes of measuring cross-community support in Assembly votes under the relevant provisions above.

7. The Chair and Deputy Chair of the Assembly will be elected on a cross-community basis, as set out in paragraph 5(d) above.

8. There will be a Committee for each of the main executive functions of the Northern Ireland Administration. The Chairs and Deputy Chairs of the Assembly Committees will be allocated proportionally, using the d'Hondt system. Membership of the Committees will be in broad proportion to party strengths in the Assembly to ensure that the opportunity of Committee places is available to all members.

9. The Committees will have a scrutiny, policy development and consultation role with respect to the Department with which each is associated, and will have a role in initiation of legislation. They will have the power to:

- consider and advise on Departmental budgets and Annual Plans in the context of the overall budget allocation;
- approve relevant secondary legislation and take the Committee stage of relevant primary legislation;
- call for persons and papers;
- initiate enquiries and make reports;
- consider and advise on matters brought to the Committee by its Minister.

10. Standing Committees other than Departmental Committees may be established as may be required from time to time.

11. The Assembly may appoint a special Committee to examine and report on whether a measure or proposal for legislation is in conformity with equality requirements, including the ECHR/Bill of Rights. The Committee shall have the power to call people and papers to assist in its consideration of the matter. The Assembly shall then consider the report of the Committee and can determine the matter in accordance with the cross-community consent procedure.

12. The above special procedure shall be followed when requested by the Executive Committee, or by the relevant Departmental Committee, voting on a cross-community basis.

13. When there is a petition of concern as in 5(d) above, the Assembly shall vote to determine whether the measure may proceed without reference to this special procedure. If this fails to achieve support on a cross-community basis, as in 5(d)(i) above, the special procedure shall be followed.

Executive Authority

14. Executive authority to be discharged on behalf of the Assembly by a First Minister and Deputy First Minister and up to ten Ministers with Departmental responsibilities.

15. The First Minister and Deputy First Minister shall be jointly elected into office by the Assembly voting on a cross-community basis, according to 5(d)(i) above.

16. Following the election of the First Minister and Deputy First Minister, the posts of Ministers will be allocated to parties on the basis of the d'Hondt system by reference to the number of seats each party has in the Assembly.

17. The Ministers will constitute an Executive Committee, which will be convened, and presided over, by the First Minister and Deputy First Minister.

18. The duties of the First Minister and Deputy First Minister will include, inter alia, dealing with and co-ordinating the work of the Executive Committee and the response of the Northern Ireland administration to external relationships.

19. The Executive Committee will provide a forum for the discussion of, and agreement on, issues which cut across the responsibilities of two or more Ministers, for prioritising executive and legislative proposals and for recommending a common position where necessary (e.g. in dealing with external relationships).

20. The Executive Committee will seek to agree each year, and review as necessary, a programme incorporating an agreed budget linked to policies and programmes, subject to approval by the Assembly, after scrutiny in Assembly Committees, on a cross-community basis.

21. A party may decline the opportunity to nominate a person to serve as a Minister or may subsequently change its nominee.

22. All the Northern Ireland Departments will be headed by a Minister. All Ministers will liaise regularly with their respective Committee.

23. As a condition of appointment, Ministers, including the First Minister and Deputy First Minister, will affirm the terms of a Pledge of Office (Annex A) undertaking to discharge effectively and in good faith all the responsibilities attaching to their office.

24. Ministers will have full executive authority in their respective areas of responsibility, within any broad programme agreed by the Executive Committee and endorsed by the Assembly as a whole.

25. An individual may be removed from office following a decision of the Assembly taken on a cross-community basis, if (s)he loses the confidence of the Assembly, voting on a cross-community basis, for failure to meet his or her responsibilities including, inter alia, those set out in the Pledge of Office. Those who hold office should use only democratic, non-violent means, and those who do not should be excluded or removed from office under these provisions.

Legislation

26. The Assembly will have authority to pass primary legislation for Northern Ireland in devolved areas, subject to:

- (a) the ECHR and any Bill of Rights for Northern Ireland supplementing it which, if the courts found to be breached, would render the relevant legislation null and void;
- (b) decisions by simple majority of members voting, except when decision on a cross-community basis is required;
- (c) detailed scrutiny and approval in the relevant Departmental Committee;
- (d) mechanisms, based on arrangements proposed for the Scottish Parliament, to ensure suitable co-ordination, and avoid disputes, between the Assembly and the Westminster Parliament;
- (e) option of the Assembly seeking to include Northern Ireland provisions in United Kingdom-wide legislation in the Westminster Parliament, especially on devolved issues where parity is normally maintained (e.g. social security, company law).

27. The Assembly will have authority to legislate in reserved areas with the approval of the Secretary of State and subject to Parliamentary control.

28. Disputes over legislative competence will be decided by the Courts.

29. Legislation could be initiated by an individual, a Committee or a Minister.

Relations with other institutions

30. Arrangements to represent the Assembly as a whole, at Summit level and in dealings with other institutions, will be in accordance with paragraph 18, and will be such as to ensure cross-community involvement.

31. Terms will be agreed between appropriate Assembly representatives and the Government of the United Kingdom to ensure effective co-ordination and input by Ministers to national policy-making, including on EU issues.

32. Role of Secretary of State:

    (a) to remain responsible for NIO matters not devolved to the Assembly, subject to regular consultation with the Assembly and Ministers;

    (b) to approve and lay before the Westminster Parliament any Assembly legislation on reserved matters;

    (c) to represent Northern Ireland interests in the United Kingdom Cabinet;

    (d) to have the right to attend the Assembly at their invitation.

33. The Westminster Parliament (whose power to make legislation for Northern Ireland would remain unaffected) will:

    (a) legislate for non-devolved issues, other than where the Assembly legislates with the approval of the Secretary of State and subject to the control of Parliament;

    (b) to legislate as necessary to ensure the United Kingdom's international obligations are met in respect of Northern Ireland;

    (c) scrutinise, including through the Northern Ireland Grand and Select Committees, the responsibilities of the Secretary of State.

34. A consultative Civic Forum will be established. It will comprise representatives of the business, trade union and voluntary sectors, and such other sectors as agreed by the First Minister and the Deputy First Minister. It will act as a consultative mechanism on social, economic and cultural issues. The First Minister and the Deputy First Minister will by agreement provide administrative support for the Civic Forum and establish guidelines for the selection of representatives to the Civic Forum.

Transitional Arrangements

35. The Assembly will meet first for the purpose of organisation, without legislative or executive powers, to resolve its standing orders and working practices and make preparations for the effective functioning of the Assembly, the British–Irish Council and the North/South Ministerial Council and associated implementation bodies. In this transitional period, those members of the Assembly serving as shadow Ministers shall affirm their commitment to non-violence and exclusively peaceful and democratic means and their opposition to any use or threat of force by others for any political purpose; to work in good

faith to bring the new arrangements into being; and to observe the spirit of the Pledge of Office applying to appointed Ministers.

Review

36. After a specified period there will be a review of these arrangements, including the details of electoral arrangements and of the Assembly's procedures, with a view to agreeing any adjustments necessary in the interests of efficiency and fairness.

Annex A
Pledge of Office
To pledge:

(a) to discharge in good faith all the duties of office;
(b) commitment to non-violence and exclusively peaceful and democratic means;
(c) to serve all the people of Northern Ireland equally, and to act in accordance with the general obligations on government to promote equality and prevent discrimination;
(d) to participate with colleagues in the preparation of a programme for government;
(e) to operate within the framework of that programme when agreed within the Executive Committee and endorsed by the Assembly;
(f) to support, and to act in accordance with, all decisions of the Executive Committee and Assembly;
(g) to comply with the Ministerial Code of Conduct.

Code of Conduct
Ministers must at all times:

• observe the highest standards of propriety and regularity involving impartiality, integrity and objectivity in relationship to the stewardship of public funds;
• be accountable to users of services, the community and, through the Assembly, for the activities within their responsibilities, their stewardship of public funds and the extent to which key performance targets and objectives have been met;
• ensure all reasonable requests for information from the Assembly, users of services and individual citizens are complied with; and that Departments and their staff conduct their dealings with the public in an open and responsible way;
• follow the seven principles of public life set out by the Committee on Standards in Public Life;
• comply with this code and with rules relating to the use of public funds;
• operate in a way conducive to promoting good community relations and equality of treatment;
• not use information gained in the course of their service for personal gain; nor seek to use the opportunity of public service to promote their private interests;
• ensure they comply with any rules on the acceptance of gifts and hospitality that might be offered;
• declare any personal or business interests which may conflict with their responsibilities. The Assembly will retain a Register of Interests. Individuals must ensure that any direct or indirect pecuniary interests which members of the public might reasonably think could influence their judgement are listed in the Register of Interests.

Strand Two

North/South Ministerial Council

1. Under a new British/Irish Agreement dealing with the totality of relationships, and related legislation at Westminster and in the Oireachtas, a North/South Ministerial Council to be established to bring together those with executive responsibilities in Northern Ireland and the Irish Government, to develop consultation, co-operation and action within the island of Ireland—including through implementation on an all-island and cross-border basis—on matters of mutual interest within the competence of the Administrations, North and South.

2. All Council decisions to be by agreement between the two sides. Northern Ireland to be represented by the First Minister, Deputy First Minister and any relevant Ministers, the Irish Government by the Taoiseach and relevant Ministers, all operating in accordance with the rules for democratic authority and accountability in force in the Northern Ireland Assembly and the Oireachtas respectively. Participation in the Council to be one of the essential responsibilities attaching to relevant posts in the two Administrations. If a holder of a relevant post will not participate normally in the Council, the Taoiseach in the case of the Irish Government and the First and Deputy First Minister in the case of the Northern Ireland Administration to be able to make alternative arrangements.

3. The Council to meet in different formats:

   (i) in plenary format twice a year, with Northern Ireland representation led by the First Minister and Deputy First Minister and the Irish Government led by the Taoiseach;
   (ii) in specific sectoral formats on a regular and frequent basis with each side represented by the appropriate Minister;
   (iii) in an appropriate format to consider institutional or cross-sectoral matters (including in relation to the EU) and to resolve disagreement.

4. Agendas for all meetings to be settled by prior agreement between the two sides, but it will be open to either to propose any matter for consideration or action.

5. The Council:

   (i) to exchange information, discuss and consult with a view to co-operating on matters of mutual interest within the competence of both Administrations, North and South;
   (ii) to use best endeavours to reach agreement on the adoption of common policies, in areas where there is a mutual cross-border and all-island benefit, and which are within the competence of both Administrations, North and South, making determined efforts to overcome any disagreements;
   (iii) to take decisions by agreement on policies for implementation separately in each jurisdiction, in relevant meaningful areas within the competence of both Administrations, North and South;
   (iv) to take decisions by agreement on policies and action at an all-island and cross-border level to be implemented by the bodies to be established as set out in paragraphs 8 and 9 below.

6. Each side to be in a position to take decisions in the Council within the defined authority of those attending, through the arrangements in place for co-ordination of

executive functions within each jurisdiction. Each side to remain accountable to the Assembly and Oireachtas respectively, whose approval, through the arrangements in place on either side, would be required for decisions beyond the defined authority of those attending.

7. As soon as practically possible after elections to the Northern Ireland Assembly, inaugural meetings will take place of the Assembly, the British/Irish Council and the North/South Ministerial Council in their transitional forms. All three institutions will meet regularly and frequently on this basis during the period between the elections to the Assembly, and the transfer of powers to the Assembly, in order to establish their modus operandi.

8. During the transitional period between the elections to the Northern Ireland Assembly and the transfer of power to it, representatives of the Northern Ireland transitional Administration and the Irish Government operating in the North/South Ministerial Council will undertake a work programme, in consultation with the British Government, covering at least 12 subject areas, with a view to identifying and agreeing by 31 October 1998 areas where co-operation and implementation for mutual benefit will take place. Such areas may include matters in the list set out in the Annex.

9. As part of the work programme, the Council will identify and agree at least 6 matters for co-operation and implementation in each of the following categories:

(i) Matters where existing bodies will be the appropriate mechanisms for co-operation in each separate jurisdiction;

(ii) Matters where the co-operation will take place through agreed implementation bodies on a cross-border or all-island level.

10. The two Governments will make necessary legislative and other enabling preparations to ensure, as an absolute commitment, that these bodies, which have been agreed as a result of the work programme, function at the time of the inception of the British–Irish Agreement and the transfer of powers, with legislative authority for these bodies transferred to the Assembly as soon as possible thereafter. Other arrangements for the agreed co-operation will also commence contemporaneously with the transfer of powers to the Assembly.

11. The implementation bodies will have a clear operational remit. They will implement on an all-island and cross-border basis policies agreed in the Council.

12. Any further development of these arrangements to be by agreement in the Council and with the specific endorsement of the Northern Ireland Assembly and Oireachtas, subject to the extent of the competences and responsibility of the two Administrations.

13. It is understood that the North/South Ministerial Council and the Northern Ireland Assembly are mutually inter-dependent, and that one cannot successfully function without the other.

14. Disagreements within the Council to be addressed in the format described at paragraph 3(iii) above or in the plenary format. By agreement between the two sides, experts could be appointed to consider a particular matter and report.

15. Funding to be provided by the two Administrations on the basis that the Council and the implementation bodies constitute a necessary public function.

16. The Council to be supported by a standing joint Secretariat, staffed by members of the Northern Ireland Civil Service and the Irish Civil Service.

17. The Council to consider the European Union dimension of relevant matters, including the implementation of EU policies and programmes and proposals under consideration in the EU framework. Arrangements to be made to ensure that the views of the Council are taken into account and represented appropriately at relevant EU meetings.

18. The Northern Ireland Assembly and the Oireachtas to consider developing a joint parliamentary forum, bringing together equal numbers from both institutions for discussion of matters of mutual interest and concern.

19. Consideration to be given to the establishment of an independent consultative forum appointed by the two Administrations, representative of civil society, comprising the social partners and other members with expertise in social, cultural, economic and other issues.

Annex

Areas for North/South co-operation and implementation may include the following:

1. Agriculture— animal and plant health.
2. Education—teacher qualifications and exchanges.
3. Transport—strategic transport planning.
4. Environment—environmental protection, pollution, water quality, and waste management.
5. Waterways—inland waterways.
6. Social Security/Social Welfare—entitlements of cross-border workers and fraud control.
7. Tourism—promotion, marketing, research, and product development.
8. Relevant EU Programmes such as SPPR, INTERREG, Leader II and their successors.
9. Inland Fisheries.
10. Aquaculture and marine matters
11. Health: accident and emergency services and other related cross-border issues.
12. Urban and rural development.

Others to be considered by the shadow North/South Council.

Strand Three
British–Irish Council

1. A British–Irish Council (BIC) will be established under a new British–Irish Agreement to promote the harmonious and mutually beneficial development of the totality of relationships among the peoples of these islands.

2. Membership of the BIC will comprise representatives of the British and Irish Governments, devolved institutions in Northern Ireland, Scotland and Wales, when established, and, if appropriate, elsewhere in the United Kingdom, together with representatives of the Isle of Man and the Channel Islands.

3. The BIC will meet in different formats: at summit level, twice per year; in specific sectoral formats on a regular basis, with each side represented by the appropriate Minister; in an appropriate format to consider cross-sectoral matters.

4. Representatives of members will operate in accordance with whatever procedures for democratic authority and accountability are in force in their respective elected institutions.

5. The BIC will exchange information, discuss, consult and use best endeavours to reach agreement on co-operation on matters of mutual interest within the competence of the relevant Administrations. Suitable issues for early discussion in the BIC could include transport links, agricultural issues, environmental issues, cultural issues, health issues, education issues and approaches to EU issues. Suitable arrangements to be made for practical co-operation on agreed policies.

6. It will be open to the BIC to agree common policies or common actions. Individual members may opt not to participate in such common policies and common action.

7. The BIC normally will operate by consensus. In relation to decisions on common policies or common actions, including their means of implementation, it will operate by agreement of all members participating in such policies or actions.

8. The members of the BIC, on a basis to be agreed between them, will provide such financial support as it may require.

9. A secretariat for the BIC will be provided by the British and Irish Governments in co-ordination with officials of each of the other members.

10. In addition to the structures provided for under this agreement, it will be open to two or more members to develop bilateral or multilateral arrangements between them. Such arrangements could include, subject to the agreement of the members concerned, mechanisms to enable consultation, co-operation and joint decision-making on matters of mutual interest; and mechanisms to implement any joint decisions they may reach. These arrangements will not require the prior approval of the BIC as a whole and will operate independently of it.

11. The elected institutions of the members will be encouraged to develop interparliamentary links, perhaps building on the British–Irish Interparliamentary Body.

12. The full membership of the BIC will keep under review the workings of the Council, including a formal published review at an appropriate time after the Agreement comes into effect, and will contribute as appropriate to any review of the overall political agreement arising from the multi-party negotiations.

British–Irish Intergovernmental Conference

1. There will be a new British–Irish Agreement dealing with the totality of relationships. It will establish a standing British–Irish Intergovernmental Conference, which will subsume both the Anglo-Irish Intergovernmental Council and the Intergovernmental Conference established under the 1985 Agreement.

2. The Conference will bring together the British and Irish Governments to promote bilateral co-operation at all levels on all matters of mutual interest within the competence of both Governments.

3. The Conference will meet as required at Summit level (Prime Minister and Taoiseach). Otherwise, Governments will be represented by appropriate Ministers. Advisers, including police and security advisers, will attend as appropriate.

4. All decisions will be by agreement between both Governments. The Governments will make determined efforts to resolve disagreements between them. There will be no derogation from the sovereignty of either Government.

5. In recognition of the Irish Government's special interest in Northern Ireland and of the extent to which issues of mutual concern arise in relation to Northern Ireland, there will be regular and frequent meetings of the Conference concerned with non-devolved Northern Ireland matters, on which the Irish Government may put forward views and proposals. These meetings, to be co-chaired by the Minister for Foreign Affairs and the Secretary of State for Northern Ireland, would also deal with all-island and cross-border co-operation on non-devolved issues.

6. Co-operation within the framework of the Conference will include facilitation of co-operation in security matters. The Conference also will address, in particular, the areas of rights, justice, prisons and policing in Northern Ireland (unless and until responsibility is devolved to a Northern Ireland administration) and will intensify co-operation between the two Governments on the all-island or cross-border aspects of these matters.

7. Relevant executive members of the Northern Ireland Administration will be involved in meetings of the Conference, and in the reviews referred to in paragraph 9 below to discuss non-devolved Northern Ireland matters.

8. The Conference will be supported by officials of the British and Irish Governments, including by a standing joint Secretariat of officials dealing with non-devolved Northern Ireland matters.

9. The Conference will keep under review the workings of the new British–Irish Agreement and the machinery and institutions established under it, including a formal published review three years after the Agreement comes into effect. Representatives of the Northern Ireland Administration will be invited to express views to the Conference in this context. The Conference will contribute as appropriate to any review of the overall political agreement arising from the multi-party negotiations but will have no power to override the democratic arrangements set up by this Agreement.

Rights, Safeguards and Equality of Opportunity
Human Rights

1. The parties affirm their commitment to the mutual respect, the civil rights and the religious liberties of everyone in the community. Against the background of the recent history of communal conflict, the parties affirm in particular:

- the right of free political thought;
- the right to freedom and expression of religion;
- the right to pursue democratically national and political aspirations;
- the right to seek constitutional change by peaceful and legitimate means;
- the right to freely choose one's place of residence;
- the right to equal opportunity in all social and economic activity, regardless of class, creed, disability, gender or ethnicity;
- the right to freedom from sectarian harassment; and
- the right of women to full and equal political participation.

United Kingdom Legislation

2. The British Government will complete incorporation into Northern Ireland law of the European Convention on Human Rights (ECHR), with direct access to the courts, and remedies for breach of the Convention, including power for the courts to overrule Assembly legislation on grounds of inconsistency.

3. Subject to the outcome of public consultation underway, the British Government intends, as a particular priority, to create a statutory obligation on public authorities in Northern Ireland to carry out all their functions with due regard to the need to promote equality of opportunity in relation to religion and political opinion; gender; race; disability; age; marital status; dependants; and sexual orientation. Public bodies would be required to draw up statutory schemes showing how they would implement this obligation. Such schemes would cover arrangements for policy appraisal, including an assessment of impact on relevant categories, public consultation, public access to information and services, monitoring and timetables.

4. The new Northern Ireland Human Rights Commission (see paragraph 5 below) will be invited to consult and to advise on the scope for defining, in Westminster legislation, rights supplementary to those in the European Convention on Human Rights, to reflect the particular circumstances of Northern Ireland, drawing as appropriate on international instruments and experience. These additional rights to reflect the principles of mutual respect for the identity and ethos of both communities and parity of esteem, and—taken together with the ECHR—to constitute a Bill of Rights for Northern Ireland. Among the issues for consideration by the Commission will be:

- the formulation of a general obligation on government and public bodies fully to respect, on the basis of equality of treatment, the identity and ethos of both communities in Northern Ireland; and
- a clear formulation of the rights not to be discriminated against and to equality of opportunity in both the public and private sectors.

New Institutions in Northern Ireland

5. A new Northern Ireland Human Rights Commission, with membership from Northern Ireland reflecting the community balance, will be established by Westminster legislation, independent of Government, with an extended and enhanced role beyond that currently exercised by the Standing Advisory Commission on Human Rights, to include keeping under review the adequacy and effectiveness of laws and practices, making recommendations to Government as necessary; providing information and promoting awareness of human rights; considering draft legislation referred to them by the new Assembly; and, in appropriate cases, bringing court proceedings or providing assistance to individuals doing so.

6. Subject to the outcome of public consultation currently underway, the British Government intends a new statutory Equality Commission to replace the Fair Employment Commission, the Equal Opportunities Commission (NI), the Commission for Racial Equality (NI) and the Disability Council. Such a unified Commission will advise on, validate and monitor the statutory obligation and will investigate complaints of default.

7. It would be open to a new Northern Ireland Assembly to consider bringing together its responsibilities for these matters into a dedicated Department of Equality.

8. These improvements will build on existing protections in Westminster legislation in respect of the judiciary, the system of justice and policing.

Comparable Steps by the Irish Government

9. The Irish Government will also take steps to further strengthen the protection of human rights in its jurisdiction. The Government will, taking account of the work of the All-Party Oireachtas Committee on the Constitution and the Report of the Constitution Review Group, bring forward measures to strengthen and underpin the constitutional protection of human rights. These proposals will draw on the European Convention on Human Rights and other international legal instruments in the field of human rights and the question of the incorporation of the ECHR will be further examined in this context. The measures brought forward would ensure at least an equivalent level of protection of human rights as will pertain in Northern Ireland. In addition, the Irish Government will:

- establish a Human Rights Commission with a mandate and remit equivalent to that within Northern Ireland;
- proceed with arrangements as quickly as possible to ratify the Council of Europe Framework Convention on National Minorities (already ratified by the UK);
- implement enhanced employment equality legislation;
- introduce equal status legislation; and
- continue to take further active steps to demonstrate its respect for the different traditions in the island of Ireland.

A Joint Committee

10. It is envisaged that there would be a joint committee of representatives of the two Human Rights Commissions, North and South, as a forum for consideration of human rights issues in the island of Ireland. The joint committee will consider, among other matters, the possibility of establishing a charter, open to signature by all democratic political parties, reflecting and endorsing agreed measures for the protection of the fundamental rights of everyone living in the island of Ireland.

Reconciliation and Victims of Violence

11. The participants believe that it is essential to acknowledge and address the suffering of the victims of violence as a necessary element of reconciliation. They look forward to the results of the work of the Northern Ireland Victims Commission.

12. It is recognised that victims have a right to remember as well as to contribute to a changed society. The achievement of a peaceful and just society would be the true memorial to the victims of violence. The participants particularly recognise that young people from areas affected by the troubles face particular difficulties and will support the development of special community-based initiatives based on international best practice. The provision of services that are supportive and sensitive to the needs of victims will also be a critical element and that support will need to be channelled through both statutory and community-based voluntary organisations facilitating locally-based self-help and support networks. This will require the allocation of sufficient resources, including statutory funding as necessary, to meet the needs of victims and to provide for community-based support programmes.

13. The participants recognise and value the work being done by many organisations to develop reconciliation and mutual understanding and respect between and within communities and traditions, in Northern Ireland and between North and South, and they see such work as having a vital role in consolidating peace and political agreement. Accordingly, they pledge their continuing support to such organisations and will positively examine the case for enhanced financial assistance for the work of reconciliation. An essential aspect of the reconciliation process is the promotion of a culture of tolerance at every level of society, including initiatives to facilitate and encourage integrated education and mixed housing.

Economic, Social and Cultural Issues

1. Pending the devolution of powers to a new Northern Ireland Assembly, the British Government will pursue broad policies for sustained economic growth and stability in Northern Ireland and for promoting social inclusion, including in particular community development and the advancement of women in public life.

2. Subject to the public consultation currently under way, the British Government will make rapid progress with:

  (i) a new regional development strategy for Northern Ireland, for consideration in due course by the Assembly, tackling the problems of a divided society and social cohesion in urban, rural and border areas, protecting and enhancing the environment, producing new approaches to transport issues, strengthening the physical infrastructure of the region, developing the advantages and resources of rural areas and rejuvenating major urban centres;

  (ii) a new economic development strategy for Northern Ireland, for consideration in due course by the Assembly, which would provide for short and medium term economic planning linked as appropriate to the regional development strategy; and

  (iii) measures on employment equality included in the recent White Paper ('Partnership for Equality') and covering the extension and strengthening of anti-discrimination legislation, a review of the national security aspects of the present fair employment legislation at the earliest possible time, a new more focused Targeting Social Need initiative and a range of measures aimed at combating unemployment and progressively eliminating the differential in unemployment rates between the two communities by targeting objective need.

3. All participants recognise the importance of respect, understanding and tolerance in relation to linguistic diversity, including in Northern Ireland, the Irish language, Ulster-Scots and the languages of the various ethnic communities, all of which are part of the cultural wealth of the island of Ireland.

4. In the context of active consideration currently being given to the UK signing the Council of Europe Charter for Regional or Minority Languages, the British Government will in particular in relation to the Irish language, where appropriate and where people so desire it:

  • take resolute action to promote the language;
  • facilitate and encourage the use of the language in speech and writing in public and private life where there is appropriate demand;

- seek to remove, where possible, restrictions which would discourage or work against the maintenance or development of the language;
- make provision for liaising with the Irish language community, representing their views to public authorities and investigating complaints;
- place a statutory duty on the Department of Education to encourage and facilitate Irish medium education in line with current provision for integrated education;
- explore urgently with the relevant British authorities, and in co-operation with the Irish broadcasting authorities, the scope for achieving more widespread availability of Teilifís na Gaeilge in Northern Ireland;
- seek more effective ways to encourage and provide financial support for Irish language film and television production in Northern Ireland; and
- encourage the parties to secure agreement that this commitment will be sustained by a new Assembly in a way which takes account of the desires and sensitivities of the community.

5. All participants acknowledge the sensitivity of the use of symbols and emblems for public purposes, and the need in particular in creating the new institutions to ensure that such symbols and emblems are used in a manner which promotes mutual respect rather than division. Arrangements will be made to monitor this issue and consider what action might be required.

Decommissioning

1. Participants recall their agreement in the Procedural Motion adopted on 24 September 1997 'that the resolution of the decommissioning issue is an indispensable part of the process of negotiation', and also recall the provisions of paragraph 25 of Strand 1 above.

2. They note the progress made by the Independent International Commission on Decommissioning and the Governments in developing schemes which can represent a workable basis for achieving the decommissioning of illegally-held arms in the possession of paramilitary groups.

3. All participants accordingly reaffirm their commitment to the total disarmament of all paramilitary organisations. They also confirm their intention to continue to work constructively and in good faith with the Independent Commission, and to use any influence they may have, to achieve the decommissioning of all paramilitary arms within two years following endorsement in referendums North and South of the agreement and in the context of the implementation of the overall settlement.

4. The Independent Commission will monitor, review and verify progress on decommissioning of illegal arms, and will report to both Governments at regular intervals.

6. Both Governments will take all necessary steps to facilitate the decommissioning process to include bringing the relevant schemes into force by the end of June.

Security

1. The participants note that the development of a peaceful environment on the basis of this agreement can and should mean a normalisation of security arrangements and practices.

2. The British Government will make progress towards the objective of as early a return as possible to normal security arrangements in Northern Ireland, consistent with the level of threat and with a published overall strategy, dealing with:

    (i) the reduction of the numbers and role of the Armed Forces deployed in Northern Ireland to levels compatible with a normal peaceful society;

    (ii) the removal of security installations;

    (iii) the removal of emergency powers in Northern Ireland; and

    (iv) other measures appropriate to and compatible with a normal peaceful society.

3. The Secretary of State will consult regularly on progress, and the response to any continuing paramilitary activity, with the Irish Government and the political parties, as appropriate.

4. The British Government will continue its consultation on firearms regulation and control on the basis of the document published on 2 April 1998.

5. The Irish Government will initiate a wide-ranging review of the Offences Against the State Acts 1939–85 with a view to both reform and dispensing with those elements no longer required as circumstances permit.

Policing and Justice

1. The participants recognise that policing is a central issue in any society. They equally recognise that Northern Ireland's history of deep divisions has made it highly emotive, with great hurt suffered and sacrifices made by many individuals and their families, including those in the RUC and other public servants. They believe that the agreement provides the opportunity for a new beginning to policing in Northern Ireland with a police service capable of attracting and sustaining support from the community as a whole. They also believe that this agreement offers a unique opportunity to bring about a new political dispensation which will recognise the full and equal legitimacy and worth of the identities, senses of allegiance and ethos of all sections of the community in Northern Ireland. They consider that this opportunity should inform and underpin the development of a police service representative in terms of the make-up of the community as a whole and which, in a peaceful environment, should be routinely unarmed.

2. The participants believe it essential that policing structures and arrangements are such that the police service is professional, effective and efficient, fair and impartial, free from partisan political control; accountable, both under the law for its actions and to the community it serves; representative of the society it polices, and operates within a coherent and co-operative criminal justice system, which conforms with human rights norms. The participants also believe that those structures and arrangements must be capable of maintaining law and order including responding effectively to crime and to any terrorist threat and to public order problems. A police service which cannot do so will fail to win public confidence and acceptance. They believe that any such structures and arrangements should be capable of delivering a policing service, in constructive and inclusive partnerships with the community at all levels, and with the maximum delegation of authority and responsibility, consistent with the foregoing principles. These arrangements should be based on principles of protection of human rights and professional integrity and should be unambiguously accepted and actively supported by the entire community.

3. An independent Commission will be established to make recommendations for future policing arrangements in Northern Ireland including means of encouraging widespread community support for these arrangements within the agreed framework of principles reflected in the paragraphs above and in accordance with the terms of reference at Annex A. The Commission will be broadly representative with expert and international representation among its membership and will be asked to consult widely and to report no later than Summer 1999.

4. The participants believe that the aims of the criminal justice system are to:

- deliver a fair and impartial system of justice to the community;
- be responsive to the community's concerns, and encouraging community involvement where appropriate;
- have the confidence of all parts of the community; and
- deliver justice efficiently and effectively.

5. There will be a parallel wide-ranging review of criminal justice (other than policing and those aspects of the system relating to the emergency legislation) to be carried out by the British Government through a mechanism with an independent element, in consultation with the political parties and others. The review will commence as soon as possible, will include wide consultation, and a report will be made to the Secretary of State no later than Autumn 1999. Terms of Reference are attached at Annex B.

6. Implementation of the recommendations arising from both reviews will be discussed with the political parties and with the Irish Government.

7. The participants also note that the British Government remains ready in principle, with the broad support of the political parties, and after consultation, as appropriate, with the Irish Government, in the context of ongoing implementation of the relevant recommendations, to devolve responsibility for policing and justice issues.

Annex A. Commission on Policing for Northern Ireland
Terms of Reference

Taking account of the principles on policing as set out in the agreement, the Commission will inquire into policing in Northern Ireland and, on the basis of its findings, bring forward proposals for future policing structures and arrangements, including means of encouraging widespread community support for those arrangements.

Its proposals on policing should be designed to ensure that policing arrangements, including composition, recruitment, training, culture, ethos and symbols, are such that in a new approach Northern Ireland has a police service that can enjoy widespread support from, and is seen as an integral part of, the community as a whole.

Its proposals should include recommendations covering any issues such as re-training, job placement and educational and professional development required in the transition to policing in a peaceful society.

Its proposals should also be designed to ensure that:

- the police service is structured, managed and resourced so that it can be effective in discharging its full range of functions (including proposals on any necessary arrangements for the transition to policing in a normal peaceful society);

- the police service is delivered in constructive and inclusive partnerships with the community at all levels with the maximum delegation of authority and responsibility;
- the legislative and constitutional framework requires the impartial discharge of policing functions and conforms with internationally accepted norms in relation to policing standards;
- the police operate within a clear framework of accountability to the law and the community they serve, so:
  - they are constrained by, accountable to and act only within the law;
  - their powers and procedures, like the law they enforce, are clearly established and publicly available;
  - there are open, accessible and independent means of investigating and adjudicating upon complaints against the police;
  - there are clearly established arrangements enabling local people, and their political representatives, to articulate their views and concerns about policing and to establish publicly policing priorities and influence policing policies, subject to safeguards to ensure police impartiality and freedom from partisan political control;
  - there are arrangements for accountability and for the effective, efficient and economic use of resources in achieving policing objectives;
  - there are means to ensure independent professional scrutiny and inspection of the police service to ensure that proper professional standards are maintained;
- the scope for structured co-operation with the Garda Síochána and other police forces is addressed; and
- the management of public order events which can impose exceptional demands on policing resources is also addressed.

The Commission should focus on policing issues, but if it identifies other aspects of the criminal justice system relevant to its work on policing, including the role of the police in prosecution, then it should draw the attention of the Government to those matters.

The Commission should consult widely, including with non-governmental expert organisations, and through such focus groups as they consider it appropriate to establish.

The Government proposes to establish the Commission as soon as possible, with the aim of it starting work as soon as possible and publishing its final report by Summer 1999.

Annex B. Review of the criminal justice system
Terms of Reference

Taking account of the aims of the criminal justice system as set out in the Agreement, the review will address the structure, management and resourcing of publicly funded elements of the criminal justice system and will bring forward proposals for future criminal justice arrangements (other than policing and those aspects of the system relating to emergency legislation, which the Government is considering separately) covering such issues as:

- the arrangements for making appointments to the judiciary and magistracy, and safeguards for protecting their independence;
- the arrangements for the organisation and supervision of the prosecution process, and for safeguarding its independence;
- measures to improve the responsiveness and accountability of, and any lay participation in, the criminal justice system;

- mechanisms for addressing law reform;
- the scope for structured co-operation between the criminal justice agencies on both parts of the island; and
- the structure and organisation of criminal justice functions that might be devolved to an Assembly, including the possibility of establishing a Department of Justice, while safeguarding the essential independence of many of the key functions in this area.

The Government proposes to commence the review as soon as possible, consulting with the political parties and others, including non-governmental expert organisations. The review will be completed by Autumn 1999.

Prisoners

1. Both Governments will put in place mechanisms to provide for an accelerated programme for the release of prisoners, including transferred prisoners, convicted of scheduled offences in Northern Ireland or, in the case of those sentenced outside Northern Ireland, similar offences (referred to hereafter as qualifying prisoners). Any such arrangements will protect the rights of individual prisoners under national and international law.

2. Prisoners affiliated to organisations which have not established or are not maintaining a complete and unequivocal ceasefire will not benefit from the arrangements. The situation in this regard will be kept under review.

3. Both Governments will complete a review process within a fixed time frame and set prospective release dates for all qualifying prisoners. The review process would provide for the advance of the release dates of qualifying prisoners while allowing account to be taken of the seriousness of the offences for which the person was convicted and the need to protect the community. In addition, the intention would be that should the circumstances allow it, any qualifying prisoners who remained in custody two years after the commencement of the scheme would be released at that point.

4. The Governments will seek to enact the appropriate legislation to give effect to these arrangements by the end of June 1998.

5. The Governments continue to recognise the importance of measures to facilitate the reintegration of prisoners into the community by providing support both prior to and after release, including assistance directed towards availing of employment opportunities, re-training and/or re-skilling, and further education.

Validation, Implementation and Review
Validation and Implementation

1. The two Governments will as soon as possible sign a new British–Irish Agreement replacing the 1985 Anglo-Irish Agreement, embodying understandings on constitutional issues and affirming their solemn commitment to support and, where appropriate, implement the agreement reached by the participants in the negotiations which shall be annexed to the British–Irish Agreement.

2. Each Government will organise a referendum on 22 May 1998. Subject to Parliamentary approval, a consultative referendum in Northern Ireland, organised under the terms of the Northern Ireland (Entry to Negotiations, etc.) Act 1996, will address the question: 'Do you support the agreement reached in the multi-party talks on Northern Ireland and set out in

Command Paper 3883?'. The Irish Government will introduce and support in the Oireachtas a Bill to amend the Constitution as described in paragraph 2 of the section 'Constitutional Issues' and in Annex B, as follows: (a) to amend Articles 2 and 3 as described in paragraph 8.1 in Annex B above and (b) to amend Article 29 to permit the Government to ratify the new British–Irish Agreement. On passage by the Oireachtas, the Bill will be put to referendum.

3. If majorities of those voting in each of the referendums support this agreement, the Governments will then introduce and support, in their respective Parliaments, such legislation as may be necessary to give effect to all aspects of this agreement, and will take whatever ancillary steps as may be required including the holding of elections on 25 June, subject to parliamentary approval, to the Assembly, which would meet initially in a 'shadow' mode. The establishment of the North–South Ministerial Council, implementation bodies, the British–Irish Council and the British–Irish Intergovernmental Conference and the assumption by the Assembly of its legislative and executive powers will take place at the same time on the entry into force of the British–Irish Agreement.

4. In the interim, aspects of the implementation of the multi-party agreement will be reviewed at meetings of those parties relevant in the particular case (taking into account, once Assembly elections have been held, the results of those elections), under the chairmanship of the British Government or the two Governments, as may be appropriate; and representatives of the two Governments and all relevant parties may meet under independent chairmanship to review implementation of the agreement as a whole.

Review procedures following implementation
5. Each institution may, at any time, review any problems that may arise in its operation and, where no other institution is affected, take remedial action in consultation as necessary with the relevant Government or Governments. It will be for each institution to determine its own procedures for review.

6. If there are difficulties in the operation of a particular institution, which have implications for another institution, they may review their operations separately and jointly and agree on remedial action to be taken under their respective authorities.

7. If difficulties arise which require remedial action across the range of institutions, or otherwise require amendment of the British–Irish Agreement or relevant legislation, the process of review will fall to the two Governments in consultation with the parties in the Assembly. Each Government will be responsible for action in its own jurisdiction.

8. Notwithstanding the above, each institution will publish an annual report on its operations. In addition, the two Governments and the parties in the Assembly will convene a conference 4 years after the agreement comes into effect, to review and report on its operation.

Agreement between the Government of the United Kingdom of Great Britain and Northern Ireland and the Government of Ireland
The British and Irish Governments:
Welcoming the strong commitment to the Agreement reached on 10th April 1998 by themselves and other participants in the multi-party talks and set out in Annex 1 to this Agreement (hereinafter 'the Multi-Party Agreement');

Considering that the Multi-Party Agreement offers an opportunity for a new beginning in relationships within Northern Ireland, within the island of Ireland and between the peoples of these islands;

Wishing to develop still further the unique relationship between their peoples and the close co-operation between their countries as friendly neighbours and as partners in the European Union;

Reaffirming their total commitment to the principles of democracy and non-violence which have been fundamental to the multi-party talks;

Reaffirming their commitment to the principles of partnership, equality and mutual respect and to the protection of civil, political, social, economic and cultural rights in their respective jurisdictions;

Have agreed as follows:

Article 1
The two Governments:

  (i) recognise the legitimacy of whatever choice is freely exercised by a majority of the people of Northern Ireland with regard to its status, whether they prefer to continue to support the Union with Great Britain or a sovereign united Ireland;

 (ii) recognise that it is for the people of the island of Ireland alone, by agreement between the two parts respectively and without external impediment, to exercise their right of self-determination on the basis of consent, freely and concurrently given, North and South, to bring about a united Ireland, if that is their wish, accepting that this right must be achieved and exercised with and subject to the agreement and consent of a majority of the people of Northern Ireland;

(iii) acknowledge that while a substantial section of the people in Northern Ireland share the legitimate wish of a majority of the people of the island of Ireland for a united Ireland, the present wish of a majority of the people of Northern Ireland, freely exercised and legitimate, is to maintain the Union and accordingly, that Northern Ireland's status as part of the United Kingdom reflects and relies upon that wish; and that it would be wrong to make any change in the status of Northern Ireland save with the consent of a majority of its people;

 (iv) affirm that, if in the future, the people of the island of Ireland exercise their right of self-determination on the basis set out in sections (i) and (ii) above to bring about a united Ireland, it will be a binding obligation on both Governments to introduce and support in their respective Parliaments legislation to give effect to that wish;

  (v) affirm that whatever choice is freely exercised by a majority of the people of Northern Ireland, the power of the sovereign government with jurisdiction there shall be exercised with rigorous impartiality on behalf of all the people in the diversity of their identities and traditions and shall be founded on the principles of full respect for, and equality of, civil, political, social and cultural rights, of freedom from discrimination for all citizens, and of parity of esteem and of just and equal treatment for the identity, ethos and aspirations of both communities;

 (vi) recognise the birthright of all the people of Northern Ireland to identify themselves and be accepted as Irish or British, or both, as they may so choose, and accordingly confirm that their right to hold both British and Irish citizenship is accepted by both Governments and would not be affected by any future change in the status of Northern Ireland.

Article 2

The two Governments affirm their solemn commitment to support, and where appropriate implement, the provisions of the Multi-Party Agreement. In particular there shall be established in accordance with the provisions of the Multi-Party Agreement immediately on the entry into force of this Agreement, the following institutions:

  (i) a North/South Ministerial Council;
  (ii) the implementation bodies referred to in paragraph 9 (ii) of the section entitled 'Strand Two' of the Multi-Party Agreement;
  (iii) a British–Irish Council;
  (iv) a British–Irish Intergovernmental Conference.

Article 3

(1) This Agreement shall replace the Agreement between the British and Irish Governments done at Hillsborough on 15th November 1985 which shall cease to have effect on entry into force of this Agreement.

(2) The Intergovernmental Conference established by Article 2 of the aforementioned Agreement done on 15th November 1985 shall cease to exist on entry into force of this Agreement.

Article 4

(1) It shall be a requirement for entry into force of this Agreement that:

  (a) British legislation shall have been enacted for the purpose of implementing the provisions of Annex A to the section entitled 'Constitutional Issues' of the Multi-Party Agreement;
  (b) the amendments to the Constitution of Ireland set out in Annex B to the section entitled 'Constitutional Issues' of the Multi-Party Agreement shall have been approved by Referendum;
  (c) such legislation shall have been enacted as may be required to establish the institutions referred to in Article 2 of this Agreement.

(2) Each Government shall notify the other in writing of the completion, so far as it is concerned, of the requirements for entry into force of this Agreement. This Agreement shall enter into force on the date of the receipt of the later of the two notifications.

(3) Immediately on entry into force of this Agreement, the Irish Government shall ensure that the amendments to the Constitution of Ireland set out in Annex B to the section entitled 'Constitutional Issues' of the Multi-Party Agreement take effect.

In witness thereof the undersigned, being duly authorised thereto by the respective Governments, have signed this Agreement.

Done in two originals at Belfast on the 10th day of April 1998.

For the Government of the United Kingdom   For the Government of Ireland
of Great Britain and Northern Ireland

Annex 1
The Agreement Reached in the Multi-Party Talks

Annex 2
Declaration on the Provisions of Paragraph (vi) of Article 1 In Relationship to Citizenship

The British and Irish Governments declare that it is their joint understanding that the term 'the people of Northern Ireland' in paragraph (vi) of Article 1 of this Agreement means, for the purposes of giving effect to this provision, all persons born in Northern Ireland and having, at the time of their birth, at least one parent who is a British citizen, an Irish citizen or is otherwise entitled to reside in Northern Ireland without any restriction on their period of residence.

Note: Square brackets in this document are reproduced from the original and do not represent editorial intervention. The Irish version of the Agreement specified the Irish language text as follows:

[to be substituted for Articles 2 and 3 of the Irish text:]

'**Airteagal 2**

Tá gach duine a shaolaítear in oileán na hÉireann, ar a n-áirítear a oileáin agus a fharraigí, i dteideal, agus tá de cheart oidhreachta aige nó aici, a bheith páirteach i náisiún na hÉireann. Tá an teideal sin freisin ag na daoine go léir atá cáilithe ar shlí eile de réir dlí chun bheith ina saoránaigh d'Éirinn. Ina theannta sin, is mór ag náisiún na hÉireann a choibhneas speisialta le daoine de bhunadh na hÉireann atá ina gcónaí ar an gcoigríoch agus arb ionann féiniúlacht agus oidhreacht chultúir dóibh agus do náisiún na hÉireann.

Airteagal 3

1. Is í toil dhiongbháilte náisiún na hÉireann, go síotheach cairdiúil, na daoine go léir a chomhroinneann críoch oileán na hÉireann i bpáirt lena chéile, in éagsúlacht uile a bhféiniúlachtaí agus a dtraidisiún, a aontú, á aithint gur trí mhodhanna síochánta amháin le toiliú thromlach na ndaoine, á chur in iúl go daonlathach, sa dá dhlínse san oileán, a dhéanfar Éire aontaithe a thabhairt i gcrích. Go dtí sin, bainfidh na dlíthe a achtófar ag an bParlaimint a bhunaítear leis an mBunreacht seo leis an limistéar feidhme céanna, agus beidh an raon feidhme céanna acu, lenar bhain na dlíthe, agus a bhí ag na dlíthe, a d'achtaigh an Pharlaimint a bhí ar marthain díreach roimh theacht i ngníomh don Bhunreacht seo.'

2. Féadfaidh údaráis fhreagracha faoi seach na ndlínsí sin institiúidí ag a mbeidh cumhachtaí agus feidhmeanna feidhmiúcháin a chomhroinntear idir na dlínsí sin a bhunú chun críoch sonraithe agus féadfaidh na hinstitiúidí sin cumhachtaí agus feidhmeanna a fheidhmiú i leith an oileáin ar fad nó i leith aon chuid de.'

[to be added to the Irish text of Article 29:]

'8. Tig leis an Stát dlínse a fheidhmiú taobh amuigh dá chríoch de réir bhunrialacha gnáth-adhmaithe an dlí idirnáisiúnta.'

Sources: United Kingdom (1998); Irish text from Ireland (1998).

6

The Good Friday Agreement, 1998: Implementation

6.1. Introduction

The months and years that followed the Good Friday Agreement were to see the governments and parties undertake the implementation of its provisions, building the institutions that it sketched and working within them. They were also to witness exhaustive negotiation of many matters that the Agreement had covered only in broad brushstrokes, or ambiguously, or hardly at all. Sometimes these negotiations were in the form of set-piece all-party and high-level meetings, as in Weston Park in 2001 and Leeds Castle in 2004. Sometimes decisions were reached by informal canvassing and agreement in the process of implementation itself. Sometimes they involved the implementation of commission reports, most importantly the Independent Commission on Policing for Northern Ireland in 1999. But implementation issues were to persist well into the twenty-first century.

The implementation process was marked by recurrent crises, changing political loyalties among voters, and the breakdown of devolved government from 2002 (see the chronological outline in Table 6.1). Only when a new all-party conference at St Andrews, Scotland, was called as a review of the Good Friday Agreement in 2006 was a revised agreement reached. A new phase of devolution began in 2007, with Revd Ian Paisley of the DUP and Martin McGuinness of Sinn Féin becoming, respectively, First Minister and Deputy First Minister. The witness seminar in this chapter deals with the initial phase of implementation in 1998–2003; the interviews address the background to the St Andrews Agreement of 2006; while this introduction also refers briefly to the subsequent period of devolution, 2007–17.

Debates on the functioning of the Agreement have focused on issues of consociational politics, public attitudes, and electoral competition.[1] The processes of implementation have drawn less attention, notwithstanding important contributions in respect of particular sectors, such as policing reform and equality legislation.[2] The creation of the complex administrative apparatus of power-sharing

---

[1] Garry (2016); Hayes and McAllister (2013); McCulloch and McGarry (2017); Mitchell, O'Leary, and Evans (2001, 2009); O'Leary (2019: vol 3); Shirlow et al. (2011); Taylor (2009); Tonge et al. (2014).
[2] On government policies and practices, Coakley, Laffan, and Todd (2005); on policing reform, Doyle (2010); Mulcahy (2006); on equality, McCrudden et al. (2009); Todd and Ruane (2012); on other legal aspects, Morison (1999, 2001).

Negotiating a Settlement in Northern Ireland, 1969–2019.
John Coakley and Jennifer Todd, Oxford University Press (2020). © John Coakley and Jennifer Todd.
DOI: 10.1093/oso/9780198841388.001.0001

Table 6.1. Important political developments, 1998–2019

22 May 1998	Referendum endorses Agreement (71% in Northern Ireland, 94% in Republic)
25 June 1998	Election to Northern Ireland Assembly
1 July 1998	Assembly meets in 'shadow' form; David Trimble and Seamus Mallon elected as First Minister and Deputy First Minister Designate
15 August 1998	Bomb in Omagh by dissident republicans kills 29 people
18 December 1998	Parties agree structure of government and North-South bodies
8 March 1999	British and Irish governments sign treaties establishing North-South and East-West bodies
6 September 1999	George Mitchell returns to help with implementation issues, especially decommissioning; review concludes, 18 November
9 September 1999	Patten report recommends radical overhaul of Royal Ulster Constabulary (renamed Police Service of Northern Ireland, 2001)
2 December 1999	New devolved institutions within Northern Ireland, North-South bodies and East-West bodies come into formal existence; Northern Ireland Executive takes office
11 February 2000	Collapse of executive over decommissioning; direct rule re-installed; executive restored, 30 May
23 October 2001	First act of decommissioning of weapons by IRA (other acts follow on 8 April 2002 and 21 October 2003; final act on 26 September 2005)
14 October 2002	Collapse of executive after controversial police raid on Sinn Féin offices in Stormont; direct rule reintroduced
26 November 2003	Assembly election: DUP and Sinn Féin replace Ulster Unionist Party and SDLP as the largest parties; no agreement on executive
28 July 2005	IRA formally announces end to armed campaign
13 October 2006	St Andrews Agreement: minor changes to Good Friday agreement
22 November 2006	Northern Ireland (St Andrews Agreement) Act, 2006, implements Agreement; makes additional changes agreed by the DUP and Sinn Féin
7 March 2007	Assembly election: increase in support for DUP and Sinn Féin
8 May 2007	Ian Paisley and Martin McGuinness take office as First and Deputy First Ministers; new executive takes office
5 February 2010	Hillsborough Castle Agreement permits devolution of policing and security powers
23 December 2014	Stormont House Agreement seeks to resolve legacy issues (confirmed by 'Fresh Start' agreement, 17 November 2015)
16 January 2017	Executive collapses due to DUP-Sinn Féin tensions
24 July 2019	Boris Johnson appointed prime minister; pledges to leave the EU on 31 October 2019 with or without a deal

governance in Northern Ireland remains largely unexplored. The consociational structure was criticized—as other consociational structures have been criticised—as cumbersome and as inimical to effective decision-making.[3] Little is known about how it was built, and how institutional inertia in the Northern Irish, British, and Irish civil services was overcome. That is the subject of the witness seminar that follows, which focuses on the period 1998–2002, when the architecture of the new institutions of government was put in place.

The process of implementation was bound to be difficult, for three reasons.

First, from the outset there were conflicting political interpretations of the provisions and principles underlying the Agreement. Key differences in the understanding of what followed from British sovereignty were never resolved. They led to major intergovernmental disagreements. One early example was in February 2000, when the British government unilaterally suspended the Assembly. The Irish view was that this was incompatible with the provisions of the Good Friday Agreement (see Section 6.7.2). Indeed, it appeared to undermine the constitutional significance of the Agreement by showing that the British government could unilaterally revise its provisions. This difference in interpretation also led to party political conflict—for example, over policing reforms in 1999 and later. Unionists, and David Trimble in particular, expected that nationalist acceptance of the 'consent' principle in the Good Friday Agreement would carry over into acceptance of the dominance of British symbols and cultural norms. As the biographer of the First Minister put it: 'This confirmation of Ulster as part of British sovereign territory, Trimble reasoned, would inevitably have consequences for symbols, in the police and elsewhere' (Godson 2004: 472). Nationalists took a diametrically opposed interpretation.[4]

Second, party political disagreement was intensified by the nature of the consociational arrangements, which prioritized the main ethnonational cleavage over other cleavages and gave the main bloc parties a small but important advantage. Indeed, the main unionist and nationalist party-political and public views moderated considerably over time (Mitchell et al. 2001, 2009). But neither the smaller parties, which had played an important mediating role in the negotiations, nor civil society actors, who highlighted other forms of class and gender exclusion, were afforded many platforms in the new regime. The consociational formula had the potential to evolve with changing public preferences, but in the meantime it weighted debates and decisions on oppositional ethnonationalist lines (see the contributions in McCulloch and McGarry 2017).

Third, the Agreement was explicitly a package of interdependent provisions, such that the functioning of one institution was likely to change as other provisions

---

[3] See Dixon (2008); Taylor (2009); Wilford and Wilson (2006).

[4] On the differing interpretations among governments, parties, and paramilitaries, see Farrington (2006); Ruane (1999, 2016); Ruane and Todd (2001); Shirlow et al. (2011); Todd (2017); Tonge et al. (2014).

were implemented and as party-political aims and strategies themselves changed through working within the new structures.[5] In particular, the functioning of the consociational representative institutions was dependent on developments within other institutions—changes in policing and security, evolution in the North–South institutions, marginalization and eventual demise of the Civic Forum, and the changing roles and assessments of British and Irish governments, for instance.[6]

Which of these factors was important in the initial sequence of political crises, and in what combination? The witness seminar on the first years of implementation shows how civil servants and politicians perceived each of these challenges and coped with them, in particular in respect of strand two, but also in respect of strand one of the Agreement.

The chapter goes on to trace the collapse of the executive, and the path taken by the governments to broker agreement in St Andrews in 2006. Between 1998 and 2002, the British government had done its best to back David Trimble and the UUP. During these years, government policies fluctuated: for example, on the contentious issue of policing reform, the British government responded to pressure by the unionists at one point in time, and to the arguments of nationalists and of the Irish government at another. After the defeat of the UUP by the DUP and of the SDLP by Sinn Féin in the 2003 elections, British–Irish strategy had to change. In the extracts from interviews reproduced in this chapter, Bertie Ahern, Irish Taoiseach 1997–2008, and Peter Hain, British Secretary of State for Northern Ireland, 2005–7, discuss how they perceived the new political situation, some of their strategies for engaging the parties in discussions, and their view of the St Andrews Agreement.

6.1.1. Nationalist–Unionist Cohabitation

The Good Friday Agreement won wide popular support; it was endorsed by 71.1 per cent of those voting in a referendum in Northern Ireland on 22 May 1998, and the proposed changes to the Irish constitution were supported by 94.4 per cent of voters in the Republic on the same day (see Table 6.1 for an outline of developments).[7] At elections for the new Assembly on 25 June 1998,

---

[5] For example, apart from its first meeting in 1999, the Intergovernmental Conference met only during periods of suspension of the executive. The practice of regular meetings ended on the reintroduction of devolved government in 2007, but, following the prolonged absence of devolved institutions after the collapse of the executive in January 2017, it met again on 25 July and 2 November 2018 and 8 May 2019; see Coakley (2014), and Chapter 7.

[6] The Civic Forum—provided for in the Good Friday Agreement—met between 2000 and 2002, when it was suspended at the same time as the Assembly. It was not reinstated.

[7] An opinion poll in June 1998 showed overwhelming Catholic support for the Agreement (99% of those saying how they had voted), with Protestant attitudes more lukewarm (60% in support). The level of Protestant support fell in later surveys. See Coakley (2008: 105).

pro-Agreement parties won all seats on the nationalist side and a bare majority (thirty out of fifty-eight) on the unionist side, where there were two important anti-Agreement parties, the DUP and the UK Unionist Party (see Table 6.2). The centre ground was occupied by the Alliance Party and by a small but significant party, the Women's Coalition, which had played an important role in negotiating the Agreement and which fought vigorously to defend its principles.

Yet power-sharing government did not come about for another eighteen months. The election of First and Deputy First Ministers Designate—respectively David Trimble of the UUP and Seamus Mallon of the SDLP—took place on 1 July 1998. In December of that year, agreement was reached on the areas within which North–South implementation bodies would be created, and on those in which structured North–South cooperation would take place. Unionists, however, re-fused to enter government with Sinn Féin prior to decommissioning, and the IRA refused to decommission prior to the full implementation of the Agreement. An Independent International Commission on Decommissioning under the chair-manship of General de Chastelain had been set up in advance of the Agreement, on 26 August 1997, but IRA engagement with it was very slow, as was the response of other paramilitary groups.[8]

Meanwhile, David Trimble was faced with a series of challenges to his leader-ship, and, when he finally entered government in December 1999, it was on the understanding that decommissioning would follow, and with a commitment to his party that he would resign should this not occur. His resignation in February 2000 triggered a British suspension of the Assembly, and, while power-sharing government was restored in May 2000, it was subject to a series of crises over the next two years. These were exacerbated by an ongoing conflict over policing following submission of the report of the Independent Commission on Policing. Established on 3 June 1998 and chaired by a senior Conservative politician, Chris Patten, it delivered a report on 9 September 1999 that proposed a renaming and a fundamental overhaul of the RUC, an outcome that was strongly opposed by unionists.

Implementing the Agreement was a lengthy process. The decommissioning issue was a central one for unionists, but it was not until October 2001 that the first set of IRA weapons was put beyond use (an event prompted by US reaction to the militant Islamic attacks on New York and Washington on 11 September 2001). It took until September 2005 for all IRA weapons to be decommissioned. Never-theless, the executive entered into office on 2 December 1999, and the North–South institutions and the British–Irish Council came into formal existence the same day. Progress on other aspects of the Agreement proceeded at varying speeds. Prisoner releases, equality legislation, and the formation of the Equality,

---

[8] The Commission issued its final report only on 28 March 2011.

Table 6.2. Results of elections to Northern Ireland Assembly, 1998–2017

Party	Share of first preference votes						Number of seats					
	1998	2003	2007	2011	2016	2017	1998	2003	2007	2011	2016	2017
Ulster Unionist Party	21.3	22.7	14.9	13.2	12.6	12.9	28	27	18	16	16	10
Democratic Unionist Party	18.1	25.7	30.1	30.0	29.2	28.1	20	30	36	38	38	28
UK Unionist Party	4.5	0.8	1.5	.	.	.	5	1	.	.	.	.
Progressive Unionist Party	2.6	1.2	0.6	0.2	0.9	.	2	1	1	.	.	.
Traditional Unionist Voice	.	.	.	2.5	3.4	2.6	.	.	.	1	1	1
Other unionists	.	.	.	0.6	1.5	.	.	.	.	.	1	1
Alliance Party	6.5	3.7	5.2	7.7	7.0	9.1	6	6	7	8	8	8
Women's Coalition	1.6	0.8	.	.	.	.	2	.	.	.	.	.
Green Party	0.1	0.4	1.7	0.9	2.7	2.3	.	.	1	1	2	2
People Before Profit	.	.	.	0.8	2.0	1.8	.	.	.	.	2	1
Others	5.7	4.2	4.6	3.0	4.7	3.4	3	1	1	1	.	.
SDLP	22.0	17.0	15.2	14.2	12.0	11.9	24	18	16	14	12	12
Sinn Féin	17.6	23.5	26.2	26.9	24.0	27.9	18	24	28	29	28	27
Total	100.0	100.0	100.0	100.0	100.0	100.0	108	108	108	108	108	90

Source: Computed from ARK (2019); Electoral Office of Northern Ireland (2019).

Human Rights, and Community Relations Commissions proceeded apace. Other aspects of implementation were, like decommissioning, slower. Implementation of the Patten report was a gradual process, with the symbolically important renaming of the RUC as the Police Service of Northern Ireland taking place on 4 November 2001. Demilitarization (the removal of British army installations from the countryside and reduction in the army presence in Northern Ireland to peacetime garrison levels) was slow, with the programme completed only in August 2007. Notwithstanding years of work on the formulation of a bill of rights for Northern Ireland, no bill was ever enacted. Progress on certain North–South institutions was also slow or non-existent: the planned North–South consultative forum never appeared, and the proposed North–South parliamentary forum was set up only in 2012, and then in the looser form of a North–South Inter-Parliamentary Association.

The slow pace of this process led to some disillusion with the Agreement. A major challenge was posed by differences on the unionist side. Although the DUP had rejected the Agreement, the party took up its ministerial posts, but refused to attend meetings of the executive. As a result of continuing tensions with Sinn Féin and pressures from within his party, Ulster Unionist leader and First Minister David Trimble finally brought the executive down in October 2002, resulting in a renewal of direct rule from London.[9]

6.1.2. The Rise of the DUP and Sinn Féin

Fresh elections in 2003 achieved little, beyond recording the fact that the DUP was now the leading party on the unionist side, with Sinn Féin overtaking the SDLP as the main nationalist party (see Table 6.2). The electoral defeat of the more moderate parties—the Ulster Unionists and the SDLP—by their more extreme competitors—the DUP and Sinn Féin—had not been expected in 1998.[10] The British and Irish governments responded to this new reality by changing their strategies to prioritize decommissioning, demilitarization, and implementation of police reform, hand in hand with negotiations to reinstate power-sharing government.

The process of brokering an agreement between these two newly dominant parties was long and hard. It involved resolving the issue of decommissioning, and the removal of British military installations in such areas as South Armagh. It also

---

[9] The end of the executive was triggered by a dramatic police raid on the Sinn Féin offices in Parliament Buildings, Stormont, and the arrest of Sinn Féin's chief administrator, Denis Donaldson, on charges of intelligence-gathering; it emerged later that Donaldson had been a long-time British agent.

[10] For the evolution of the nationalist parties at this time, see Murray and Tonge (2005); and for detailed studies of the DUP and of the UUP, respectively, see Tonge et al. (2014) and Hennessey et al. (2019).

entailed thoroughgoing reform of the police service and of the criminal justice system that unionists found difficult to accept. However, acceptance of the deal was driven in part by threats of worse to come should agreement not be reached. As one (unattributable) Irish source reported to one of the authors, the British and Irish governments had a 'plan B' should devolution fail to be agreed, but the content of that plan would depend on who brought down the negotiations. Both the DUP and Sinn Féin saw positive opportunities in the new power-sharing arrangement, though they presented this in utterly contrasting ways to their own supporters.[11]

The stalemate was brought to an end following a new agreement reached at St Andrews, Scotland, on 13 October 2006. This amended the Good Friday Agreement primarily in its provisions for the devolution of policing to Northern Ireland (the police service had by now been radically reformed), and in changed rules for the selection of First Minister and Deputy First Minister.[12] It also included a British commitment to repeal the Northern Ireland Act, 2000, which permitted British suspension of the Assembly (see Subsection 6.7.2) and made other minor changes. Following further Assembly elections on 7 March 2007, the devolved institutions in Belfast were restored, with the DUP's Ian Paisley as First Minister and Sinn Féin's Martin McGuinness as Deputy First Minister. However, it was almost three years later—after the Hillsborough Castle Agreement of February 2010—that policing and the administration of justice were devolved to the Northern Ireland Executive. At that stage, many—but still not all—of the provisions of the Good Friday Agreement had been implemented, and it appeared that the institutions were functioning well (Conley 2013; McEvoy 2015; O'Connor 2013). Queen Elizabeth's state visit to the Republic of Ireland in 2011, and the reciprocal state visit to the UK by President Higgins in 2014, symbolized the newly cooperative character of British–Irish relations. The new phase of power-sharing, with the DUP and Sinn Féin as the dominant partners, continued until January 2017. From 2012, however, it was—unexpectedly—beset by crises, public protests, and contention. We assess these in Chapter 7.

---

[11] For analysis of why the DUP changed its position, agreed to a modified institutional package at St Andrews, and decided to enter government with Sinn Féin, see Tonge et al. (2014: 35–61, 220–6). For analysis of the earlier shift in the republican position, see Brams and Togman (2000).

[12] The Good Friday Agreement provided for election of the First Minister and Deputy First Minister by cross-community vote in the Assembly. The St Andrews Agreement modified this by providing that the post of First Minister would go automatically to the largest party in the largest designation, with the deputy post going to the largest party in the second-largest designation, thus removing the need for DUP Assembly members to vote for a Sinn Féin Deputy First Minister. However, when the Agreement was being given legal effect, following a further DUP–Sinn Féin deal, this formula was quietly changed: the post of First Minister would now go the largest party, regardless of designation, opening the way for a Sinn Féin First Minister; see Northern Ireland (St Andrews Agreement) Act 2006, s. 16A (4) and s. 16C (6).

6.1.3. Witness Seminar and Interviews

The witness seminar, which took place on 9 December 2008 in Newman House, St Stephen's Green, Dublin, addressed the institutional aspects of implementation—building institutions and implementing new laws—rather than addressing the tense security issues involving decommissioning, demilitarization, and policing that proceeded alongside these processes. The participants in the witness seminar whose contributions are reported here included Seán Farren, a negotiator on behalf of the SDLP and later a minister in the executive; Tony McCusker, a Northern Ireland civil servant who played a key role in implementation from the northern side; Hugh Logue and Colm Larkin, advisors in the Office of First Minister and Deputy First Minister in the first period of devolution; and Walter Kirwan, formerly of the Department of the Taoiseach, who was involved in the negotiation of the Good Friday Agreement and the early phase of implementation. Academic questioners included Michael Anderson, John Coakley, Christopher Farrington, and Jennifer Todd.

Peter Hain, former Secretary of State for Northern Ireland, and Bertie Ahern, former Irish Taoiseach, worked to restore the power-sharing executive. The discussion that follows shows how they worked towards a new agreement, and how they viewed the St Andrews Agreement and its relation to the Good Friday Agreement. It is drawn from separate interviews with each, with excerpts approved and amended for this book.[13]

6.2. Implementing the Good Friday Agreement

6.2.1. Participant Roles

HUGH LOGUE: My name is Hugh Logue. I was seconded from the European Commission in September 1998 to be a special advisor in the Office of the First and Deputy First Ministers (OFM/DFM), and I was there until May 2003. I was one of the EU officials sent to Northern Ireland by EU President Delors after the 1994 ceasefires to consult widely and make recommendations for the creation of the EU Peace and Reconciliation Fund for Northern Ireland and the Border Regions.

COLM LARKIN: I am Colm Larkin. I was appointed by the European Commission to the OFM/DFM Office in October 1998. Prior to that I was Director of the Commission Representation in Ireland. I stayed at OFM/DFM until Seamus

---

[13] The interview with Peter Hain was conducted by Christopher Farrington in May 2009, and the interview with Bertie Ahern was conducted by Jennifer Todd in December 2017.

Mallon's resignation, and I'm still involved in a number of things, including the Northern Ireland Human Rights Commission and the Economics Research Institute.

WALTER KIRWAN: I am Wally Kirwan. I was involved with Northern Ireland since 1 February 1974. I was a member of the Irish government negotiating team on the all-party talks from the beginning to the end. In terms of the implementation, I headed the group from the Irish government that was negotiating the working out of strand two and to a certain extent strand three as well. I then moved back to the European side. I alternated a bit between Northern Ireland and Europe. I moved back to being involved in the National Forum on Europe in the autumn of 2001 and retired in 2004.

SEÁN FARREN: At the start of 1998 I was a member of the SDLP's negotiating team and I was elected to the Assembly in the elections that took place in June following the Agreement. I served as a minister in the power-sharing executive until 2002, when, after several suspensions, we reached the big one in October of that year. I stayed a member of the Assembly, or of 'proto' or 'shadow' assemblies, in the interim period to March 2007. I'm retired from the Assembly now. I am a visiting professor at the UNESCO Centre, University of Ulster in Coleraine.

TONY McCUSKER: Tony McCusker. I came into this work in 1998, when I was appointed as a sort of an advisor for Mo Mowlam just before the Good Friday Agreement. I was the link between the Northern Ireland civil service and the home civil service. At that stage I was primarily involved in the negotiations. After the Agreement I was heavily involved in the referendum work. Wally and I jointly chaired the negotiations on the North–South bodies. I was also involved in the work around establishing the new departments in the executive. I was the Director of the Office of First Minister and Deputy First Minister and, unusually, also attended the Executive meetings. I moved into the Department of Agriculture in 2000, to the beginning of 2002, and then I retired in 2005. Since then I have been doing various things, including chairing the Community Relations Council and the Community Foundation of Northern Ireland.

6.2.2. The Post-Agreement Context

Q: What did you see as the main challenges facing the Agreement in 1998?

WALTER KIRWAN: Different groups of us were involved in different issues. What you might call the most politically sensitive stuff, especially involving contacts with the republican movement around issues like decommissioning and so on, was dealt with by a very small group of civil servants: Dermot Gallagher, Paddy

Teahon, and Tim Dalton.[14] Even though I was heading the Northern Ireland Division in the Taoiseach's Department, I didn't know much about what was going on there.

I suppose you could say that decommissioning, and all the issues around it, turned out to be the most difficult and most sensitive issue in the fullness of time. I suppose we were all conscious at the time that what was in the Good Friday Agreement around decommissioning was a bit of a fudge. We were all conscious of the side letter that came from Tony Blair and the significance of that at the final stage in the negotiations.[15] We knew this was a neuralgic issue, but I think, speaking for myself anyway, we probably did not foresee that it was going to be quite so neuralgic and so drawn-out an issue as it turned out to be. I often say 'we reached the Agreement practically in spite of ourselves', in the sense that the degree of interaction between delegations was very, very low. I think another colleague used to have a lot of contact with the Progressive Unionist Party. In terms of dealings with the official Unionists as delegations, as distinct from background contacts, that might take place in some other place. The degree of contact was very little and we probably didn't have a very good or lively knowledge of the state of opinion within the Unionist delegation—never mind the wider unionist community.

I suppose we were expecting the implementation of strands two and three to be a much more difficult process than it turned out to be. It wasn't the commanding heights of the economy, so it wasn't going to be a major source of worry for the unionists.

We did an exhaustive exercise over months, even before the negotiation of the Agreement started, when we went around all the southern departments, and in effect negotiated with our own departments what would be our bid in terms of the North–South dimension. The feeling we had was that our bid was supposed to be a maximal bid; that was the feeling we were getting from the political level. There would have to be a nationalist dimension in the Agreement, mainly to strand two, so we were going to go for a maximal position.

I remember one time that Paddy Teahon said to me 'we'd be satisfied if we got six good ones', as he put it, and that meant six North–South bodies. I remember being profoundly shocked, because it seemed to run counter to everything that had come to us over months and years from the political level. But I think it probably was realistic. We were anticipating a difficult political context around strand two, and I suppose we were also focused on the fact that there might be a

---

[14] Dermot Gallagher was a senior official in the Department of Foreign Affairs, Secretary General of the Department of the Taoiseach, 2000–1, and Secretary General of the Department of Foreign Affairs, 2001–9; Paddy Teahon was Secretary General in the Department of the Taoiseach, 1993–2000; and Tim Dalton was Secretary General of the Department of Justice, 1993–2004.

[15] See Subsection 5.3.2.

lot of difficult technical issues. The setting-up of the bodies straddling the border was a novel thing. How was it going to be done legislatively? What was going to be the personnel situation? There were all sorts of technical matters like that. We were conscious that these were going to be difficult.

We didn't anticipate too many problems about strand three. There were certain people at the top of the civil service who hadn't got much enthusiasm for strand three. To some extent the job of those of us who had to implement strand three was to deliver a strand three that was going to be just about acceptable to the unionists.

SEÁN FARREN: The Good Friday Agreement, as I reflect on it, was probably one of the most pre-cooked agreements that you're ever likely to come across. Virtually everyone knew the broad parameters within which it was going to be set. Obviously there was detail which had to be negotiated with respect to strand one, strand two, and maybe even less detail about strand three. But, with respect to the difficulties that could have been anticipated at the time, there's no doubt that decommissioning was the big one.

It's difficult in my mind to understand how people underestimated the significance of decommissioning. Unionists never campaigned for power-sharing, they never campaigned for North–South bodies, and only latterly did they campaign for the British–Irish Council-type arrangement. For them the big issue to be resolved was: would the war be over, would the siege be lifted. If it was, then they were prepared to pay all of the other prices that they had to pay. They knew that power-sharing was essential, they knew some form of North–South structures were going to be required, and they knew that they would have to deal with all or most of the issues that fall under what we might call the confidence-building measures agenda.

But in return for all of that they needed to be clearly guaranteed that the war was over. Of course, we had the IRA ceasefires, but they were only ceasefires, and they had no guarantee, except a promise in some kind of vague way, that the political road would be the road that the republicans would henceforth take and, as Wally says, the language in the decommissioning section of the Good Friday Agreement was a fudge.

However much Sinn Féin protested that all it required was 'best efforts' to try and influence the achievement of decommissioning, rather than a com-mitment to achieve decommissioning by a certain time, I certainly understood that the commitment, insofar as it was stated in the Agreement, would actually be met. The uncertainties that followed are all related to the failure on the IRA's part to honour what I believe was an essential requirement if the unionists were going to be kept in.

I do think that perhaps from the Irish government side there was a feeling, 'well, let's hope we can have the guns put in the thatch; the unionists should be satisfied with the silence of the guns; that is all that we're going to be able to get', and that that should be sufficient.[16] But, after all, we had established the international body on decommissioning after the executive was formed in early December 1999 with a commitment that there would be meetings between representatives of the IRA and the decommissioning body.[17] In the words of General de Chastelain himself, all they did was come and take tea and talk about the weather, and not much else, and there was no 'give'. So it wasn't surprising that we ran into trouble very quickly, and that trouble reappeared, and reappeared, until eventually it was resolved.

TONY McCUSKER: The summer of 1998 was a funny time. I think the Northern Ireland civil service wasn't geared up for what was going to happen. After the Agreement was signed, the first things people were reaching into were the elections and the referendum. There were some interesting issues during the referendum. Clearly, Trimble was unhappy campaigning during the referendum, and there was a point in time when the DUP were actually winning the unionist propaganda war, and if you remember they had some startling ads appearing in the paper about old people facing into a bleak future, and the Ulster Unionists were doing absolutely nothing about it.

I can remember when Paul Murphy,[18] who was Mo [Mowlam]'s deputy, brought Trimble in, and Trimble's response was that they'd no money to campaign. Murphy said to me 'what do we do about it?', and I said 'we can't pay them any money'. Rowntree[19] gave the Ulster Unionists £25,000 the day after for the campaign, and from that point on the Ulster Unionists' ads started to change.

The DUP made a mistake. I think the DUP over-frightened people at that point in time. The unionists started to pull around a bit, and the referendum took its course. I can remember the day of the referendum up in the King's Hall, and everybody was gathered in the Thrupenny Bit waiting for the results, and Mo of course was fairly euphoric about the result.[20] She went out to do the press conference, and somebody was asking about a rerun under different

---

[16] This refers to an image in nationalist folklore in which, since the 1798 rebellion, whenever rebels had been defeated militarily they had not surrendered their weapons (pikes), but instead hidden them in their thatched roofs, to be potentially used another day.

[17] The IRA's failure to make any movement on decommissioning after the formation of the institutions in December 1999 was attributed by Sinn Féin to unionist pressure in Trimble's resignation letter. Brinkmanship followed, with offers and undertakings later withdrawn, until—under unprecedented US pressure after the attacks of 11 September 2001—a first act of decommissioning was verified and announced by the Decommissioning Commission on 23 October 2001. Two other such acts following on 8 April 2002 and 21 October 2003, with completion of the decommissioning process on 26 September 2005. For the political significance of the process, see Subsection 6.1.1.

[18] See Ch. 5, n. 63.

[19] The Joseph Rowntree Charitable Trust is a UK-based Quaker philanthropic body; www.jrct.org.uk (accessed 12 May 2019).

[20] The King's Hall in Balmoral, South Belfast, a complex which also housed the Thrupenny Bit, was the venue at which the counting of referendum votes took place.

circumstances, and Mo's famous reply was: 'You don't get a replay when you've won 3–1.' So then, after all that, things sort of died down.

It was a long time from the summer of 1998 through to December 1999.[21] It was a long time to keep things going, keep things motivated. It was hard to pull the civil service around on it, especially on the North–South bit. I think there were two issues, really.

One was a natural reluctance to lose power, and I think that you in the South faced that within your departments. A department rarely wanted to give away functions and power.

There was a deeper issue in the Northern Ireland civil service, which was to try and minimize any sense of power going into an all-Ireland situation. The dilemma for us in some of the negotiations was how you could deal with this situation in the civil service with, on the one hand, Trimble trying to minimize the North–South dimension, and, on the other hand, the SDLP wanting to maximize it; and the civil service was always going to be seen to be leaning towards the Trimble view.

There was one famous occasion—I can't actually date it now—when the Irish government came up North to meet the parties to talk about progress and so forth, particularly on the North–South issues. This was happening, I think on the Monday. On the Friday before, the Department of Foreign Affairs delivered their desired list for the North–South bodies, which was probably totally beyond where we had ever been in any conversation before that.

Over the weekend, the Northern Ireland civil service was trying to work out reasons why we would oppose taking them. For example, one of the proposals was that the two industrial development boards would merge into a single body. So, then, everybody came up on the Monday, and of course during all the briefing what emerged was Trimble sitting quite pretty, thinking 'the civil service backs me'.

The Irish government and the SDLP were absolutely livid, believing the civil service was apparently trying to thwart the outcome of the North–South bodies. It was a bad time in the relationship between the two civil services. It was bad enough the politicians claiming that the civil service in the North was whatever it was, but when you see the civil service of the South almost jumping on the bandwagon, it was hard to take. Those were the bits that were the sort of underground where nobody knew what you were dealing with, in terms of trying to bring the system around.

The funny thing was that when we got to negotiations—and bear in mind, on the North–South negotiations, it was the northern administration who were supposed to be negotiating, not the British government—the NIO had

---

[21] On 2 December 1999 power was formally devolved to Northern Ireland and the institutions provided for by the Good Friday Agreement began to be put in place.

difficulty accepting them because they [the NIO] had been so much out front all the time.[22] Suddenly it was the Northern Ireland civil service who were out front, and when we got into that stage of the joint meetings in the North and the joint meetings in Dublin, you couldn't have kept the Northern Ireland civil service out of Dublin.

Everybody wanted to be involved in the process. Suddenly it became a situation to be involved in. There still was a lot of background reluctance to push towards a united Ireland, but there was a certain attractiveness about the international negotiations that were going on.

I think one of the big failures on our part was we simply didn't get ready for the shadow period (1998–9) when Trimble and Mallon were elected as the Shadow First and Deputy First Ministers, and, appallingly, we had no infra-structure ready for them whenever they took up office.[23] I think neither Trimble nor Mallon ever forgave us for that—probably rightly. We had always assumed that the shadow service just meant they were named as ministers, but they wouldn't effectively operate an office. But suddenly these two guys appeared a day afterwards saying 'where's my office, where's my staff?', and nobody had done anything about it, and they saw that as tantamount to an apathy in the civil service in relation to political structures.

Q: How do you explain that gap: was it an oversight or was it apathy?

TONY McCUSKER: I honestly think it was just an oversight. Senior members of the civil service were not politically attuned at all. They sat weekly and they debated all the policy stuff, but never really reflected on the politics. One permanent secretary boasted about never reading a newspaper.

SEÁN FARREN: What would have happened if we had formed an executive immediately?

TONY McCUSKER: The funny thing was, that would have been easy, because it was the 'shadow' nature that the people couldn't comprehend. If you went formally into the executive, all the stuff was waiting; Central Secretariat became the Office of the First Minister, all the departmental private offices folded over into ministerial offices. The only thing you would have had to have done was create the new departments, if there were new ones to be created. So, ironically, it would have been easier, I think, for the system to respond to the real thing than to a shadow one.

---

[22] The Northern Ireland civil service was the domestic body responsible for supporting the work of the devolved government and its departments, and would be answerable to the new executive. The Northern Ireland Office, created in 1972, was a branch of the (central) UK civil service, answerable to the Secretary of State for Northern Ireland, and had borne the main burden during the political negotiations. See Subsections 1.4.1, 1.4.2,

[23] David Trimble and Seamus Mallon had been elected First Minister Designate and Deputy First Minister Designate on 1 July 1998, but the executive functioned in 'shadow' form until 2 December 1999.

And another thing: there was a serious breakdown between the Northern Ireland Office and the Northern Ireland civil servants, because the Northern Ireland civil servants were in a sense kept out of all the negotiations and all the debate, to a large extent. So that move between direct rule in Northern Ireland, where the Northern Ireland Office was the key part of the civil service, to a situation where the Northern Ireland civil service assumed that role, wasn't really managed at all.

HUGH LOGUE: I think the twenty years of direct rule had affected the Northern Ireland civil service. Each had a department, and my impression was that they were quite literally little czars themselves and had a lot of authority. There was very little oversight from London. I could be wrong, but there was certainly a resistance. Later in 1998 the Northern Ireland civil service first resisted the appointment of special advisors at all, either by David Trimble or by Seamus Mallon, and very specifically objected to the arrival of Mallon's team of advisors from Europe, saying that this would undermine them and create difficulties for the Northern Ireland civil service; that there were things that we couldn't be told because of our links with Europe.

Mallon later told us that he went both to Ahern and to Blair, and to Mo, to get our appointments, and he had to threaten his own resignation before the Northern Ireland civil service relented.

COLM LARKIN: I would be happy to say something about the relationships of the Northern Ireland civil service. Others are right to say that the initial treatment of Mallon and Trimble shocked them very much, and perhaps they traded on it, but they often told anecdotes about not knowing what office they were in, and that they had to ask for a phone, and so on.

The structure which was set up was that there were two people appointed to liaise between Mallon, Trimble, and the rest of the civil service. So, we were meant to pass messages to them, who would then pass messages to the civil service, so if you wanted, say, a brief on housing policy or the budget, they would collect and bring it back to us. This was an attempt to square the fact that there was no executive up and running, but that there was still this functioning civil service.

The effect of it was to leave Mallon and Trimble isolated, and it didn't really help their prestige or their capacity to take control of the system. I also got the impression that civil servants, because Hugh and I mixed a lot with them and had one-to-one meetings with them and so on, were quite afraid of the politics of the situation. They were scared really to engage with this rather difficult new structure and this really difficult Trimble–Mallon relationship.

There was a nervousness there that surprised me. I personally was quite surprised at the level of hostility from the Unionists towards the civil service. I kind of expected that from the SDLP, but the Unionists often would tell you that civil servants were totally untrustworthy, and worked with the British, and had undermined them time after time.

The other thing the civil service was very nervous about was the underlying issue about the number of departments. When we went in, there were six departments, and the Good Friday Agreement had allowed for the creation of up to ten, so there was quite a lot of lobbying about which departments you could split and what could be done—so there was a very fluid period for them, but what you can say in hindsight was that there was no real systemic help in building up a strong OFM/DFM in the transition period, so it wasn't a very good start.

TONY McCUSKER: There's not an awful lot I would disagree with. I think the issue around the six departments going to ten and all the issues around that, it's probably not unusual, because in some departments, for example, in the Department of the Environment, we were actually going to create three departments out of what was one department. For the department secretary at that stage, now that was a huge shift and challenge, but also in the sense that you were then becoming a much lesser permanent secretary than you previously were. It was hard to see these people as permanent secretaries in the Whitehall context, because they were at a level which was probably at about one or two levels down the tier in a Whitehall context.

COLM LARKIN: There was more concern about this type of issue than laying out 'this is what OFM/DFM should be doing, these are the challenges facing us'.

TONY McCUSKER: Unionists never trusted those civil servants who worked in the NIO. I think it was a difficult time for the civil service, but I think that there were many civil servants at a senior level who just avoided politics; they just avoided politics, and part of the consequences of that was that the Northern Ireland Office never involved them in what was going on at an overall political level, from the Anglo-Irish Agreement onwards. They just opted out.

HUGH LOGUE: And that came across as well, I think, in terms of how the Deputy First Minister would later deal with the civil service. Senior civil servants were just very, very nervous every time, and were ready to do all their bidding at that stage. But I think they reserved much of their respect and their time for the meetings with the Secretary of State and with the officers and officials.

6.3. The Context of Implementation

6.3.1. The North–South Bodies

HUGH LOGUE: The NIO was the real power around that time, rather than the Northern Ireland civil service. In terms of what was said earlier about the setting-up of the North–South bodies, I think that the SDLP felt that the game was lost at the early stage, and that the Unionists won the North–South debate insofar as the construction of the list being a long, narrow list of small tasks, from which they could pick Waterways, Irish Language, Food Safety, those kinds of things, rather than a short, fat list where it might have been Health or Commerce or Environment or Education. It allowed the Unionists to render the North–South dimension pretty ineffectual, or have North–South bodies which had no great substance. Trimble said 'we got the architecture right'—a list he could live with.

COLM LARKIN: What I found very interesting was that, when Hugh and I arrived, if my memory is right, the proposal on North–South bodies was to be agreed on by OFM/DFM—by the incoming Northern Ireland Executive. We found in September–October 1998, in Trimble, perhaps more appetite for North–South bodies than had been the case at the time of the Good Friday Agreement, perhaps because he'd got the architecture right, and perhaps also because he felt safe because this arithmetical idea, that you get to pick six, allowed all kinds of games: he would pick three at the bottom, and we would pick three at the top, and then each would say the one you've picked is ridiculous, and so on.

Interestingly we pushed very hard to reopen the Industrial Development Authority (IDA), the North–South IDA, and with that push we ended up with the Intertrade Body, which had not been foreseen at the time of Good Friday—it wasn't on the list.[24] Equally we pushed very hard for a European Union Body, which was also not on the list, but, again, emerged.

WALTER KIRWAN: And then there was a push about tourism.

COLM LARKIN: Exactly, Wally. We were still unhappy with the six that were coming out. Quite a good deal was done on tourism as a kind of a 'seventh' body—but not quite a seventh.[25] I thought at the time Trimble showed more flexibility in October 1998 than he was showing back in May. I personally regretted very much the fact that Sinn Féin had booked an Irish language North–South body. I could see no case for that in terms of interaction between unionism and nationalism, but the Irish government was quite content with that, so that was one of the six gone already.

I think a lot of us felt that was a wasted opportunity. It wasn't that we had any dislike of the Irish language, but it was wasteful of a meaningful economic body. The surprising thing was that Sinn Féin seemed to be surprised when Trimble said 'no problem', because he could see as well that it had actually no real significance in terms of his own constituency or in terms of

---

[24] This refers to a proposal to merge the southern Industrial Development Authority and its northern counterpart, the Industrial Development Board.

[25] Tourism Ireland was established on 11 December 2000 to succeed Tourism Brand Ireland, a joint marketing initiative that had been set up in November 1996 by the British and Irish governments to link the Irish tourist board (Bord Fáilte) and the Northern Ireland Tourist Board. It is a publicly owned limited company; though resembling an implementation body, it is not so classified.

North–South relations, and then he managed to parallel it with the Ulster Scots Agency.

WALTER KIRWAN: Well, a couple of points. First about how fat the list was at the beginning of the week. For a reason that I can't remember now, I do remember us working under great pressure, and very late that Monday.

Why we were working under such pressure that night I can't quite remember, because, certainly in the Irish system at one level, there was work going on that the people at the very top weren't paying enough attention to, because, I would think, they were concentrating on stuff to do with Sinn Féin. They were operating in separate compartments.

But, on the other hand, we'd had a whole series of memos for government, and the Irish government position had been endorsed at government level three or four times and, as I recall it, honed in a series of memos to them. We'd had all these meetings of the liaison group, going on often in lunch down here, downstairs here, bringing this forward.[26] So I can't quite remember why we were working under such pressure.

Just on the Irish language, it's worth mentioning—I was a strong proponent of the Irish language all my life, so when we came onto that Irish language body I was conscious of the fact that, in a sense, it had been visited on us by Sinn Féin, that it was highly likely that the unionists would use the existence of a North–South body to, as it were, undermine the Irish language and generally make it difficult to make any progress with the Irish language.

I spent an awful lot of energy trying to make sure that these two bodies within the language body were totally isolated from each other practically, and that Foras na Gaeilge was totally isolated from the wider body and was able to run the Irish language independently. But from talking to people involved in the Irish language over the years, I have more or less come to the conclusion that I didn't succeed, because at a minimum you had to agree the budget, the budget for the overall body had to be agreed by the two administrations.

So the budget gave leverage, and later on we had people trying to cause problems, and use the Ulster Scots thing as leverage to trip up the Irish language, and so on. We didn't fully succeed in that; even though I'm an Irish language proponent, I fully concur with what Hugh and Colm say—that it was a waste, and, again, it was Sinn Féin optics. They were entirely focused on their own agenda, about the release of prisoners and stuff like that.

TONY McCUSKER: There were a couple of opportunities missed. The food body was, and remains, a nonsense. At the same time you were actually creating a Food

---

[26] A reference to the Commons Restaurant in the basement of Newman House, St Stephen's Green, where participants had frequently met for lunch.

Standards Agency; it was further advanced in the South. We hadn't actually established one in the North. So, we ended up in this curious position.

COLM LARKIN: With three bodies.[27]

TONY McCUSKER: With three bodies, but not only that: the northern body is a UK body; it is part of a UK government agency. It ended up with the most bizarre outcome on a piece of devolved policy that you could ever imagine, and what actually happened was, when you got into the first executive meeting, that was the point in time when they were setting up the UK Food Standards Agency, so the proposal was do you have a Northern Ireland one or does Northern Ireland join the UK one. Trimble wanted the Northern Ireland one, and people rolled over. So you had three bodies, and the Northern one not even under the auspices of the Northern administration. It was actually under the UK government; it was controlled from London, anyway.

HUGH LOGUE: Again, there was similar confusion on Irish Lights.

TONY McCUSKER: Loughs and Irish Lights were a gimmick, because Trimble just smiled and said 'well, Loughs is already a cross border body' and Irish Lights— nobody even knew what Irish Lights did. It was controlled from London anyway.[28]

SEÁN FARREN: Well, I suppose in a general sense the SDLP's ambitions were unbounded in this regard; we wanted as much as we could possibly get. We were very dependent on the Irish government as to what in fact you were going to be prepared to offer, because obviously we had nothing over which we had any control. We had a lot of ideas and recommendations, but yourselves were our mentors in terms of guiding us as to where it was practical.

WALTER KIRWAN: In that regard, on an informal level, from a fairly early stage somebody like Hugh was very much interacting with us, and we were very much taking on board ideas that were coming from Hugh.

SEÁN FARREN: There is one issue there, Wally, that reflected a dilemma for us, and for me in particular, which was that a lot of the dialogue that was going on between you and the SDLP was quite clear and took place also on the margins with Sinn Féin as well. The dilemma, then, was how you actually interacted with the Unionists, because to some extent I was forced to be in a position to reflect the Unionists' view back into those discussions because they weren't

---

[27] While the Food Safety Promotion body (now Safefood) came into formal existence on 2 December 1999, it acquired permanent physical shape only when its new headquarters opened in Cork on 24 November 2001. Two new bodies overshadowed it: the Food Safety Authority of Ireland, established under an Act of July 1998, and the (UK) Food Standards Agency in Northern Ireland, being created at the same time.

[28] The Foyle, Carlingford, and Irish Lights Commission was to comprise two agencies: the Loughs Agency, which replaced the Foyle Fisheries Commission, established in 1952, and the Commissioners of Irish Lights, dating from 1786, and operating under its present name since 1867. The latter body operates, however, in the context of UK-wide rather than devolved legislation.

really getting involved in that sort of dialogue. It was actually quite uncomfortable at times.

HUGH LOGUE: Trimble was quite clever, I thought, insofar as he wanted ineffectual bodies, and he wasn't that concerned. On the other hand, some of the unionists concerned—and one example would be John Taylor—didn't give a damn how powerful they were as long as they had a low profile.[29]

I'll give you an example. We went to Brussels at this stage, and I was asked at the dinner to sit beside Taylor to try and sort Taylor out on tourism. Taylor made it quite clear to me that there was no way that they could possibly agree to tourism, and that his constituents liked that map of Northern Ireland that looked like Australia, and hadn't got the rest of Ireland involved, and that he was going to be keeping that, come what may.

I was then saying, 'well, the alternative is the EU body, and it will have a lot of funds and a lot of money', and he said his constituents knew zero about how the EU worked. He didn't give a damn, they could have billions as far as he was concerned, it was something inside the offices of the government that nobody understood in his constituency. He certainly had no difficulty with the EU body if the alternative was tourism, and that was one of the areas, whereas I think that Trimble would have been more concerned about the EU body than he would have been about tourism.

HUGH LOGUE: Tourism was a big surprise. I mean when tourism emerged I couldn't actually believe that Trimble overruled Taylor on it because de facto it was a seventh body.

SEÁN FARREN: It was of course. My recollection concurs with Hugh's. I got the impression Trimble was willing to go further, and that Taylor had led a revolt on it.

Q: I am puzzled, because Tourism Ireland was set up under a process which preceded the Agreement, and of course tourism was written in as one of the areas for North–South cooperation—but the actual movement towards establishing this body began in 1996 or 1997?

SEÁN FARREN: The architecture was essentially maintaining two tourist boards, but off-the-island marketing was down to the new body, essentially.

Q: The other question had to do with the famous long, thin list. As far as I recall, it contained something between forty and sixty proposed areas for cooperation. I'm just wondering about the process by which that was whittled down. Was it simply cast aside after Taylor's comment, and did it possibly begin anew, or were items selectively dropped?

---

[29] John Taylor, Deputy Leader of the Ulster Unionist Party and member of the party's negotiating team, was an experienced politician, a former member of the Northern Ireland House of Commons, a former Northern Ireland government minister, and MP for Strangford, 1983–2001; he was made a life peer as Baron Kilclooney in 2001.

WALTER KIRWAN: How did it go from the long list down to the particular twelve that appeared in the list? I think it's worth saying that Paddy Teahon said to me in his office, and that was months before this, I can't quite put a date on it, 'but we'd be doing well if we got six-plus'. So in one way, at the top level officially on the Irish side, I think there was an understanding from a relatively early stage that they were going to go for a rather restricted number.

It's at least arguable that it wasn't actually a particularly effective process— to come out with a very long list, and then to come down to twelve, with a view to getting six plus. Again, in my perception the people at the top of our departments were very heavily focused on the republican dimension around decommissioning, and didn't specifically, in hindsight, engage with most of us who were working on cooking up this list.

SEÁN FARREN: Faced with the 'forty-foot barge pole' reaction to the long list, and looking like there was going to be no agreement on North–South and therefore no agreement at all, I think the decision was to go with what was eventually a framework.[30] The nationalist side would get a framework for North–South relations, including an institutional framework for North–South cooperation, for the first time.

WALTER KIRWAN: That idea was actually put forward by the Unionists on the Tuesday. I remember at a meeting there with Ken Maginnis, in fact Ken Maginnis came forward with that idea.[31]

Q: But how were those particular twelve issues selected?

WALTER KIRWAN: I recall that Bertie and Blair were sitting down there on an afternoon, which may have been Thursday afternoon, I'm not sure, and some of us were going in and out and doing a bit of arbitrage around this list.

Q: Why did tourism continue to be on the list because that was already an area of very substantial cooperation—substantial controversial cooperation?

WALTER KIRWAN: It was to do it within the framework.

SEÁN FARREN: Not really the framework of the North/South Ministerial Council; the only things that could be in the framework of the North/South Ministerial Council were those that were included in that list.

WALTER KIRWAN: And it wasn't intended that the list would always relate to things that were completely new, because in many of these areas there was a background of some cooperation. Another thing I thought is worth mentioning is, picking up the thing about the Northern Ireland civil service, those of us from Dublin weren't very well placed to observe what Colm, Tony, and Hugh have been talking about, but it is worth mentioning that some of us did have, over

---

[30] As the negotiations entered their final stages and the draft list of areas for potential North–South cooperation became known, John Taylor famously stated that he would not touch them 'with a 40-foot barge pole' (*Irish Independent*, 8 April 1998). See discussion in Subsections 5.4.1 and 5.4.2.

[31] Ken Maginnis was a member of the Ulster Unionist negotiating team and MP for Fermanagh and South Tyrone, 1983–2001; he was made a life peer as Baron Maginnis in 2001.

the years, a certain amount of exposure to permanent secretaries and senior Northern Irish civil servants. One held a job as liaison between North and South going back to a process that was started up by Jim Callaghan and Jack Lynch in 1978.

Then, on the Advisory Committee of the International Fund for Ireland, some of us had contact with senior Northern Ireland civil servants, so we had developed a certain friendly relationship with these people from working with them around the table.[32] While we probably would have been conscious, of course, that their approach would have been the opposite of ours, from the point of view of coming up with the maximal list and all that, nevertheless we had a better talking relationship to these Northern civil servants than we had with the actual Unionist delegation. The process in Castle Buildings was woeful in terms of what you might call social interaction.[33]

6.3.2. The Executive

SEÁN FARREN: Can I ask Tony a question about the northern civil servant perspective on the formation of the ten departments? When the Agreement allowed for ten, it was quite obvious that the parties were going to go for ten. The elections made it clear that the four main parties would all have at least one if not two ministries, and there were very intense inter-party negotiations—at which I don't think civil servants were present—as to the division of the different areas. Hugh and Colm will recall one of the nights when we were in intense discussions, the night that Seamus had to go off for his operation, and he left instructions, clearly written instructions, that we were not to agree anything in his absence. And lo and behold, at one o'clock in the morning or maybe an hour later, Eddie McGrady came down and headed a press conference where we announced that we had reached agreement on the division.[34] How was that perceived and received within the civil service? Was it seen as making any sense, and what were the initial reactions to having to prepare for ten departments?

TONY McCUSKER: It wasn't totally without civil-service involvement; there were a few discussions. I can remember being there that night after Seamus had left. There's a mixed thing, some of the combinations of departments are illogical. There's no doubt about that. When questioned about it then, Mark Durkan

[32] The International Fund for Ireland was established by the British and Irish governments in 1986 following the Anglo-Irish Agreement; see Ch. 3, n. 40.

[33] Reference to the multi-party negotiations, which took place in Castle Buildings, Stormont.

[34] See Ch. 3, n. 55.

said that he forced departments to cooperate better, because if the thing was too logical they would all sit in silos.

I don't think it worked, because departments are natural silos anyway. And there was an element of how do you divide this up in a way that at least gives tenable departments, and so forth. So there was a feeling about the illogicality of some of them. But, on the other side of it, you were creating four extra departments and solid jobs; it was four new permanent secretaries; it was four sets of under-secretaries; the jobs that flowed from that meant the civil service did awfully well. And, then, if you added in the Assembly, the impact on career opportunities for civil servants around that time was actually very, very significant. So any sort of thoughts about the illogicality of it . . .

WALTER KIRWAN: Vanished with the size of the salary?

TONY McCUSKER: When people saw it all—because, you know, in reality every permanent secretary's post is downsized by virtue of spreading out into eleven—they made a clear decision that there would be no differentiation between responsibilities; everybody would be paid on exactly the same scale; there would be no differentiation.

WALTER KIRWAN: And there is differentiation down here.

TONY McCUSKER: There is differentiation down here, and there's differentiation down in Whitehall. With the Northern Ireland civil service, the civil servants themselves, the senior civil servants, took the clear decision that there couldn't be differentiation, and so that was the balance. In terms of the preparation, it was certainly better prepared for than the 'shadow' period, in that all the departments were ready, all the private offices were ready. So all the staffing was in place. There was difficulty, actually, in holding it in place for so long because people needed to be doing things.

COLM LARKIN: Well, my memory of that period was that Trimble played that very hard. We were trying to persuade him both to increase the number of departments and to have decent North–South bodies. I remember the main political calculation was if there were ten departments then there would be two Sinn Féin in the executive; if there were six there would be only one. Ten would be a confidence-building measure and help decommissioning to speed up and so on. Trimble was quite resistant to that.

TONY McCUSKER: He wanted to isolate the DUP as well.

COLM LARKIN: I think yes. I think he was not at all persuaded that it was that helpful to bring in the DUP and Sinn Féin; the balance of six and ten was quite different in terms of their position there, so I would be interested to know why they shifted to ten and what kind of calculations, or who spoke to them at that time.

HUGH LOGUE: I think we should also take account of the dynamics outside Stormont at that time. The Omagh bomb came in the midst of that summer, and that brought Mallon and Trimble, I think, closer together than they had been because they both shared and went through different things. I had forgotten there was also Drumcree that summer, and Ballymoney, and then the Quinns—that was in July.[35]

COLM LARKIN: I think that's right. I think certainly Mallon and Trimble during that summer were much more bound together than before or after.

6.3.3. Interdependence of Institutions

TONY McCUSKER: Just one question on the North–South area, maybe. There was a big issue towards the end on the 'sunset clause'. Trimble was insisting that if the Assembly and the executive went down, then all the institutions that were created would collapse as well, and nobody was prepared to write into the North–South papers in the legislation that there would actually be a 'sunset clause' in it.[36] And it was got out of in the same way as everything else was got out of—there was a letter that was exchanged.

But you remember that wasn't enough for Trimble, and at the very end a letter was exchanged. Remember, Trimble came under attack from McCartney about the 'sunset' bit, and there was something in the preamble, but it wasn't considered to be enough.[37] He got a letter that Saturday. But he was still under huge pressure from McCartney, and then the Foreign Office, that Saturday.

HUGH LOGUE: Just to comment on the North–South bodies. Early on, from the list, Colm and I were tasked with 'fattening up' the bodies as much as we could, and it was really going to be an issue, since the nationalist–republican side were going to have three and Trimble and the unionist side were going to have three. We really only had an opportunity to fatten two, as one had already been given away in terms of Irish language. The ones that we were looking at were trade—and we added things like science and technology, research development, innovation, anything we could manage at all to get into the terms of it, and they were added to it. Then we spent a bit of time on the EU body, trying to widen its remit beyond just the traditional Interreg and the different funding bodies.

The other side, then, was to try and get—just not let go of—tourism. I think one of the people who managed to get Taylor quietened on this was

---

[35] In June 1998 the newly established Parades Commission banned an Orange march from proceeding from Drumcree church down the mainly Catholic Garvaghy Road in Portadown. The march had been a source of conflict for several years (see Ch. 5, n. 40). When the march on 5 July was blocked by the army and police, there were protests elsewhere in Northern Ireland. On 12 July three children aged between 9 and 11, the Quinn brothers, were killed in a loyalist firebomb attack on their home in Ballymoney. On 15 August a car bomb planted by dissident republicans in Omagh killed twenty-nine people.

[36] This refers to a provision of the Agreement that the institutions are interdependent.

[37] Robert McCartney was leader of the small UK Unionist Party and a strong critic of the Agreement.

Reg Empey.[38] Reg actually could see that the tourism body made sense, and he was also being lobbied by the hotel federations and the hotel industry, and he was ready to do tourism as he called it, as far as possible, so I think that was another aspect of it.

I think we should say that we had a very good working relationship with David Trimble's advisors at the time. I think we have to put on the record that it's a pity that none of them is here.

COLM LARKIN: Oh, yes, Hugh is absolutely right; we had a good open and very decent working relationship with them. I've nothing but good memories of working with them; they were correct, and they were open, and they were very good colleagues.

6.3.4. Decommissioning

COLM LARKIN: Before you move on, can I just go back to the decommissioning issue? The impression I got of Mallon at that period was that he was extremely anxious to get the executive up and running, and I think he detected that Trimble was not at all sure that he wanted to go through with the whole process; Trimble had signed up to the Agreement, but would he take the next step?

Mallon was very anxious; it was very, very urgent that we had to get things up and going: 'what's holding it up?' and 'what's the next problem?' I think even by the time I joined in October 1998 we'd already missed one deadline, which had been set out in the Good Friday Agreement. Mallon made a speech at the SDLP Conference in November in which he stated that we should go ahead and form the executive immediately, and, if within the two years set out in the Agreement there had not been decommissioning, he would move to exclude Sinn Féin from the executive, and this was the offer to Trimble.

I remember at the time it was discreetly but badly received by the DFA, and we were told that this was not realistic, or practical, or in line with political realities in relation to decommissioning, and it also had not been cooked in any way with Trimble, so Trimble did not respond to it; Trimble did not bite on it. But I remember as an interesting lesson that decommissioning was not to be subject to ordinary political cut and thrust, and offers and counter-offers; it was very much a closed circle being run in a very, very tight way indeed.

Q: Was your perception that Unionists actually wanted to engage, but couldn't because of decommissioning, or did they not want to engage and decommissioning was just a flag?

---

[38] Member of the Assembly and a leading member of the Ulster Unionist negotiating team; later leader of the UUP, 2005–10. See also Subsection 5.4.2.

SEÁN FARREN: I think they wanted to engage when the Agreement had been signed, but they were under tremendous pressure. Remember that Trimble's party was divided; his community was divided. I think it was the night he lost the election a few years ago, paying tribute in a sense to him I said 'would John Hume or Gerry Adams have made a deal with their parties as divided and their communities as divided as Trimble's was?' I think the answer clearly is 'no'.

In many respects, Trimble was the hero of the day because he took the biggest risks and he was therefore held to bring it as far forward as possible, but decommissioning was the big issue for them. It was their community that had suffered; it was their policemen who were being shot, and the UDR were from their community mostly, the business people whose businesses were burnt and bombed were mainly from the unionist community, and, however much the IRA might have said it was a war against the British presence, for unionists it was a war against the unionists, and the only way in which they could see that there was real sincerity there was that guns had been given up.

The silence was not sufficient; it was necessary, but it wasn't sufficient. Therefore it's not surprising that that became the issue on which the whole process was to be logjammed, and it was only after it was resolved in recent years, and with it support for the PSNI from Sinn Féin, that the DUP were free, in a sense, to move forward. Those of us who said the silence of the guns was sufficient, I think, were wrong at the time. Even a token decommissioning— they might have got away with a token decommissioning in the very beginning, in the very early days after the Agreement, that might have been possible.

COLM LARKIN: It was talked about in 1999.

SEÁN FARREN: Some kind of big explosion, or whatever, or something that was verifiable; but after that I think it had to be all or nothing.

TONY McCUSKER: I remember Trimble made the point that it was the British government who forced them into the position over decommissioning, and it got to a point where the Unionists couldn't actually soften on decommissioning.[39]

HUGH LOGUE: He also repeated it in Paris when we met President Chirac. He put the decommissioning issue very much as an issue that was a monkey on his back. Incidentally, Chirac left no one in any doubt about President Clinton's commitment to Ireland, telling us, almost as an aside, that, no matter what issue in the global world, and there were many, when he was in telephone discussion with President Clinton, Clinton never let the discussion close without an exhortation to him to help the Irish peace process in Europe and with the British.[40]

---

[39] The reference is to Sir Patrick Mayhew's 'Washington Three' statement in March 1995 in Washington, which declared some actual decommissioning to be a precondition for Sinn Féin to join talks; see Subsection 5.1.1.

[40] This refers to a meeting, on 31 January 2001, in the Elysée Palace in Paris between Trimble, Mallon, and President Chirac as part of a drive for foreign investment in Northern Ireland.

However, the pressure wasn't coming on Sinn Féin at that time on decommissioning; the pressure was on Trimble to ignore it for the time being, and
that pressure wasn't just from Dublin and from London. I remember being at
the meeting when President Clinton came—I think it was the first week of
September—and Clinton, at the meeting with Trimble, putting him under
pressure as well, insofar as Martin McGuinness had been appointed to act as
interlocutor with the de Chastelain Commission, and Clinton saying to Trimble 'well, you've got the right person now, at least you have', and selling the
appointment of Martin McGuinness to the de Chastelain Commission to be
interlocutor with the Commission as a big deal.[41]

In hindsight it wasn't, but there, again, Trimble was under pressure from the
Americans to do something. And ultimately, if you look back, or even not
looking back, at the time you had one of two options: (1) get the executive up
and going, and let it work its way, or (2) wait for decommissioning. As it
turned out, getting the executive up and going, and then pulling it down time
after time because decommissioning wasn't occurring, brought the whole
thing down. It was fraught in the end. If more pressure had been put on
Sinn Féin, they probably couldn't have done it at the time, but they might have
done it earlier. Ultimately the DUP were the people who got the prize for
putting Sinn Féin under so much pressure that they succumbed in a dramatic
way to decommissioning.

SEÁN FARREN: But realizing that there was an expectation there that something
would happen, a process had to start; it wasn't sufficient that McGuinness and
whoever else went to see the decommissioning people and sat and simply took
tea. Here's where the political judgement of Sinn Féin is very, very open to
question—what on earth were they thinking they were going into by arranging
a meeting with de Chastelain and not discussing anything substantial with
respect to the main issue on the agenda? And there was only one issue on the
agenda. What on earth did they think they were at? Did they hope against hope
that simply forming the executive was sufficient, even though Trimble, after
all, when he agreed to form it said 'I'm jumping, Gerry, now you follow'? So
they couldn't have expected nothing to happen by virtue of their doing
nothing; there was a need to follow on, and that was a huge, huge mistake.
Well, maybe the movement wasn't ready, but the Agreement had been signed,
so what was in their minds when the section of the Agreement on decommissioning was drawn up and they subscribed to it? What did they expect, that we
would just use our best efforts?

WALTER KIRWAN: My perception throughout the whole thing was that the Irish
government and the people who counted in the Irish government in terms

---

[41] President Clinton visited Northern Ireland on 3 September 1998 at a time when Trimble was
being put under pressure to be less insistent on the question of decommissioning.

of both officials and ministers had made the calculation from early on that you had to play decommissioning long. I think that even at the time of the negotiations, before Sinn Féin came in and all that, I recall Seán Ó hUiginn very much of the mind that it's about decommissioning mindsets, all this stuff, that you could replace the weapons, it's not a real issue and all that.

People like Paddy Teahon and Tim Dalton and so on definitely carried that view, I think, throughout. I think Bertie Ahern would have been of that view, and it would have reflected back to the old business about dumping arms, and all that, back in the 1920s, and so on. They definitely had the view all the time that any deal—like that in Central America—which brought arms into some central place or something was totally out the window so far as what was saleable with the republican community in Northern Ireland.

COLM LARKIN: To go back to your earlier question, did Trimble really believe in the Good Friday Agreement? I've often wondered about it. I think he was ambivalent about it, I think there were bits he would love to renegotiate, and love to have changed, but on balance he went for it. But don't forget, throughout that period his party was not happy. Numbers of them resigned and joined the DUP. You must never underestimate the old, totally understandable, unionist wish to keep the unionist family together. So, he signed up to the Agreement, and he did his best to implement it, but it was very, very difficult for him, very difficult.

Q: About Mallon's offer of exclusion of Sinn Féin, why was it that the UUP didn't pick that up and run with it?

COLM LARKIN: I think they didn't believe, when the time came two years down the road, that Mallon would actually move to exclude Sinn Féin.

SEÁN FARREN: Mallon had no support from the Irish government.

TONY McCUSKER: Nor did he have that much support within. I mean John Hume was opposed to it.

SEÁN FARREN: After that speech we were having a drink in the evening of the conference and John Hume was expressing his own unhappiness with what had been said. He was also telling me that he had been told by Sinn Féin that some of the things I had been writing—there were a few articles for the *Irish Times* and the *Irish News* on decommissioning—he was telling me quietly that Sinn Féin weren't happy with it. Of course, they were written to make Sinn Féin unhappy.

WALTER KIRWAN: Well, Mallon was always much tougher on Sinn Féin.

COLM LARKIN: You see, Mallon had the day-to-day meetings with Trimble. Mallon knew where it was hurting, and he had to do something about it; that was the big difference.

SEÁN FARREN: But Dublin was never supportive of Seamus confronting on decommissioning. Playing long is one thing; they wanted it sidelined altogether, really, I think.

COLM LARKIN: By 1998–9 Trimble had great implicit trust in Blair, and in Blair's ability to take him through the situation. Now that did cause some tensions with Mallon, in that Trimble had a very privileged relationship with Blair and met him, I'd say, every fortnight, or very frequently, and he got a lot of comfort and support from Blair, and I think it took him a long time to realize that Blair couldn't deliver everything that he thought he could get delivered.

HUGH LOGUE: Blair indulged Trimble personally, but indulged Sinn Féin politically at that stage too.

TONY McCUSKER: The other side was his officials; his advisors were in Downing Street every week. I mean they had unparalleled access to the Advisory Committee.

HUGH LOGUE: That's what I mean by indulging him personally, but they didn't get anything out of it.

TONY McCUSKER: No, but it still meant that whatever your issue was, it was always there at the top table. Nobody had the access to the Irish government that Trimble had to Number 10—he was amazing. Even after Trimble went out of office, his advisors continued to have very regular contact with Number 10.

WALTER KIRWAN: The British government basically made the same calculation—to drag out the decommissioning thing and to trust that it would come right in the end, and not to put too much pressure on Sinn Féin. I doubt that there's ever going to be enough evidence to provide a definitive judgement on that.

SEÁN FARREN: Let me ask you a question, what do you think your colleagues, what did they think the Provos were going to do on the basis of the decommissioning section of the Agreement?

WALTER KIRWAN: I don't know, but I would think that it would be a bit like the process that occurred in the South in the 1920s. There would be a gradual process of politicization, a gradual process of absorption into the political stream of democracy—non-violence and so on.

SEÁN FARREN: Not one big act?

WALTER KIRWAN: Not one big act—but in the same way with lots of fits and starts as it had worked out in the 1920s in the South.

SEÁN FARREN: One final question: what was the risk of putting more pressure on Sinn Féin? To my mind there was really no big risk of a return to violence after the Agreement had been signed.

WALTER KIRWAN: Well, there was some risk. If we look at it, the quartermaster general of the IRA went off and set up his own outfit. How much of a calculation would you make that others wouldn't have gone in that direction as well?

HUGH LOGUE: I think John Hume was of that view as well. I think he never really and never fully brought decommissioning into the equation, and was therefore ready to indulge Sinn Féin further as well.

Q: What is the long view of the British government?

TONY McCUSKER: I think they played it long, because within the NIO I can remember Joe Pilling, who was the permanent secretary in the NIO at that stage, calling a sort of a seminar one day for the people. Basically, it was 'how the hell do we get out of this decommissioning mess?', and everybody was encouraged to brainstorm the most outrageous ways of how you could actually get some sort of closure on it. But one of the few things that emerged in that was that all the advice that was coming in from the security side was that decommissioning wasn't worth a toss. It's a non-issue, it's an issue which it wouldn't matter a toss whether you got rid of all the guns tomorrow because people could re-arm very rapidly the following day. So, as a security issue it was a non-issue.

It was about trust, and it was a political issue, and clearly Blair and Powell and company were playing it very long.[42] They had shifted the dynamic from where it was in the Mayhew–Major times: that had changed quite dramatically, and I think they were totally going, as Wally says, with the Irish government.

SEÁN FARREN: They had to wake up and realize that the Unionists were for real on this issue. At the end of the day Paisley cracked the whip and Paisley got what he asked for.

And you could also ask the question that, if Trimble had got the final deal on decommissioning, and that happened, would Paisley have been satisfied, and the answer almost certainly would have been 'no'. But what issue would he have raised? What more, in a sense, could Paisley begin to demand, except that they're not going to deal with Sinn Féin?

TONY McCUSKER: Trimble did all the heavy lifting and at the end of the day in Scotland, St Andrews, there wasn't an awful lot of lifting to be done. You know, Trimble had done it all for them.

Q: Was it not the case that Sinn Féin needed some kind of fig leaf, the fig leaf being holding on to their weapons or putting their weapons in the thatch, rather than being forced, in addition to what they'd already agreed to, to decommission their weapons?

SEÁN FARREN: It raises another issue, and that is could we have replaced decommissioning by another issue, or could we have helped unionism? And that then brings up the issue of policing, and again they [Sinn Féin] were indulged. John Hume wanted to indulge them, Seamus Mallon didn't; Dublin wanted to indulge them in the difficulties they would have on policing. If we had moved faster on policing, and had forced Sinn Féin to move on policing at

---

[42] Jonathan Powell, a former Foreign Office diplomat, was chief of staff in the Prime Minister's Office, 1997–2007, and was centrally involved in the negotiations in Northern Ireland (see Powell 2008).

some stage, could we have probably saved Trimble and saved the Agreement? That is another issue that you probably have to raise.

COLM LARKIN: Well, I think there's a very simple, crude, read of all this, which is to say, well, Sinn Féin and the DUP were willing to compromise and turn away from their previous stances in return for electoral success, and majority positions within their communities. The argument is that only when the DUP became the major unionist party and Sinn Féin the major nationalist party, and they saw the promise of power and prestige and so on that went with it, were they then willing to do deals. They weren't willing to do it when they were in a less favourable position.

TONY McCUSKER: I think just after the Good Friday Agreement, after the referendum, there must be a strong argument that Trimble and the Ulster Unionists just didn't see how they could celebrate what they'd actually achieved. Sinn Féin went out and drove the taxis around West Belfast—I mean what was Sinn Féin actually celebrating? They'd absolutely nothing to celebrate, and yet they did. Unionists, on the other hand, all they could do at this point was point up what the remaining negatives were rather than what they'd actually achieved.

SEÁN FARREN: Well, Trimble did say that the Agreement secures the Union; that was almost one of the first phrases out of his mouth when he started.

TONY McCUSKER: He didn't do much more after that.

6.3.5. Agreeing the New Institutions

Q: There's an argument in the literature that much of this is just choreography and there weren't real issues involved—that everybody knew it was going to get resolved after a while. What's your immediate reaction to that?[43]

WALTER KIRWAN: But what happened wasn't rehearsed.

TONY McCUSKER: But I think Seán made the point earlier on that everybody knew when there was an outcome what the shape of the outcome would be.

SEÁN FARREN: We didn't know that we were going to get there.

COLM LARKIN: It's worth spending five or ten minutes on December 1998, since we all have different perspectives on it. My recollection of it was that Seamus Mallon had to go off for an operation, but there was the possibility that there could be, after months of pressure, agreement on the formation of the ten departments and the North–South bodies. So, we were getting close to some kind of agreement on it.

Mallon wanted to ensure that this wouldn't happen in his absence; but Trimble decided that he wanted to go ahead with discussions, and believed he

---

[43] For the most developed argument to this effect, see Dixon (2018).

was ready to do it. As far as I can remember, it was because he had got word that there would be some loyalist decommissioning, and he felt that, if he could associate that with the loyalist decommissioning breakthrough at the time, it would give some new impetus or incentive.

To me that always seemed to be a rather fragile basis on which to have this negotiation, especially in the absence of Mallon and against his wishes, but negotiate they did. I suppose what I remember most about it, which is a personal reminiscence, is that it kind of went out of the reach of the parties, and Dublin came up and London engaged, and it was like the old team was back again. I remember running across one or two senior Irish civil servants, and it was very much 'we are doing this and we'll let you know what's happening'. So it was almost as if they had been out of practice for a couple of months, but they were quite glad to get in and have another little run around the field.

So they came out with what they came out with. I suppose the thing that bemused me at the time was that they came out with this idea for an economic policy unit in OFM/DFM, which threw into some imbalance the whole working of the executive; it caused an awful lot of tension and difficulties. The interesting thing is that apparently it has now been abolished, or is no longer operating in OFM/DFM. Mallon inherited the deal that was done that night, and then had to work it as best he could.

I suppose, looking back on it, the thing is to try to analyse why Trimble moved when he moved, and why were people so anxious to do a deal when it was done, and I've never really got a satisfactory view on that. I mean, a deal had to be done at some stage, but why it was judged so important to do it then I never really understood.

TONY McCUSKER: I don't know what the background was, but I can remember all the debate that night about the policy, which in a sense was quite blatantly the Unionists putting in a watching mechanism on the SDLP, who were obviously going to take the Department of Finance. Reg Empey made clear that he wasn't going to take the Department of Finance, and Trimble was going to bow to him. So, if the SDLP were taking Finance, they were seeking some sort of oversight. What they were doing was building it into OFM/DFM: joint control, an oversight mechanism, and I think I remember that night we were trying to work around the draft with one of Trimble's advisors. But what happened that night was that a fundamental part of the new department was created almost on a whim, and the fundamentals of it were put in place in a couple of hours.

COLM LARKIN: No build-up to it. As it happened, it worked out quite well, mainly because the people who ran the EPU [Economic Policy Unit] were able to get a *modus vivendi*, but it really was a very debatable decision to take at that time.

SEÁN FARREN: My memories of the night are hazy, but we had been closeted up in Stormont for several days, and long hours during each of those days. I'm not so aware of the external developments, such as the possibility of loyalist decommissioning, and to what extent that was a factor, but I do remember there were parallel processes going on preparing for what happened. Mark [Durkan] and myself, up in my room in Stormont, drafting something on the Economic Policy Unit in order to ensure that it conformed as much as possible to what we wanted out of it. Then, later on, there was a quite intense number of meetings with people like Fred Cobain, Reg Empey, and I can't remember who else on the unionist side over the structure, over the different functions, of the different departments that we were going to create.[44] Eddie McGrady was part of our team because he was in charge when Seamus left, and we did come to an agreement.

TONY McCUSKER: But that was actually seen as being a big night, because the following day all of the senior civil service, all of us, got a handwritten and hand-delivered note from Blair, because he had seen it as one of the big breakthroughs in the discussions. Blair wasn't there, but everybody else was there.

SEÁN FARREN: Sinn Féin were irate at being excluded, and I was dispatched up to their room to brief Bairbre de Brún and whoever else was up there, and I had to take the brunt of their displeasure at being excluded.

COLM LARKIN: And Adams put out lots of press releases saying that he is actively involved in all these negotiations.

WALTER KIRWAN: Yes, but again it sort of illustrates the point that I was making earlier, that these things worked in compartments. The SDLP were very heavily involved in all the things to do with structures, like strand two and strand three; and Sinn Féin were more or less out of that, and had almost nothing to do with it. When it came down to stuff like prisoners, decommissioning, or whatever, it was always Sinn Féin. The SDLP had nothing to do with it.

In a certain sense, within the Irish government, different teams dealt with different stuff, but on this particular occasion this was an exception to that, because Paddy Teahon was leading there for the Irish government in that particular discussion to try and pull it together. But I suppose the answer was this stuff had been going on for months; people were anxious to bring it to a head.

HUGH LOGUE: Well, Dublin was keen. I can still see Paddy Teahon and Dermot Gallagher[45] coming down the corridor with purpose, and, speaking to them briefly, it was clear that they were determined to go ahead with it. They headed, I think, straight to Trimble's room at that stage.

WALTER KIRWAN: I think it's worth making a more general point here: that, in many ways, all of these agreements have been built on concepts that were developed by

---

[44] Fred Cobain was an UUP MLA for North Belfast.
[45] The most senior Irish civil servants; see n. 14.

John Hume, but at so many of the crucial times, in terms of actually delivering the concept in some form that would work, it was Seamus Mallon who was the key person who had to be got on board, and who constructively made the compromise, and who carried the burden of the negotiations. John set the big picture, but he was up there, he wasn't down in the trenches at all during these negotiations. I think that's a very important point.

Q: What was the point of the Economic Policy Unit?

WALTER KIRWAN: It was to mark the Department of Finance. The SDLP were clearly going to get the Department of Finance and this was the Unionists trying to, as it were, mark the Department of Finance and have a counterbalancing force.

COLM LARKIN: Trimble decided—having argued in the May negotiations that they should be separate ministries—once he was in OFM/DFM he wanted a strong centralizing control, and so Gudgin looked at the Office of Budget Management, I think, which was in the President's Office in the USA, and they thought this would be very good.[46] I think the theory was that all policy proposals had to be vetted and agreed by EPU, so it immediately clashed with the Department of Finance and Personnel, who were roughly already doing that kind of thing. I personally think it wasn't properly drafted at all in the terms of reference, but it worked better than it could have had, because of the person running it.

It could have raised awful difficulties, but in fact it didn't. It worked better than it could have done. It wasn't a good bit of negotiation.

TONY McCUSKER: The last thing of that night was tourism.

SEÁN FARREN: Where would tourism go?

TONY McCUSKER: It wasn't about tourism, because I mean tourism automatically should go into an economic department, but the big issue that night was do you want to end up with two North–South bodies in one department. There wasn't a structural argument that you could really have advanced that night to say, well, tourism can go into another department.

SEÁN FARREN: We tried to get it into Culture, Arts, and Leisure.

6.4. The Process of Implementation

6.4.1. Relations between Negotiators

Q: The impression you get when you're looking just at the statements from the parties is that the SDLP was, through those years, doing more strategic economic thinking, and the Unionist Party just didn't say anything?

---

[46] Dr Graham Gudgin, an economist, was special advisor to the First Minister (David Trimble), 1998–2002.

SEÁN FARREN: If you go through the discussions that were taking place during the negotiations, I remember we put forward an economic document one day when economy was on the agenda and I think we were the only party. We were churning out the stuff.

WALTER KIRWAN: It's also interesting to reflect that there was a lot of this work going on—about doing papers and so on—but, if you looked at it, there were so many cases where the actual thing that was decided wasn't something that was all worked out in a paper three months in advance; it was something that was decided in ten minutes on the back of an envelope, just like with this EPU.

There's a certain dimension about that, if you think how long we had to ruminate about this problem, and to draw on the resources of political science. One of the things that struck me reading Robin Wilson's thesis recently was, where he did interviews with both British and Irish officials, I was interested to see that almost all the Irish officials said the same thing as I said myself—that we didn't study the theory of consocation.[47] We did it at college years ago, but we didn't study that theory at all and, in a sense, the things happened through kind of a practical application of something that would work in terms of political balance. I was amazed to see the British officials were all quoted as more or less saying almost exactly the same thing—that it sort of all worked out through a political parallelogram of forces in a pressured situation, and there's an awful lot in that.

SEÁN FARREN: You're detailing a framework that is in existence. The framework is there, the framework has been agreed, and so you're working in from the outside, from the margins. Your actions are being restricted.

6.4.2. Executive Formation

Q: What about that first time they tried to run D'Hondt on 15 July 1999, where none of the Unionists turned up? What were the repercussions of that?[48]

SEÁN FARREN: I don't have a very clear recollection, except to say that it was quite clear that it was going to be a non-event in terms of producing anything.

HUGH LOGUE: Trimble hadn't indicated to Mallon that he wouldn't turn up.

SEÁN FARREN: And if he did, he wouldn't nominate. Did we not know that he wouldn't nominate even if he turned up?

---

[47] See Wilson (2008).

[48] Over a year after the election of David Trimble and Seamus Mallon to the positions of First Minister Designate and Deputy First Minister Designate (see n. 23), an effort was made on 15 July 1999 to nominate the other ministers to the executive. Only the SDLP and Sinn Féin participated, so the nominations were ineffective, as they were not compatible with standing orders.

HUGH LOGUE: That was still in the balance.

SEÁN FARREN: I thought that he clearly wasn't going to nominate. Well, again, because the SDLP didn't have any leverage over the decommissioning process, we were simply part players there. There's not an awful lot of light that I can throw on the hard negotiations, because we weren't material to those. We turned up, and George Mitchell could almost read our script for us, because he knew what we were going to say—that we really wanted to see this happen and that we had no influence over the process.

We went to London and we had a big meeting there at Wingfield House, the American ambassador's residence, and again I felt that we were just part of the process, because, though we were one of the parties, we weren't influential or significant. But what he did succeed in doing was drawing us closer to the point where Trimble felt sufficiently confident to go before the Ulster Unionist Council meeting to say that he was going to jump.

COLM LARKIN: Some of Trimble's people came back to me and said 'we've got explicit promises from Sinn Féin', there and then.

SEÁN FARREN: Well, I feel that he felt he had. In other words, there was a commitment there to engage with the decommissioning body, once Trimble had committed formally to the executive. But there was no way, of course, that he was going to extract from them how they were going to engage, what would transpire between them. He got them through the door or, if you like, just inside the door of decommissioning, but he had no control, and he couldn't extract from them what they would say. This was, I suppose in a sense, the weakness; but absent from the Agreement, or absent immediately thereafter, was some kind of indication as to what kind of process would be required in order to satisfy particularly the Unionists that decommissioning was in train. As I did say earlier, if there had been some indication that there was a process, we might have been spared an awful lot of the trouble.

6.4.3. Policing: The Patten Report

Q: What was the impact of the Patten report on policing in September 1999?

SEÁN FARREN: The UUP hope was that they would mobilize sufficient Conservative opposition once the bill came before parliament, and that was a second bite at the cherry. OK, these were recommendations, but there was a long way to go yet, and you have to see the draft bill, and of course we had umpteen more meetings, and we were very dissatisfied as the drafts of the bill became available. So, there was still a long road to go.

WALTER KIRWAN: The implementation was, if I recall correctly, in a sense of the follow-up, Patten was tailored, if you like, to try and mitigate Trimble's difficulties. It was so tailored that it was in danger of losing the SDLP, never mind Sinn Féin.[49]

HUGH LOGUE: Well, there had been a fair bit of tick-tacking. Seamus was virtually, on a daily basis at that stage, tick-tacking with Dublin and Daithi Ó Ceallaigh, who later went on to be ambassador in London, and that was very close: exactly what you were looking for, how you would respond.[50] Dublin were keen—they seemed to be indifferent to what Sinn Féin were doing, because Sinn Féin were lobbying us. I had a couple of meetings with Tom Hartley and Jim Gibney at that stage; they were saying all kinds of dire things would happen if the SDLP moved ahead of Sinn Féin.[51] It came to a point where Seamus said just not to meet them any more, or say anything more to them, and he went to Dublin on it. I remember Patten coming out the weekend of the British–Irish conference.[52] Patten was at Oxford, as was Trimble, and that was a set-to like few others. Trimble went ballistic, and Patten, who had immense charm and reserve, took the gloves off immediately.[53]

I remember him being incredibly impressive that day, particularly taking Trimble apart in front of his own people—in front of his own supporters as it were—on the issue of victims, and what had been done, because they were criticizing what had been done, and Patten responding by describing meeting with the RUC widowed spouses and pointing out that he was the first one to do anything for them, and that they had been around for thirty years and that so little had been done for them, and it was a devastating performance by Patten, and I think Trimble, certainly that weekend, didn't recover from it.

WALTER KIRWAN: I don't know in detail much about the generation of the Patten Commission reports, but later I had a lot to do with Maurice Hayes, and I've no doubt that Maurice Hayes was very influential in the development of the Patten recommendations, and certainly that would also be my observation over the years.[54] Maurice Hayes was also very closely associated with Dermot Gallagher, and the two of them would have tick-tacked quite a bit. I had little doubt that as the Patten recommendations were coming to a head that a kind of a quadrilateral, if you like, involving Dermot Gallagher, Maurice Hayes, Daithi Ó Ceallaigh, and Seamus Mallon, were sort of playing out, and

[49] The bills designed to implement the Patten report adopted only some of the recommendations of the report, rejected others, and pushed yet others into the future.

[50] See Ch. 3, n. 56.

[51] Tom Hartley was a republican activist and a Sinn Féin councillor on Belfast City Council, 1993–2015: in 2008–9 he was Lord Mayor of Belfast. Jim Gibney was an important republican strategist.

[52] The annual conference of the British–Irish Association took place at Oxford on 9–11 September 1999 and included an opening session, attended by David Trimble, in which Chris Patten discussed his report.

[53] See Ch. 3, n. 50.

[54] Maurice Hayes (1927–2017), a member of the Irish Senate, was appointed to the Patten Commission; he was a former senior Northern Ireland civil servant and was very active in public life.

definitely, I would say, the recommendations of the Patten Commission didn't come as any surprise to either the Dublin government or Seamus Mallon.

6.4.4. Executive Nomination Process

SEÁN FARREN: Earlier that day [29 November 1999] there had been an effort made to try to find out what options in particular the Ulster Unionists and indeed Sinn Féin might go for in terms of choice of portfolios in the D'Hondt mechanism.[55]

It didn't come to an awful lot. No other parties were keen to reveal their hand, but I suppose we did have some indications. We knew that Reg Empey would be nominated for Commerce, and then that Mark Durkan would be nominated for Finance. Then it would fall to the DUP, and the question was whether or not they would take Education. The DUP were third. They went for Regional Development and, of course, with that Sinn Féin went for Education, and there were some gasps of surprise at that.

TONY McCUSKER: We were sitting in the gallery that day when Sinn Féin did that, and there was a collective 'Oh, f***'.

SEÁN FARREN: The DUP took time out; I think they were the only ones who explicitly took time out. Am I right in that? So, then the process went on from there. The first round was the significant one, because it gave indications as to where parties were staking themselves out politically, and with education going to Sinn Féin, that was something that was almost inevitable once the DUP passed it up. And why the DUP passed it up I suppose you can only ascertain by asking the DUP. I've never really understood why they did, because they were only storing trouble up for themselves and for everybody else, but, nonetheless, maybe they saw that there was more to be gained by being minister in charge of Regional Development.

WALTER KIRWAN: Regional Development did involve a lot of infrastructure investment and all that, didn't it?

SEÁN FARREN: Education is the second biggest spender.

TONY McCUSKER: I accept that. But you could also argue, and some did, that leaving Education for Sinn Féin was also creating such a groundswell of opposition. Trimble based his approach on the North–South bodies.

SEÁN FARREN: He based it on whichever department controlled the most North–South bodies and Enterprise, Trade, and Investment controlled two.

---

[55] The designation of ministers according to the D'Hondt procedure took place on 29 November 1999, and the ministers-designate formally assumed office on 2 December 1999.

TONY McCUSKER: So that drove Trimble into DCAL—culture—because he was scared stiff of Sinn Féin becoming the Department of Culture.[56]

SEÁN FARREN: Compulsory Irish! In fact, they controlled 60 per cent of the budget—20 per cent of it went to their areas in Education and 40 per cent of the budget went to Health, and so the rest of the budget was divided up between eight. Well, the department that I first controlled was the next in terms of budget; it was 10 million or 15 million.

HUGH LOGUE: That was part of Sinn Féin's spin afterwards. Nobody wanted Health. Health was a poisoned chalice at that stage, and it came to them. It was either that or Agriculture, and they picked Health, and then left with Education and Health. The first thing they did was count up the sums and say 'well, get out the spin right away that it was 60% of the budget'.

SEÁN FARREN: That's right, and so after that we dusted ourselves down and introduced ourselves to our permanent secretaries and private offices.

6.5. The Institutions at Work

6.5.1. Preparing for Government

Q: How soon did actual policymaking start—did you do much in those first days?

COLM LARKIN: I think the first big task we all had was to do a programme for government.

TONY McCUSKER: All the institutions had to meet within a period of time, so you had the executive, the North/South Ministerial Council, the British–Irish Council and the British–Irish Intergovernmental Conference—all had to meet before Christmas, which was a very short period of time. There was a huge amount of work just to actually fulfil that part of the infrastructure.

SEÁN FARREN: You see, December was virtually taken up. The ministers, etc., were settling into the departments and getting briefings, and all of that. But in the centre of things everybody was focused on all those first meetings, writing speeches for the North/South Ministerial Council and writing speeches for the British–Irish Intergovernmental Conference, and we had two of those in the one day, remember? We had the British–Irish Council in Lancaster House, and then we went to 10 Downing Street for the British–Irish Intergovernmental Conference, where we famously had the goose Christmas dinner that Bertie Ahern had requested.

TONY McCUSKER: In all that there was a huge learning exercise for everybody as to how the thing would actually run. We were still fairly naive about how the

[56] The Department of Culture, Arts, and Leisure, the third ministry selected by Trimble and taken up by Chris McGimpsey.

parties were going to run the executive, so issues like would advisors attend the executive, how many officials would attend it, all those sorts of things we hadn't really thought about suddenly started to appear as critical issues. I think that first month was predominantly taken up with that. The North/South Ministerial Council was an interesting thing in itself.

There was a great historical moment in Armagh, but in the middle of it there were these odd things happening.[57] At the start there was a row over the membership of and the appointments to the North–South ministerial bodies, and particularly over Intertrade Ireland, because the South wanted to appoint the head of the IDA, and there was a row over this.

SEÁN FARREN: So, before the meeting started, Reg Empey and Mary Harney had to get into a huddle to clear the issue on that, and the procedure that was going to happen then was that the First Minister and Deputy First Minister would nominate chairs to the North–South bodies and we were then going to formally nominate and approve the membership and the chairs. And then Bairbre de Brún, who had heard about this, objected strenuously to one of the proposed chairs of one of the bodies.[58]

TONY McCUSKER: Anyway, so Bairbre only found out about this nomination before the meeting started. As the meeting started, I mentioned this to her permanent secretary, who was there, and I said 'look, you just need to be aware of this'. So he spoke to Bairbre, and told her, and the next thing there was a note that came up the table that got to me. It went up the side and the back and got to me and said 'if this happens, I'm leaving'.

So, I went over between Trimble and Mallon, and I said we've got a wee problem when we get to this bit of nominating chairs, and so Trimble and Mallon said 'what are we going to do?', and we said 'well, we can leave it and do it at the next meeting—it doesn't have to be done, it can be done at any meeting, it doesn't have to be a full one'.

Anyway, when it got to that point, Bertie Ahern was chairing that part of the agenda, they just moved seamlessly on, but nobody else knew what had happened, so everybody was scrabbling with all their papers, wondering had they missed something at this particular point.

Well, of course, the turnout of your [the Irish] cabinet was astonishing. It was hard enough to get all the Unionist ministers to come to that meeting, never mind, but every [Irish] cabinet minister was there.

WALTER KIRWAN: In all these things there was exhaustive attention paid to the rule of 'no surprises', trying to have everything pre-agreed so that nothing could go

[57] The North/South Ministerial Council formally came into existence on 2 December 1999 and held its first meeting in Armagh, where its secretariat was based, on 13 December 1999.

[58] Bairbre de Brún was a member of the Sinn Féin negotiating team, an MLA for West Belfast, 1998–2004, and Minister for Health, 1999–2002.

wrong, and still there was sufficient edginess around, so that these kinds of hiccups arose. It was almost impossible to foresee everybody that had to be consulted about everything.

HUGH LOGUE: The silly one, which should have been anticipated, was the snake of limousines coming through the mist; it was like a Mafia funeral.[59]

TONY McCUSKER: There must have been about twenty of these limousines, black Mercs, all snaking down the drive, and of course there was a big bank of photographers there thinking 'oh God, this is brilliant', and photographs appeared all over the place the next day of all these cars.

WALTER KIRWAN: There was a very good atmosphere at that meeting, and then there was a very good atmosphere at the meeting in London of the British–Irish Council that followed afterwards.

TONY McCUSKER: One of the interesting little things that happened was in relation to the British–Irish Intergovernmental Conference; in a sense the Northern administration was a side player in that, the main players essentially being the British and Irish governments.[60] Nobody had really thought through how we would actually play our part in that in terms of just the logistics, how you sat at the table. So, in your early discussions, the two, Britain and the South, had sort of seen us as being on the margins of the meeting or as witnesses to it.

Of course, Seamus and Trimble were adamant that we would be up front on it. So there were a lot of negotiations around just the simple things of who actually sat where at what meeting, and what the order of things was. But those ones in December were critical in terms of just getting all those things done up until December. Then it was really into January where you started to get down to some of the real business, starting to look at the programme for government and all that, and the budget.

6.5.2. The Executive at Work

TONY McCUSKER: The issue about policymaking wasn't actually a big issue, because to a large extent there was an awful lot of learning going on at both advisor level and ministerial level, and the actual amount of significant new policy or significant new legislation was quite limited. It was very, very limited.

---

[59] Journalists were much taken by the enthusiastic and very visible presence of southern ministers. For example, alongside a photograph of the fleet of cars, the *Irish Times* (14 December 1999) commented that it was 'some sight. A fleet of 99-D and 98-D registered Mercedes lined up bumper to bumper on the driveway to the Church of Ireland Primate's former palace in Armagh, now the headquarters of the North–South Council'.

[60] The Agreement provided for the attendance of 'relevant' members of the executive at meetings of the conference but made it clear that decisions would be by agreement of the two governments.

HUGH LOGUE: Well, I remember Mallon being frustrated at that stage, and to an extent Trimble was as well, and when they rounded on the civil service they were quite a combination. I remember, someone protested about the amount of time that it takes to draft legislation, and there was a shortage of parliamentary drafts people, I think, at that stage, and Trimble saying: 'Let's get them, let's get them!'

TONY McCUSKER: One of the things is they also took the decision to adopt the Cabinet Office model that the only civil servant who attended the cabinet was the cabinet secretary, there was no other civil servant. I think it was about after the second meeting that Seamus insisted on me coming in to balance that part of it. That was the big change, actually: having two people at the cabinet table, and advisors in the cabinet as well, and in the room.

COLM LARKIN: Not ministerial advisors?

TONY McCUSKER: Yes, on OFM/DFM, not individual ministerial advisors.

COLM LARKIN: Were permanent secretaries in then?

TONY McCUSKER: They were brought in for specific issues.

COLM LARKIN: Well, just a couple of points about the operation of the executive. The programme for government took a long time and was largely aspirational, but it was a fairly consensual exercise, and it was a good building of a corporate view of things. It wasn't particularly contentious or divisive. My memory of the executive was that it worked relatively well during that period. The main decisions were budgetary reallocation decisions, which were difficult, but Mark Durkan of the Department of Finance was very skilful in keeping everyone happy and making the reallocations.

The main burden, I felt, fell on OFM/DFM, in that they had to chair the meeting and had to agree between them on the proposal put forward, so once they'd agreed it was then very difficult for their party colleagues to take another position. What often used to happen was that we could get Trimble to sign off on stuff, but when his ministers saw the actual proposals the day or two before the executive they'd panic, and there would be a huge reorientation a day or two before the actual executive to get things organized. Seamus was slightly better organized, in that he had a meeting a few days prior to the executive with his colleagues.

So there's a lot of management stress put on OFM/DFM to make the thing work. I found the executive—I was at most of the meetings—pretty temperate and pretty workmanlike. The big politics of decommissioning, and so on, very seldom came in through the door.

SEÁN FARREN: The only standoff that I can remember, I think, was probably at the very first executive meeting, if not the second, when we had to decide the location for the North–South bodies in the North. Although the Loughs Agency already had its base in Derry, John Hume had lobbied very hard: Derry must be seen to have something new coming out of the new arrangement, and of course Trimble was very anxious that some of the unionist constituencies, particularly in Belfast, would have something. Seamus already had Newry earmarked for the Intertrade Body, and on top of that the headquarters had to be in Armagh.

I remember we had to adjourn the meeting for about twenty minutes or half an hour for each of the parties to come back and try and get their own act together, because there were tensions, and different locations being proposed, so one of the compromises was Omagh for the headquarters of the EU Body.

HUGH LOGUE: Seamus had already had much of this, as it were, pre-cooked without telling anyone else. We knew for weeks, or days anyway, that the headquarters was going to be in Armagh and that the new Intertrade body was going to be in Newry, but we were committed to silence on it. Trimble knew that Enniskillen was going to be the Waterways.

SEÁN FARREN: The big frustration in that executive was that, while it obviously did good enough work, every time Trimble and Mallon would make a press conference to announce that they'd allocated money to a hospital or some-thing—the questions would only be about decommissioning. We just could not get the agenda on to nuts and bolts, and they could never satisfactorily handle the press conference to defuse it. Trimble would say too much, and it was very difficult, so they never really got ordinary devolved government out ahead of the big picture.

TONY McCUSKER: The other thing is, and it's always going to be there, it is actually very difficult to have a two-headed office. To get two people to agree on things, it's not easy at all. It's a complicated and very pressurized environment. Then, when you add two junior ministers to it, it became more of a nightmare; you're seeing four people in one department at official and advisor level because the advisor role would run into this big-time.

HUGH LOGUE: Seamus's relationship with Mo Mowlam was very good, and they could think in each other's heads a lot of the time, and Mallon was always confident that he could persuade Mo, whereas Trimble was infuriated by her. She didn't have to speak, and Trimble would just get very, very upset. On the other hand, Mandelson's relationship with Mallon quickly deteriorated, and Trimble had quite a good relationship with Mandelson. But I remember Mandelson at the Downing Street lunch, which followed the inaugural British–Irish Intergovernmental Conference [17 December 1999] appearing enraptured by Trimble and Mallon, particularly Mallon. As you say, that meeting was intended to have the British and Irish governments centre stage, but it was very much Trimble and Mallon who were the stars.

SEÁN FARREN: And Mallon came out of it way ahead of anybody else. There was a famous shot just the day after Mandelson was appointed, and Trimble going into Castle Buildings, and he was carrying the book 'Mandy'.

6.5.3. Policymaking and Civil Servants

SEÁN FARREN: Can I just say one thing? It's more a personal reflection on relationships as a minister with the Northern Ireland civil service. Obviously I was very much a greenhorn going in there, but, contrary to the general perception that the department was there in a sense to stop you doing things— I served in two departments, but my experience, I suppose, was mostly within the Department of Employment and Learning as it is now, or Higher and Further Education, Training, and Employment, the rather cumbersome title that it had then—what I found was that there was a release of energy within the department. Here was a local minister prepared to take some initiatives.

Of course, that gave the department incentives to rise to the bait and to start to advise as to how this might be done, rather than what may have been the situation before.

Within a week or two, one of the main things that I was to review, because it was party policy, was the whole student finance package. Even though there was nothing materially achieved before the first suspension, we had a review committee established, and, by the time we came back in the early summer, a lot of the work had been done, because it didn't stop.[61] In fact, it continued; there were some very, very good civil servants involved, and they had a lot of the work done.

So when I came back we were virtually ready with a set of recommendations to go. I found that here, and indeed in other areas, further education was due for a significant investment in order to meet the kind of challenges of the time, including the whole Training and Employment Agency, the equivalent of FÁS down here.[62] Those areas were ripe for investment and moving ahead. I found that the quality of senior civil servants, the ones I dealt with on a regular basis, was high, and they were only too anxious to find themselves working with a minister who was prepared to take some initiatives.

I don't overblow the initiatives that I took, because the time wasn't very long while we were there, but nonetheless there was that release of energy, and the commitment I found was genuine. So, my experience of the civil service was generally quite a positive experience.

WALTER KIRWAN: People like Garret FitzGerald often make out that the southern departments are very strongly partitionist in mentality. But when myself and

---

[61] In addition to two 'technical' twenty-four-hour suspensions on 10 August and 21 September 2001, designed to allow extra time for further inter-party negotiations, there were open-ended suspensions on 11 February 2000 (ending on 30 May 2000), 14 October 2002 (ending on 8 May 2007), and 9 January 2017 (still in force in November 2019). The work of the civil service continued during the periods of suspension.

[62] Foras Áiseanna Saothair (FÁS), referred to in English as the Training and Employment Authority, existed between 1988 and 2013. It was replaced by SOLAS, the Republic's agency for further education and training.

others were going around first of all cooking for the North–South strand, I have to say, in the same vein as Seán, that we found a very cooperative spirit from the departments, and each department set up a kind of a North–South person with specific responsibility. They were all dedicated people who didn't have other responsibilities, and obviously to some extent, then, the success of their job, for those people, was dependent on taking action and taking initiative.

We had a committee that used to meet every so often, which was made up of all the departments which were concerned both with the North–South bodies and with the areas of cooperation. It used to come together under Foreign Affairs chairmanship to discuss the common issues that might have arisen, maybe around personnel policy, or all the different things that were cross-cutting across the different areas of cooperation and the North–South bodies. My experience was that they did enter in a spirit of activity and innovation and enthusiasm. In general I wouldn't agree that it was a very partitionist mentality, and that they wanted to hold back or avoid cooperating with their Northern counterparts; my experience was the opposite.

HUGH LOGUE: I'm not sure that was reciprocated. Mind you, I always felt that the Northern Irish civil service had little enthusiasm for North–South. Yourself excepted, Tony, there wasn't a great deal of enthusiasm, and I think that became more evident when it went into direct rule. There certainly was, in any of the departments that the DUP or Unionist ministers were in, very little enthusiasm. I remember how lethargic they had become—and senior civil servants telling me 'if I do nothing on North–South nothing will happen to me; if I do something on it I could well put my career at risk'. Whereas the South had managed to put together, as it were, a North–South desk within each department, nothing like that was done in the North.

COLM LARKIN: My impression of the civil service was this. I came from a very policy-rich institution, the European Commission, where anyone worth his salt has a ten-point plan in the back of his pocket to give to a minister or commissioner, and ideas about the remaking of the world, night and day. So I went from a policy-rich atmosphere to a policy-poor atmosphere, where you said to people 'what are your ideas about the environment?', and the reply came 'what do you think?', or 'what does the minister want?'

There was very little creative thinking, at least initially, and a lot of the work that was done, like the review of public administration, was terribly slow and terribly elaborate, and very much dragged down with procedures. Having said that, which is obviously critical and negative, I found all civil servants immensely loyal to the executive and immensely trustworthy. They weren't playing politics. I am aware of very little tension between the ministers of a particular political party and their senior officials; I think all that worked extremely well, and that they were all genuinely doing their best to make the executive work, and were very loyal to the executive in their dealings with the UK Treasury, and so on.

I think over time they became a bit better in creating policy. You remember various things we had, like executive programmes and so on, that were quite creative putting together things. So I found it a mixed bag, but I think the main thing I would have feared, and didn't discover, was disloyalty: there was a great loyalty towards the executive and its ministers—I think especially to Sinn Féin ministers.

TONY McCUSKER: I don't recall there being a complaint from any minister in the executive about any senior civil servant for the duration of that. The issue about policy is absolutely right, and it's still probably an issue, because if you look at the period of the first executive, now, there actually has been a dearth of serious, imaginative new policies starting to emerge. Part of the explanation for that is that during twenty-seven to thirty years of direct rule essentially everything was a read-across to the UK, to Britain, and very little was done on a new basis.

Scotland, for example, was completely different; they were into new policy. When I moved after 2002 to the Department of Agriculture, I saw it there, because when I went into that department they were very reluctant to do something which was different from what Britain would do, or even what the Republic would do. They tended to want to keep agricultural policies, so whenever we did the CAP reform in 2004 we came out of those discussions with the UK, on one hand, and the Irish government, on the other hand, saying 'you have to follow the same direction we're going on CAP reform'.[63]

We went down a different path, and it worked. The department was prepared to actually think and say, well, what specifically does this region need that is different from what the South needs, which is different from what Britain needs. You look at the Department for the Environment, for example, during all those years there was a huge failure to implement EU directives. Part of that was it was just caught up on other stupid stuff, and never said 'we really need to get these in place', and there was a huge backlog of stuff.

WALTER KIRWAN: The same has been true to a degree in the South, especially around the intersection of the environment and agriculture.

TONY McCUSKER: What legislation did emerge tended to be the implementation of the EU Directives, which had to be done, or copying UK legislation. There was no imaginative stuff starting to emerge, doing a new piece of law on women or children, or whatever. One institution around which there was a lot of apathy was the Civic Forum, mainly because the main parties didn't really want the Civic Forum. It was a proposal of the Women's Coalition. Nobody was really

---

[63] The EU's Common Agricultural Policy (CAP) has undergone a series of attempts at reform since the 1960s. The reform mentioned here involved the decoupling of subsidies from particular crops.

quite clear, first, about the representational nature, and how you could actually get that sort of civic society adequately represented on it. Secondly, I think there was a problem when it was formed: there was a clear difference of opinion as to whether it is a third chamber which is actually mirroring the executive, or whether it was just a body that picked up a number of issues that it would do a detailed examination on.

Nobody in the government end gave a toss, really, other than to keep it off our back. It never really got any sort of sense of clear direction as to what it could really be.

WALTER KIRWAN: It's probably worth saying something about the British–Irish Council. I was gone out of that whole area by 2001, so I didn't have that huge experience of it, but I think it's fair to say that, when that whole thing was being discussed originally, some senior Irish civil servants would have had very little enthusiasm for that, and would have foreseen some risk that it would have brought us back into the ambit of the UK, and so on.

Now some of us always felt that the UK government was least likely to show much interest in it, and that it wasn't going to be a risk to us, and that's the way it turned out. I think now it's very, very hard to get a meeting of the British–Irish Council that Gordon Brown will turn up at. It will always be the Northern Ireland Secretary, or somebody like that, so far as the UK level is concerned. The most enthusiastic people for it, I think, turned out to be the Scots, maybe.

Obviously all the suspensions, again, in the North kept interfering with the meetings of the British–Irish Council. So this thing was invented to suit David Trimble, and at David Trimble's instance, but it very quickly got to the stage where David Trimble was annoying his colleagues in Scotland, Wales, and London with the fact that they couldn't organize the meetings and stick to timetables that had been agreed. I don't think it's amounted to a huge amount.

Q: I've always been struck by OFM/DFM: you go into their website and there are loads and loads of policies and reports?

SEÁN FARREN: Well, there's no shortage of reports on this, that, and the other. One of the things that we were accused of was consulting too frequently and too widely, and taking too long to make decisions. I suppose it was inevitable, just on that general point, that people coming into a new regime would want to review some of the key areas that they had responsibility for. Otherwise, they were simply going to inherit and keep administering what was there already. The only way to inform yourself as to a better way to go forward was somehow or other to have the issues reviewed.

So I think it was almost inevitable that there would be quite a plethora of views initiated from within the departments, certainly in the first run around, and what was frustrating was that we didn't have the time, or the opportunity, to take decisions. Some of the decisions were taken for us afterwards—the major review by the Department of Finance. To a certain extent Mark [Durkan] started the ball rolling, and when I picked it up it was the whole rates review situation, and that led to an unholy row after the report was adopted by the direct rule government. I think we would have adopted the same report, and the same recommendations, had we still been there.

Q: What about the *Shared Future* document, where there was always the allegation—I'm not sure whether it was OFM/DFM or whether it was just the First Minister's Office—of reluctance to address this issue, and it took the suspension and it took the British government releasing that document to get the ball rolling? [64]

TONY McCUSKER: It's now sent back to what it was, because Sinn Féin and the DUP refused to acknowledge it as a policy document of theirs. There is an issue over community relations and between the two parties, because they both have completely different ideas as to what the agenda should be on the community-relations strategy. The DUP, to my way of thinking, don't actually have any sense of a joined-up society here at all. I think Sinn Féin are not that far away from that either. They actually see community relations mainly in terms of equality, which is a fairly late jumping on that particular bandwagon for them, because the debate around a Commission for Racial Equality was in the 1970s and 1980s.

So it's not about relations; it's about equality, and they've actually shifted quite dramatically. Sinn Féin are sort of back there now. But if you took what various people on both sides of the parties were saying about the future of society, it's hard to actually see, to any extent, what they envisage as a joined-up society at all. A differentiated and segregated society seems to be almost a prerequisite.

COLM LARKIN: Having said that, Trimble and Mallon were relatively courageous, if not very successful, but they got to close grips with Drumcree. They got to close grips with North Belfast, the Holy Cross standoff.[65] They did actually engage quite a lot of time seeing could they be helpful, and appointed specific officials and task forces. So, while there certainly was no great appetite to tackle the big picture of community relations, especially, in my recollection, on Trimble's side, they were willing to engage in flashpoints and particular circumstances. The North Belfast efforts were quite commendable, the effort that they put into that.

TONY McCUSKER: They put a lot of time and energy and money into it.

---

[64] *A Shared Future: Policy and Strategic Framework for Good Relations in Northern Ireland* was a consultative document launched in March 2005 (see Office of the First Minister and Deputy First Minister 2005).

[65] The 'Holy Cross' dispute, 2001–2, involved local Protestants protesting against Catholic schoolgirls and their parents walking to their primary school in a deeply divided area of North Belfast.

HUGH LOGUE: Following what Colm said, I think Trimble had a lot of guts there, maybe too much insofar as at Drumcree he'd been the hero of it at a previous time.[66] It was in the middle of his constituency. It was one of the few areas that his advisors used to exercise us steadily about: to allow Harold Gracey and people like that some room for manoeuvre.[67] It was a constant irritant for Trimble, and yet he coped with it, and he eventually realized that what was being sought on the Garvaghy Road wasn't available, and came to terms with it. So I think Trimble knew where he was coming from, and came to recognize where that was, and whatever sectarianism was in him, it had by and large evaporated.

TONY McCUSKER: I must say he gave interesting signals—he appointed a private secretary who was an Irish-speaking *Gaeilgeoir* from Coalisland, and everybody sort of blinked. He did put in a number of clear markers that showed that he was prepared to take a different approach, and that behaviour would change dramatically.

COLM LARKIN: Yes, he had quite a lot of discipline, and I found, for example, that he chaired the executive meetings very skilfully and showed great ability to take points from Sinn Féin and the SDLP. He was a very uneven performer, but he had a lot of capacities as well, very positive capacities.

6.6. Overall Assessments

6.6.1. Performance of Parties

Q: Did Trimble achieve more than the DUP is presently achieving?

WALTER KIRWAN: Tony touched a moment ago on the business about the nature of society in the North and the nature of the future evolution of society, and again it's interesting, looking at Robin Wilson's thesis, and looking at the comments that are expressed in that by officials from both the British and the Irish sides. Basically, every last one of them, practically, is quoted as saying we had to set this thing up, we had all sort of checks and balances in it, and so on, but we were all hoping that over time it would evolve, and that what Hume referred to as a healing process would come into effect, and that over time one could evolve towards a system that didn't need so many checks and balances, which obviously had their downsides in terms of potential deadlocks, and so on.

---

[66] David Trimble had—arm in arm with the Revd Ian Paisley—led one of the Orange protests at Drumcree in 1995.

[67] Harold Gracey was District Master of Portadown District Loyal Orange Lodge No. 1, and one of the leaders of the campaign to allow the Drumcree march to proceed down the Garvaghy Road.

So, I suppose anybody looking forward would have seen that, if you reached a situation where the DUP were the primary party on the unionist side, and you could argue just as much whether Sinn Féin were the primary party on the other, that the chances of evolving in that way were going to be very severely diminished. I'm not quite sure if people were—if the British people were—thinking that far ahead, or if they were just managing the situation from month to month. But I think it is a slightly bleak prospect, as one looks forward, if we have the present situation perpetuated indefinitely.

TONY McCUSKER: If Trimble had tried to do what the DUP did last year, he would have been destroyed completely. I never quite understood where the magical change was that allowed the DUP to go into government with Sinn Féin and actually get away with it. Trimble had taken the thing so far, and he had left unionism completely divided, but it seemed to be divided on quite specific issues, and suddenly you come to 2007 and you have this agreement to go into government, and it's never quite clear what was the magic.

HUGH LOGUE: I think it was pretty clear, the DUP got—instead of 'not an ounce, not a bullet'—they got every ounce and every bullet.[68]

TONY McCUSKER: Did anybody seriously believe that they got every ounce and every bullet?

HUGH LOGUE: Well, they certainly, the IRA, led them to believe that they got every ounce and every bullet, and there haven't been too many since then.

TONY McCUSKER: What I mean is, there would have been a view around unionism that, even if you'd got the Archbishop of Canterbury verifying that everything was away, you would never get into government with Sinn Féin; then suddenly Ian Paisley sits in beside them.

HUGH LOGUE: The question is about London and Trimble for three years. The only game in town really was, for a long time, saving David, and you find this very much in Jonathan Powell's book,[69] and this was the reason they saved David all the time: they didn't feel there was anybody else strong enough within unionism to carry through the mandate, or to carry through Blair's will.

COLM LARKIN: I agree with that, but just one nuance to it, and Mallon used to say it. I always regarded it as quite significant that in 1998 the DUP took their seats in the executive as opposed to staying out, and they showed an appetite for running departments; Robinson and others were in their full pomp as ministers. I kind of felt, from that, the seed of hunger had grown there, and at some stage they would want to come in.

TONY McCUSKER: They probably participated more than people actually thought they were.

COLM LARKIN: Yes, so they were tempted, they ate the forbidden fruit.

---

[68] See Ch. 5, n. 47.
[69] See Powell (2008: *passim*).

HUGH LOGUE: I think in hindsight it was a mistake of the executive to not require them to turn up; I think that was a fundamental mistake. I think the DUP would have been a far less attractive option for many of the unionists if they had been denied power. In other words, you turn up or you're not in.

SEÁN FARREN: It would have required legislation; it wasn't in the pledge of office.[70]

COLM LARKIN: But also Trimble was always very hesitant about it because he didn't want to be totally isolated on the executive. He wanted unionists around him, but I think the fact that they participated in 1998 showed that in the long run you could bring them in from the cold.

Q: Were they any good as ministers—the DUP?

TONY McCUSKER: Oh, they were good, yes. I mean Robinson and Dodds were excellent ministers.

HUGH LOGUE: So was Gregory Campbell.[71]

COLM LARKIN: Gregory Campbell was good, and then they had Morrow. They were very, very committed; they worked very hard.

TONY McCUSKER: It was a nuisance for everybody that they changed ministers—I mean administratively it was an awful mess, because every so often you're going to bring in some new ministers and get them up to speed.

SEÁN FARREN: But as Minister for Finance I had to deal with them maybe on almost a more regular basis than any other minister in the executive, and I always found them very supportive.[72] And indeed proposals, particularly coming up to the establishment of the Strategic Investment Body, they certainly accepted that in principle and had comments to make about it.[73] So, in a sense, they participated by correspondence, but didn't participate by their physical presence.

TONY McCUSKER: Most people would say that all the ministers that came out of the administration were very good, and certainly in comparison to any direct-rule ministers they'd no reason to feel in any way inferior.

SEÁN FARREN: We were there every day in that sense.

TONY McCUSKER: I don't think you would have any senior civil servant on any occasion ever feeling sort of ashamed of their minister in a public forum, whereas you couldn't have said that about all the direct-rule ministers, I have to say. But the intriguing thing with Trimble was at what point was it—when he lost the election, or before—that the British governments switched off the lights on him a bit, and then moved towards the DUP. Hard to know.

---

[70] Provision was made in the Good Friday Agreement for a pledge of office to be taken by ministers, binding them to a code of conduct.

[71] Peter Robinson, Nigel Dodds, Gregory Campbell, and Maurice Morrow were senior DUP politicians and ministers in the Northern Ireland Executive.

[72] Seán Farren took over as Minister for Finance when Mark Durkan became Deputy First Minister in succession to Seamus Mallon on 14 December 2001.

[73] This body was planned in 2002 as a mechanism to coordinate investment and public services.

SEÁN FARREN: Well, I think the time to give them most support was obviously after the Mitchell Review and when the executive was established, but more particularly when we came back after the first suspension, which was a three-month-long suspension, and everybody felt that things were going to happen then. I thought that was when the republican movement was more vulnerable than ever before to pressure, and maybe pressure was applied, but the intended effect wasn't achieved.

So from there on we were living on borrowed time, because we went into two more technical suspensions, twenty-four-hour suspensions, and it's amazing that the executive lasted from the summer of 2000 to October 2002. It's quite amazing; the raid on Stormont just brought things to a head. It was the straw that broke the camel's back.[74]

COLM LARKIN: And it has never been fully explained why that raid happened; it has never been explained.

TONY McCUSKER: It's extraordinary how it happened. I remember ringing the head of security in the Northern Ireland Office, and I said 'Do you know about this?', and he said 'I got a phone call that morning'. I said 'What did you do about it?' He says 'Well, it was the police.' I said 'this will be leading to the downfall of the executive, what do you do?' And just everybody was in denial. I swing different ways on it, whether—did the police at a senior level actually realise that in doing that they were going to bring down the executive? You could work out a conspiracy theory so easily on it.

HUGH LOGUE: And let's remember whose office they raided, Donaldson's.[75]

SEÁN FARREN: There's just one general question, it's more a question maybe for your researchers to consider. Arising out of the discussion you had there on policy or the lack of policymaking, and legislation and the lack of legislation, are we heading more for a form of dressed-up administrative devolution than devolution with a bite? In other words, are we simply heading, over the longer term, [for] a devolution which will essentially, with a little bit of work in the margins, implement UK legislation that would have had to be implemented anyway, or are you really going to make a difference? And what flexibility is there for the institutions to make a real difference? Maybe those opportunities are more constrained now in the economic climate.

TONY McCUSKER: I often wondered whether the outcome of an involuntary coalition was always going to be the lowest common denominator. You can't actually see them coming through with an education policy. And some of the large economic policies have such a sectarian edge to them. I can never understand why we never really got into significant policy change or policy

---

[74] A reference to the police raid on 4 October 2002 that destabilized the executive; see n. 9.

[75] It emerged in December 2005 that Denis Donaldson had been working for British intelligence for twenty years. He was murdered in Donegal in April 2006.

innovation. I just wonder whether people had decided that we needed to have a longish period of low-key stuff before you get into significant policy change.

COLM LARKIN: I think, as Seán knows better than anyone, there's very little economic autonomy, and in many ways the DUP and people before have done as much as they can with the rates and so on, which is the only thing that they have got control over.[76] It's administrative devolution, I think.

HUGH LOGUE: There was a stage when politics was like that in the South, where you left much of the decision-taking to the civil service and the importance of being a minister—and Sinn Féin are very good at it—is out glad-handing the electorate. There's not a farm mart that Michelle Gildernew hasn't been in, there wasn't a school that Martin McGuinness didn't go to.[77]

So there's not very much by way of ministerial achievement, and in terms of economics it's interesting that when the most recent hiatus existed we saw what Sinn Féin's agenda was: policing, Long Kesh, and the Irish language.[78] None of them gave a hint of economic policy at all, so they still see themselves as serving a constituency in which those three issues are dealt with: policing, the Irish language, and having Long Kesh immortalized. And one would have thought that, given the heavy lifting that the SDLP had done on North–South, given the republican ideal of a united Ireland, that one would have seen North–South, or strengthening of North–South, and its various forms, you'd have thought that that might have been on the agenda in this recent standoff, but nothing of that was there at all.

TONY McCUSKER: If you go way back to the formation of OFM/DFM, apart from the Economic Policy Unit, the fact is that the equality unit was established, and in a sense was almost the alternative to having a department of equality. That was a big option that Sinn Féin had wanted at that particular point in time, and into that then dropped community relations as well.

COLM LARKIN: The single equality bill is just stuck because of political tension in OFM/DFM.[79]

TONY McCUSKER: Although people have a perception that all the equality issues are either sorted out or being addressed, there are actually still quite significant differentials that haven't really changed that dramatically, particularly in west Belfast. Look at Belfast itself—it's still the city centre and the east taking priority; the north and west are still hugely left behind in terms of any sort

[76] Rates, local taxes on property based on valuation, were among the few revenue-generating areas under the control of the devolved administration.

[77] At the time, Michelle Gildernew of Sinn Féin was Minister for Agriculture and Martin McGuinness was Minister for Education in the Northern Ireland Executive.

[78] The reference is to policing reform, the creation of a heritage centre at the old Long Kesh/Maze prison, and proactive government measures to protect and recognize the Irish language.

[79] A single equality bill to make coherent the patchwork of equality legislation in Northern Ireland was considered in 2005–6, but not followed up; see Potter (2011).

of investment. But, having said that, you don't get the impression that it's a big issue being confronted by OFM/DFM.

6.6.2. Later Changes

Q: How far was the British and Irish governments' joint declaration of 2003 a continuation or a change of policy? And St Andrews, how far was it simply the Good Friday Agreement amended?

WALTER KIRWAN: I only recently became actively aware that one of the features of St Andrews was that any three ministers could call for something to be made the subject of a cross-community vote. Given the composition of the executive at the present time, one was a bit conscious that this was reinforcing the potential for deadlock, and for inhibiting the emergence of any kind of worthwhile economic and social policy from these two parties.

SEÁN FARREN: St Andrews kind of added, in terms of some of the issues that Wally has been pointing to, to what Mark Durkan called (at the last British–Irish meeting) some of the ugly scaffolding of the Agreement, by which I think he was talking about all of the protections, as it were, which have been included, to the point where gridlock is more likely in many situations than something more positive. It does invite the question as to whether or not we're going to be able to see the time when some of that ugly scaffolding can be dismantled.

Now, obviously, part of what Mark was thinking about was the possibility that we might move to a more voluntary coalition-type arrangement. A voluntary coalition would always have to be conditional on at least one party being from each community, and of course that invites the question as to whether or not it would be a party other than Sinn Féin, let's say—or other than the DUP—sufficiently strong to enable the coalition to be put together without one or other of those two parties who may be seen as the non-desirables. The present electoral arithmetic wouldn't lead you to be too sanguine about that.

HUGH LOGUE: I think we have to be careful here that we don't say that things are going to get worse, but I actually do think the institutions will stay in place. I think that it will be more administering British rule. I think there are already parallels going with Edinburgh and Cardiff in the British mind in terms of how the three are governed.

COLM LARKIN: Well, I suppose for me the question is if the British and Irish governments had acted differently from 1998 onwards on the decommissioning issue, could we now be in a situation where we have the UUP and the SDLP as majority partners or did they, by allowing Sinn Féin such a central position, inevitably go to the outcome we now have. That's a very difficult judgement to call. We're certainly better placed now than we were twenty or fifteen years ago, but my own instincts are that we could have saved the middle, and we would have had a better system of government as a result, but time will tell.

WALTER KIRWAN: I think that is the big question, and that it is very hard to know. The government put Sinn Féin so much in the centre, and then later on, I suppose to a slight degree, the DUP. It went against all my grain in terms of what I'd been involved in over my career, and at the same time I find it difficult to reach a definitive judgement that they were wrong to do it, because it's much better to rest on an agreement that you have, rather than getting into a kind of unstructured situation.

HUGH LOGUE: It seems to me weird to think that the first law of politics is to be there, and we allowed an institution to be created where you didn't have to be there. That in many ways indulged the DUP, by allowing them to participate in government. I think that was obviously a fundamental flaw, an error, and they had to be there. On the other hand, Sinn Féin was indulged in terms of decommissioning, and they had the Irish government, the British government, the American government, and the SDLP all ready to agree with them.

TONY McCUSKER: One issue I often wondered about, which came into my head when I saw Paisley and McGuinness—the extent to which, if Trimble and Mallon had actually got on better, there might have been a slightly different outcome. I just have this view that personal relationships are almost as critical as some of the big policy issues.

COLM LARKIN: I don't buy that, because Trimble's issues were not really with Mallon; they were with Sinn Féin and decommissioning. It's very hard to list the things where Trimble said 'Mallon is wrong on this', and Mallon has said 'Trimble is wrong'. You are right; the chemistry was not good, but it wasn't that that was cracking up the executive.

TONY McCUSKER: There were times that you almost felt that they were doing things to irritate each other rather than take any principled decisions. In the United States, the year I went to the United States with them, here were two men on an adventure to meet Colin Powell, the Secretary of State. Not once during the trip did they actually talk to each other. I ended up travelling alternately in different cars, so there wasn't any issue. Having said that, we went in to Colin Powell and they gave the performance of their life, the two of them, they were brilliant. Colin Powell would not have known that there was the slightest issue between the two of them.

6.7. The St Andrews Agreement

After the suspension of the devolved institutions in 2002, and the 2003 elections, the British and Irish governments made concerted efforts to restore devolution. Lord

Hain was Secretary of State for Northern Ireland in 2005–7. Bertie Ahern was Taoiseach in 1997–2008.

6.7.1. A British perspective

Q: What were the main problems and what were your tasks and priorities when you became Secretary of State for Northern Ireland?

PETER HAIN: Funny thing is that Tony Blair never said to me, 'I really want you to settle this.' He said, 'You know this is a huge job, and it's at a critical time, but it always is a critical time and I think you're the best person to take it forward,' or words to that effect. There was a real mood of pessimism when I came in because you'd had the failure of the comprehensive negotiations the previous autumn–winter of 2004.[80] You'd had the Northern Bank robbery, which put a sort of dagger through the heart of the whole process.[81] It destabilized the DUP, including Ian Paisley, but also others who had been keen to do the deal at the time. So there was all of that, and then on top of that the general election had seen a very good DUP performance and a very good Sinn Féin performance. The centre had got squeezed; the Ulster Unionist Party and the SDLP had got squeezed very severely.

So what I found was a Northern Ireland Office, which I came to rate very highly—they are probably among the very best civil servants anywhere in Whitehall, and I've worked with some of the top ones as Leader of the Commons, the Cabinet Office, and also the Foreign Office. I thought they were absolutely top notch. But they were very pessimistic. Number 10 was very pessimistic. It was in the doldrums of the process, and the very fact that Paisley's DUP and Adams's Sinn Féin had squeezed the opposition out of sight almost, and it left most people feeling that you were not going to make any progress.

I very quickly came to take exactly the opposite view, partly because of my experience in South Africa. I did give an interview, I think in *The Times*, a few months after getting the job; Philip Webster, the political editor, did it.[82] I think it was the first time I used this analogy; the South African experience was a settlement ultimately between the two most polarized positions. The Afrikaner apartheid rulers that had imprisoned Nelson Mandela and

---

[80] British–Irish attempts to broker a 'comprehensive agreement' between the DUP and Sinn Féin finally broke down in winter 2004 after a set of talks at Leeds Castle ended without agreement. See Subsection 6.7.2.

[81] The Northern Bank robbery of 20 December 2004 involved the theft of £26.5 million in sterling and other currencies from the Donegall Square West branch of Northern Bank in Belfast. The British and Irish authorities claimed that the IRA were responsible.

[82] See Peter Webster, 'Hain Urges Ulster to go a "final mile"', *The Times*, 27 June 2005.

oppressed his people, and virtually eliminated the African National Congress (ANC) at one point, literally physically; it was between the ANC and the Nationalist government that did the deal.

I remember saying it to my officials 'we are going to do this, and I want to do this, and I think we can do this, because you now are in a situation where if you do a deal between Sinn Féin and the DUP it's going to stick, because there isn't really anybody either side of them significant, there are those either side but nobody significant'.

So, I was very optimistic, pretty much from day one, that these were the right conditions to do it, but you needed obviously to do an absolute mountain of work and of negotiation, and there needed to be some pretty seismic changes from both Sinn Féin and the IRA in respect of its military activity, and also, on the other hand, the DUP, to get there.

Q: So did you have a strategy?

PETER HAIN: Well obviously you get into a series of meet and greets and early contact meetings, that was kind of routine. I set out to build a very close personal relationship with Ian Paisley from very early on in 2005, and in 2006 with his son, Ian Junior, and I'll come back to that. That was critically important in the end. The DUP were polite and courteous mostly, but also suspicious of any British Secretary of State. Sinn Féin similarly so, although there was less hostility, curiously.

In my own case I'd known Adams and McGuiness during my Labour Party activity and I'd met them in previous years. I didn't know them very well, but I knew them. They knew that I came at this not from the standpoint of a traditional British Secretary of State; I came at it with a record of anti-apartheid activity, and Sinn Féin were very close to the ANC. They knew I had a record, prior to the Good Friday Agreement, of strong public advocacy of a united Ireland as an objective. They knew that they were not dealing with anybody who was from the traditional mould. So, there was a relatively easy process of building links there, and building a certain amount of trust was relatively easy. We had very severe arguments and fall-outs later on, as is inevitably the case, given the different roles.

But, with the DUP, I thought several things. I thought that I needed to get close to Ian Paisley, as I've said. The DUP, I felt, needed to be made to feel not just that they were top dogs, but that they were being treated as such, that they were being treated properly by the British government. They had had a history of being outsiders. They needed to get themselves into a frame of mind where they were no longer just oppositionists but they were the key actors alongside Sinn Féin, but on the unionist side of the fence. They needed to be made to feel that they were the key actors in moving everything forward and that it wasn't in their interests to keep saying 'no', because somebody would take their place. They had to be the party that said 'yes' on their terms, but did say 'yes'. This was something they'd never been prepared to do before, although you got a sort of a sniff of that in the comprehensive agreement talks process. So I, in a sense, I thought that they had to be given a lot of respect and I said to my team of ministers: 'Whatever the pattern has been in the past, you've got to deal with the leadership of the DUP, Paisley, and Robinson and the others, as if they were equal to ministers.'

Q: Did you think that the DUP wanted a deal?

PETER HAIN: I was very clear that they wanted a deal, but they were absolutely intransigent—and in my view they were right to be—that Sinn Féin had to sign up to policing, that the IRA had to end its war, which of course it did at the end of July 2005. That in itself was an interesting process to be involved in.

By the autumn I remember Ian Paisley asking me whether I'd have some of his 'boys', as he called them, his senior team—they were all 'boys'—to dinner at Hillsborough Castle, to get to know them, which I did. He said, 'some of them are very suspicious of you, Peter,' and he had to leave early, I think to go and preach somewhere. I walked him downstairs, and out to his car and I said to him, as I'd said in one-to-one meetings: 'Well, you've got to be First Minister, at some point.' And he'd always laugh it off and say, 'ah, you know, you're trying to manoeuvre me and manipulate me, and I won't have that'—but in a jocular fashion, it was that kind of banter. This time I said to him: 'How do you think you'll do the job?' And much to my astonishment, and this was autumn 2005, he said: 'Well, I want to do it, Peter, I'm telling you this privately, but I will only want to do it for a relatively short time because then I think my job will have been done, but provided I have set everything right so the country can go forward in peace then I think that will be my job done.'

So, that process continued through the September, to the autumn, the various ups and downs. Around February, March, April 2006, was his eightieth birthday, and I had the idea of inviting him to dinner at Hillsborough Castle with his entire family, in the sort of rather stately dining room there. There were his children, his grandchildren as well, so it was actually quite a nice occasion. But that was the courteous thing to do in any case; it was about building that relationship, and with the others I had built up a very strong, and I think reasonably trusting, relationship with Peter Robinson, and had a lot of one-to-ones with him. I saw Jeffrey Donaldson a bit as well, but I also spoke to some of the others, like Gregory Campbell, David Simpson, and Sammy Wilson, and people like that, who would often have a go at me. Well, that's fine, that's politics, but I wanted them to know that on an individual relationship basis, they were being given the proper respect that they were entitled to, and that they could have a relationship.

Q: Was the leadership constrained by what their constituency was telling them?

PETER HAIN: I don't think the constituency was ready at that time, but I thought it would be in due course, as indeed it was. The DUP, at that stage, and increasingly subsequently, was quite a complex animal, with people like Peter Robinson, Jeffrey Donaldson, and others, who wanted to do the deal. They realized that there was actually a relatively short window for them. Then there were a lot of others, you know, Willie McCrea. He was most fiery about it all.

I thought that Paisley had a kind of uncanny ability to have his finger on the pulse of unionist opinion. He kept saying to me, 'they want me to do it, Peter, the people who are behind me, they're saying, "Big Man we want you to get in there and be there for us."' We got to the point, actually, where Paisley, having been behind in his leadership, leapt in front of it to some extent, even ahead of people like Robinson, and Donaldson, and others who wanted the deal done.

Q: Were you trying to create trust between yourself and the parties as a proxy for the trust that wasn't there between the DUP and Sinn Féin?

PETER HAIN: Well yes, but that had been the role of previous secretaries of state. In this case it was between the DUP and Sinn Féin, so I don't think there is anything particularly new. Everybody understood that you are the conduit both ways, as it were, because they wouldn't talk directly to each other. The other thing that I did was to get them to come to me fairly early on with what they called confidence-building measures, a whole string of things.

Q: You said that you thought that there was a relatively short timeframe?

PETER HAIN: In the early meetings I just said to them both, and particularly to the DUP: 'Look, you've got a series of things converging. Tony Blair has already said he's not going to serve a full term. You have got elections due.' So I said: 'Well, let's deal with Blair first. You've got a prime minister who's given this his personal attention, with Jonathan Powell, who is also very important in all of this, in a way that none of his predecessors had done, and I'm telling you now, his successor is likely to be Gordon Brown, who won't do either. The caravan will move on. If you can't solve this now, you're probably talking about many, many years.' I particularly said this to Ian, because he'd of course had a real health scare. I said: 'You've got a couple of years to do this.' This is what I started saying in 2005.

There was that factor, that the longer the peace held, the less interest there was in Northern Ireland amongst the public, amongst the politicians, amongst the media, outside Northern Ireland, outside Ireland and the island of Ireland, and therefore you needed to maximize your strength. So, those are the main things I said. The other thing I also said, is: 'I don't know how long Bertie Ahern is going to last. There's a general election coming up there. You've got somebody who's gone the extra mile compared with any Taoiseach before him.' So, you've got these series of factors.

Q: So it was time running out?

PETER HAIN: There were two things I did; one was on the domestic policy side of Northern Ireland, which had never been done before, and the other was on the timing. I started to say, around about the autumn of 2005: 'We cannot have elections again to an Assembly that doesn't exist. The people won't wear it.' I started to say that 'I cannot see the justification for politicians continuing to draw their salaries and their allowances when they're not doing their jobs'. This caused huge resentment on Stormont Hill, understandably, and kick-backs against me, but if you're not willing to be tough in these jobs, and stand your ground, then you shouldn't be doing them.

I started to pursue quite radical domestic policy changes, such as banning the 11+ entrance exam for secondary education, pushing ahead with water charges, coming up with what had been an independent recommendation for seven unitary councils, to replace the twenty-six, which was a ridiculous number for the size of Northern Ireland.[83] To introduce water charges, I just said: 'My constituents pay water charges, what's the justification for you not to?' So what you had was a much more, as it were, radical domestic policy, which reflected my own values—doing other things like pushing forward with renewable energy projects and energy efficiency schemes, and free solar panels on the roofs of pensioners on benefit, and things like that. They were all things that I thought could be defended as in the public interest, and reflected what I believed in—in terms of what any sensible government would actually do.

They were also things that were controversial in domestic-policy terms—particularly so in the unionist community. But in some cases they were generally opposed, I mean everybody opposed water charges, who wants water charges? Only Sinn Féin supported the reduction to seven councils from twenty-six, though I didn't do it for that reason, I did it because I thought it was the right thing.[84] I reformed education and health in quite radical ways as well. I kept saying to people: 'Well, the solution to your grievance on this is very simple. I'm not accountable to you. I'm governing in the interest of Northern Ireland, and I'm governing in what I judge to be the best interests of you, the citizens of Northern Ireland. But if you don't like what I'm doing, the remedy is in your hands. Instruct your politicians to start doing their jobs, and get into government and take these decisions themselves.'

Just to cut a long story short, that whole process culminated in the election in February–March of last year.[85] I remember meeting Ian Paisley a couple of weeks into the campaign and chatting to him, I think it was in an Orange Order ceremony—I was the first Secretary of State to be invited to the headquarters—and him saying: 'You know Peter, the public are not interested in all the things I thought they were going to be, they just want us to get you out and get the water charges out with you.' So, that vindicated that approach.

---

[83] The reference is to local government councils; some argued that the existing number of bodies (twenty-six) was too large for Northern Ireland.

[84] The initial proposal to reduce the number of councils to seven was replaced by a reduction to eleven councils. The new system eventually came into operation on 1 April 2015.

[85] A reference to the Assembly election of 7 March 2007.

The other thing I did, I firmly asked Tony Blair and Jonathan Powell to always have me present when they met Adams, McGuiness, and Paisley, because that had not been the case for any of my predecessors. In the key negotiating crisis meetings they were not there. I just said: 'I can't do my job if I'm not there.' There was a bit of initial reluctance and then I did attend all those meetings. Actually, the DUP particularly noticed it. I think that showed them (a) that I was serious about the process, and (b) that Tony Blair had his full trust in me and that he was delegating to me.

Q: Were you making a break with the way secretaries of state had governed Northern Ireland in the past?

PETER HAIN: So yes, in short I did make a break with the past role of the Secretary of State. But I don't want people to think that I did it crudely or gratuitously. I did these things because in the case of water charges, and rates reform, the existing system of local finance was unsustainable. In the case of the 11+ it was more a personal mission. I disagreed with deciding a kid's future on the basis of a couple of hour exams at the age of 11. I was also quite forceful in banning discrimination around sexuality. I made a big hoo-ha around that in 2006–7.

Among the Conservatives, David Liddington was my opposite number, and somebody I had a lot of respect for. He is very diligent, knew his stuff, frequent visitor to Northern Ireland, and so on. So he was a conscientious opponent. But the Tory party in my view, including under Cameron—it didn't funda-mentally change, and it behaved in a disgraceful way. They effectively acted as outriders for the DUP. If you just go look at what they say, they would vigorously nod to everything the DUP did. They had a half-hearted partisan-ship, and they didn't really understand republicanism. I don't think the Tories ever did.

Just on that point you can say, OK, the talks were initiated in Heath's time and contact was maintained under Thatcher, and John Major did start the process that led to the Good Friday Agreement, but the Conservatives didn't fundamentally understand republicanism and its legitimacy in the politics in the island of Ireland, including in Northern Ireland. When I say its legitimacy, it's got a respectable historical heritage there that you cannot ignore. You can't just box it in a corner marked 'terrorists', and this was absolutely and frus-tratingly the case. In the period I was the Secretary of State, the Tories could have actually adopted a much more progressive position. That would have had more of an effect on the DUP moving.

Q: What did you see as the republican strategy?

PETER HAIN: It was very evident to me that Adams and McGuinness wanted to do the deal. But not at a price where they couldn't take their people with them. I always felt when I was talking to Gerry Adams that this is somebody who was well versed in the history of Irish republicanism and knew that if he got out too far ahead of his followers he probably wouldn't stay alive. Similarly with McGuinness, and you know Adams would say things like, 'You know, I don't want my children to go through what we've been through,' and it was almost like a generational thing. This is not an original observation, other people have made this point, but it was pretty evident to me. He came to say this explicitly by 2007, that, if they couldn't achieve it this time, I think he might have passed the baton to somebody else, but I was very clear that he did want the IRA to end its armed campaign, which of course they did. On the question of policing, there was much more ambivalence, because it was actually more difficult in many respects. But I was very clear in my mind that they wanted to do the deal, and that from their point of view time was running out.

Q: Did you need to put pressure on them in the same way that you might have put pressure on the DUP?

PETER HAIN: Well, I was putting pressure on both all the time, but in respect of Sinn Féin I think the biggest pressure I put on them was over policing around the St Andrews process both before it and after it, to the point where Adams and McGuiness came very close to falling out with me, and complaining to No. 10 at one point and threatening not to have anything to do with me. I just said to them: 'Look, if you sign up for policing, and particularly if you sign up for the pledge in the legislation to support the rule of law of policing when you take ministerial office, and as Assembly members, if you sign up to that, I think Paisley will do the deal.'

I was basically pressuring them in a way that the PM wasn't, although he was standing behind me. So things got quite fraught with him towards the end of 2006. I've had a reasonably long experience in politics and as a trade-union official as well as a negotiator, so I know about negotiations. McGuinness and Adams are probably two of the most professional and finest political negotiators I've come across. So they would up the ante when it suited them, they would shout and threaten and so on when it suited them. Not that they were being insincere or false, but they could turn the temperature up or wind it down, as befitted the necessity.

Q: And so the actual agreement at St Andrews, how did you get that?

PETER HAIN: Well, I'll probably tell the story in my own way at some point, probably in my own book.[86] Deadlines had been set but they'd lost credibility. My deadlines, however, were set in legislation, deliberately, so if there hadn't been a broad agreement at St Andrews, I'd have closed Stormont down.

---

[86] See the extended discussion in Hain (2012: 310–53). Some further background detail on the St Andrews agreement is available in Hain (2015: 524–41) and on the DUP–Sinn Féin agreement to form an executive in Hain (2015: 572–6).

I remember Ian [Paisley] saying to me 'You'll really do this?' I said: 'Yes, I will, because there's no point in continuing.'

Q: How did you see the role of the Irish government?

PETER HAIN: I had a tremendous respect for both the Aherns, for Dermot, with whom I formed a very good relationship, and Bertie, whom I thought was tremendously creative.[87] The relationship between Bertie Ahern and Tony Blair was crucial. You could see that at St Andrews whenever we got together, they were as one. I thought that the Irish government officialdom in the foreign-affairs ministry was, on the one hand, admiring of the fact that I was always pushing the boat out, in terms of talking about an Island of Ireland economy, for example. I don't think any Secretary of State had done that beforehand. I don't think they had had that sort of perspective on things, like putting the pressure on the DUP.

So they were a bit worried initially, like my officials were, about my radical domestic reform programme, but then came to see that it was producing results. They were initially worried about the deadlines, and Bertie Ahern was very keen on the deadlines. Officials were a bit worried about it, so I think they had a sort of ambivalent attitude toward me. Sometimes I had to do things which didn't involve all the bureaucratic consultation that their officials would have liked, so I found a bit of resentment there. But I never encountered that from Dermot, and I certainly didn't encounter it from Bertie—he went out of his way personally one-to-one, and also in public, to praise the role that I was performing. I think this came out of the fact that the Good Friday Agreement meant to the officials, for the first time, that London and Dublin were moving together as one, but that meant they had to be bureaucratically consulted and agree on every little move.

To make a final comment, I thought their approach to cross-border relations was too bureaucratic, as was the nationalist community in Northern Ireland. Adams and McGuinness were not, but the others were. You know these cross-border bodies, all fine and dandy, but actually don't amount to a row of beans if all they're doing is the whole process of bureaucratic meetings. The really important things were Tourism Ireland, Rally Ireland, some of the Southern economic links, the cross-border links that were built up between the unionist community and the business community and the business community in the South, which I encouraged. The business community in the North came to see me, because I was pursuing a radical reform programme. They were saying things like 'this economy is not sustainable with the size of the public sector, ahead of the private sector'. I was more interested in that than I was in the cross-border body for whatever.

---

[87] See Ch. 5, n. 24.

6.7.2. An Irish perspective

This extract begins with a discussion of the difficulties of implementing the Good Friday Agreement.

BERTIE AHERN: In fairness to the unionists, they saw an awful lot of things happening on the nationalist or republican side, and they didn't see as much happening on their side. So, I think that's why they were aggrieved, and I suppose that's why we had two or three breakdowns of the executive in the early years, because they said 'well, this is all about the republican agenda, this is about them getting everything, us getting little'.

That didn't make life easy for the unionists, it didn't make life easy for Tony Blair and myself, and that's why we had so many of those meetings in Leeds Castle, and going through the legislation for policing.[88] There was a huge amount of change. David Trimble, who's a good man, was finding that he was under pressure because they still hadn't got decommissioning. So, that put a lot of pressure on him in 2001, 2002, and 2003 as we worked away.

We did a great job, I think, on the Patten Commission and its recommendations for policing reform. We didn't do such a good job on decommissioning. We hadn't satisfied anyone that we had completed it, and all these other things were happening, so it was a difficult period. Then you had the switch of voters away from the SDLP, away from the UUP, towards the DUP and towards Sinn Féin.[89] In the middle of it all, there was a change in the dominant parties, and we had to deal with that, and of course that changed the dynamics quite a lot.

Q: Wasn't it in February 2000 that Mandelson suspended the Assembly, and that looked as if there was a difference between the British and Irish governments?

BERTIE AHERN: We disagreed with that. Brian Cowen and I were dealing with that, with Mandelson and Blair on the other side. We did not accept that they had the right under the Good Friday Agreement to suspend the institutions. That was our position. I know they rushed through legislation as an order through Westminster,[90] but we questioned very vociferously their right to suspend the institutions, and we never did agree on that. We continued that argument for some considerable time. I think from an Irish point of view we finally won that argument. We felt that the way that Mandelson did it was wrong, and it was

---

[88] Ahern and Blair had a series of meetings in an attempt to produce a comprehensive agreement (see Section 6.1 and Subsection 6.7.1); through this period there was also continuous discussion about legislation on policing reform that would follow the Patten recommendations (see Subsections 6.1.1 and 6.4.3).

[89] See Subsection 6.1.2 and Table 6.2.

[90] This refers to the first suspension, in February 2000. Under direct rule, most Northern Ireland legislation has been adopted by order in council rather than by statute, a mechanism that does not ensure very full consideration of measures adopted.

legally incorrect. It wasn't just wrong, it was not in either the legal spirit or within the terms of the Good Friday Agreement.

Q: How did you win it eventually?

BERTIE AHERN: It took time. We didn't win it on that first round because they brought in legislation that permitted them to suspend the Assembly. We continued over many years to say that this isn't something that they can do. The difficulty was that the Good Friday Agreement was an international agreement, a UN-registered agreement, signed by two governments, and here was one government taking ad hoc action without the agreement of the other. And I think, over time, the British government accepted that was wrong. You have seen in recent weeks (October–November 2017) how they have done everything to avoid suspending the institutions. And that is the correct way to do it. Mandelson was a tough-minded guy and he met his match in Brian Cowen. The two of them had some fierce debates over that issue and other issues.

Q: Were there other things that you and Tony Blair disagreed about?

BERTIE AHERN: Tony Blair and I had a great relationship, a great friendship, and we worked together; but there were many issues that we would disagree on. We had a lot of debate about aspects of the whole Patten Commission, and how its report could be dealt with, and how we could get back to half nationalists, half unionists in the police service.[91] That was very difficult to do, but we worked out good compromises, I think. We had long debates about taking down the watchtowers, and getting the military and the security forces off the streets, to demilitarize the situation. We had lots of hard negotiations over that.

Q: I read somewhere that in 2005 you were on the phone practically every week about that?

BERTIE AHERN: It was certainly every week. At this stage there was no violence; maybe a small number of dissidents, but since 1998 the Provisional IRA and the Army Council were holding very solemnly to the ceasefire. But still we had the border crossings, the big military watchtowers, still we had a high degree of militarization.[92] I was adamant that there had to be a reward for honouring the ceasefire, and that reward had to be demilitarization. My view of it was that Tony Blair was not against moving faster, but that the authorities in the UK, including MI5 and MI6, were against doing so. And in the end, Tony Blair, to his credit, went and discussed it directly with the military people and the

---

[91] The recommendation in the report for changing the composition of the police service proposed a policy of ensuring that 50% of new recruits would be Catholic and 50% Protestant and undetermined for a period of at least ten years; see Independent Commission on Policing in Northern Ireland (1999: 88).

[92] The reference is to the British watchtowers and installations that were a particular focus of contention in South Armagh.

chief of staff, the GOC.[93] That is what moved the process on. That was very helpful in bringing an end to the potential violence in South Armagh and East Tyrone and South Derry and places like that—places that were once hotspots, you know.

Q: When Trimble was ousted by the DUP, what did you think at that time?

BERTIE AHERN: I was sorry for him. I think Trimble was very brave. I built up a very good relationship with David Trimble.

Q: Would he have moved faster than Paisley eventually did?

BERTIE AHERN: I think at that time he was moving as fast and as much as he could. He still didn't have decommissioning, and he had several challenges to his leadership. There were regular Saturday morning party conferences with these challenges, and he won most of those votes,[94] but it was tough on him, and within unionism the campaign against him was growing—by the DUP and others. It was undermining him, but he was trying his best, I think, to implement the agreement as best he could.

Now, the institutions had fallen a few times and that didn't help him. Remember, after the Agreement, there was the Omagh bombing,[95] and he went to visit the families of the Catholics that were killed as well as the Protestants and others. I think he was doing his very best to make progress. But he was losing that battle within his own unionist family. I felt sad for him when he was pushed out. It was almost the same time that John Hume and Seamus Mallon of the SDLP were losing support.[96] They had done such a brilliant job down through the years, from the time I was a young guy watching the two of them fight the constitutional nationalist line. So, I was genuinely sorry for Trimble, I'd built up a good relationship with him, a good friendship with him. I understood why he couldn't move quickly.

So then the dynamic changed, and we had to see how we were going to do business with Dr Paisley. I always wanted an inclusive process, and the only one outside by that stage was the DUP. The PUP and the UDP, the Women's Coalition, the Alliance Party, the UUP, Sinn Féin, the SDLP, had all been inside the talks process. The only one we hadn't got inside was the DUP. So I always knew we had to try to work to get Paisley on side. The election took place in 2003, they had a manifesto, and I think Peter Robinson very much influenced that manifesto. We saw issues in the manifesto that we could negotiate on. I came up with the idea that the Good Friday Agreement said that there could be a review: that if the other parties were prepared to have a

---

[93] The General Officer Commanding, Northern Ireland, who headed military forces there.

[94] David Trimble faced a series of challenges to his leadership within the Ulster Unionist Council and the party executive.

[95] See n. 35.

[96] In the 2003 Assembly elections, Sinn Féin overtook the SDLP to become the largest nationalist party; see Table 6.2.

review we could do so, and I nailed down the areas in which I thought we could have a review.

They signed up to that, and we got into a very long process of meetings. Some of them were good, some of them were bad, we were making good progress at Leeds Castle in 2005. That collapsed. It was a pity, because we were making good progress. I think we would have made more progress, but we had to get out at lunchtime on the third day because there was a wedding; if there hadn't been a wedding, we might have been able to continue later, but like all these things we had to end up abruptly. But then we did a lot of preparatory work in the spring and summer of 2006, which led to the St Andrews discussions on 12, 13, and 14 October 2006, and that led to the St Andrews Agreement. It wasn't signed at St Andrews. The two governments agreed the terms at St Andrews, but it took that winter before we got the parties to sign.

Q: So St Andrews was a review of the Good Friday Agreement, it wasn't an alternative to it? Or a replacement of it?

BERTIE AHERN: It was a relatively minor review. It was significant for the DUP, and it was significant insofar as it brought the DUP inside. It may not be fair to say it was minor, but it wasn't by any means a fundamental alteration of the Good Friday Agreement. And as you know, it's not an international agreement in the same sense as the Good Friday Agreement, so it is almost seen as an annex to the Good Friday Agreement.

After 1998, I think the DUP felt isolated; they were the only ones who hadn't been at the talks or signed up to the Good Friday Agreement. That's why they were anxious to get back in. It took them maybe eight years to do so, but I think they realized that, if they wanted to share power and to be involved in going forward and to modernize their party, they had to change their position, and they did that under Peter Robinson. He was politically astute in the way he moved his party from being anti-Good Friday Agreement to coming in. I mean there was that famous time when Paisley came down to protest about the Good Friday Agreement and he was hammered by the loyalists: the loyalists were outside and he had to run out of the place. They realized they were losing ground, though; it took them eight years to get back on side.[97]

Q: In retrospect, if you were doing it again, would you do any of it differently?

BERTIE AHERN: I think negotiating the Agreement was fairly good. We started intense negotiations on 1 September 1997 and we finished them on 10 April 1998, so that was huge in negotiations of that kind. The implementation process was painfully slow. I've talked to people in lots of countries that have been involved in peace processes over the last twenty years, and I've

---

[97]   On the eve of the Agreement, on the night of 9 April 1998, Ian Paisley used his status as a political leader to insist on entry to the talks venue at Castle Buildings, Stormont, but was loudly heckled by loyalists accusing him of having led them into battle before then abandoning them.

said, the more items you include in the settlement the better. The more detail you put onto those items the better, and the more you put realistic timescales onto those provisions, even better again.

Decommissioning turned out to be a nightmare for us. The amount of hours that Tony Blair and I put in to try to bring a resolution to decommissioning was horrendous. If you were doing it again, I think you'd be more prescriptive of how in the name of God you're going to bring decommissioning about, because it caused us and the other parties so much pressure. Sinn Féin, in fairness, if they were here they would say they didn't drag it out, they just couldn't get the IRA to do it until they were happy that other things were done, but I would say that there's give and take in these things and it was too slow, it was done too slowly.

Q: By 2007, would you say that there was parity of esteem in the North?

BERTIE AHERN: Yes. By 2007, we had a new criminal justice bill, we had an equality act, we had the oversight commissioners, we had the ombudsperson, we might not have had the Civic Forum, and that was a pity—the Women's Coalition, Monica McWilliams and the others, had played a great role and they drifted out of the scene, which was a pity because they were very constructive and very helpful all the way through. I think since 2007 you don't hear about problems in the courts in the North, or policing. It's strange that now all the issues about policing are down here.

Q: A bill of rights didn't get agreed. Would that have helped?

BERTIE AHERN: Yes, I think so. And it's still an item to be completed, together with the Civic Forum. Probably a lot of things that would be in the bill of rights are already included in other legislation, but I think it would still be a good thing to do. I always argue for the full implementation of the Agreement. Now, most of the provisions of the Agreement have been implemented, but it's an international agreement, two governments supported it, it got huge support from the public north and south, it got huge support internationally from the European Union and from the UN and all around the world, Kofi Annan used it as a beacon for hope in other places. So I always think that everything in it should be implemented, including the bill of rights.

Documents

Document 6.1. Texts of Agreements, Treaties, and Legislation

- Agreement reached in the multi-party talks (Good Friday Agreement) (10 April 1998), <https://peacemaker.un.org/uk-ireland-good-friday98> (accessed 19 May 2019).
- Agreement between the United Kingdom of Great Britain and Northern Ireland and Ireland establishing a North/South Ministerial Council (8 March 1999), <https://peacemaker.un.org/uk-ireland-ministerial-council99> (accessed 19 May 2019).

- Agreement between the United Kingdom of Great Britain and Northern Ireland and the Government of Ireland Establishing Implementation Bodies (8 March 1999), <https://peacemaker.un.org/uk-ireland-implementation-bodies98> (accessed 19 May 2019).
- Agreement between the Government of the United Kingdom of Great Britain and Northern Ireland and the Government of Ireland establishing a British-Irish Council (8 March 1999), <https://peacemaker.un.org/uk-ireland-council99> (accessed 19 May 2019).
- Agreement between the British and Irish Governments [on establishment of Independent Monitoring Body] (1 April 2003), <https://peacemaker.un.org/uk-ireland-agreement2003> (accessed 19 May 2019).
- Agreement at St Andrews (13 October 2006), <https://peacemaker.un.org/unitedkingdom-ireland-standrews2006> (accessed 19 May 2019).
- Hillsborough Castle Agreement (5 February 2010), <https://www.gov.uk/government/publications/hillsborough-castle-agreement> (accessed 19 May 2019).
- Stormont House Agreement (23 December 2014), <https://www.gov.uk/government/publications/the-stormont-house-agreement> (accessed 19 May 2019).
- A Fresh Start for Northern Ireland (Fresh Start Agreement, 17 November 2015), <https://www.gov.uk/government/news/a-fresh-start-for-northern-ireland> (accessed 19 May 2019).
- Northern Ireland Act, 1998 c. 47 (19 November 1998), <https://www.legislation.gov.uk/ukpga/1998/47/contents/enacted> (accessed 19 May 2019).
- Northern Ireland (St Andrews Agreement) Act, 2006 c. 53 (22 November 2006), <https://www.legislation.gov.uk/ukpga/2006/53/contents> (accessed 19 May 2019).
- British-Irish Agreement Act (no. 1 of 1999) (22 March 1999), <http://www.irishstatutebook.ie/eli/1999/act/1/enacted/en/html> (accessed 19 May 2019) [see also amending acts: no. 16 of 1999, no. 32 of 2006 and others on the Irish side].

7

Conclusion: Benchmarks from the British–Irish Process

7.1. Introduction

This book has shown how the British and Irish governments opened a path to peace and settlement in Northern Ireland. While the Good Friday Agreement represented the high point in this process, it had been prefigured by an earlier series of negotiations and agreements, and it was by no means the last word. In earlier chapters, senior British and Irish civil servants and politicians have described how they negotiated successive agreements, and why they did so—their proximate goals, their assumptions, and their constraints. We have outlined the political, economic, and institutional context in which they worked, the radically different contexts and political interests of successive governments in the United Kingdom and the Republic of Ireland, the conflicting objectives and interpretations of the parties in Northern Ireland, and the impact of successive British–Irish negotiations and agreements on political relations in Northern Ireland. We have also provided additional documentation to aid in the understanding and assessment of the different perspectives.

What patterns can be discerned in the process? This chapter explores the significance of the evidence presented and the processes discussed in previous chapters. We ask three general questions. What were the achievements in the period that led from Sunningdale to St Andrews? How were agreements reached, put in place, and sustained? To what extent have the agreed institutions in Northern Ireland proven resilient to new and unexpected shocks? Bringing the story up to 2019 allows us to distinguish the lasting achievements from apparent failures (such as commitments that were made but never implemented) and from more ephemeral successes (such as arrangements that were later reversed). It lets us test the robustness of these achievements and to assess the stress points at which they are vulnerable. This in turn highlights the significance of the British–Irish process for the understanding of negotiated agreements more generally, and the lessons it offers about the manner in which such agreements may be reached and about the determinants of their durability.

This concluding chapter, then, benchmarks the partial successes of the sequence of British–Irish negotiations. Our aim is to provide a provisional audit of the achievements of the process as it was outlined in earlier chapters, and of the principles and policy paradigms that underpinned it. We examine the extent to

Negotiating a Settlement in Northern Ireland, 1969–2019.
John Coakley and Jennifer Todd, Oxford University Press (2020). © John Coakley and Jennifer Todd.
DOI: 10.1093/oso/9780198841388.001.0001

which these were institutionally embedded in such a way as to shape future relations, or were instead products of passing conjunctures. We build on the evidence of the earlier chapters, while reframing it in more general concepts, so as to allow it to inform wider comparative and theoretical debates, and to let these in turn inform assessments of past policy.

We address three broad questions in the three sections that follow. The first has to do with the mechanisms that facilitated agreement and affected its impact in Northern Ireland: shifts in British and Irish policy and in its implementation, a redefinition of the relationship between the British and Irish governments, and the restoration of a functioning political system in Northern Ireland. We also note the stress points in this system. The impact of Brexit on these points of tension was to lead to a partial unravelling of the settlement.

The second question concerns the significance of the British–Irish negotiations and agreements for wider scholarly debates on the mechanisms of conflict-management and peace-building. We focus on the ways in which conflicts over sovereignty, democracy, and inequality were resolved (at least partially) and the extent to which the changes that followed were securely embedded. We explore the degree to which incremental reform led to a lasting transformation of political relations.

Third, we seek to draw policy lessons from the process. We assess the achievements of the British–Irish engagement and discuss the wider lessons that emerge from it for peace processes more generally. To what extent, we ask, might the Irish peace process provide a model for the future in other divided societies or trans-frontier conflicts?

7.2. Processes and Patterns of British and Irish Engagement

The contrast between Northern Ireland in the 1960s and half a century later in 2019 could hardly be starker. At the beginning of the 1960s, Northern Ireland was isolated from its relatively poor southern neighbour. Edward Heath was struck by the contrast when he crossed the Irish border: in the South, 'the countryside was simpler and less cultivated, the houses smaller and more dated, the roads narrower and far less modern'.[1] At this time, and into the late 1960s, Northern Ireland appeared to be more firmly embedded than ever within the structures of the British state, notwithstanding periodic expressions of dissent from its Catholic minority, the first civil-rights protests, and occasional outbursts by politicians in the Republic, whose constitution defined Northern Ireland as part of its own

---

[1] Heath (1998: 420) recalled being smuggled across the border into Donegal in 1960 covered by a blanket in the back seat of a car. At the time he was an MP and a senior politician, but not yet leader of the Conservative Party (1965–75) or prime minister (1970–4).

national territory. Within Northern Ireland, a majoritarian system of devolved government with relatively autonomous policymaking, lightly regulated and generously funded by the British government, sustained a deeply unequal and divided society. British policymakers seemed incapable of tackling problems of uneven access to resources, including unionist monopoly of political power and dominance in public culture, serious intercommunal inequality in every sector of the economy, discriminatory practices in the allocation of public-sector housing, and rampant bias in the make-up and behaviour of the security forces. Neither the British nor the Irish government had any realistic strategy to tackle the problems; there was limited communication between them; and intergovernmental policy convergence was entirely lacking. Both governments, in Noel Dorr's words, reacted to the outbreak of conflict 'in an outdated way'.[2]

By 2019, a set of fundamental changes had taken place. Economically, the Republic was now the more prosperous part of the island; thanks to shared membership of the European Union, the border was now almost invisible. Within Northern Ireland, all major parties had agreed to a power-sharing settlement; a new constitutional agreement appeared to satisfy nationalists in both parts of the island as well as unionists in Northern Ireland; significant economic reforms and an overhaul of the security forces and of the criminal justice system had been undertaken; and communal inequality in employment and housing had been substantially eliminated. The British and Irish governments had engaged in over two decades of closely cooperative conflict management and peace-building, developing imaginative constitutional and institutional mechanisms to achieve agreement in Northern Ireland. From the 1990s to the 2010s, communication between the two governments was immediate, and relations were close.

How did this happen? In this section we review the major mechanisms that facilitated change. We look in turn at the changing policy paradigms in Ireland and the United Kingdom, the pattern of British–Irish convergence and its contribution to ultimate agreement, and the quest to institutionalize a new, more inclusive political order in Northern Ireland. We also review the countervailing tendencies and pressure points in these arrangements and analyse the ways in which the British decision to leave the EU has placed increasing strain on this new political order.

7.2.1. Changing Policy Paradigms

In the half century since civil unrest began in Northern Ireland, the goals and practices of British and Irish governments in respect of the region have changed significantly. Political leaders—successive prime ministers and taoisigh—determined

---

[2] See Subsection 2.2.3.

the broad goals of policy, and their civil servants prepared the ground for negoti-ations, narrowed the options for political choice, and invented frameworks and formulations through which otherwise incompatible British and Irish views could be accommodated. In this way, they participated in changing the policy framework or paradigm, which, following Hall (1993: 279), we understand as 'a framework of ideas and standards that specifies not only the goals of policy and kind of instru-ments that can be used to attain them, but also the very nature of the problems they are meant to be addressing'. We trace here changes in the manner in which British and Irish elites understood the processes, and their assessments of how the Northern Ireland conflict could and should be managed, focusing on the exhaustion of old strategies and the gradual forging of a shared British–Irish approach in the mid-1980s.

At the start, neither the British nor the Irish governments had articulated any clear policy paradigm. For the British government, Northern Ireland was its jurisdiction, part of its sovereign territory in which the Irish government had no role; equally, until the civil-rights crisis, the British parliament itself had in effect surrendered any role in the internal affairs of Northern Ireland. If it had a policy paradigm, it was to leave well enough alone. Nor was the Irish government initially clear on what it could or should accomplish. If it had a policy paradigm, it was one of modernization: contact between economically modernizing taoiseach, Sean Lemass, and economically modernizing prime minister of Northern Ireland, Terence O'Neill, would gradually bring change.

In the early 1970s, faced with conflict in Northern Ireland and few practical options for tackling the problems it posed, politicians and civil servants in the Republic of Ireland began to work out new policy paradigms based on an incremental path towards greater North–South integration and possible future Irish unity. This process of policy formation and reformulation was institutionally embedded. The Anglo-Irish division in the Department of Foreign Affairs was created at this time (see Appendix 1.3) and was later to become a key locus of policy thinking. At the same time, Dermot Nally provided policy continuity on British–Irish and Northern Irish affairs in the Department of the Taoiseach for well over twenty years, and a Northern Ireland Division was created there too (see Appendix 1.4). These developments for the first time allowed for the definition of viable proximate policy goals. In the early 1970s, the Irish government was strongly in favour of power-sharing and an 'Irish dimension'; by the early 1980s, its focus had turned to reform of the security services and of their operating procedures, and to the need for Irish government input into Northern Ireland; and, by the 1990s, it participated in the planning of a new constitutional settle-ment that incorporated all of these elements, and more.

The evolution of Irish government policy was shaped by interaction with the SDLP (in particular with John Hume) and by close collaboration between civil-service departments and political leaders. In the early period—in the 1970s—civil servants drafted the speeches which defined policy. In the witness seminars, the Irish participants emphasized the evolution of policy, starting with initial layers (the 'Irish dimension' and power-sharing), to which were later added new ones, which in turn led to the further development of the original layers.[3] The early 1970s saw the initiation of what would become a familiar two-pronged strategy: to achieve nationalist inclusion in government in Northern Ireland and an 'Irish dimension'. The latter was understood both as a symbolic resource for nationalists and as an institutional layer—a Council of Ireland—that could promote North–South integration and at some indefinite future stage evolve into an all-Ireland locus of policymaking. The limits within which the Irish government had to work were clarified by government-commissioned studies on the capacity of the defence forces to cope with violence spilling over from the North. These showed conclusively that loyalist mobilization against Irish unity, should it occur, would overwhelm the military and security capacity of the state.[4] For this reason, Irish government policy immediately after the fall of Sunningdale in 1974 was supportive of the continued British presence in Northern Ireland, for only the British state had the security strength to prevent full-blown civil war. The Irish government, like the SDLP, emphasized the need for security-force reform from an early stage, but only very slowly added an emphasis on economic inequality—although by the 1990s its policy incorporated a stronger emphasis on equality and rights.

Politically, the Irish strategy from the early 1970s to the late 1980s was to strengthen moderate nationalists in the SDLP while marginalizing militant republicans—'seeing off the streets'.[5] In the 1980s, against a background of electoral gains by Sinn Féin, the government adopted an Anglo-Irish focus as the way to achieve its aims. This strategy rested on the assumption that peace and stability would come about when it was proven that moderate, peaceful strategies could bring significant change in Northern Ireland. This new focus was only partly successful; although significant advances were made in the area of equality, there were clear limits to the extent of advance in other areas, especially that of policing and security.[6] By the 1990s, a new framework of understanding had emerged within the Irish government. This rested on a conviction that a lasting settlement would come about only with the end of violence and the incorporation of republicans in democratic politics. Irish negotiators thus increasingly argued for a formula for including republicans in negotiations and in power-sharing government. Their aim became one of ending republican violence by creating an inclusive polity in Northern Ireland, one where unionists would no longer have a veto either on internal change or on the engagement of the Irish government in Northern Ireland, and where a peaceful path to Irish unity became a realistic option.

---

[3] See Subsections 2.4.2 and 3.6.2.   [4] See Subsection 2.4.2.
[5] See Subsection 4.2.2.   [6] See Subsection 3.5.2.

British policy paradigms evolved in a different manner. As conflict escalated, and as it became impossible to restore order under a reformed unionist government, British direct rule was instituted in 1972. At this point, the primary aim of the British government was to restore devolution in Northern Ireland, but now with a measure of power-sharing, while containing violence. But in effect the British government also underwrote a society of gross inequality on the basis of religion and nationality (Smith and Chambers 1991). Successive governments were slow to recognize the extent of inter-communal inequality in Northern Ireland, its capacity to aggravate conflict, and their own role in reproducing this inequality. In the 1970s, British security practices disproportionately targeted nationalists rather than unionists (Ní Aoláin 2000: 72–134). State bias occurred by default as much as by intent. In 1974, for example, the newly formed Labour government assumed that Sunningdale was doomed because of unionist dissatisfaction, but its own resulting inaction helped to translate this dissatisfaction into support for armed loyalist mobilization (Craig 2010: 176–80). The prime minister, Harold Wilson, was willing to consider withdrawal from Northern Ireland, but unwilling to consider restructuring society there to make possible social relations that did not involve domination by one community.

Policy paradigms changed through the evident inefficacy—indeed exhaustion—of the old policies. Through the 1970s, successive British governments continued to defend the existing social order and to toughen security policy, while intermittently calling for a new devolved settlement. This proved incapable of stopping the violence, or even reducing its intensity; it brought no progress on power-sharing, and political support for Sinn Féin rose. In the 1980s, senior British and Irish officials, with the general support of Margaret Thatcher and Garret FitzGerald, began to formulate a new approach that emphasized the British–Irish axis as key to conflict management.[7] For the Irish, this would allow the creation of a society more acceptable to nationalists by institutionalizing enforceable principles of equality and inclusiveness. Importantly, it would also be impossible for unionists and loyalists to veto this, as they had done in 1974. For the British, it promised an enhancement of security force successes. The Anglo-Irish Agreement of 1985 superimposed a new institution onto the existing state institutions—an Anglo-Irish Intergovernmental Conference that promised an influential role to the Irish government in the internal affairs of Northern Ireland. This created new incentives for unionists to negotiate and led to an acceleration of the reform programme, particularly in the economy. It also resulted in some restrictions on Orange marches through Catholic areas.

As the witness seminar on the Anglo-Irish Agreement details, however, reform of security was much slower.[8] This was not simply a function of the ongoing

---

[7] See Chapter 3.   [8] See Subsection 3.5.2.

violence and the technical needs of the security forces: senior British civil servants acknowledged the need for reform. Margaret Thatcher, however, was unwilling to overrule the security establishment, or even to appear to do so. This may have reflected a British interest in keeping bargaining counters available if and when the republicans became ready for a peaceful path, but if so our participants did not mention it. The 'frustration' of both British and Irish elites at the slow pace of progress within the framework of the Anglo-Irish Agreement was clear. This led to further change in goals and paradigms in the 1990s, in the quest for an inclusive and far-reaching constitutional settlement: in Quentin Thomas's words 'you can't see off the street; the street has to be co-opted', with a 'comprehensive cast-list' and a 'comprehensive agenda'.[9] Increasingly, the changing policy paradigms took place in the context of intergovernmental negotiations, which radically increased in intensity in the 1990s.

A major outcome of these negotiations was the creation of a set of principles, ground rules, and institutions designed to resolve conflicts over sovereignty, democracy, and inequality that could win multi-party acceptance in Northern Ireland. These came to inform British and Irish policymaking and institution-building in Northern Ireland, although they were only partially legally articulated and embedded, and the governments—and particularly the British—sometimes fell back to the earlier drive for political inclusion, to the detriment of this new, broader set of provisions. This, as we will see, became particularly problematic in the 2010s.

To conclude, it is clear that British and Irish policy paradigms evolved and changed in the light of new circumstances, constraints, and opportunities. It is also clear that agreement in Northern Ireland required the new general paradigm of political inclusion to be articulated and translated into a set of principles and institutional provisions which could achieve such inclusion; this was done in a set of agreements from 1993 to 2006.

7.2.2. British–Irish Convergence

British–Irish negotiations were initially rather narrow in range. The two states worked on the basis of very different assumptions, principles, and aims, and their relationship was highly asymmetrical in respect of power and influence on policy. The formal positions of the two sides—defending the union and securing Irish unity—were quickly supplemented, and eventually replaced, by less ambitious short-term policy goals. State perspectives gradually began to converge, first in the aims of ameliorating and reforming rather than resolving or transforming

[9] See Subsection 4.2.2.

the issues in conflict. But initial British–Irish policy convergence in restoring devolution, this time with power-sharing and a 'Council of Ireland' agreed at the Sunningdale conference of December 1973, was short-lived. The British refusal to confront the UWC strikers who sought to bring down the Sunningdale Agreement, and the Labour government's later security policy, were seen by the Irish government as deeply problematic and conflict-generating. The sole convergence was on the need for the British to remain in Northern Ireland. Even this, though, was briefly challenged in late 1974 when Harold Wilson contemplated a British withdrawal from Northern Ireland, a reversal that ironically saw the British and Irish sides temporarily swapping policy positions.

By the early 1980s, however, the Irish government saw an opportunity for a new joint approach to conflict management and the British were open to engagement. Senior civil servants in the two states were at the heart of the British–Irish negotiation process, and in the 1980s they came to see this as a collaborative problem-solving exercise. They drafted the Anglo-Irish Agreement of 1985, which facilitated British–Irish co-management of the conflict, despite opposing British and Irish constitutional views. The Anglo-Irish Intergovernmental Conference created by the Agreement was not an executive body, for that would have conflicted with Margaret Thatcher's strong notion of British sovereignty. But it was not merely consultative either, for that would have offered the Irish government insufficient influence over the shape of reforms designed to ameliorate the conditions of nationalists, and an insufficiently robust role for the Irish government would not create sufficient incentives for the parties—and especially the unionists—to negotiate. Thus the Conference was defined by both governments as 'more than consultative but less than executive'; a key provision, article 2 (b), stated that 'determined efforts shall be made through the Conference to resolve any differences' (see Documents 3.5 and 3.6).

The Anglo-Irish Agreement relied on the political will of the two governments to allow it to work. That political will was, however, limited, particularly in matters of security, where the British did not implement agreed reforms. After several years of stalemate, frustration on both sides, reinforced by a perception that republican strategies were changing, led to the development of a new intergovernmental approach that aimed to reach an inclusive settlement.[10] This was driven forward by prime ministers Major and Reynolds, and later Ahern and Blair. It generated intense activity in the 1990s among a wide range of British and Irish civil servants and advisors, who attest to its value in learning about 'the mindsets and the constraints under which the other side operated' and—for the British—in learning about 'nationalist sensitivities'.[11] There were limits to convergence,

---

[10] See Subsection 4.2.2.   [11] See Subsections 4.6.1 and 4.6.2.

but the negotiating teams and political leaders were able to find small windows where principled disagreements could be bypassed.

One important illustration of the success of this mode of negotiation was the process by which the text of the Downing Street Declaration was agreed in 1993. The British insisted only on the 'principle of consent' to constitutional change, while the Irish emphasized the need for the British to incentivize unionist acceptance and republican engagement.[12] In the context of ongoing multi-party talks, proxy and direct contacts with the IRA, and talks between John Hume and Gerry Adams, the British and Irish teams sketched a constitutional and institutional framework that would permit multi-party agreement *and* peace in Northern Ireland.[13] This in turn led to ceasefires by the paramilitaries and engagement by a very wide range of Northern Ireland parties. The Framework Documents of 1995, intended as a blueprint for new institutions that would secure wide agreement, spelled out some of the implications of the Declaration.

The Good Friday Agreement of 1998 elaborated ideas and provisions already sketched in the Downing Street Declaration and Framework Documents. The civil servants of the two states, in the name of their governments, collaborated in producing the successive drafts of the text in light of their assessments of what the parties could accept. The parties negotiated on the drafts of agreement already set out by the governments. Close engagement by Prime Minister Tony Blair and Taoiseach Bertie Ahern pushed the process to agreement, in particular in the tense final days. Ambiguities and gaps (whether intentional or inadvertent) remained in the text, and unofficial promises by the leaders were necessary to broker agreement.[14]

British–Irish cooperation continued in the process of implementing the Good Friday Agreement. In some sectors—the most obvious being the British–Irish Intergovernmental Conference that replaced the Anglo-Irish Intergovernmental Conference—that cooperation was fully institutionalized. In others, it was formalized, but the British and Irish governments were just two of several sitting around the same table (as in the case of the British–Irish Council), or the role of the British government was reduced to that of offering benevolent support, especially during times of crisis (as in the case of the North/South Ministerial Council). Most important of all for concerted policy, collaboration took place informally through meetings and telephone calls between taoiseach and prime minister, and—after the fall of the first power-sharing executive in 2002—in a range of more-or-less coordinated strategic actions designed to incentivize agreement between the parties.[15]

This significant enhancement in British–Irish cooperation and the distinct improvement in inter-state relations in turn increased policy impact. If, in the

[12] See Subsection 4.6.2.   [13] See Subsection 5.2.1.
[14] See Subsection 5.3.2.   [15] See Subsection 6.7.2.

1970s, British–Irish cooperation was uncertain and this hampered peace-building, after 1985 the co-management of conflict provided a coherence and focus in efforts at settlement, and this was augmented in the 1990s. This prevented internal Northern Irish conflicts from being magnified into British–Irish ones, and it meant that each state was able to put pressure on its 'own' client groups in Northern Ireland. The Irish government's new role after 1985 ushered in a period of much greater British sensitivity to the needs of the nationalist population. Public policy became considerably more egalitarian and began to undo long-term economic and, to a lesser extent, cultural inequalities and to create a more open and equal arena for political interaction in Northern Ireland. As Northern Ireland unionists and republicans began to contemplate a more comprehensive settlement, British–Irish conflict management took on new efficacy. As two of the prime ministers who contributed to this book noted, close intergovernmental relations allowed for more focused negotiations and more concerted policy outcomes.[16] Through the 1990s this British–Irish collaboration increasingly created trans-border links and institutions, and provided a dual focus of loyalty for the people of Northern Ireland. Thus it blurred or bypassed what appeared to be incompatible constitutional standpoints. New links across the Irish border and across the Irish Sea, more clear-cut and extensive definition of rights, and harmonized equality legislation, all provided for in the Good Friday Agreement, made any future constitutional choice much less momentous in its consequences than it had previously been.

Even at its most effective, however, British–Irish intergovernmental cooperation did not so much resolve as sidestep the issues in dispute between the governments and the parties. Even after 1998, its efficacy depended on political will. This facilitated very effective cooperation between the two governments in the run-up to the St Andrews Agreement in 2006. But the force of British–Irish agreements tended to vary with wider British interests. The asymmetry of power between the Irish and British states, the impossibility of effective international enforcement even of formal British–Irish agreements, and the lack of any written British constitution meant that the Irish government had to rely on personal relationships and persuasion where conflicts existed. The excellent relations between Major and Reynolds and between Blair and Ahern provided a quick and effective channel for tackling any difficulties that arose. But these good relations were products of common goals and projects as well as of temperamental compatibility. Indeed, reliance on such informal networks had an unintended consequence: it led to a de-institutionalizing of British–Irish cooperation. The British–Irish Intergovernmental Conference was seen as more cumbersome than direct communication, and it stopped meeting altogether in 2007 once the

---

[16] See Subsections 5.2.1 and 5.2.2.

devolved institutions began to function again. This was to have major consequences when relations and policy convergence later deteriorated.[17]

7.2.3. Building an Agreed Northern Ireland

The Good Friday Agreement sketched provisions and principles that appeared to resolve long-standing conflicts over sovereignty, democracy, and inequality. These were accepted and confirmed in simultaneous referenda North and South, starting a phase of institution-building in the North, and confirming constitutional change in the South. In Northern Ireland, the civil service was reorganized to reflect the increased responsibilities devolved to this executive, and departmental responsibilities were reorganized to match an enlarged and more inclusive team of ministers.[18] Six North–South 'implementation bodies' under the auspices of the North/South Ministerial Council were created. Strong equality and rights provisions were introduced. The police service was radically reformed and renamed and the criminal justice system was overhauled, but it took longer to resolve the remaining sensitive areas of security. Although the IRA had completed the process of decommissioning its weapons by 2005 and Sinn Féin had agreed fully to endorse the police service in the St Andrews Agreement of 2006, it was not until the Hillsborough Castle Agreement of 2010 that policing and justice powers were devolved.

Each phase of implementation was highly contested by the parties in Northern Ireland. By the St Andrews Agreement of 2006 many of the issues in dispute had been addressed, if not fully resolved.[19]

- The *constitutional dispute* between the British and Irish governments had been settled in a way that was broadly acceptable to the Northern Ireland parties. The Irish state, and all the main nationalist parties, recognized that Northern Ireland would remain part of the United Kingdom for as long as this was the will of a majority in Northern Ireland, and most Catholics were prepared to accept this.[20] The British committed to facilitate constitutional change to a united Ireland should this become the will of a majority in Northern Ireland. Meanwhile, the full legitimacy of nationalist aspirations for a united Ireland (to be achieved democratically) was accepted. But, while

---

[17] When the British Irish Intergovernmental Conference eventually met again in 2018, it was in the context of the collapse of the devolved institutions in Northern Ireland and deterioration in British–Irish relations in the course of the Brexit negotiations.

[18] See Subsection 6.2.2.   [19] See Subsection 1.2.5.

[20] A significant minority of Catholics had always reported in attitude surveys that they supported remaining in the United Kingdom as a long-term policy. However, after 2007 (when the option of devolution in Northern Ireland under the Good Friday Agreement was added), a plurality of Catholics positively preferred the Union (either direct rule or devolution); see <www.ark.ac.uk/nilt/> (accessed 19 May 2019).

this defined the mechanisms for determining which state would exercise sovereignty over Northern Ireland, the implications of state sovereignty remained unresolved. The settlement did not articulate clearly the constraints on state power in relation to Northern Ireland, the strength of the voice given to the Irish government in influencing how this was exercised, or the manner in which this would be marked symbolically in public culture (for example, in the display of flags).

• The *legitimacy of power-sharing government* in Northern Ireland was very widely accepted, and almost universally so among Catholics and nationalists, who had refused to recognize the legitimacy of Northern Ireland governments in the past.[21] The difficulties of agreeing policy within the power-sharing executive remained very challenging, however.

• *Discrimination and gross intercommunal inequality* had successfully been tackled in the economy, in political life and in the security sphere, thanks to a reform programme driven by the British government from 1989 onwards. There was now public recognition of the legitimacy of nationalist aims and more acceptance of the public expression of Irish culture and symbols, but unionists strongly resisted full cultural equality between nationalism and unionism. No bill of rights for Northern Ireland which might have defined the principle of 'parity of esteem' had been accepted.[22]

Meanwhile, the security problems had largely been overcome by the decommissioning of paramilitary weapons, the removal of British military installations from the border area and reduction in troop levels, and reform of the police. Remaining security dangers—the continuing existence of dissident republicans, and the persistence of loyalist organizations—could realistically be seen as marginal in the early twenty-first century. Most attention had for long been given to republican weapons and violence, while loyalist violence was generally assumed to be a reaction to this.[23] This assumption would be tested in the 2010s.

The implementation of the provisions of the Agreement was far from complete, and in some respects it was clearly reversible. The Civic Forum, intended to give civil society a voice in politics, was quickly sidelined by the parties in the Assembly and has not met since 2002. The proposed North–South parliamentary forum came into existence only in 2012, and then as a looser 'parliamentary association'. The proposed North–South consultative forum never came into existence.

---

[21] The Northern Ireland Life and Times Survey showed that in 2003 92% of Catholics and 78% of Protestants agreed that 'any Northern Ireland government should have to ensure that Protestants and Catholics share power'; see <www.ark.ac.uk/nilt/> (accessed 19 May 2019).

[22] Such a bill of rights had been foreseen in the Good Friday Agreement ('Rights Safeguards and Equality of Opportunity', paras 4, 5) as one of the tasks for consideration by the new Northern Ireland Human Rights Commission. However, while 'parity of esteem' was understood as involving equality of respect and recognition for nationalists and unionists, this was never codified.

[23] See Subsection 4.5.5.

As already mentioned, the British–Irish Intergovernmental Conference disappeared altogether from view for eleven years. The planned bill of rights never appeared. Unresolved issues remain in the area of cultural equality and in respect of certain legacy issues (see Chapter 6). But other provisions were more deeply embedded: equality, security, and justice provisions were institutionalized and came to define practice in these fields, shaping social relations in ways that would be hard to undo.

As all significant parties and their supporters came to accept the Agreement, their positions softened (Mitchell, Evans, and O'Leary 2009). The St Andrews Agreement brought the once-militant parties, the DUP and Sinn Féin, into power-sharing government in 2007, with Revd Dr Ian Paisley of the DUP and Martin McGuinness of Sinn Féin as First Minister and Deputy First Minister respectively. Thus it appeared that a final political hurdle had been overcome: the DUP had now accepted the set of institutions agreed in 1998 and slightly amended in 2006. The last piece of the jigsaw seemed to have been put in place by the Hillsborough Castle Agreement in 2010 with the devolution of responsibility for policing and justice to the Northern Ireland executive.

7.2.4. Stability and Stress

The formation of the new devolved power-sharing executive in May 2007 appeared to signal the emergence of 'normal' politics. The new system seemed sufficiently robust to survive leadership change and political challenge: in June 2008 Ian Paisley was replaced by Peter Robinson as leader of the DUP and as First Minister.[24] The Assembly's functioning—for example, in its capacity to question the executive—appeared healthy (Conley 2013; Wilford 2010). Political elites seemed to be adapting to new, more consensual modes of conducting their business, both in the Assembly and at local government level in Belfast city council (O'Connor 2013). This apparent 'normalization' extended to the British–Irish relationship, where the governments appeared to have entered a new phase of amicable cooperation by the 2010s. This was reflected in Queen Elizabeth's state visit to the Republic of Ireland in 2011 (the first-ever visit of the monarch to independent Ireland), and the reciprocal state visit to the UK by President Higgins in 2014. To some degree, these positive developments disguised the fragile character of the Northern Ireland settlement; effective cooperation within the power-sharing government depended on continued British–Irish insistence on the provisions of the Agreement, and was sustained only by a new British financial package.

---

[24] There had been tensions within his party over Paisley's allegedly too amicable relationship with the Deputy First Minister, Martin McGuinness, but the changeover took place with little fuss.

Subsequent developments exposed the vulnerability of the new institutions and their reliance on the British–Irish axis. Shifts in this axis were already taking place. The challenges of the Irish economic crisis of 2008–11, together with rotation of governments in London and Dublin, brought in new prime ministers with different priorities who had no strong commitment to the Blair–Ahern project: David Cameron took over as head of a new Conservative-led government in 2010, and Enda Kenny took charge of a Fine Gael-led coalition in 2011. The Irish government was preoccupied with the aftershock of the economic crash of 2008. Cameron's view from the start of his premiership was that the peace process was over, and that it was time for normal government in Northern Ireland. In 2012, the two prime ministers announced a new phase of British–Irish cooperation, focusing now on the direct British–Irish relationship rather than on Northern Ireland (Coakley 2014: 81–2). Cameron in particular was averse to any further intervention to broker agreement between the Northern parties. In response to the new language and practice in London and Dublin, underlying conflicts came to the fore in Northern Ireland (Todd 2017). Once British–Irish support had been removed, the power-sharing government survived, but there was policy stasis. This was illustrated by the impact of the 'flag protest' movement of 2012–13.[25] Popular unionist mobilization and resultant tension led to an escalation in conflict between the DUP and the nationalist parties and increasing paralysis of power-sharing government from 2013.

The British and Irish governments were slow to intervene to manage these problems, seeing this as a matter for the parties themselves. A process of institutional drift ensued, with British–Irish inaction encouraging internal unionist criticism of the direction of policy, and making the institutions increasingly vulnerable to crisis. The collapse of the executive was avoided by an agreement reached at Stormont House in December 2014, which provided, *inter alia*, for a commission on cultural issues and an oral archive of the 'troubles'. Neither this, nor a later 'Fresh Start' agreement in November 2015, which reiterated it, restored any momentum to the executive. Arlene Foster took over from Peter Robinson as First Minister in January 2016, and, following continuing conflicts over symbolic issues and 'the past', and over a corruption scandal about a mismanaged clean energy scheme, the power-sharing government collapsed in January 2017.

Ongoing tensions within Northern Ireland were exacerbated by the shock of Brexit. Although the Brexit proposal was narrowly supported in the United

---

[25] Belfast City Hall had for long displayed the Union Jack every day, but the non-unionist majority in the council resolved that the flag would be flown only on fifteen 'designated' days annually. This resulted in a popular unionist protest, which at its height won the support of almost half of all Protestants (Nolan et al. 2014). The agreed days are officially designated as ones on which the Union Jack should be displayed on government buildings throughout the United Kingdom, and include eight royal birthdays, three other royal commemorative events, Commonwealth Day, Europe Day, and Remembrance Sunday, and, uniquely in Northern Ireland, St Patrick's Day; see Suchenia (2013: 12).

Kingdom (by 52 per cent to 48 per cent), this balance was reversed in Northern Ireland, where 44 per cent voted in favour of leaving and 56 per cent against. Voting patterns broke down largely along traditional communal and partisan lines. Opinion polls showed that the 'remain' position had been supported by 41 per cent of Protestants and by 85 per cent of Catholics (Coakley and Garry 2017). Among the major Northern Ireland parties, only the DUP campaigned for Brexit; the Ulster Unionist Party was divided on the issue, though officially supporting the remain position; while the three other large parties supported the 'remain' position. Following the result, the British Conservative government, led by Theresa May since July 2016, committed itself to Brexit for the whole United Kingdom, overriding predominant opinion in Northern Ireland and Scotland.

The British government later made clear what it meant by leaving the EU: not just giving up its representation in the various governing institutions, but also leaving the customs union and the single market. The implications of this for the Good Friday Agreement were far-reaching: if the full Brexit programme were to come into force, a 'hard' border between Northern Ireland and the Republic in respect of the movement of goods and people would be inevitable, undermining the central assumptions of the Agreement. In response, the Irish government intensified its own diplomatic efforts within the EU to defend the Agreement. The EU insisted that nothing should be done to jeopardize the Good Friday Agreement, and the withdrawal agreement drafted by EU and UK negotiators and accepted by the British government on 24 November 2018 made provision for a Northern Ireland 'backstop' (European Commission 2018). This was a device that would ensure avoidance of a 'hard' border by keeping Northern Ireland (and, in a later variant, Great Britain too) within the customs union unless and until an alternative solution was found. Later, during intensive negotiations in October 2019, an alternative to the 'backstop' was negotiated by the new Johnson government. This would avoid a hard border on the island of Ireland: Northern Ireland would remain legally in the UK customs union while in practice working within EU customs rules, and conforming to single market regulations (European Commission 2019).

Fallout from the indecisive results of a snap general election in June 2017 added to political instability. Although the Conservative Party remained the largest party in Westminster, it lost its overall majority, and eventually signed up to a 'confidence and supply' agreement with the DUP, which the DUP was able to exploit as divisions over Brexit deepened. The party became an increasingly committed defender of Brexit at Westminster, notwithstanding the probable consequences for the Irish border, and strongly resisted the notion of a 'backstop'. The years of the Brexit debate saw an increased insistence within the Conservative Party and the DUP on British 'sovereignty', and on the need to assert this against the creeping encroachments of Brussels. This newly assertive articulation of British nationalism undermined the constitutional understanding that had underlain the Northern Ireland settlement.

By 2019, the failure to restore devolution in Northern Ireland, the threat of a hard border, and the growing commitment to sovereignty in the United Kingdom and on the part of the DUP raised question marks about the survival of the Good Friday Agreement and its institutions. In retrospect, the failure sufficiently to institutionalize and provide a legal framework for its provisions under propitious British–Irish circumstances has permitted a partial unravelling when those geo-political circumstances changed.

7.3. Principles and Mechanisms of Peace-Building

The processes of negotiation and the pathways towards agreement detailed in this book are of importance not only for an understanding of the peace process in Northern Ireland, but also for wider debates on the principles of peace-building that are relevant across different societies. First, there are different perspectives on how to manage issues of contested sovereignty and on the principles needed to go beyond zero-sum nationalist conflict. Second, there are enduring debates about the nature of democracy and, more specifically, about the types of power-sharing institutions that can help manage conflict, and the mechanisms by which they do so. Third, there are questions about the role of equality measures in peace processes and about the forms of equality that aid or hinder settlement. In addition, we explore a fourth metalevel debate: about the efficacy of reform in situations of protracted conflict, and the mechanisms by which incremental institutional change can have transformative effects. We explore how each of these debates helps make sense of the issues at the heart of the Northern Ireland conflict, and the extent to which they have been resolved. We show how evidence from the British–Irish and Northern Irish case can contribute to the more general scholarly debates in these areas.

7.3.1. Debates about Sovereignty

Sovereignty, in the classical Hobbesian sense, refers to the ultimate governing authority, the sovereign state. Sovereignty as thus understood is singular, for there cannot be more than one supreme authority over a territory or a people. The institutional base of sovereign authority, however, may vary from one political system to another—in the United Kingdom, the traditional understanding is that sovereignty lies in the 'Crown in Parliament'.[26] This concept of sovereignty makes for zero-sum conflict when sovereign authority is challenged. The Irish (later, Northern Irish) conflict has typically been understood precisely as such a zero-sum conflict over which state—Irish or British—should be sovereign.

---

[26] For contemporary discussion of the British constitution, see variously Bogdanor (2009); Hazell (1999, 2008); Norton (1989); on Ireland, see MacMillan (1993); Ward (1994).

This conflict came substantially to an end with the 1998 Good Friday Agreement. Now it was accepted by nationalists that the legitimacy of British state sovereignty in Northern Ireland depended on the vote of a majority in Northern Ireland, and that a move to Irish sovereignty would be legitimate if and only if such a majority so voted in Northern Ireland and in the Republic of Ireland. Both the British and Irish governments affirmed this understanding in a formal international agreement. On the traditional concept of sovereignty, this provided a mechanism (the so-called principle of consent) by which state sovereignty would be changed only by majority vote in each part of the island.[27]

In practice, this absolute concept of sovereignty oversimplifies the options facing two claimants of sovereignty over a disputed territory, and it does not grasp the complexity of the arrangements agreed in 1998. There are ways in which sovereignty may be shared, and there are devices by which territories may be partitioned, and each of these arrangements undermines the zero-sum character of dispute (Coakley 2017b: 380–3). Both of these alternatives were featured on the menu of British–Irish negotiations. In the mid-1980s, a form of joint sovereignty over Northern Ireland was one of three institutional options identified by the New Ireland Forum, and a specific model of this was presented to the British in the 'Nally Proposals' of May 1984 (see Document 3.2). At the same time, forms of repartitioning Ireland were being considered by the British government, and the 'Armstrong Proposals' of March 1984, which proposed the creation of a new cross-border security zone, contained elements of this (see Document 3.1).[28] The multi-party negotiations of 1997–8 also considered various forms of territorial and non-territorial autonomy.[29]

Contemporary constitutional theorists have gone further to argue that the early modern concept of state sovereignty is conceptually as well as practically flawed.[30] Walker distinguishes 'really-existing sovereignty' (the actual state, which currently exercises legitimate authority) from the sovereign principles of legitimacy and authority, which govern the actions of this (or any future) state-in-control. These latter can be seen as principles embedded in legal provisions and public expectations that constitute popular allegiance, such that, were a state to abrogate them,

[27] The 'principle of consent' was important not in its advocacy of popular consent for constitutional change—this had long been the basis of self-determination claims—but in its definition of the units in which the 'people' would consent, in this case Northern Ireland and the Republic of Ireland. Alternative units for a democratic vote might be the island of Ireland (the basis of the traditional nationalist claim for self-determination) or the unionist people (who themselves traditionally resisted the nationalist claim by asserting their own right to self-determination); see Gallagher (1990). The subjective character of territorial selection in collective decision-making was put vividly by Sir Ivor Jennings (1956: 55–6) in his critique of US President Woodrow Wilson's advocacy of the principle of national self-determination: 'On the surface it seemed reasonable: let the people decide. It was in fact ridiculous because the people cannot decide until somebody decides who are the people.' See Chapter 4 and Subsection 5.3.1.

[28] A review by the Northern Ireland Office of research by Paul Compton of Queen's University Belfast into the implications of repartition concluded that this was not feasible owing to the extent to which the population was intermingled: 'one has to give up large areas of territory to achieve small gains in homogeneity' ('Repartition', report by Northern Ireland Office, 6 June 1984, TNA: PREM 19/1286).

[29] See Subsections 5.3.1 and 5.4.2.

[30] See Carolan (2009); Keating (2001); Walker (2006, 2013).

this would provoke a major public outcry and political crisis. These principles may be transnational, and there may be overlapping principled sources of authority on different issues, with potential conflicts governed procedurally by agreed processes of negotiation. Thus sovereignty is not necessarily unitary but may be shared, and it may transcend the state (Keating 2001). These ideas have led several constitutional theorists to argue that the Good Friday Agreement provides a new democratic, authoritative, and legitimate frame for politics, with the question of the locus of sovereignty (whether this is British or Irish or both) as a secondary one (Harvey 2001; Meehan 2014; Morison 2001).

On this understanding, the Good Friday Agreement sketches a radically new constitutional configuration. If Britain remains the state-in-control, the principles outlined in the Agreement ensure that it is no longer the ultimate authority, able unilaterally to overrule provisions enshrined in the Agreement or indeed to overrule the will of the people of Northern Ireland (and the Republic of Ireland in the case of a will for Irish unity) as the locus of legitimate sovereignty. The very agreement that had given a new legitimacy to the state-in-control also defined the principles—including parity of esteem—which that state had to follow. Nationalists accepted the Good Friday constitutional settlement, arguing, in the reported words of Irish foreign minister Brian Cowen, that, 'beyond the constitutional acceptance that Northern Ireland remains part of the United Kingdom, there should be no further evidence of Britishness in the governance of Northern Ireland'.[31] From this perspective, legitimacy was conferred by agreement in 1998, with no implications that the British state's presence or its actions in Northern Ireland before that were legitimate or should have been accepted. The Agreement reconciled nationalists with the present status of Northern Ireland, not its past status, and this was later to become the basis of the politicization of 'the past' by unionists.

Most unionists, however, took the Agreement as confirming a more traditional understanding of British sovereignty, past and present. They held to the traditional view that British sovereignty has cultural impact, such that policing, public symbolism, and flags should reflect the British character of the state, and that the norms in contemporary Great Britain should apply in Northern Ireland. While almost all nationalists had accepted the legitimacy of *de facto* British state sovereignty, they had not accepted the traditional British and unionist understanding of sovereignty, past and present. Thus the basis for new disagreements arose on what followed from the Good Friday Agreement: for the limits on British power unilaterally to suspend aspects of the Agreement, such as the Assembly[32]; for governance and public culture, not least flags and anthems; for the value of cultural capital and the public recognition of the Irish language; and for how disagreements on these matters would be adjudicated.

---

[31] *Irish Times*, 11 May 2000.   [32] See Subsection 6.7.2.

On one reading the Good Friday Agreement itself—incorporated in a formal British–Irish agreement—defined the sovereign principles that would thereafter govern the behaviour of the British state. On this reading, British sovereignty in Northern Ireland was consistent with transborder institutions, which could (with political consent) radically increase in strength, with a harmonization of rights and equality legislation between North and South, and with parity of esteem for nationalist and unionist culture and political aspirations. On another reading, the internal affairs of Northern Ireland remained governed by British law and custom, after the Good Friday Agreement as before, and in particular by the 1998 Northern Ireland Act and its successors. Following British law and precedent, and on traditional interpretations of the (unwritten) British constitution, the Good Friday Agreement left British sovereignty unchanged.

The Northern Ireland anomaly was rooted in the disparities between domestic British law and the international British–Irish (Good Friday) Agreement.[33] In this respect it was analogous to the much older 'Scottish anomaly', rooted in the different Scottish and English legal understanding of the Anglo-Scottish Act of Union (1707), which gave rise to different Scottish and English interpretations as to the basis of British sovereignty (Kidd 2008; MacCormick 1998). The Northern Irish anomaly, like the Scottish, was a source of political stability, for it allowed the different parties to uphold the same political settlement on very different grounds. But this held only as long as the British state's policies in Northern Ireland did not contradict the provisions or principles of the Good Friday Agreement. Since some of these provisions and many of the principles were themselves contested, this was not an easy task. The governments chose not to try to articulate the principles more clearly. Thus the anomaly survived, but never came to inform public culture. Many unionists continued to adhere to the earlier tradition of British sovereignty as singular, unconstrained, rooted in the Crown in Parliament, and inconsistent with parity for nationalism. Thus, when the two governments failed to uphold the anomaly after 2010, political conflict between the Northern Ireland parties escalated (Todd 2017).

This had consequences for the outworking of the Agreement. As British government assumptions swung back to a more traditional notion of sovereignty in the 2010s, so too did loyalists and unionists begin to unpick the Northern Ireland anomaly in a series of actions: in the flags dispute, in backing off from (at least tacit) agreements over the Irish language and the proposed Maze Heritage Centre, and in conflicts over 'the past' (Lawther 2015; Nolan 2014; Nolan et al. 2014).

---

[33] It should be noted that what is conventionally labelled as the Good Friday Agreement in fact comprises two agreements. One, formally entitled *The Agreement Reached in the Multi-Party Negotiations 10 April 1998*, includes as an annex the text of an 'Agreement between the Government of the United Kingdom of Great Britain and Northern Ireland and the Government of Ireland', which itself incorporates as an annex *The Agreement Reached in the Multi-Party Negotiations*; see Document 5.4.

7.3.2. Debates about Democracy

In a world where the notion of democracy as the only appropriate form of government reigns supreme, it is worth recalling that this concept has been intensely debated in Northern Ireland, where British political cultural models were for long taken for granted. These extended to the 'Westminster model' of democracy in its fullest sense: a majoritarian system of representative democracy, with elections conducted on the plurality ('first-past-the-post') system, and a winner-takes-all formula for government formation, where a bare-majority cabinet faces a powerless opposition. The fact that this delivered an overwhelmingly unionist parliament in Stormont and an exclusively unionist cabinet from 1921 to the early 1970s reinforced its attractiveness to unionists.

As debates about political reform began in the early 1970s, an alternative model presented itself: power-sharing or 'consociational' democracy. The power-sharing formula was quickly adopted by the non-unionist parties and the British and Irish governments as their favoured system of government. It was seen as both fairer and more inclusive than the Westminster system, since it required proportional representation in elections and cross-community coalition government. Power-sharing government has since become the international norm for governing post-conflict societies (Hartzell and Hoddie 2015). It is commonly extended to include other consensus-building devices, to produce a governing formula that has been labelled 'consociational democracy'. This entails the inclusion of significant minority groups not just in government but at all levels of the public sector, including the civil service and the security forces, as well as a proportional distribution of economic, social, and cultural resources.[34] The notion of consociation is also usually seen as incorporating group autonomy—a misleading term, since the groups between which power is shared in countries conventionally described as 'consociational' typically enjoy little if any autonomy. Consociation is not without its critics: its capacity to heal divisions has been queried, its sustainability over time has been questioned, and there are disputes over the most effective types of power-sharing in different socio-political contexts.[35]

The long but intermittent experience of power-sharing in Northern Ireland since 1973 provides a useful test case of the conditions under which different types of power-sharing institutions work effectively, and the circumstances under which they are likely to break down. Early debates in Northern Ireland saw political

---

[34] For recent overviews of power-sharing and consociation and other contributions to the debate, see Cochrane, Loizides, and Bodson (2018); Jakala, Kuzu, and Qvortrup (2018); McCulloch (2014); McCulloch and McGarry (2017); McEvoy (2015); McEvoy and O'Leary (2013); Walsh (2017); Wolff and Cordell (2016).

[35] For a more critical literature, see Horowitz (2000); O'Flynn and Russell (2005); Reilly (2001); Taylor (2009).

leaders and activists, together with their academic supporters, present two stark models for the future government of Northern Ireland, consociational and majoritarian.[36] From the early 1970s, the British government came to recognize that any settlement in Northern Ireland had to include nationalists as well as unionists in government. In 1973, a particular form of power-sharing government was agreed—a coalition of moderate nationalists, moderate unionists, and the cross-community Alliance Party. This was described as a form of 'partnership' government. Unlike the 1998 arrangements, it was the Northern Ireland Secretary who was to determine whether a particular coalition met the appropriate conditions for power-sharing—it was required to satisfy the not entirely objective condition that it would be 'likely to be widely accepted throughout the community'. The 1973 Sunningdale settlement divided unionist opinion, and gave unionist opponents of power-sharing a target against which they could mobilize. Unionists used their position of advantage in respect of power resources—not least in the electricity industry—to bring down the executive. The majoritarian ideology which had justified the old Stormont system, reformulated in the report of the Constitutional Convention of 1975–6, continued to be a core ingredient in unionism down to the late years of the twentieth century.

After a series of unsuccessful initiatives, another form of power-sharing government, this time more clearly consociational, was agreed in 1998 and came into effect in 1999. The executive was based on proportional assignment of seats to parties depending on their strength in the Assembly. The new agreement provided for still greater inclusion across the range of institutions, from the economy to policing. It was based not so much on a concept of partnership government, as in 1974, as on a concept of 'parity of esteem' and proportionality in representation. As near-parity between the nationalist and unionist communities was reached at the demographic level, this was reflected also at the political level, and the First Minister and Deputy First Minister were elected on a basis that would ensure equality between the blocs.

The contrast between the fate of the 1973 agreement (which lasted less than five months) and the 1998 agreement (which has lasted for more than twenty years, despite intermittent collapses of the power-sharing executive) is instructive. In 1974, the future of executive power-sharing depended crucially on the wider social context, and it was highly vulnerable to exogenous shock—in this case, an election to the British House of Commons changed the wider political power balance and incentivized unionist counter-mobilization. In the absence of British intervention, the anti-power-sharing unionists had the ideological, economic, and military

---

[36] For the background on this debate, see Coakley (2011). Both approaches were vigorously proposed at an early stage of the debate on Northern Ireland's constitutional future: a strong case for consociational principles was made by the doyen of research in this area (Lijphart 1975), but a leading democratic theorist dismissed this on the ground that it 'may make things worse' (Barry 1975: 395).

resources to bring the new institutions down, and with them the entire package agreed at Sunningdale with which it was inextricably linked.

The Good Friday Agreement was designed to be more resilient, and it proved to be so. It was an international agreement between two states, and it continued to be supported by them. The settlement as a whole proved capable of surviving the recurrent crises and fractures in power-sharing government. Continued British–Irish support of the Agreement did not ensure the survival of the power-sharing executive, but it facilitated its later restoration after breakdown. The reforms in the economy, in policing, and in the criminal justice system, and the much more even balance of power resources in part brought about by the Agreement, meant that neither community could easily unpick the new institutional framework, and the incentive to try to do so was weak.

Executive power-sharing remained vulnerable, and dependent on the wider political context. The emergence of a more strongly nationalist Conservative government in Britain, unwilling to take a proactive role in Northern Ireland, gave a boost to unionist and loyalist assertiveness. In historical institutionalist terminology, change in the wider institutional context led to 'drift', in which once-functional institutional rules became dysfunctional and ineffective (see Mahoney and Thelen 2009). Institutional provisions such as bloc vetoes, which in benign circumstances function as bloc safety nets, were used to promote group assertion and polarization. Liberal nationalist norms of respect for each identity and tradition, which in the past were used to moderate classic nationalist aims, were now used to pursue classic unionist ones of the right to traditional marches (even against local nationalist protest) and to the continuous flying of the Union Jack on public buildings (never the Irish flag), since this was the unionist identity and tradition, which should be respected. This set the scene for more radical subversion of the Agreement when a new policy paradigm—in this case, a British return to insistence on national sovereignty in its relations with the EU after the 2016 vote for Brexit—led to a subsumption of the Good Friday institutions within this paradigm ('displacement', in historical institutionalist terminology). Drift and displacement work slowly; change in the functioning of the institutions set in place in 1998 represents a bigger danger than a unilateral British disavowal of the Good Friday Agreement.

In conclusion, the Northern Ireland case illustrates the dependence of executive power-sharing on the wider social and political context. In the 1990s, processes of reform and equalization across the economy, education, and—more tentatively—cultural expression paved the way for agreement, which in turn furthered these processes. Moreover, the broader political framework redefined the preference structures in sections of the population: unionists moved towards acceptance of power-sharing and transborder institutions in part as a way of ruling out an Irish government role in the governance of Northern Ireland and in part as a way of having a say in their own future. But, when wider political opportunities changed, so, slowly, did unionist preferences, setting in motion a change in the way in which the institutions functioned.

7.3.3. Debates about Equality

Horizontal inequality, understood as inequality on the basis of cultural characteristics, and encompassing economic, political, and cultural dimensions, is highly correlated with conflict (Cederman, Weidmann, and Gleditsch 2011; Stewart 2008). But little comparative research has been carried out on how remedying it— whether by 'group equality', forms of affirmative action, or universalistic policies and rights—affects conflict. Brown, Langer, and Stewart (2012: 2) note that 'there is a remarkable dearth of serious comparative work on affirmative action'. There is still less work on how interventions to remedy low cultural status affect conflict.

In these respects, the Northern Ireland case is particularly revealing, since communal inequality was deep and historically entrenched on several dimensions, and was only very slowly remedied, and because the systematic efforts to secure equality preceded rather than followed settlement. In the 1980s—with the help of a range of allies in the USA, and assisted by emerging international equality norms—nationalists increasingly gained from strong economic equality measures, and by the 1990s had moved close to a position of equality in employment. Since 1998, as already outlined, there has been a political settlement on the basis of substantive equality in representation and participation while leaving the constitutional question open for the future.

Despite its importance in the politics of Northern Ireland, the question of equality features relatively little in the witness seminars and interviews that form the core of this book. To be sure, the Irish participants were aware of the imbalances. In the early 1980s, remedying the conditions of northern nationalists was one of the motivations of the Irish negotiators.[37] By the 1990s, senior British politicians and civil servants were also taking equality issues seriously: in the words of Sir Roderic Lyne, they were 'trying to make it a smaller and less heated conflict'.[38] However, cultural inequality was mentioned only occasionally—for example, in the form of 'equal institutional recognition and respect' for each

---

[37] So, e.g., Peter Barry, Minister for Foreign Affairs 1982–7, and closely involved in the negotiation and implementation of the Anglo-Irish Agreement, noted: 'You see, we were fighting from a long way back. We wanted to get the point of view of Irish nationalists catered for in the North of Ireland education system, health system, court system, everything' (interview with Christopher Farrington and Susan McDermott, Cork, 1 January 2007, lodged in John Whyte Archive, UCD). See Subsections 3.3.1 and 3.4.1.

[38] Interview with Jennifer Todd, London, 1 July 2011, lodged in John Whyte Archive, UCD.

identity and tradition, in the liberal nationalist paradigm expressed in the New Ireland Forum Report of 1984.[39]

Even in Northern Ireland itself, mobilization over inequality was intermittent. For example, communal economic inequality was highlighted in the early civil-rights movement, then sidelined as first security concerns and later nationalist political demands came to prominence. The early hopes that 'good government' by the British would resolve questions of discrimination and economic inequality were shattered by the findings of the 1981 census and of other research that showed no improvement in the relative economic position of Catholics.[40] By the mid-1980s, economic inequality came to symbolize the lack of will or capacity of the British state even to ensure fair treatment, much less equality of opportunity or equality of condition. At the same time, policy instruments were becoming available to achieve equality of opportunity and—later again—equality of condition, and nationalists and their allies campaigned effectively to ensure that such policies were enacted.

The 1989 Fair Employment Act was more ambitious and much more effective than earlier Northern Ireland legislation, and it went beyond all existing legislation in the United Kingdom (Osborne and Shuttleworth 2004: 5–6). As outlined in Chapter 1, it took as its model recent Canadian legislation, which abjured quotas but incorporated strong monitoring requirements. It outlawed indirect as well as direct discrimination. It gave greater powers of enforcement to the newly named Fair Employment Commission (FEC) and broadened the range of legally acceptable compensatory measures—for example, the targeting of specific groups in job advertising and training programmes. It made monitoring of the religious composition of the workforce a requirement (and extended this to the monitoring of job applications in the case of public-sector and large private firms), and it set up a new Fair Employment Tribunal to hear individual cases of discrimination. There followed swiftly a set of measures designed to ensure equality of condition, in particular in areas of social need, and after 1998 equality was 'mainstreamed' in all public policy (McCrudden 1999).

As Chapter 1 shows, Catholics quickly reached equality in employment. The improvement, however, was not simply a matter of legislation. Todd and Ruane (2012: 202) argue that 'it is more accurate to see the marked relative improvement in Catholics' economic position as a product of multiple determinants operating over different time scales'. These determinants included deindustrialization (which hollowed out or restructured large sectors in which Protestants had traditionally worked) and later security reform (which led to greater competition for fewer jobs in another traditionally Protestant sector) and trends in education

[39] New Ireland Forum (1984: paras 4.15, 4.16).
[40] For discussion and analysis of the census and other available data, see Eversley (1989: 56–238). For discussion of the extent of inequality, see Smith and Chambers (1991: 152–234).

and migration (themselves products of changing political expectations). Whatever the causal processes, and despite continuing pockets of poverty disproportionately within Catholic neighbourhoods, economic inequality was depoliticized both at the popular level and by nationalist and republican politicians.[41]

Cultural inequality remained stubbornly politicized. From the 1990s, this took the form of the repoliticization of public space and loyalist assertion of the right to march past Catholic areas. A set of small-scale symbolic contests took place through the 2000s (McCall 2006), with major contention focusing on the symbolism of policing (Doyle 2010: 189–93). Flags became an issue in dispute— republicans and nationalists called for a ban on national flags, while loyalists and unionists argued for the prominence of the British flag. The absence of agreed legislation or principles of 'parity of esteem' in a bill of rights kept the issues open. By the 2010s they became highly contentious. Paradoxically (since British symbolism continued to predominate in the public sphere), they were politicized by Protestants in the name of cultural equality: any reduction in the flying of British flags, or in the restriction of marches, was perceived as a lack of (equal) respect for their cultural identity.

In conclusion, equalization in the economic and political spheres reduced the intensity of conflict; by the 2000s a threshold was passed after which inequality was no longer politicized. The same did not happen in the cultural sphere. Without clear guidelines institutionalized in a bill of rights, the concept of cultural equality was used to assert, rather than to reflect upon and amend, oppositional cultural traditions.

7.3.4. Understanding Institutional Change

In protracted conflicts where the state is one of the conflict actors, there is often intense debate as to whether incremental reform within the state has the capacity to transform social and political divisions, or whether this can be achieved only by regime transformation or constitutional change. This is a special case of the general debates on institutional change within the field of comparative historical analysis (Mahoney and Thelen 2015). The British–Irish negotiations and their impact on Northern Ireland are directly relevant to these debates, providing rich material that illustrates how institutional change proceeds, when and how it becomes cumulative and lasting, and the conditions under which it becomes transformative.

The British–Irish process discussed in this book involved changing policy paradigms, which were carried forth in increasingly cooperative interstate

---

[41] See Nolan (2014: 82–3), who shows that the poorest Belfast neighbourhoods are still disproportionately Catholic.

relations, eventually leading to the institutionalization of far-reaching reforms. One may hypothesize that institutional changes, especially those legally enforced and expressing norms common across a range of institutions, are likely to be more difficult to reverse than are policy paradigms, while changes in intergovernmental relations are likely to be most ephemeral.[42] Tracing the process up to the present allows us to assess which forms of change were lasting, and which were more easily reversed.

Coakley (2017a, b) has argued that the Irish state made major changes in its aims, strategies and practices over the period discussed here, culminating in significant qualification of its aim of a united Ireland, with the principle of dual consent for unity (of a majority in the North and a majority in the South) now locked into the Irish constitution. These changes began early and were a direct response to Irish powerlessness in the face of the Northern Irish crisis. They were rooted in the state's interest in maintaining its own legitimacy and stability, and, much later, in its interest in maintaining an international reputation enhanced by its conflict-management success. The civil-service departments became centres where this thinking would be transmitted and would come to inform elite assumptions and practices, and latterly it was embedded in the constitution itself. It would be very difficult for any future Irish government to reverse this stance and work for Irish unity without consent.[43]

Some of the changes in the Republic of Ireland were, however, less embedded, and some much more ephemeral. With the gradual qualification of the aim of a united Ireland came a shift in policy paradigm, expressed most coherently in the New Ireland Forum Report of 1984, which portrayed the Northern Ireland conflict not simply as a national problem, but as one where two communities or two traditions were in conflict and both had to be respected. This liberal nationalist (or pluralist) approach was to inform the Irish strategy of conflict management. It proved to be effective as an argument for nationalist equality and parity of esteem in Northern Ireland. More recently, however, it has failed to provide a criterion for resolving ongoing conflicts between the Northern Ireland parties, or within the Northern Ireland executive (Todd 2018: 219–22).

There is further debate on the extent to which and the manner in which the British state changed its institutions, policy paradigms, and structures. Certainly there were continuities from the 1970s to the 1990s: a desire to prevent discrimination, an openness on the part of sections of the state apparatus to engage in discussions with republicans, and a willingness on the part of some of the political elite to contemplate a united Ireland (Craig 2012). But there were also changes in

---

[42] Capoccia (2016), e.g., argues that institutions 'bite', that is, have causal impact, when the same categories (and implicitly rules) are common across a wide range of institutions.

[43] The development of units of special expertise in the civil service is described in Appendices 1.3 and 1.4.

policy paradigms, beginning in the 1980s and developing more radically in the 1990s. By the mid-1980s, senior British civil servants and successive prime ministers became more open to Irish involvement in a 'more than consultative' way. Later they engaged with all parties, including republicans, not simply (as in the past) in order to reduce the level of British involvement in Northern Ireland, but with the aim of reconstructing Northern Ireland as a now more equal and stable society. For a period, the most important British policymakers had little interest in securing traditional British sovereignty of 'the Crown in Parliament', but rather worked to construct a viable, multilevelled mode of governance for Northern Ireland that respected international as well as internal linkages and that could lead to a settlement. Senior civil servants, leading Conservative politicians (John Major, Peter Brooke, and Chris Patten) and 'new' Labour leaders (Tony Blair, Mo Mowlam, and Peter Hain) were comfortable thinking in these terms. This understanding, quite far removed from traditional concepts of state sovereignty, was seldom made explicit; it was a mode of practice rather than a formal principle.

The process involved some institutional continuities. The Secretary of State for Northern Ireland and the Northern Ireland Office (created in 1972) were central in carrying through the new strategies. They were helped by a range of other institutions. Important examples are the Standing Advisory Commission on Human Rights (formed in 1973, subsumed within the Northern Ireland Human Rights Commission in 1998) and the Fair Employment Agency (founded in 1976, later renamed the Fair Employment Commission, and in 1998 subsumed into the Equality Agency). While the institutional forms were continuous, the resources assigned them, their remit, their legal powers, and their policy impact increased dramatically over time. There were also new institutions, notably the Anglo-Irish Intergovernmental Conference of 1985, which for a period played an important role in agenda-setting and which had a lasting impact in convincing key British politicians and civil servants of the value of joint British–Irish conflict management. The main institutional innovations took place in Northern Ireland and in North–South relations—the reconstruction of the processes of fair employment (1989–98), policing (1999–2010) and criminal justice (since 2000), and the new North–South institutions after 1998—although in the context of wider British changes in territorial management (including in particular devolution for Scotland and Wales) and amendment of articles 2 and 3 of the Irish constitution.

British-sponsored institutional change in Northern Ireland was indeed radical, and for the most part it has remained in place and continues to be effective.[44] In contrast, the changes in policy paradigms by British leaders and civil servants in the central British state took place in a 'post-sovereigntist' moment in the 1990s

---

[44] For some critical discussion of the lack of progress of policing reform after 2010, see Gray et al. (2018: 114–25).

and 2000s, when interstate interdependencies were emphasized internationally and throughout Europe (Keating 2001). They were only thinly embedded in the central institutions of the British state. In the 2010s, this paradigm was being replaced by a return to a more traditional British perspective, defensive of state sovereignty and emphasizing the unconstrained power of the 'Crown in Parliament'. Most ephemeral of all, the policy convergence and friendly relations between Britain and Ireland throughout the period were much more a product of temporarily convergent state interest than of a process of normalization. They quickly deteriorated when state interests diverged in the Brexit negotiations of 2016–19. The question remains how long the institutional reforms can survive these changes.

7.4. The Wider Lessons

This book is based on witness seminars and interviews with members of the British, Irish, and Northern Irish political elites—in particular with very senior civil servants and politicians. This inevitably limits the comparative and theoretical conclusions that can be reached. The limited number of participants and the inevitably selective emphasis of their discussions means that oral evidence of this kind, like any data, must be measured against other evidence and analysis (Natow 2019). It is for this reason that we add some of the main documents discussed so that readers may themselves assess the evidence.[45]

Yet the witness seminars and interviews also reveal in a striking and immediate way the manner in which these officials and politicians understood the British–Irish process and the resulting British–Irish agreements, the differences and tensions between the British and the Irish positions, and the ways in which these differences were overcome. It provides insight into how a protracted conflict was brought to an end through interstate agreements that gave incentives to the political parties in conflict to change their strategies. If we construct a benchmark from these slow processes of strategy development and negotiation, it centres on this positive feedback pattern that characterized the later 1990s and much of the early 2000s.

Despite vested interests, the slow pace of IRA decommissioning, and internal unionist divisions, the early years of the twenty-first century witnessed substantial

---

[45] For example, in discussing the negotiations leading to the Downing Street Declaration, the participants were clear that there was a political drive to remove Gerry Adams's 'fingerprints' from the final version of the Declaration. But it is also clear that there are some continuities between the successive drafts, from the first (John Hume's version of 6 October 1991) to the longer and more developed version announced on 15 December 1993 (see Documents 4.3, 4.4, 4.5, 4.6, and 4.8). Mallie and McKittrick (1996: 119) point out that Hume's original draft, following his discussions with Adams, 'contained many of the key features of what would, after many changes, become the Downing Street Declaration'. This no doubt increased the likelihood that republicans would accept the document.

progress in the direction of political 'normalization'. British–Irish co-management of conflict promoted interrelated processes of structural transformation in the direction of equality, changing party-political policies and increasing compromise, and a softening in public attitudes. That momentum allowed the institutions of the agreement to function tolerably well, and kept alive some of the hopes of the 1990s. It provides a standard by reference to which we can assess the impact on Northern Ireland of change in British and Irish practices and priorities since 2007, in particular during the difficult negotiations over Brexit.

7.4.1. Learning from the Past

The story told by the respondents in the earlier chapters of this book is of developing sets of policy paradigms, embedded in political and institutional practice. The Irish respondents describe an iterative Irish strategy, initially focusing on North–South relations (an 'Irish dimension') and power-sharing government. The Irish side was able to take advantage of those periods when the more powerful British state was open to new policy paradigms and new institutional experiments. As British–Irish negotiations began in earnest, especially in the early 1980s, there developed a repertoire of negotiation that found narrow windows of agreement—often themselves open to different interpretations—which became the focus for cooperative and collaborative conflict management. A cumulative approach was adopted, so that one set of agreements built on at least some of the provisions of the previous agreements. In the 1990s, for example, the Good Friday Agreement built on the Framework Documents, which built in turn on the Downing Street Declaration. The Declaration and the Framework Documents built on the practice and institutions of British–Irish joint conflict management initiated by the Anglo-Irish Agreement, even while taking a new, more inclusive tack. The Anglo-Irish Agreement, in turn, built on the foundations of the relationship between British and Irish officials developed at the time of the Sunningdale Agreement.

By the 1980s, the Irish were beginning to emphasize the need for far-reaching reform, and in dialogue with the British there developed a slow convergence on this and on a set of policy interventions in Northern Ireland (in particular in the area of substantive equality in employment) that produced major structural change. These changes, first in the economy, and much later in the security forces and criminal justice system, gave credibility to the claim that there was a new British strategy that would lead to the full inclusion of nationalists and republicans on an equal basis. During the most productive period of the 1990s and 2000s, a benign feedback loop developed: state-sponsored reforms led to changes in party political preferences within the nationalist and unionist blocs and the initiation of inclusive negotiations that led in turn—after the Good Friday Agreement—to further reconstruction of policing and justice in Northern Ireland.

The closest cooperation occurred during the 1990s and 2000s when transborder linkages and institutions were emphasized globally, and when the political will, interests, and paradigms of British and Irish leaders converged, permitting a complex process of peace and settlement building. In this period, the emphases on power-sharing government, thorough reforms towards equality, a rights culture, and an innovative constitutional framework—which up to this time had been only intermittently and partially pursued—began to be institutionalized.

In some other respects, however, the process was less benign. Women were present only as a minority, albeit—for example, in the multi-party negotiations of 1997–8—one that played an important role. Democratic participation was minimal, except for elections and occasional referenda. In important ways this was a top-down process familiar to observers of consociational government, and, if political parties also played a part, the public did not. Most important of all, the normative principles that underlay the Good Friday Agreement itself were not articulated by the two states and thus did not embed themselves in public attitudes. Implementation was painfully slow. For example, the task of articulating a bill of rights for Northern Ireland was left to the Northern Ireland Human Rights Commission, when, in retrospect, the only actors able clearly to articulate and decide a normative framework for the future were the very governments which had successfully drafted the set of agreements themselves. Indeed, had the principles of inclusivity and equality been formally articulated, these would have provided a basis for further inclusion on gender and democratic grounds. Without such clearly articulated principles, conflict in Northern Ireland continued over each new issue, the implementation of the Good Friday Agreement was crisis ridden, and conflict between the Northern Ireland parties escalated where agreement had not already been reached (notably on culture and on 'the past'). As the wider framework of British–Irish convergence and cooperation weakened, so too did some of the achievements of the Good Friday Agreement begin to look vulnerable. This danger has intensified with Brexit.

In a wider comparative perspective, the British–Irish process provides a revealing model of peace-building. It shows executive power-sharing as one part—an important one to be sure—of a complex, multilayered process of settlement that was substantially consociational. Indeed, there was a complex causal nexus. Equality reforms served to show the credibility of the governments' promises, and thus incentivized agreement on the constitutional framework. This in turn allowed stronger action on security-related issues—policing and justice—and eventual demilitarization and decommissioning, which in turn enabled broader agreement in 2006. Yet the process even after 2006 was far from complete: it remained stable only through continued work by the British and Irish governments, and, when this ceased, the settlement became vulnerable to external pressures, most particularly to those associated with Brexit.

This story highlights a benign dynamic of peacemaking, albeit a temporary one. At the same time, it reveals the inherently changeable character of inter-state relations and modes of understanding, particularly problematic when the states are asymmetric in respect of power. Thus it shows the need to embed the institutions and principles of settlement quickly, while the wider inter-state context favours it, so that the prospects of their long-term durability are maximized, and they are ring-fenced against unexpected international changes.

7.4.2. Looking to the Future

As Brexit approached in 2019, and in particular as the prospect of a 'no-deal' Brexit increased, growing divergence on issues of rights and equality and the undermining of cross-border institutions seemed likely. Moreover, there was a new uncertainty about future governance if devolution were not restored. Would the British government attempt to return to direct rule as it was before the Anglo-Irish Agreement? Might it settle for the formula by which the Irish government had been given a meaningful voice after 1985? Might it be prepared to give the Irish government a greater say in the absence of devolution, as had been threatened in 2006? How might the status of Northern Ireland be affected by whatever deal accompanied the Brexit process? Could a British government committed to traditionalist concepts of sovereignty involve the Irish government in co-management of conflict? If it attempted a return to direct rule as it was in the past, would this not be a breach of the 1998 Agreement, and a reversal of the agreement at St Andrews in 2006 to remove this option from the statute book?

Brexit also stimulated popular and political debate, with shifts in public opinion in Northern Ireland. It re-engaged the interest of the Irish government in matters north of the border, a border that it pledged to keep as invisible as possible. It also highlighted for many unionists the potential damage to the Northern Ireland economy that was likely to be inflicted by new barriers to the movement of goods and people. Opinion polls showed massive nationalist support for 'special status' for Northern Ireland; many unionists also supported this, and some began to contemplate the prospect of Irish unity. But institutional vehicles to build on these public changes were now absent: neither the Assembly nor the North/South Ministerial Council was available to articulate and elaborate on shared interests.[46]

[46] The last meeting of the North/South Ministerial Council on 18 November 2016 appeared to register an island-wide shared perception of threats arising from Brexit. The subsequent joint communiqué tersely recorded that, 'in taking forward their discussions, the Northern Ireland Executive and the Irish Government will be guided by some common principles' <www.northsouthministerialcouncil. org/publications/twenty-third-plenary-joint-communique-18-november-2016-0> (accessed 19 May 2019). The eight principles were not publicly specified, but dealt with areas where Brexit was likely to have a particular impact and noted seven specific areas that would be affected (higher education, energy, sport, telecommunications, fisheries, security, and criminal justice ('Common Principles

Thus by 2019 it appeared that the progress achieved in the years following the Agreement was being rolled back. Central to this was a change in policy paradigms, which began slowly in 2012, and accelerated in Britain, so that by 2019 earlier assumptions had been reversed. By the latter part of the 2010s, a new generation of British Conservative politicians (and many of their Labour counterparts) appeared to turn their back on the principles, institutions, and policies that had underpinned the Northern Ireland settlement, at times appearing to be willing even to abandon the Good Friday Agreement itself. This perspective has threatened to undermine the credibility of British commitments to Northern Ireland, including those expressed in solemn international agreements.

In the Republic of Ireland, in contrast, a new generation of politicians was more actively engaged with matters relating to the Irish border, reflecting the fundamental challenge that Brexit posed to both parts of the island of Ireland. In a way that would have been unthinkable in the 1990s and 2000s, it is the EU rather than the UK or the USA that has become the effective guarantor of the Good Friday Agreement in the new world of Brexit.

The ultimate outcome of the Brexit process and its impact on Northern Ireland remained uncertain in November 2019. Whatever settlement emerges, it will have a signficant impact on the Good Friday Agreement. Already, the Brexit debate has encouraged a reassessment of relationships within these islands on the part of nationalists and Catholics, it has sharpened divisions over constitutional matters among unionists and Protestants, and it has offered a major challenge to the sustainability of the complex balance that the Agreement set in place. These threats have been aggravated by the growing divergence in policy perspectives and the sharp deterioration in political relations between the British and Irish governments. Upholding the principles of the Agreement while its provisions are reconfigured to cater for a redefined geopolitical reality is likely to remain a major challenge in a post-Brexit world.

7.5. Conclusion

The extent of change in political institutions and political culture over the period covered in this book is clear when we look at the evolution of the three principles on which conflict has been recurrent: sovereignty, democracy, and equality. In 1969, two conflicting absolute claims over the territory of Northern Ireland separated the Irish and British governments; fifty years later, these had been

---

Agreed at the NSMC', annex A to 'Special Status within the EU', document in the authors' possession). The collapse of the Executive a few weeks later brought this channel of cooperation to an end, and for the DUP the focus shifted to Westminster. The areas identified as vulnerable to Brexit were, however, incorporated in section 13.1 of the draft British withdrawal agreement, together with a number of other areas (European Commission 2018: 319).

replaced by agreement on the legitimacy of British sovereignty in Northern Ireland and on the modalities of changing this, and on the complex relationship between the people of Northern Ireland and the two states. In 1969, the majoritarian model of democracy facilitated the complete political dominance of the Unionist Party; by 2019, there was near-universal support for power-sharing government. In 1969, there was striking communal inequality in all fields; fifty years later there was substantial equality between the two communities at socio-economic level, and some movement towards recognizing the cultural rights of both.

Yet in important respects these achievements were uneven and incomplete. There was no agreement on what British sovereignty entailed for state powers or for public symbolism, nor was there agreement on the basis of its present legitimacy, on its past legitimacy, or on the legitimacy of republican armed resistance in the past. There was agreement on the necessity of power-sharing, but there was no process (other than British and Irish pressure) by which agreement within the executive could be reached. While significant communal equality had been achieved, the politicization of equality of cultural rights, traditions, and interpretations of the past was at the centre of political crisis. Nor did the undermining of agreement take place simply or primarily in Northern Ireland: in 2019, the main voices questioning the importance of the Good Friday Agreement and its principles came from within the British parliament.

These setbacks do not take away from the important achievements documented in this book, nor from the capability and perseverance of the politicians and civil servants who made them. Rather, they highlight the difficulties faced and overcome in earlier periods when negotiations took place against a backdrop not just of political opposition but also of violent conflict. These recent setbacks, however, give reason to look back at some of the principles and policy paradigms that evolved through the most fruitful periods of British–Irish cooperation, and they invite us to consider whether these might have been more fully developed, or more effectively implemented, with a view to promoting greater resilience into the future. They also invite us to reconsider how political progress towards sustainable peace may be reasserted, notwithstanding the immense strains imposed by the Brexit challenge. This book provides much of the material necessary for re-evaluation of this kind, and for reflection on the most promising pathways towards peaceful coexistence in an era of social, cultural and political division.

References

Adams, Gerry (2003). *Hope and History: Making Peace in Ireland*. Dingle: Brandon.

Ahern, Bertie, with Richard Aldous (2009). *Bertie Ahern: The Autobiography*. London: Hutchinson.

ARK (2019). *Northern Ireland Elections*, <www.ark.ac.uk/elections/> (accessed 19 May 2019).

Arthur, Paul (2000). *Special Relationships: Britain, Ireland and the Northern Ireland Problem*. Belfast: Blackstaff.

Aughey, Arthur (1989). *Under Siege: Ulster Unionism and the Anglo–Irish Agreement*. London: Hurst.

Aughey, Arthur (1999). 'A New Beginning? The Prospects for a Politics of Civility in Northern Ireland', in Joseph Ruane and Jennifer Todd (eds), *After the Good Friday Agreement: Analysing Political Change in Northern Ireland*. Dublin: University College Dublin Press, 122–44.

Aughey, Arthur (2005). *The Politics of Northern Ireland: Beyond the Belfast Agreement*. Abingdon: Routledge.

Aughey, Arthur, and Cathy Gormley-Heenan (2011) (eds). *The Anglo-Irish Agreement: Rethinking its Legacy*. Manchester: Manchester University Press.

Aunger, Edmund A. (1975). 'Religion and Occupational Class in Northern Ireland', *Economic and Social Review*, 7/1: 1–18.

Barry, Brian (1975). 'The Consociational Model and its Dangers', *European Journal of Political Research*, 3/4: 393–412.

Bew, John, Martyn Frampton and Iñigo Gurruchaga (2009). *Talking to Terrorists: Making Peace in Northern Ireland and the Basque Country*. London: Hurst.

Bew, Paul (1998). 'The Unionists Have Won, They Just Don't Know It', *Sunday Times*, 17 May.

Bew, Paul, and Gordon Gillespie (1999). *Northern Ireland: A Chronology of the Troubles 1968–1999*. New edn. Dublin: Gill and Macmillan.

Bew, Paul, Peter Gibbon, and Henry Patterson (1996). *Northern Ireland 1921–1996: Political Forces and Social Classes*. London: Serif.

Blair, Tony (2010). *A Journey*. London: Hutchinson.

Bloomfield, David (1998). *Political Dialogue in Northern Ireland: The Brooke Initiative, 1989–92*. Basingstoke: Palgrave Macmillan.

Bloomfield, David (2001). *Developing Dialogue in Northern Ireland: The Mayhew Talks*. Basingstoke: Palgrave Macmillan.

Bloomfield, Sir Kenneth (1994). *Stormont in Crisis: A Memoir*. Belfast: Blackstaff.

Bloomfield, Sir Kenneth (2007). *A Tragedy of Errors: The Government and Misgovernment of Northern Ireland*. Liverpool: Liverpool University Press.

Bogdanor, Vernon (2009). *The New British Constitution*. Oxford: Hart.

Brams, Steven, and Jeffrey M. Togman (2000). 'Agreement through Threats: The Northern Ireland Case', in Fioravante Patrone, Ignacio García-Jurado, and Stef Tijs (eds), *Game Practice: Contributions from Applied Game Theory*. New York: Springer Science+Business Library, 35–52.

Bric, Maurice J., and John Coakley (2004) (eds). *From Political Violence to Negotiated Settlement: The Winding Path to Peace in Twentieth-Century Ireland*. Dublin: University College Dublin Press.

Brown, Graham, Arnim Langer, and Frances Stewart (2012) (eds). *Affirmative Action in Plural Societies: International Experiences*. London: Palgrave Macmillan.

Bulpitt, Jim (1983). *Territory and Power in the United Kingdom: An Interpretation*. Manchester: Manchester University Press.

CAIN (2019). *Conflict Archive on the Internet: Conflict and Politics in Northern Ireland*, <cain.ulster.ac.uk/index.html> (accessed 19 May 2019).

Callaghan, James (1973). *A House Divided: The Dilemma of Northern Ireland*. London: Collins.

Cameron, David (2019). *For the Record*. London: William Collins

Campbell, Alastair (2013). *The Irish Diaries (1994–2003)*, ed. Kathy Gilfillan. Dublin: Lilliput.

Campbell, Alastair, and Bill Hagerty (2010–12). *The Alastair Campbell Diaries*. 4 vols. London: Hutchinson.

Capoccia, Giovanni (2016). 'When do Institutions "Bite"? Historical Institutionalism and the Politics of Institutional Change', *Comparative Political Studies*, 49/8: 1095–1127.

Carolan, Eoin (2009). *The New Separation of Powers*. Oxford: Oxford University Press.

Cederman, Lars-Erik, Nils B. Weidmann, and Kristian Skrede Gleditsch (2011). 'Horizontal Inequalities and Ethno-Nationalist Civil War: A Global Comparison', *American Political Science Review*, 105/3: 478–95.

Choudhry, Sujit (2008) (ed.). *Constitutional Design for Divided Societies: Integration or Accommodation?* Oxford: Oxford University Press.

Clancy, Mary-Alice (2010). *Peace without Consensus: Power Sharing Politics in Northern Ireland*. London: Routledge.

Clinton, Bill (2004). *My Life: The Early Years*. New York: Random House.

Coakley, John (2005). 'The North–South Relationship: Implementing the Agreement', in John Coakley, Brigid Laffan, and Jennifer Todd (eds), *Renovation or Revolution? New Territorial Politics in Ireland and the United Kingdom*. Dublin: University College Dublin Press, 110–31.

Coakley, John (2008). 'Has the Northern Ireland Problem Been Solved?', *Journal of Democracy*, 19/3: 98–112.

Coakley, John (2009a). '"Irish Republic", "Eire" or "Ireland"? The Contested Name of John Bull's Other Island', *Political Quarterly*, 80/1: 49–58.

Coakley, John (2009b). 'The Political Consequences of the Electoral System in Northern Ireland', *Irish Political Studies*, 24/3: 253–84.

Coakley, John (2009c). 'Implementing Consociation in Northern Ireland', in Rupert Taylor (ed.), *Consociational Theory: McGarry and O'Leary and the Northern Ireland Conflict*. London: Routledge, 122–45.

Coakley, John (2011). 'The Challenge of Consociation in Northern Ireland', *Parliamentary Affairs*, 64/3: 473–93.

Coakley, John (2012). 'The Prehistory of the Irish Presidency', *Irish Political Studies*, 27/4: 539–58.

Coakley, John (2014). 'British Irish Institutional Structures: Towards a New Relationship', *Irish Political Studies*, 29/1: 76–97.

Coakley, John (2017a). 'Adjusting to Partition: From Irredentism to "Consent" in Twentieth-Century Ireland', *Irish Studies Review*, 25/2: 193–214.

Coakley, John (2017b). 'Resolving International Border Disputes: The Irish Experience', *Cooperation and Conflict*, 52/3: 377–98.

Coakley, John (2017c). 'The Sunningdale Agreement: A Step too Far?', in David McCann and Cillian McGrattan (eds), *Sunningdale, the Ulster Workers' Council Strike and the Struggle for Democracy in Northern Ireland*. Manchester: Manchester University Press, 55–71.

Coakley, John, and John Garry (2017). *Northern Ireland: The Challenge of Public Opinion*. Belfast: Queen's University Policy Engagement; online, <http://qpol.qub.ac.uk/public-opinion-challenge-ni/> (accessed 19 May 2019).

Coakley, John, and Jennifer Todd (2014a) (eds). *Breaking Patterns of Conflict in Northern Ireland: The British and Irish States*. London: Routledge.

Coakley, John, and Jennifer Todd (2014b). 'Breaking Patterns of Conflict in Northern Ireland: New Perspectives, *Irish Political Studies*, 29/1: 1–14.

Coakley, John, Brigid Laffan, and Jennifer Todd (2005) (eds). *Renovation or Revolution? New Territorial Politics in Ireland and the United Kingdom*. Dublin: University College Dublin Press.

Cochrane, Feargal (1997). *Unionist Politics and the Politics of Unionism since the Anglo-Irish Agreement*. Cork: Cork University Press.

Cochrane, Feargal (2013). *Northern Ireland: The Reluctant Peace*. New Haven: Yale University Press.

Cochrane, Feargal, Neophytos Loizides, and Thibaud Bodson (2018). *Mediating Power-Sharing: Devolution and Consociationalism in Deeply Divided Societies*. London: Routledge.

Conley, Richard S. (2013). 'The Consociational Model and Question Time in the Northern Ireland Assembly: Policy Issues, Procedural Reforms and Executive Accountability, 2007–2011', *Irish Political Studies*, 28/1: 78–98.

Cooper, James (2017). *The Politics of Diplomacy: US Presidents and the Northern Ireland Conflict, 1967–1998*. Edinburgh: Edinburgh University Press.

Cox, Michael, Adrian Guelke, and Fiona Stephen (2006) (eds). *A Farewell to Arms? Beyond the Good Friday Agreement*. 2nd edn. Manchester: Manchester University Press.

Craig, Anthony (2010). *Crisis of Confidence: Anglo-Irish Relations in the Early Troubles*. Dublin: Irish Academic Press.

Craig, Anthony (2012). 'From Backdoors and Back Lanes to Backchannels: Reappraising British Talks with the Provisional IRA, 1970–1974', *Contemporary British History*, 26/1: 97–117.

Cunningham, Michael (2001). *British Government Policy in Northern Ireland, 1969–2000*. Manchester: Manchester University Press.

Currie, Austin (2004). *All Hell Will Break Loose*. Dublin: O'Brien Press.

Darby, John (1976). *Conflict in Northern Ireland: The Development of a Polarised Community*. Dublin: Gill and Macmillan.

De Bréadún, Deaglán (2008). *The Far Side of Revenge: Making Peace in Northern Ireland*. New edn. Cork: Collins.

Devlin, Paddy (1993). *Straight Left: An Autobiography*. Belfast: Blackstaff.

Dixon, Paul (2008). *Northern Ireland: The Politics of War and Peace*. 2nd edn. Basingstoke: Palgrave Macmillan.

Dixon, Paul (2018). *Performing the Northern Ireland Peace Process: In Defence of Politics*. Basingstoke: Palgrave Macmillan.

Donoughue, Bernard (1987). *Prime Minister: The Conduct of Policy under Harold Wilson and James Callaghan*. London: Jonathan Cape.

Donoughue, Bernard (2006). *Downing Street Diary: With Harold Wilson in No. 10*. London: Pimlico.

Dorr, Noel (2011). *A Small State at the Top Table: Memories of Ireland on the UN Security Council, 1981–1982*. Dublin: Institute of Public Administration.

Dorr, Noel (2017). *Sunningdale: The Search for Peace in Northern Ireland*. Dublin: Royal Irish Academy.

Doyle, John (2010). 'The Politics of the Transformation of Policing', in John Doyle (ed.), *Policing the Narrow Ground: Lessons from the Transformation of Policing in Northern Ireland*. Dublin: Royal Irish Academy, 167–211.

Doyle, John, and Eileen Connolly (2017). *Brexit and the Future of Northern Ireland*. Working Paper no. 1–2017. Dublin: Brexit Institute, Dublin City University.

Duignan, Seán (1995). *One Spin on the Merry-Go-Round*. Dublin: Blackwater Press.

Dunnigan, John P. (1995). *Deep-Rooted Conflict and the IRA Ceasefire*. London: University Press of America.

Electoral Office for Northern Ireland (2019). *Elections*, <www.eoni.org.uk/Elections/> (accessed 19 May 2019).

Elliott, Marianne (2007) (ed.). *The Long Road to Peace in Northern Ireland*. Liverpool: Liverpool University Press.

Elliott, Sydney (1973). *Northern Ireland Parliamentary Election Results 1921–1972*. Chichester: Political Reference Publications.

Elliott, Sydney, and W. D. Flackes (1999). *Northern Ireland: A Political Directory, 1968–1999*. 5th edn. Belfast: Blackstaff.

English, Richard (2003). *Armed Struggle: The History of the IRA*. London: Macmillan.

Equality Commission for Northern Ireland (2002–17). *Monitoring Report No.12 [No. 13, 14, . . . 27]: A Profile of the Northern Ireland Workforce*. Belfast: Equality Commission for Northern Ireland.

European Commission (2018). *Draft Agreement on the Withdrawal of the United Kingdom of Great Britain and Northern Ireland from the European Union and the European Atomic Energy Community, as Agreed at Negotiators' Level on 14 November 2018*. Brussels: European Commission.

European Commission (2019). *Protocol on Ireland/Northern Ireland*. Brussels: European Commission

Eversley, David (1989). *Religion and Employment in Northern Ireland*. London: Sage.

Executive Office (2018). *Labour Force Survey Religion Report 2016: Annual Update— January 2018*. Belfast: Northern Ireland Statistics and Research Agency.

Farrell, John A. (2011). *Tip O'Neill and the Democratic Century*. Boston: Little, Brown.

Farren, Seán, and Robert Mulvihill (2000). *Paths to a Settlement in Northern Ireland*. Gerrards Cross: Colin Smythe.

Farrington, Christopher (2006). *Ulster Unionism and the Peace Process in Northern Ireland*. Basingstoke: Palgrave Macmillan.

Faulkner, Brian (1978). *Memoirs of a Statesman*. London: Weidenfeld and Nicolson.

Finlay, Fergus (1998). *Snakes and Ladders*. Dublin: New Island Books.

FitzGerald, Garret (1991). *All in a Life: An Autobiography*. Dublin: Gill and Macmillan.

FitzGerald, Garret (2006). 'The 1974–5 Threat of a British Withdrawal from Northern Ireland', *Irish Studies in International Affairs*, 17: 141–50.

FitzGerald, Garret (2010). *Just Garret: Tales from the Political Front Line*. Dublin: Liberties Press.

Gallagher A. M., R. D. Osborne, and R. J. Cormack (1995). *Fair Shares? Employment, Unemployment and Economic Status*. Belfast: Fair Employment Commission.

Gallagher, Michael (1990). 'Do Ulster Unionists Have a Right to Self-Determination?', *Irish Political Studies*, 5: 11–30.

Garry, John (2016). *Consociation and Voting in Northern Ireland: Party Competition and Electoral Behavior*. Philadelphia: University of Pennsylvania Press.

Gay, Oonagh (1998). *The Northern Ireland Bill: Implementing the Belfast Agreement*. Research Paper 98/76, 20 July. London: House of Commons Library.

Gay, Oonagh, and Bryn Morgan (1998). *Northern Ireland: Political Developments since 1972*. Research Paper 98/57, 20 May. London: House of Commons Library.

Gibbons, Ivan (2018). *Drawing the Line: The Irish Border in British Politics*. London: Haus.

Gilligan, Chris, and Jon Tonge (1997) (eds). *Peace or War? Understanding the Peace Process in Northern Ireland*. Aldershot: Ashgate.

Godson, Dean (2004). *Himself Alone: David Trimble and the Ordeal of Unionism*. London: Harper Perennial.

Gray, Ann Marie, Jennifer Hamilton, Gráinne Kelly, Brendan Lynn, Martin Melaugh, and Gillian Robinson (2018). *Northern Ireland Peace Monitoring Report—Number Five*. Belfast: Community Relations Council.

Guelke, Adrian (1988). *Northern Ireland: The International Dimension*. Dublin: Gill and Macmillan.

Hadfield, Brigid (1998). 'The Belfast Agreement, Sovereignty and the State of the Union', *Public Law* (Winter), 599–616.

Hain, Peter (2012). *Outside In*. London: Biteback.

Hain, Peter (2015). *The Hain Diaries 1998–2007*, ed. Matthew Ward. London: Biteback.

Hall, Peter A. (1993). 'Policy Paradigms, Social Learning, and the State: The Case of Economic Policymaking In Britain', *Comparative Politics*, 25/3: 275–96.

Harbison, Jeremy, and William Hodges (1991). 'Equal Opportunities in the Northern Ireland Civil Service', in Robert J. Cormack and Robert D. Osborne (eds), *Discrimination and Public Policy in Northern Ireland*. Oxford: Clarendon Press, 177–98.

Hartzell, Caroline A., and Matthew Hoddie (2007). *Crafting Peace: Power-Sharing Institutions and the Negotiated Settlement of Civil Wars*. University Park, PA: Pennsylvania State University Press.

Hartzell, Caroline A., and Matthew Hoddie (2015). 'The Art of the Possible: Power Sharing and Post-Civil War Democracy', *World Politics*, 67/1: 37–71.

Harvey, Colin (2001) (ed.). *Human Rights, Equality and Democratic Renewal in Northern Ireland*. Oxford: Hart.

Harvey, Colin (2018). 'Leaving the Union: Brexit and Complex Constitutionalism in Northern Ireland', in Fiona de Londras and Siobhan Mullally (eds), *Irish Yearbook of International Law*, 11–12 (2016–17), Oxford: Hart, 5–22.

Hayes, Bernadette C., and Ian McAllister (2013). *Conflict to Peace: Politics and Society in Northern Ireland over Half a Century*. Manchester: Manchester University Press.

Hayes, Maurice (1995). *Minority Verdict: Experiences of a Catholic Public Servant*. Belfast: Blackstaff.

Hayward, Katy, and Mary C. Murphy (2018). 'The EU's Influence on the Peace Process and Agreement in Northern Ireland in Light of Brexit', *Ethnopolitics*, 17/3: 276–91.

Hayward, Katy, and David Phinnemore (2018). *The Northern Ireland/Ireland Border, Regulatory Alignment and Brexit: Principles and Options in Light of the UK–EU Joint Report of 8 December 2017*. Briefing Paper 3. Belfast: Queen's University Brexit Briefing Series.

Hazell, Robert (1999) (ed.). *Constitutional Futures: A History of the Next Ten Years*. Oxford: Oxford University Press.

Hazell, Robert (2008) (ed.). *Constitutional Futures Revisited: Britain's Constitution to 2020*. Basingstoke: Palgrave Macmillan.

Heath, Edward (1998). *The Course of my Life: An Autobiography.* London: Hodder and Stoughton.

Hennessey, Thomas (2000). *The Northern Ireland Peace Process: Ending the Troubles?* Dublin: Gill and Macmillan.

Hennessey, Thomas (2015). *The First Northern Ireland Peace Process: Power-Sharing, Sunningdale and the IRA Ceasefires 1972–76.* Basingstoke: Palgrave Macmillan.

Hennessey, Thomas, Máire Braniff, James W. McAuley, Jonathan Tonge, and Sophie A. Whiting (2019). *The Ulster Unionist Party: Country before Party?* Oxford: Oxford University Press.

Hermon, John (1997). *Holding the Line: An Autobiography.* Dublin: Gill and Macmillan.

Horowitz, Donald L. (2000). *Ethnic Groups in Conflict.* Berkeley and Los Angeles: University of California Press.

Humphreys, Richard (2018). *Beyond the Border: The Good Friday Agreement and Irish Unity after Brexit.* Dublin: Irish Academic Press

Hurd, Douglas (2003). *Memoirs.* London: Little, Brown.

Independent Commission on Policing in Northern Ireland (1999). *A New Beginning: Policing in Northern Ireland. The Report of the Independent Commission on Policing for Northern Ireland.* Belfast: Independent Commission on Policing in Northern Ireland.

International Body (1996). *Report of the International Body on the Decommissioning of Arms, 22 January 1996.* Dublin, Belfast: International Body.

Ireland (1967). *Report of the Committee on the Constitution.* Pr. 9817. Dublin: Stationery Office.

Ireland (1973). *Northern Ireland: Agreed Communiqué Issued Following the Conference between the Irish and British Governments and the Parties Involved in the Northern Ireland Executive (designate) on 6th, 7th, 8th, and 9th December 1973.* Dublin: Government Information Services.

Ireland (1985) *Agreement between the Government of Ireland and the Government of the United Kingdom.* Dublin: Stationery Office.

Ireland (1993). *Joint Declaration by An Taoiseach, Mr. Albert Reynolds, T.D., and the British Prime Minister, The Rt. Hon. John Major, M.P.* Dublin: [Stationery Office].

Ireland (1998). *The Agreement Reached in the Multi-Party Negotiations 10 April 1998.* Dublin: Stationery Office.

Ivory, Gareth (2014). 'Fianna Fáil, Northern Ireland and the Limits on Conciliation, 1969–1973', *Irish Political Studies*, 29/1: 522–46.

Jakala, Michaelina, Durukan Kuzu, and Matt Qvortrup (2018) (eds). *Consociationalism and Power-Sharing in Europe: Arend Lijphart's Theory of Political Accommodation.* London: Palgrave Macmillan.

Jarrett, Henry (2018). *Peace and Ethnic Identity in Northern Ireland: Consociational Power Sharing and Conflict Management.* London: Routledge.

Jennings, Sir Ivor (1956). *The Approach to Self-Government.* Cambridge: Cambridge University Press.

Jones, Tom (1971). *Whitehall Diary*, iii. *Ireland 1918–1925*, ed. Keith Middlemas. London: Oxford University Press.

Keating, Michael (2001). *Plurinational Democracy: Stateless Nations in a Post-Sovereignty Era.* Oxford: Oxford University Press.

Keating, Michael (2018). 'Brexit and the Territorial Constitution of the United Kingdom', *Droit et société*, 98: 53–69.

Kelly, Stephen (2016a). *'A Failed Political Entity': Charles Haughey and the Northern Ireland Question 1945–1992.* Dublin: Merrion Press.

Kelly, Stephen (2016b). 'An Opportunistic Anglophobe: Charles J. Haughey, the Irish Government and the Falklands War, 1982', *Contemporary British History*, 30/4: 522–41.

Kennedy, Michael (2000). *Division and Consensus: The Politics of Cross-Border Relations in Ireland, 1925–1969*. Dublin: Institute of Public Administration.

Keogh, Dermot (2008). *Jack Lynch: A Biography*. Dublin: Gill and Macmillan.

Kerr, Michael (2006). *Imposing Power-Sharing: Conflict and Coexistence in Northern Ireland and Lebanon*. Dublin: Irish Academic Press.

Kerr, Michael (2011). *The Destructors: The Story of Northern Ireland's Lost Peace Process*. Dublin: Irish Academic Press.

Kidd, Colin (2008). *Union and Unionisms*. Cambridge: Cambridge University Press.

Kissane, Bill (2011). *New Beginnings: Constitutionalism and Democracy in Modern Ireland*. Dublin: Irish Academic Press.

Knight, James (1974). *Northern Ireland: The Elections of 1973*. London: Arthur McDougall Fund.

Knight, James, and Nicolas Baxter-Moore (1973). *Northern Ireland Local Government Elections, 30th May 1973 by the Single Transferable Vote System of Proportional Representation*. London: Arthur McDougall Fund.

Law Enforcement Commission (1974). *Report to the Minister for Justice of Ireland and the Secretary of State for Northern Ireland*. Prl. 3832. Dublin: Stationery Office.

Lawrence, R. J., S. Elliott, and M. J. Laver (1975). *The Northern Ireland General Elections of 1973*. London: HMSO.

Lawther, Cheryl (2015). *Truth, Denial and Transition: Northern Ireland and the Contested Past*. London: Routledge.

Lijphart, Arend (1975). 'Review Article: The Northern Ireland Problem: Cases, Theories, and Solutions', *British Journal of Political Science*, 5/1: 83–106.

Lillis, Michael (2009). 'Footnotes to the Anglo-Irish Agreement of 1985', in Jane Conroy (ed.), *Franco-Irish Connections: Essays, Memoirs and Poems in Honour of Pierre Joannon*. Dublin: Four Courts Press, 197–215.

Lillis, Michael (2016) (ed.). 'Bunker Days', *Dublin Review of Books*, 84, <www.drb.ie/essays/bunker-days> (accessed 19 May 2019).

Lillis, Michael, and David Goodall (2010). 'Edging towards Peace', *Dublin Review of Books*, 16, <www.drb.ie/essays/edging-towards-peace> (accessed 19 May 2019).

Lynch, John M. (1972). 'The Anglo-Irish Problem', *Foreign Affairs*, 50/4: 601–17.

McAlpine, Alistair. (1998). *Once a Jolly Bagman: Memoirs*. London: Phoenix.

McCall, Cathal (2006). 'From "Long War" to "War Of The Lilies": "Post-Conflict" Territorial Compromise and the Return of Territorial Politics', in Michael Cox, Adrian Guelke and Fiona Stephen (eds), *A Farewell to Arms: Beyond the Good Friday Agreement*. 2nd edn. Manchester: Manchester University Press, 302–16.

McCann, David, and Cillian McGrattan (2017) (eds). *Sunningdale, the Ulster Workers' Council Strike and the Struggle for Democracy in Northern Ireland*. Manchester: Manchester University Press.

MacCormick, Neil (1998). 'The English Constitution, the British State and the Scottish Anomaly', *Scottish Affairs*, 25/2: 129–45.

McCrudden, Christopher (1999). 'Equality and the Good Friday Agreement', in Joseph Ruane and Jennifer Todd (eds), *After The Good Friday Agreement: Explaining Change In Northern Ireland*. Dublin: University College Dublin Press, 96–121.

McCrudden, Christopher, Raya Muttarak, Heather Hamill, and Anthony Heath (2009). 'Affirmative Action without Quotas in Northern Ireland', *Equal Rights Review*, 4: 7–14.

McCulloch, Allison (2014). *Power-Sharing and Political Stability in Deeply Divided Societies*. London: Routledge.

McCulloch, Allison, and John McGarry (2017) (eds). *Power-Sharing: Empirical and Normative Challenges*. London: Routledge.

McEvoy, Joanne (2015). *Power-Sharing Executives: Governing in Bosnia, Macedonia and Northern Ireland*. Philadelphia: University of Pennsylvania Press.

McEvoy, Joanne, and Brendan O'Leary (2013) (eds). *Power Sharing in Deeply Divided Places*. Philadelphia: University of Pennsylvania Press.

McGarry, John (2017). 'Conclusion: What Explains the Performance of Power-Sharing Settlements?', in Allison McCulloch and John McGarry (eds), *Power-Sharing: Empirical and Normative Challenges*. London: Routledge, 268–92.

McGarry, John, and Brendan O'Leary (1995). *Explaining Northern Ireland: Broken Images*. Oxford: Blackwell.

McGarry, John, and Brendan O'Leary (2004). *The Northern Ireland Conflict: Consociational Engagements*. Oxford: Oxford University Press.

McGarry, John, and Brendan O'Leary (2008). 'Consociation and its Critics: Northern Ireland after the Belfast Agreement', in Sujit Choudhry (ed.), *Constitutional Design for Divided Societies: Integration or Accommodation?* Oxford: Oxford University Press, 369–408.

McGarry, John, and Brendan O'Leary (2017). 'Power-Sharing Executives: Consociational and Centripetal Formulae and the Case of Northern Ireland', in Allison McCulloch and John McGarry (eds), *Power Sharing: Empirical and Normative Challenges*. London: Routledge, 63–86.

McGrattan, Cillian (2010). *Northern Ireland 1968–2008: The Politics of Entrenchment*. Basingstoke: Palgrave Macmillan.

McIntyre, Anthony (1995). 'Modern Irish Republicanism: The Product of British State Strategies', *Irish Political Studies*, 10: 97–122.

McIvor, Basil (1998). *Hope Deferred: Experiences of an Irish Unionist*. Belfast: Blackstaff.

McKittrick, David (2012). *Making Sense of the Troubles: A History of the Northern Ireland Conflict*. Rev. edn. London: Viking.

McLaughlin, Mitchel (2001). *Redefining Republicanism: A Political Perspective*. IBIS Working Papers, no. 5. Dublin: Institute for British–Irish Studies, University College Dublin.

McLoughlin, P. J. (2010). *John Hume and the Revision of Irish Nationalism*. Manchester: Manchester University Press.

MacMillan, Gretchen (1993). *State, Society and Authority in Ireland: The Foundation of the Modern State*. Dublin: Gill and Macmillan.

Mahoney, James, and Kathleen Thelen (2009) (eds). *Explaining Institutional Change: Ambiguity, Agency and Power*. Cambridge: Cambridge University Press.

Mahoney, James, and Kathleen Thelen (2015) (eds). *Advances in Comparative Historical Analysis*. Cambridge: Cambridge University Press.

Major, John. (1999). *John Major: The Autobiography*. London: Harper Collins.

Mallie, Eamonn, and David McKittrick (1996). *The Fight for Peace: The Secret Story behind the Irish Peace Process*. London: Heinemann.

Mallon, Seamus, with Andy Pollak (2019). *A Shared Home Place*. Dublin: Lilliput Press.

Mandelson, Peter (2010). *The Third Man: Life at the Heart of New Labour*. London: HarperPress.

Mansergh, Martin (2003). *The Legacy of History for Making Peace in Ireland: Lectures and Commemorative Addresses*. Cork: Mercier Press.

Mars, Sylvia de, Colin Murray, Aoife O'Donoghue, and Ben Warwick (2018). *Bordering Two Unions: Northern Ireland and Brexit*. Bristol: Policy Press.

Maudling, Reginald (1978). *Memoirs: Reginald Maudling*. London: Sidgwick and Jackson.

Meehan, Elizabeth (2014). 'The Changing British–Irish Relationship: The Sovereignty Dimension', *Irish Political Studies*, 29/1: 58–75.

Mitchell, David (2015). *Politics and Peace in Northern Ireland: Political Parties and the Implementation of the 1998 Agreement*. Manchester: Manchester University Press.

Mitchell, George J. (2000). *Making Peace*. Berkeley and Los Angeles: University of California Press.

Mitchell, Paul, Brendan O'Leary, and Geoffrey Evans (2001). 'Northern Ireland: Flanking Extremists Bite the Moderates and Emerge in their Clothes', *Parliamentary Affairs*, 54/4: 725–42.

Mitchell, Paul, Geoffrey Evans, and Brendan O'Leary (2009). 'Extremist Outbidding in Ethnic Party Systems Is not Inevitable: Tribune Parties in Northern Ireland', *Political Studies*, 57/2: 397–421.

Moore, Charles (2015). *Margaret Thatcher: The Authorized Biography*, ii. *Everything She Wants*. London: Allen Lane.

Morgan, Austen (2000). *The Belfast Agreement: A Practical, Legal Analysis*. London: Belfast Press.

Morison, John (1999). 'Constitutionalism and Change: Representation, Governance and Participation in the New Northern Ireland', *Fordham International Law Journal*, 22/4: 1608–27.

Morison, John (2001). 'Democracy, Governance and Governability: Civic Public Space and Constitutional Renewal in Northern Ireland', *Oxford Journal of Legal Studies*, 21/2: 287–310.

Mowlam, Mo (2002). *Momentum: The Struggle for Peace, Politics and the People*. London: Hodder and Stoughton.

Mulcahy, Aogán (2006). *Policing Northern Ireland: Conflict, Legitimacy and Reform*. Cullompton: Willan.

Murphy, Mary C. (2014). *Northern Ireland and the European Union: The Dynamics of a Changing Relationship*. Manchester: Manchester University Press.

Murphy, Mary C. (2018). *Europe and Northern Ireland's Future: Negotiating Brexit's Unique Case*. Newcastle upon Tyne: Agenda Publishing.

Murray, Gerard and Jonathan Tonge (2005). *Sinn Fein and the SDLP: From Alienation to Participation*. Dublin: O'Brien Press.

Natow, Rebecca S. (2019). 'The Use of Triangulation in Qualitative Studies Employing Elite Interviews', *Qualitative Research*. Electronic preprint, doi:10.1177/1468794119830077.

New Ireland Forum (1984). *Report*. Dublin: Stationery Office.

New Ulster Movement (1971). *The Reform of Stormont*. Belfast: New Ulster Movement.

Ní Aoláin, Fionnuala (2000). *The Politics of Force: Conflict Management and State Violence in Northern Ireland*. Belfast: Blackstaff.

Nolan, Paul (2014). *Northern Ireland Peace Monitoring Report—Number Three*. Belfast: Community Relations Council.

Nolan, P., D. Bryan, C. Dwyer, K. Hayward, K. Radford, and P. Shirlow (2014). *The Flag Dispute: Anatomy of a Protest*. Belfast: Institute for the Study of Conflict Transformation and Social Justice, Queen's University Belfast.

Northern Ireland Constitutional Convention (1975). *Report, together with the Proceedings of the Convention and Other Appendices*. London: HMSO.

Northern Ireland General Register Office (1975). *Census of Population 1971: Religion Tables*. Belfast: HMSO.

Northern Ireland Life and Times (1998–2017). *Northern Ireland Life and Times Surveys*, 1998–2017 <www.ark.ac.uk/nilt/> (accessed 19 May 2019).

Northern Ireland Office (1972). *The Future of Northern Ireland: A Paper for Discussion*. London: HMSO.

Northern Ireland Office (1973). *Northern Ireland Constitutional Proposals*. Cmnd 5259. London: HMSO.

Northern Ireland Registrar General (1984). *The Northern Ireland Census 1981: Religion Report*. Belfast: HMSO.

Northern Ireland Statistics and Research Agency (2018). *Equality Statistics for the Northern Ireland Civil Service Based on Staff in Post at 1 January 2018*. Belfast: Northern Ireland Statistics and Research Agency.

Northern Ireland Statistics and Research Agency (2019). *Census 2011*, <www.nisra.gov.uk/statistics/census/2011-census> (accessed 26 January 2019).

Norton, Philip (1989). 'The Glorious Revolution of 1688: Its Continuing Relevance', *Parliamentary Affairs*, 42/2: 135–47.

Ó Beacháin, Donnacha (2019). *From Partition to Brexit: The Irish Government and Northern Ireland*. Manchester: Manchester University Press.

Ó Cinnéide, Colm (2013). 'A Common Floor of Rights Protection? The Belfast Agreement, "Equivalence of Rights" and the North–South Dimension', in Cillian McGrattan and Elizabeth Meehan (eds), *Everyday Life after the Irish Conflict*. Manchester: Manchester University Press, 135–49.

Ó Dochartaigh, Niall (2015). 'The Longest Negotiation: British Policy, IRA Strategy and the Making of the Northern Ireland Peace Settlement', *Political Studies*, 63/1: 202–20.

O'Brien, Conor Cruise (1999). *Memoir: My Life and Themes*. Dublin: Poolbeg.

O'Clery, Conor (1996). *The Greening of the White House: The Inside Story of how America Tried to Bring Peace to Ireland*. Dublin: Gill and Macmillan.

O'Connor, Karl (2013). 'Belfast Revisited: Everyday Policymaking in a Contested Environment', *Irish Political Studies*, 28/1: 58–77.

O'Duffy, Brendan (2007). *British–Irish Relations and Northern Ireland: From Violent Politics to Conflict Regulation*. Dublin: Irish Academic Press.

O'Flynn, Ian, and David Russell (2005) (eds). *Power Sharing: New Challenges for Divided Societies*. London: Pluto Press.

O'Kane, Eamon (2007). *Britain, Ireland and Northern Ireland since 1980: The Totality of Relationships*. London: Routledge.

O'Leary, Brendan (1995). 'Afterword: What Is Framed in the Framework Documents?', *Ethnic and Racial Studies*, 18/4: 862–72.

O'Leary, Brendan (2005). 'Mission Accomplished? Looking back at the IRA', *Field Day Review*, 1/1: 216–46.

O'Leary, Brendan (2019). *A Treatise on Northern Ireland*. 3 vols. Oxford: Oxford University Press.

O'Leary, Brendan, and John McGarry (1996). *The Politics of Antagonism: Understanding Northern Ireland*. 2nd edn. London: Athlone Press.

O'Leary, Cornelius, Sydney Elliott and Richard A. Wilford (1988). *The Northern Ireland Assembly, 1982–1986*. London: Hurst.

Office of the First Minister and Deputy First Minister (2005). *A Shared Future: Policy and Strategic Framework for Good Relations in Northern Ireland*. Belfast: Community Relations Unit, Office of the First Minister and Deputy First Minister

Osborne, Robert D., and Ian Shuttleworth (2004). *Fair Employment in Northern Ireland: A Generation On*. Belfast: Blackstaff.

Owen, Lord David (2007). 'The Resolution of Armed Conflict: Internalization and its Lessons, Particularly in Northern Ireland', in Marianne Elliott (ed.), *The Long Road to Peace in Northern Ireland*. 2nd edn. Liverpool: Liverpool University Press, 22–40.

Patten, Chris (2017). *First Confession: A Sort of Memoir*. London: Allen Lane.

Phinnemore, David, and Katy Hayward (2017). *UK Withdrawal ('Brexit') and the Good Friday Agreement*. Luxembourg: Publications Office of the European Union.

Police Service of Northern Ireland (2019). *Security Situation Statistics*, online, <www.psni.police.uk/inside-psni/Statistics/security-situation-statistics/> (accessed 19 May 2019).

Potter, Michael (2011). *Equality and Human Rights Legislation in Northern Ireland: A Review*. Research Paper 75/11. Belfast: Northern Ireland Assembly Research and Information Service.

Powell, Jonathan (2008). *Making Peace in Northern Ireland*. London: The Bodley Head.

Prince, Simon (2018). *Northern Ireland's '68: Civil Rights, Global Revolt and the Origins of the Troubles*. New edn. Dublin: Irish Academic Press.

Prior, James (1986). *A Balance of Power*. London: Hamish Hamilton.

Purdie, Bob (1990). *Politics in the Streets: The Origins of the Civil Rights Movement in Northern Ireland*. Belfast: Blackstaff.

Rees, Merlyn (1985). *Northern Ireland: A Personal Perspective*. London: Methuen.

Reilly, Ben (2001). *Democracy in Divided Societies: Electoral Engineering for Conflict Management*. Cambridge: Cambridge University Press.

Reynolds, Albert, with Jill Arlon (2009). *My Autobiography*. London: Transworld Ireland.

Rose, Peter (2000). *How the Troubles Came to Northern Ireland*. Basingstoke: Palgrave Macmillan.

Rose, Richard (1971). *Governing without Consensus: An Irish Perspective*. London: Faber and Faber.

Ruane, Joseph (1999). 'The End of (Irish) History? Three Readings of the Current Conjuncture', in Joseph Ruane and Jennifer Todd (eds), *After the Good Friday Agreement*. Dublin: University College Dublin Press, 145–69.

Ruane, Joseph (2016). 'Modelling Ireland's Crises: North, South and North–South Intersections', in Niall Ó Dochartaigh, Katy Hayward and Elizabeth Meehan (eds), *Dynamics of Political Change in Ireland: Making and Breaking a Divided Island*. London: Routledge, 93–109.

Ruane, Joseph, and Jennifer Todd (1996). *The Dynamics of Conflict in Northern Ireland: Power, Conflict and Emancipation*. Cambridge: Cambridge University Press.

Ruane, Joseph, and Jennifer Todd (1999). 'The Belfast Agreement: Context, Content, Consequences', in Joseph Ruane and Jennifer Todd (eds), *After the Good Friday Agreement*. Dublin: University College Dublin Press, 1–29.

Ruane, Joseph, and Jennifer Todd (2001). 'The Politics of Transition? Explaining Political Crises in the Implementation of the Belfast (Good Friday) Agreement', *Political Studies*, 49/5: 923–40.

Ruane, Joseph, and Jennifer Todd (2007). 'Path Dependence in Settlement Processes: Explaining Settlement in Northern Ireland', *Political Studies*, 55/2: 442–58.

Ruane, Joseph, and Jennifer Todd (2014). 'History, Structure and Action in the Settlement of Complex Conflicts: The Northern Ireland Case', *Irish Political Studies*, 29/1: 15–36.

Shirlow, Peter, Jonathan Tonge, James McAuley, and Catherine McGlynn (2011). *Abandoning Historical Conflict? Former Paramilitary Prisoners and Political Reconciliation in Northern Ireland*. Manchester: Manchester University Press.

Sinn Féin (1987). *A Scenario for Peace: A Discussion Paper*. Dublin: Sinn Féin.

Sinn Féin (1992). *Towards a Lasting Peace in Ireland*. Belfast: Sinn Féin.

Sinn Féin (1994). *Setting the Record Straight: A Record of Communications between Sinn Féin and the British Government October 1990 – November 1993*. Dublin: Sinn Féin.

Smith, David J., and Gerald Chambers (1991). *Equality and Inequality in Northern Ireland*. Oxford: Clarendon Press.

Social Democratic and Labour Party (1972). *Towards a New Ireland: Proposals by the Social Democratic and Labour Party*. Belfast: Social Democratic and Labour Party.

Spencer, Graham (2015) (ed.). *The British and Peace in Northern Ireland: The Process and Practice of Reaching Agreement*. Cambridge: Cambridge University Press.

Stevenson, Jonathan (2017). 'Does Brexit Threaten Peace in Northern Ireland?', *Survival*, 59/3: 111–28.

Stewart, Frances (2008) (ed.). *Horizontal Inequalities and Conflict: Understanding Group Violence in Multiethnic Societies*. London: Palgrave.

Suchenia, Agnieszka (2013). *The Union Flag and Flags of the United Kingdom* [Standard Note SN/PC/04474]. London: House of Commons Library.

Sweeney, George (1993). 'Irish Hunger Strikes and the Cult of Self-Sacrifice', *Journal of Contemporary History*, 28/3: 421–37.

Tannam, Etain (2018). 'Intergovernmental and Cross-Border Civil Service Cooperation: The Good Friday Agreement and Brexit', *Ethnopolitics*, 17/3: 243–62.

Taylor, Rupert (2009) (ed.). *Consociational Theory: McGarry and O'Leary and the Northern Ireland Conflict*. London: Routledge.

Thatcher, Margaret (1993). *The Downing Street Years*. London: HarperCollins.

Todd, Jennifer (2011). 'Institutional Change and Conflict Regulation: The Anglo-Irish Agreement of 1985 and the Mechanisms of Change in Northern Ireland', *West European Politics*, 34/4: 838–58.

Todd, Jennifer (2014). 'Thresholds of State Change: Changing British State Institutions and Practices in Northern Ireland after Direct Rule', *Political Studies*, 62/3: 522–38.

Todd, Jennifer (2015). 'The vulnerability of the Northern Ireland settlement: British Irish relations, political crisis and Brexit', *Études Irlandaises*, 40/2, 61–73.

Todd, Jennifer (2017). 'Contested Constitutionalism? Northern Ireland and the British–Irish Relationship since 2010', *Parliamentary Affairs*, 70/2: 301–32.

Todd, Jennifer (2018). *Identity Change after Conflict: Ethnicity, Boundaries and Belonging in the Two Irelands*. Basingstoke: Palgrave Macmillan.

Todd, Jennifer and Joseph Ruane (2012). 'Beyond Inequality: Assessing the Impact of Fair Employment, Affirmative Action and Equality Measures on Conflict in Northern Ireland', in Graham Brown, Arnim Langer and Frances Stewart (eds), *Affirmative Action in Plural Societies: International Experiences*. London: Palgrave Macmillan, 182–208.

Tonge, Jonathan (2002). *Northern Ireland: Conflict and Change*. London: Prentice Hall.

Tonge, Jonathan (2005). *The New Northern Irish Politics?* Basingstoke: Palgrave Macmillan.

Tonge, Jonathan (2017). *The Impact and Consequences of Brexit for Northern Ireland*. Luxembourg: Publications Office of the European Union.

Tonge, Jonathan, Máire Braniff, Thomas Hennessey, James W. McAuley, and Sophie A. Whiting (2014). *The Democratic Unionist Party: From Protest to Power*. Oxford: Oxford University Press.

Tonge, Jonathan, Peter Shirlow, and James McAuley (2011). 'So why did the Guns Fall Silent? How Interplay, not Stalemate, Explains the Northern Ireland Peace Process', *Irish Political Studies*, 26/1: 1–18.

United Ireland Association (1972). *Stormont: An Assessment*. N.p.: United Ireland Association.

United Kingdom (1995). *Frameworks for the Future*. Belfast: HMSO.

United Kingdom (1998). *The Agreement: Agreement Reached in the Multi-Party Negotiations* [Good Friday Agreement]. Belfast: Northern Ireland Office.

Walker, Neil (2006) (ed.). *Sovereignty in Transition*. Oxford: Hart.

Walker, Neil (2013). 'Sovereignty Frames and Sovereignty Claims', in Richard Rawlings, Peter Leyland, and Alison Young (eds), *Sovereignty and the Law*. Oxford: Oxford University Press, 18–33.

Walsh, Dawn (2017). *Independent Commissions and Contentious Issues in Post-Good Friday Agreement Northern Ireland*. Basingstoke: Palgrave Macmillan.

Ward, Alan J. (1994). *The Irish Constitutional Tradition: Representative Government and Modern Ireland, 1782–1992*. Dublin: Irish Academic Press.

White, Timothy J. (2017) (ed.). *Theories of International Relations and Northern Ireland*. Manchester: Manchester University Press.

White, Timothy J. (2018). 'Consociation, Conditionality, and Commitment: Making Peace in Northern Ireland', in Michaelina Jakala, Durukan Kuzu, and Matt Qvortrup (eds), *Consociationalism and Power-Sharing in Europe: International Political Theory*. Basingstoke: Palgrave Macmillan, 85–102.

Whitelaw, William (1989). *The Whitelaw Memoirs*. London: Aurum.

Whyte, John (1990). *Interpreting Northern Ireland*. Oxford: Clarendon Press.

Wilford, Richard (2001) (ed.). *Aspects of the Belfast Agreement*. Oxford: Oxford University Press.

Wilford, Rick (2010). 'Northern Ireland: The Politics of Constraint', *Parliamentary Affairs*, 63/1: 134–55.

Wilford, Rick, and Robin Wilson (2006). *The Trouble with Northern Ireland: The Belfast Agreement and Democratic Governance*. Dublin: New Island.

Williamson, Daniel C. (2017). *Anglo-Irish Relations in the Early Troubles: 1969–1972*. London: Bloomsbury Academic.

Wilson, Andrew J. (1995). *Irish America and the Ulster Conflict 1968–1995*. Belfast: Blackstaff.

Wilson, Harold (1979). *Final Term: The Labour Government 1974–1976*. London: Weidenfeld and Nicolson; Michael Joseph.

Wilson, Robin (2008). 'Ethnonationalist Conflicts, Consociationalist Prescriptions and the Travails of Politics in Northern Ireland'. PhD thesis. Belfast: Queen's University Belfast.

Wolff, Stefan (2001). 'Context and Content: Sunningdale and Belfast Compared', in Rick Wilford (ed.), *Aspects of the Belfast Agreement*. Oxford: Oxford University Press, 11–27.

Wolff, Stefan (2005). 'Between Stability and Collapse: Internal and External Dynamics of Post-Agreement Institution Building in Northern Ireland', in Sidney Noel (ed.), *From Power-Sharing to Democracy: Post-Conflict Institutions in Ethnically Divided Societies*. Montreal: McGill University Press, 44–66.

Wolff, Stefan, and Karl Cordell (2016). 'Consociationalism', in Karl Cordell and Stefan Wolff (eds), *The Routledge Handbook of Ethnic Conflict*. 2nd edn. London: Routledge, 289–300.

Wright, Frank (1987). *Northern Ireland: A Comparative Analysis*. Dublin: Gill and Macmillan.

Ziegler, Philip (2010). *Edward Heath: The Authorised Biography*. London: HarperPress.

Index

Note: Tables and figures are indicated by an italic '*t*' and '*f*', respectively, following the page number.

For the benefit of digital users, indexed terms that span two pages (e.g., 52–53) may, on occasion, appear on only one of those pages.

Wilson, President Woodrow 539n.27
Wilson, Robin
    doctoral thesis 488, 502
Wilson, Sammy 511
Wingfield House 489
witness seminars
    limitations of 550
    organization of 23
    participants in 23

potential value of 550
    role of civil servants 456
women *see also* Northern Ireland Women's
    Coalition
    and political parties 344–5, 457, 499
    role of 26–7, 552

Yemen
    partition of 248n.53